HANDBOOK OF

Clinical Family Therapy

HANDBOOK OF
Clinical Family Therapy

Edited by Jay L. Lebow

WILEY

John Wiley & Sons, Inc.

Published by John Wiley & Sons, Inc., Hoboken, New Jersey.
Published simultaneously in Canada.

Library of Congress Cataloging-in-Publication Data:

Handbook of clinical family therapy / edited by Jay L. Lebow.
    p. cm.
  ISBN-13 978-0-471-43134-3 (cloth)
  ISBN-10 0-471-43134-6 (cloth)
  1. Family therapy. 2. Marital psychotherapy. 3. Adolescent psychotherapy. I. Lebow, Jay.
RC488.5.H3262 2005
616.89'156—dc22

                                 2004063708

Printed in the United States of America

10 9 8 7 6 5 4 3 2 1

To my wife, Joan, and daughter, Ellen,
who demonstrate to me daily how much family matter

Contents

PART II
Problems in Adults

PART III
Couple Relationship Difficulties

PART IV
Relationship Difficulties in Families

Contributors

James F. Alexander, PhD
University of Utah
Salt Lake City, UT

Michael Barnes, PhD, LMHC
Bayside Center For Behavioral
    Health—Sarasota Memorial
    Hospital
Sarasota, FL

Brian Baucom, MA
University of California, Los Angeles
Los Angeles, CA

Donald H. Baucom, PhD
University of North Carolina
Chapel Hill, NC

Steven R. H. Beach, PhD
University of Georgia
Athens, GA

Dorothy S. Becvar, PhD
Saint Louis University
St. Louis, MO

Gary R. Birchler, PhD
University of California, San Diego
San Diego, CA

L. Elizabeth Bodnar, MA
American University
Washington, DC

James H. Bray, PhD
Baylor College of Medicine
Houston, TX

Andrew Christensen, PhD
University of California, Los Angeles
Los Angeles, CA

James C. Coyne, PhD
University of Pennsylvania Health
    System
Philadelphia, PA

Gayle A. Dakof, PhD
University of Miami School of
    Medicine (D93)
Miami, FL

Guy S. Diamond, PhD
Children's Hospital of Philadelphia
Philadelphia, PA

William Fals-Stewart, PhD
Research Triangle International
Research Triangle Park, NC

Charles R. Figley, PhD
Florida State University
Tallahassee, FL

Mona DeKoven Fishbane, PhD
Chicago Center for Family Health
Chicago, IL

Peter David Goldberg, MS
Reston, VA

Kristina Coop Gordon, PhD
University of Tennessee-Knoxville
Knoxville, TN

Maya Gupta, MS
University of Georgia
Athens, GA

Alan S. Gurman, PhD
University of Wisconsin Medical School
Madison, WI

Scott W. Henggeler, PhD
Medical University of South Carolina
Charleston, SC

Viviana E. Horigian, MD
University of Miami
Miami, FL

Mark A. Hubble, PhD
Institute for the Study of Therapeutic
   Change
Basking Ridge, NJ

Susan M. Johnson, EdD
Ottawa University
Ottawa Couple and Family Institute
   (OCFI)
Ottawa, Canada

Elda Kanzki, LMHC
University of Miami School of
   Medicine
Miami, FL

Jay L. Lebow, PhD, ABPP
Family Institute at Northwestern
Northwestern University
Evanston, IL

Howard A. Liddle, EdD, ABPP
University of Miami School of
   Medicine
Miami, FL

Lisa D. Locke, MS
Virginia Tech
Falls Church, VA

Francoise A. Marvel, BA
University of Miami School of
   Medicine
Miami, FL

Carla C. Mayorga, BA
University of Miami School of
   Medicine
Miami, FL

Barry W. McCarthy, PhD
American University
Washington, DC

Eric E. McCollum, PhD
Virginia Tech–Northern Virginia
   Center
Falls Church, VA

Susan H. McDaniel, PhD
University of Rochester Medical
   Center
Rochester, NY

William R. McFarlane, MD
Maine Medical Center
Portland, ME

David Mee-Lee, MD
DML Training and Consulting
Davis, CA

Scott D. Miller, PhD
Institute for the Study of Therapeutic
   Change
Chicago, IL

Victoria B. Mitrani, PhD
University of Miami School of
    Medicine
Miami, FL

Timothy J. O'Farrell, PhD, ABPP
Harvard Medical School Department
    of Psychiatry at the VA Boston
    Healthcare System
Brockton, MA

Anthony R. Pisani, PhD
University of Rochester Medical
    Center
Rochester, NY

William Plum, LADC
University of Minnesota-Duluth
    Medical School
Duluth, MN

Michael S. Robbins, PhD
University of Miami School of
    Medicine
Miami, FL

Rosemarie A. Rodriguez, MS
University of Miami School of
    Medicine
Miami, FL

Karen H. Rosen, EdD
Virginia Tech
Falls Church, VA

Sonja K. Schoenwald, PhD
Medical University of South Carolina
Charleston, SC

Thomas L. Sexton, PhD
Indiana University
Bloomington, IN

Douglas K. Snyder, PhD
Texas A&M University
College Station, TX

Sandra M. Stith, PhD
Virginia Tech
Falls Church, VA

Lourdes Suarez-Morales, PhD
University of Miami
Miami, FL

José Szapocznik, PhD
University of Miami School of
    Medicine
Miami, FL

Karen C. Wells, PhD
Duke University Medical Center
Durham, NC

Scott R. Woolley, PhD
Alliant International University
San Diego, CA

Jean C. Yi, MS
University of Washington
Seattle, WA

Mónica Zarate, MEd LMHC
University of Miami School of
    Medicine
Miami, FL

Preface

Edited volumes and texts that strive to represent the most prominent methods of family therapy have typically adhered to the same format since the earliest days of the field. Chapters typically each describe a similar core group of therapies: structural, strategic, Bowenian, behavioral, psychoanalytic, experiential, and so on. These ways of organizing the material present a fine historical view of the branches of development in the field of family therapy, yet also reify a structure for the field that reflects its earliest being rather than its evolution. Some of the approaches described in those volumes are almost never encountered today; a few are no longer even followed by their developers.

This volume looks to present approaches to family therapy in a much different manner. First, it presents prominent family therapy approaches without regard to fitting them into a structure of the first generation schools of family therapy. As I describe in the first chapter, today's approaches typically assume an integrative stance rather than one based on the categorizations of the older schools. A generic core of strategies and interventions derived from the first generation of models serves as the basis for all of these therapies.

Second, the chapters in this volume are organized around the treatment of specific individual and relational difficulties. In recent years, the cutting edge of model development has moved away from universal theories of how families operate to a more limited focus on how to best operate in a more limited sphere. This volume follows that movement in emphasizing how to best use family therapy in the context of specific difficulties.

Yet, paradoxically, given this focus on specificity of approach, what emerges for the reader prepared to digest all of these approaches is the foundation for a generic family therapy (see Chapter 1). As the twenty-first century begins, family therapy is moving to include a widely accepted range of strategies and interventions that are useful across many specific contexts.

The approaches summarized in the chapters in this volume were chosen following a series of criteria. Approaches needed to focus on one or more specific disorders or relational difficulties. Some of these problems are the age-old Diagnostic and Statistical Manual (DSM) individual problems such as depression and Attention-Deficit Disorder, but equally important in this volume is the presentation of methods that aim at relational difficulties, such as couple distress or problems in family connection. Approaches also needed to be prominent and highly regarded. The approaches also needed to have at least some modicum of support through empirical and clinical testing and to be consistent with the emerging literature on families experiencing that type of specific difficulty. Because specific family therapies for many difficulties are still in the early stages of model development, the standard for evidence for the efficacy of approaches has been kept relatively low. The reader can judge the degree of support for each approach from the brief section in each chapter on empirical support.

In pursuing this method for the organization of this volume a few striking observations emerge. There are many well-developed family therapies for treating some difficulties, such as adolescent delinquency and substance abuse, and none for others, such as most of the anxiety disorders. We decided to make this a volume that tracked the best of family therapy, rather than one aimed to be comprehensive at the cost of including what were more preliminary efforts at developing an approach that were based mostly in musings about what might be effective. Therefore, there are four chapters in this volume describing a range of methods for intervening with acting-out adolescents and none dealing with Generalized Anxiety Disorder. In the next edition of this volume, we hope there will be approaches to fill in the gaps.

We included couple therapies as well as family therapies. Couple and family therapies are often intermixed in the treatment of specific difficulties. In some recent categorizations, couple therapy has begun to be split off from family therapy as a separate entity. Yet, the overlap in these methods far exceeds the differences. As the chapters on couple therapy for couple distress in this volume attest, the strategies and interventions utilized bear striking similarity to those in the family therapies.

We did not include special chapters on culture, social class, or sexual orientation. This decision was based on the desire to keep these issues in central focus in each chapter rather than have them segregated to a special section. Each author was asked to speak to issues of culture that have importance in his or her particular domain and how that therapy needs to be adapted in specific contexts.

The authors for this volume were asked to follow a specific outline, with instructions to include:

1. A description of the problem area that includes a brief statement describing the problem, its importance, and what is known about it.

2. The roots of the treatment approach that includes a brief description of the theoretical and practical roots of the treatment approach, with special attention focused on the relevance of couple and family intervention for the problem in focus.

3. Specific intervention strategies for treating this problem that includes providing a step-by-step guide that readers can use as a generic blueprint for treatment: how to utilize assessment, how to formulate treatment goals, what are viewed as curative factors, a specific description of the treatment strategies and how these strategies connect to the special nature of the presenting problem, how decisions are made about which interventions to employ and how to sequence these interventions, and typical issues that need to be addressed in the course of treatment and how to address those issues.

4. Special considerations in the treatment of this problem, including any aspects of the treatment approach that require special attention.

5. Research evidence supporting the approach, including a paragraph or two that provide a sense of how much evidence there is about the efficacy and effectiveness of the approach and any important process data about it.

6. A clinical example, including a brief example of how the treatment is implemented.

And authors were given the following additional directions:

- Think of your core reader as a professional in practice or an advanced clinical graduate student or professional.

- Describe the special aspects of the problem area on which you are focusing and the unique aspects of couples and families in this domain. What are the key aspects of these relationship systems that need to be addressed?

- As you describe the treatment, be sure to accentuate the aspects of your approach that especially are connected to treatment of those with this particular difficulty. For example, establishing a strong therapeutic alliance probably will be an important aspect in every treatment covered in the volume, but it will be more valuable to speak to the special issues in establishing alliances in the domain you are addressing than to describe generic methods of establishing treatment alliances. What special mediating and ultimate goals and methods of accomplishing those goals need to be highlighted in couples/families in the domain you are addressing?

- If the method you are describing involves both individual and couple/family therapy interventions, accentuate the couple/family aspects of the treatment, providing a brief summary of the individual-focused methods.

- Emphasize what specifically is done in treatment.

- Research relevant to the approach should be presented in a brief section in a manner that will be understandable by the typical clinician.

I believe this volume conveys the excitement of the new family therapy that is emerging. This therapy is no longer a radical opponent to other approaches, but instead is a fairly well-established, mature set of intervention strategies that are dependable and effective, and are increasingly simply a well-established part of good practice. In bringing these approaches together in this book, I hope this volume can serve to further the movement to a widely disseminated, evidence-based generic family therapy that families can count on wherever they are located and whoever they see.

Finally, I'd like to thank Patricia Rossi, Jennifer Simon, Isabel Pratt, and Peggy Alexander at John Wiley and Sons and Becca Uhlers, Jane Kinsman, Danielle Shannon, Michelle Factor, and Jennifer Nastasi at the Family Institute at Northwestern University for their help with preparing the manuscript.

JAY LEBOW, PhD

CHAPTER 1

Family Therapy at the Beginning of the Twenty-first Century

Jay L. Lebow

This volume marks a watershed in the development of couple and family therapy. We have entered an era in which the most prominent models of practice no longer primarily accentuate disparate, broad visions of how families operate and how people change, as they did a generation ago, but instead draw from a core set of well-established strategies to create pragmatic, effective ways of working with specific difficulties and life situations. In the newest generation of family therapies, generic family-based strategies of intervention are shaped to most successfully fit and impact on the specific clinical context.

Today's state-of-the-art methods in couple and family therapy, although diverse in their specific focus and their particular blueprint for intervention, share many core attributes. A number of transcendent core characteristics readily emerge from deconstructing the ingredients of the kinds of twenty-first-century family therapies exemplified in this volume. These core characteristics are summarized in the following sections.

SYSTEMIC FOCUS

Today's state-of-the-art methods have a systemic focus. Drawing upon the preeminent core concept of the early family therapy movement (Haley, 1963), these approaches accentuate the importance of understanding the family as a system and the core properties of such social systems. Systemic concepts are apparent in the fabric of these approaches, manifested in such aspects as the significance assigned to mutual ongoing influence, the view that the whole is more than the sum of its parts, the importance assigned to feedback in interpersonal process, and the power of the dueling forces moving toward homeostasis and morphogenesis.

However, it is very much a twenty-first-century version of systems theory that is evident in these approaches, rather than earlier variants of systems theory that were more closely linked to the properties of inanimate systems. In this newer view of social systems, families are seen as more than simply the product of inevitable systemic forces. This systems theory allows room for understandings of causal processes, for the differential impact of different individuals on the mutual systemic process, for influences on the system that reside within the inner selves of individuals, and for the impact of the larger system on the family.

Within such a framework, pathways of mutual influence move well beyond the idealized, circular causality that was posited to be at work in an earlier generation of family therapies (Bowen, 1966; Whitaker, 1992). Following the core insight first presented by Virginia Goldner (Goldner, 1998) in the context of examining couple violence, this includes an understanding that sometimes one person's influence is greater than another's on their mutual process, even though the action of each has some impact. As Goldner (1998) suggested, patterns of couple violence may show circular arcs of influence, but typically the individual personality of the abuser has much more impact on the initiation and continuation of abuse than that of the abused partner. This viewpoint provides a crucial example of the refinement of the systems theory that has occurred in light of the pragmatic knowledge gained from a half century of clinical experience and research. There are few findings in the social sciences as well demonstrated as the mutual influence of family and individual behavior (Snyder & Whisman; 2003; Pinsof & Lebow, 2005), but this mutual influence is mediated and moderated by numerous factors. The simplistic application of systems theory derived from observations primarily about inanimate objects and animals has been refined in the context of observations and research about the properties of human systems.

BIOBEHAVIORAL-PSYCHOSOCIAL FOUNDATION

These approaches have a biobehavioral-psychosocial underpinning. Social systems exert influence, but are not the only factors in the lives of individuals. Whereas early family-therapy models eschewed individual psychology (the biological basis of behavior, social psychology, and principles of learning), most of the emerging models embrace these sets of ideas.

The last few decades have been a time in which the biological basis of behavior has come to be well established. In the earliest versions of family systems therapies, notions of a biological basis were dismissed for even the most severe problems in individual functioning, such as schizophrenia or Bipolar Disorder (Haley, 1997). In that era, leaders in the field of family therapy mustered strong arguments against the primitive biological theories of the time (which had little basis in evidence) as part of their argument for the supremacy of a systemic viewpoint. These arguments were the systemic equivalent of Watson's landmark statement of behaviorism, denying biology any significant role in the development of mental health or pathology.

However, a generation of investigation has very much changed this picture. Although biological theories of the origins of behavior are still often grossly overstated and reductionistic, the impact of biology on individual functioning and on family processes is now well established. Biology has been demonstrated to affect the genesis and development of many specific behavioral patterns and disorders (see, for example, the chapters in this volume by McFarland and Wells) and has become incorporated as a factor to assess and deal with in many of today's state-of-the-art models. The emerging bodies of knowledge in biology, genetics, and neuroscience influence the most recent models of family intervention in a multitude of ways. These include: suggesting risk factors to mitigate through intervention, as in the treatments designed to reduce expressed emotion in the treatment of families with members with severe mental illness (e.g., see the chapter by McFarland in this volume), suggesting solutions such as medication, as in the use of stimulants as part of the treatment of Attention-Deficit Disorder in children (see the chapter by Wells in this volume), suggesting ways of helping families understand syndromes through psychoeducation, such as in the treatment of schizophrenia and Bipolar Disorder (see the chapter by McFarland in this volume), and suggesting ways of coping with problematic states of autonomic arousal in processes such as couple conflict (see the chapters by Wooley, Johnson, and B. Baucom, Christensen, & Yi in this volume). The importance of understanding and responding to the biological basis of behavior is most apparent in those treatments dealing with psychological disorders with the strongest biological bases for disorder (e.g., those dealing with severe mental illness and Attention-Deficit Disorder), but also is apparent across a wide range of difficulties, including medical disorders such as juvenile diabetes and congestive heart failure, and even in everyday normal couple and family process. It's also notable that when Minuchin and colleagues wrote *Psychosomatic Families* (Minuchin, Rosman, & Baker, 1978), the focus at that time in the interface between biology and family was on the influence of family on biology; today's approaches are as likely to work with the important understandings from the biology of such diseases as juvenile diabetes (e.g., see the chapter in this volume by Pisani & McDaniel).

Behavioral and social psychological understandings have also become well established and integrated into the majority of these models. The last 20 years has seen the emergence of a far better grasp of the patterns of learning and of social exchange that occur in families, and how they impact on family process. Classical conditioning, operant conditioning, modeling, covert processes of learning, and social psychological principles of exchange have all clearly emerged as central processes in shaping the lives of family members. And the understandings of the importance of these processes has led to the development of numerous interventions that draw on behavioral and social psychological principles that have been proven to have considerable impact. Technologies for helping with specific interpersonal skill sets in couples and families, such as communication, intimacy, problem solving, and social exchange, that have been part of clinical practice for many years, have been refined and augmented. These intervention strategies stand as key ingredients in almost all of the state-of-the-art methods in family therapy.

Individual psychological process is also a focus for intervention in most of these approaches. Cognition and affect are crucial human processes and powerfully impact on each of the various difficulties addressed in this volume. As a result, cognitive and affect-focused interventions are typically part of today's state-of-the-art approaches. Numerous approaches accentuate working with cognitions through examining thoughts (e.g., see the chapter in this volume by B. Baucom, Christensen, & Yi) and several prominent approaches (e.g., see the chapters in this volume by Wooley, Johnson, and Diamond) focus on methods centered on processing affect. And whereas traditional psychodynamic viewpoints are encountered less often today than a generation ago, the essential core psychodynamic notions of the importance of working through individual past history and inner conflicts, and of establishing working alliances with all family members, can be found in most approaches (e.g., see the chapter by Fishbane).

Applying Generic Strategies of Change

Although the technology for approaching problems grows and becomes more refined each year, paradoxically most of the state-of-the-art methods in family therapy today draw from the same generic set of methods. Although the theoretical lens focusing across these approaches and the language for describing the methods for intervention may vary, almost all of these approaches include strategies that work with family structure; strategies that are based on behavioral principles of learning, exchange, and task assignment; strategies that work with cognitions, narratives, or attributions; strategies based in psychoeducation; strategies for working with affect; and strategies for working with meaning. The specific interventions utilized to carry out these strategies similarly draw from a generic catalog of interventions.

Accenting Broad Curative Factors

Today's state-of-the-art approaches don't simply accentuate technique, but also emphasize the creation of the so-called non-specific conditions for change in psychotherapy. Almost all of these approaches emphasize such factors as enabling client engagement, building alliances with each family member, and the creation of hope and positive expectations for change. Almost without exception, these approaches look to build strong treatment alliances as a key ingredient in treatment. A transcendent understanding has emerged—treatments can only be as effective as they are able to engage clients. Some of these approaches, such as Brief Strategic Family Therapy, described in this volume by Horigian and colleagues, and the Outcome-Informed approach of Miller and colleagues center a considerable part of their methods on alliance building, and have offered significant refinements in creating alliances. Clearly, couple and family therapies can only be effective if alliances can be created and maintained that enable participation in therapy.

Shaping Strategies Relative to Specific Difficulties

Another core characteristic of these approaches is that they shape strategies of change in relation to the core difficulty or life issue that is in focus. Increasingly, family approaches are grounded in the ecological nexus of the problem area to which they are addressed. Although these methods build from a generic set of strategies and techniques, those strategies and techniques are adapted in relation to the knowledge available about the particular problem area. For example, although psychoeducation is an important intervention in many of the therapies described in this volume, the specific focus of psychoeducation and the content of that psychoeducation will vary with the problem. And, so will the expected affective states likely to be encountered, the behavioral skills likely to be deficient and useful to augment, the most typical problems with family structure and the most useful interventions for working with that structure, and the most helpful cognitive formulations, potential narratives, and reframes. The present state-of-the-art methods of intervention have developed following idiosyncratic pathways, but in almost every instance these models have evolved out of some sort of dialectic between a broad conceptual framework and the pragmatics of working with a particular focal problem.

Labeling Problems

In today's state-of-the-art approaches, problems are labeled as problems, but sensitivity is maintained regarding the social meaning of labels. The early models of family therapy largely took an ideological stand against the existence of "individual" problems. In the wake of the version of systems theory then popular, clients with difficulties were seen as "identified patients," that is, the carrier of the symptoms of the problem for the system (Minuchin, 1974; Whitaker, 1992). Today's approaches almost never speak of an identified patient. Instead, the individual or individuals who bear problems are viewed as having an individual difficulty, even if there is some basis for that problem in the social system (e.g., see Gupta, Beach, & Coyne's discussion of depression in the context of marital difficulty in this volume). And yet today's state-of-the-art approaches strongly emphasize the context for the generation and maintenance of difficulty, and make considerable effort to limit the possibly deleterious effects of the labeling of individual difficulties through a careful use of language and a nonjudgmental and sympathetic view of problems. Thus, diagnosis has a role in these approaches, but it is a kinder, gentler diagnosis.

Building on Empirical Foundations

Today's state-of-the-art strategies of change are based in empirical knowledge about families and the problem area in focus, and empirically testing the efficacy of the approach to intervention. Today's state-of-the-art methods are anchored in the empirical knowledge available about family processes, individual development, individual personality and psychopathology, and about the particular life circumstance around which the approach has been honed. These approaches are heir to several decades of research assessing broadly applicable principles of family and individual process and assessing those family and individual processes in the context of specific life circumstances. And, almost all of the state-of-the-art models in family therapy are the product of a honing of these methods through clinical and research testing, and are in the process of being clinically tested.

Perhaps the most prominent finding that serves as the foundation for these methods is the now very well-established relationship between family functioning and individual functioning, cited in almost every chapter of this volume—one of the most replicated findings in psychological research. Yet, the body of findings that provides the basis for these methods moves well beyond those documenting this simple relationship. We are now heir to a great deal of prominent research that describes the complex relationships within families in the context of various relational difficulties, life transitions, and individual disorders. This research has informed today's approaches about the typical ways problems develop, the ways problems are maintained, and the pathways that distinguish movement toward greater difficulty or resilience. As an example, the various approaches to the treatment of adolescent delinquency, substance use disorder, and other acting out delineated in this volume are the heir to the complex understandings of such processes developed by Paterson and others over three decades (Dishion & Patterson, 1999).

Today's state-of-the-art approaches are far from simplistic renditions of the old syllogism that all individual problems must be rooted in family difficulty. Instead, reflecting the contemporary understanding of these issues, families are primarily seen as potential resources for helping with problems and developmental challenges, rather than as the cause of these problems. And, the specific mechanisms that have been identified in the basic research on couple and families often have become the focus for intervention, be those mechanisms parental monitoring of child behavior, parental structure, parental depression, couple attachment, or couple communication.

It is also becoming clear that for treatment approaches to make claims for effectiveness, these approaches must be demonstrated to be efficacious through empirical testing. Most of the approaches in this volume have a strong base of empirical testing that not only demonstrates efficacy but has allowed for the rehaping of methods in relation to the data that emerge. In summary, the evidence offered for the impact of couple and family approaches in relation to a wide range of specific individual and relational difficulties points to the considerable evidence for their impact for couple and family therapy (Sprenkle, 2002).

Today's family therapy can be more scientific because of the emergence of a true science of couple and family relationships. Research now has vital implications for practice, which it did not have a generation ago. Striking developments in the world of research have important implications for methods of practice. The sources of this change include:

1. *An increase in the volume of research.* The quantity of research in family psychology has vastly expanded over the last 20 years. Whereas earlier there were very few findings in family psychology that were well established enough to affect intervention, there are innumerable, highly usable findings that can help guide clinical practice and public policy.

2. *More research on both broad aspects of family process and on specific disorders and/or problems.* There is one tradition in family research that begins with the family and another that begins with the individual. In the former, the primary focus is on a family process (for example, cohesion) and its effect in the individual. In the latter, the research is anchored in an individual issue or problem, such as depression, and family variables are examined in relation to that problem. What we see in current research is a coming together of the two approaches. Whether the figure is the individual or the family, the same family processes are now studied, typically utilizing similar methodologies, and the findings about the relationship between the individual and the family are remarkably consistent.

3. *A general acceptance of the power of the circular relationship between family process and individual functioning.* In every area of investigation, the importance of the relationship between family process and individual functioning has become well established. If there was a clinical trial about whether the family and the individual affect one another powerfully in their ongoing mutual influence, that trial could be stopped, since the findings so consistently point in this direction.

4. *Attention to the importance of other systems.* Early research in families ignored systems other than the family. Today's research considers the impact of a range of systems, including peers and aspects of the macrosystem in which the family is situated.

5. *Much-improved methodology.* Perhaps the most marked change in research relevant to couple and family therapy is the vast improvement in the technology in the research. Family research has now been underway for over 40 years, and with that time span have come the development of the infrastructure of instruments and methods (and, one might add, investigators) that could speak to the complexities involved in this research. Measures take many years to develop and refine. The breadth of investigation in family psychology now provides numerous measures and procedures for assessing complex family processes. And, the technology for studying interpersonal process and for the complex statistical analyses needed for studying sequential processes have vastly improved over that time.

6. *Multimethod research.* The research in family psychology has moved more and more to a multitrait multimethod matrix. It is no longer unusual for a range of methods to be utilized in a single study with a range of focuses, some on the individual and some on the family. Quantitative and sophisticated qualitative methods are also mixed readily. For example, in Gottman's landmark research (Gottman, 1994) on couples, complex analyses of couples' behaviors are derived from ratings of interactions, augmented with physiological measures and a qualitative life history taken from the subjects.

7. *Patience.* Some aspects of family process can only be studied over time and, unfortunately (unlike fruit flies), generations of families require over 15 years (and sometimes over 40!). Research in family psychology now has the good fortune to begin to benefit from the information from longitudinal studies conducted over generations. Studies like those of the Oregon Social Learning group, led by Gerald Patterson, have now been ongoing for 40 years (Patterson & Fagot, 1967).

8. *Increasing links between process research and treatment research.* There was a time when the questions about family process bore little relation to the questions asked in treatment research. Today, in contrast, we see far greater linkage. The processes that evolve in research on families become the focus of treatment, and the treatment research informs the family process as well. As an example, Gupta, Beach, and Coyne's chapter in this volume highlights how research suggesting the linkage between depression and family process has crucial meaning for treatment development, and how treatment research that is conducted feeds back into the base of information about this problematic constellation.

9. *Research grounded in theory.* Research does not occur in a vacuum. The best research is anchored in relation to theory. Although there have always been theories about the essential processes in families, the development of theories grounded in empirical findings requires the iteration between theory and research that only can occur over time. Early in the history of family therapy, numerous theories were suggested. Some of them have turned out to be entirely wrong, such as the double bind theory of schizophrenia (Bateson, Jackson, Haley, & Weakland, 1956) or the psychosomatic family theory stated by Minuchin and colleagues (Minuchin, Rosman, & Baker, 1978), while others have emerged as remarkably accurate, such as Minuchin's

theory of family structure (Minuchin, 1974). At this time, we are seeing the blossoming of theories grounded in research that can help guide treatment development.

10. *An awareness of cultural diversity.* The issue of external validity was once the Achilles' heel in family research. Findings would be presented and conclusions drawn, only to be followed by the belated understanding that the subjects in the research were all middle-class caucasian-Americans, severely truncating the meaning of the conclusions drawn. Issues around the generalizability of findings remain. Funds are often limited for research and study samples are small. But we are at least seeing a broad acknowledgment of the problem, and we are seeing many more efforts to examine processes in diverse populations.

11. *A focus on prevention.* Research that identifies family processes related to the emergence of difficulties easily translates into mandates for programs designed to ameliorate these processes. We've seen the emergence of many such programs, and the research emerging from prevention programs has contributed to the knowledge base about intervention.

Maintaining A Multisystemic Focus

Drawing on the term Henggeller (Henggeler, Schoenwald, Borduin, Rowland, & Cunningham, 1998) uses to describe his specific approach, today's state-of-the-art strategies maintain a multisystemic focus. Instead of centering only on the family, these approaches extend their view to other systems as well, and to a range of system levels: individual, couple or other dyad, nuclear family, multigenerational family, and macrosystems, such as schools and community. Intervention typically focuses on multiple levels, and sometimes the family is not the principal focus for intervention. And yet these are family approaches. Family intervention is in the fabric of each method of intervention, and in most cases the family is the principal vehicle for the change process.

Maintaining a Realistic Frame

These approaches build a realistic frame for the change process. Some approaches to psychotherapy are highly optimistic, suggesting that change is a simple, easy process. Other approaches are more pessimistic, emphasizing the difficulties in changing deeply rooted problems. The earliest family therapies were accompanied by strong statements about the power of homeostasis, incumbent in the system, to derail the change process (Haley, 1963). Later versions of systems theory grafted the more optimistic core of humanistic therapy to family treatment. This generation of approaches finds a midpoint, able to both recognize the difficulty in changing some conditions (e.g., marital distress, major mental illness, adolescent substance abuse), yet possess the optimism that change can occur, given an effective approach.

Enhancing the Durability of Change

Today's state-of-the-art approaches emphasize concern about achieving lasting change. Family approaches have proven to be highly effective, but, like all other approaches in mental health treatment, have been shown to have difficulties in the maintenance of such a change over time (Lebow & Gurman, 1995). The kinds of approaches summarized in this volume typically build on this understanding, looking for ways to actively work to maintain change. Often, processes intended to maintain treatment gains by setting tasks for the time after termination are invoked to reduce recidivism.

Length of Treatment

Almost invariably, today's state-of-the-art treatments are time limited. As Alan Gurman has noted, family therapy is by its nature a short-term therapy, given the need for multiple family members to make themselves available for treatment over time (Gurman, 2001). Yet, these therapies are also a far cry from the talk of one- or two-session cures of a generation ago. Most of these therapies look to a time frame of 3 to 12 months for intervention. And in the face of severe problems, some therapies, in order to achieve their goals, are enormously intensive (e.g., Multisystemic Therapy), while others look to ways to structure client engagement that promote continuing self-help over longer periods (as in the multifamily groups described in this volume by McFarland).

Stages of Change

Another frequent theme in these approaches is working with some notion of client readiness to change. Clients differ in many ways; one of the most important is where they are in what Prochaska and DiClemente have termed "stages of change" (Prochaska, Norcross, & DiClemente, 1995). Prochaska and colleagues differentiate those who didn't realize they had a problem (*in precontemplation*), those who realized they had a problem but were not yet ready to do something about it (*in contemplation*), those who were actively trying to change (*in action*), and those working to keep the changes they had already undergone (*in maintenance*). Although some of the approaches in this volume explicitly refer to Prochaska and DiClemente's stages while others do not, most of these approaches share an implicit focus to look to different ways to intervene with people at different points along this continuum.

Mixing Individual, Couple, and Family Session Formats

Today's cutting-edge methods mix individual, couple, and family session formats. Twenty-first-century approaches are highly pragmatic in defining who is seen in treatment at various points. Whereas earlier generations of therapy reified certain formats for therapy as the most useful therapy format, with some family therapists even refusing to see subsystems when the whole family was not available (Whitaker & Napier, 1977), contemporary approaches mostly mix session formats, accentuating the best use of various formats for various kinds of work. Paired with this mix are both pragmatic and ethical understandings of the meanings of mixing session formats, so as to reduce the likelihood of iatrogenic effects of such blends.

A More Limited Worldview

These approaches, although based solidly on evidence, tend to be more humble than their progenitors and to have a less grandiose worldview. The modernist concept of one solution for all has been replaced with the more limited notion of working at problem areas and life difficulties and achieving growth. The specter of those clients for whom goals remain unmet, despite the best efforts of the therapist, remains omnipresent, leading to a greater awareness of the difficulties in the task at hand.

Understanding and Building on Personal Narratives

Twenty-first-century family therapies have moved beyond the vision of the family as an entity to include a focus on understanding the individual narratives of family members and to ensure that all members of the family can be heard. Some of this thread in family therapy emerges from the strong postmodern influence in the field, but as much can be traced to simple pragmatics; if family members don't feel heard, they don't engage in strong alliances, or do as well in achieving treatment goals (see, for example, the chapters in this volume by Fishbane and Becvar).

Utilizing Solution-Oriented Language

Solution-oriented language and reframes that help family members more readily accept directives and that diminish resistance to change are almost universally included in these approaches. The product of generations of research in social psychology and clinical experience with families, such framings help increase client motivation to change and increase the likelihood of treatment success (see, for example, the chapter in this volume by Sexton and Alexander).

Building on Family Strengths

Today's state-of-the-art family therapies consider strengths as much as liabilities (Walsh, 1998). Whereas an earlier generation of family therapies were predicated on accentuating family difficulties, most of these approaches clearly identify and build on client strengths.

Considering Client Goals

Today's state-of-the-art approaches accentuate client goals. People enter family therapy for a variety of reasons. Many do so to solve individual problems, such as the behavior of an adolescent. Others do so to resolve a family crisis or negotiate a transition in family development. Some of the chapters in this book emphasize using family therapy to help resolve individual difficulties, often as one method in a multimethod treatment. Other chapters accentuate changing family process. In general, these approaches are highly responsive to client goals.

Tracking Outcomes

Although Miller, Mee-Lee, Plum, and Hubble alone in this volume describe a specific technology for tracking and feeding back outcome information to clients as therapy progresses, explicitly focusing on client outcome is a core ingredient of most of these models. As Miller and his colleagues point out in their chapter, tracking outcomes improves the levels of success in psychotherapy.

Attachment

Attachment is an explicit focus in only a few of the models in this volume—most prominently, Diamond's approach, aimed at childhood depression, and Wooley and Johnson's Emotionally Focused Couples Therapy. Yet, working toward stable attachments that support family members is also a generic goal shared by most twenty-first-century approaches. Attachment is the foundation of the relational nexus that makes the family a healing entity rather than a source of stress.

Attending to Culture

One of the major insights of the last 20 years in the field of family therapy has been the vast importance that culture has on the process and outcome of therapy. Families live in different cultures, and the same intervention may have vastly different meanings to families from differing backgrounds. State-of-the-art methods in family therapy are also very much informed by an understanding of culture. Clearly, culture makes for vast differences in what constitutes normal family life and what constitutes health and pathology. In many of these approaches, specific methods have been developed in the context of particular cultures for working with those cultures (e.g., see the chapter by Horrigian et al. in this volume).

Ethical Considerations

Family therapy is by its nature more complex than other forms of intervention. With more people participating, there are additional difficult decisions about who to regard as the client, about confidentiality, about goal setting, and about innumerable other issues (Margolin, 1982). Contemporary family therapies don't simply describe how to intervene—they think about and offer suggestions about how to deal with these dilemmas. And, while in some instances there are simple answers to questions of ethics (e.g., clients are each entitled to confidentiality), in many instances there are no perfect answers to such complex questions. What is essential is that family therapists understand the ethical issues likely to emerge and be thoughtful about their resolution.

CONCLUSION: TOWARD ONE FAMILY THERAPY

Family therapy is becoming more a single therapy than any time since its beginning. In their early reviews of research on family therapy, Gurman and Kniskern (Gurman & Kniskern, 1992) pointed out that there were family therapies rather than a method that might be called family therapy. They suggested that the striking differences in approach across treatments rendered it less useful to group these treatments together as if they constituted one entity. Although that logic certainly aptly described family therapy as conducted at that time, today's state-of-the-art family therapy is moving much closer to being a generic therapy with a shared foundation adapted to particular contexts.

With the movement toward the utilization of multimethod strategies for intervention that cross the boundaries of schools of family therapy, the emergence of what now can much better be regarded as a single family therapy, in which there are multiple variants, seems much more appropriate than at any time since the earliest beginnings of family treatment, before there were schools of family therapy. And though the boundaries between couple and family therapy have grown as a product of the ways these methods are presented as separate entities in course-work, workshops, and writing, the methods employed in couple and family therapy show much more resemblance to one another than differences. Clearly, there are aspects of couple and of family therapy that are unique to one of these domains (e.g., sex as an aspect of couple therapy), but the similarities in focus, strategies of intervention, and techniques vastly outweigh differences across most of today's current methods.

To point out the emerging common ground shared by this new generation of family therapies is not to suggest there aren't differences between family therapies. For example, in as complex an endeavor as family therapy there will always be outliers who work from very different positions. And a close reading of the approaches in this volume will uncover numerous differences, even among the approaches included here, but the emerging commonalities far outweigh those differences.

This emerging consensus stands in contrast to the family therapies of earlier eras. In that era, there were numerous competing systems for understanding and intervening in couples and families. Each of these systems accentuated a different aspect of family life. Whether the goal was to impact on the structural foundation of the family, to develop a rapier-sharp intervention strategy, to differentiate individual selves from the family, to connect with family, to leave home, to fully experience, to establish fairness in the balance of power, or to explore the inner selves of the psychodynamics of family members depended on the view of the beholder. Strong opinions existed, leading to many acrimonious arguments. Following in the psychoanalytic tradition of dueling institutes, training accentuated how to work according to the model of a particular master therapist rather than how to work with particular kinds of clients. Little research was also brought to bear in relation to these questions. Persuasion and charismatic charm were the major forces in generating a school of approach.

A footnote here; in describing the strengths of the new generation of family therapies, I do not mean to minimize the contribution of that first generation of pioneers of couple and family therapy who created this field of endeavor. It is much easier to bring tools of analysis and assimilation to a method after its central core thesis has become well established. When the first generation of couple and family therapists began to develop their methods, they were heirs to a 100 years of focus on the individual. Almost no one thought in terms of family process, or grasped the vital importance of the social nexus to the inner lives of individuals. Juxtaposing the systemic and cybernetic metaphors from physics and biology to families was nothing short of a paradigm shift, and the resistance to this shift in the world outside of the community of family therapists was powerful. The present generation of the kinds of family therapies described in this volume could only be constructed building on the foundations of the systemic insights of the earlier generations of therapists.

And what ideas! The core systemic understanding was nothing less than one of the brilliant insights of the twentieth century. Thousands of research studies have subsequently confirmed the central wisdom of noticing how people are affected by the social system in which they live, and how the behaviors of individuals have profound effects on the behaviors of others, at least in part influenced by circular causal pathways. And there probably is no single idea, strategy, or intervention in this volume that was not in some shape or form stated in the early writings and presentations of those pioneers. Both the theoretical concepts invoked (for example, the importance of structure in families) and the techniques most frequently described in this volume, such as reframing, communication training, alliance building, and challenging cognitions can all be traced back to an origin in this earlier potpourri of approaches.

What was missing, however, from this early generation of therapies was the ability to borrow from one another, to engage in an iteration with individual personality and psychopathology, and to explore the realm of how approaches work in the context of specific problems. Pride and belief in the ultimate wisdom of their particular approach—and the needs that evolved from trying to build a constituency for a family viewpoint—transcended all else. There was little search for common ground, or testing and shaping of approaches in specific contexts. The transcendent, core belief was that in helping resolve the central aspect of family life that was in focus in a particular approach, all would change around it.

The approaches in this volume have been built on the foundations of those earlier approaches and these current methods are both more comprehensive and more limited. Twenty-first-century family approaches have been able to integrate and sift the powerful ideas and methods offered by their progenitors. And they have had the additional advantage of drawing from the accumulated knowledge of the last quarter century and the empirical testing of methods that could occur over that period of time. It is an exciting time in the field of family therapy, in which we can point to a diversity of successful methods for helping those with range of difficulties, in addition to an underlying set of strategies and techniques and understandings about families that transcend the specific problem or method in focus.

REFERENCES

Bateson, G., Jackson, D. D., Haley, J., & Weakland, J. (1956). Toward a theory of schizophrenia. *Behavioral Science, 1,* 251–264.

Bowen, M. (1966). The use of family theory in clinical practice. *Comprehensive Psychiatry, 7,* 345–374.

Dishion, T. J., & Patterson, G. R. (1999). Model building in developmental psychopathology: A pragmatic approach to understanding and intervention. *Journal of Clinical Child Psychology, 28,* 502–512.

Goldner, V. (1998). The treatment of violence and victimization in intimate relationships. *Family Process, 37,* 263–286.

Gottman, J. M. (1994). *What predicts divorce? The relationship between marital processes and marital outcomes.* Hillsdale, NJ: Lawrence Erlbaum Associates.

Gurman, A. S. (2001). Brief therapy and family/couple therapy: An essential redundancy. *Clinical Psychology: Science and Practice, 8,* 51–65.

Gurman, A. S., & Kniskern, D. P. (1992). The future of marital and family therapy. *Psychotherapy, 29,* 65–71.

Haley, J. (1963). *Strategies of psychotherapy.* New York: Grune & Stratton.

Haley, J. (1997). *Leaving home: The therapy of disturbed young people* (2nd ed.). Philadelphia: Brunner/Mazel.

Henggeler, S. W., Schoenwald, S. K., Borduin, C. M., Rowland, M. D., & Cunningham, P. B. (1998). *Multisystemic treatment of antisocial behavior in children and adolescents.* New York: Guilford.

Lebow, J. L., & Gurman, A. S. (1995). Research assessing couple and family therapy. *Annual Review of Psychology, 46,* 27–57.

Margolin, G. (1982). Ethical and legal considerations in marital and family therapy. *American Psychologist, 37,* 788–802.

Minuchin, S. (1974). *Families and family therapy.* Cambridge, MA: Harvard University Press.

Minuchin, S., Rosman, B. L., & Baker, L. (1978). *Psychosomatic families: Anorexia nervosa in context.* Cambridge, MA: Harvard University Press.

Patterson, G. R., & Fagot, B. I. (1967). Selective responsiveness to social reinforcers and deviant behavior in children. *Psychological Record, 17,* 369–378.

Pinsof, W. M., & Lebow, J. L. (Eds.). (2005). *Family psychology: The art of the science.* New York: Oxford.

Prochaska, J. O., Norcross, J. C., & DiClemente, C. C. (1995). *Changing for good.* New York: Avon.

Snyder, D. K. & Whismon, M. A. (Eds.). (2003). *Treating difficult couples.* New York: Guilford.

Sprenkle, D. H. (Ed.). (2002). *Effectiveness research in marriage and family therapy.* Alexandria, VA: American Association for Marriage and Family Therapy.

Walsh, F. (1998). *Strengthening family resilience.* New York: Guilford.

Whitaker, C. A. (1992). Symbolic experiential family therapy: Model and methodology. In Zeig, J. K. (Ed)., *The evolution of psychotherapy: The second conference* (pp. 13–23). Philadelphia: Brunner/Mazel.

Whitaker, C. A., & Napier, A. Y. (1977). Process techniques of family therapy. *Interaction, 1,* 4–19.

PART I

Problems in Children and Adolescents

CHAPTER 2

Attachment-Based Family Therapy for Depressed and Anxious Adolescents

Guy S. Diamond

―――――――――――――― **Case Study** ――――――――――――――

Sally is a 14-year-old, referred by a psychiatrist who in frustration recently changed her diagnosis from Major Depression to Bipolar Disorder and started her on a course of lithium. School failure, family conflict, intense sibling rivalry, and a fascination with death-rock music were increasing. Six months ago the depression had remitted somewhat, so Sally's psychiatrists recommended that the mother make more behavioral demands about school performance and cooperation at home. Conflict and isolation escalated.

Sally, her 16-year-old sister, and her mother attended the first therapy session. She wore all-black, heavy eye make-up, a metal choker, and several piercings in her ears. For the first 20 minutes she remained silent, only making insinuating gestures and groans of disagreement while the mother compassionately complained about her daughter's unpredictable behavior, indifference about school, fascination with death, and her own frustration over her failure to help her daughter.

Hoping to redirect the conversation from a focus on Sally to shared family struggles, the therapist asked about the father's death 10 years ago. Sally immediately asserted that she was glad he died, which raised protests from her sister and mother. Once the therapist showed some sincere interest in Sally's feelings about her father, Sally revealed that the father had become a depressed alcoholic who physically abused her mother. After some minimizing statements, the mother admitted to the violence and how bad things had been. The therapist pointed out that Sally's hatred toward her dad also expressed protectiveness toward her mom. Over this, Sally began to cry and express worries about her mom, then and now. The mother seemed uncomfortable with her daughter's empathy toward her. Perceiving her mother's discomfort, Sally returned to complaining about the father. The therapist redirected Sally back to her more vulnerable feelings by noting how hard it was to show love and concern for her mom. Sally's mood softened again and she began to discuss how they had grown apart, and rarely spent time together. Mother said she assumed her daughter was no longer interested in that, to which Sally responded, "I will never be too old for that." At this juncture, the therapist complimented Sally's willingness to discuss difficult issues that others wanted to avoid and punctuated Sally's feelings of missing her mom. The therapist also empathized with the mother's confusion about how to be close to her daughter while also establishing expectations. Finally, the therapist suggested that the first goal of treatment focus on getting reconnected with each other. This way, they would understand each other better, not feel so alone, and Sally would have someone to talk to when she was depressed or suicidal. Both the mother and Sally agreed to this initial treatment focus.

This first session embodies many of the principles and goals of attachment- based family therapy (ABFT; Diamond, G. S., Reis, B. F., Diamond, G. M., Siqueland, & Isaacs, 2002). Depressed adolescents usually come to therapy feeling hopeless, alone, and angry at their parents for misunderstanding their despair. Parents, with their own ambivalence about, and struggle with, attachment and intimacy, feel frustrated over their failure to help their child. However, the generationally-shared wounds caused by attachment failures are often obscured by conflicts over behavioral problems. It is safer to argue about chores or homework than abuse, abandonment, and/or neglect. Even families that display closeness and open communication struggle with maintaining these strengths in the face of a major depressive episode. Identifying and discussing relational ruptures, and the painful emotions associated with them, creates an experience of shared vulnerability and authenticity that can rekindle the natural desire for attachment (adolescent) and caregiving (parent). Empathic, nonaccusatory conversations about attachment failures become the context for teaching and practicing more effective conflict management and affect regulation skills, expressing contrition and forgiveness, and renewing trust between family members.

This chapter provides a brief overview of the ABFT approach. It begins with a description of the theoretical foundations of the model. Then, a detailed description of the five treatment tasks, along with the logic underlying each, is provided. Empirical support for ABFT with depressed adolescents is briefly reviewed. Next, the adaptation of ABFT to working with anxious adolescents is offered, and preliminary pilot data are presented. Because ABFT has been tested primarily with inner-city African American clients, this chapter also provides a brief discussion of some cultural issues that inform the application of the model. We conclude with a brief summary of the next few sessions of the case previously presented.

THE THEORETICAL BASE

Attachment Theory

Attachment Theory (Bowlby, 1969) offers an alternative theory base to general systems or cybernetic theory for understanding the interpersonal dynamics of family life. These models were critical in helping therapists shift their focus from individuals to systems and from symptoms to interaction. While revolutionary at the time, these theories assumed that families functioned as biological or mechanical systems. Family therapists in search of more relationship-based models have turned to attachment theory to better explain human motivations, emotions, and behaviors (Johnson & Whiffen, 2003; Wood, 2002).

Attachment theory rests on the assumption that a child's sense of security in life depends on parents being available and protective. When a parent appropriately responds to this need, the child generally develops a secure attachment style. This attachment/caregiving system is essential for survival and thus is a hardwired, biological instinct. While much of the attachment research has focused on infants and young children, the importance of appropriate attachment throughout the lifespan has been well-theorized and documented (Ainsworth, 1989; Steinberg, 1990). For adolescents in particular, secure attachment nurtures healthy development, while insecure attachment has repeatedly been associated with depression and other kinds of functional problems (Kobak & Sceery, 1988; Rosenstein & Horowitz, 1996).

For adolescents, attachment is maintained (and possibly revived) when three interpersonal elements exist. Adolescents must feel they have access to caregivers when needed. They must also feel free to openly communicate without the fear of rejection or judgment. And, adolescents must feel that parents can protect them, not just from physical harm, but from emotional harm as well (Kobak, Sudler & Gamble, 1991). When these conditions are met, adolescents are more likely to feel secure and safe. With this foundation in place, adolescents show greater autonomy seeking behavior, positive peer relations, and higher self-esteem (Allen & Land, 1999). They also freely express negative or vulnerable emotions (e.g., fear, anger, distress) with the expectation of acceptance and comfort, rather than criticism and abandonment. In fact, Kobak and Duemmler (1994) found that secure attachment leads to more direct communication, which fosters perspective-taking and problem-solving skills. In this regard, adolescent attachment theory parallels the now empirically supported view that an appropriate balance of connection to and independence from the family is the central task of adolescent development (Allen & Land, 1999).

One challenge in an attachment-based family intervention approach is in building the parents' capacity for providing security-promoting parenting. Many parents of depressed adolescents were denied adequate parenting as children and consequently have insecure attachment styles themselves. These parents often feel ambivalent, anxious, or incapable of providing comfort, soothing, and reassurance. In these families, the expression of negative, vulnerable feelings is unwelcome and unsafe. When caretakers are unavailable and/or unresponsive, particularly at critical moments, they can become a source of emotional injury rather than a foundation of safety and support (Kobak & Mandelbaum, 2003).

Lacking confidence in the safety of interpersonal relationships, adolescents fail to develop effective problem-solving skills. Instead of addressing conflict and disappointment directly, they protect themselves with conflict avoidance, denial, and other cognitive distortions. Emotional energy becomes preoccupied with preserving fragile and dysfunctional relationships. In fact, depressed adolescents often protect parents from angry or sad feelings, fearing that honesty would overburden their parents or lead to further rejection (Diamond & Siqueland, 1998). Consequently, adolescents express anger about core attachment failures indirectly, through conflicts over day-to-day behavioral problems (e.g., chores, curfew, or other issues). Depressed adolescents also have a tendency to blame themselves for these attachment failures, and view themselves as unworthy of love and affection. This can promote a negative schema of self and others, putting them at greater risk for depression (Cicchetti, Toth & Lynch, 1995).

Repairing Attachment

In contrast to the psychoanalytic tradition, Bowlby posited that internal working models, although persistent, were open to revision across the lifespan (Bowlby, 1969, 1988; Waters, Kondo-Ikemura, Posada & Richters, 1991). Not only can negative life experience damage one's felt security, but positive life experience can help rebuild it. Several studies have now found that good parenting, a loving marriage, or a positive therapeutic experience increases one's sense of felt security (Cicchetti & Greenberg, 1991; Weinfeld, Sroufe, & Egelund, 2000). Main and Goldwyn (1988) characterized this process as "earned security." Individuals victimized by negative parenting can earn security by working through and "coming to terms" with these experiences. Interestingly, adults with earned security remain as susceptible to depression as adults with insecure attachment styles, but they have parenting practices similar to adults with secure attachment thereby. Good parenting thus buffers against the negative impact of the parents' depression (Pearson, Cohn, Cowan & Cowan, 1994). In this way, parents or adolescents who can resolve these attachment failures can develop interpersonal skills and strengths that promote healthier living.

While adult attachment research has primarily focused on the consequences of negative internal working models, how to earn a secure attachment style has not been well spelled out. Research and theory on forgiveness and trauma resolution provide some insight into this process. The process of forgiveness has been characterized as (1) experiencing strong emotions, (2) giving up the need for redress from the perpetrator, (3) seeing the offender as distinct and separate from one's needs and identity, and (4) developing empathy for the offender (McCullough, Pargament, & Thoresen, 2000). Although ABFT focuses on exoneration rather than forgiveness, these processes characterize many of the therapeutic domains traversed during the attachment task. Herman's (1992) model of trauma recovery also delineates several steps toward resolving trauma experiences. These steps include (1) restoring a sense of control, (2) establishing safety, (3) telling the trauma story in detail, (4) mourning losses, and (5) reconnecting with self and community. ABFT helps family members collaboratively participate in conversations that achieve similar goals.

Studies on adolescent affect regulation and family interaction also offer insights into the process of earned security (Allen, Hauser, & Borman-Spurrell, 1996). In particular, Kobak and Sceery (1988) suggest that while behavioral interactions between parents and children shape early attachment security, given adolescents' emerging cognitive capacity, conversation increasingly becomes the mechanism through which attachment security is experienced and negotiated (Kobak & Duemmler, 1994). Thus, the ABFT model proposes that direct conversations about relational failures may be a key vehicle or mechanism through which family members earn or develop a secure attachment style.

Conversations about relational trauma become the enactment within which families have a corrective attachment experience. Children who have been treated unjustly, be it physical or psychological abuse, internalize a model of self as unworthy of love, and of other as untrustworthy (Bartholomew & Horowitz, 1991). Therefore, rather than appropriately seeking redress for interpersonal injustices, they act out destructively toward themselves or others. Alternatively, helping adolescents identify, articulate, and appropriately talk about these relational ruptures challenges their hopelessness and helplessness, increases their tolerance for emotional conflict, and promotes an appropriate sense of entitlement to healthier relationships. For parents, these conversations offer an opportunity to provide effective caregiving (sensitivity, emotional protection, empathic listening). If successful, these intense, emotionally charged encounters offer an opportunity to provide comfort and protective parenting. This helps the adolescent rebuild trust in the parents' capacity to provide a secure base. In ABFT, like contextual therapy, repairing trust and reestablishing fairness between family members is a primary therapeutic target (Boszormenyi-Nagy & Spark, 1973). These kinds of corrective-attachments, experienced directly with caretakers (and ideally with sustained improvement in parenting behavior), may alter both day-to-day interactions between family members and parents' and adolescents' interpersonal schemas about self and other (see Weinfeld, Sroufe & Egelund, 2000).

CLINICAL FOUNDATION

ABFT is rooted in the structural tradition, with some recasting of the basic concepts. For instance, reestablishing hierarchy in the traditional sense (e.g., parental control) is not the driving theme. Rather, promoting authoritative parenting skills, such as warmth, acceptance, demanding behaviors, and clear expectations (Baumrind, 1991), and a more age-appropriate, mutual communication, serves as one primary treatment goal. Reframing and enactment remain primary intervention strategies. Reframing aims to restructure how patients think about or explain a problem, ideally leading to cognitions that promote more positive behavior. In ABFT, reframing has a specific goal: shifting the family's focus from the patient as the problem to the family as the cure. Enactment may be the most innovative contribution from the structural tradition. Rather than clients resolving interpersonal conflict through transference with the therapist, family therapists facilitate conversations directly between the family members themselves. In ABFT, enactments are engineered to specifically and systematically focus on specific content and affect—family trauma and vulnerable emotions.

Clearly, the most profound impact on ABFT has come from multidimensional family therapy (MDFT), developed by Howard Liddle (Liddle, 1999; Liddle, Dakof, Parker, Diamond, Barrett, & Tejada, 2001). MDFT also emerges from the structural tradition, but brings to family therapy the informative knowledge base of family and clinical psychology. In this regard, interventions in MDFT are informed by research on child and adolescent development and psychopathology, parenting, cognitions, emotions, social learning theory, attachment theory, and other specialty psychological disciplines. This empirical and theoretical orientation provides a new depth and understanding to the change processes involved in family therapy. In many ways, MDFT offers a system of thought about family treatment that can be used to understand any family intervention model. MDFT also provides one of the first developmentally informed approaches to working with adolescents. Traditional structural family therapy focused on establishing parental hierarchy as the first, if not ultimate, goal of therapy. Appreciating the adolescents' developmental need to feel respected and understood, MDFT therapists set out to actively engage adolescents in the treatment processes as the first agenda of treatment (Liddle & Diamond, 1991). Helping adolescents identify problems that are meaningful to them, and helping parents take these concerns seriously, is a hallmark of MDFT and a fundamental principle in ABFT.

Focus on affective engagement, education, and processing is an essential tool in ABFT. In the last decade, many individual and family therapists have begun to write about the importance and use of emotions in therapy. Emotionally focused therapy (EFT; Greenberg & Johnson, 1988) has been at the forefront of understanding and using emotion as the core intervention mechanism. Relying on contemporary research on emotion, EFT therapists assume that while the expression of affect may be cathartic, it is also a primary signaling system that serves a communication function (Greenberg & Safran, 1987). For example, anger usually makes others defensive, and thus creates distance and separation. On the other hand, sadness and pain communicate the need for support and thus can evoke protection and compassion. Clearly, affect and cognition are linked. Core emotions develop in tandem with cognitions that emerge from strong (positive or negative) experiences. Core traumatic experiences generate a cognitive-affective schema that can organize future behavior. Creating conversations where these "hot cognitions" are re-evoked creates a profound learning environment for the inspection, clarification, and modification of these affect-laden, core events.

Hot cognitions arise from core conflicts that drive underlying anger and animosity ("I still hate you for what you did to our family." "If you treated him better, Dad might not have left." "Even though you are sober now, I will never forgive you for being drunk all those years."). When these kinds of affectively charged memories and cognitions haunt the family, avoiding them in therapy may derail or stall treatment. In particular, a focus on behavioral goals (e.g., parental supervision, rules and expectations) often fails if adolescents hold an emotional grudge against their parents for past injustices. In fact, adolescents often use behavioral conflicts to punish parents for past attachment failures and betrayals. Although families often avoid these topics, they usually feel relieved to finally address them in therapy—like the unburdening of a secret that everyone knows but never discusses. In many families, merely identifying and acknowledging these topics helps diffuse tension and distrust.

At the skill-building level, sustained discussion of vulnerable and painful emotions creates a learning environment within which to exercise new interpersonal skills that have been promoted throughout the therapy. Parents have the opportunity to provide empathy, compassion, understanding, and reassurance—the core competencies of attachment-promoting caregiving. Simultaneously, adolescents practice putting emotions into words, addressing difficult problems in a direct and mature manner, tolerating difficult emotions, and discovering that relationships can withstand emotional challenges. In this regard, these conversations create a corrective attachment experience.

Clinical Structure of ABFT

Based on the theoretical formulation previously described, ABFT treatment focuses first on helping the family identify and discuss past and present conflicts that have violated the attachment bond and damaged trust. Once some of these issues have been diffused, if not resolved, the family can serve as a secure base from which to promote adolescent autonomy (e.g., improving school performance and/or attendance, finding a job, developing or returning to social activities). To achieve these goals, five treatment tasks have been developed. A *task* is a discrete episode with a defined set of therapist procedures for addressing specific patient problem states. Tasks may occur in a single session or, if needed, evolve over several sessions. In ABFT, the full or partial success of each task forms a foundation for future tasks (Diamond & Diamond, 2002). Although the ABFT model provides a recommended order and unique structure for each task, implementation requires constant assessment, judgment, and flexibility by the therapist. For example, relationship and trust building can occur between a child and a primary caregiver, be it a single parent, a grandparent, or a foster parent. We briefly summarize the five tasks and then provide more detail on each.

The Relational Reframe Task sets the foundation of treatment by shifting the family's focus from fixing the patients to improving family relationships (Diamond & Siqueland, 1998). *The Adolescent Alliance Building Task* usually occurs alone with the patient in order to strengthen the therapist-patient bond, develop meaningful individual and family-focused treatment goals, and convince the adolescent to discuss core conflicts with his or her parents. *The Parent Alliance Building Task* explores personal stressors and family-of-origin history that may affect parenting (Diamond, Diamond, & Liddle, 2000). When parents feel and receive empathy for their own history of attachment failures, they become more compassionate toward their child's traumas and felt injustices. In this softened state, they are more receptive to learning the emotional coaching parenting skills (Gottman, Katz, & Hooven, 1996) needed to facilitate the attachment-repairing task.

These first three tasks set the foundation for *The Attachment Task* (Diamond & Stern, 2003). In this task, the adolescent discloses his or her concerns, while the parent responds with sensitivity and empathy. Monologue turns to dialogue as adolescent and parent develop a new, more mature capacity for conversation. This discussion fosters mutual acceptance of the other's failings as well as a shared commitment to future respect and communication. Finally, *The Competency Promoting Task* helps the adolescent rebuild his or her life at school and with peers, using the parents as a new, secure base from which the adolescent can explore his or her autonomy and competency.

THE CLINICAL MODEL

Task One: Relational Reframing

The relational reframe shifts the goal of therapy from a focus on blaming the depression or the adolescent as the cause of the problem to strengthening family relationships as the solution to the problem. Essentially, this redefines the initial focus of the therapy, from fixing the child or the depression to rebuilding the adolescent's attachment to parents and reviving parents' caregiving instincts. The intent of the reframe is to develop problem definitions that (1) reduce parental blaming and criticism, (2) increase parental support and concern (e.g., he or she is not a bad kid but a sad kid), and (3) put the responsibility for change on all family members.

Helping family members accept relationship building as the initial goal of treatment can be a formidable task. Parents often want to blame their child (e.g., he or she is lazy, mean, or selfish) or view depression as an excuse for negative behavior. Even when parents understand the depression, they often assume they have little ability or responsibility for changing it (i.e., "It's a medical problem. He should just take his medicine."). Simultaneously, the adolescent's depression reinforces isolation, distrust, and indifference, mood states that thwart relationship building. Adolescents also complain that parents are impatient, controlling, critical, and overbearing. More importantly, long-standing interpersonal conflicts and attachment failures have often resulted in deep-seated resentment and disappointment. Consequently, many adolescents have given up on having a relationship with their parents, either out of resentment or self-protection. Given these dynamics, parents and adolescents are, at best, ambivalent about reattachment. Therefore, the process of developing this therapeutic agenda must be focused and strategic.

The initial session follows many of the procedures and goals that characterize many family therapy models. These goals begin with building multiple alliances. First, the therapist must help each family member feel that his or her unique opinions and needs will be taken seriously. Second, the session or task focuses on reframing the problem definition. In general, reframing refers to helping the family develop a more constructive definition of the problem that brought them to therapy. For ABFT, reframing specifically refers to helping the family adopt a more systemic or relational goal for the therapy. Rather than fixing the patients, treatment will focus on repairing family trust and communication. This goal is framed as the family's initial step toward helping the adolescent manage and reduce depression and suicide ideation. Finally, the session should end with the establishment of a therapy contract. This is essentially a punctuation of the reframe; the family members agree to work on rebuilding relationships.

Typically, the therapist begins the session by orienting the family to the overall therapy process and specific goals for the first session. Clarity about the structure, the timeline, and the expected goals of treatment convey competency and authority. Families want to work with therapists who know what they are doing. The therapist then focuses on joining and getting acquainted with each family member. Time is spent talking with each family member about his or her individual lives, independent of the problems that brought them to therapy (e.g., work, hobbies, relationships). These questions help the family begin to feel comfortable, acknowledge that families are more than just their problems, and reveal interesting details about family members that can be used later in treatment.

With a clear shift in intention, the therapist then elicits a description of the problems that have brought the family to treatment. Initially, the therapist focuses on fact finding: the specifics of the depression, when it started, who has been involved, the most recent events, and previous attempts to manage the problem. The therapist must always have a systemic perspective in mind and focus on how the quality of relationships and patterns of interaction contribute to the depression. For example, the therapist might ask each family member his or her opinions about what different family members do and feel in response to the depression. The therapist also tries to examine and gather information about the wider context of both the family's problems and supports. The therapist asks about the family's involvement with extended family, church, school, community, social services, and the legal system.

Once the therapist has a general understanding of the depression and how it affects the family, he or she begins to set the foundation for the reframe. To accomplish this, the therapist begins to shift the discussion from fact finding to an understanding of the family's attributions about the problem. The pacing of this switch depends on multiple factors, including the condition of the alliance with each family member and the family's general readiness to consider how family relationships may cause and help resolve the depression. However, therapists should not be too timid in guiding the process in the desired direction; families are looking for professional leadership.

The pivotal moment of the relational reframe interventions generally begins with some version of the following question from the therapist: "When you feel so depressed or suicidal, why don't you go to your parents for help? Why can't you use them as a resource?" This question directs the discussion away from a focus on the patient and symptoms and toward a focus on the quality of the relationship between family members. Adolescents often report that parents are not good listeners, always try to fix things, or just don't care. Rather than feeling comforted and reassured, adolescents feel unheard, dismissed, or invalidated. To circumvent the inevitable parental defensiveness, therapists identify and amplify the adolescent's primary emotions beneath the frustration and blame—typically loneliness and abandonment. For instance, the therapist might say, "Although you sound angry, you also seem a bit sad."

Aiming to remain focused on more vulnerable emotions, the therapist may ask the parent, "Did you know your child feels alone most of the time?" Parents may claim awareness of these feelings, but complain that the adolescent refuses to discuss them. Here the therapist can acknowledge the parent's efforts and empathize with the difficulties of raising a depressed adolescent. If the parent does too much, they are perceived as controlling. If the parent does too little, they are perceived as abandoning. It can feel like a no-win situation. The therapist must contain the parent's feelings of anger and frustration and amplify feelings of disappointment and loss. Focusing parents on vulnerable emotions activates their biologically hardwired caretaking, empathy and protection (Gottman et al., 1996, Johnson & Whiffen, 2003).

In some cases, the conversation can continue. However, often the therapist may want to lay more groundwork before exploring this further. The session culminates by the therapist punctuating that repairing this relational disconnect may provide some support and comfort for the adolescent when he or she is faced with future depressive or suicidal thoughts. In this instance the relational failure is not touted as the cause of the depression (though sometimes it is), but rather that repairing these ruptures is one important step toward reducing the depression. At the end of the hour, the therapist may punctuate the session with some version of the summary and request, as in the following.

> It sounds like many things are contributing to your depression. Certainly, your struggles with schoolwork, reading, and math are frustrating. We want to figure out how to help you with that. And, you seem very isolated, like you have lost all your friends. . . . Life gets very hard when you're depressed, right? (Patient nods her head in agreement.) But there are also some painful things between you and your mom, almost too painful for you to discuss. The deep love you two feel for each other has been buried under a lot of pain and resentment. Would you agree? (Nods her head again.). It is OK if you are not ready to talk about this. After all, we have just met. But I wonder if you would meet alone with me next week, and help me understand what those tears are about. Do you think we could talk about that together without mom here? (She agrees, but continues to hold her head down).
>
> Good. Once we understand that better, we can think together about what gets in the way of talking to your mom and dad about these things. Because I firmly believe that (turns to mother) when kids are depressed, parents can be a tremendous help to them. I think your daughter feels very alone, with a lot of pain. She has no one to talk with, to cry with, and to share all the things that are on her mind. Instead it just builds up.
>
> And it sounds like you (mom and dad) have tried to be helpful, but it is hard to know how to help (they agree). I would like our first goal of treatment to be helping the three of you reconnect. Help you two (parents) work better as a team and help your daughter talk with you about what has gotten in the way of trusting you. I want your daughter to feel safer at home. Would you be willing to work with me on this?

Task Two: Building Alliance with the Adolescent

The alliance-building task with the adolescent is a critical goal in and of itself and is the setup for future tasks. Unlike younger children, whom parents can easily bring to treatment, adolescents make a strong contribution to whether they attend and engage in treatment. Therefore, if adolescents feel the therapist can understand, support, and even defend them, they will more likely give treatment a chance. However, alliance formation is not about being nice. It is about being perceptive, incisive, and knowledgeable. Alliance develops when a therapist knows what he or she is doing, remains focused in the face of chaos, empathetically speaks the truth, and has high expectations for change.

To build this alliance, the initial phase of treatment focuses on the adolescent as a victim of circumstance. We intentionally side with the adolescent's feeling of abuse, neglect, disrespect, being put down, and/or blamed. In doing this, we connect with a side of the adolescent that has rarely been acknowledged (Liddle &

Diamond, 1991). Depressed teens can be complainers, irritable, and noncommunicative, which often makes it hard for parents to take their claims of injustice seriously. Consequently, depressed adolescents often feel compelled to fight in order to be heard. Therefore, therapists must identify and acknowledge these felt injustices in order to free the adolescent from the battle for recognition. Until the depressed adolescent feels heard, understood, and appreciated, he or she will often not allow a therapist or parent to challenge or hold him or her accountable for behavior. In this regard, although we initially join with them as victims, once we are in, we challenge the adolescent to respond to these stressors in more direct, productive, and less depressogenic ways.

As a general guideline, this task consists of three components. Based on Bordin's (1979) tripartite definition of the therapeutic alliance, the three phases of the alliance-building process are: (1) establishing a bond, (2) identifying meaningful treatment goals, and (3) agreeing on the tasks that will achieve these goals. For each of these components, the therapist has specific outcomes. The ultimate goal of the session is for the adolescent to admit to being unhappy, express a desire for change, and agree to address these conflicts with his or her parents.

There are three different elements to forming a bond. First, the therapist focuses on getting to know the world of the adolescent (Liddle, 1999). The therapist shows curiosity about the teen's interests, hobbies, friends, music, and his or her thoughts and feelings about these subjects. Problem areas like depression, family conflict, or school failure are reserved for later discussion, and in fact, are often avoided (e.g., "I'm interested in that, but let me hear a bit more about your dance performance!"). Depressed adolescents (and many therapists) overly focus on problems. A focus on positive aspects is surprising and refreshing. Second, the therapist wants to identify and highlight strengths. Amplifying strengths and skills makes these aspects of the adolescent more accessible to the therapist. Third, the therapist seeks to shift the adolescent's view of the therapist from an authority figure to an ally. In this regard the therapist will serve as a transitional relationship, renewing the adolescent's hope that a helpful and mutually satisfying relationship with adults is possible.

The second component of alliance building focuses on establishing the adolescent's goals for treatment. This begins by asking about the adolescent's concerns, worries, and goals for treatment. To help engage a passive and depressed adolescent, the therapist must transform the usual complaints into more meaningful and substantial themes. For example, wanting more freedom to choose their clothes or keep their room a mess is interpreted as needs for autonomy and respect. In general, the therapist is always looking to identify the broader interpersonal themes that help make the specific details more meaningful (Diamond & Liddle, 1996, 1999).

Details about the depression remain important. Therapists may ask about symptom severity and diversity, duration, suicidal ideation, and impact on home, school, and social functioning. This can serve two goals. Therapists can use this information to punctuate and acknowledge the adolescent's pain (e.g., "So you are more unhappy than your parents know."). In addition, the therapist can use this information to help combat denial and resistance (e.g., "So even though you said things were OK, you are really unhappy."). Once the misery is clearly understood, the therapist can introduce a pivotal question: "So, given how unhappy you are, how interested are you in trying to change this? *How* to change is another question, and we will get to it. What I want to know at this point is whether you want things to be different?" Ambivalence or resistance to change is countered by reminding the adolescent of the misery he or she just described. Ideally, his or her unhappiness becomes the motivation for change, rather than external pressures. When hopelessness about change is encountered, the therapist must inspire more hope and optimism by saying things like: "I am not hopeless. I am an expert in helping kids like you! I know how to get these things done!" The desired outcome of this phase is that the adolescent says, "Yes, I would like things to be different." Acknowledgment of this desire provides leverage against later resistance, whereby the therapist can say, "Remember two weeks ago, you said you wanted things to change? Well, that is what we are trying to do now. Don't give up so easily! Fight for what you want!" The therapist can also use vulnerable emotions to help combat this resistance (e.g., "You are saying it doesn't matter, but I can see the pain and disappointment in your face.").

Next, the therapist gently moves the conversation toward repairing attachment. The therapist might ask the following: "Do your parents know about or understand how much you are suffering? When you feel this bad, why don't you turn to them for help? What events have happened in the past that have damaged trust between you and your parents?" These questions are pivotal in moving the conversation from an intrapersonal focus to an interpersonal focus. In response, adolescents will often identify critical events (i.e., abuse, abandonment, neglect) or processes (i.e., overly critical or controlling). Associating these problems with the adolescent's depression is ideal, but defining them as pivotal causes of damaging trust is the essential goal of the session.

Once some of the affectively charged trauma experiences have been identified, the therapist can introduce the central question of the session: "Have you ever told your parents about these problems?" If the answer is no, then the therapist can explore further the distrust and the anticipation of what would happen if they did. Adolescents often fear that parents will not listen or be interested. The therapist can then recap the logic of the conversation to help the adolescent agree to the task. Some version of the following statement might be said.

> "Look, you told me that you are miserable, right? That you are so unhappy with your life that you sometimes think about killing yourself. . . . You also said that you wanted things to change. . . . You also said that the things that you have done in the past to try to create change did not work and that maybe you do not know how to make things better by yourself, right? . . . Well, I have some new ideas for you to try. For instance, I think your parents need to know the things that you are telling me. They have a very different understanding of the situation. They think you are the problem and until you can be honest and direct with them, they never have to take you seriously. Does that make sense? I think we should plan for a meeting together where you talk and they listen. They need to hear these things and you need to get them off your chest. What do you think about this? What do you have to lose?"

The logic set out above is the centerpiece of the adolescent-alone alliance-building session. All the previous discussions have lead to this moment. If the groundwork has been well laid, then this recommendation is just the natural conclusion to a long conversation. If the adolescent agrees to the task, the therapist might spend time preparing him or her for the conjoint session. If the adolescent remains resistant, the therapist reworks themes from earlier in the session. The most common resistance is that mom or dad will not listen or care or they have tried in the past and it has not worked. Again, the therapist must lend optimism by saying, "Yes, but you have never done this with me before. I can help them listen. I will prepare them. I can get them ready." If agreement still cannot be made, the therapist may scale back his or her goals, and merely ask the adolescent to think about this over the week and come to the next session.

Task Three: Building Parent Alliance

The alliance-building task with parents alone is an essential component of the attachment-repairing process and the therapy in general. If nothing more, alliance with the parent increases the likelihood that a family will remain in treatment (Shelef, Diamond, Diamond, & Liddle, in press). The parent, not the adolescent, typically initiates treatment, pays for treatment, and brings the adolescent to treatment. Therefore, if the parent-therapist alliance is weak, the parent is more likely to give in to the natural resistance voiced by the adolescent.

In addition to retention, the parent-therapist alliance sets the essential foundation for future attachment-repairing work. Therefore, in ABFT, parents are the client as well as is the adolescent. Parents of depressed adolescents often have insecure attachment styles resulting from their own history of attachment failures: inadequate parental care, neglect, or abuse. This, compounded with other potential problems, such as marital distress, psychiatric problems, or financial stress, compromises natural caregiving instincts and skills (Kobak & Mandelbaum, 2003). Although the ABFT therapist does not attempt to launch a full course of individual treatment for the parents, the parents' current and past attachment insecurity become leverage for the current treatment goals. Helping parents acknowledge and sympathize with their own losses, disappointments, and pain prepares them to be more empathetic to their adolescent's current experience.

Like the adolescent alliance task, the parent alliance tasks can also be conceptualized as consisting of bonds, goals, and tasks. The bond phase has three goals. First, the therapist must set a tone of support and empathy. This is especially important given that early sessions tend to side with the adolescent's concerns. This imbalance can be addressed directly early in the session (e.g., "I am glad we have a chance to meet alone. I know it appears that I have sided a bit with your son, but we find this is often necessary to engage an adolescent in treatment. Does that make sense?") After this is discussed, the therapist turns to a focus on the parent (e.g., "I would like to spend a little time getting to know you a bit more, you know, what is going on in your life"). As with the adolescent, the therapist should try to identify strengths and resources that will provide a broader definition of the parent, both as a parent and as an independent adult. As parents feel admired and recognized as competent, they are more willing to share their vulnerabilities.

The therapist begins to explore the stressors that impact general functioning and parenting specifically. Discussions usually focus on depression, substance use or other psychiatric problems, marital distress, stressful life events, or financial problems. The therapist explores the impact of these stressors on the parenting process, if not the adolescent's depression itself. The therapist might probe with statements like, "It must be hard to raise a depressed teenager when you are struggling with all this," or "Do you think your depression or marital conflicts are affecting your daughter?") These questions must not be perceived as blame, but must be experienced as empathic explorations. The goal is not to necessarily resolve these issues, but to show interest, express empathy, and offer some recommendations (e.g., referral for therapy or case management). For many parents, this is more support than they usually receive or would have sought for themselves independent of their adolescent. In addition, the therapist's empathy increases the likelihood that the parent's vulnerable emotions associated with these challenges will surface. In this softened state, parents become more likely to empathize with the adolescent's concerns.

In the bond phase of the session, discussions also focus on the parent's own experience of being parented. These conversations begin with questions like, "So, what kind of relationships did you have with your parents?" If trust has been established, parents willingly describe the strengths or limitations of their own childhood experience. While this conversation could be endless, the therapist is guided by the goal of identifying information that will create parental sympathy for the adolescent. For instance, if the parent had a good relationship with his or her parents, the therapist might say the following, "You know how rewarding this kind of closeness can be. It must be disappointing that you don't have that with your child." Alternatively, when parents had an insecure attachment experience, the therapist might say, "So you know how painful it is for a child to feel estranged from his or her parent. I wonder if this is how your daughter feels?"

The bond phase sets the foundation for the goal phase. Ideally, the parent is in a softened, self-reflective mood, with a deeper appreciation of how relational failures can negatively impact a child. The discussion then turns to how current or past stressors in the parent's life may impact his or her emotional availability for the child. The intent here is not to blame the parent, but to express empathy for how difficult it is to parent a depressed adolescent when one is overwhelmed, depressed, or has never experienced adequate parenting him- or herself. With this foundation, the therapist can introduce the goal of the attachment task with the following kind of statement: "You know . . . you have had many disappointments in your life. Some you have survived well and others have scarred you for life. Worst of all, you have had few people to turn to for help and support. Right? . . . I think your daughter is struggling with some similar things. Feeling hurt and alone. I wonder if you would like to rescue her from the darkness that you have struggled with. You could reach out to her in ways your mother never did." This invitation offers parents an opportunity to interrupt the generational pattern of neglect and emotional isolation. It does not blame the parents, but promotes them as capable of soothing the child's despair and hopelessness.

The challenge here, however, is that many of the core concerns and complaints from the adolescent may be directed at the parents themselves. The sell to the parent is that the adolescent's strong feelings about these relational failures keep him or her from talking to or trusting the parent. Helping the adolescent to get these feelings off his or her chest (regardless of their accuracy) may serve to diffuse some of the tension between them. When this phase is executed successfully, parents express willingness to listen to their adolescent's grievances, in the hope that it will open communication.

If parents sign on to the goal, the remainder of the session is spent preparing for the task. What role should the parents have? Do they say anything or just listen? Do they defend themselves or tell their side of the story? To deliver an answer to these questions, the ABFT therapist uses the framework of the emotional coach promoted by Gottman and colleagues (1996). Emotional coaching essentially teaches parents empathic listening skills. Discussions begin with a focus on the parents' meta-emotions: their theories, beliefs, feelings, and attitudes toward emotions in general and negative emotions in particular. This discussion may again have an intergenerational focus by exploring how emotions were handled in the previous generation. After understanding the parents' past approach to emotions, the therapist begins to educate parents about the value of emotions and children's need to learn how to identify, express, and manage them. Better emotional functioning encourages cooperation and problem solving, builds self-esteem, facilitates the learning of communication skills, serves as the foundation for intimacy, improves one's capacity to manage stress, and even improves social, academic, and physical health (Gottman et al.).

Once this philosophical battle is won, the therapist can teach some concrete, specific, and simple emotional coaching skills to help the parent during the attachment conversation. Give your child full attention. Do not be distracted. Listen to your child and try to understand what is being said from his or her point of view. Ask questions rather than make statements. Show curiosity. Accept whatever emotions he or she expresses. Do not try to talk him or her out of how he or she is feeling. Try to listen for vulnerable emotions underneath anger. Help him or her label emotions. Use reflective listening; say back what you have heard. Share simple observations and, in a limited fashion, share examples from your own life.

By promoting attachment-based caregiving skills, the therapist accomplishes three goals. First, the therapist transforms the parents' intention (motivation) to criticize, blame, or fix the adolescent into a desire to offer protection and comfort. Second, the therapist uses this opportunity to teach or broaden parenting skills to include empathy and warmth. Third, the expression of appropriate caregiving skills creates a new, and unfamiliar, yet sorely needed, moment of intimacy between the parent and adolescent. Therefore, this discussion serves to momentarily resuscitate the attachment/caregiver bond that is typically tarnished in these families.

Task Four: The Attachment Task

This task builds on the foundation established in the earlier tasks. Previous sessions have developed new problem attributions, established strong alliances with all family members, identified core conflict themes, and solidified the commitment to engage in a dialogue about attachment failures. With this foundation set, the therapist initiates the attachment task at the outset of the session. If the foundation is unstable, the therapist may postpone the enactment of this conversation.

Alternatively, the conversation itself may solidify the foundation. This task can be conceptualized as three phases: adolescent disclosure, parent brief disclosure, and parent-adolescent dialogue (Diamond & Stern, 2003).

If willing, the adolescent begins the session by presenting his or her grievances. This usually concerns chronic family conflicts or traumas, such as abandonment, abuse, or neglect. Although challenging for parents, the adolescent's direct expression of anger is often welcomed over their typical avoidant, flat, or withdrawn presentation. The therapist encourages the parent to elicit details of the adolescent's grievances, while the therapist helps him or her articulate these concerns in a mature, direct, and emotionally managed manner. The therapist and parents elicit thoughts, feelings, and memories in order to explore every nuance of these experiences.

The therapist helps the parents resist the temptation to gloss over these conflicts, offer solutions too quickly, or become defensive. Instead, the therapist coaches the parents to interview the adolescent and express interest in and curiosity about his or her subjective experience. Parents should remain empathic and supportive. If parents become overbearing or too protective, adolescents may feel infantilized and cut off communication. Respecting the adolescent as mature and autonomous, yet still lovable and in need of support and empathy provides the appropriate balance of nurture and protection that fosters secure attachment. In general, this first phase of the conversation should last as long as possible. Family members may never address these issues again, and parents and adolescents are learning to work through and tolerate emotionally charged, conflict-focused conversations.

In the second phase of this conflict-resolution task, the parent is given a chance to express his or her side of the story. Prior to this phase, the therapist has delicately blocked the parent's attempts to explain or apologize for his or her past behavior. Once the adolescent's memories, feelings, and attributions have been thoroughly explored, however, the therapist encourages the parent to present his or her own perspective on, and experience of, the rupture events. Parent's explanations may include descriptions of mitigating circumstances or personal weaknesses. Remorse and contrition are common (e.g., "I was depressed and did the best I could, but I see it was not enough"). The therapist coaches the adolescent to ask difficult questions regarding the parent's behaviors, motives, and regrets. However, the therapist is careful not to let the parent's disclosure invalidate the adolescent's experience or elicit the adolescent's caretaking behavior.

The importance of the parent's disclosure appears counterintuitive, given the focus on the adolescent. Nevertheless, our studies suggest that a brief and discrete period of parent sharing and vulnerability fosters an atmosphere of reciprocity that promotes the rebuilding of trust and the renewal of an adolescent's desire for closeness. It is as if, for a few moments, this conversation is between two mature adults, sharing their own experiences and offering each other understanding and empathy. The adolescent sees his or her parent as an autonomous, distinct person with his or her own strengths, weaknesses, and challenges, rather than simply as the parent who failed him or her. Obviously, too much sharing, or sharing with the intent of defending or guilt-inducing, is inappropriate. The therapist must watch, listen closely, and be ready to redirect the conversation if these negative directions begin to appear. The therapist should help the adolescent appreciate his or her parent's perspective, yet restrain the adolescent from overprotecting the parent or becoming parentified.

The adolescent and parent disclosure phase lays the foundation for a more mutual dialogue and developmentally appropriate family interaction. The parent, aided by the therapist, invites the adolescent to explore his or her own reactions to the parent's disclosure. Often the parent's explanation and apology can stir up deeper and more vulnerable emotions for the adolescent (e.g., sadness or remorse). The therapist helps the adolescent to explore and accept mixed feelings (e.g., empathy and resentment) toward his or her parent and to struggle with whether, when, and how to forgive the parent.

At the end of the conversation, the therapist compliments the family for sustaining such an intense, honest, and revealing conversation. Rather than encouraging the family to summarize or draw conclusions (i.e., intellectualize) about the session, the therapist punctuates the integrity shown by each family member during the conversation, as well as the collective mood of intimacy and accomplishment.

Critical to the success of the session is the therapist's own presence and state of mind: focused, intense, and affectively attuned. The therapist must follow every nuance of conversation in order to keep the family on track and find doorways that lead to deeper and more profound and honest communication. The therapist's vision keeps the conversation meaningful, fluid, and often unexpected. The therapist must expect and extract the best from each family member, orchestrating a melody of honesty, grief, self-reflection, and humility. When therapists themselves are in this zone, families are much more likely to follow.

Task Five: Promoting Competency

The fifth treatment task focuses on promoting the adolescent's perceived and actual competency. The three primary goals of this task are to (1) increase the quantity and quality of competency experiences, (2) decrease social isolation, and (3) help parents become an effective resource for the adolescent. During this task, the therapist increases his or her attention to behavioral and organizational changes, both inside and outside the home. These behavioral changes are supported by the interpersonal strengths and skills developed in the first half of treatment. In fact, solving current behavioral problems becomes an exercise in using the newly found trust and mutual respect experienced in earlier sessions. In particular, the therapist now encourages parents to appropriately challenge and support the adolescent to become more motivated and courageous. Similarly, the therapist encourages the adolescent to stop blaming his or her parents, take his or her life more seriously, and accept greater responsibility for his or her behavior. In these sessions, family members thereby practice and solidify their new interpersonal skills, competencies, maturity, and trust while working through the more concrete behavioral problems of life. Therefore, this task requires the therapist to keep his or her eye on both interpersonal processes (e.g., how family members talk to each other) and behavioral goals (e.g., returning to school).

The therapist encourages the family to discuss and develop expectations about normative activities such as chores, curfews, dating, and allowance, as well as problems related to school, peers, violence, drugs, relationships, and sex. Parents are encouraged to support the adolescent's small steps toward autonomy and competency (e.g., new clothes, hairstyles, make-up, ear piercing). Since depressed adolescents are often out of step with their peer group, supporting age-appropriate behavior can help them feel more adjusted. Within limits, the therapist encourages parents to show interest in the adolescent's activities without being overinvolved or controlling (i.e., adolescent teaches parent about rock and roll music). Simultaneously, parents must become less tentative about setting appropriate goals and expectations. Without expectations, adolescents have no standards or vision (Baumrind, 1991). But the expectations need to be realistic. For some adolescents, remaining in an honors program or even finishing school may be a self-defeating goal. Ideally, the adolescent should be involved in the negotiation of these decisions and plans. This enhances confidence, communication skills, and a sense of agency.

An important step in promoting competency is to increase or improve the quality of the adolescent's (and parents') connections to social supports or resources. Especially in the context of a brief treatment, therapists must make immediate contact (often within the first week) with important extended family members, school personnel, and social service providers (e.g., probation officers and social workers). These support systems provide a broader, ecological context to the family, and assist in identifying important treatment goals. The therapist may invite important persons to attend a session, go on a home or school visit, or keep other professionals updated by phone. Whenever possible, adolescents and parents should participate in planning these larger systems interventions. Adolescents should take an active role in these events and not be a bystander. Parents should advocate for their adolescent while continuing to appropriately challenge him or her.

We have begun integrating cognitive-behavioral therapy (CBT) into the ABFT framework (see anxiety treatment, following). Thus far, CBT has been used after the initial goals of the family treatment are accomplished. This sequence diffuses family tension and builds family trust. Once secure attachment is on the mend, CBT skills can be taught without the family conflict spoiling the learning environment.

EMPIRICAL SUPPORT

ABFT has garnered empirical support from clinical and process research studies. In the first outcome study (Diamond et al., 2002), funded by the National Institute of Mental Health (NIMH), 32 adolescents were randomized to 12 weeks of treatment or a 6-week waitlist control. Of the 16 treatment cases, 13 (81%) no longer met criteria for Major Depressive Disorder (MDD) post treatment, while only 9 (56%) of the patients on the waiting list no longer met criteria for MDD post-waitlist (χ^2 [1] = 4.05, p < .04). Clinical improvement was also significantly better in the treatment group, where 62% of the adolescents treated with ABFT had a Beck Depression Inventory (BDI) of 9 or less compared to 19% of adolescents in the waitlist condition (BDI < 9, (2 [1] = 6.37, p = .01). Patients treated with ABFT also showed more improvement on anxiety, family conflict, attachment to mothers, hopelessness, and suicidal ideation. Similar results were maintained at 6 months. Although this first study is small, it is promising and warrants more research. In addition, several process research studies have also been carried out that explore the specific processes and proposed mechanism of each ABFT task (see Diamond, Siqueland, & Diamond, 2003).

Three new studies are currently underway. One study focuses on suicidal adolescents presenting in a primary care setting. This study aims to integrate a brief (6 week) ABFT model into the primary care setting. A second study provides brief family treatment in combination with antipsychotic medication for adolescents with psychotic depression. Finally, we are developing an ABFT psychoeducational parenting program to be used with children of depressed parents in community mental health settings. These studies will help broaden the application of ABFT to other populations and provide more empirical support for its effectiveness.

ABFT for Anxious Adolescents (ABFT-A)

We have begun to adapt ABFT to working with anxious adolescents (Siqueland, Rynn, & Diamond, 2005). This approach combines ABFT with individual cognitive-behavioral treatment. Although the basic structure of the five tasks is retained, some modifications are made to the clinical model. ABFT-A targets four primary processes: parental beliefs about anxiety, family modeling of anxious behavior, encouragement of avoidance, and psychological control related to communication and negotiation of conflict. Overall, family treatment focuses on granting autonomy as the central challenge to the parents and adolescents. These targets are briefly explained in the following.

In families with an anxious child, family beliefs about parenting and anxiety can seriously impact the adolescent's ability to cope with life challenges. Many parents view anxiety as threatening—something to be avoided at all costs. Consequently, they strive to protect their adolescent (and themselves) from these experiences. This leads to parenting behaviors that promote avoidance and dependency. Possibly more subtle is the parent's use of psychological control. Here, parents discourage different viewpoints, feelings, and experiences within the family, especially regarding negative affect (e.g., anger or sadness). These families often believe that the expression of differences or conflict will damage, or lead to the loss of their intimate relationships. Therefore, open negotiation of conflict is blocked, which derails the normative task of autonomy development. These dynamics reinforce adolescents' dependency on parents, which reinforces a self-concept of incompetence. Unfortunately, anxious adolescents have become so dependent on parents that they contribute to the maintenance of these dynamics as much as the parents.

In our first pilot study with this population, families received an initial family session to help set the frame of therapy (Siqueland et al., 2005). How does the family feel about and handle the adolescent's anxious behavior, and can they be a better resource to the adolescent as he or she attempts to reduce or overcome these problems? Session two is an alliance-building session with the adolescent alone. After the general bonding phase, the therapist explores individual desires, fears, and barriers about autonomy. Family issues usually revolve around adolescents' concerns about protecting or upsetting their parents, discomfort with conflict, or feeling that their parents do not understand them. This alliance-building, problem-identification session is followed by three or four individual CBT skill sessions.

The alliance-building session with the parents alone occurs sometime during the CBT sessions with the adolescent. The session focuses on identifying parents' own anxieties and fears and how these worries might lead to parents restricting the adolescent's autonomy and encouraging his or her avoidance. The therapist helps the parents reexamine their view of the adolescent as frail, and challenges the parents' tendency to protect the adolescent from danger and encourages him or her to avoid challenges. The therapist helps parents understand that promoting psychological autonomy means encouraging the adolescent to express opinions, differences, or conflicts, and learning to rely on him- or herself for self-soothing and coping.

The remaining eight or so sessions involves combinations of parent-adolescent, adolescent alone or parent alone sessions as determined by the particular case. The sessions focus on CBT, exposure therapy, and family themes identified in individual adolescent and parent sessions. Discussions can directly address family beliefs or focus on current problems; both provide opportunities to alter interactional patterns that reinforce psychological control and restrain autonomy building.

Parents are also included in in vivo exposure exercise, where they are coached to provide support while promoting the adolescent's independence in the task. In this way, CBT training not only serves to build skills to buffer anxiety, but also offers an additional context for prompting parent support and protection of the adolescent.

An initial open pilot study was conducted with eight families receiving ABFT-A (with the CBT sessions). This pilot allowed us to refine the treatment manual and carry out an initial test of the approach. The results show significant change over time with a majority of patients reporting Hamilton Anxiety ($88\% \leq 12$) and Beck Anxiety Inventory (BAI) scores ($88\% \leq 18$) in the nonclinical range. We then conducted a randomized pilot trail with 11 families receiving either ABFT-A or CBT alone. Ninety-one percent completed 12 of the 16 sessions and 55 percent completed the full 16 sessions. There were no significant treatment differences on diagnosis, anxiety, or depression rating scales at posttreatment or 6 months follow-up. There was a trend finding for adolescents' report of psychological control posttreatment ($F(1, 11) = 2.2, p = .18$), with adolescents in CBT reporting an increase in psychological control and adolescents in ABFT-A reporting a decrease in psychological control.

The lack of difference in these preliminary findings is not surprising given the small sample size. The main goals of a treatment development project such as this are model development, testing feasibility, acceptability, and gathering pilot data. On these fronts the project has been successful, and we are pursuing funding for a larger study to more fully test effectiveness of ABFT for this population.

Low Income, Minority Patients

Much of the treatment development work of ABFT has been with inner-city, often African American families. Therefore, many clinical features have been designed to meet the needs of this population. First, ABFT focuses on trauma and loss, extremely common experiences for inner-city populations. The inner city has been called a war zone, where most children are exposed to, witness, or experience loss due to violence (Garbarino, Kostelny, & Dubrow, 1991). However, youth and families often identify these as critical events, which can exacerbate underlying psychiatric conditions. Second, the ABFT therapist focuses heavily on engagement and reduction of treatment barriers. Lack of mental health insurance, financial constraints, stigma regarding mental health, and mistrust of systems have been noted as barriers to mental health service for African Americans (U.S. Department of Health and Human Services, 2001). We address these barriers not only logistically (e.g., phone calls, occasional home visit, bus tokens, child care) but also by explicitly developing trust and respect. Third, this population is likely to experience adversity and hardships, have limited resources, live in chaotic neighborhoods, and experience societal oppression. Consequently, ABFT therapists are selectively, but ecologically, oriented in their case conceptualization and treatment plan. Contacts with schools, social service providers, probation officers, neighbors, and extended family members are necessary activities when working with poor, urban families. Fourth, treatment themes focus on several topics that are salient when working with this population. These topics include racism, loss of fathers, community violence, religion, teen pregnancy, and drug use. In addition, guidelines are given about cultural etiquette (e.g., using last names, respecting the role of elders, or encouraging families to discuss racial differences between themselves and the therapist, if necessary). Finally, ABFT's emphasis on brief treatment with specific-problem focus is culturally congruent with African Americans, who tend to prefer an action-oriented therapeutic approach with short-term goals (Sue & Sue, 1999).

--- **Case Study** ---

A brief summary of the case described at the beginning of this chapter exemplifies how ABFT unfolds over the early phase of treatment. As described, in the first session, with some elicitation of vulnerable emotions, Sally (the daughter) expressed her feelings of rejection and abandonment by her mom and her memories of an abusive father, both of which her mother had minimized and discounted. In the second session, the therapist met alone with Sally. After discussions of her interest in music and art, the conversation turned to her relationship with her mother. Sally returned to her initial protest—that she was no longer interested in being close to her. The mother was too strict, only concerned about Sally's schoolwork, and uninterested in helping with her life challenges (depression, boys, alienation from friends). The therapist reminded the daughter of her tears from the last session and wondered what happened to her feelings of loneliness and the deep desire for her mom's love. Sally continued to protest until the topic of the father resurfaced.

A long conversation ensued that depicted deep ambivalence about her father. On the one hand, she was dad's favorite and she loved the attention. On the other hand, once his depression had set in, she despised his irritability, drinking, and abusive behavior toward her mother. When asked how often she had discussed these events with her mother, Sally reported that mom had made this topic off limits. Then, in loyalty to her mother, Sally agreed to avoid these topics and "just try to get on with her life." But the therapist was empathically steadfast, saying, "Your memories of him *are* your life. He is in your music, your art, and your fears of being bipolar like him. His ghost lives with you every day." The therapist did not believe that exorcising dad's ghost was the key to Sally's recovery. But he did believe that the denial or avoidance of these feelings and events by the family was indicative of the emotionally constraining climate in this family. After some more tears, Sally agreed that discussing these issues with mom might have some value.

In the following session, the therapist met alone with the mother. Initially, the mother was surprisingly guarded, and gave brief answers to the therapist's empathic inquiries about her life. Eventually, the therapist commented about the tension in this conversation, saying, "You know, you seem less trusting of me today. Have I done something to upset you?" The mother then revealed that she worried that the therapist was looking for evidence of her bad parenting in order to take her daughter away from her. The therapist's shock at this seemingly irrational fear dissipated as the mother began to tell her childhood history.

Her depressive mother abandoned the family with a lover when Sally was 10 years old. This left her in charge of four other children and an alcoholic father. When dad made sexual advances toward her at the age of 16 she left home, and never spoke to her father again. She spent the next 5 years in fear of getting arrested and sent home, but by the age of 21 she got herself into college, eventually became a computer programmer, and was now the director of a larger data management service at a local hospital. The therapist expressed admiration for her tenacity and resilience, and also empathy for the loneliness of her "don't look back" approach toward life. What had allowed her to survive came with the price of emotional isolation. While the mother fought back tears, the therapist offered her the opportunity to protect her daughter from a similar fate. The therapist said, "You know what it is like to be abandoned by a parent, to be so cut off that you have no one to turn to or trust. . . . Your daughter needs you. She wants to feel she can come to you for help and support." In this vulnerable state, the mother could appreciate the therapist's intent. But still she feared that she could not provide the kind of emotional attention that her daughter craved. The therapist offered to meet alone with the mother again to discuss the basic skills of emotional coaching.

When Sally and her mother came back together, they were both cautious. However, with the therapist's gentle guidance, the daughter initiated a conversation about her father. Knowing very little about her father, Sally began by asking questions about his work and hobbies and eventually about his depression. She asked about his history of depression and the aneurysm that killed him, and she shared her fear of being bipolar like him. The mother compassionately offered any information she could. Then Sally began to talk about her ambivalence toward him, both loving and hating him. She started to cry when she shared her guilt over her wishes that he would die, as if that had killed him. In response, mother moved next to her daughter, held her, and said soothing statements as she stroked her hair. Sally willingly gave in to her mother's comfort and continued to cry for several minutes. The issues with her father were far from resolved, but a breakthrough had occurred in Sally's tolerance for emotional distress and in a mutual trust between her and her mother.

The next several sessions continued to focus on family history. Gradually, Sally and her mother were becoming better friends. As Sally gained insight into her mother's relational and emotional history, she felt less compelled to blame her and more accepting of her mother's emotional constriction. As Sally acted more maturely in the session, mother came to appreciate that her little girl was an emerging woman. This led to more mature negotiations about expectations in the home and privileges outside the home. Mother offered Sally the guitar lessons she had previously denied her. (Mom survived as a musician in her adolescent years, and had not wanted that life for her daughter.) Treatment was reduced to every other week for 6 more months. The family had several crises along the way, and Sally's depression had similar cycles. New medications were tried, with varying responses. Sally ended her long distance phone relationship of one year, because she now felt ready for a more substantial connection with someone. As the treatment ended, she had fallen in love with a new boy (one mom approved of), and had become the singer in a punk rock garage band (which mom reluctantly supported). Occasionally, the therapist received e-mails from Sally, with a few pictures or a new poem or song. Sally went off medication and was doing fine (with a few low periods). A year later the family came back, over a crisis in school. The therapist helped them get back on the same team, and the family resolved the school issue on their own.

REFERENCES

Ainsworth, M. D. S. (1989). Attachment beyond infancy. *American Psychologist, 44,* 709–716.

Allen, J. P., Hauser, S. T., & Borman-Spurrell, E. (1996). Attachment theory as a framework for understanding sequelae of severe adolescent psychopathology: An 11-year follow-up study. *Journal of Consulting and Clinical Psychology, 64,* 254–263.

Allen, J. P., & Land, D. (1999). Attachment in adolescence. In P. R. Shaver and J. Cassidy (Eds.), *Handbook of attachment: Theory, research, and clinical applications* (pp. 319–335). New York: Guilford Press.

Bartholomew, K., & Horowitz, L. (1991). Attachment styles among young adults: A test of a four-category model. *Journal of Personality and Social Psychology, 61,* 226–244.

Baumrind, D. (1991). The influence of parenting style on adolescent competency and substance abuse. *Journal of Early Adolescence, 11,* 56–95.

Bordin, E. S. (1979). The generalizability of the psychoanalytic concept of working alliance. *Psychotherapy: Theory, Research and Practice, 16,* 252–260.

Boszormenyi-Nagy, I. & Spark, G. M. (1973). *Invisible loyalties: Reciprocity in intergenerational family therapy.* Oxford, England: Harper & Row.

Bowlby, J. A. (1969). Disruption of affectional bonds and its effects on behavior. *Canada's Mental Health Supplement, 59,* 12.

Bowlby, J. A. (1988). *A secure base: Parent-child attachment and healthy human development.* New York: Basic Books.

Cicchetti, D., & Greenberg, M. T. (1991). The legacy of John Bowlby. *Development and Psychopathology, 3,* 347–350.

Cicchetti, D., Toth, S. L., & Lynch, M., (1995). Bowlby's dream comes full circle: The application of attachment theory to risk and psychopathology. *Advances in Clinical Child Psychology, 17,* 1–75.

Diamond, G. M., Diamond, G. S., & Liddle, H. A. (2000). The therapist-parent alliance in family-based therapy for adolescents. *Journal of Clinical Psychology, 56,* 1037–1050.

Diamond, G. S., & Liddle, H. A. (1996). Resolving a therapeutic impasse between parents and adolescents in multidimensional family therapy. *Journal of Consulting and Clinical Psychology, 64,* 481–488.

Diamond, G. S., & Liddle, H. A. (1999). Transforming negative parent-adolescent interactions in family therapy: From impasse to dialogue. *Family Process, 38,* 5–26.

Diamond, G. S., & Diamond, G. M. (2002). Studying mechanisms of change: A process research agenda for family-based treatments. In H. Liddle, R. Leant, & J. Bray (Eds.), *Family Psychology Intervention Science* (pp. 41–66). Washington, DC: American Psychological Association Press.

Diamond, G. S., Reis, B. F., Diamond, G. M., Siqueland, L., & Isaacs, L. (2002). Attachment-based family therapy for depressed adolescents: A treatment development study. *Journal of the American Academy of Child and Adolescent Psychiatry, 41,* 1190–1196.

Diamond, G. S., & Siqueland, L. (1998). Emotions, attachment and the relational reframe: The first session. *Journal of Systemic Therapies, 17,* 36–50.

Diamond, G. S., Siqueland, L., & Diamond, G. M. (2003). Attachment-based family therapy for depressed adolescents: Programmatic treatment development. *Clinical Child and Family Psychology Review, 6,* 107–127.

Diamond, G. S., & Stern, R. (2003). Attachment based family therapy for depressed adolescents: Repairing attachment by addressing attachment failures. In S. Johnson (Ed.), *Attachment: A family systems perspective* (pp. 191–215). New York: Guilford Press.

Garbarino, J., Kostelny, K., & Dubrow, N. (1991). *No place to be a child: Growing up in a war zone.* San Francisco: Jossey-Bass.

Gottman, J. M., Katz, L. F., & Hooven, C. (1996). Parental meta-emotion philosophy and the emotional life of families: Theoretical models and preliminary data. *Journal of Family Psychology, 10,* 243–268.

Greenberg, L. S., & Safran, J. D. (1987). *Emotion in psychotherapy: Affect, cognition, and the process of change.* New York: Guilford Press.

Greenberg, L. S., & Johnson, S. M. (1988). *Emotionally focused therapy for couples.* New York: Guilford Press.

Herman, J. L. (1992). *Trauma and recovery.* New York: Basic Books.

Johnson, S. M., & Whiffen, V. E. (2003). *Attachment process in couples and family therapy.* New York: Guilford Press.

Kobak, R., & Duemmler, S. (1994). Attachment and conversation: Toward a discourse analysis of adolescent and adult security. In D. Perlman & K. Bartholomew (Eds.), *Attachment processes in adulthood: Advances in personal relationships: Vol. 5* (pp. 121–149). Bristol, PA: Jessica Kingsley Publishers.

Kobak, R., & Mandelbaum, T. (2003). Caring for the caregiver: An attachment approach to assessment and treatment of problematic child behavior. In S. Johnson (Ed.), *Attachment Processes in Couples and Family Therapy* (pp. 144–164). New York: Guilford Press.

Kobak, R., & Sceery, A. (1988). Attachment in late adolescence: Working models, affect regulation, and representations of self and others. *Child Development, 59,* 135–146.

Kobak, R., Sudler, N., & Gamble, W. (1991). Attachment and depressive symptoms during adolescence: A developmental pathways analysis. *Development and Psychopathology, 3,* 461–474.

Liddle, H. A. (1999). Theory development in a family-based therapy for adolescent drug abuse. *Journal of Clinical and Child Psychology, 28,* 521–533.

Liddle, H. A., Dakof, G. A., Parker, K., Diamond, G. S., Barrett, K., & Tejada, M. (2001). Multidimensional family therapy for adolescent drug abuse: Results of a randomized clinical trial. *American Journal of Drug and Alcohol Abuse, 27,* 651–687.

Liddle, H. A., & Diamond, G. S. (1991). Adolescent substance abusers in family therapy: The critical initial phase of treatment. *Family Dynamics of Addictions Quarterly, 1,* 55–68.

Main, M., & Goldwyn, R. (1988). Adult attachment classification system. Version 3.2. Unpublished manuscript. Berkeley, University of California.

McCullough, M. E., Pargament, K. I., & Thoresen, C. E. (2000). The psychology of forgiveness: History, conceptual issues, and overview. In K. I. Pargament & M. E. McCullough et al. (Eds.), *Forgiveness: Theory, research, and practice* (pp. 1–14). New York: Guilford Press.

Pearson, J. L., Cohn, D. A., Cowan, P. A., & Cowan, C. P. (1994). Earned and continuous-security in adult attachment: Relation to depressive symptomatology and parenting styles. *Development and Psychopathology, 6,* 359–373.

Rosenstein, D. S., & Horowitz, H. A. (1996). Adolescent attachment and psychopathology. *Journal of Consulting and Clinical Psychology, 64,* 244–253.

Shelef, K., Diamond, G. M., Diamond, G. S., & Liddle, H. L. (in press). Adolescent and parent alliance and treatment outcome in multidimensional family therapy. *Journal of Consulting and Clinical Psychology.*

Siqueland, L., Rynn, M., & Diamond, G. S. (2005). Cognitive behavioral and attachment based family therapy for anxious adolescents: Phase I and II studies. *Journal of Affective Disorders.*

Steinberg, L. (1990). Autonomy, conflict and harmony in the family relationships. In S. S. Feldman and G. R. Elliot (Eds.), *At the threshold: The developing adolescent* (pp. 255–276). Cambridge, MA: Harvard University Press.

Sue, D. W., & Sue, D. (Eds.), (1999). *Counseling the culturally different: Theory and practice* (3rd ed.). New York: John Wiley & Sons.

U.S. Department of Health and Human Services (2001). *Mental health: Culture, race, and ethnicity—A supplement to mental health: A report of the Surgeon General.* Rockville, MD: U.S. Department of Health and Human Services.

Waters, E., Kondo-Ikemura, K., Posada, G., & Richters, J. E. (1991). Learning to love: Mechanisms and milestones. In M. R. Gunnar & L. A. Sroufe (Eds.), *Self processes and development. The Minnesota symposia on child psychology: Vol. 23* (pp. 217–255). Hillsdale, NJ: Lawrence Erlbaum Associates.

Weinfeld, N. S., Sroufe, L. A., & Egelund, B. (2000). Attachment from infancy to early adulthood: A twenty-year longitudinal study. *Child Development, 71,* 684–689.

Wood, B. (2002). Introduction to special issue on attachment theory and family systems therapies. *Family Process, 41,* 3–5.

CHAPTER 3

Family Therapy for Attention-Deficit/Hyperactivity Disorder (ADHD)

Karen C. Wells

Attention-Deficit/Hyperactivity Disorder is a chronic and impairing disorder that spans childhood through adulthood. In childhood, epidemiological studies indicate that between 3 percent to 5 percent of youth meet criteria for ADHD (Angold, Erkanli, Egger, & Costello, 2000; Jensen et al., 1999). Although various labels have been used historically to describe the disorder, clinical descriptions have remained remarkably stable with regard to what are now considered to be its cardinal features: inattention, hyperactivity, and impulsivity (American Psychiatric Association, 1994). In the current version of the Diagnostic and Statistical Manual of Psychiatric Disorders (DSM-IV), there are three subtypes of the disorder: ADHD, Predominantly Inattentive Type; ADHD, Predominantly Hyperactive-Impulsive Type, and ADHD-Combined Type (a combination of inattentive and hyperactive-impulsive symptoms).

Dimensional approaches to the study of ADHD have repeatedly identified two distinct behavioral dimensions that underlie the behavioral symptoms of the disorder. One of these is characterized by symptoms reflective of inattention; the other is reflective of disinhibition (behaviors of both hyperactivity and impulsivity). Recent studies have lent evidence to the discriminant validity of these two dimensions (Lahey & Willcutt, 2002). For example, the disinhibition dimension is more strongly associated than is inattention with both Conduct Disorder and with Oppositional Defiant Disorder, with indicators of impairment such as accidental injuries, teacher-reported lack of self-control, aggression and disruptiveness, and peer-rejection problems related to disruption and aggression. On the other hand, inattention is more strongly associated with anxiety and depressive symptoms and with academic underachievement, use of special-education services, and peer relationship problems related to shyness and social withdrawal. These dimensions seem to follow a different developmental course, with hyperactive/impulsive behaviors arising at an earlier age (3 to 4 years old) and inattentive behaviors arising around ages 5 to 7. Likewise, the hyperactive/impulsive behaviors associated with disinhibition decline with age, whereas inattention remains relatively stable through childhood, declining later in adolescence (Barkley, 2003). However, neither returns to entirely normal levels, and as we will see, impairing symptoms of

ADHD persist into adolescence and adulthood in a significant percentage of cases diagnosed in childhood.

In addition to their primary problems with inattention, hyperactive, and impulsive behaviors, ADHD children and adolescents may also suffer from additional comorbid conditions and functional deficits that add to the impairment picture and complicate assessment and treatment. Chief among the complicating comorbid conditions are Oppositional Defiant Disorder (35 to 60 percent of ADHD cases in clinical and epidemiological samples) and Conduct Disorder (30 to 50 percent). Other comorbid conditions that may also be present are specific learning disabilities (10 to 26 percent of ADHD cases when conservative estimates of learning disability (LD) are employed); anxiety (25 to 40 percent; Barkley, 1996; Biederman, Faraone, & Lapey, 1992; Hinshaw, 1992; Conners & Erhardt, 1998); mood disorders (between 20 percent and 30 percent; Biederman et al., 1992; Fischer, Barkley, Smallish, & Fletcher, 2002) and, as these children grow into adolescence and young adulthood, Substance Abuse Disorders (current estimates range from 12 percent to 27 percent; Fischer et al., 2002; Mannuzza, Klein, Bessler, Malloy, & LaPadula, 1993; Mannuzza, Klein, Bessler, Malloy, & LaPadula, 1998; Quinn, 1997; Wilens & Lineham, 1995). Much of the association of ADHD with substance abuse disorders and with mood disorders seems to be mediated by the co-occurring presence of Conduct Disorder, (Angold, Costello, & Erkanli, 1999; Molina, Smith, & Pelham, 1999) making this an even more important target for treatment when it is present.

In addition to these associated psychiatric conditions, more recent research has focused on functional outcomes that place ADHD children at additional risk. ADHD children have been shown to be more accident-prone than normal controls, with up to four times more accidents related to impulsive behaviors (Taylor, Sandberg, Thorley, & Giles, 1991; Barkley, 2003). ADHD teens and adults also have more automobile crashes than non-ADHD teens, and are more likely to get speeding tickets and to have their driver's licenses suspended (Barkley, Murphy, DuPaul, & Bush, 2002). Not only does this place the ADHD individual at greater risk of injury or even death, it also places an exceptional burden of additional stress on the families of these individuals, who are left with the practical, emotional, and financial aftermath.

Clinically, ADHD youth have difficulty at both home and school in persisting at work (especially tedious or boring work), without giving up or changing activities, or completing tasks such as chores or school assignments, or at sustaining play. They become distracted more easily in work and at play than age peers, and have more difficulty following through on instructions or house rules. Parents and teachers perceive them as not listening well, not concentrating, failing to finish assignments, and being forgetful. Those who also have problems with disinhibition are more motorically active and fidgety, less able to remain seated at school or at home (e.g., at the dinner table), are noisy, talk excessively, verbally interrupt teachers, parents, and peers, and have difficulty taking their turn or waiting in line. In short, these youth can be difficult and annoying to be around, and they try the patience of their parents, teachers, caregivers, and friends.

In addition to these aspects of the clinical picture, those ADHD youth who have coexisting oppositional or conduct disorders display major difficulties with noncompliant, defiant, and rule-breaking behavior. They do not listen to their parents or comply with their parents' instructions at an age-appropriate level. Many, if not most, instructions by parents meet with verbal defiance or behavioral avoidance of the request. Older children and adolescents with these additional problems may violate major family and community rules, such as lying, stealing, truanting from school, violating curfew, hanging out with deviant peers, and, later, substance use and abuse. These difficulties of noncompliance with parental and family rules are problems in their own right and also make it more difficult for parents and teachers to work with the primary problems of inattention and impulsivity. A child who will not follow directions will not be able to profit from his or her parents' or teachers' instructions to "sit down, raise your hand, wait your turn, stop running around the dinner table, lower your voice," and so on. Thus, problems with noncompliance rob parents and teachers of an essential social tool in trying to help the ADHD child. Adolescents who engage in major family and community rule violations, and/or abuse illegal substances, place themselves at greater risk of poor adult outcomes.

ADHD AS A FAMILY ILLNESS

Family Interactions and Dysfunction

Not surprisingly, family interactions within a family with members who have ADHD are characterized by higher levels than normal of discord and disharmony. Children with ADHD are less compliant to their parents' instructions, sustain their compliance for shorter time periods, are less likely to remain on task, and display more negative behavior than their normal, same-age counterparts. In what Johnston (1996) labeled a "negative-reactive" response pattern, mothers and fathers of ADHD children display more directive, commanding behavior, more disapproval, less rewards that are contingent on the child's prosocial and compliant behaviors, and more overall negative behavior than the parents of normal children (Anderson, Hinshaw, & Simmel, 1994; Barkley, Karlsson, & Pollard, 1985; Befera & Barkley, 1984; Cunningham & Barkley, 1979; Mash & Johnston, 1982; Tallmadge & Barkley, 1983).

Studies of ADHD adolescents and their parents show continuation of elevated levels of negative interactions, angry conflicts, and less positive and facilitative behavior toward each other, relative to normal adolescents and their families (Barkley, Anastopoulos, Guevremont, & Fletcher, 1992; Barkley, Fischer, Edelbrock, & Smallish, 1991; Edwards, Barkley, Laneri, Fletcher, & Metevia, 2001). Elevated rates of reciprocal, negative behaviors characterize these teen-parent interactions.

When a child has ADHD, family life is characterized by more parenting stress and a decreased sense of parenting self-competence (Fischer, 1990; Mash & Johnston, 1990; Podolski & Nigg, 2001; Whalen & Henker, 1999), more parent alcohol consumption (Pelham & Lang, 1993, 1999), increased rates of maternal depression and marital conflict, separation, and divorce (Befera & Barkley, 1984; Barkley, Fischer, Edelbrock, & Smallish, 1990; Barkley et al., 1991; West, Houghton, Douglas,

Wall, & Whiting, 1999). Although the presence of comorbid Oppositional Defiant Disorder (ODD) is associated with much of the parent-child interactional conflicts and stress in ADHD families (Barkley et al., 1992; Podolski & Nigg, 2001), parents and youth with ADHD alone still display interactions that are deviant from normal (Fletcher, Fischer, Barkley, & Smallish, 1996; Johnston, 1996; Johnston & Mash, 2001).

Recent evidence from longitudinal studies suggests that for some ADHD youth, dysfunctions in parenting may play a role in the origins of ADHD (Campbell, 1994; Carlson, Jacobvitz, & Sroufe, 1995; Pierce, Ewing, & Campbell, 1999). In addition, the careful, systematic work of Patterson and his colleagues has clearly documented the etiologic significance of disrupted parenting in childhood aggression and oppositional behavior which have high comorbidity rates with ADHD (Dishion & Patterson, 1999; Patterson, Reid, & Dishion, 1992). There is evidence that aggression and other signs of conduct disorder mediate the increased risk for later substance abuse, criminality, and antisocial spectrum disorders in adulthood (Lynskey & Fergusson, 1995; Hinshaw, 1994; Klein & Mannuzza, 1991). In addition, high rates of negativity in parent-child interactions are related to dysfunction across domains of functions and settings (Anderson et al., 1994).

Associated Problems in the ADHD Family

The previously reviewed literature documents the nature of ADHD, its associated conditions, and the family interactions and family dysfunction that can characterize families in which there is an ADHD child or adolescent. However, family assessment and intervention must extend beyond interactions of the parent-child dyad. Contrary to earlier theories that ADHD was a developmental disorder confined to prepuberty, longitudinal follow-up studies as well as studies of adult ADHD now confirm that ADHD spans the developmental continuum. Studies examining adolescent outcome have assessed persistence of symptoms as well as presence of the diagnosis of ADHD in adolescents. When persistence of symptoms is the criteria, 70 to 80 percent of ADHD children continue to display significant symptoms of ADHD into adolescence. Studies utilizing full diagnostic criteria have shown that a substantial proportion of ADHD children will continue to meet diagnostic criteria in adolescence (68 percent to 85 percent across studies of 10- to 15-year-olds). Studies of older adolescents (16- to 19-year-olds) have shown slightly lower persistence rates (30 percent to 50 percent). This may simply reflect that older adolescents (and adults) have outgrown some of the diagnostic criteria that were developed for children, but the adult form of the disorder may still be present (Barkley, 2003). More work needs to be done on assessment of diagnostic criteria in developmental contexts appropriate to adolescents and adults in order to clarify this issue.

Studies of ADHD in adulthood have similarly shown that a substantial majority (50 percent to 70 percent) of formerly ADHD children show persistence of significant ADHD symptoms into adulthood. When adult diagnosis (rather than symptoms) based on self-report only of the young adult has been studied, the rates of formal diagnosis extending into adulthood are substantially lower. However, when the report of parents of the young adult is included, rates are higher than with self-report only, and when an empirical definition is used based on dimensional measures administered to parents of young adults, the rates rise to 68 percent. Thus, it appears that a very substantial proportion of persons diagnosed with ADHD in childhood will continue to display significant symptoms of the disorder into adulthood. In studies looking at point-prevalence rates of adult ADHD in community (i.e., not clinic-referred) samples, 2.5 percent of adult subjects have been found to exceed the first standard deviation on adult rating scales (Weyandt, Linterman, & Rice, 1995), and in one study a total of 4.7 percent met diagnostic criteria for three subtypes of ADHD in DSM-IV (Murphy & Barkley, 1996a). Thus, adult prevalence ranges from 2.5 to about 5 percent.

What this means is that about eight million adults in the United States have ADHD, making it the second most common adult psychiatric disorder (after depression). Because only in recent years has adult ADHD even been recognized by the professional community, only a small proportion of these adults know that they have the illness. Most of these adults probably suffered from ADHD as children (whether it was diagnosed in childhood or not) and many of these adults now have children of their own. In a study by Biederman, Faraone, et al. (1995) that sampled 84 parents with childhood onset of ADHD, 57 percent of their children had ADHD. In this sample, 84 percent of the parents had at least one child with ADHD. In many families more than one child has ADHD (Faraone, Beiderman, Mennin, Gershon, & Tsuang, 1996). Other studies have shown that about one quarter of children presenting with ADHD will have an ADHD parent (Faraone, 1997). These and other studies have also documented the family transmission of ADHD. Thus, ADHD is truly a family illness in the sense that it is more likely than chance that when a child in a family has ADHD (and possible associated conditions) one or both parents may suffer from ADHD as well, or vice versa—and it is often undiagnosed.

Complicating the family illness picture even further, adults (who may now be parents and spouses) with ADHD often have associated comorbid conditions and functional impairments themselves. Clinic-referred adults diagnosed with ADHD have higher rates of Oppositional Defiant Disorder, Conduct Disorder, and not surprisingly, given the first two, alcohol dependence or abuse disorders (especially marijuana) than control samples (Barkley, Murphy, & Kwasnik, 1996a; Barkley, Fischer, Smallish, & Fletcher, 2004; Biederman et al., 1997). Although the association of adult ADHD with anxiety is relatively weak and may reflect a referral bias when it occurs, adult ADHD is significantly associated with major depression (16 percent to 31 percent) and dysthymia (Biederman et al., 1993; Murphy & Barkley, 1996b). Marital functioning is problematic in ADHD adults, who are twice as likely to have divorced and remarried, and report less marital satisfaction in their current marriages (Murphy & Barkley, 1996a; Biederman et al., 1993). In one longitudinal follow-up study (Weiss & Hechtman, 1993) 20 percent of the childhood ADHD group also reported sexual adjustment problems in adulthood, compared to only 2.4 percent for the control group, although the nature of these sexual problems was not specified. As with ADHD adolescents, ADHD adults are also involved in more automobile accidents involving bodily injury and are more likely to receive speeding tickets and to have their licenses suspended or revoked

(Barkley, Murphy, & Kwasnik, 1996b). In addition, adults diagnosed with ADHD are significantly more likely to be fired from their job, or to have performed poorly or quit their job, than clinic-referred non-ADHD adults (Murphy & Barkley, 1996b). Taking all of these aspects of the functioning of child and adult ADHD into account, the clinical picture that emerges of daily life in a family with ADHD children and adults is one of disorganization and resulting chaos, noise, uncooperativeness, rule violations, annoyance, anger and/or frustration, irritability among family members, interpersonal conflict, disruption in almost all aspects of family role functions (e.g., parenting, marital), occupational disruption, possibly depression and substance use and/or abuse, and a high stress burden.

ADHD and Family Structure

The primary diagnosis of adult and child ADHD, with its associated comorbidities and functional impairments, can have a profound impact on the ability of parents and other family members to arrive at an adaptive family structure and organization. In adaptive family functioning, there is a structural organization that promotes the healthy development of all family members. A hierarchical organization exists, defining lines of authority in the family. In a two-parent family, the parents occupy the top level of the hierarchy. In this regard, they assume primary responsibility for creating overall structural patterns and rules that govern daily life. If the parental subsystem is functioning well, the parents are able to communicate and problem-solve together; they cooperate in sharing responsibility for family management and the nurturance and discipline of the children. If the parents are married or in an adult couples relationship, they also have the shared roles involved in intimate couples relating; supporting, comforting, sharing, enjoying, and confiding in each other, as well as sharing the many instrumental tasks and burdens of adult and family life. In a well-functioning family, the roles involved in these two subsystems (parental subsystem and marital subsystem) support and complement each other. Couples who are confiding, intimate, and supportive of each other in their couples relationship are less likely to be depressed, are more satisfied in their marriages, and have an easier time communicating and cooperating as coparents with each other. When the couple's relationship is distant, disengaged, and/or conflicted, the ability to work together as parents is often also affected.

Another aspect of family structure has to do with the boundaries that define patterns of closeness and distance; who participates with whom, when, and how. In families with diffuse boundaries, family members are intrusively involved with one another. There are no rules that place limits on the children's access to and involvement with the parents or with each other. Family members interrupt and talk over each other, take unchallenged liberties with each other's space and belongings, and do not respect personal privacy. There is a premium placed on family closeness at the expense of age-appropriate independence and autonomy. In families with rigid boundaries, family members are disengaged and have little interaction with each other. In these families, independence is emphasized at the expense of closeness and mutual support. In families with permeable boundaries, children have age-appropriate access to parents, as needed, to support their sense of attachment and belonging; however, there are also rules that define when access is limited, such as when the parents' bedroom door is closed, or when parents are on the telephone. In the ideal situation, parents and children are involved with each other in ways that support closeness and a sense of attachment, and parents also set limits on violations of boundaries when needed. Children learn how and when to expect contact and closeness with parents and also learn to accept the limits on contact and closeness.

The presence of ADHD (and the associated comorbidities and impairments with which it is often associated) in family members presents a real challenge to the ability of the family to establish a functional and adaptive family structure, with well-functioning marital, parental, and child/sibling subsystems. In addition, the principles of reciprocity and transactional family influence are operative in ADHD families just as they are in normal family process. That is, the presence of ADHD symptoms and behaviors provokes dysfunctional responses from other family members that feed back in a reciprocal-influence process that exacerbates and escalates the original symptomatic behaviors, and also spills over to influence interactions within other family subsystems.

To take an example, the ADHD child with symptoms of inattention, impulsivity, and motor drivenness displays behaviors at home that are irritating and frustrating to parents. Especially if the child also displays oppositional symptoms, the parents' attempts to control the child's behavior are met with resistance, stubbornness, and emotional reactivity by the child. Such a reaction provokes the parents to respond with even more negative emotional and behavioral reactions (anger, explosiveness) that further exacerbate the child's resistance, noncompliance, and anger. The picture is even further complicated if the parent also has ADHD, with its associated behavioral and emotional dysregulation. Such a parent has even less patience with the child, and is even more likely to respond negatively and reactively in behavior and emotions. These patterns of escalating, discordant interchange not only exacerbate the under-regulated behavior of the child, but are etiologic in the development and maintenance of secondary oppositional comorbidity (Patterson et al., 1992).

Adult ADHD is also often associated with deficits in executive functions that result in (among other things) disorganization and difficulty with proactive planning and action toward the future (Murphy, Barkley, & Bush, 2001). As it relates to parenting, this means that ADHD parents will have more difficulty than normal in establishing a well-functioning family structure and a proactive approach to family management and discipline. Such things as time schedules, family routines, rituals, and preestablished expectations and rules governing social behavior among family members are more difficult for ADHD parents to establish and maintain. Establishing age-appropriate boundaries (e.g., do not interrupt when mom is on the phone; do not go into your sister's room when her door is closed; do not take other family members' things without asking)—already a challenge with an impulsive, hyperactive, ADHD child, is even more difficult when the parent also has ADHD. Thus, chaos is likely to rule, and there is more likelihood that when the ADHD child behaves disruptively, the ADHD parent will erupt reactively in the absence of a proactively established plan.

Inattentiveness and impulsivity associated with adult ADHD also makes it more difficult for these parents to display the nurturing and monitoring functions that are associated with supportive parenting of children. ADHD parents often report how difficult it is to sit quietly with an infant while feeding, engage with a young child in childlike games and activities, or help an older child with homework, without becoming quickly distracted or bored and unable to sustain positive attention to the child. Parental inattentiveness also makes it relatively more difficult for parents to remain engaged and to conduct the monitoring that is so crucial to guiding the young child's socialization. For example, if an ADHD parent gives an ADHD child an instruction to clean up his or her room, the parent's own inattentiveness and distractibility may result in the parent failing to monitor whether the child in fact performs the instruction. This failure to monitor the child's performance of instructions and adherence to rules will result in a lack of appropriate follow-through by the parent to child compliance or noncompliance. Over time, children learn that their noncompliant behavior will not be met with any consequences, resulting in escalating rates of child noncompliance. As the child becomes more and more noncompliant, the ADHD parent's lack of impulse control makes it more likely that the parent will erupt reactively with negative emotions and behavior (e.g., loud verbal outbursts, yelling, anger) that further exacerbate the child's negative behavior and emotions. Thus, parent and child ADHD together drive an escalating spiral of negative family interactions and emotions and child behavior problems.

Adult ADHD also potentially impacts on the ability of the parent to cooperate with treatment of the ADHD child, most importantly regarding stimulant medication and parent management training. Because many ADHD children are treated with stimulant medications, it is important that parents dispense pills according to the schedule prescribed by the doctor. Optimally, parents also may be asked to fill out daily ratings of the child's behavior or to coordinate teacher ratings of the child at school, in order to establish the correct dose and monitor maintenance of effects. Because of the disorganization and inattentiveness of the ADHD parent, she or he may have a more difficult time following through with these tasks, with the result that the child does not receive an adequate trial of the medication (Weiss, Hechtman, & Weiss, 2000). Adult ADHD also can impact the ability of parents to cooperate with parent training programs, which are another essential element of treatment for child ADHD. Two recent studies (Harvey, Danforth, McKee, Ulaszek, & Friedman, 2003; Sonuga-Barke, Daley, & Thompson, 2002) have documented a relationship between parent ADHD, negative child behaviors, and the outcomes of parent training. Harvey et al. (2003) showed that a high level of mothers' inattention disrupts both baseline parenting as well as the implementation of new parenting techniques. Sonuga-Barke et al. (2002) extended these findings by demonstrating the impact of parent ADHD on child outcomes following parent training. In this study ADHD children were divided into three groups: those with mothers who were themselves high, medium, or low on adult ADHD symptoms. All groups received parent management training. Children of mothers in the high-ADHD group displayed no improvement after parent management training, whereas the levels of ADHD symptoms of the children of mothers in either the medium or low adult ADHD groups reduced substantially. Thus, adult ADHD can impact significantly on the ability of the parent to implement the two major treatment approaches for the child's ADHD—medication and parent management training.

Finally, as mentioned earlier, adult ADHD is associated with a greater-than-chance co-occurrence of depression and substance abuse, and these conditions themselves have been associated with disrupted parenting. For example, depressed mothers display significantly higher levels of negative and/or hostile behavior alternating with disengaged behavior, and significantly lower levels of praise and affection than nondepressed mothers (Lovejoy, Graczyk, O'Hare, & Neuman, 2000). Likewise, in laboratory studies, alcohol consumption has been shown to reduce appropriate parenting behaviors such as positive attending and listening, and to increases in commands and indulgence. The impact of these parent behaviors on ADHD children may be to increase the negative and/or hostile interchange that is associated with escalating levels of child misbehavior, and to reduce the degree to which parents monitor children and supply appropriate positive and negative consequences to child behavior.

ADHD: Gender and Ethnicity Considerations

The scientific literature on ADHD historically has focused almost exclusively on male populations. Females with ADHD, and the impact of gender differences on understanding and treatment of the disorder have been largely neglected—until very recently. This state of affairs is related to the epidemiology of the disorder and its expression in population-based versus clinical samples. There is a substantial discrepancy in male-female ratios between clinic-referred samples (which provide subjects for most scientific studies) where the ratio has been estimated at around 9:1, and community samples, where the ratio is closer to 3:1. What this suggests is that ADHD females are underidentified, under-referred, and therefore undertreated relative to ADHD males. And yet, based on combined and sex-specific prevalence rates, over one million girls and women in the United States are estimated to have the disorder. Some researchers have presented data suggesting that one reason for this underidentification is because ADHD in females is characterized by a preponderance of symptoms of inattention over those of hyperactivity and impulsivity, and is less likely to be associated with comorbid, disruptive behaviors that impact negatively on others, such as parents, teachers, and schools (Abikoff et al., 2002; Biederman et al., 1999; Newcorn et al., 2001). It is the disruptive and aggressive behaviors that drive referral in males, resulting in their higher rate of presentation to clinics. Thus, only girls with the most substantial levels of impairment are referred for treatment.

In recent years, researchers have begun to investigate the expression and impairment associated with ADHD in females in studies that have begun to highlight the severity of the disorder in this population. Biederman et al. (1999) compared clinic-referred ADHD girls to pediatric clinic control girls and found a higher rate of primary symptoms of ADHD, especially inattention, and a far higher rate of disruptive (ODD and CD) and mood and anxiety disorders in the ADHD girls (although the rates of disruptive behavior were lower than those typically reported in boys). In addition, a higher rate of Substance Use Disorders in the ADHD female adolescents compared to control adolescents was found. Even so, 55 percent of the ADHD girls had no comorbidity. ADHD girls also had higher rates of school and family dysfunction than female controls. Hinshaw (2002) and his colleagues have refined and extended these findings, showing that ADHD girls attending a summer camp program displayed higher rates of primary ADHD symptoms and higher rates of ODD and CD than non-ADHD comparison girls (with the highest rates in Combined Type relative to Inattentive Type). In addition, higher rates of mood and anxiety disorders were noted compared to comparison girls (with no differences between the ADHD subtypes). ADHD girls also showed more intellectual impairment, more dysfunction in parents' parenting skills, and more dysfunction in peer relationships (Blachman & Hinshaw, 2002; Hinshaw, 2002). Interestingly, combined type ADHD girls were more likely to have a history of physical and sexual abuse than inattentive subtype or control girls.

These important studies have demonstrated that ADHD in girls is, as in boys, a serious disorder, associated with significant psychiatric, psychological, and family impairment. Recent reviews of studies of gender differences in ADHD have shown that, compared with ADHD boys, ADHD girls display greater intellectual impairment, but lower levels of hyperactivity and lower rates of externalizing behavior (Gaub & Carlson, 1997; Gershon, 2002). In addition, Gershon (2002) found higher rates of internalizing problems in ADHD girls than ADHD boys. Thus, comorbid conditions such as depression and anxiety may be more problematic for ADHD females. These findings taken together corroborate that ADHD in females presents as a more subtle illness than in males—but one that is impairing in multiple domains and is more likely to be associated with internalizing pathology.

Just as is the case with gender, a scientific void exists with regard to the relationship between ADHD and ethnicity in the United States. Of the thousands of ADHD studies that exist, only a handful examine this topic. The few studies that have looked at differences between African American and European American school-age populations have generally found a higher prevalence of ADHD and higher mean ratings of ADHD, as rated by parents and school personnel, in African American boys and girls (Epstein, March, Conners, & Jackson, 1998; Reid, Casat, Norton, Anastopoulos, & Temple, 2001; Samuel et al., 1997). However, it is not clear whether these findings represent real differences in behavior, rater biases, halo effects, or the effects of socioeconomic status (SES) as confounded with ethnicity. For example, Reid et al. (2001) reported that African American teachers rate African American children somewhat lower than European American teachers do on ADHD ratings. Studies that have examined Mexican American children have generally reported no differences in ratings of ADHD compared to European American children. It is unknown whether patterns of comorbidity differ for ADHD children across different ethnic groups.

Treatment studies of both ADHD females and ADHD African American children with stimulant medication are few, but those that exist tend to show equivalent treatment effects as those obtained with Caucasian males (Samuel et al., 1997; Sharp et al., 1999). However, African American children may be more at risk for hypertension with medication treatment (Samuel et al., 1997). One uncontrolled study (Smith & Barrett, 2000) examined the effects of parent training with three

ADHD girls, and showed similar improvements in child compliance as well as similar symptoms of ADHD as are generally obtained with male clients. Interestingly, in this study, improvements were also seen in emotional functioning (symptoms of anxiety and depression), and these improvements were noticeably larger than behavioral improvements, even though they were not the direct targets of treatment. Since ADHD girls are more likely to experience emotional difficulties than boys, this unanticipated effect of parent training is encouraging. Arnold (1996) has noted that since parent training programs have historically primarily targeted the disruptive and aggressive comorbidity that is more prevalent in boys than in girls, parent training programs for girls may need redefinition so as to target inattention, self-organization, and internalizing symptoms more so than for boys. Finally, Arnold et al. (2003) examined ethnicity as a moderator of treatment outcome in the Multimodal Treatment Study of Children with Attention-Deficit/Hyperactivity Disorder (MTA) of unimodal and multimodality treatments of ADHD (MTA Cooperative Group, 1999). In this study, whereas the overall findings showed no superiority of combined treatment (medication plus behavior therapy) over medication alone on most symptoms (MTA Cooperative Group, 1999), ethnic minority families cooperated with and benefited significantly more from combination treatment compared with medication alone (Arnold et al., 2003). The authors conclude that treatment for lower socioeconomic status, minority ADHD children, especially if comorbid, should combine medication and behavioral treatment. While these studies and suggestions provide interesting speculation for clinical modifications to standard treatment for ADHD, more research clearly is needed of the effects of both gender and ethnicity on epidemiology and on treatment of ADHD.

TREATMENT OF ADHD AS A FAMILY ILLNESS

The literature reviewed above indicates that a diagnosis of ADHD in a child can have far-reaching implications for family assessment and treatment. Far from being confined to the primary symptoms of ADHD per se, the presence of this diagnosis implies the possible presence of other associated comorbidities and impairments in the child him- or herself. In addition, diagnosis in a child implies the possible presence of ADHD, other psychiatric comorbidities, and other functional impairments in the parent(s), and, if there is a couple, the marital/couple pair. These conditions can impact on family structure, family role functions, family interactional dynamics, and the ability of the parents to implement the kind of comprehensive plan that the child may need to treat this serious and chronic condition. In addition, the functional impairments (e.g., job loss and/or change, accidents) can place a terrific stress on an already overburdened family system. If treatment is to be sensitive, responsive, adaptive to the child's and family's needs, and maximally effective, it must address these broader issues in the family system.

As these comments imply, the family treatment plan for ADHD will be guided by an assessment for the presence of ADHD, associated comorbidities and functional impairments in the child and in the parents, and possibly in other family members. Comprehensive diagnostic assessment of child and adult ADHD and other psychiatric comorbidities is beyond the scope of this chapter, and the reader is referred to several excellent texts (Johnson & Conners, 2002; Mash & Terdal, 1997; Murphy & Gordon, 1998). Suffice it to say that if the child or adolescent does not come to the family therapist with a complete diagnostic report, then the first order of business may be to refer the individual for such an assessment, so that the elements of the clinical picture will be clear to the therapist. Likewise, in conducting an initial evaluation for family therapy, the therapist should observe the parents and ask them about the presence of possible ADHD and other psychiatric conditions in themselves, siblings, and even other family members (such as grandparents). If the family therapist suspects the presence of adult ADHD, screening tools are available (Goldstein & Ellison, 2002; Weiss, Hechtman, & Weiss, 1999) that can be used to discuss a possible referral of the parent(s) for their own evaluation. A good adult diagnostic evaluation will also pinpoint the presence of other adult psychiatric comorbidities (such as depression) and functional impairments (such as severe marital conflict) that may be important to address or treat as part of the comprehensive family treatment plan. My experience is that the earlier in the process that these conditions can be identified the better, as the success of treatment for the child's symptoms will rise or fall on the ability of the parents and entire family to cooperate with therapy. Much better to identify and treat parent ADHD or depression early, rather than to leave it unaddressed while implementing a parent training intervention, only to have the parent(s) fail, drop out of treatment, and lose confidence in themselves or the treatment system and its ability to help them. Likewise, if severe marital conflict is present, the therapist is well advised to at least know about it at the onset of therapy. Even if marital therapy is not undertaken first, the therapist can incorporate knowledge of the fact that there is marital conflict into the strategy for working with the parents in parent management training.

To illustrate these points, Evans, Vallano, and Pelham (1994) reported a case study in which an ADHD mother of an ADHD child initially failed to benefit from an attempt at parent training due to her own difficulties with consistency, completing tasks, accurately dispensing medication to the child, and keeping accurate records. Following stimulant medication of the mother, her parenting behaviors improved, as did the child's behaviors. Likewise, in an interesting randomized clinical trial with disruptive children and depressed mothers, one group of families received parent training alone and another received parent training plus cognitive therapy procedures for adult depression. Both treatments were equally effective in reducing mothers' depression and children's disruptive behavior at immediate posttreatment. However, at the 6-month follow-up, more families who received the parent training plus cognitive behavior therapy (CBT) for maternal depression, compared to parent training alone, showed continued reliable reductions in maternal depression and child disruptive behavior (Sanders & McFarland, 2000). Although it is not certain that these results would generalize to children with primary diagnoses of ADHD, it is likely that similar results would be found in ADHD children who share many of the oppositional and conduct problems seen in the disruptive children in this study. These two studies lend support to the clinical recommendation that treatment of ADHD and depression in parents will result in better child as well as parent outcomes when parent training is implemented as a treatment for the ADHD child.

For all of these reasons, screening and referral for evaluation and treatment of ADHD or depression in the parents must be thoughtfully considered by the family therapist. In general, the earlier this can occur in the process the better. However, clinical judgment must be exercised in making this decision. If the therapist believes that confronting the parent with his or her own possible psychopathology too early in the process will drive the parents away from treatment, then this discussion might be delayed until more trust has been established, and/or more clinical material relevant to the impact of parent psychopathology on the course of family treatment is available.

The issue of if and when to introduce stimulant medication (or other medication) treatment for the child also must be given consideration in the family treatment plan. Some clinicians/researchers in the field of ADHD consider stimulant medication the first line of treatment for child ADHD; certainly, its effectiveness for the primary symptoms of ADHD cannot be disputed at this point (MTA Cooperative Group, 1999). Other clinicians/researchers believe that behavioral/ family intervention should be instituted first, and stimulant medication added later, if needed (Fabiano & Pelham, 2002). In clinical practice, issues of medication effectiveness for the child's particular clinical profile and medication palatability and acceptability all enter into this decision. These issues have been discussed in detail in Wells (2004), to which the reader is referred. Suffice it to say here that for ADHD children and adolescents, the issue of if and when to introduce stimulant medication should be carefully discussed with the child and parents and their physician, early in the family treatment plan. In the likely event that the family therapist is not also a physician, the therapist should refer the family for medication evaluation and treatment as indicated, and work closely with the physician prescribing the medicine throughout the course of family therapy.

FAMILY INTERVENTION

Once the clinical profile of the referred patient with ADHD and relevant family members is identified, the family-oriented therapist must then proceed with a treatment plan to address the various elements in that family's clinical profile. Since there may be several potential targets of intervention, prioritizing treatment goals becomes important. If the assessment has revealed the presence of substance abuse in the target child/adolescent or parent who will be involved in treatment, or any dangerous or out-of-control behavior, these become the top priority for the initial phase of treatment. Frequent substance use/abuse by the child can be dangerous, can cloud the symptom picture, and make it difficult or impossible to track the effectiveness of the treatment on other symptoms. Substance abuse by a parent may also be dangerous, and can effect the ability of the parent to participate and cooperate actively in the treatment. A decision must be made early in the initial phase of treatment whether to refer the substance user to a substance abuse treatment center. Then, family intervention for ADHD can occur concurrently with or subsequent to the substance abuse treatment.

Sometimes, parents who are substance abusers are reluctant to embark on their own substance abuse treatment when it is their child whom they have brought for therapy. In that case, I sometimes proceed with family therapy targeted at the child's problems, with full knowledge that the parent(s)' substance abuse will almost certainly interfere with their ability to participate fully in the therapy. When this inevitably happens, I can then talk with the parents, using concrete examples from the therapy sessions or failed attempts at homework assignments of how their substance abuse is interfering with their child's treatment (e.g., parents who pass out on the couch every evening will not be able to comply with parenting homework assignments to conduct special-time sessions with their child, or monitor the child's performance of school-assigned homework). Parents are often more likely to accept a referral for their own substance abuse treatment when they are gently confronted with evidence of the impact of their substance abuse on their children.

If there is evidence of other dangerous or out-of-control behavior (e.g., child abuse, serious family aggression) then age-appropriate intervention designed to restore safety and control in the family should be undertaken. In the case of child abuse, state regulations regarding referral of the family to child protective services must be followed. In the case of serious child or adolescent aggression, the first priority for family intervention should be establishing or restoring parental controls. Principles and techniques from behavioral parent management training and behavioral family therapy can be used to help the parents gain immediate control. For example, with younger children who are aggressive toward siblings it may be necessary to immediately implement careful monitoring and time-out procedures every time there is an aggressive act. Parents may need to establish a clear house rule that "hitting other family members is not allowed" and then observe or listen carefully whenever the child and siblings are in the house together. Any time the child displays an aggressive action, no warning or verbal reprimand is given; the parent swiftly removes the child to a preestablished location for an isolation time-out. With adolescents who are aggressive, a hierarchical safety plan may need to be negotiated, in which every aggressive act by the adolescent is met with immediate consequences (e.g., removal of all privileges, such as access to car or phone). If adolescents escalate their aggression or attack the parents, then parents are coached in how to call the police in order to keep family members safe. Adolescents who react to in-home attempts at parental control by escalating their aggression may need to be referred to inpatient or residential treatment. Due to the phenomenon of extinction burst, children and adolescents can be expected to display transient increases in some of their aggressive behavior when parents first attempt to reestablish control. If the baseline rate of aggression is already high, the family may understandably not be able to tolerate this temporary burst due to safety concerns. Therefore, it is important for the family therapist to predict this, and to help the family anticipate and establish a very concrete plan for responding to high or intolerable levels of aggressive behavior with police intervention or out-of-home placement.

Once urgent issues involving safety or dangerousness have been addressed, the family therapist can proceed with an outpatient family treatment plan that may address several treatment targets, depending on the family's clinical profile. However, in almost every case, the treatment will begin with psychoeducation about ADHD. While this is especially important for the person(s) with ADHD it is also important that all family members, not just the person(s) with ADHD, be included in this psychoeducation process. It is often a tremendous relief for ADHD families to hear the message that their affected family member(s) suffers from a neuropsychological, brain-based disorder, and not from laziness, meanness, or stupidity, or other pejorative labels that the family may have been using to characterize their affected member. This can be the first step in relieving some of the guilt and shame experienced by ADHD persons about themselves, and in alleviating some of the anger, resentment, and hostility experienced by family members. This, in turn, sets the stage for increased acceptance and cooperation among family members for what is to follow.

Psychoeducation can occur in initial outpatient family therapy sessions as well as throughout therapy, and can include all family members. Age-appropriate explanations should be given of the core symptoms of ADHD (inattention, impulsivity, and hyperactivity) and how these manifest in the presenting problem. It is important to relate the symptoms of ADHD to the everyday interactions and behaviors of the affected member, especially where these have a negative impact on other family members, and to problematic areas of life functioning (e.g., completing homework, completing household tasks, keeping commitments and appointments in a timely manner). The neurobiological nature of the disorder and its chronicity throughout the lifespan should be explained to the family. This can assist in repairing the self-esteem of the individual and reducing hostility in family members. It is useful to present the frame that while the disorder is not the individual's fault, it *is* the individual's and the family's responsibility to develop and pursue realistic goals for improvement. In addition, information on family transmission of ADHD (ADHD can run in families) is important, and can set the stage for raising the possibility that the diagnosis may be present in other family members (e.g., one or both parents), whose ability to assist with the family treatment plan for the target individual may be compromised. If comorbidity is present, then this should also be discussed with the family, especially as it is linked to elements of the treatment plan, to prognosis, or to implications for treatment. Likewise, if other psychopathology or functional impairment is present in key family members who will have an important role in treatment (e.g., a depressed mother), then this should be noted, and a plan discussed for how it will be addressed. Even if these family members are not willing initially to address the problem, noting it early allows for reopening the discussion as treatment proceeds and the impact of the problem on the treatment process becomes more evident.

After these basic facts about symptoms, etiology, family transmission, and comorbidity have been discussed, a treatment plan should be recommended to the family. This may include referral to other professionals as part of a collaborative, multidisciplinary approach (e.g., school professionals for children with academic problems, or life-skills coaches for adults with job problems, or physicians for medication treatment). The family therapist should collaborate with these professionals in a comprehensive treatment plan. Likewise, individual sessions with the ADHD person might occur, especially if comorbid conditions are present. For example, while individual cognitive behavior therapy has not been found to be useful in improving the primary symptoms of ADHD, it may be useful for ADHD children with comorbid anxiety (March et al., 2000). Individual therapy sessions would focus on cognitive behavioral strategies for anxiety management involving exposure and response prevention. Then, in parent training sessions, anxiety management targets might be included in a home token economy implemented by the parents in order to provide incentives to the child to practice exposure tasks. In all likelihood, intervention with the family, either its subsystems and/or as a whole, will be an important component of that treatment plan, in addition to individual therapy or medication, and it is to those elements of treatment that we now turn.

Possible Components of Family Intervention for ADHD

Parent Management Training for Preadolescent ADHD

For families with a preadolescent child who has ADHD, especially if the child also has comorbid ODD or CD, Parent Management Training (PMT) will almost certainly be one of the central components of family intervention. Although a number of clinical researchers have employed parent training programs with families of children with behavior problems, the investigators most associated with this approach for use with ADHD populations are Russell Barkley (1998) and Wells and colleagues (1996; 2000). Barkley adapted an 8- to 10-session intervention for use with ADHD children from the parent training program first developed by Constance Hanf. Wells and colleagues developed an extended parent training program that incorporated many of Barkley's adaptations, but embellished and extended the basic program to include attention to school and other parent factors that are often issues in ADHD families. Each of these will be described briefly.

In Barkley's version of parent training for ADHD, treatment begins with psychoeducation, including a review of information on ADHD as well as causes of oppositional and defiant behavior, including diagnosis, theories of etiology, and principles of social learning theory that are relevant to parent-child interactions. Once this background has been discussed with parents, presentation of parent management skills begins, starting first with increasing positive parental attention to children during a 10- to 20-minute "special time" every day. After parent attention has been established as a reinforcer, parents are taught how to apply their positive attention to two critical target behaviors for ADHD children: compliance to parent instructions and independent play. Parents are taught to "catch the child being good" (i.e., compliant) and also to attend and praise the child when the child is playing independently while the parent is engaged in some other activity (such as working or cooking).

Compliance to parental instructions is felt to be a critical target behavior to increase in ADHD children, especially those comorbid for ODD or CD. Noncompliance is the keystone characteristic of Oppositional Defiant Disorder, and decreasing this comorbidity is important in the clinical management of these children. However, even in children with pure ADHD, improving compliance to parental instructions is often key if parents are to assist the child with managing his or her inattentive, impulsive, and overactive behaviors. That is, management of these behaviors can only be accomplished via parental instructions to the child (e.g., "sit down at the table and don't get up again until dinner is finished"), and establishment of house rules (e.g., "grabbing your sister's toys without asking is not permitted"). If the child cannot or will not follow these instructions and house rules, then the parent will be unsuccessful in assisting the child with his or her overactive and impulsive behaviors. Likewise, independent play is felt to be a critical target behavior in these children, since staying on task for an age-appropriate amount of time is a frequent, primary problem behavior.

For young children, improving positive parent attention may be sufficient. For older children, the next step is establishing a home token economy, which sets up a reward system for compliance, as well as an expanded array of target behaviors, such as social behaviors related to impulsivity (e.g., hitting, swearing), age-appropriate chores, and other responsibilities. Later, parents are taught a time-out procedure to use as a mild punishment procedure for decreasing noncompliance and later, other disruptive behaviors that may still be occurring (violations of house rules, etc.).

In the final stage of the basic parent training program, attention is paid to establishing generalization of treatment effects across settings and time. Parents are taught procedures for managing disruptive behavior in public places and at school, using the home-school Daily Report Card (DRC). The DRC is an index card or other monitoring form that lists school target behaviors (negotiated in cooperation with the teacher) and monitoring intervals (such as class periods). The teacher checks off on the child's card the occurrence or nonoccurrence of the target behaviors in each specified interval and the child brings the card home each day to the parent, who delivers backup rewards at home. In a final session, the focus is on anticipation and planning for management of future behavior problems. A booster session is then held 1 month after the final intensive phase session, to review treatment goals and consolidate treatment gains.

The parent training program developed by Wells and colleagues (1996, 2000) was used in the MTA study of multimodal treatment of ADHD. This program is a 27-session treatment program that incorporates adaptations of the 8- to 12-session program described previously, but extends well beyond the basic program. It provides more discussion of clinical nuances that arise in treatment of ADHD families, and more step-by-step instructions of basic procedures. However, beyond embellishments to the basic program, the parent training program of Wells et al. (1996) was designed more intensively and comprehensively to address multiple settings and domains of child and family functioning in ADHD. First, great emphasis is placed on intervention in the school setting, since most ADHD children display considerable difficulties related to primary ADHD symptoms in school. Many sessions are devoted to discussing, modeling, and role-playing with parents, both in therapy sessions as well as in visits to the school, and to developing parent advocacy and teacher consultation skills. Other innovations include training parents in cognitive strategies for changing their own maladaptive cognitions and attributions related to parenting a child with ADHD (e.g., "my child is bad; I must be a very bad parent"), as well as stress management strategies, including calming self-talk and relaxation skills, to use in disciplinary encounters with the child. These innovations were added to address findings from empirical research, reviewed earlier, that have shown that parents of ADHD children experience more parenting stress, anger, and irritability, and a decreased sense of parenting self-competence compared to other parents.

Since 1980, there have been several controlled studies in the published literature that have examined parent training as a single treatment or as a component of a clinical behavior therapy package for youth with ADHD. These studies have shown that parent training produces reductions in inattention and overactivity (Anastopoulos, Shelton, DuPaul, & Guevremont, 1993; Dubey, O'Leary, & Kaufman, 1983; Sonuga-Barke, Daley, Thompson, Laver-Bradbury, & Weeks, 2001) in child noncompliance and conduct problems (Pisterman et al., 1989; Pollard, Ward, & Barkley, 1983; Sonuga-Barke et al., 2001) and in child aggression (Anastopoulos et al., 1993). As would be expected, improvements in parenting skills (Pisterman et al., 1989, 1992) also have been found. Some studies also have reported reductions in parent stress and improvements in parent self-esteem with parent training (Anastopoulos et al., 1993; Sonuga-Barke et al., 2001; Pisterman et al., 1992). Effect sizes for parent training for ADHD of 1.2 have been reported on ADHD symptoms. Anastopoulos et al. (1993) reported that 64 percent of their sample demonstrated clinically significant changes in terms of percentage of children no longer in the clinical range on the ADHD rating scale with parent training, compared with 27 percent for a waitlist control group.

Other studies have examined multicomponent behavior therapy programs of which parent training is one component. The most typical combination involves parent training plus teacher consultation. In teacher consultation, the therapist works with the teacher to set up a DRC focusing on classroom behavior and academic performance, and may also consult with the teacher on classroom-wide behavior management strategies as well. Several studies have combined parent training and teacher consultation (Horn, Ialongo, Greenberg, Packard, & Smith-Winberry, 1990; Horn et al., 1991; Pelham et al., 1988) and compared them to medication, with results generally showing that the combination of parent training plus teacher consultation results in significant improvement in children's home and school behavior. Even greater improvements are noted when parent training and teacher consultation are combined with stimulant medications (Pelham et al., 1988).

The two largest scaled, randomized clinical trials in the published literature each included parent training as one component of comprehensive behavior therapy programs, and compared behavior therapy to medication alone and their combination (Klein & Abikoff, 1997; MTA Cooperative Group, 1999). While the effects of parent training alone cannot be elucidated from these studies, they are instructive when considering the best multimodal treatment for ADHD children. In both studies, medication outperformed behavior therapy alone on several measures of ADHD children's functioning. However, on some measures, the combination of medication and behavior therapy (including parent training) resulted in greater improvement than medication alone (Klein & Abikoff, 1997), or than community-treated controls—whereas medication alone did not result in greater improvement than community-treated controls (MTA Cooperative Group, 1999). Full normalization on objective classroom measures was only achieved with combination treatment (Klein & Abikoff, 1997); parents were more satisfied with behavior therapy alone and with combination treatment, rather than with medication alone (MTA Cooperative Group, 1999). These results suggest that a comprehensive behavior therapy approach that includes parent training will be most effective (on some but not all symptoms) and result in greater normalization of ADHD children. All of these studies confirm that parent training is and will remain an important component of the treatment armamentarium for the families of children with ADHD, and should be considered to be an essential leg in the three-legged-stool comprising treatment of these children (i.e., stimulant medication, parent training, and school intervention). These studies also illustrate the importance of multidisciplinary collaboration in which family/parent interventions delivered by the family therapist must be coordinated with interventions delivered with the child in individual or group contexts and/or with school intervention specialists. This multisystemic, collaborative perspective can be expected to result in the greatest positive outcomes for children with ADHD, and in the greatest chance at normalization.

Family Intervention with Adolescent ADHD

For families with an adolescent with ADHD, especially if there are high levels of oppositional or conduct disorder symptoms, and/or high levels of parent/teen conflict, some form of family intervention will be indicated. The clinician/researcher most noted for family intervention with adolescent ADHD is Arthur Robin, who has written about a combined behavioral/systems approach (Robin, 1998). Robin describes a 10- to 20-session approach to family intervention that begins with psychoeducation, which, in addition to all the elements described earlier, also includes information on adolescent development and the normal tasks of adolescents that may be driving some of the current parent/teen conflict (e.g., the drive toward independence fueling conflict over later curfew). Understanding teen behavior in an adolescent development framework assists in reducing the hostility that parents may bring to later discussions. Treatment then progresses to sessions in which cognitive restructuring strategies are used to help parents and adolescents adhere to reasonable expectations. Then, communications skills training with parents and teens occurs, in order to reduce the negative communication habits that are characteristic of families with high levels of parent/teen conflict. Negative communication habits, such as calling each other names, interrupting, criticizing, lecturing, and dredging up the past are directly targeted as bad habits to eliminate both in sessions and at home; more positive communication habits, such as expressing anger directly, listening even when one disagrees, and sticking to the present are agreed to and practiced. The final major strategy is family problem-solving, in which parents and teen learn a step-by-step framework to use in discussions of conflict areas to be negotiated (such as curfew, chores, etc.). Once these skills are learned, they are applied to discussions in therapy sessions and ultimately at home. Robin also describes the need for structural family interventions, targeted at restoring a united parental subsystem, in families in which one parent has been disengaged and the other enmeshed with the adolescent, or in families in which the parents and adolescent together have colluded in transforming disciplinary efforts into marital disputes.

One study has evaluated this approach to family intervention with adolescent ADHD and compared it to two other approaches: behavioral parent training, such as that described earlier for younger children (modified for adolescents), and a structural family therapy approach, in which families were helped to identify and alter maladaptive family interaction patterns, such as transgenerational coalitions, scapegoating, and triangulation, by targeting family boundaries, alignments, and power. In this study (Barkley, Guevremont, Anastopoulos, & Fletcher, 1992), all three approaches to family intervention resulted in significant improvement on most measures of internalizing and externalizing symptoms as well as family conflict, from before to after treatment, with further gains in many cases at 3-month follow-up. However, relatively few families moved into the normal range (5 percent for behavioral parent training, 19 percent for behavioral/systems intervention, and 10 percent for structural intervention) in this study, and the lack of any type of control group leaves open the question of whether the change observed in any of the groups was due to placebo or measurement effects or simply the passage of time. A subsequent family intervention study by Barkley, Edwards, Laneri, Fletcher, and Metevia (2001) with ADHD adolescents comorbid for ODD compared the behavioral/systems approach described previously to behavioral parent management, followed by the systems approach. While both approaches produced significant improvements on rating of parent-teen conflict, there were no differences between the two approaches at mid- or posttreatment. However, in this study 31 percent to 70 percent of families were normalized on measures of family conflict (no differences between the groups on most measures). These studies, taken together, suggest that principles and techniques of behavioral parent training, modified to be developmentally appropriate for adolescents, as well as principles and techniques of problem solving, communication training, and cognitive restructuring, are promising although not maximally effective approaches to the difficulties in families of ADHD adolescents. In addition, because a structural family therapy approach resulted in similar levels of improvement when used as a comparison treatment, this approach also merits consideration when treating ADHD adolescents and their families. However, empirical evidence is scant as there are only these two studies in the published literature and further work is needed in this area.

Marital Therapy for Adult ADHD

Beyond the studies reviewed earlier documenting the higher rates of marital conflict, sexual difficulties, divorce, and multiple marriages in parents of ADHD youth, as well as in adult ADHD populations, there is very little empirical research characterizing the contributors to marital conflict and dissatisfaction in these groups. Likewise, I know of no controlled studies of marital or couples intervention in adult ADHD. Therefore, what is presented is limited and comes from my own observations and from anecdotal reports of therapists working with couples in which one partner has ADHD. However, because marital dysfunction threatens the integrity of the family and the ability of the adults to work together in supporting the adaptive development of the children, this is an area of critically important family functioning to which family therapists must direct therapeutic attention.

The symptoms and behaviors of ADHD can influence the couple/marital relationship in a variety of ways that present to the family therapist as marital complaints. The non-ADHD spouse often presents as angry and resentful, or alternatively as resigned but disengaged, as a result of the years of insult to the marital relationship that result from ADHD symptoms. Symptoms of inattention and motor restlessness make for a spouse who is a poor listener, who cannot sit still, and who may even walk out of the room while the spouse is talking. Inattention and impairments in verbal working memory and sense of time seen in ADHD adults also can affect areas of relationship functioning such as timely performance of duties, completing household tasks, and completing parenting responsibilities in a timely fashion (e.g., picking up the children after school or sports practice, arriving home on time for dinner with the family, monitoring and performing household tasks that need to be done, following through on a promise to stop at the grocery store). Symptoms of impulsivity and difficulties with emotional self-regulation result in impulsive verbal outbursts and inappropriate management of anger, leading to irritable, reactive comments that are experienced by the spouse as hostile and hurtful. The restlessness of the ADHD spouse can make it difficult to sit still and engage in problem-solving discussions about bills, household management, and coparenting. All of these symptoms can also impact the bonding and intimacy that are important in anchoring a marriage.

Any or all of these relationship difficulties, prompted by the symptoms and impairments associated with adult ADHD, produce feelings of hurt, resentment, anger, and frustration in the spouse. Initially a distancer-pursuer interactional dynamic may occur, in which the non-ADHD spouse pursues (often in the form of nagging) the ADHD spouse to be more attentive, caring, involved, and collaborative with the tasks and responsibilities of the relationship and family life. However, over time, if the symptoms do not improve, and the marriage does not disintegrate early, the non-ADHD spouse eventually adapts, by taking on more and more of the family responsibilities. This stabilizes the family but results in ever more resentment in the non-ADHD spouse, and eventually results in the disengagement in the marital dyad. Due to difficulties with attentiveness to social cues and the inability to sit quietly and listen, the ADHD spouse may be unaware of the feelings of the partner, or alternatively may feel that he or she can do nothing right. Intimacy is affected under the accumulated weight of the attachment injuries that result from these assaults to the relationship, as the couple becomes more and more disengaged.

There are no controlled studies of marital therapy for ADHD. However, a consideration of the previously described interactional processes and their resulting outcomes suggests several potentially important ingredients in marital therapy. First, marital therapy will have the best chance of succeeding if preliminary changes are made in the primary ADHD symptoms. Because stimulant medications are effective on the primary symptoms of ADHD with a large proportion of adults, strong consideration should be given to referral to a physician for evaluation and treatment. As I have repeatedly emphasized in other sections, psychoeducation about ADHD, and especially about how the symptoms impact on relationship behaviors, is also important as an initial step in therapy. Both spouses must understand the impact of adult ADHD on the person trying to manage it in him- or herself, and on the spouse who is affected by it. This may provide an alternative explanation for the individual as well as for the spouse about the origin of the behaviors and can provide the first step along the road to relationship repair ("He forgets your birthday because of inattention and poor time tracking, not because he doesn't love you;" "She feels guilty and ashamed when she forgets to pick up the children, even though she impulsively reacts only with anger when confronted about it"). It is also important, as part of this process, to emphasize that although ADHD is not the individual's fault, it is nevertheless his or her responsibility to take whatever action is possible to address the problems, especially as they impact negatively on other people. Failure to take personal responsibility for change by the affected adult must be challenged at every turn, in order to not saddle the non-ADHD spouse with additional relationship burdens and to keep him or her engaged in the process.

As a further step toward initial relationship repair, the non-ADHD spouse should be helped to verbalize his or her accumulated hurts and frustrations and the ADHD spouse should be supported to listen without defending. This may be difficult in the beginning, and initial training in communications skills may be necessary for the ADHD spouse to be able to listen and reflect what his or her spouse is saying about his or her experience without criticizing or deflecting. My experience, however is that behavioral problem solving and contracting designed at negotiating a new, shared balance and greater attentiveness in the relationship will not move forward until the partner has had a chance to verbalize his or her accumulated negative feelings without being tuned out or discounted by the ADHD spouse. The therapist will need to provide a great deal of skills training, prompting, and support to the ADHD spouse in this process. Concepts and strategies from Emotionally Focused Couples Therapy (Johnson, 1996) may also be particularly well suited to this stage of therapy.

Other steps in marital therapy may involve strategies from behavioral marital therapy (Epstein & Baucom, 2002) aimed at negotiating constructive solutions to ongoing areas of relationship difficulty. For example, using problem-solving strategies, couples can be helped specifically to plan and structure their time with prompts built into the system for the ADHD spouse (e.g., the PDA is programmed to beep as a reminder to the ADHD spouse when relationship activities are to occur). Concrete structures are discussed as ways of insuring that commitments are adhered to (e.g., a running grocery list is kept on the refrigerator; spouses take weekly turns in going to the grocery). The importance and nature of caring and intimacy is also discussed, and the therapist helps the partners to share and specifically plan activities and exchanges that nurture the fundamental attachment in the relationship.

It is important not to move too quickly and to introduce no more than one or two areas of relationship change at a time. However, my experience is that for a couple whose relationship has not been irrevocably damaged by the time they appear for therapy—and who each retain some commitment to the marriage—these approaches can help gradually to reverse relationship-damaging interactions, and facilitate a closer and more satisfying marriage for both members.

Case Study

Brandon S. is an 8-year-old Caucasian male who was referred to the family therapy clinic from a psychologist who had completed a comprehensive assessment of

Brandon and his family. Brandon had been referred for assessment by his school third grade class, where his teacher reported that he was disruptive in class, didn't follow class rules involving staying in his seat, raising his hand before talking, and finishing his work on time. In addition, he was aggressive on the playground with other kids who frequently reported that Brandon was pushing, shoving, and hitting them. At home, he was defiant with his mother, although less so with his father. The teacher's initial efforts to manage Brandon had not resulted in much improvement. Brandon's mother presented as tearful and depressed when she discussed Brandon as well as her strained relationship with her husband, who was frequently absent from the home, working long hours and critical of her for "not being able to control Brandon." The testing revealed a diagnosis of ADHD, Combined Type, and Oppositional Defiant Disorder in Brandon, maternal depression, and marital distress.

Although the father did not come to the initial session, the family therapist called specifically to invite the father to the next session. In this session, the therapist began by asking the family members (mother, father, and Brandon) what they understood about the diagnosis of ADHD. Brandon said that he thought it meant that he was "dumb;" his father said he thought Brandon just needed some good hard discipline. The therapist spent the remainder of the session providing education to all three about the nature of ADHD, emphasizing the neuropsychological basis for the disorder and also the way in which the symptoms impact on school functioning and family life. The therapist emphasized that children with ADHD present special parenting challenges and require "more than the ordinary amount of good parenting skills." He also emphasized the special importance of parents working together on behalf of an ADHD child. Brandon had started taking a stimulant medication, and some improvement in school behavior had been noticed—but little improvement in home behavior. The therapist therefore recommended a course of parent training, and emphasized the importance of both parents attending. Mother's depression was noted, but a decision was made to begin parent training and keep checking in with mother regarding her depression. During parent training sessions the marital conflict became apparent. This was noted in sessions, and the interference of the conflict on their ability to cooperate on parenting their child was discussed. The therapist contracted with the couple to continue with parent training for six sessions, until some improvement in Brandon's oppositional behavior was achieved, and then to embark on marital therapy sessions. This course was chosen because of the functional relationship of Brandon's oppositional behavior to the high level of criticism in the marriage as well as to mother's depression. Couples sessions focused on the lack of intimacy and mutual support in the marriage and the resulting feelings of anger and loneliness experienced by both partners. After eight sessions of couples therapy, the focus changed back to parenting issues, where the couple were now more able to work together cooperatively and with the teacher on establishing a home-school DRC system. Father was put in charge of receiving Brandon's DRC each day and delivering backup rewards to him at home every evening. Brandon's behavior showed gradual improvement at home and further improvement at school with the combination of medication and parent training. At the end of 18 sessions, mother's depression was reassessed and found to be greatly improved, an outcome that is sometimes achieved as a result of both parent training and marital therapy. For this reason, mother was not referred specifically for treatment of depression, but was advised to notice any future upsurge in depressed feelings as a possible cue that parenting or marital issues were once again resurfacing, or a cue that it was time to seek treatment for depression. She was encouraged to call the therapist to help with this assessment if needed. At the end of therapy the family was advised that periodic booster visits (at least once a year) were frequently helpful with ADHD children—to reassess behavioral and family adjustment and to intervene early as new behavioral or developmental issues arise.

CONCLUSIONS

In this chapter I have presented ADHD as a family illness, in the sense that the disorder can have a major impact on family interactions and family structure and role functions, and in the sense that it is an illness that runs in families. That is, when one member of a family has ADHD it is more likely than chance that other members will also have ADHD. It is also an illness that lends itself to systems and/or interactional perspectives. Although there is certainly a fundamental neuropsychological basis to the etiology of the core symptoms of ADHD, those symptoms provoke reactions and responses from the system (e.g., family, school) that can function to escalate primary symptoms further and have negative spillover effects onto other areas of individual and family functions. These, in turn, feed back to the ADHD person, further exacerbating and extending his or her symptoms, comorbidities, and impairments. By the time a family with one or more members who have ADHD presents for treatment, there may be multiple comorbidities (e.g., ODD, CD, substance abuse), and/or areas of maladaptive functioning in individuals (e.g., maternal depression) or subgroups (e.g., the marital pair) of the family. Because family interventions have been demonstrated to be useful for many of these areas, the overall family treatment plan may include several components of family intervention aimed at those symptom and impairment areas.

I have presented a general strategy for conceptualizing and treating ADHD with family interventions. This strategy starts with an assessment to pinpoint the major areas of psychological and functional impairment that are present in individuals and subsystems in the family. This is done not just for purposes of general diagnosis, but specifically with an eye toward understanding how these areas of impairment impact on family role functions (such as parenting or marital relating). Areas requiring urgent or emergency intervention are identified and become the first priority for treatment. Thereafter, a treatment strategy is identified, consisting of components of family intervention that address the major areas of individual or subgroup impairment that have been demonstrated to be related to ADHD symptoms or to affect the ability of the family to cooperate with treatment of ADHD. Often this will require that the family therapist work collaboratively in a multidisciplinary approach with other treatment providers who have expertise in affected areas (e.g., school psychologist, life-skills coach, or physician). The purview of the family therapist is to provide those treatment components from the literature on family interventions that have evidence for effectiveness in areas of family dysfunction.

I have outlined several of the major family treatment components for ADHD and have provided suggestions throughout for the ordering of treatment components. Treatment should always start with psychoeducation about ADHD with all family members, if this has not already been done by a physician or the psychologist who performed the initial assessment. Even if it has, the family therapist should begin by asking the family what their understanding is of the diagnosis of ADHD, what causes it and how it impacts on their family roles and relationships. Subsequently, the order in which treatment components are implemented is a matter of clinical judgment based on the exigencies of each case. Ideally, when a child with ADHD is the identified patient, psychopathology or marital dysfunction in the parents should be identified and treated as early in the process as possible—before working with the parents in parent management training targeted at the child's symptoms. However, the ideal situation is not always possible, most notably when parents are resistant to the idea of treating their own problems. Often, parents will become more receptive over time if treatment begins by focusing on the identified patient whom they have brought for services. As they see that the treatment is beginning to be helpful, develop a sense of trust in the therapist, and as the therapist gently but firmly points out to them in sessions the way in which their own psychopathology interferes with their ability to be the most effective parents for their child, they may become more open to accepting additional treatment recommendations or components for themselves. Finally, throughout family treatment, families should be educated about the chronic nature of ADHD and the need for ongoing follow-up and booster intervention, especially as children go through their various stages of development. New issues and challenges will arise at the different developmental stages, and treatments will need to be adjusted and modified accordingly. The dental model of a once-a-year checkup is useful, to introduce families to a way of instilling the importance of ongoing monitoring, with occasional booster interventions along the way.

REFERENCES

Abikoff, H. B., Jensen, P. S., Arnold, L. L. E., Hoza, B., Hechtman, L., Pollack, S., Martin, D., Alvir, J., March, J. S., Hinshaw, S., Vitiello, B., Newcorn, J., Greiner, A., Cantwell, D. P., Conners, C. K., Elliott, G., Greenhill, L. L., Kraemer, H., Pelham, W. E., Severe, J. B., Swanson, J. M., Wells, K., & Wigal, T. (2002). Observed classroom behavior of children with ADHD: Relationship to gender and co-morbidity. *Journal of Abnormal Child Psychology, 30,* 349–359.

American Psychiatric Association. (1994). *Diagnostic and statistical manual of mental disorders* (4th ed.). Washington, DC: Author.

Anastopoulos, A. D., Shelton, T., DuPaul, G. J., & Guevremont, D. C. (1993). Parent training for attention deficit hyperactivity disorder: Its impact on parent functioning. *Journal of Abnormal Child Psychology, 21,* 581–595.

Anderson, C. A., Hinshaw, S. P., & Simmel, C. (1994). Mother-child interactions in ADHD and comparison boys: Relationships with overt and covert externalizing behavior. *Journal of Abnormal Child Psychology, 22,* 247–265.

Angold, A., Costello, E. J., & Erkanli, A. (1999). Co-morbidity. *Journal of Child Psychology and Psychiatry, 40,* 57–88.

Angold, A., Erkanli, A., Egger, H. L., & Costello, E. J. (2000). Stimulant treatment for children: A community perspective. *Journal of the American Academy of Child and Adolescent Psychiatry, 39,* 975–994.

Arnold, L. E. (1996). Sex differences in ADHD: Conference summary. *Journal of Abnormal Child Psychology, 24*(5), 555–569.

Arnold, L. E., Elliott, M., Sachs, L., Bird, H., Kraemer, H. C., Wells, K. C., Abikoff, H. B., Comarda, A., Conners, C. K., Elliott, G. R., Greenhill, L. L., Hechtman, L., Hinshaw, S. P., Hoza, B., Jensen, P. S., March, J. S., Newcorn, J. H., Pelham, W. E., Severe, J. B., Swanson, J. M., Vitiello, B., & Wigal, T. (2003). Effects of ethnicity on treatment attendance, stimulant response/dose, and 14-month outcome in ADHD. *Journal of Consulting and Clinical Psychology, 71,* 713–727.

Barkley, R. A. (1996). Attention-deficit/hyperactivity disorder. In E. J. Mash & R. A. Barkley (Eds.), *Child psychopathology* (pp. 63–112). New York: Guilford Press.

Barkley, R. A. (1998). *Attention-deficit hyperactivity disorder: A handbook for diagnosis and treatment.* (2nd ed.). New York: Guilford Press.

Barkley, R. A. (2003). Attention-deficit/hyperactivity disorder. In E. J. Mash & R. A. Barkley (Eds.), *Child psychopathology.* (2nd ed.). (pp. 75–143). New York: Guilford Press.

Barkley, R. A., Anastopoulos, A. D., Guevremont, D. G., & Fletcher, K. F. (1992). Adolescents with attention deficit hyperactivity disorder: Mother-adolescent interactions, family beliefs and conflicts, and maternal psychopathology. *Journal of Abnormal Child Psychology, 20,* 263–288.

Barkley, R. A., Edwards, G., Laneri, M., Fletcher, K., & Meteva, L. (2001). The efficacy of problem-solving communication training alone, behavior management training alone, and their combination for parent-adolescent conflict in teenagers with ADHD and ODD. *Journal of Consulting and Clinical Psychology, 69,* 926–941.

Barkley, R. A., Fischer, M., Edelbrock, C. S., & Smallish, L. (1990). The adolescent outcome of hyperactive children diagnoses by research criteria: I. An 8-year prospective follow-up study. *Journal of the American Academy of Child and Adolescent Psychiatry, 29,* 546–557.

Barkley, R. A., Fischer, M., Edelbrock, C. S., & Smallish, L. (1991). The adolescent outcome of hyperactive children diagnoses by research criteria: III. Mother-child interactions, family conflicts, and maternal psychopathology. *Journal of Child Psychology and Psychiatry, 32,* 233–256.

Barkley, R. A., Fischer, M., Smallish, L., & Fletcher, K. (2004). Young adult follow-up of hyperactive children: Antisocial activities and drug use. *Journal of Child Psychology and Psychiatry, 45,* 195–211.

Barkley, R. A., Guevremont, D. C., Anastopoulos, A. D., & Fletcher, K. E. (1992). A comparison of three family therapy programs for treating family conflicts in adolescents with attention-deficit hyperactivity disorder. *Journal of Consulting and Clinical Psychology, 60,* 450–462.

Barkley, R. A., Karlsson, J., & Pollard, S. (1985). Effects of age on the mother-child interactions of hyperactive children. *Journal of Abnormal Child Psychology, 13,* 631–638.

Barkley, R. A., Murphy, K. R., Dupaul, G. J., & Bush, T. (2002). Driving in young adults with attention deficit hyperactivity disorder: Knowledge, performance, adverse outcomes, and the role of executive functioning. *Journal of the International Neuropsychological Society, 8,* 655–672.

Barkley, R. A., Murphy, K. R., & Kwasnik, D. (1996a). Psychological adjustment and adaptive impairments in young adults with ADHD. *Journal of Attention Disorders, 1,* 41–54.

Barkley, R. A., Murphy, K. R., & Kwasnik, D. (1996b). Motor vehicle driving competencies and risks in teens and young adults with attention deficit hyperactivity disorder. *Pediatrics, 98,* 1089–1095.

Befera, M., & Barkley, R. A. (1984). Hyperactive and normal girls and boys: Mother-child interactions, parent psychiatric status, and child psychopathology. *Journal of Child Psychology and Psychiatry, 26,* 439–452.

Biederman, J., Faraone, S. V., & Lapey, K. (1992). Co-morbidity of diagnosis in attention-deficit hyperactivity disorder. In G. Weiss (Ed.), *Child and adolescent psychiatric clinics of North America: Attention-deficit hyperactivity disorder* (pp. 335–360). Philadelphia: Saunders.

Biederman, J., Faraone, S. V., Mick, E., Spencer, T., Wilens, T., Kiely, K., Guite, J., Ablon, J. S., Reed, E., & Warburton, R. (1995). High risk for attention deficit hyperactivity disorder among children of parents with childhood onset of the disorder: A pilot study. *American Journal of Psychiatry, 152,* 431–435.

Biederman, J., Faraone, S. V., Mick, E., Williamson, S., Wilens, T. E., Spencer, T. J., Weber, W., Jetton, J., Kraus, I., Pert, J., & Zallen, B. (1999). Clinical correlates of ADHD in females: Findings from a large group of girls ascertained from pediatric and psychiatric referral sources. *Journal of the American Academy of Child and Adolescent Psychiatry, 38,* 966–975.

Biederman, J., Faraone, S. V., Spencer, T., Wilens, T., Norman, D., Lapey, K. A., Mick, E., Lehman, B. K., & Doyle, A. (1993). Patterns of psychiatric co-morbidity, cognition, and psychosocial functioning in adults with attention deficit hyperactivity disorder. *American Journal of Psychiatry, 150,* 1792–1798.

Biederman, J., Wilens, T., Mick, E., Faraone, S. V., Weber, W., Curtis, S., Thornell, A., Pfister, K., Jetton, J. G., & Soriano, J. (1997). Is ADHD a risk factor of psychoactive substance use disorders? Findings from a four-year prospective follow-up. *Journal of the American Academy of Child and Adolescent Psychiatry, 36,* 21–29.

Blachman, D. R., & Hinshaw, S. P. (2002). Patterns of friendship among girls with and without attention-deficit/hyperactivity disorder. *Journal of Abnormal Child Psychology, 30,* 625–640.

Campbell, S. B. (1994). Hard-to-manage preschool boys: Externalizing behavior, social competence, and family context at two-year follow-up. *Journal of Abnormal Child Psychology, 22,* 147–166.

Carlson, E. A., Jacobvitz, D., & Sroufe, L. A. (1995). A developmental investigation of inattentiveness and hyperactivity. *Child Development, 66,* 37–54.

Conners, C. K., & Erhardt, D. (1998). Attention-deficit hyperactivity disorder in children and adolescents. In A. S. Bellack & M. Herse (Eds.), *Comprehensive clinical psychology* (pp. 487–525). New York: Pergamon.

Cunningham, C. E., & Barkley, R. A. (1979). The interactions of hyperactive and normal children with their mothers during free play and structured tasks. *Child Development, 50,* 217–224.

Dishion, T. J., & Patterson, G. R. (1999). Model building in developmental psychopathology: A pragmatic approach to understanding and intervention. *Journal of Clinical Child Psychology, 28,* 502–512.

Dubey, D. R., O'Leary, S. G., & Kaufman, K. F. (1983). Training parents of hyperactive children in child management: A comparative outcome study. *Journal of Abnormal Child Psychology, 11,* 229–246.

Edwards, G., Barkley, R. A., Laneri, M., Fletcher, K., & Metevia, L. (2001). Parent-adolescent conflict in teenagers with ADHD and ODD. *Journal of Abnormal Child Psychology, 29,* 557–572.

Epstein, J. N., March, J. S., Conners, C. K., & Jackson, D. L. (1998). Racial differences on the Conners Teacher Rating Scale. *Journal of Abnormal Child Psychology, 26,* 109–118.

Epstein, N. B., & Baucom, D. H. (2002). *Enhanced cognitive-behavioral therapy for couples: A contextual approach.* Washington, DC: American Psychological Association.

Evans, S. W., Vallano, G., & Pelham, W. (1994). Treatment of parenting behavior with a psychostimulant: A case study of an adult with attention-deficit hyperactivity disorder. *Journal of Child and Adolescent Psychopharmacology, 4,* 63–69.

Fabiano, G. A., & Pelham, W. E. (2002). Comprehensive treatment for attention-deficit/hyperactivity disorder. In D. T. Marsh & M. A. Fristad (Eds.), *Handbook of serious emotional disturbance in children and adolescents* (pp. 149–174). New York: John Wiley & Sons.

Faraone, S. V. (October, 1997). *Familial transmission of attention-deficit/hyperactivity disorder and co-morbid disorders.* Paper presented at the Annual Meeting of the American Academy of Child and Adolescent Psychiatry, Toronto.

Faraone, S. V., Beiderman, J., Mennin, D., Gershon, J., & Tsuang, M. T. (1996). A prospective four-year follow-up study of children at risk for ADHD: Psychiatric, neuropsychological, and psychosocial outcome. *Journal of the American Academy of Child and Adolescent Psychiatry, 35,* 1449–1459.

Fischer, M. (1990). Parenting stress and the child with attention deficit hyperactivity disorder. *Journal of Clinical Child Psychology, 19,* 337–346.

Fischer, M., Barkley, R. A., Smallish, L., & Fletcher, K. (2002). Young adult follow-up of hyperactive children: self-reported psychiatric disorders, co-morbidity, and the role of childhood conduct problems and teen CD. *Journal of Abnormal Child Psychology, 30,* 463–475.

Fletcher, K. E., Fischer, M., Barkley, R. A., & Smallish, L. (1996). A sequential analysis of the mother-adolescent interactions of ADHD, ADHD/ODD, and normal teenagers during neutral and conflict discussions. *Journal of Abnormal Child Psychology, 24,* 271–297.

Gaub, M., & Carlson, C. L. (1997). Gender differences in ADHD: A meta-analysis and critical review. *Journal of the American Academy of Child and Adolescent Psychiatry, 36,* 1036–1045.

Gershon, J. (2002). A meta-analytic review of gender differences in ADHD. *Journal of Attention Disorders, 5,* 143–154.

Goldstein, S., & Ellison, A. T. (2002). *Clinician's guide to adult ADHD: Assessment and intervention.* San Diego, CA: Elsevier Science.

Harvey, E., Danforth, J. S., McKee, T. B., Ulaszek, W. R., & Friedman, J. L. (2003). Parenting of children with attention-deficit/hyperactivity disorder (ADHD): The role of parental ADHD symptomatology. *Journal of Attention Disorders, 7,* 31–42.

Hinshaw, S. P. (1992). Academic underachievement, attention deficits, and aggression: Co-morbidity and implications for intervention. *Journal of Consulting and Clinical Psychology, 60,* 893–903.

Hinshaw, S. P. (1994). *Attention deficits and hyperactivity in children.* Thousand Oaks, CA: Sage.

Hinshaw, S. P. (2002). Preadolescent girls with attention-deficit/hyperactivity disorder: I. Background characteristics, co-morbidity, cognitive and social functioning, and parenting practices. *Journal of Consulting and Clinical Psychology, 70,* 1086–1098.

Horn, W. F., Ialongo, N., Greenberg, G., Packard, T., & Smith-Winberry, C. (1990). Additive effects of behavioral parent training and self-control therapy with attention deficit hyperactivity disordered children. *Journal of Clinical Child Psychology, 19,* 98–110.

Horn, W. F., Ialongo, N. S., Pascoe, J. M., Greenberg, G. A., Packard, T., Lopez, M., Wagner, A., & Puttler, L. (1991). Additive effects of psychostimulants, parent training, and self-control therapy with ADHD children. *Journal of the American Academy of Child and Adolescent Psychiatry, 30,* 233–240.

Jensen, P. S., Kettle, L., Roper, M. T., Sloan, M. T., Dulcan, M. K., Hoven, C., Bird, H. R., Bauermeister, J. J., & Payne, J. D. (1999). Are stimulants over prescribed? Treatment of ADHD in four U.S. communities. *Journal of the American Academy of Child and Adolescent Psychiatry, 38,* 797–804.

Johnson, D. E., & Conners, C. K. (2002). The assessment process: Conditions and comorbidities. In S. Goldstein and A. T. Ellison (Eds.), *Clinician's guide to adult ADHD: Assessment and intervention* (pp. 71–83). San Diego, CA: Elsevier Science.

Johnson, S. M. (1996). *The practice of emotionally focused marital therapy: Creating connection.* Philadelphia: Brunner/Mazel.

Johnston, C. (1996). Parent characteristics and parent-child interactions in families of nonproblem children and ADHD children with higher and lower levels of oppositional-defiant behavior. *Journal of Abnormal Child Psychology, 24,* 85–104.

Johnston, C. & Mash, E. J. (2001). Families of children with attention-deficit/hyperactivity disorder: Review and recommendations for future research. *Clinical Child and Family Psychology Review, 4,* 183–207.

Klein, R. G., & Abikoff, H. (1997). Behavior therapy and methylphenidate in the treatment of children with ADHD. *Journal of Attention Disorders, 2,* 89–114.

Klein, R. G., & Mannuzza, S. (1991). Long-term outcome of hyperactive children: A review. *Journal of the American Academy of Child and Adolescent Psychiatry, 30,* 383–387.

Lahey, B. B., & Willcutt, E. G. (2002). Validity of the diagnosis and dimensions of attention deficit hyperactivity disorder. In P. S. Jensen & J. R. Cooper (Eds.), *Attention deficit hyperactivity disorder: state of the science; best practices* (pp. 1-1–1-23). Kingston, NJ: Civic Research Institute.

Lovejoy, M. C., Graczyk, P. A., O'Hare, E., & Neuman, G. (2000). Maternal depression and parenting behavior: A meta-analytic review. *Clinical Psychology Review, 20,* 561–592.

Lynskey, M. T., & Fergusson, D. M. (1995). Childhood conduct problems, attention deficit behaviors, and adolescent alcohol, tobacco, and illicit drug use. *Journal of Abnormal Child Psychology, 23,* 281–302.

Mannuzza, S., Klein, R. G., Bessler, A., Malloy, P., & LaPadula, M. (1993). Adult outcome of hyperactive boys: Educational achievement, occupational rank, and psychiatric status. *Archives of General Psychiatry, 50,* 565–576.

Mannuzza, S., Klein, R. G., Bessler, A., Malloy, P., & LaPadula, M. (1998). Adult psychiatric status of hyperactive boys grown up. *American Journal of Psychiatry, 155,* 493–498.

March, J. S., Swanson, J. M., Arnold, L. E., Hoza, B., Conners, C. K., Hinshaw, S. P., Hechtman, L., Kraemer, H. C., Greenhill, L. L., Abikoff, H. B., Elliott, L. G., Jensen, P. S., Newcorn, J. H., Vitiello, B., Severe, J., Wells, K. C., & Pelham, W. E. (2000). Anxiety as a predictor and outcome variable in the multimodal treatment study of children with ADHD (MTA). *Journal of Abnormal Child Psychology, 28,* 527–541.

Mash, E. J., & Johnston, C. (1982). A comparison of the mother-child interactions of younger and older hyperactive and normal children. *Child Development, 53,* 1371–1381.

Mash, E. J., & Johnston, C. (1990). Determinants of parenting stress: Illustrations from families of hyperactive children and families of physically abused children. *Journal of Clinical Child Psychology, 19,* 313–328.

Mash, E. J., & Terdal, L. G. (1997). *Assessment of childhood disorders* (3rd ed.). New York: Guilford Press.

Molina, B. S. G., Smith, B. H., & Pelham, W. E. (1999). Interactive effects of attention deficit hyperactivity disorder and conduct disorder on early adolescent substance use. *Psychology of Addictive Behavior, 13,* 348–358.

MTA Cooperative Group (1999). A 14-month randomized clinical trial of treatment strategies for Attention Deficit Hyperactivity Disorder (ADHD). *Archives of General Psychiatry, 56,* 1073–1086.

Murphy, K. R., & Barkley, R. A. (1996a). Attention deficit hyperactivity disorder adults: Co-morbidities and adaptive impairments. *Comprehensive Psychiatry, 37,* 393–401.

Murphy, K. R., & Barkley, R. A. (1996b). Prevalence of DSM-IV symptoms of ADHD in adult licensed drivers: Implications for clinical diagnosis. *Journal of Attention Disorders, 1,* 147–161.

Murphy, K. R., Barkley, R. A., & Bush, T. (2001). Executive functioning and olfactory identification in young adults with attention deficit hyperactivity disorder. *Neuropsychology, 15,* 211–220.

Murphy, K. R., & Gordon, M. (1998). Assessment of adults with ADHD. In R. A. Barkley (Ed.), *Attention-deficit hyperactivity disorder: A handbook for diagnosis and treatment* (2nd ed., pp. 345–369). New York: Guilford Press.

Newcorn, J. H., Halperin, J. M., Jensen, P. S., Abikoff, H. B., Arnold, L. E., Cantwell, D. P., Conners, C. K., Elliott, G. R., Epstein, J. N., Greenhill, L. L., Hechtman, L., Hinshaw, S. P., Hoza, B., Kraemer, H. C., Pelham, W. E., Severe, J. B., Swanson, J. M., Wells, K. C., Wigal, T., & Vitiello, B. (2001). Symptom profiles in children with ADHD: Effects of co-morbidity and gender. *Journal of the Academy of Child and Adolescent Psychiatry, 40,* 137–146.

Patterson, G. R., Reid, J. B., & Dishion, T. J. (1992). *Antisocial boys.* Eugene, OR: Castalia.

Pelham, W. E., & Lang, A. R. (1993). Parental alcohol consumption and deviant child behavior: Laboratory studies of reciprocal effects. *Clinical Psychology Review, 13,* 763–784.

Pelham, W. E., & Lang, A. R. (1999). Can your children drive you to drink?: Stress and parenting in adults interacting with children with ADHD. *Alcohol Research and Health, 23,* 292–298.

Pelham, W. E., Schnedler, R. W., Bender, M., Nilsson, D., Miller, J., Budrown, M., Ronnei, M., Paluchowski, C., & Marks, D. (1988). The combination of behavior therapy and methylphenidate in the treatment of attention deficit disorder: A therapy outcome study. In L. M. Bloomingdale (Ed.), *Attention deficit disorder* (vol. 3, pp. 29–48). Oxford, UK: Pergamon.

Pierce, E. W., Ewing, L. J., & Campbell, S. B. (1999). Diagnostic status and symptomatic behavior of hard-to-manage preschool children in middle childhood and early adolescence. *Journal of Clinical Child Psychology, 28,* 44–57.

Pisterman, S., Firestone, P., McGrath, P., Goodman, J. T., Webster, I., Mallory, R., & Goffin, B. (1992). The role of parent training in treatment of preschoolers with ADHD. *American Journal of Orthopsychiatry, 62,* 397–408.

Pisterman, S., McGrath, P., Firestone, P., Goodman, J. T., Webster, I., & Mallory, R. (1989). Outcome of parent-mediated treatment of preschoolers with attention deficit disorder with hyperactivity. *Journal of Consulting and Clinical Psychology, 57,* 628–635.

Podolski, C.-L., & Nigg, J. T. (2001). Parent stress and coping in relation to child ADHD severity and associated child disruptive behavior problems. *Journal of Clinical Child Psychology, 30,* 503–513.

Pollard, S., Ward, E., & Barkley, R. A. (1983). The effects of parent training and Ritalin on the parent-child interactions of hyperactive boys. *Child and Family Therapy, 5,* 51–69.

Quinn, P. (1997). *Attention deficit disorder: Diagnosis and treatment from infancy to adulthood.* New York: Brunner/Mazel.

Reid, R., Casat, C. D., Norton, H. J., Anastopoulos, A. D., & Temple, E. P. (2001). Using behavior rating scales for ADHD across ethnic groups: The IOWA Conners. *Journal of Emotional and Behavioral Disorders, 9,* 210–219.

Robin, A. L. (1998). *ADHD in adolescents: Diagnosis and treatment.* New York: Guilford Press.

Samuel, V. J., Curtis, S., Thornell, A., George, P., Taylor, A., Brome, D. R., Beiderman, J., & Faraone, S. V. (1997). The unexplored void of ADHD and African-American research: A review of the literature. *Journal of Attention Disorders, 1,* 197–207.

Sanders, M. R., & McFarland, M. (2000). Treatment of depressed mothers with disruptive children: A controlled evaluation of cognitive behavioral family intervention. *Behavior Therapy, 31,* 89–112.

Sharp, W. S., Walter, J. M., Marsh, W. L., Ritchie, G. F., Hamburger, S. D., & Castellanos, F. X. (1999). ADHD in girls: Clinical comparability of a research sample. *Journal of the American Academy of Child and Adolescent Psychiatry, 38,* 40–47.

Smith, M., & Barrett, M. S. (2000). Parent training for families of girls with attention deficit hyperactivity disorder: An analysis of three cases. *Child and Family Behavior Therapy, 22,* 41–54.

Sonuga-Barke, E. J. S., Daley, D., Thompson, M., Laver-Bradbury, C., & Weeks, A. (2001). Parent-based therapies for preschool attention-deficit/hyperactivity disorder: A randomized, controlled trial with a community sample. *Journal of the American Academy of Child and Adolescent Psychiatry, 40,* 402–408.

Sonuga-Barke, E. J. S., Daley, D., & Thompson, M. (2002). Does maternal ADHD reduce the effectiveness of parent training for preschool children's ADHD? *Journal of the American Academy of Child and Adolescent Psychiatry, 41,* 696–702.

Tallmadge, J., & Barkley, R. A. (1983). The interactions of hyperactive and normal boys with their fathers and mothers. *Journal of Abnormal Child Psychology, 11,* 565–580.

Taylor, E., Sandberg, S., Thorley, G., & Giles, S. (1991). *The epidemiology of childhood hyperactivity.* Oxford: Oxford University Press.

Weiss, G., & Hechtman, L. T. (1993). *Hyperactive children grown up: ADHD in children, adolescents, and adults.* New York: Guilford Press.

Weiss, M., Hechtman, L. T., & Weiss, G. (1999). *ADHD in adulthood: A guide to current theory, diagnosis, and treatment.* Baltimore: Johns Hopkins Press.

Weiss, M., Hechtman, L. T., & Weiss, G. (2000). ADHD in parents. *Journal of the American Academy of Child and Adolescent Psychiatry, 39,* 1059–1061.

Wells, K. C. (2004). Treatment of ADHD in children and adolescents. In P. M. Barrett & T. H. Ollendick (Eds.), *Handbook of interventions that work with children and adolescents: Prevention and treatment* (pp. 343–368). West Sussex, England: John Wiley & Sons.

Wells, K. C., Abikoff, H., Abramowitz, A., Courtney, M., Cousins, L., Del Carmen, R., Eddy, M., Eggers, S., Fleiss, K., Heller, T., Hibbs, T., Hinshaw, S., Hoza, B., Pelham, W., & Pfiffner, L. (1996). *Parent training for attention deficit hyperactivity disorder: MTA study.* Unpublished manuscript.

Wells, K. C., Pelham, W. E., Kotkin, R. A., Hoza, B., Abikoff, H. B., Abramowitz, A., Arnold, L. E., Cantwell, D. P., Conners, C. K., Del Carmen, R., Elliott, G., Greenhill, L. L., Hechtman, L., Hibbs, E., Hinshaw, S. P., Jensen, P. S., March, J. S., Swanson, J. M., & Schiller, E. (2000). Psychosocial treatment strategies in the MTA study: Rationale, methods, and critical issues in design and implementation. *Journal of Abnormal Child Psychology, 28,* 483–505.

West, J., Houghton, S., Douglas, G., Wall, M., & Whiting, K. (1999). Levels of self-reported depression among mothers of children with attention-deficit/hyperactivity disorder. *Journal of Attention Disorders, 3,* 135–140.

Weyandt, L. L., Linterman, I., & Rice, J. A. (1995). Reported prevalence of attentional difficulties in a general sample of college students. *Journal of Psychopathology and Behavior Assessment, 17,* 293–364.

Whalen, C. K., & Henker, B. (1999). The child with attention-deficit/hyperactivity disorder in family context. In H. C. Quay & A. E. Hogan (Eds.), *Handbook of disruptive behavior disorders* (pp. 139–156). New York: Kluwer Academic.

Wilens, T. E., & Lineham, C. (1995). ADD and substance abuse: An intoxicating combination. *Attention, 3,* 24–31.

CHAPTER 4

Brief Strategic Family Therapy for Adolescents with Behavior Problems

Viviana E. Horigian, Lourdes Suarez-Morales, Michael S. Robbins, Mónica Zarate, Carla C. Mayorga, Victoria B. Mitrani, and José Szapocznik

Behavioral problems in adolescence interfere with youths' ability to master normal developmental skills and to function effectively in their environment. Disruptive behaviors, including defiance of authority, violation of personal and property rights of others, and substance use are a great concern to parents, school staff, and society as a whole. Many individual, familial, and social factors have been implicated as critical variables in the evolution and treatment of adolescent behavior problems. However, no single factor has received as much attention as the family. Clinical theory and research have helped to identify specific family interactional patterns that are linked to adolescent behavior problems, and to develop family-based intervention strategies that specifically target these patterns. (Marin & Marin, 1991; McGoldrick, 1989; Szapocznik, Scopetta, & King, 1978).

This chapter presents Brief Strategic Family Therapy (BSFT), an empirically supported intervention designed to target behavioral problems and drug abuse by working with the family. We present the basic principles and goals of BSFT and provide a description of specific clinical interventions. First, definitions of behavioral problems and a brief overview of BSFT are provided. Second, we present a specific approach to the assessment of dysfunctional family interactions. Third, we discuss common treatment challenges faced by professionals working with these families. Fourth, we summarize the research evidence supporting BSFT. Finally, we describe a clinical case that illustrates the principles and strategies of BSFT.

BEHAVIORAL PROBLEMS IN ADOLESCENCE

Problem Definition and Clinical Characteristics

The term 'behavior problems' is often used to characterize the constellation of acting out and externalizing-type behaviors manifested by youth during adolescence. The American Psychiatric Association has identified clusters of these problem behaviors as symptoms of various disorders (American Psychiatric Association,

1994), including Oppositional Defiant Disorder (ODD), Conduct Disorder, and substance abuse and dependence disorders. BSFT has been studied with adolescents that present with many symptoms of these disorders. A more detailed description of these disorders is presented in the following, to illustrate the types of behaviors that BSFT addresses.

Oppositional Defiant Disorder

Symptoms of Oppositional Defiant Disorder (ODD) are frequently identified during the preschool years and persist into adolescence. The hallmark signs of ODD are negativistic and defiant behaviors and disobedience toward authority figures. Other key behaviors of ODD include frequent temper tantrums, excessive arguing with adults, defiance and refusal to comply with adult requests and rules, deliberate attempts to annoy or upset people, blaming others for one's own mistakes or misbehavior, irritability, anger, and resentment, and being spiteful and vindictive (APA, 1994; American Academy of Child and Adolescent Psychiatry [AACAP], 2004). The symptoms are usually seen in multiple settings, but may be more noticeable at home or at school. Five to fifteen percent of all school-age children are diagnosed with ODD (AACAP, 2004).

Conduct Disorder

The Diagnostic and Statistical Manual of Mental Disorders-Fourth Edition (APA, 1994) breaks down the symptoms of conduct disorder into four categories of disruptive behaviors, including aggression toward people and animals (e.g., physical fights or bullying; use of weapons; cruelty to animals; forced sexual activity), destruction of property (e.g., arson), deceitfulness or theft (e.g., breaking into house or car; shoplifting), serious violations of rules (e.g., truancy, stays out at night). Children with conduct disorder also repeatedly violate the personal or property rights of others and the basic expectations of society.

Delinquency

Children and adolescents with conduct or oppositional defiant disorder may also experience problems with the law. When disruptive behaviors have legal constraints, they are referred to as delinquent. These behaviors typically come to the attention of the police or juvenile justice system. Status offenses (e.g., truancy, running away from home) are behaviors that are only considered illegal because the adolescent is a minor. Nonstatus offenses or index crimes cover the range of illegal behavior, from misdemeanors to first degree murder (Moore & Arthur, 1989).

Substance Abuse

Although findings from recent research studies indicate that there has been a general improvement in rates of marijuana, ecstasy, LSD, inhalants, amphetamines, alcohol, and tobacco use, serious drug use continues to represent a major problem for our nation's teenagers (National Institute on Drug Abuse [NIDA] 2004). When the youth's alcohol or drug use interferes with major roles and obligations at school, home or work, the youth may meet criteria for diagnosis of substance abuse. When drug use results in tolerance, withdrawal, and compulsive use of the drug(s), the youth may meet criteria for substance dependence.

In summary, BSFT has been studied with adolescents that present with many symptoms of the disorders described above. It should be noted that in actual clinical practice, adolescents often present with symptoms from some (and even all) of these problems. For example, in a recent study with drug-using Hispanic and African American adolescents, we documented high rates of co-occurring behavior problems (Robbins, Kumar, Walker-Barnes, Feaster, Briones, & Szapocznik, 2002). This overlap among behavior problems is common among adolescents with disruptive behavior problems (Jessor & Jessor, 1977). One strength of BSFT, the clinical model reviewed here, is that the model was developed and refined with clinical samples that presented with high rates of co-occurring behavior problems. As we describe below, BSFT is primarily concerned with targeting the maladaptive patterns of relationships in the family that are associated with the occurrence of behavior problems. By working to improve family relationships, BSFT simultaneously addresses multiple behavioral domains. As such, BSFT consistently maintains a focus on family relationships irrespective of the different clinical manifestations of adolescent behavior problems.

Family Characteristics

The evolution of BSFT has been influenced by research demonstrating that families play a large role in allowing or preventing adolescent behavior problems (Szapocznik & Coatsworth, 1999). Some of the most prominent family problems that have been linked to adolescent behavior problems include: parental drug use or other antisocial behavior, parental under- or overinvolvement, poor quality of parent-child communication, lack of clear rules and consequences, lack of consistency in application of rules and consequences, inadequate monitoring of peer activities, and a weak parent-adolescent bond (Hawkins, Catalano, & Miller, 1992). High levels of family conflict often characterize the families of behavior problem adolescents. Effective management of conflict and reduction in conflict is a specific target of BSFT. Research has provided evidence about the critical role that families play in the lives of adolescents. We present the key theoretical principles of BSFT in the following.

OVERVIEW OF BSFT

The theory and specific techniques of BSFT have been developed over the past 3 decades through a rigorous program of clinical implementation and research evaluation. The primary goal of BSFT is to improve family relationships and relationships between the family and other important systems that influence the youth (e.g., school, peers). By strategically targeting maladaptive family interactions, BSFT is intended to reduce adolescent behavior problems (e.g., drug use, conduct problems, association with antisocial peers, aggressive and violent behaviors) by improving maladaptive family interactions.

Theoretical Background

Systems

The family is a system that must be viewed as a whole organism rather than merely as the composite sum of the individuals who compose it. In BSFT, this view of the family system is evident in the following assumptions:

1. The family is a system with interdependent/interrelated parts.
2. Each family member's behavior influences the family and the family influences each of its members.
3. The behavior of one family member can only be understood by examining the context (i.e., family) in which it occurs.
4. Interventions must be implemented at the family level and must take into account the complex relationships within the family system.

Structure

While the concept of systems tells us that family members are interdependent, structure helps us to explain the patterns of behaviors among family members composing a family system. In BSFT, structure is defined as the linked behavioral interactions among individuals that tend to recur and to create patterns of interaction among family members. This view of structure is evident in the following assumptions:

1. Repetitive patterns of interactions occur in any family.
2. Repetitive interactions (i.e., ways family members behave with one another) are either successful or unsuccessful in achieving the goals of the family or its individual members.
3. BSFT targets those repetitive patterns of interactions (i.e., the habitual ways in which family members behave with one another) that are directly related to the youth's behavior problems.

Strategy

BSFT is a strategic approach that uses pragmatic, problem-focused, and planned interventions. This strategic approach emerged from an explicit focus on developing an intervention that was quick and effective in eliminating symptoms. In BSFT, this strategic approach is evident in the following assumptions:

1. Interventions are practical. That is, interventions are tailored to the unique characteristics of families and their needs.
2. Interventions are problem focused. A problem-focused approach targets first those patterns of interactions that most directly influence the youth's psychosocial adjustment and antisocial behaviors, and targets one problem at a time.
3. Interventions are well planned, meaning that the therapist determines what

seem to be the maladaptive interactions (directly related to the youth's behavior problems), determines which of these are most amenable to change, and establishes a treatment plan to help the family develop more effective patterns of interaction.

CLINICAL INTERVENTION STRATEGIES FOR ADOLESCENTS WITH BEHAVIORAL PROBLEMS

There are three sets of steps in BSFT: joining, diagnosing, and restructuring. These are discussed in the following. Throughout these descriptions, we have inserted clinical examples to provide exemplars of each of the intervention domains in BSFT. Because of our rich experience developing BSFT with Hispanic populations, many of these exemplars include material relevant to this ethnic group.

Establishment of a Therapeutic Relationship—Joining

Engaging adolescents and family members into treatment is usually a challenge in itself. The first step in working with a family is to establish and build a working therapeutic relationship. The construction of this relationship begins from the very first contact. The ultimate goal of the joining process is for the therapist to form a new system—a therapeutic system that is made up of the whole family and the therapist (Szapocznik, Hervis, & Schwartz, 2003).

The challenge is to establish a therapeutic alliance with several individuals who have a shared history, and who come into therapy usually in conflict with each other. Successfully joining the family system requires that the therapist simultaneously attend to the thoughts, feelings, and goals of individual family members as well as the patterns of interaction that govern the family system. Thus, joining occurs at two levels: at the individual level, in which joining involves establishing a relationship with each participating family member; and at the family level, in which the therapist must recognize, respect, and maintain the family's characteristic interaction patterns. At the individual level, this requires that the therapist be able to find ways to support the individuals on either side of the conflict. A creative therapist may be able to establish an alliance around the common goal of ridding the family of its undesirable problem and of the stress that it is experiencing. For example, in the case of the family with a rebellious adolescent, the therapist may have to offer the mother what she wants—"I'll help you get more support from your husband in handling Tania;" the therapist may have to offer the father figure what he wants—"I'll help you handle the rebellious behavior of your daughter;" and the therapist may have to offer Tania what she wants—"I'll help you get your parents to stop fighting with you." By offering each family member something she or he would like to achieve, the therapist is able to establish a therapeutic alliance with the family—a governing coalition—in which they are all committed to working together to improve things. Simultaneously, at the family level, the therapist may recognize that the adolescent dictates family process and seems to hold the power in the family. Thus, while the therapist provides support to each individual family member for the purpose of joining the system, the therapist validates the powerful member of the family—the adolescent.

The desired qualities of the therapeutic relationship are respect, empathy, and commitment to working toward achieving the goals formulated between the therapist and the family. Strategies suggested to maintain the quality of the therapeutic relationship with individuals in family therapy include validating or supporting family members, formulating goals that are personally meaningful to family members, and attending to each client's experience (Diamond & Liddle, 1996; Diamond, Liddle, Hogue, & Dakof, 1999).

At the family level, the therapist must be simultaneously paying attention to the various contexts in which these individual therapeutic relationships are being formed. For example, the therapist must be careful to enter the family system in a manner that maintains or supports the family's organization, rather than challenging the family too early. That is, the therapist works her or his way into the family through the existing structure to become a special temporary member of the family for the purpose of treatment. In contrast, challenging the existing structure prematurely will interfere with the therapist's ability to join the family, and may even result in a failure to effectively engage families into treatment.

Besides affording each family member a personal experience of the therapist's regard and commitment to her or his well-being, it is of crucial importance that the family perceive the therapist as the leader of the therapeutic system. Families come for help with problems that they have not been able to resolve by themselves. They expect, need, and are entitled to a therapist who will lead them in a new and more effective direction. Therefore, in the therapeutic system the therapist is both a member and its leader. To earn this position of leadership, the therapist must offer clear rules that serve the needs of all family members, and the therapist must show respect for all family members—in particular, for powerful family members.

It is by respecting and accepting the family that the therapist eventually earns the family's trust and becomes accepted as its leader. It is also by gaining the family's trust and blending with it that the therapist is able to observe how the family functions so that she or he can diagnose the system's problems. But, being accepted is not a permanent position. Acceptance can be lost at any moment, and thus it has to be earned repeatedly throughout the entire therapy process. Joining takes place when therapy begins, when each session begins, and after each change maneuver has been successfully completed.

Diagnostic Assessment of the Family

Behavioral problems in adolescents are directly linked to enabling patterns of family interactions. In BSFT, diagnosis refers to the identification of the patterns of family interaction that allow and encourage or are responsible for the problematic youth behavior. To derive a diagnosis of the family, family interactions are assessed along five dimensions: organization, resonance, developmental stage, identified patienthood, and conflict resolution. Accurate diagnosis along these dimensions can only be achieved through direct observation. The therapist's first goal in the diagnosis process is to create opportunities for family members to interact directly with one another, with minimal interference from the therapist. Content plays a minimal role in the diagnostic and therapeutic process. That is, what family members say is considered to be less important than what they do. For the BSFT therapist to identify the nature of the family interactions, the therapist must avoid getting trapped in attending to content. Moreover, when attending to process, the BSFT therapist does not interpret to the family the process she or he perceives. Rather, the BSFT therapist uses the maladaptive interactional patterns perceived to determine her or his intervention strategy (Szapocznik, Hervis, & Schwartz, 2003; Szapocznik & Kurtines, 1989).

Creating Enactments

Diagnosis of family interactions is based on what families do in the therapy sessions—not what they report they do at home. BSFT therapists must create a therapeutic context wherein family members are free to interact in their typical style. These enactments permit the therapist to directly observe how the family behaves at home (outside the session) and are critical for accurately identifying the family's characteristic patterns of interaction. In other words, enactments permit the therapist to gather information that is outside the family's awareness, and therefore cannot be gathered by asking questions (Mitrani & Perez, 2003). Facilitating enactments is difficult. The challenge lies in how to bring about enactments. The expectation of the family about the therapy situation will cause the family to centralize the therapist, so that the family will attempt to direct all their communications to the therapist. Family members often come into therapy with the view that their job is to tell the therapist what happened. Most families, in fact, might think of a therapist as somewhat of a judge; each side presents their evidence and the judge renders a judgment. To achieve an enactment and remain decentralized, the therapist needs to redirect these family members' verbalizations to each other. Thus, when a family member speaks to the therapist about another family member who is present, the therapist must ask the family member who is speaking to repeat what was said, directing the communication now at the family member about whom it was said. For example, an older sister may say, "I am home before my mom so I am in charge of the kids until mom gets home. Frank locks himself up in the bedroom and won't come out for hours. I can't get him to come out and do his homework." An individual-focused intervention might involve the therapist querying the sister about how that makes her feel. However, in BSFT, therapists use these statements as opportunities for encouraging the family members to speak directly with one another about this issue. For example, the therapist might ask the older sister, "Would you tell Frank how it makes you feel when he closes himself up in the bedroom and won't come out?" This type of directive question creates an opportunity for the siblings to interact with one another in the session. Family members often have difficulty with these types of directives and require considerable encouragement to interact with one another, rather than with the therapist. If the enactment breaks down the therapist either comments on what went wrong, or urges them to continue. It is the therapist's responsibility to facilitate enactments that provide important information about the family's usual, routine, habitual behavior patterns.

Dimensions of Family Functioning

This section presents the five dimensions of family functioning along which repetitive patterns of family interactions are diagnosed.

Organization

Repetitive patterns of interactions give the family a specific form, conceptualized as its organization. Organization in a family can be examined through three aspects: leadership, subsystem organization, and communication flow. Leadership is defined as the distribution of authority and responsibility within the family. In functional two-parent families, leadership is in the hands of the parents. In modern societies, both parents or parent figures usually share authority and decision-making. Frequently, in one-parent families, the parent shares some of the leadership with an older child. In the case of a single parent living within an extended family framework, leadership may be shared with a cousin, uncle, or grandparent.

In assessing whether leadership is adaptive, BSFT therapists look at hierarchy, behavior control, and, guidance. Guiding questions to help the therapist identify leadership are, "Who is in charge of directing the family? Who are the family members in positions of authority? Is this leadership in the appropriate hands? Is it shared between (or among) the appropriate people? Is hierarchy assigned appropriately with respect to age, role, and function within the family?" When the therapist evaluates the existing hierarchy of the family, leadership should be with the parental figures, although some leadership can be delegated to older children, as long as such delegation is not overly burdensome, is age-appropriate, and is delegated, not usurped. Therapists evaluate if parents are in charge of maintaining behavior control by observing who keeps the order in the family, who disciplines, and whether these attempts to discipline are successful or are ignored. Therapists should also learn who provides advice in the family, who are the "family teachers," and if the advice has an impact on family interactions. In general, parent figures should be responsible for providing guidance, although some of this responsibility can be delegated to other family members.

In working with Hispanic families, a common organization pattern is that of an adolescent, or young child, who, because of his or her increased English fluency, is inadvertently placed in an authority role, having to communicate and serve as translator between parents and other authority figures, such as teachers. The centralization of adolescents in this communication process does not necessarily indicate that there is a serious dysfunction in family processes; however, there are times when this is the case. The BSFT therapist, of course, only observes what happens within the session. Often these youths become family leaders, so that either parent shows an overreliance on the youth, and/or the youth takes a leadership role in the family, even when language is not an issue. Of course, a Spanish-speaking therapist that permits the parents to speak directly to the therapist without the youth translating can only assess this pattern of family organization.

Families have both formal subsystems (e.g., spouses, siblings, grandparents) and informal subsystems (e.g., the older women, the people who manage the money, the ones who do the housekeeping, the ones who play chess). Spouse and sibling subsystems must have a certain degree of privacy and independence. BSFT therapists are concerned with the adequacy or appropriateness of the subsystems that exist in a family. BSFT therapists also assess the nature of the coalitions that give

rise to these subsystems. Covert alliances, especially those that violate generational and role definitions, are often at the core of dysfunctional behaviors.

To assess the family's subsystem organization, the BSFT therapist looks at alliances, triangulation, and subsystem membership. Alliance between parental figures should be strong, whereas problematic alliances tend to occur between adult
and child, particularly when a parent is left out of the alliance or when they are
formed to oppose the other parent. Triangulation typically occurs when two
parental authority figures have a disagreement and drag in a third, less powerful
person to diffuse the conflict, rather than resolving the disagreement between
themselves. Triangles are maladaptive because they prevent the resolution of a
conflict between two authority figures. This unresolved conflict becomes an ongoing source of frustration, irritation, and anger for all involved family members.
The triangulated child typically receives the brunt of much of the unhappiness of
his or her parents and frequently becomes the family's symptom-bearer.

The final category of organization looks at the nature of communication. In
functional families, communication flow is characterized by directness and specificity. Good communication involves each family member communicating directly,
rather than via intermediaries, and communicating specifically with each other.
"You kids are all rotten," is neither direct nor specific. In contrast, "Lila, I don't
like it when you come home late," is both direct and specific. In the second example, Lila knows exactly what is expected of her.

Resonance

Resonance is defined as the sensitivity and/or connection of family members to
one another. *Resonance* defines the emotional and psychological accessibility or
distance between family members. When assessing family resonance, therapists
evaluate interpersonal boundaries, which is a way of denoting where one person
or group of persons ends and where the next one(s) begins. Family boundaries reflect how connected or disconnected family members are with each other. Family
members overreact to one another when emotional and psychological boundaries
are weak. The term coined to define this is *enmeshment.* On the opposite end of
the resonance spectrum are families where members are not engaged at all, and
do not react to one another; they ignore each other. For these family members,
emotional and psychological boundaries are excessively distant. This is defined as
disengagement. Disengagement can be part of the usual order of things in a family, or it can emerge, for example, when adolescents become attached to peers and
begin to separate from the family. Although this separation is a normative aspect
of adolescent development, it may go too far, or be perceived by other family
members as a rejection of the family, thus feeding a growing cycle of alienation.

Family members with the proper (i.e., moderate) degree of engagement react to
one another while maintaining their separate individuality. The notion of resonance
and strength of boundaries applies not only to the relationship between family
members, but also to the relationship between a particular subsystem (such as the
marital couple) and the rest of the family. As noted, *closeness and distance refer to
emotional and psychological distance.* The psychological and emotional distance

between family members is brought about by, as well as reflected in, the interactions that are permitted. For example, a marital couple that has little privacy and weak boundaries is more likely to permit their child to sleep with them at night.

BSFT therapists look for certain behaviors in a family that are clear signs of either enmeshment (high resonance) or disengagement (low resonance). Obviously, some of these behaviors may happen in any family. However, when a large number of these behaviors occur, or some occur in extreme form, they are likely to reflect problems in the family patterns of interactions. Examples of high resonance—that is, weak boundaries, or enmeshment include mind reading, mediated responses (one family member speaks to another family member on behalf of a third family member), simultaneous speeches, interruptions, continuations (one family member completes the statement of another family member), personal control (one family member assumes she or he is able to control the thoughts, feelings, or behaviors of another family member), physical loss of distance (one family member controls the behaviors of another through physical means), joint affective reactions (family members share the same emotions even when not appropriate), engagement reactions (the reactions of one family member trigger the reactions of another). An example of disengagement is when no one talks with or about a family member who is attending the session, as if he or she was not present. Both enmeshment and disengagement may signal a problem in the family. Most families and relationships can be characterized more on one dimension than the other; however, problems emerge when the patterns become rigid and extreme. It should be noted that some cultures have a tendency toward more or less-interpersonal engagement. For example, Hispanics are more likely to be engaged than White Americans from New England. Regardless of whether engagement or disengagement is cultural, if it is linked to symptoms in the family, it needs to be targeted in therapy.

Developmental Stage

Individuals go through a series of developmental stages, ranging from infancy to childhood, adolescence, young adulthood, middle age, and old age. Each stage typically involves different roles and responsibilities. Families are composed of multiple individuals who are often at different stages of development. It is not always understood, however, that *families* also go through a series of developmental stages; in order for its members to continue to function in a healthy way, family members need to behave in ways that are appropriate at each developmental level. As families grow and develop, changes occur in family composition, as well as in the behaviors in which family members are expected to engage. For example, families must reorganize to adapt to major developmental milestones, such as when a child is born, when children leave home to live on their own, when a partner retires, when there is a death or serious illness of any family member; the breakup of parents' marriages, the temporary custody of children by one or another parent, a grandparent, or foster parent, the reunification of portions of a family—and the many other permutations that families undergo as members are added and subtracted. All of these milestones bring stress and require that the family adapt to the new circumstances. As noted above, one feature of family interactions that must be recalibrated as the family goes through developmental changes is the nature of boundaries. For example, a new couple needs to establish a strong boundary that separates it from the family of origin. These same boundaries need to be loosened (yet maintained) when a new child comes into the family. Failure to adapt (i.e., establish new interactional patterns) may lead to the emergence of maladaptive symptoms.

One of the most common developmental problems for adolescents involves parents continuing to treat an adolescent as if she or he were a younger child. In this example, the family behaviors that were adaptive at one time (when the adolescent was a child) become maladaptive when circumstances change. During adolescence, parents must be able to continue to be involved and monitor the adolescent, but now from a distinctly different perspective that allows for increasing autonomy in the youth. The family's flexibility will have a profound impact on its ability to adapt to new circumstances, including those new circumstances caused by developmental shifts. In general, flexible families are healthier families, and consequently their members are less likely to develop symptoms.

When a family's developmental stage is observed, four major sets of tasks and roles are assessed: parenting tasks and roles, marital tasks and roles, sibling tasks and roles, and the extended family's tasks and roles. How each of these family subgroups is functioning is evaluated in reference to what is normative or expected at that stage of individual and familial development. Examples of maladaptive patterns include immature parenting behaviors, children that are treated or act too young and are given few opportunities for responsible behavior, or when the child is overloaded with adult tasks, such as parental or confidante roles. A variation of a child who is overwhelmed with adult tasks occurs in Hispanic families in which a child is not only asked to translate, but then is asked by the parent to make a family decision—"because the child understands better how things work in this country." When a child is placed in such a powerful family role, if the child chooses to disobey his parents, they will be unable to set limits.

Identified Patienthood

Adolescents with behavior problems often are the repository for all the family's blame. Sometimes, it is easier for a parent to blame a child for her or his own troubles; in families, it is natural for less powerful persons to be subjected to blaming. Thus, adolescents referred to treatment are often viewed by the family as the sole cause of all of the family problems. That is, they are the family's "identified patient."

Although the identified patient is usually the target of family negativity, the identified patient may also receive considerable support from one or more family members. One parent, for example, may support or nurture inappropriate behaviors, failing to provide needed sanctions or consequences. Irrespective of the level of negativity, identified patients are easy to identify because they are often the centerpieces of family discussions. That is, family interactions tend to revolve around the identified patient. The more that family members blame and centralize the adolescent, the more difficult it will be to change the family's repetitive, maladaptive interactions.

Conflict Resolution

While solving differences of opinion is always challenging, it is much more challenging when done in the context of a history of highly conflictive relationships. Disagreements are natural and all families experience them. A family can approach and attempt to manage conflicts (i.e., disagreements) in five ways: denial, avoidance, diffusion, conflict emergence without resolution, and conflict emergence with resolution. For a family to function well, it must use the full range of styles in solving conflicts. Different styles may work well at different times. For example, a couple that fully discusses and negotiates to resolution every difference of opinion would not have time to do anything else. Hence, priorities need to be established to determine which conflicts deserve full attention and negotiation and which should be set aside for a more appropriate or convenient time. Similarly, diffusion of a conflict at a time when the parties are not in a good frame of mind can pave the way for more constructive discussions when tempers have cooled. Furthermore, it can prevent a total breakdown of communications. Timely diffusion thus facilitates later successful negotiations.

Ideally, a well-functioning family uses all conflict management styles, according to the needs of the situation. Emergence of the conflict with a subsequent resolution is generally considered to be the best solution in areas of conflict that are of significant importance to the family's functioning. Separate accounts and opinions regarding a particular conflict are clearly expressed and confronted. Then, the family is able to negotiate a solution that is acceptable to all family members involved. Conflicts go unresolved however, when family members are stuck in a conflict resolution style that does not permit bringing to resolution crucial differences of opinion.

Clinical Formulation

Assessment refers to the process of conducting a systematic review of family interactions to identify specific qualities in the patterns of interaction of each family. That is, assessment identifies the strengths and weaknesses of family interactions. In contrast, *clinical formulation* refers to the process of integrating the information obtained through assessment into *molar* processes that characterize the family's interactions (Szapocznik & Kurtines, 1989). In individual psychodiagnostics, clinical formulation explains the presenting symptom in relationship to the individual's psychodynamics. Similarly, clinical formulation in BSFT explains the presenting symptom in relationship to the family's characteristic patterns of interaction.

In BSFT, the same family domains (described earlier) are assessed in every case and serve as the primary base for all clinical formulations. Thus, every family will present with unique configurations and patterns of interaction. The therapist uses the domains noted previously to derive a systemic diagnosis of the family and to design interventions that systematically address these patterns of interaction. In this sense, every family is handled in a unique and specialized manner. However, the same strategies for assessing family interactions, making clinical formulations, and implementing treatment plans are applied in every case. For example, in BSFT, the therapist's clinical formulation will always include an articulation of the way in which disturbances in family interactions (i.e., structure, resonance) give rise to or maintain problem behaviors.

Treatment Goals: Restructuring

The main goal in BSFT is to help the family change the maladaptive interactional patterns that are identified during the diagnostic process. The therapist plans how she or he will intervene to help the family move from its present way of interacting, and the undesirable symptoms it produces, to a more adaptive and successful way of interacting that will eliminate these symptoms. By joining the family, the therapist is able to work as an insider. In this role, the therapist is able to encourage the family to behave as it usually does. This permits the therapist to diagnose the family and to develop a focused treatment plan that will facilitate the establishment of new skills in the family.

The interventions used to help families move from their maladaptive patterns of interactions to healthier patterns are called *restructuring*. The four restructuring techniques described here will give the beginning therapist the basic tools needed to carry out the work of helping the family change its patterns.

Working in the Present: Process versus Content

One of the hallmarks of BSFT is a sustained focus on family relationships in the here-and-now. As noted earlier, in the section on enactments, the therapist is explicitly concerned with attempting to engage family members in active discussions in treatment, rather than relying on their reports about what has happened in the past. In BSFT, the present focus is almost exclusively about family interactions, that is, process focus. This present/process focus becomes the primary mechanism through which the therapist diagnoses and restructures family interactions. In fact, it is the therapist's ability to focus on process rather than content that is the essence of BSFT. Therefore, the therapist needs to focus on what is happening *here and now,* rather than getting trapped in the content (reasons the family provide) of what happened there and then. A process focus enables the therapist to identify and restructure repetitive, maladaptive patterns of family interaction that are directly linked to the adolescent's problem behaviors.

The BSFT therapist understands the process of a family system by attending to *behaviors* that are involved in an interaction. It is the *how* of what people do, and the *what happens* in an interaction. *Process* describes the flow of actions and reactions between family members. The repetitive actions and reactions between and among family members become the focus of planned interventions in BSFT.

Content is easier and more obvious to observe. Most therapists have some experience eliciting content from family members. Training programs provide information and experiences that help therapists learn techniques for helping individuals share information about their current experience and personal history. Content is what people are actually saying when they are interacting. Content refers to the specific or concrete *facts* used in the communication. Content includes the reasons families give for a particular interaction. Families will try to engulf the therapist with historical descriptions that are rich in content. Despite all the efforts of families to trap the therapist in ornate content, it is crucial, as previously noted, that the therapist maintains focus on the here-and-now and on the patterns of the interactions that arise.

Reframing

Reframing is the formulation of a different perspective or frame of reality than the one within which the family has been operating. The therapist presents this new frame to the family in a manner that sells it to the family. The new frame is then used to facilitate change. It is important to note that in BSFT the goal of reframing is *not* to change individual cognition. Rather, the goal is to disrupt rigid, maladaptive family interaction patterns and create a new context in which more adaptive family interactions can occur. Reframing is typically used to disrupt negative affect, based on negative perceptions, by offering positive alternatives to the family. This shift from negative affect to positive affect creates a window of opportunities that the therapist must open to make new interactions happen.

For example, families with a drug-abusing adolescent often enter treatment describing the identified patient as disobedient, rebellious, and disrespectful. Family members are usually angry and rejecting of the identified patient, blaming the adolescent for all of the pain in the family. There are no signs of warmth or caring for her or him as an individual. Reframing in these circumstances is usually critical for reducing negativity and identified patienthood in these families. Expanding the family's view of the adolescent from the simple perspective—that this is a misbehaving, or even evil child—to one that also considers him or her as a vulnerable child who is in pain can profoundly influence family interactions. Such an expansion in focus is not easy to attain, because families are invested in their current frame. For example, to perceive their child as not merely problematic, but also suffering, can induce a sense of guilt in parents, and may lead them to react defensively to such a reframe. Therapists must use convincing reframes that are timed to the family's readiness. For example, if a parent does not "buy" the child in pain, the therapist might modify the reframe to suggest that "I did not realize that you [the parent] are so hurt by your child"—the reframe here is from anger to the hurt and pain of the parent.

Reframing is a very safe intervention; that is, it does not require challenging and does not have to include directives; as such, we encourage therapists to use it liberally. Reframing is an intervention that usually does not cause the therapist any loss of rapport. For that reason, the therapist should feel free to use it, particularly in the most explosive of situations. An experienced therapist is always equipped with some standard reframes that he or she can access in various situations: anger as pain or loss (underlying the anger), highly conflictive relationships as close or passionate, crises as opportunities (e.g., to pull the family closer, to become a stronger person), feeling overwhelmed as a signal that one must recharge one's batteries, impulsiveness as spontaneity, and insensitivity as 'telling it as it is' (Mitrani, Szapocznik, & Robinson-Batista, 2000).

Reframing interventions are also important in helping the therapist to overcome therapeutic impasses. Every family exhibits some reluctance to change. This reluctance may occur during any phase of treatment and often signifies a return to the family status quo. One way this return is often noted is through a return to high levels of conflict as the family fails to experience new ways of relating with one another. Therapists should be prepared for these minifailures in carrying out the tasks of treatment, and should continue to reframe family members in a positive light to keep them focused on the change process.

Working with Boundaries and Alliances

Family members must form alliances to carry out important functions in the family. For example, a strong parental alliance is essential to maintain effective behavior control and nurturance of children. Much of the work in BSFT involves helping family members establish adaptive alliances that meet the needs of the family and its individual members. This often involves disrupting harmful alliances.

An alliance basically denotes the existence of a subsystem, which has boundaries around it. To change the nature of an alliance, the therapist shifts the boundaries that connect some family members, and those that keep others apart. This is called *shifting boundaries*. For example, in the case of an overinvolved mother-daughter subsystem, the therapist may ask the father to engage in a fun task with the daughter in order to strengthen the daughter-father alliance. As the daughter develops a relationship with her father, her overreliance in mom weakens.

The parenting subsystem is central in nearly all BSFT interventions. Building a strong leadership subsystem with clear boundaries and the power to carry out leadership functions is critical for the life of the family. Membership in the parental subsystem is flexible, and can include two parents (married or separated) or a single parent and grandparent or older sibling if authority is delegated. In working with behavior problem adolescents, it is important that the therapist recognize that members of the parental subsystem have complex relationships that involve more than parenting functions. Issues from other aspects of the relationship often interfere with effective parenting. Although these other issues (such as marital conflict) can be addressed in treatment, BSFT is not intended to resolve all of the problems encountered by the marital couple. Because of the strategies and the problem-focused nature of BSFT, the therapist tries to resolve only those aspects of their difficulties with each other that are interfering with their ability to approach their problems with their youth. In the example above, once father develops an interest in daughter, the therapist can take advantage of the common interest between dad and mom to initiate parenting conversations. In this way the most sensitive marital couple issues are side stepped to focus strategically on parenting functions.

Boundary shifting also involves the clear demarcation of the perimeter around a subsystem. There are times, for example, when children interfere with interactions between parents. In this example, boundaries between the generations are weak and need to be more clearly marked. The therapist can make it understood that parents have a right to a certain amount of privacy to achieve a clearer demarcation of limits between the generations. In the same way, the sibling subsystem has the right to a certain amount of privacy, and it is often necessary to mark the boundaries or limits of how much parents should intrude in sibling life, or in the interactions among siblings.

Shifting alliances may also be a very useful strategy for addressing problems that arise in therapy sessions and that interfere with the therapist's success in addressing family interactions. For example, when a family gets stuck in a session, the therapist can expand the focus of the current discussion to include other family members in the discussion. The therapist may also strategically choose to connect with a family member with whom they have a stronger alliance and use this relationship to move the family to a new place. Likewise, the therapist can choose to connect with the person or persons that appear to be the most reluctant. Either way, the therapist strategically uses relationships between family members and between the family and her- or himself to move the family forward.

Behavioral contracting is also a strategy for setting limits to both parent and youth. At times in which there is constant battle between parents and adolescents as a result of vague and inconsistent rules, the therapist will recommend the use of behavioral contracting to help parent(s) and youth agree on a set of rules and their resulting consequences. Thus, the setting of clear rules and consequences helps to develop the demarcation of boundaries between parent(s) and child(ren). In these cases, helping parents establish boundaries for themselves in relationship to their child through the use of behavioral contracting is of tremendous therapeutic value, because it means that parents can no longer respond to the child's behavior/misbehavior according to how they feel at the time (lax, seductive, frustrated, or angry). Rather, the parent has committed to respond according to agreed-upon rules.

As the therapist will learn through experience with families that have problems with boundaries, the most difficult part of the job is to get parents to stick to their side of the contract. We expect that the youth will *not* keep his or her side of the contract (i.e., improved behavior), but rather, will instead try to test whether the parents will stick to their side of the contract (i.e., consequences). And test they will! When the misbehavior occurs, parents will want either to do less or to do more than the contract calls for, or the parents will disagree as to how to manage the adolescent's breach of contract. The therapist's job is to encourage and support the parents and help them support each other in keeping to their side of the contract. Once this is achieved, most youth's misbehavior quickly diminishes. From a BSFT point of view, it is very important that the therapist has begun to help the parents develop adequate boundaries with their behavior problem youths.

Assignment of Tasks

The use of tasks is central to all work with families. Tasks are used both inside and outside the therapy sessions as a basic tool for orchestrating change. Because our emphasis is on promoting new skills among family members, both at the level of individual behaviors and of family interactional relations, tasks are the vehicle through which therapists compose opportunities for the family to behave differently.

It is a general rule that the BSFT therapist must first assign a task to be performed within the session, where the therapist has an opportunity to observe, assist, and facilitate the successful conduct of the task. The therapist's aim is to create a successful experience for the family. Thus, the therapist should start with easy tasks and work up to the more difficult ones, slowly building a foundation of successes with the family, before attempting truly difficult tasks. Guidelines for the therapist to follow include: do not try to accomplish too much in a single leap, move step by step without skipping steps, and move from tasks performed *inside the session* to the same tasks *outside the session*. A task should never be assigned for outside the session before the family has successfully completed the same or very similar task within the therapy session. For example, in the session, the therapist may help the family set priorities for the children's schoolwork. The task at home could be for the family to set priorities for the children's house and work assignments. Some classic examples of in-session tasks are asking the parents to talk together to determine an appropriate curfew; asking mother and daughter to decide on an activity that they would like to share; asking a father to retrieve a son who has stormed out of the therapy room. Examples of homework tasks are having the family carry out a plan that was worked out in the therapy session, such as the mother-daughter activity; having the mother call the school to make an appointment with a counselor; having parents spend an hour alone together, in which they don't discuss the children.

Therapists should not expect the family to accomplish the assigned tasks flawlessly. In fact, if the family were skillful enough to successfully accomplish all assigned tasks, they would not need therapy. When tasks are assigned, therapists should always hope for the best, but be prepared for the worst. After all, a task represents a new behavior for the family. It represents a behavior that is very different from what the family has been doing for years. As the family attempts a task, the therapist should assist the family in overcoming obstacles to accomplishing the task. However, even then, in spite of the therapist's best efforts, the task is not always accomplished.

Therapists should not become discouraged at this stage. Their mission now is to *identify the obstacle(s)* and then help the family to overcome it (or them). Actually, failed tasks are usually a great source of new and important information about what happens such that a family cannot do what is best for them. The most important question in therapy is, "What interactions prevent some families from doing what is best for them and how do we change them?"

Termination of Treatment

Termination occurs when it is clear that the family has met the goals of the treatment plan; that is, family functioning has improved and adolescent behavior problems have been reduced or eliminated. Thus, termination is not determined by the number of sessions provided, but by the improvement in identified behavioral criteria. BSFT is designed to be delivered in 12 to 16 directive and active sessions, with booster sessions implemented as needed. A good prognostic sign of readiness for termination is the family's ability to effectively manage a crisis without therapist intervention. The family is empowered by the knowledge that even when behavior problems reoccur (as they naturally will), they are equipped to rein in their adolescent's behavior. After successful termination, families may encounter some of the old or even some new problems for which they may receive booster sessions. At this point, even a troubled situation for the family is different from previous times, because each member has already enjoyed the benefits of a better-functioning family.

SPECIAL CONSIDERATION IN TREATMENT

Engagement of Hard-to-Reach Families.

Engagement and retention in child and adolescent treatment is difficult (Kazdin, 1994); however, these problems are even more pronounced with families that present with a behavior problem adolescent. Thus, therapists should expect that engaging adolescents and family members into treatment will be challenging. In our prior clinical research, we have spent considerable time and effort to identify specific family-level obstacles to engagement, and we have developed specific strategies for engaging resistant families—BSFT Engagement (Szapocznik, Perez-Vidal, Hervis, Brickman, & Kurtines, 1990; Szapocznik & Kurtines, 1989).

The central theme that guides our engagement strategies is that resistance is not an individual problem. In BSFT, resistance is viewed systemically, and is understood only within the context of the family member's and therapist's actions and reactions in relation to each other. Therefore, resistance occurs when the therapist is unable to change her or his behavior to the family's usual way of behaving. The solution in BSFT Engagement is to change the therapist's behavior—to enable the therapist to get around the family's usual pattern of interaction long enough to bring the family into treatment. The therapist must identify family interaction patterns that may interfere with engagement and then adjust her or his own behavior.

Therapists must recognize that the engagement process begins with the first call. Do not expect all family members to show up at the first session after a single conversation with a single family member, particularly families with drug-abusing adolescents. In this section, we provide guidance to therapists about some of the most common types of family interaction that may interfere with engagement into treatment, and provide guidelines about how therapists can adjust their engagement strategies based on these patterns. Note that here we are referring to our work and findings with Hispanic families in Miami; it is possible that with other groups very different patterns may emerge. Therapists should be aware that the goal of the strategic interventions described in the following is to engage family members into treatment; these interventions are *not* intended to restructure family interactions. In fact, it is by respecting and accepting while at the same time getting around the family's patterns of behavior that the therapist is able to join the family (or individual family members), and influence family members' participation in treatment.

We have identified four general patterns of family interaction that interfere with engagement into treatment in Hispanic families with a problem behavior adolescent. These four patterns are discussed following, in terms of how the resistant patterns of interactions are manifested, and how they come to the attention of the therapist.

Powerful Identified Patient

With behavior problem adolescents, the most frequently observed pattern of family interaction that interferes with engagement is a powerful identified patient. This is particularly a problem in cases that are not court mandated; therefore, the adolescent identified patient has no reason to engage in therapy. These families are characterized by an adolescent identified patient who is in a powerful position in the family, and whose parents, conversely, are unable to influence the adolescent. Powerful parents are able to bring such an adolescent into therapy without having to lie about where they are taking him or her. This is not the case for these families. Very often, the parent of a powerful identified patient will admit that her or his son or daughter flatly refuses to come to therapy. The identified patient may resist therapy because it threatens her or his position of power and moves her or him to a problem-person position—or, it is the parent's agenda to come to therapy, and thus if the youth agrees to the parent's agenda, this would strengthen the parent's power.

To bring these families into treatment, the youth's power in the family is not directly challenged, but rather it is accepted and tracked by the therapist. The therapist allies her- or himself with the powerful adolescent so that she or he may later be in a position to influence the adolescent to change. This often requires a direct outreach of the therapist to the adolescent, frequently in person. The purpose of such a meeting is to give the youth a convincing reason to want to come to treatment. The initial goal is to form an alliance with the powerful adolescent and to reframe the need for therapy in a manner that allows the adolescent to perceive her- or himself in a powerful way and her or his position in the family in a non-threatened way. The kind of reframing that is most useful with powerful adolescents involves transferring the symptom from the powerful identified patient to the family system. For example, "I want you to come into therapy to help me change some of the things that are going on in your family." Later, however, once the adolescent is in therapy, her or his position of power will be challenged. This is one of the clearest uses of a practical intervention that characterizes strategic interventions.

It should be noted that in cases of powerful adolescents who have less powerful parents, forming the initial alliance with the parents is likely to be ineffective because the parents are not strong enough to bring their adolescent into therapy. Their failed attempts to bring the adolescent into therapy would render the parents even weaker, and the family would fail to enter therapy. Furthermore, the youth is likely to perceive the therapist as being the parent's ally, which would immediately be translated into distrust for the therapist and qualifying the therapist as powerless. This does not mean that therapists ignore building a relationship with parents. Therapists must be respectful of all family members' roles and responsibilities, and should be empathic and understanding of each person's thoughts, feelings, and behaviors. However, by giving proper respect to power and making an early deal with power, the therapist will have power on her or his side to bring the family into treatment.

Caller Protecting the Symptom

A parent who protects the family's maladaptive patterns of interaction characterizes the second most common type of resistance to entering treatment. These families are identified when the person making the agency contact (usually a mother) to request help is also the person protecting the unwillingness of other family members to enter therapy. The mother, for example, might give contradictory messages to the therapist: "I want to take my family to therapy but my son couldn't come to the session because he forgot, and my husband has so much work he doesn't have the time."

To bring these families into treatment, the therapist must first acknowledge the mother's frustration in wanting to get help, yet not getting any cooperation from the family member(s). The therapist will then ask the mother's permission to contact the other family members, "even though they are busy," and the therapist acknowledges how difficult it is for them to become involved. With the mother's permission, the therapist calls the other family members and "separates" them from the mother around the issue of coming to therapy. The therapist does this by developing her or his own relationship with other family members about each family member's own interest in coming to therapy. By the therapist developing his or her own relationship with these other family members, he or she circumvents the mother's protective behaviors. Once in therapy, the mother's overprotection of the adolescent's misbehavior, and her overprotection of the father's lack of involvement (and the adolescent's and father's eagerness that mother continue to protect them) will be restricted, as maladaptive patterns of interactions related to the adolescent's presenting problem behaviors.

Disengaged Parent

These family organizations are characterized by little or no cohesiveness or alliance between the parents or parent figures as a subsystem. One of the parents, usually the father, refuses to come to therapy. This is typically a parent and or father who has remained disengaged from the problems at home. Parent disengagement not only protects the parent from having to address adolescent behavior problems, but it also often protects the parents from having to deal with marital aspects of the relationship. In many circumstances, the engaged parent may be overinvolved (enmeshed) with the identified patient and may be inadvertently supporting the adolescent's problem behaviors. Consequently, in this family both overinvolvement and disengagement coexist with perfect complementarities.

To engage these families into treatment, the therapist must engage the caller (usually the mother). The therapist then begins to direct the mother's interactions with the father, changing their patterns of interaction so as to improve, at least temporarily, their cooperation in bringing the family into treatment. The therapist gives mother tasks to do with her husband that pertain *only* to the issue of taking care of their son's (or daughter's) problems by getting the family into treatment. The therapist assigns tasks and coaches the mother to act in such a way that is least likely to spark the broader marital conflict. These tasks are intended to change the marital couple's interaction only around the whole family coming to treatment. To set up the task, the mother may be asked what she believes is the real reason her husband does not want to come in. Once this is ascertained, she is coached to present coming to treatment in a way that the husband can accept. For example, if he doesn't want to come because he has given up on the son, she may be coached to present it to him as coming to help her cope with the situation. Although the pattern is similar to that of the contact person protecting the family's organization, in this instance the challenge emerges differently. In this case, the mother does not excuse the father's distance but, quite the contrary, she complains about his disinterest; this mother is usually eager to do something to involve her husband, given some direction. This is one of the very unusual situations when a task is given before it has been successfully done in session.

Fear of Therapy as an Expose

Sometimes therapy is threatening to one or more individuals, who are afraid of secrets being revealed. The therapist must reframe the goal of therapy in a way that respects this person's wishes to keep her or his secret. One example is to assure this person that therapy does not have to go where she or he does not want it to go. The therapist will make every effort to focus on the behavior problems of the youth, and will not focus on the issues that might concern the unwilling family member (which could be the youth or another family member). The individual is also assured that in the session, "we will deal only with those issues that you want to deal with." In our experience, however, sometimes the frightening secrets will be revealed in therapy, because others already knew or because the person with the secret chooses to open up.

Therapists should keep in mind that many other family patterns likely may interfere with engagement. The important frame is that therapists pay attention to identifying family patterns from the first contact, and that she or he adjust the engagement strategy to maximize chances for bringing family members to treatment. Also, therapists are reminded not to attempt to restructure while engaging. In our experience, it can backfire. Thus, while engaging, the therapist must not try to fix the maladaptive interactions, but must just get around them.

Working with Individual Family Members: One Person BSFT

Engaging the whole family in treatment is one of the most challenging aspects of working with youth with behavior problems and their families. Thus, it was necessary to develop strategies for achieving the goals of BSFT (i.e., changes in maladaptive family interactions and symptomatic adolescent behavior), without requiring the whole family to be present in treatment. The approach we developed to meet this goal, One Person BSFT (Szapocznik, Foote, Perez-Vidal, Hervis, & Kurtines, 1983; Szapocznik, Kurtines, Foote, & Perez-Vidal, 1986; Szapocznik & Kurtines, 1989; Szapocznik, Kurtines, Perez-Vidal, Hervis, & Foote, 1990), capitalizes on the systemic concept of complementarity, which suggests that when one family member changes, the rest of the system responds by either restoring the family process to its old ways or adapting to the new changes (Minuchin & Fishman, 1981). In One Person BSFT, family interactional patterns are the focus of treatment. The therapist focuses exclusively on family interactions, not on the individual adolescent. The goal of One Person BSFT is to change the drug-abusing adolescent's participation in maladaptive family interactions that include her or him. These changes often create a family crisis, as the family attempts to return to its old ways, and crisis is used as the golden opportunity to engage reluctant family members.

RESEARCH EVIDENCE

Outcome research findings for BSFT are briefly presented below, including the impact of BSFT on: (1) adolescent drug use, (2) engagement and retention, (3) behavior problems, and (4) family functioning. Three studies (Santisteban et al., 2003; Szapocznik, Perez-Vidal et al., 1988; Szapocznik, Kurtines, Foote, Perez-Vidal, & Hervis, 1986) were conducted to examine the impact of BSFT on adolescent drug abuse.

Marijuana

Santisteban and colleagues (2003) found that for adolescents who abused marijuana, 60 percent showed reliable improvement and 15 percent showed reliable deterioration in the BSFT condition, whereas 17 percent showed reliable improvement and 50 percent showed reliable deterioration in a group control condition.

Engagement and Retention

In three separate studies (Coatsworth, Santisteban, McBride, & Szapocznik, 2001; Santisteban et al., 1996; Szapocznik et al., 1988) the efficacy of specialized BSFT Engagement strategies in engaging and retaining drug-abusing adolescents and their families in treatment have been demonstrated. Szapocznik, Perez-Vidal and colleagues (1988) demonstrated that 93 percent of families that received the specialized BSFT Engagement condition were successfully engaged, as compared to 42 percent that did not receive these engagement interventions. Moreover, the utilization of the same specialized engagement strategies to retain cases in treatment resulted in 77 percent of families in the specialized engagement condition receiving a full dose of therapy, compared to 25 percent of families that did not receive these interventions.

Externalizing Behaviors

Externalizing behaviors, as measured by the Revised Behavior Problem Checklist (Rio, Quay, Santisteban, & Szapocznik, 1989) and reported by a parent or guardian, have also been investigated in these outcome studies (Santisteban et al., 2003; Santisteban et al., 1997; Szapocznik et al., 1986). Results indicated that participants in BSFT showed significantly greater reduction in behavior problems than group controls. In the most recent study (Santisteban et al., 2003), analyses of clinical significance in Conduct Disorder showed that in the BSFT condition 44 percent showed reliable improvement, 26 percent were classified as recovered, and 5 percent showed reliable deterioration. In the group control condition 11 percent showed reliable deterioration, and no case was classified as reliably improved or recovered. A similar pattern was seen for Socialized Aggression.

Family Interactions

BSFT theory is based on the assumption that the family is considered to play a critical role in the development, maintenance, and treatment of adolescent behavior problems. Studies examining the impact of BSFT on family interactions (Szapocznik et al., 2002) have shown significant impact of BSFT on family functioning (as measured among the five diagnostic dimensions described earlier). The most recent study (Santisteban et al., 2003) demonstrated that when compared to a group control condition, BSFT produced significant improvement in adolescent-reported family cohesion and improvements in observer-reported family functioning.

――――――――――――――――――――― **Case Study** ―――――――――――――――――――――

Jessica is a 15-year-old White American high school sophomore living with her maternal grandparents and 11-year-old brother, Jonathan. Jessica was 9 years old when her grandparents obtained custody of her and her brother, when it was determined that their mother could not take care of her children because of her prolonged drug use and involvement in prostitution. Jessica's mother's numerous attempts to receive treatment were unsuccessful, and she was never able to regain custody of her children, despite strong efforts by both her family and family services. The children's biological father left the family shortly after Jonathan was born, and has had minimal contact with the family.

Jessica and Jonathan seemed initially to adjust well to life with their grandparents. Their grandparents made every effort to provide a loving and caring home. They wanted to do a good parenting job, but discovered that parenting their grandchildren was not an easy task. Their grandmother became the disciplinarian in the home; their grandfather occasionally set limits, but was less consistent, and often contradicted grandmother's efforts to control their behavior. Jessica did her chores and was helpful and often took care of Jonathan, pretending he was her own child.

After she was arrested for injuring a student during a fight in school, family services was notified and the family was referred for family therapy.

The BSFT therapist contacted the grandmother to schedule the first appointment with the family. During this call, the therapist let the grandmother share some of her frustration about the current circumstances in the family. However, the therapist redirected the grandmother to gather information about who played key roles in the family and to identify any potential barriers to getting key people into treatment. The grandmother assured the therapist that all family members would attend the session, but when the therapist arrived at the home, only Jessica and her grandmother were present. The grandfather was not present because he had been arguing with his wife earlier that day and his wife had not insisted that he participate in the session. Also, the grandparents forgot to tell Jonathan about the session, and he was out with his friends. The first session involved joining with Jessica and her grandmother—supporting and connecting with each one in an effort to develop a therapeutic system that will help bring the rest of the family into the session. Some of the joining behaviors of the therapist included: (1) demonstrating respect and acceptance for Jessica and her grandmother; (2) validating their statements, positions, and feelings; and (3) blending in with their relaxed style and sense of humor.

The therapist also spent the session exploring with Jessica and her grandmother how to engage Jonathan and the grandfather for the next session. Jessica immediately took charge of the conversation, expressing her concerns about her grandfather's irritable behavior and recent lack of involvement in the family. Her grandmother agreed with Jessica that her husband often seemed angry and uninvolved, and expressed that this is the case of grandma protecting—therefore maybe it was not a good idea for him to attend. The family expressed that they would not be able to get the grandfather to come to the session after all, and diffused their discussion to other family problems. The therapist guided the grandmother and Jessica back to the discussion about engaging grandfather, highlighting how important it was for grandmother because she needs the additional support to overcome the current problems in the family. The therapist explored strategies for framing therapy to the grandfather, and practiced in the session how she would approach him to invite him to the next session. Jessica was given the task of inviting her younger brother to the session. These interventions were successful, and all family members were present for subsequent sessions.

Throughout the first three sessions with the entire family, the therapist joined with all of the individual family members by providing opportunities for each person to become involved in the session and by validating each family member's perspective. The therapist also maintained a less central role, encouraging family members to interact with one another whenever possible. These in-session family interactions, or enactments, helped the therapist to develop diagnostic formulations along the five dimensions previously discussed. These early formulations were:

Organization—Jessica and her grandmother seemed to have a strong alliance. There was also evidence that this alliance often resulted in Jessica engaging in conflicts with her grandfather. This cross-generational alliance appeared to keep the grandfather excluded from family interactions, and it prevented the grandparents from dealing with their own conflicted relationship. This triangle caused a great deal of stress for Jessica; conflict with her grandfather often preceded her own acting-out behaviors. In addition to issues in the marital relationship, the therapist also noted problems in the executive subsystem, such as unbalanced leadership and inconsistent and inappropriate behavior control attempts.

Resonance—The therapist observed evidence of enmeshment behaviors between Jessica and her grandmother, such as mind readings, finishing each other's sentences (continuations), and joint affective reactions (both laughing inappropriately at the same time). The therapist also noted that the grandfather often withdrew from interactions, particularly following sequences where he became embroiled in a conflict with Jessica.

Developmental Stage—The therapist noted that the family is facing two important developmental challenges. The first is the grandparents' change in role from an extended, supportive role to a parenting role. The second is the children's transition into adolescence. Successful adaptation to these transitions will determine healthier family functioning.

Identified Patienthood—The family identified multiple concerns leading to family problems. The focus was not on any one person and negativity seemed minimal initially.

Conflict Resolution—The therapist identified diffusion as the family's conflict resolution pattern. Family members often diverted their conflicts and rarely reached resolution.

The diagnostic process continued as therapy progressed and the therapist directly observed additional problems in family interactions. Based on information obtained from later sessions, the therapist amended the diagnostic map to include grandparents' serious difficulties in sharing authority and decisionmaking, ineffective and inappropriate behavior control attempts, and unclear rules and consequences. Also, the change from the grandparents' role to the role of parenting figures began to have an effect in the spousal alliance. Their arguments became more frequent and increasingly hostile, further compounding their difficulty to parent together. The enactments also confirmed conflict in the sibling subsystem and further revealed sibling aggression.

Once the therapist was able to assess the family's interactional pattern and develop a working diagnostic map of the family, she developed a treatment plan that targeted the maladaptive patterns of interaction that were identified from the interactional diagnosis. The therapist formulated the following treatment plan, organizing it around the five BSFT diagnostic categories:

Organization: To address the difficulties in hierarchy and in the executive subsystem, the therapist worked toward balancing the leadership and establishing an effective decisionmaking subsystem, wherein the grandparents worked collaboratively to offer guidance, direction, and support to Jessica and Jonathan. The therapist began this process by assigning the grandparents the task of working together to develop an effective behavior control plan in collaboration with the children. To facilitate this working collaboration, the therapist introduced and reiterated themes about effective business management and teamwork. These frames appealed to the grandfather's own experiences and served to activate existing leadership skills. The grandmother resonated to the notion of teamwork and quickly responded positively to her husband's supportive behaviors.

The therapist then guided the grandparents to develop plans, rules, and consequences for behaviors in the home. The therapist encouraged the grandparents to complete the task on their own as much as possible, intervening when they were stuck or to reinforce and/or highlight adaptive interactions. The therapist focused only on the process of how the task was accomplished, and focused specifically on using restructuring strategies, such as reframing and highlighting, to produce the desired treatment goal of establishing a strong and supportive parental alliance. The therapist also made sure to highlight interactions that offered guidance, direction, and support to the children, and also made sure to ask the grandparents to talk together about how to implement the plan effectively and consistently. Throughout this process the therapist made every effort to remain decentralized, permitting the new family interactions to emerge. The therapist was often faced with the challenge that family members wanted to speak to her directly and to avoid direct communication with each other. The therapist frequently redirected communications so that they would occur among family members, directly opening up opportunities for new interactions to occur (i.e., "Talk to your granddaughter and let her know how concerned you are; let your grandfather know what is bothering you; tell your grandson how much you appreciate his support"). After successful completion of the task the therapist praised the family's accomplishments. Establishing a collaborative, supportive alliance between the grandparents had an expectedly positive effect on the spousal alliance and reduced conflict. To address triangulation the therapist guided the grandparents to deal with conflicts directly and to discourage Jessica's involvement. For instance, when the grandparents were doing the task of discussing how to implement their behavior control plan effectively the discussion became a little heated and a conflict ensued between them. Jessica quickly got involved in their discussion, expressing her alliance to her grandmother. The moment the therapist observed this she intervened in the interaction and asked the grandparents to let Jessica know that even though they appreciated her input as a way of offering support, they would prefer to resolve the situation on their own. In this way, the therapist guided the grandparents to deal with the triangulation effectively without putting Jessica off, and thus they were then able to resolve their differences directly and effectively. The BSFT therapist seized the opportunity to intervene in the here-and-now, guiding family members to do for themselves instead of having the therapist doing for them. Reframing Jessica's interfering in the argument as a way of expressing her support instead of as an acting-out behavior or a nuisance gently pulled Jessica out of the triangle without resistance, and the grandparents were able to resolve their conflict. In the process of breaking up triangles—as the family was gaining mastery in dealing with conflicts directly—the therapist was faced with the challenge of dealing with the family's attempts to triangulate her. Jessica often made attempts to get the therapist to ally with her against her grandfather or grandmother at different stages in the therapy. To avoid getting triangulated and risking being ineffective as a therapist, she quickly redirected the conflict back to the persons involved, thus placing the focus of the interaction back on the family. The therapist also worked on strengthening the sibling subsystem to decrease conflicts and reestablish caring behaviors. To accomplish this the therapist gave the siblings the task of coming up with an activity that they would both enjoy together. The therapist guided the siblings to complete the task, intervening strategically by highlighting caring behaviors when they were expressed, and guiding them to reach resolution if differences of opinion emerged. At different points in time in this process the therapist was faced with some resistance from the siblings to work together. She addressed this by using reframes that emphasized the importance of the sibling relationship, now and in the future. After successful completion of the task the therapist praised the siblings' accomplishments and punctuated their ability to work together as a team.

Resonance: To address enmeshment behaviors the therapist worked with the family; to develop more firm boundaries while still allowing permeability for shared experiences. The therapist discouraged mind readings, continuations, mediated responses, and any other behaviors that prevented family members from maintaining their separateness and individual differences. To address the grandfather's disengagement, the therapist focused on involving him more in family activities and encouraging direct dialogue with family members. She reinforced the grandfather's leadership role in the family, guiding him to participate more actively in managing the children's behavior and offering his wife support.

Developmental Stage: The therapist worked with the grandparents in the process of adapting to their new role as parents, validating their concerns and offering guidance and support. The therapist incorporated in her therapy a psychoeducational component to address developmental issues during adolescence and the impact these changes have on parenting functions. To achieve this goal, the therapist engaged the family in a discussion focusing on identifying changes that have affected the family as a result of the normal process of growth in the children and the transition into adolescence. The therapist facilitated the exploration of how these changes have affected parenting practices, and worked with the family to uncover dysfunctional patterns and restructure them. Some of the questions that the therapist posed to the family included the following: (1) How are parental rules negotiated and/or implemented differently now than when the children were younger? (2) How flexible are they, as parents, in changing as the children grow and develop? (3) In what ways is it easier or more difficult for them to be flexible? (4) Are there aspects of parenting that become more difficult or, conversely, are facilitated by being older parents? During the discussion, as enactments emerged, the therapist seized opportunities to create change in dysfunctional interactional patterns of behavior in the moment, linking family members in more effective and adaptive interactions.

Identified Patienthood: The therapist worked toward decreasing negativity in the family, and guided the family to develop a more interactive perspective. The therapist achieved this by using reframes, thus creating different perspectives or frames of reality for the family that were positive, and transforming adversarial interactions into ones that allowed opportunities for better communication and more adaptive interactions to take place. Several themes were used to reduce negativity. First, Jessica's behaviors were normalized within her own developmental trajectory. For example, by reframing and validating her desire for autonomy, it was possible to challenge the means with which she was attempting to gain independence. Second, intergenerational differences were blamed for much of the family's difficulty in understanding one another. The additional generation gap was used whenever a difference emerged in the session. This frame made it possible to disrupt negative sequences, and helped the family to redirect the conversation.

Conflict Resolution: To address the family's diffusion and avoidance patterns the therapist worked with the family to focus on individual conflict situations and bring resolution through negotiation. The therapist facilitated negotiations sufficiently to allow for a new set of conflict resolution skills to be practiced.

With a well-developed treatment plan in hand the therapist was able to intervene—to help the family move from a maladaptive way of interacting that sustains symptoms to a more adaptive and successful way of interacting. Some of the restructuring techniques that the therapist used to achieve the therapeutic goals included the following: working in the present—using enactments to capture the essence of the maladaptive interactions, and orchestrating new interactions within the therapy session to give the family a new experience of a more adaptive way of relating; offering the family new perspectives of reality by offering reframes to facilitate change (e.g., reframing Jessica's anger to an expression of pain or hurt); shifting boundaries to restore the balance of power in the family, bringing the parental figures together and breaking up destructive triangles; and using tasks as a basic tool for orchestrating change (e.g., asking the grandparents to work together to develop a behavior contract with their grandchildren). Tasks were performed within the therapy session, thus giving the therapist the opportunity to observe, assist, and facilitate interactions so as to give the family the experience of successfully completing the task and in the process relating in a more adaptive way.

RECOMMENDED READINGS

Szapocznik, J., Hervis. O. E., & Schwartz, S. (2003). *Brief strategic Family Therapy for Adolescent Drug Abuse* (NIDA *Therapy Manuals for Drug Addiction* Series). Rockville, MD: NIDA.

Szapocznik, J., & Kurtines, W. (1989). *Breakthroughs in family therapy with drug abusing problem youth.* New York: Springer.

REFERENCES

American Academy of Child and Adolescent Psychiatry (AACAP). Children with Oppositional Defiant Disorder. The Facts for Families© series. http://www.aacap.org/publications/factsfam/72.htm. [January 9, 2004].

American Psychiatric Association. (1994). *Diagnostic and statistical manual of mental disorders* (4th ed.). Washington, DC: Author.

Coatsworth, J. D., Santisteban, D. A., McBride, C. K., & Szapocznik, J. (2001). Brief strategic family therapy versus community control: Engagement, retention, and an exploration of the moderating role of adolescent symptom severity. *Family Process, 40,* 313–332.

Diamond, G., & Liddle, H. A. (1996). Resolving a therapeutic impasse between parents and adolescents in multidimensional family therapy. *Journal of Consulting and Clinical Psychology, 64,* 481–488.

Diamond, G. M., Liddle, H. A., Hogue, A., & Dakof, G. A. (1999). Alliance-building interventions with adolescents in family therapy: A process study. *Psychotherapy: Theory, Research, Practice, Training, 36,* 335–368.

Hawkins, J. D., Catalano, R. F., & Miller, J. Y. (1992). Risk and protective factors for alcohol and other drug problems in adolescence and early adulthood: Implications for substance abuse prevention. *Psychological Bulletin, 112,* 64–105.

Jessor, R., & Jessor, S. (1977). *Problem behavior and psychosocial development: A longitudinal study of youth.* New York: Academic Press.

Kazdin, A. E. (1994). Interventions for aggressive and antisocial children. In L. D. Eron & J. H. Gentry (Eds.), *Reason to hope: A psychosocial perspective on violence and youth* (pp. 341–382). Washington, DC: American Psychological Association.

Marin, G., & Marin, B. V. (1991). *Research with Hispanic populations.* Newbury Park, CA: Sage.

McGoldrick, M. (1989). Ethnicity and the family life cycle. In B. Carter & M. McGoldrick (Eds.), *The changing family life cycle: A framework for family therapy* (2nd ed., pp. 70–90). Needham Heights, MA: Allyn & Bacon.

Minuchin, S., & Fishman, H. C. (1981). *Family therapy techniques.* Cambridge, MA: Harvard University Press.

Mitrani, V. B., & Perez, M. A. (2003). Structural-strategic approaches to couple and family therapy.

The ecosystemic lens to understanding family functioning. In T. L. Sexton, G. Weeks, and M. S. Robbins (Eds.), *Handbook of family therapy* pp. 177–200. New York, NY: Brunner Routledge.

Mitrani, V. B., Szapocznik, J., & Robinson-Batista, C. (2000). Structural ecosystems therapy with HIV+ African American women. In W. Pequegnat & J. Szapocznik (Eds.), *Working with families in the era of HIV/AIDS* (pp. 3–26). Thousand Oaks, CA: Sage.

Moore, D. R., Arthur, J. L. (1989). Juvenile delinquency. In T. H. Ollendick & M. Hersen (Eds.), *Handbook of psychopathology* (2nd ed., pp. 197–217). New York: Plenum Press.

National Institute on Drug Abuse. Johnston, L. D., O'Malley, P. M., & Bachman, J. G. (2001). *Monitoring the future: National results on adolescent drug use. Overview of key findings.* Bethesda, MD: NIDA: NIH Publication No. 01-4923.

Rio, A. T., Quay, H. C., Santisteban, D. A., & Szapocznik, J. (1989). A factor analytical study of a Spanish translation of the Revised Behavior Problem Checklist. *Journal of Clinical Child Psychology, 18,* 343–350.

Robbins, M. S., Kumar, S., Walker-Barnes, C., Feaster, D. J., Briones, E., & Szapocznik, J. (2002). Ethnic differences in comorbidity among substance-abusing adolescents referred to outpatient therapy. *Journal of the American Academy of Child and Adolescent Psychiatry, 41,* 394–401.

Santisteban, D. A., Coatsworth, J. D., Perez-Vidal, A., Kurtines, W., Schwartz, S. J., LaPerriere, A., & Szapocznik, J. (2003). Efficacy of brief strategic family therapy in modifying Hispanic adolescent behavior problems and substance abuse. *Journal of Family Psychology, 17,* 121–133.

Santisteban, D. A., Coatsworth, J. D., Perez-Vidal, A., Mitrani, V., Jean-Gilles, M., & Szapocznik, J. (1997). Brief structural strategic family therapy with African American and Hispanic high risk youth: A report of outcome. *Journal of Community Psychology, 25,* 453–471.

Santisteban, D. A., Szapocznik, J., Perez-Vidal, A., Kurtines, W. M., Murray, E. J., & LaPerriere, A. (1996). Efficacy of intervention for engaging youth and their families into treatment and some variables that may contribute differential effectiveness. *Journal of Family Psychology, 10,* 35–44.

Szapocznik, J., & Coatsworth, J. D. (1999). An ecodevelopmental framework for organizing the influences on drug abuse: A developmental model of risk and protection. In M. D. Glantz & C. R. Hartel (Eds.), *Drug abuse: Origins and interventions* pp. 331–366. Washington, DC: American Psychological Association.

Szapocznik, J., Hervis, O. E., & Schwartz, S. (2003). *Brief Strategic Family Therapy for Adolescent Drug Abuse* (NIDA *Therapy Manuals for Drug Addiction* Series). Rockville, MD: NIDA.

Szapocznik, J., & Kurtines, W. (1989). *Breakthroughs in family therapy with drug abusing problem youth.* New York: Springer.

Szapocznik, J., Kurtines, W. M., Foote, F., & Perez-Vidal, A. (1983). Conjoint versus one-person family therapy: Some evidence for effectiveness of conducting family therapy through one person. *Journal of Consulting and Clinical Psychology, 51,* 889–899.

Szapocznik, J., Kurtines, W. M., Foote, F., & Perez-Vidal, A. (1986). Conjoint versus one-person family therapy: Further evidence for the effectiveness of conducting family therapy through one person. *Journal of Consulting and Clinical Psychology, 54,* 395–397.

Szapocznik, J., Kurtines, W., Perez-Vidal, A., Hervis, O., & Foote, F. H. (1990). Interplay of advances between theory, research, and application in treatment interventions aimed at behavior problem children and adolescents. *Journal of Consultation and Clinical Psychology, 58,* 696–703.

Szapocznik, J., Perez-Vidal, A., Brickman, A. L., Foote, F. H., Santisteban, D., Hervis, O., & Kurtines, W. M. (1988). Engaging adolescent drug abusers and their families in treatment: A strategic structural systems approach. *Journal of Consulting and Clinical Psychology, 56,* 552–557.

Szapocznik, J., Perez-Vidal, A., Hervis, O. E., Brickman, A. L., & Kurtines, W. M. (1990). Innovations in family therapy: Strategies for overcoming resistance to treatment. In R. A. Wells & V. J. Giannetti (Eds.), *Handbook of the brief psychotherapies* (pp. 93–114). New York: Plenum.

Szapocznik, J., Robbins, M. S., Mitrani, V. B., Santisteban, D., Hervis, O., & Williams, R. A. (2002). Brief strategic family therapy with behavior problem Hispanic Youth (pp. 83–109). In J. Lebow (Ed.) *Integrative and Eclectic Psychotherapies* (Vol. 4). In F. Kaslow (Ed.) *Comprehensive Handbook of Psychotherapy,* New York: Wiley & Sons.

Szapocznik, J., Scopetta, M. A., & King, O. E. (1978). Theory and practice in matching treatment to the special characteristics and problems of Cuban immigrants. *Journal of Community Psychology, 6,* 112–122.

CHAPTER 5

Multisystemic Therapy for Adolescents with Serious Externalizing Problems

Sonja K. Schoenwald and Scott W. Henggeler

Recent reports from the United States Surgeon General explicated the high personal and societal costs of youth violence (U.S. Public Health Service, 2001) and serious emotional disturbance (U.S. Department of Health and Human Services, 1999). For example, experiencing such problems during childhood and adolescence is associated with many concurrent problems, as well as increased risk for future (1) mental health and substance abuse problems, (2) educational and vocational difficulties, (3) relationship difficulties (e.g., divorce, child maltreatment), and (4) health-related problems. On a societal level, youths with serious emotional and behavioral problems can consume considerable treatment resources, including expensive and iatrogenic out-of-home placements. Moreover, such youths are less likely to become productive taxpayers and more likely to consume societal resources, through the criminal justice, social welfare, and health care systems. Thus, the development of effective interventions for these youths and their families has the potential to produce cascading benefits.

As also noted in the surgeon general's reports, as well as by many leading reviewers (e.g., Loeber & Farrington, 1998; McBride, VanderWaal, Terry, & Van-Buren, 1999), the development of effective interventions can be guided by an extensive knowledge base that has already been developed. Decades of correlational, longitudinal, and experimental research has shown that serious clinical problems in children and adolescents are associated with multiple factors within and between the key systems in which children are embedded—family, peer, school, and neighborhood. For example, parenting practices have been associated with virtually all aspects of childhood behavior, ranging from academic achievement and moral development to youth violence and substance abuse. As such, this literature can be used to guide the focuses of family-based interventions (e.g., increasing caregiver monitoring and supervision to decrease risk of adolescent antisocial behavior). Similarly, investigators have examined variables that influence parents' capacity to interact effectively with their children. Here, variables such as parental social support, mental health and substance abuse problems, and behavioral skills are important influences on parenting; therefore, effective family-based interventions require the capacity to address these problems as well. As a final example, the research literature is very clear that association with problem peers is a powerful predictor of behavior problems in adolescents. Yet, traditional family therapy models have rarely extended their reach beyond the family system. As described throughout this chapter, a key aspect of Multisystemic Therapy (MST) is its capacity to address established risk factors across family and extrafamilial systems.

THEORETICAL AND CONCEPTUAL FOUNDATIONS

As described more than 20 years ago (Henggeler, 1982) and updated in more recent clinical texts (Henggeler, Schoenwald, Borduin, Rowland, & Cunningham, 1998; Henggeler, Schoenwald, Rowland, & Cunningham, 2002), the development of MST has been based on the social ecological theory of human development (Bronfenbrenner, 1979), more pragmatically oriented family therapy approaches, and the extensive research on the determinants of behavior problems in children and adolescents noted previously.

Theory of Social Ecology

The fundamental tenet of the social ecological framework (Bronfenbrenner, 1979) is that individuals are embedded in multiple systems that have direct and indirect influences on behavior. This conceptualization provides an excellent fit with the known determinants of antisocial behavior in children and adolescents described previously. That is, research has shown how adolescent behavior is influenced by variables at the family, peer, school, and community level of analyses. Moreover, as first emphasized by Bell (1968), interactions among these systems are reciprocal in nature. For example, adolescents influence their parents and, in turn, parents influence their children. Hence, behavior is embedded within systems of reciprocal influence. This conceptualization has clear implications for clinical interventions. To be fully effective, interventions must have the capacity to address a broad array of risk and protective factors across the key systems in which youths are embedded.

Pragmatic Family Therapies

The development of MST also owes much to the early work of strategic (Haley, 1976) and structural (Minuchin, 1974) family therapy theorists. Specifically, several key aspects of MST are based on commonalities of these approaches. The models (1) are problem-focused and change-oriented, (2) recognize the principle of equifinality (i.e., many different paths can lead to the same outcomes), (3) assume that the therapist should take an active and directive role in treatment, (4) develop interventions within the context of the presenting problem, and (5) view changing interpersonal transactions as essential to long-term behavior change.

Empirical Support

MST is the most extensively validated family-based treatment for adolescents presenting serious clinical problems. Leading academic reviewers (e.g., Elliott, 1998; Kazdin & Weisz, 2003), the U.S. Surgeon General (U.S. Department of Health and Human Services, 1999; U.S. Public Health Service, 2001), the National Institute on Drug Abuse (NIDA, 1999), and consumer groups (e.g., National Alliance for the Mentally Ill, 2003) have identified MST as demonstrating considerable promise in the treatment of youth criminal behavior, substance abuse, and emotional disturbance. As summarized next, these conclusions are based on findings from nine published clinical trials, and at least a dozen additional clinical trials are in progress.

Juvenile Justice Outcomes

The first MST outcome study was conducted with inner-city juvenile offenders (Henggeler et al., 1986); findings from three subsequent randomized trials with serious juvenile offenders (Borduin et al., 1995; Henggeler, Melton, Brondino, Scherer, & Hanley, 1997; Henggeler, Melton, & Smith, 1992) and one with substance abusing offenders (Henggeler, Clingempeel, Brondino, & Pickrel, 2002) showed that MST significantly reduced the criminal activity of these juvenile offenders for as long as 4 years following treatment. Importantly, MST also greatly reduced rates of incarceration, which has resulted in considerable cost savings (Aos, Phipps, Barnoski, & Lieb, 1999). More recently, such favorable outcomes have been replicated in a randomized trial of MST conducted in Norway (Odgen & Halliday-Boykins, 2004).

Juvenile Sex Offender Outcomes

In a small randomized trial, Borduin and his colleagues (Borduin, Henggeler, Blaske, & Stein, 1990) showed that MST was significantly more effective at decreasing recidivism over a 3-year follow-up than was individual therapy. These findings were recently replicated in a larger study with juvenile sex offenders that included a 9-year follow-up (Borduin, Schaeffer, & Heiblum, 2004). Currently, a major randomized trial of MST with juvenile sex offenders is being conducted in Chicago.

Substance Abuse Outcomes

Aforementioned trials of MST with serious juvenile offenders also demonstrated significant decreases in alcohol and drug use for youths in the MST conditions (Henggeler et al., 1991). In a trial that focused specifically on substance abusing and dependent juvenile offenders (Henggeler, Clingempeel et al., 2002; Henggeler, Pickrel, & Brondino, 1999; Schoenwald, Ward, Henggeler, Pickrel, & Patel, 1996), MST produced significant reductions in out-of-home placements, and 4-year reductions in drug use. Currently, MST is being evaluated in the context of juvenile drug court, and preliminary findings regarding treatment effects on substance use and incarceration are favorable.

Mental Health Outcomes

Although MST reduced the psychiatric symptoms of juvenile offenders in trials noted previously, the most significant mental health-related outcome research pertains to a recently completed study of MST as an alternative to the psychiatric hospitalization of youths presenting mental health emergencies. Short-term clinical outcomes were favorable regarding reduced symptoms, improved family relations, and school attendance (Henggeler, Rowland et al., 1999); decreased out-of-home placements (Schoenwald, Ward, Henggeler, & Rowland, 2000); and decreased suicide attempts (Huey et al., 2004). Favorable short-term outcomes, however, generally dissipated by 16-month follow-up (Henggeler, Rowland et al., 2003). Several studies that attempt to enhance long-term mental health outcomes for MST are currently underway.

Maltreatment Outcomes

One of the first MST outcome studies was conducted with maltreating families (Brunk, Henggeler, & Whelan, 1987). Findings supported the capacity of MST to improve aspects of family interactions that are associated with maltreatment. A major MST trial with maltreating families is currently being conducted in Charleston, South Carolina.

Mediators of Outcomes

Most of the studies cited previously also examined variables that are hypothesized mediators (e.g., family relations, peer relations, school performance, individual symptomatology) of key outcomes such as crime reduction (Weersing & Weisz, 2002). As summarized in a recent meta-analysis of MST (Curtis, Ronan, & Borduin, 2004), MST has demonstrated its largest effects on family relations. In the one of the few formal tests of mediational processes in the field, Huey and his colleagues (Huey, Henggeler, Brondino, & Pickrel, 2000) showed that MST therapist effects on family functioning and association with deviant peers mediated decreases in delinquent behavior.

Moderators of Outcomes

Moderators of treatment outcomes examined in completed trials include the severity and chronicity of youth problems and youth and family demographic variables. To date, these variables have not been found to moderate the outcomes of MST. The majority of youths and families participating in completed trials have been African American and Caucasian, as have the MST therapists. Treatment retention and outcomes have not varied as a function of either family or therapist ethnicity in these trials (Brondino, Henggeler, Rowland, Pickrel, Cunningham, & Schoenwald, 1997) nor have treatment processes been found to vary among African American and Caucasian client families (Cunningham, Foster, & Henggeler, 2002). And, the outcomes of a recently completed randomized trial of MST in Norway are both favorable and associated with therapist adherence (Ogden & Halliday-Boykins, 2004). Evidence emerging from research on the transportability of MST to ethnically diverse communities in the United States, however, suggests that caregivers rate therapist adherence more favorably when the therapist and caregiver are from the same ethnic group (Schoenwald, Halliday-Boykins, & Henggeler, 2003); and that ethnic match is associated with greater improvements in youth psychosocial functioning and discharge status (Halliday-Boykins, Schoenwald, & Letourneau, in press). Accordingly, quality improvement and research efforts are now beginning to focus on the identification of aspects of treatment implementation in dissemination sites that may vary in ethnically matched and unmatched caregiver-therapist pairs (Halliday-Boykins et al., in press). Finally, evidence from MST dissemination sites suggests that both therapist adherence and the organizational climate and structure of the service provider organization are associated with youth outcomes, and that therapist adherence moderates the effects of the organization's influence on youth outcomes (Schoenwald Sheidow, Letourneau, & Liao, 2003).

IMPLEMENTING MST

The purpose of this section is to convey what it means to "do MST" by describing the treatment principles and analytic process that guide MST assessment and intervention strategies, and illustrating their application in a case example. MST interventions focus on the specific individual, family, peer, school, and social network variables that contribute to a youth's presenting problems, and on interactions between these factors linked with the presenting problems. The combination of intervention techniques applied and the expected impact of intervention procedures varies in accordance with the circumstances of each youth and family. Thus, step-by-step or session-by-session guides are not used to implement MST. Instead, to balance adequate specification of the model with responsiveness to the needs and strengths of each youth and family, principles are used to guide the MST assessment and intervention process. In addition, a scientific method of hypothesis testing, referred to as the Analytic Process (also known as "Do-Loop"; see Figure 5.1) encourages clinicians to generate specific hypotheses about the combination of factors that sustain a particular problem behavior, provide evidence to support the hypotheses, test the hypotheses by intervening, collect data to assess the impact of the intervention, and use that data to begin the assessment process again. The sources of information from which hypotheses are drawn are: the knowledge base on the individual; family, peer, school, and neighborhood factors that contribute to serious clinical problems; observations and reports of the youth, family members, and key members of the social context.

MST Treatment Principles and Process

Principles

The nine principles that guide the MST assessment and intervention process are enumerated in the following.

Principle 1. The primary purpose of assessment is to understand the fit between the identified problems and their broader systemic context.

Principle 2. Therapeutic contacts should emphasize the positive and should use systemic strengths as levers for change.

Principle 3. Interventions should be designed to promote responsible behavior and decrease irresponsible behavior among family members.

Principle 4. Interventions should be present-focused and action-oriented, targeting specific and well-defined problems.

Principle 5. Interventions should target sequences of behavior within and between multiple systems that maintain the identified problems.

Principle 6. Interventions should be developmentally appropriate and fit the developmental needs of the youth.

Principle 7. Interventions should be designed to require daily or weekly effort by family members.

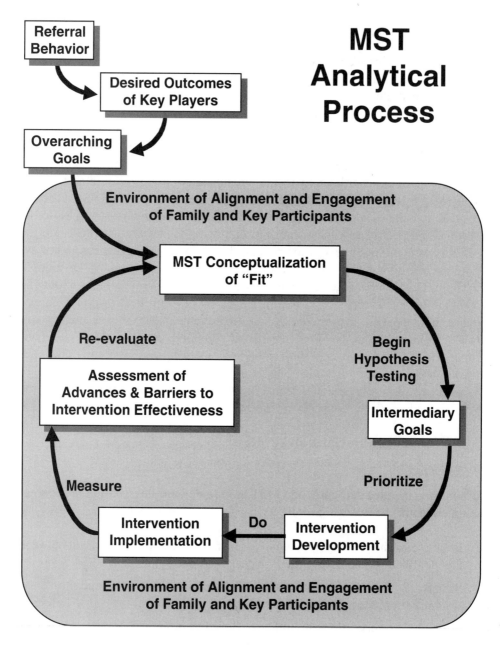

Figure 5.1   MST Analytic Process (Do-Loop)[1]

Principle 8. Intervention efficacy is evaluated continuously from multiple per-spectives, with providers assuming accountability for overcoming barriers to successful outcomes.

Principle 9. Interventions should be designed to promote treatment general-

[1] From *Multisystemic Treatment of Antisocial Behavior in Children and Adolescents* (p. 47) by S. W. Henggler, S. K. Schoenwald, C. M. Borduin, M. D. Rowland, & P. B. Cunningham, New York: Guil-ford Press. Copyright 1998 by Guilford Press. Reprinted with permission.

ization and long-term maintenance of therapeutic change by empowering caregivers to address family members' needs across multiple, systemic contexts.

These principles embody the specificity of problem definition, present-focused, and action-oriented emphases of behavioral and cognitive-behavioral treatment techniques; the contextual emphases of pragmatic family systems therapies; and, the importance of client-clinician collaboration and treatment generalization emphasized in system of care and consumer philosophies. In MST, however, these evidence-based interventions, which have historically focused on a limited aspect of the youth's social ecology (e.g., the cognitions or problem-solving skills of the individual youth, the discipline strategies of a parent, family interactions [but not interactions between family and other systems]), are integrated into a social ecological framework. Moreover, MST interventions are delivered where the problems and their potential solutions are found: at home, at school, and in the neighborhood, rather than in a therapist's office. MST interventions are tailored to the specific strengths and weaknesses of each youth's family, peer, school, and community contexts. Throughout the 4 to 5 months of MST treatment, interventions are strategically selected and integrated in ways hypothesized to maximize synergistic interaction. For example, parents with permissive parenting practices often need instrumental and emotional support from spouses, kin, and/or friends to change parenting practices in the face of significant protests from the youth. Thus, therapist and parent might work together to mend fences between the parent and an estranged relative before trying to implement new rules and consequences for a youth, so that the relative can actively support the parent when she or he first tries to implement new rules and consequences.

Do-Loop

The MST analytic process, or "Do-Loop," entails interrelated steps that connect the ongoing assessment of the fit of referral problems with the development, implementation, and evaluation of interventions. From initial case formulation through discharge from treatment, therapists are encouraged to engage in hypothesis testing as they try to identify the causes and correlates of a particular problem in a family, the reasons that improvements have occurred, and barriers to change. As depicted in Figure 5.1, the ongoing MST assessment and intervention process begins with a clear understanding of the *reasons for referral.* To gain that understanding, MST therapists meet with family members and other key figures in the ecology (e.g., probation officers, teachers) to identify the problem behaviors that led to the referral. Common examples of problems identified include behaviors such as criminal activity, fighting with peers, physical and verbal aggression toward family members, school truancy, suspension, or expulsion, and drug abuse.

The next task is to develop *overarching treatment goals* that reflect the goals of the family and other key stakeholders in the youth's ecology, such as probation officers and teachers. Following the development of overarching treatment goals, a preliminary multisystemic conceptualization of the fit of the referral problems—of how each referral problem makes sense within the ecology of the youth—is developed. This *initial conceptualization of fit* encompasses strengths and weaknesses observed in each of the systems in the youth's ecology, and becomes more detailed as the clinician gathers information and observations about interactions within and between each system that directly and indirectly influence the referral behaviors. Next, *intermediary treatment goals* that are logically linked to overarching goals are developed. The intermediary goals reflect steps toward achieving overarching goals that are achievable in the short term. When initial intermediary goals are defined, the therapist identifies the range of modalities and techniques that might be used to achieve the goals and tailors these to the specific strengths and weaknesses of the client system and to interactions between those systems (family, parent-child, parent-teacher).

As *interventions are implemented* and their success is monitored, *barriers* to intervention effectiveness may become evident at several levels. For example, at the family level, previously unidentified parental difficulties such as marital problems, parental depression, or parental drug use might emerge. Similarly, clinician limitations such as inexperience with cognitive behavioral interventions for depression in adults or with the management of marital conflict may present barriers to change. Then, in an iterative process, *strategies for overcoming the barriers* are defined and implemented. Common barriers to intervention success include: faulty or incomplete conceptualizations of the fit of the problem targeted for a particular intervention; intermediary goals that do not reflect the most powerful and proximal predictors of the target behavior, such that interventions designed to achieve these goals miss the mark; appropriate intermediary goals, but interventions that do not follow logically from the goals; and, failure of the clinician to implement the intervention correctly or completely, or to assure that the individuals (parent, grandparent, teacher) who were to implement the intervention had sufficient understanding and competency to do so. Each of these factors, in turn, may be influenced by a combination of case-specific, clinician-specific, and supervision-specific issues. That is, at any juncture of MST, it may be helpful—indeed, necessary—to consider not only the details of the particular case, but the extent to which the clinician, team, and supervisor are engaging in the behaviors necessary to help families achieve their treatment goals. Thus, the MST treatment process is self-reflexive for clinicians and supervisors, who continuously consider their own behavior as factors that contribute to intervention success and failure. The nature of the MST team, clinical supervision, and other quality assurance mechanisms needed to support therapist implementation of MST are described in the special considerations section of this chapter.

Implications of Principles and Process for MST Intervention Strategies

The nature and combination of intervention strategies developed in accordance with MST principles draw from strategic and structural family therapies, behavioral parent management training, cognitive-behavioral approaches to treatment, and pharmacotherapy. The extent to which strategic, structural, or behavioral parent-training techniques are applied is determined by the degree to which interaction patterns and skill deficits are sustaining the behavior problem targeted for intervention. If, for example, observational and interview evidence suggest that a parent has the skills needed to establish effective rules and consequences but cannot use the skills in the midst of negative interactions with another parent, the youth, or others in the ecology, then the negative interaction patterns are addressed before or while the behavioral parent-training techniques are used. However, if the parent does not have the knowledge or skills needed to implement an effective behavior plan for a youth, then behavior parent-training interventions would likely be attempted first. Generally, individual interventions (i.e., behavioral or cognitive-behavioral interventions designed to address the thoughts, feelings, or behaviors of an individual) are attempted only after interventions designed to alter interaction patterns among family members (e.g., parent-child and/or marital conflict) or between family members and others (e.g., teachers, parents of peers) that reinforce a youth's problem behavior are implemented. The precise nature, mix, and order of interventions implemented in MST, however, is tailored to the strengths and needs of each youth and family and to the social ecology in which the family is embedded. Thus, it is difficult to describe, a priori, which classes of intervention strategies (e.g., structural or strategic family therapy, behavior parent training) and techniques within an intervention approach (e.g., thought-stopping or relaxation training used in cognitive-behavioral treatment) might be implemented in a given case. The following case example is designed to illustrate the application of the MST principles and analytic process to the selection, adaptation, development, and sequencing of intervention techniques in the treatment of one youth and family.

———————————————— Case Study ————————————————

Dale Hunter was a 13-year-old youth of mixed Caucasian and Native American heritage referred to an MST program following his arrest for threatening a teacher at school with physical harm. Dale had a history of truancy and school suspensions for fighting with peers and verbally threatening teachers. He had been arrested twice previously, once with a group of older teens in a police raid of a trailer thought to be a methamphetamine lab, and once for possession of marijuana. In the latter case, the charges were dropped when an older cousin came forward and confessed to having asked Dale to transport the marijuana for him. Dale lived with his mother, Ann, age 29, and two brothers, aged 11 and 9, in a trailer park at the edge of town. When Dale was 6, Ann separated from his father, whose substance abuse problems contributed to domestic violence, harsh discipline practices, and unemployment. A maternal uncle lived with them periodically. Ann's mother, several adult cousins, and their children lived on a reservation 2 hours from town.

Referral reasons. The therapist began her first meeting with Dale and his mother by obtaining a clear understanding of the reasons Dale was referred for treatment and of the treatment outcomes they desired. After this initial meeting, the therapist met with the probation officer and school principal to obtain their perspectives on the reasons for referral and desired treatment outcomes. The therapist documented her understanding of the referral reasons on the Initial Contact Sheet depicted in Table 5.1.

Initial goals/desired outcomes. Also presented in Table 5.1 are the initial goals and desired outcomes of the family members and referral agents. There was some, but not complete, consensus about desired outcomes. Ann wanted Dale to attend school, stop fighting with peers, and listen to his teachers. The principal wanted Dale expelled and placed in an alternative school for troublesome youth. Dale

Table 5.1   MST Initial Contact Sheet For Dale

Family: <u>Hunter</u>	Therapist: <u>Jones</u>	Date: <u>November 18, 2003</u>

Reasons for Referral

Arrested for verbally threatening to harm a teacher. The teacher was trying to break up a fight between two groups of boys, one of which included Dale. In addition, although charges from two past drug-related arrests were dropped, the judge, probation officer, and school principal suspect drug use.

Truancy, suspensions, and poor performance when in school. Dale skips school with others, engages in bullying activity with others, and is verbally aggressive with teachers who try to correct his behavior. When he is in class he is often inattentive, and sometimes mutters under his breath. When teachers try to deal with this behavior, he "talks back."

Initial Goals/Desired Outcome

Participant	Goal
Ann	Wants Dale to go to school, stop fighting there, and mind teachers; also wants to be sure Dale does not use drugs
Dale	Wants to go to alternative school
Principal	Wants Dale to go to alternative school
Judge	Wants Dale to get substance abuse treatment at a local outpatient clinic
Probation Officer	Wants Dale to get substance abuse treatment at a local outpatient clinic

Overarching Treatment Goals

1. Attend regular (not alternative) school daily (eliminate truancy).
2. Decrease physical aggression with peers.
3. Decrease association with deviant peers and increase association with prosocial peers.
4. Assess ADHD and take medication as prescribed if such is indicated.
5. Ensure Dale does not use drugs or alcohol.

Systemic Strengths	Systemic Weaknesses\Needs
Individual:	
Handsome	Dale was diagnosed with ADHD at age 10 but
Big and strong for his age	is not on medication. Drug use is suspected but
Likes sports and has some athletic talent	not confirmed
Gets along fairly well with younger brothers	
Family:	
Mother loves her children	Financial stresses and no health insurance
Mother tries to use rules and consequences	Mother has a permissive parenting style
Mother left abusive marriage when children were young	Lack of parental monitoring
	Uncle and other kin live with family occasionally
Family occasionally does fun things together	Mother and grandmother conflict about parenting
Mother's mother (Dale's grandmother) tries to be helpful	Grandmother and kin object to medication for ADHD
Relatives live 2 hours away	
Dale baby-sits younger brothers when asked	
School:	
Principal is willing to postpone expulsion if MST is "on call"	"Zero tolerance" policy requires expulsion
Football coach would like Dale to play	Negative school-family interactions
Some teachers suspect ADHD and think Dale could perform at grade level	

Table 5.1   (*Continued*)

Peers:	
Dale has typically had a few prosocial friends	Dale hangs out with drug-using and aggressive peers
Football team includes prosocial youth	
Two agemates at the reservation are prosocial	Dale hangs out with a 16-year-old cousin known to use drugs

Neighborhood/Community:	
Recreational sports leagues are available and some scholarships are available	Some trailer park occupants use alcohol and drugs
One neighbor in the trailer park may be a monitoring resource	Trailer park is at the edge of town, nearly a mile from the nearest bus stop
Reservation has some prosocial activities for youth	Gas and convenience store between trailer park and bus stop attracts teens looking for cigarettes and alcohol

interpreted the principal's goal as his rationale for not returning to the regular school. In addition, Ann, the judge, the probation officer, and the therapist agreed that Dale should not use drugs. But, they defined the related treatment goal differently. The judge had ordered Dale to outpatient treatment at the local substance abuse center, while the MST therapist wanted the judge to suspend the order pending her assessment of Dale's drug use and an opportunity to implement substance use interventions in the context of MST. Dale denied use and did not want to include that goal at all.

Initial understanding of the fit of referral problems. Within the first week of treatment, the therapist conducted an initial assessment of strengths and weaknesses in Dale's social ecology. The week's worth of interviews and observations at home, school, in the trailer park, and on the reservation suggested specific family, peer, and school factors might be contributing to the referral problems, and revealed numerous strengths as well. These strengths and weaknesses are documented in Table 5.1.

At the level of the individual, Dale had been diagnosed with Attention-Deficit/Hyperactivity Disorder when he was 10, but had not been reevaluated since then, and had only intermittently taken Ritalin during the intervening years. Although he denied drug use, his previous arrests and association with drug-using peers prompted his mother and his probation officer to think he used marijuana and may have tried methamphetamine. At the family level, lack of parental monitoring, permissive parenting style, conflict between mother and grandmother about parenting, and the disruption of daily routines created when relatives lived with the family were apparent. At school, a zero tolerance policy contributed to the now-imminent placement of Dale in an alternative school. In addition, Ann perceived the principal and teachers as talking down to her when they made contact, which generally occurred only when Dale was in trouble. The school perceived Ann as slow to respond to their calls and notes about Dale's behavior. With respect to the peer system, Dale had begun to skip school with other youth shortly after starting middle school, and some of these were known to school personnel to use drugs. On the reservation, Dale liked to hang out with the 16-year-old son of a cousin of Ann's who used marijuana and tried other drugs. Within the neighborhood and community, some occupants of the trailer park were known drug users, and there were no agemates for Dale and his brothers in the park. In addition, the trailer park was almost half a mile from the nearest bus stop, and a gas station and convenience store that attracted teen drivers looking for cigarettes and adults to buy alcohol for them lay between the park and that bus stop. Finally, Ann did not appear to have friends or acquaintances in town to provide either emotional or practical support.

The therapist also identified considerable strengths in the social ecology that could be used as levers for change (Principle 1). Dale was big for his age and handsome, loved to play football, and baby-sat for his brothers. Several family strengths were apparent. Ann loved her children and wanted them to get a good education and good jobs. At the time of referral, Ann had just started a new job and enrolled in local community college courses. She tried to establish expectations for good behavior, rules, and consequences. She took her children to the reservation to spend time with their grandmother (her mother) and other relatives once or twice a month, and the children enjoyed these visits. At school, the principal agreed to postpone Dale's expulsion as long as the MST therapist would agree to come to the school if there was any hint of trouble brewing with Dale. A teacher who thought Dale might have ADHD believed he might be capable of at least average work if the ADHD was treated with medication. And, the math teacher who coached the football team was willing to give Dale a chance to practice with the team if the truancy and aggression problems were attenuated. Dale seemed to have at least some positive peers. He had fun with two agemates in the video arcades on the reservation when he visited there. He spoke with a few football players at school. The therapist determined she needed to further assess neighborhood strengths with Ann's permission. She noted that the new job and community classes might expose Ann to individuals who could provide, on a quid pro quo— and therefore more likely to be sustained (Principle 9)—basis, some emotional and practical support.

Treatment goals revisited—overarching treatment goals. Given the imminent risk of school expulsion and placement in an alternative school for troublesome youth, decreasing Dale's physical and verbal aggression at school was identified by Dale's mother, the school principal, and the therapist as immediate treatment priorities. In addition, the judge, probation officer, and Ann wanted to be sure that Dale did not use drugs. Given that Dale was usually with peers who were aggressive or used drugs when he got in trouble at school or with the law, the therapist suggested adding a peer-related goal to the list. And, she suggested a psychiatric evaluation for ADHD. Thus, the overarching goals for treatment were expanded, as seen in Table 5.1.

Initial assessment of the fit of the referral problems (Principle 1). Using the initial assessment of systemic strengths (Principle 2) and weaknesses as an initial platform for hypothesis development, the therapist set about trying to understand how individual youth, family, school, and peers interacted to contribute to, or to attenuate, Dale's problems. To map out the sequences of interactions within the family, school, and peer systems believed to contribute to a specific problem (Principle 5), MST therapists develop what is known as "fit circles." To develop a fit circle, the therapist describes a particular behavior, or problematic interaction between individuals, in the middle of a circle. Factors thought to contribute to the problematic behavior or interaction sequence are depicted outside the circle. The behavior or interaction in the middle of the circle should be operationally defined and observable (Principle 4), and the same should be true for the factors thought to contribute to the problem. The therapist should have (or be able to gather) evidence to support or refute the hypothesis that the factor exists, and that it contributes to the problem in the center of a circle. Fit circles are modified, and new fit circles are developed throughout treatment to reflect what has been learned about the combination of factors that contribute to the problematic behavior of a specific youth, and to assess whether MST interventions designed to address the factors are effective (Principle 8). Accordingly, fit circles are completed when a problem previously identified in the middle of a circle has attenuated. Therapists identify the combination of factors that contributed to positive changes in behaviors and interactions to ensure that treatment effects can be sustained and generalized (Principle 9).

Figure 5.2 provides an example of several fit circles and how they interacted in the Hunter case. The main referral problems are identified in bold print. In addition, behaviors and interaction patterns identified as intermediary goals for treatment, because they were powerful and proximal contributors to multiple referral problems, are identified with bold print. Association with aggressive and drug-using peers and use of ineffective discipline strategies were initially identified as contributing to Dale's physical and verbal aggression at school. Lack of parental

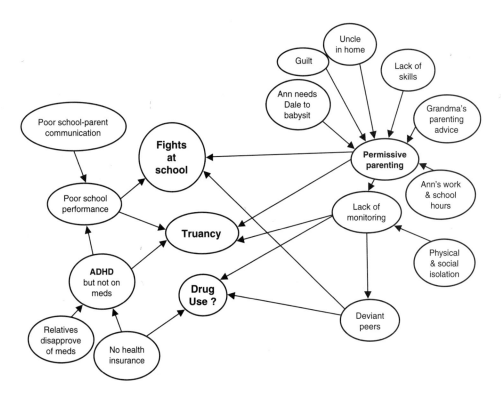

Figure 5.2   Initial Conceptualization of "Fit" for Dale

monitoring also contributed to Dale's association with deviant peers, which in turn contributed to his aggression at school. Contributing to Ann's permissive parenting style was a lack of parenting skills, guilt about the harsh discipline her ex-husband had exerted when he was using drugs, problematic parenting advice she received from her mother, the disruptions created when the uncle and others came to live with the family, and concern that Dale would not baby-sit for the younger boys if she made him angry. Contributing to the lack of monitoring were Ann's work and school hours, the demands of caring for three children and her uncle, and the remote location of the trailer park. Accordingly, the factors contributing to ineffective parenting and insufficient monitoring were early targets for intervention in the family system.

School. To meet the conditions the school had established to avert Dale's imminent expulsion, the therapist dedicated significant resources to ensuring that Dale got to school, stayed in school, and avoided fights with peers and verbal altercations with teachers. Thus, for the first week of treatment the therapist visited the school while Ann was at work to ensure that Dale stayed in school and to observe his behavior. In addition, she arranged a meeting between Ann, the principal, and Dale's teachers to establish consensus about using a daily checklist (Principle 4) to communicate about Dale's attendance and behavior in school (Principle 7). During the first week of treatment, the therapist picked Dale up from school, ensured the checklist had been completed by all teachers, and inquired about any brewing problems that could prompt the principal to consider the expulsion option. Although suboptimal from the perspective of empowering the caregiver to address family members' needs across multiple systemic contexts (Principal 9), these strategies were necessary to avoid Dale's placement during a time when the range of intra- and extrafamilial strategies needed to change Dale's behavior at home, school, and with peers had not yet been identified and implemented. By the end of the second week of treatment, however, Ann began to pick Dale up and ensure the checklist had been completed. The therapist continued to be on call to the school during the day until there was evidence that: (1) Ann could effectively tie rewards and consequences at home to Dale's school behavior, and that Dale's aggressive behavior at school decreased accordingly; (2) the teachers, principal, and Ann could communicate about Dale's progress and setbacks without undue conflict; (3) Dale took his Ritalin as prescribed; (4) progress was being made toward increasing Dale's association with positive peers and decreasing his association with peers who were physically aggressive and who used drugs.

Family. During the first weeks of treatment, the therapist met with Ann alone to introduce the rationale for the use of rules and consequences as parenting tools, identify and challenge beliefs about parenting that sustained her permissive practices (e.g., her belief that she had to make up for the harsh discipline exerted by her ex-husband; concern that Dale would not baby-sit if she exerted more parental authority), and to consider options to increase adult monitoring of Dale's whereabouts. The therapist met with Ann and Dale conjointly to identify privileges and rewards he valued and could earn, contingent upon daily school attendance and appropriate verbal behavior with teachers, as well as to specify consequences for truancy and verbal and physical aggression that he would experience as aversive. A preliminary monitoring plan was developed that heavily involved the therapist at first.

In addition, the therapist held conjoint sessions with Ann and her mother at Ann's home and at the reservation to accomplish several objectives: (1) establish Ann's role as head of the household and primary parent and grandmother's role as a wise helper rather than intermittent coparent; (2) obtain grandmother's blessing to stop taking in the uncle (grandmother's brother) and other relatives when they were down on their luck, and to establish a concrete plan for what to do when the uncle, in particular, asked to stay. Because Ann and her mother often argued about Ann's parenting practices and obligations to kin, the therapist and Ann role-played the meetings with grandmother to ensure that Ann could effectively communicate her concerns and requests for help. The therapist also met with grandmother individually before the conjoint meetings began to obtain her perspective on the strengths and needs of her daughter and grandchildren—in particular, Dale—and on how she might be of help.

As Ann began to implement rules and consequences and interventions with the school, she complained of feeling hopeless and tired, particularly when Dale reacted negatively to new rules and consequences and when negotiations with school personnel, her mother, or a relative were difficult. The therapist asked about vegetative symptoms of depression (e.g., loss of appetite, early morning waking) and suicidal thoughts, which Ann denied having. In response to the therapist's suggestion that a psychiatric evaluation for Ann's depression might be warranted, Ann said she did not want to see a "shrink," but might consider doing so if she felt worse. Thus, the therapist and Ann tracked Ann's daily subjective experience of depression and the factors that contributed to depressive thoughts and feelings daily, for a week. Contributing to Ann's depression was exhaustion from the demands of her new job, staying up late to do her homework after the kids were in bed, increased stress and parent-child conflict associated with Dale's negative responses to the new rules and consequences, worries about money, and lack of emotional support in the local community. Although she had been reluctant to give up on school because she saw it as the path to a better life, she agreed with the therapist that, at this particular time in her life, the costs of attending class, doing homework (late at night), and foregoing a full-time income outweighed the benefits of taking community college courses. She therefore dropped the course she was taking, but not before getting the names and telephone numbers of two classmates who were also single mothers, and who might be sources of emotional and instrumental assistance (e.g., babysitting, giving rides, helping to find a job).

Peers. Although Dale had never had a lot of friends and had exhibited some impulsive and aggressive behavior on the playground in elementary school, he got along well enough with a few children to be invited occasionally to their homes, on outings, and to birthday parties. During his first year in middle school, however, he started gravitating toward older kids who were bullying the younger kids. Dale was as tall and heavy as many of these older youth, and by outward appearances seemed to fit right in. When they suggested Dale skip the occasional class with them, he went along with the idea. He was with these youth at the trailer thought to be a methamphetamine lab when he was arrested for the first time. Dale also liked and looked up to a 16-year-old third cousin who lived on the reservation and, along with friends, had been arrested for possession of marijuana. Despite the drug charges levied against this cousin, there remained some pressure from relatives to retain close ties to kin despite their problems, and Ann had been reluctant to prohibit Dale from visiting with this cousin.

The therapist and Ann agreed that strategies to prohibit Dale's contact outside of school with the aggressive and drug-using peers were needed, as were strategies to increase Dale's involvement with positive peers. With respect to the latter, the therapist and Ann asked the school football coach and principal to allow Dale to attend practice, contingent upon a week's attendance at school without an aggressive incident. During the conjoint sessions between Ann and her mother about parenting practices and obligations to kin, it was agreed that Dale would not be allowed to spend time with the 16-year-old cousin unless an adult was present. Nonetheless, given Ann's work schedule and the needs of the younger boys, it was clear she would not be able to monitor Dale's association with deviant peers without help from others. So, Ann and the therapist developed a "top 5" list of youth Dale was to avoid, and asked a neighbor in the trailer park, the football coach, and teachers to report to Ann if they saw him with these youth outside of the classroom. After 3 days it became apparent that Ann needed additional monitoring help and more support to design and deliver aversive consequences when Dale affiliated with his deviant peers. Because local sources of social support had not yet been cultivated, the therapist and Ann asked Ann's mother if she would be willing to live with the family for 2 weeks to support the first steps in extracting Dale from this peer group. Given previous concerns about the disruption of daily routines and stress that occurred when relatives came to stay with Ann, and because this was not a sustainable strategy (Principle 9), the therapist continued to work hard to identify other sources of adult monitoring in the trailer park, at Ann's workplace, and at school, while the grandmother stayed with the family.

Individual. Obtaining an accurate assessment for ADHD and drug use were two priority areas for the MST therapist. The therapist's observations of Dale in school and conversations with teachers and his mother suggested he had trouble attending to instructions, organizing his work, and focusing on work when there were distractions in the room. Ann reported that his pediatrician had diagnosed Dale with ADHD when he was 10, and that she gave him Ritalin for the remainder of that school year but stopped doing so over the summer. She noted that he did not like taking the medicine, and that her mother and other relatives strongly objected to medicating children for behavior problems. Ann herself had been ambivalent about giving Dale the Ritalin, in part because she was concerned about his being labeled as abnormal by teachers, peers, and relatives. Given the escalation in Dale's behavior problems, however, Ann was willing to have him reevaluated by a child psychiatrist. Before the appointment, the therapist provided Ann with short and easy-to-read information about ADHD and its treatment, and helped Ann develop a list of questions for the psychiatrist. The therapist also asked Ann to sign a release of information at the psychiatrist's office so that the three of them could work together if any problems with dosage, medication compliance, or behavior changes cropped up.

Because Dale denied drug use, although the judge, probation officer, and Ann suspected it was ongoing, the therapist established a plan with Ann and Dale to conduct random urine drug screens for 4 weeks. The protocol for this drug screening procedure is part of a contingency management protocol being used in randomized trials of MST for substance-abusing adolescents (Cunningham et al., 2003; Randall, Halliday-Boykins, Cunningham, & Henggeler, 2001). The therapist established an agreement with Ann, the probation officer, and the judge that a dirty screen would signal the need to introduce contingency management procedures for drug use in to the MST treatment plan, rather than an automatic referral to the substance abuse outpatient clinic.

SPECIAL CONSIDERATIONS IN THE TREATMENT OF SERIOUS PROBLEMS IN YOUTH

Youth engaged in serious antisocial behavior and with other serious emotional and behavior problems are often at imminent risk of out-of-home placement in incarceration facilities, residential treatment centers, group homes, or psychiatric hospitals. The challenges they and their families face at home, in school, and in the community can be daunting for them and for therapists. And, courts and other agencies such as juvenile justice, child welfare, and mental health often have a legally mandated involvement with the youth and family that can support or interfere with treatment progress. MST is implemented within a model of service delivery and quality-assurance system designed to help therapists achieve desired clinical outcomes with youth and families facing these difficult circumstances.

Home-Based Model of Service Delivery

MST as delivered in community-based clinical trials and community-initiated programs around the country has been provided within a home-based model of service delivery. As such, MST is: (1) provided in home, school, neighborhood, and community settings; (2) intensive (2 to 15 hours of service provided per family per week); (3) flexible (clinicians are available 24 hours per day, 7 days a week); (4) time-limited (4 to 6 months); and (5) characterized by low caseloads (3 to 6 families per clinician). Intensive home-based services have increasingly been recommended as desirable alternatives to the use of restrictive and expensive placements for youth with serious behavioral and emotional problems. A basic assumption underlying most programs is that children are better off being raised in their natural families than in surrogate families or institutions (Nelson & Landsman, 1992). Thus, the family is seen as a source of strengths, even when serious and multiple needs are evident, and a common objective is to empower families to meet their needs in the future. To date, however, few home-based programs have delivered evidence-based treatments to youth and their families (Fraser, Nelson, & Rivard, 1997; Henegan, Horwitz, & Leventhal, 1997).

The intent of using a home-based model to deliver MST is to provide very intensive, clinical interventions when and where they are needed, so as to alter the youth's natural ecology in ways that will avert imminent and future out-of-home placements. MST therapists are organized into teams of 3 to 4 individuals, with a clinical supervisor; as described subsequently, the majority of clinical supervision occurs in a group format, with all therapists present. The organization of therapists into teams is designed to accomplish several purposes. First, for the complex and challenging problems that are treated with MST, more heads are better than one when it comes to case formulation and problem-solving barriers to intervention implementation and effectiveness. Second, by virtue of therapists' participation as a group in supervision and expert consultation calls, therapists are familiar enough with one another's cases to take over for each other in the event of therapist illness, need for a weekend off, or vacation. Third, the team structure supports the availability of treatment to families as needed, 24 hours a day.

Quality Assurance and Improvement System

Overview

Following the publication of promising long-term outcomes from MST, directors of state and county juvenile justice and mental health agencies contacted treatment developers in search of means by which to establish MST programs in their communities. In response to this demand, clinical training, supervision, and consultation protocols were designed to approximate for clinicians at remote locations the training, supervision, and fidelity monitoring provided to therapists in clinical trials. In addition, because factors at the organizational and service system level also affect the implementation and sustainability of specific treatment protocols, the quality assurance system encompasses these levels of the practice context as well.

The overriding purpose of the MST quality assurance system is to help therapists and supervisors achieve desired clinical outcomes for youths and families (Henggeler & Schoenwald, 1999). Described in detail elsewhere (Henggeler & Schoenwald, 1999; Henggeler, Schoenwald, Rowland et al., 2002), a graphic depiction of the MST quality assurance process appears in Figure 5.3. The first step toward quality assurance is taken before an MST program is ever established, when interested parties in a community express interest in bringing the model to their community. That step is a site assessment process designed to identify and cultivate organizational and community conditions that are conducive to the establishment of an MST program. Once these conditions are established, the training and consultation components begin. These components include a 5-day orientation training for therapists and on-site clinical supervisors; quarterly booster sessions, tailored to the clinical competencies and needs of each team; on-site, weekly clinical supervision of the MST team, provided by a master's level individual; and, weekly telephone consultation for the team and supervisor by an expert in MST, known as the MST consultant. This training and consultation is supported by manuals for clinicians (Henggeler et al., 1998; Henggeler, Schoenwald et al., 2002), clinical supervisors (Henggeler & Schoenwald, 1998), and organizations implementing MST (Strother, Swenson, & Schoenwald, 1998), as well as a manual for MST expert consultation (Schoenwald, 1998).

Feedback about the implementation of each component is both qualitative (i.e., occurs during weekly supervision and weekly consultation) and quantitative. The quantitative feedback regarding therapist and supervisor implementation of MST consists of data from validated measures of clinician adherence to MST (Henggeler & Borduin, 1992) and MST supervisory practices (Schoenwald, Henggeler, & Edwards, 1998). Linkages between caregiver-reported therapist adherence to MST principles and youth outcomes such as arrest, incarceration, and placement have

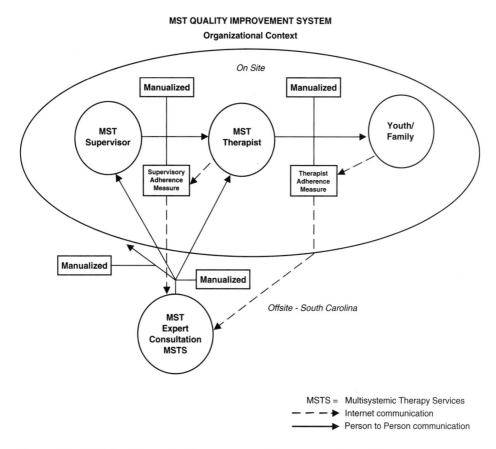

Figure 5.3 MST Continuous Quality Assurance / Improvement System[2]

been demonstrated in several clinical trials (Henggeler et al., 1997; Henggeler et al., 1999; Huey et al., 2000). Recent studies have documented linkages between therapist reports of supervisor adherence to the MST supervision protocol and caregiver reports of therapist adherence (Henggeler, Schoenwald, Liao, Letourneau, & Edwards, 2002) and between therapist reports of consultant adherence to the MST consultation protocol and caregiver reports of therapist adherence and child outcomes (Schoenwald, Sheidow, & Letourneau, 2004).

By providing multiple layers of clinical and programmatic support and ongoing feedback from several sources, the system aims to optimize the likelihood that deviations from fidelity are detected quickly, that factors contributing to these deviations are identified, and that strategies needed to enhance fidelity are implemented.

MST Supervision

The overarching objective of MST supervision is to facilitate therapists' acquisition and implementation of the conceptual and behavioral skills required to adhere to the MST treatment model. As such, supervision serves three interrelated pur-

---

[2] From *Serious Emotional Disturbance in Children and Adolescents: Multisystemic Therapy* (p. 228) by S. W. Henggler, S. K. Schoenwald, M. D. Rowland, & P. B. Cunningham, 2002, New York: Guilford Press. Copyright 2002 by Guilford Press. Reprinted with permission.

poses: (1) development of case-specific recommendations to speed progress toward outcomes for each client family, (2) monitoring of therapist adherence to MST treatment principles in all cases, and (3) advancement of clinicians' developmental trajectories with respect to each aspect of the ongoing MST assessment and intervention process. The MST supervisory manual (Henggeler & Schoenwald, 1998) is structured to orient supervisors to processes that are important to the success of MST supervision, therapist adherence, and child/family outcomes. In addition, the manual includes sections aimed at resolving difficulties that arise during supervision and dealing with barriers that arise in the treatment of families.

MST supervision typically occurs in a group format. Three to four therapists and their supervisor meet together at least once each week, for 1½ to 2 hours per session. Supervision sessions may occur two or more times weekly when clinicians and supervisors are new to MST, and three times per week when MST is used as an alternative to psychiatric hospitalization for youth in crises. Indeed, daily supervision may be needed when crisis stabilization plans are activated. In addition, all supervisors conduct periodic field supervision and reviews of therapists' audiotaped treatment sessions, to ensure that they have continued firsthand experience with clinician performance in the field. Therapists prepare summaries of each case for supervision, and supervisors develop, note, and update recommendations for each case.

Since few clinicians possess all of the clinical competencies required to execute MST, on-site supervisors, usually in collaboration with MST consultants, provide training experiences (e.g., appropriate reading, role-played exercises) to assist with the development of needed skills (i.e., marital interventions, cognitive-behavioral interventions for depressed adults, and so on).

Expert Consultation

As specified in a consultation manual (Schoenwald, 1998) and depicted in Figure 5.3, an MST expert plays an important role as a consultant who teaches clinicians and supervisors how to implement MST effectively, and how to identify and address organizational and systemic barriers to program success. Consultants are expected to be highly knowledgeable regarding the theoretical and empirical underpinnings of MST as well as the use of evidence-based child and adolescent treatments and mental health services research. Through weekly phone consultations and quarterly on-site booster sessions with therapists and supervisors, the consultant provides ongoing evaluation and feedback regarding the team's implementation of MST. In addition, considerable attention is devoted to developing the skills of the on-site supervisors. The consultant is also responsible for helping the team and the organization overcome internal and external barriers to successful implementation of MST.

Training

The core training package for formal MST programs is provided by MST Services, which has the exclusive license for the transport of MST technology and intellectual property through the Medical University of South Carolina. This package consists of pretraining organizational assessment and assistance, initial 5-day training, weekly MST clinical consultation for each team of MST clinicians, and quarterly booster trainings. The training package was developed to replicate the characteristics of clinicians, training, clinical supervision, consultation, and program support provided in the successful clinical trials of MST with serious juvenile offenders.

Prior to MST training, consultation is provided regarding the development and implementation of a successful MST program. The objectives of this assessment are to identify the mission, policies, and practices of the provider organization and of the community context in which it operates, and to specify the clinical, organizational, fiscal, and community resources needed to successfully implement MST. Assessment activities include on-site meetings with the organization's leadership and clinical staff as well as meetings with staff from agencies that influence patterns of referral, reimbursement, and policy affecting the provider organization's capacity to implement MST. A central purpose of these meetings is to identify the goals of the MST program and the outcomes for which the program will be accountable. In addition, assistance is provided in designing clinical record-keeping systems to document MST treatment goals and progress, reviewing evaluation proposals, measuring outcomes, and consulting on Requests for Proposals relevant to the development and funding of an MST program.

Organizational Support

The MST organizational manual (Strother et al., 1998) is a resource for administrators of organizations developing MST programs. The manual provides an introduction to the theory and practice of MST and describes particular areas of program administration that have been identified as important or challenging to other organizations that have developed MST programs. These areas include, for example, quality control and evaluation, program financing, staff recruitment and retention, and youth referral and discharge criteria. In addition, programmatic features central to the success of MST programs (e.g., on-call systems, intraagency communication, interagency relations) are discussed, as well as technological and practical needs (e.g., agency vehicles, insurance, cellular phones). Finally, appendices are provided that facilitate MST program development administratively. These include cost estimating forms, job descriptions, recommendations for forming a community advisory board, and so forth.

Outcome Measurement

Significant effort is directed toward helping key stakeholders in each community identify ultimate outcomes for which the MST provider will be accountable. These outcomes are specified in a document entitled "MST Goals and Guidelines," which is generated during the pretraining site assessment. This document, individualized to each provider, specifies the domains in which outcomes are to be achieved, the criteria used to measure outcome attainment, the comparison against which outcomes will be measured, and the intervals of outcomes measurement (i.e., at baseline, posttreatment, at 6, 12, or 18 months posttreatment). Desired ultimate outcomes typically include reductions in out-of-home placements and costs as well as improved individual, family, and school functioning. These outcomes reflect the domains proposed in a comprehensive model for treatment effectiveness described by Hoagwood and colleagues (Hoagwood, Jensen, Petti, & Burns, 1996) and are consistent with those endorsed by a broad constituency of policy makers, providers, consumers, and researchers (American College of Mental Health Administration, 1998).

Implications for Clinicians

Although aspects of the MST treatment and quality assurance models can provide useful templates for practitioners implementing other empirically supported treatments, the transport and dissemination of MST is currently focused at the program rather than individual clinician level. Given the extensive and intensive effort needed to address the treatment needs of youths at imminent risk of out-of-home placement, as well as evidence of associations between components of the multilayered quality assurance model (i.e., MST supervision, consultation), therapist adherence, and youth outcomes, it seems unlikely that individual practitioners operating in outpatient models of service delivery could clinically and cost-effectively implement the model with such youth. Thus, resources are not currently directed toward the development and evaluation of mechanisms to support the implementation of MST by individual clinicians operating outside the context of an MST program. Evidence from ongoing research on adaptations of the MST model for different populations and on factors affecting clinician implementation and youth outcomes will guide decisions regarding the future development and evaluation of such mechanisms. Thus, clinicians are encouraged to refer adolescents at imminent risk for out-of-home placement due to serious externalizing problems to an MST program in the vicinity rather than to attempt implementation of the model on their own. A list of licensed MST programs appears on the MST Services website (www.mstservices.com).

REFERENCES

American College of Mental Health Administration (1998). *Preserving quality and value in the managed care equation.* Pittsburgh, PA: Author.

Aos, S., Phipps, P., Barnoski, R., & Lieb, R. (1999). The comparative costs and benefits of programs to reduce crime: A review of national research findings with implications for Washington State, Version 3.0. Olympia, WA: Washington State Institute for Public Policy.

Bell, R. Q. (1968). A reinterpretation of the direction of effects in studies of socialization. *Psychological Review, 75,* 81–95.

Borduin, C. M., Henggeler, S. W., Blaske, D. M., & Stein, R. (1990). Multisystemic treatment of adolescent sexual offenders. *International Journal of Offender Therapy and Comparative Criminology, 35,* 105–114.

Borduin, C. M., Mann, B. J., Cone, L. T., Henggeler, S. W., Fucci, B. R., Blaske, D. M., & Williams, R. A. (1995). Multisystemic treatment of serious juvenile offenders: Long-term prevention of criminality and violence. *Journal of Consulting and Clinical Psychology, 63,* 569–578.

Borduin, C. M., Schaeffer, C. M., & Heiblum, N. (2004). Multisystemic treatment of juvenile sexual offenders: Effects on adolescent social ecology and criminal activity. Manuscript submitted for publication.

Brondino, M. J., Henggeler, S. W., Rowland, M. D., Pickrel, S. G., Cunningham, P. B., & Schoenwald, S. K. (1997). Multisystemic therapy and the minority client: Culturally responsive and clinically effective. In D. K. Wilson, J. R. Rodrigue, & W. C. Taylor (Eds.), *Adolescent health promotion in minority populations* (pp. 229–250). Washington, DC: APA Books.

Bronfenbrenner, U. (1979). *The ecology of human development: Experiments by design and nature.* Cambridge, MA: Harvard University Press.

Brunk, M., Henggeler, S. W., & Whelan, J. P. (1987). A comparison of multisystemic therapy and parent training in the brief treatment of child abuse and neglect. *Journal of Consulting and Clinical Psychology, 55,* 311–318.

Cunningham, P. B., Donohue, B., Randall, J., Swenson, C. C., Rowland, M. D., Henggeler, S. W., & Schoenwald, S. K. (2003). *Integrating contingency management into multisystemic therapy.* Charleston, SC: Medical University of South Carolina.

Cunningham, P. B., Foster, S. L., & Henggeler, S. W. (2002). The elusive concept of cultural competence. *Journal of Children's Services: Social Policy, Research, and Practice, 5,* 231–243.

Curtis, N. M., Ronan, K. R., & Borduin, C. M. (2004). Multisystemic treatment: A meta–analysis of outcome studies. *Journal of Family Psychology, 18,* 411–419.

Elliott, D. S. (1998). (Series Ed.). *Blueprints for Violence Prevention.* Boulder, CO: Center for the Study and Prevention of Violence, University of Colorado.

Fraser, M. W., Nelson, K. E., & Rivard, J. C. (1997). Effectiveness of family preservation services. *Social Work Research, 2,* 138–153.

Haley, J. (1976). *Problem solving therapy.* San Francisco: Jossey-Bass.

Halliday-Boykins, C. A., Schoenwald, S. K., & Letourneau, E. J. (in press). Caregiver-therapist ethnic similarity predicts youth outcomes from an empirically based treatment. *Journal of Consulting and Clinical Psychology.*

Henegan, A. M., Horwitz, S. M., & Leventhal, J. M. (1997). Evaluation of intensive family preservation programs: A methodological review. *Pediatrics, 97,* 535–542.

Henggeler, S. W., Mihalic, S. F., Rone, L., Thomas, C., & Timmons-Mitchell, J. (1998). *Blueprints for violence prevention, Book Six: Multisystemic Therapy.* Boulder CO: Center for the Study and Prevention of Violence.

Henggeler, S. W. (Ed.). (1982). *Delinquency and adolescent psychopathology: A family-ecological systems approach.* Littleton, MA: Wright-PSG.

Henggeler, S. W., & Borduin, C. M. (1992). *Multisystemic Therapy Adherence Scales.* Charleston, SC: Department of Psychiatry and Behavioral Sciences, Medical University of South Carolina. Unpublished instrument.

Henggeler, S. W., Borduin, C. M., Melton, G. B., Mann, B. J., Smith, L., Hall, J. A., Cone, L., & Fucci, B. R. (1991). Effects of multisystemic therapy on drug use and abuse in serious juvenile offenders: A progress report from two outcome studies. *Family Dynamics of Addiction Quarterly, 1,* 40–51.

Henggeler, S. W., Clingempeel, W. G., Brondino, M. J., & Pickrel, S. G. (2002). Four-year follow-up of multisystemic therapy with substance abusing and dependent juvenile offenders. *Journal of the American Academy of Child and Adolescent Psychiatry, 41,* 868–874.

Henggeler, S. W., Melton, G. B., Brondino, M. J., Scherer, D. G., & Hanley, J. H. (1997). Multisystemic therapy with violent and chronic juvenile offenders and their families: The role of treatment fidelity in successful dissemination. *Journal of Consulting and Clinical Psychology, 65,* 821–833.

Henggeler, S. W., Melton, G. B., & Smith, L. A. (1992). Family preservation using multisystemic therapy: An effective alternative to incarcerating serious juvenile offenders. *Journal of Consulting and Clinical Psychology, 60,* 953–961.

Henggeler, S. W., Pickrel, S. G., & Brondino, M. J. (1999). Multisystemic treatment of substance abusing and dependent delinquents: Outcomes, treatment fidelity, and transportability. *Mental Health Services Research, 1,* 171–184.

Henggeler, S. W., Rodick, J. D., Borduin, C. M., Hanson, C. L., Watson, S. M., & Urey, J. R. (1986). Multisystemic treatment of juvenile offenders: Effects on adolescent behavior and family interactions. *Developmental Psychology, 22,* 132–141.

Henggeler, S. W., Rowland, M. D., Halliday-Boykins, C., Sheidow, A. J., Ward, D. M., Randall, J., Pickrel, S. G., Cunningham, P. B., & Edwards, J. (2003). One-year follow-up of multisystemic therapy as an alternative to the hospitalization of youths in psychiatric crisis. *Journal of the American Academy of Child and Adolescent Psychiatry, 42,* 543–551.

Henggeler, S. W., Rowland, M. R., Randall, J., Ward, D., Pickrel, S. G., Cunningham, P. B., Miller, S. L., Edwards, J. E., Zealberg, J., Hand, L., & Santos, A. B. (1999). Home-based multisystemic therapy as an alternative to the hospitalization of youth in psychiatric crisis: Clinical outcomes. *Journal of the American Academy of Child and Adolescent Psychiatry, 38,* 1331–1339.

Henggeler, S. W., & Schoenwald, S. K. (1998). *Multisystemic therapy supervisory manual: Promoting quality assurance at the clinical level.* Charleston, SC: MST Institute.

Henggeler, S. W., & Schoenwald, S. K. (1999). The role of quality assurance in achieving outcomes in MST programs. *Journal of Juvenile Justice and Detention Services, 14,* 1–17.

Henggeler, S. W., Schoenwald, S. K., Borduin, C. M., Rowland, M. D., & Cunningham, P. B. (1998). *Multisystemic treatment of antisocial behavior in children and adolescents.* New York: Guilford Press.

Henggeler, S. W., Schoenwald, S. K., Liao, J. G., Letourneau, E. J., & Edwards, D. L. (2002). Transporting efficacious treatment to field settings: The link between supervisory practices and therapist fidelity in MST programs. *Journal of Child Clinical Psychology, 31,* 155–167.

Henggeler, S. W., Schoenwald, S. K., Rowland, M. D., & Cunningham, P. B. (2002). *Serious emotional disturbance in children and adolescents: Multisystemic therapy.* New York: Guilford Press.

Hoagwood, K., Jensen, P. S., Petti, T., & Burns, B. J. (1996). Outcomes of mental health care for children and adolescents: A comprehensive conceptual model. *Journal of the American Academy of Child and Adolescent Psychiatry, 35,* 1055–1063.

Huey, S. J., Henggeler, S. W., Brondino, M. J., & Pickrel, S. G. (2000). Mechanisms of change in multisystemic therapy: Reducing delinquent behavior through therapist adherence and improved family and peer functioning. *Journal of Consulting and Clinical Psychology, 68,* 451–467.

Huey, S. J., Henggeler, S. W., Rowland, M. D., Halliday-Boykins, C. A., Cunningham, P. B., Pickrel, S. G., & Edwards, J. (2004). Multisystemic therapy effects on attempted suicide by youth presenting psychiatric emergencies. *Journal of the American Academy of Child and Adolescent Psychiatry, 43,* 183–190.

Kazdin, A. E., & Weisz, J. R. (Eds.), (2003). *Evidence-based psychotherapies for children and adolescents.* New York: Guilford Press.

Loeber, R., & Farrington, D. P. (1998). *Serious and violent juvenile offenders: Risk factors and successful interventions.* Thousand Oaks, CA: Sage.

McBride, D. C., VanderWaal, C. J., Terry, Y. M., & VanBuren, H. (1999). *Breaking the cycle of drug use among juvenile offenders.* Washington, DC: National Institute of Justice.

Minuchin, S. (1974). *Families and family therapy.* Cambridge, MA: Harvard University Press.

National Alliance for the Mentally Ill (2003). An update on evidence-based practices in children's mental health: Multisystemic therapy. *NAMI Beginnings, 3,* pp. 8–10. Arlington, VA: Author.

National Institute on Drug Abuse. (1999). *Principles of drug addiction treatment: A research-based guide.* NIH Publication No. 99-4180. Bethesda, MD: Author.

Nelson, K. E., & Landsman, M. J. (1992). *Alternative models of family preservation: Family-based services in context.* Springfield, IL: Charles C. Thomas.

Ogden, T., & Halliday-Boykins, C. A. (2004). Multisystemic treatment of antisocial adolescents in Norway: Replication of clinical outcomes outside of the United States. *Child and Adolescent Mental Health, 9,* 76–82.

Randall, J., Halliday-Boykins, C. A., Cunningham, P. B., & Henggeler, S. W. (2001). Integrating evidence-based substance abuse treatments into juvenile drug courts: Implications for outcomes. *National Drug Court Institute Review, 3,* 89–115.

Schoenwald, S. K. (1998). *Multisystemic therapy consultation manual.* Charleston, SC: MST Institute.

Schoenwald, S. K., Halliday-Boykins, C., & Henggeler, S. W. (2003). Client-level predictors of adherence to MST in community service settings. *Family Process, 42,* 345–359.

Schoenwald, S. K., Henggeler, S. W., & Edwards, D. L. (1998). *MST Supervisor Adherence Measure.* Charleston, SC: MST Institute.

Schoenwald, S. K., Sheidow, A. S., & Letourneau, E. J. (2004). Toward effective quality assurance in evidence-based practice: Links between expert consultation, therapist fidelity, and child outcomes. *Journal of Child and Adolescent Clinical Psychology, 33,* 94–104.

Schoenwald, S. K., Sheidow, A. S., Letourneau, E. J., & Liao, J. G. (2003). Transportability of multisystemic therapy: Evidence for multilevel influences. *Mental Health Services Research, 5,* 223–239.

Schoenwald, S. K., Ward, D. M., Henggeler, S. W., Pickrel, S. G., & Patel, H. (1996). MST treatment of substance abusing or dependent adolescent offenders: Costs of reducing incarceration, inpatient, and residential placement. *Journal of Child and Family Studies, 5,* 431–444.

Schoenwald, S. K., Ward, D. M., Henggeler, S. W., & Rowland, M. D. (2000). MST vs. hospitalization for crisis stabilization of youth: Placement outcomes 4 months post-referral. *Mental Health Services Research, 2,* 3–12.

Strother, K. B., Swenson, M. E., & Schoenwald, S. K. (1998). *Multisystemic therapy organizational manual.* Charleston, SC: MST Institute.

U.S. Department of Health and Human Services (1999). *Mental health: A report of the Surgeon General.* Rockville, MD: U.S. Department of Health and Human Services, National Institutes of Health, National Institute of Mental Health.

U.S. Public Health Service (2001). *Youth violence: A report of the Surgeon General.* Washington, DC: author.

Weersing, V. R., & Weisz, J. R. (2002). Mechanisms of action in youth psychotherapy. *Journal of Child Psychology and Psychiatry and Allied Disciplines, 43,* 3–29.

CHAPTER 6

Multidimensional Family Therapy: A Science-Based Treatment for Adolescent Drug Abuse

Howard A. Liddle, Rosemarie A. Rodriguez, Gayle A. Dakof, Elda Kanzki, and Francoise A. Marvel

Substance use and abuse during adolescence is strongly associated with other problem behaviors such as delinquency, precocious sexual behavior, deviant attitudes, or school dropout . . . Any focus on drug use or abuse to the exclusion of such correlates, whether antecedent, contemporaneous, or consequent, distorts the phenomenon by focusing on only one aspect or component of a general pattern or syndrome (Newcomb & Bentler, 1989).

BACKGROUND AND OVERVIEW

Multidimensional Family Therapy (MDFT) is an outpatient, family-based approach to the treatment of adolescent substance abuse and associated mental health and behavioral problems. MDFT integrates the clinical and theoretical traditions of developmental psychology and psychopathology, the ecological perspective, and family therapy. A manualized intervention (Liddle, 2002b), MDFT uses research-derived knowledge about risk and protective factors for adolescent drug and related problems as the basis for assessment and intervention in four domains: (1) the adolescent, as an individual and as a member of a family and peer group; (2) the parent, both as an individual adult and in his or her role as mother or father; (3) the family environment and the family relationships, as evidenced by family transactional patterns; (4) extrafamilial sources of positive and negative influence. Independent reviews identify and recommend MDFT as an exemplary (Brannigan, Schackman, Falco, & Millman, 2004; Drug Strategies, 2003; Office of Juvenile Justice and Delinquency Prevention [OJJDP], 1999), best practice (DHHS, 2002), model program (Substance Abuse and Mental Health Administration [SAMHSA], 2004), and scientifically proven and effective treatment (National Institute on Drug Abuse [NIDA], 2001) for teen drug abuse. Internationally, in Rigter and colleague's (Rigter, Van Gageldonk, & Ketelaars, 2005) volume assessing the state of the science of evidence-based practice, MDFT received the highest rating of available research-based adolescent drug abuse interventions for its number and quality of controlled-outcome studies and investigations of the therapeutic process.

MDFT has been conceived, developed, and tested as a *treatment system* rather than a one-size-fits-all approach. A treatment system designs different versions of the clinical model depending on the characteristics of the adolescent clinical population (older versus younger adolescents, juvenile justice involved versus no involvement in juvenile justice systems), and treatment parameters, such as type of clinical setting and treatment dose. Our overall strategy of treatment development (Kazdin, 1994) seeks to create a clinically and cost-effective approach for teen substance abuse that can be used in a range of non-research clinical settings.

ADOLESCENT SUBSTANCE ABUSE: HOW CHARACTERISTICS OF THE CLINICAL PROBLEM SUGGEST THE NEEDED CLINICAL PARAMETERS AND INTERVENTIONS

Considerable scientific progress has been made in our knowledge about the causes and correlates of adolescent drug problems. We know a great deal about the ingredients, sequence, and interactions that predict initial and increased drug involvement, and the clinical utility of this still-expanding knowledge base has become increasingly apparent (Liddle, Rowe, Diamond, Sessa, Schmidt, & Ettinger, 2000). Adolescent substance abuse progresses along various, sometimes intersecting developmental pathways, hence its designation as a multidimensional and multidetermined phenomenon requiring interventions that address several domains of functioning (Hawkins, Catalano, & Miller, 1992). The accumulation of empirically based knowledge yields a new conceptualization of adolescent substance abuse—one that is more complex than previous historical periods. Drug problems are now understood through the filter of one or several theoretical lenses. Social-cognitive factors; psychological functioning; personality and temperament; values and beliefs; family factors; peer relationships; environmental influences, such as school and neighborhood/community; and sociocultural factors, such as norms and media influences, all have empirical links to the development and maintenance of teen drug abuse. On the basis of longitudinal and cross-sectional findings that have illuminated how drug problems develop and exacerbate over time, the treatment landscape for adolescent drug problems has been transformed, and family-based treatments have become the most researched intervention for teen drug misuse (Liddle, 2004).

MDFT focuses on understanding the risk and protective forces at multiple system levels and in different domains of functioning. Thus, intrapersonal factors (e.g., identity, self-competence), interpersonal factors (family and peer relationships), and contextual and environmental factors (school support and community influences) are all included in case conceptualization, treatment planning, and implementation. Drug abuse is seen as a deleterious deviation from healthy, adaptive development, and MDFT's therapeutic sensibility and its therapeutic interventions aim to place the adolescent on a more functional developmental trajectory.

OPERATING PRINCIPLES OF MDFT

Ten principles provide a framework for what a MDFT therapist should do (i.e., prescribed behaviors), and they also imply what she or he is not supposed to do (i.e., proscribed behaviors).

1. *Adolescent drug abuse is a multidimensional phenomenon.* MDFT clinical work is guided by an ecological and developmental perspective and corresponding research. Adolescent drug abuse problems are defined intrapersonally, interpersonally, and in terms of the interaction of multiple systems and levels of influence.

2. *Problem situations provide information and opportunity.* Current symptoms of the adolescent or other family members, as well as crises pertaining to the adolescent, provide critical assessment information and important intervention opportunities.

3. *Change is multidetermined and multifaceted.* Change emerges out of the synergistic effects of interaction among different systems and levels of systems, different people, domains of functioning, time periods, and intrapersonal and interpersonal processes. Assessment and interventions themselves give indications about the timing, routes, or kinds of change that are accessible and potentially efficacious with a particular case. A multivariate conception of change commits the clinician to a coordinated and sequential working of multiple change pathways and methods.

4. *Motivation is malleable.* We do not assume that motivation to enter treatment or to change will be present with adolescents or their parents. Treatment receptivity and motivation vary across individual family members and extrafamilial others. We understand resistance as normative. Resistant behaviors are communications about the barriers to successful treatment implementation, and they point to important processes requiring therapeutic focus.

5. *Working relationships are critical.* The therapist makes treatment possible through supportive but outcome-focused working relationships with family members and extrafamilial supports, and the facilitation and working through of personally meaningful relationship and life themes. These therapeutic themes emerge from discussions about generic individual and family developmental tasks and the case-specific aspects of the adolescent's and family's development.

6. *Interventions are individualized.* Although they have generic aspects (e.g., promoting competence of adolescent or parent inside and outside of the family), interventions are customized according to each family, family member, and the family's environmental circumstances. Interventions target known etiologic risk factors related to drug abuse and problem behaviors, and they promote protective intrapersonal and interpersonal processes.

7. *Planning and flexibility are two sides of the same therapeutic coin.* Case formulations are socially constructed blueprints that guide the therapist throughout the therapeutic process. These formulations are revised on the basis of new information, in-treatment experiences, and feedback. In collaboration with family members and relevant extrafamilial others, therapists continually evaluate the results of all interventions. Using this feedback process, a therapist alters the intervention plan and modifies particular interventions, or more general strategy, accordingly.

8. *Treatment and its multiple components are phasic.* MDFT is based on epigenetic principles specifying a sequential pattern of change. Thus, theme development, intervention plans and implementation, and the overall therapy process are organized and executed in stages. Progress in one area (therapeutic alliance, for instance), lays the foundation for the next step—formulation of content themes learned about early on. Then content themes become more focused, therapeutically oriented, and these focuses serve as a basis for change strategy and change attempts, all of which are followed by the therapist, who consistently adjusts treatment strategy and interventions per the frequent, sometimes daily, feedback about intervention outcomes.

9. *Therapist responsibility is emphasized.* Therapists accept responsibility for promoting participation and enhancing motivation of all involved individuals; creating a workable agenda and clinical focus; devising multidimensional and multisystemic alternatives; providing thematic focus and consistency throughout treatment; prompting behavior change; evaluating the ongoing success of interventions; and revising the interventions as needed according to the feedback from the interventions.

10. *Therapist attitude and behavior are fundamental to success.* Therapists advocate for both the adolescent *and* the parent. They are careful not to take extreme positions as either child savers or proponents of the "tough love" philosophy. Therapists are optimistic but not naive about change. They understand that their own ability to remain positive, committed, creative, and energetic in the face of challenges is instrumental in achieving success with adolescents and their families.

METHODS OF ASSESSMENT AND INTERVENTION IN MULTIDIMENSIONAL FAMILY THERAPY

Multidimensional Assessment

Assessment in MDFT creates a therapeutic blueprint. This blueprint directs therapists as to where to intervene in the multiple domains of the teen's life. A comprehensive, multidimensional assessment process involves identifying risk and protective factors in all relevant domains and then targeting these identified dimensions for change. The therapist seeks to answer critical questions that supply information about functioning in each MDFT target area, through a series of individual and family interviews and observations of both spontaneous and directed family interactions. The MDFT target areas of the approach are called *modules* and consist of the following: (1) adolescent, (2) parent, (3) family interaction, and (4) extrafamilial social systems. In their investigation of the MDFT target areas, the therapists ask questions based on research-derived knowledge about adolescent substance abusers and their life contexts. We attend to both the deficits and the areas of strength, so as to obtain a complete clinical picture of the unique combination of assets and weaknesses that the adolescent, family, and ecosystem bring to therapy. With a complete picture of the adolescent and family, which includes an understanding of how the current problems are understandable, given the adolescent's developmental history and current risk and protection profile, interventions aim to decrease risk and processes known to be related to dysfunction development or progression, and enhance protection, first within what the therapist finds to be the most accessible and malleable domains (i.e., essentially, a "get the ball rolling" philosophy). Assessment is an ongoing process throughout therapy. Assessment findings are grist for the mill of treatment planning, recalibration, and intervention execution and redirection.

Assessment of the Family

The assessment process typically begins with a meeting that includes the entire family, allowing the therapist to observe family interaction and to begin to identify the contribution that different individuals make to the adolescent's life and current circumstances. Assessment of family interaction is accomplished using both direct therapist inquiries and observations of enactments during family sessions, as well as individual interviews with family members. The therapist meets individually with the adolescent, the parent(s), and other members of the family within the first session or two. Individual meetings clarify the unique perspective of each family member, their different views of the current problems, and how things have gone wrong (e.g., family relationships), and what they would like to see change with the youth and in the family.

Assessment of the Adolescent

Therapists elicit the adolescent's life story, an important assessment and intervention strategy, during early individual sessions. Sharing their life experiences contributes to the teen's engagement in therapy. It provides a detailed picture of the severity and nature of his or her drug abuse, family history, peer relationships, school and legal problems, and important life events. The therapist may utilize techniques such as asking the adolescent to draw a map of his or her neighborhood, indicating where he or she goes to buy and use drugs, where friends live, the location of school, and, in general, where the action is in his or her environment. Therapists inquire about the adolescent's health and lifestyle issues, including sexual behavior. The presence and severity of comorbid mental health problems is determined through the review of previous records and reports, the clinical interview process, and psychiatric evaluations.

Assessment of the Parent(s)

Assessment with the parent(s) focuses on their functioning both as parents and as individual adults, with their own unique history and current interests, goals, and concerns. We assess the parents' strengths and weaknesses in terms of parenting skills and general parenting style, as well as parenting beliefs and emotional connection to their child. In assessing parenting knowledge and competencies, the therapist asks parents about their parenting practices and observes their limit-setting, supportive expressions and communication skills in their ways of relating with the adolescent. In discussing parenting style and beliefs, the therapist asks parents about their own experiences, including their family life when they were growing up. Considerable attention must be paid to the parent's level of commitment and emotional investment to the adolescent. How do they handle their parenting responsibilities? If parental abdication exists, therapists work diligently to elicit and rekindle even a modest degree of hope about helping their teen get back on track. What is the parent's capacity to understand what needs to change in their family and their child—are they responsive to having a role in facilitating the needed changes? A parent's mental health problems and substance abuse are also evaluated as potential obstacles to parenting and, when indicated, referrals for individual treatment of drug or alcohol abuse or serious mental health problems are also appropriate in MDFT.

Assessment of Relevant Social Systems

Finally, assessment of extrafamilial influences involves gathering information from all relevant sources and combining this information with the adolescent's and family's reports in order to compile a complete picture of each individual's functioning in relation to external systems. The adolescent's educational/vocational placement is assessed thoroughly. Alternatives are generated in order to create workable alternatives to drug use and to build bridges to a productive lifestyle. Therapists build relationships with, and work closely and collaboratively with, the juvenile court and probation officers in relation to the youth's legal charges and probation requirements. They focus the parents on the potential harm of continued negative or deepening legal outcomes, and using a nonpunitive and nonantagonizing tone, they strive to help teens adopt a reality mode about their legal situation. Assessment of peer networks involves encouraging the adolescent to talk about peers, school, and neighborhood contexts in an honest and detailed manner, and this is used to craft areas of work in treatment.

Multidimensional Interventions: Facilitating Adolescent, Parent, and Family Development

A multidimensional perspective suggests that symptom reduction and enhancement of prosocial and appropriate developmental functions occur by facilitating adaptive, risk-combating processes in important functional domains. We target behaviors, emotions, and thinking patterns implicated in substance use and abuse, as well as the complementary aspects of behaviors, emotions, and thought patterns associated with development-enhancing intrapersonal and familial functioning (Hawkins et al., 1992). Intervention targets are connected with our assessment methods. They have intrapersonal (i.e., feeling and thinking processes) and interpersonal and contextual (i.e., transactional patterns between family members or between family member and extrafamilial persons) aspects. Strategy and a logic model of what change is and how it occurs are important in multisystems clinical work. Change targets are prioritized, so that the focus for change begins in certain areas first, which are used as departure points for the next, usually more difficult, working areas for change. All roads lead to changing drug use and abuse and related problem areas. When development-enhancing interventions are effective, they create outcomes that are incompatible with previous drug using behaviors and ways of moving through life. New developmental tasks and pathways are created; they crowd out the drug-using lifestyle and replace it with a new, more adaptive way of growing up. With each case, we assess and intervene in four interdependent and mutually influencing subsystems.

Interventions with the Adolescent

Establishing a therapeutic alliance with the teenager, distinct from identical efforts with the parent, builds a critical foundation of treatment (Diamond, Liddle, Hogue, & Dakof, 1999). Sequentially applied alliance-building techniques, called Adolescent Engagement Interventions (AEI) present therapy as a collaborative process, define therapeutic goals that are meaningful to the adolescent, generate hope, and attend to the adolescent's experience and evaluation of his or her life.

The initial stage discovers and articulates treatment's focal themes. Family and peer relationships, school and the juvenile justice system, coping strategies, and identity and adaptive self expression are key areas of work (Liddle, Dakof, & Diamond, 1991). An elaboration of the youth's view of his or her friendships and social networks is also important. We help teenagers learn how to (1) communicate effectively with parents and others, (2) effectively solve interpersonal problems, (3) manage their anger and impulses, (4) enhance social competence, and (5) critically address the role of and use of drugs in their lives. Considerable work is done in individual sessions with parents and teens to prepare them to come together to talk about important issues. Individual sessions with the teen are used to assess his or her peer network and friendship patterns and to develop alternatives to impulsive and destructive coping behaviors, such as alcohol and or drug use. Core work with the adolescent involves conducting a detailed drug use history. Interventions focus on attitudes and beliefs about drugs, helping the adolescent link his or her drug use to distress or areas of dissatisfaction, learning how to deal with drug use and deviance / antisocial triggers, changing friendship networks, and developing new ways of enjoying oneself outside of a drug-using lifestyle.

Interventions with the Parent

MDFT focuses on reaching the parent as both an adult with her or his own needs and issues, and as a parent who may have lost motivation or faith in her or his ability to influence the adolescent. Parental Reconnection Interventions (Liddle, Rowe, Dakof, & Lyke, 1998) include such things as enhancing feelings of parental love and emotional connection, validating parents' past efforts, acknowledging difficult past and present circumstances, and generating hope. They are used to increase the parents' emotional and behavioral investment in their adolescent. Taking the first step toward change with the parent, these interventions facilitate the parents' motivation and, gradually, their willingness to address relationship issues and parenting strategies. Increasing parental involvement with the adolescent (e.g., showing an interest, initiating conversations, creating a new interpersonal environment in day-to-day transactions), creates a new foundation for behavioral and attitudinal change in parenting strategy. In this area of work, parenting competency is fostered by teaching and coaching about normative characteristics of parent-adolescent relationships, consistent and age-appropriate limit setting, monitoring, and emotional support—all important and research-established parental functions.

Interventions to Change the Parent-Adolescent Interaction

Family therapy originally articulated a theory and technology about changing particular dysfunctional family transactional patterns that connect to the development of problem behaviors. Following in this tradition, MDFT interventions also change development-retarding transactions. Direct changes in the parent-adolescent relationship are usually made through the structural family therapy technique of enactment (Minuchin, 1974). Enactment is both a clinical method and a set of ideas about how change occurs (Liddle, 1999). Typically, enactment involves elicitation, in a family session, of topics or themes that are important in the everyday life of the family, and preparing family members to discuss and try to solve problems in new ways. The method actively guides, coaches, and shapes increasingly positive and constructive family interactions. In order for discussions between parent and adolescent to involve problem solving and relationship healing, parents and adolescents must be able to communicate without excessive blame, defensiveness, or recrimination (Diamond & Liddle, 1996). We help teens and parents to avoid or to exit extreme, inflexible stances that create poor problem solving, hurt feelings, and erode motivation and hope for change. Skilled therapists direct and focus in-session conversations on important topics in a patient, sensitive way (Diamond & Liddle, 1999).

Although individual and interaction work with the adolescent and parent(s) is central to MDFT, other family members can also be important in directly or indirectly enabling the adolescent's drug-taking behaviors. Thus, siblings, adult friends of parents, or extended family members must be included in assessment and interventions. These individuals are invited to be a part of the family sessions, and sessions are held with them alone per MDFT session composition guidelines. Cooperation is achieved by highlighting the serious, often life-threatening circumstances of the youth's life, and establishing an overt, discussable connection (i.e., a logic model of sorts) between his or her involvement in treatment and the creation of behavioral and relational alternatives for the adolescent. This follows the general procedure used with the parents—the attempt to facilitate caring through several means, first through a focusing and detailing of the difficult and sometimes dire circumstances of the youth and the need for his or her family to help.

Interventions with Social Systems External to the Family

MDFT also facilitates changes in the ways that the family and adolescent interact with systems outside the family. Substance-abusing youth and their families are involved in multiple social systems, and their success or failure in negotiating these systems has considerable impact on their lives. Close collaboration with the school, legal, employment, mental health and health systems influencing the teen's life is critical for initial and durable change. For an overwhelmed parent, help in dealing with complex bureaucracies or in obtaining needed adjunctive services not only increases engagement, but also improves his or her ability to parent effectively by reducing stress and burden.

SPECIFIC INTERVENTION STRATEGIES FOR TREATING ADOLESCENT SUBSTANCE ABUSE WITHIN THE MDFT FRAMEWORK

This section outlines the core interventions of MDFT according to each of the three stages of treatment and each of the four target domains—adolescent, parent, parent-adolescent transactional patterns, and extrafamilial.

MDFT INTERVENTIONS

Stage 1

Adolescent Module: Build the foundation (Engagement)

1. Motivate the adolescent to engage in treatment. "There is something in this for you" is the phrase we use to capture one of therapy's first tasks. Specify how the therapist and the therapy can address some of the adolescent's specific and practical concerns. Therapists are careful not to make false promises, but, at the same time, they communicate that they are an ally and advocate for the teen. It is important to help the teen discuss the changes he or she might like to see in his or her family, and of course in his or her life generally.

2. Encourage a collaborative process. For example, "We are going to work together to formulate goals," or, "What we do here is . . ."

3. Communicate a genuine interest in knowing about the youth as an individual. The therapist endeavors to get to know them and their world. This includes personal interests, likes and dislikes (e.g., music or sports), or anything that is important to the adolescent. The tone is positive and encouraging, nonauthoritarian and nonjudgmental. Early on, no attempts are made to change the youth. It is critical to get to know the youth in a personal way, and to express a liking, respect, and interest in the teen and what he or she has to say.

4. Get the day-to-day details of the adolescent's life. How does the teen spend his or her time? What about peer relationships, girlfriends, boyfriends, parents, siblings, clubbing, and hanging out after school and on weekends? Thoughts and feelings about his or her relationships inside and outside of the family are vital to elicit. The clinician must obtain a vivid portrayal of the sights and sounds of the teen's world. Visits to the youth's school, in-home sessions, and meeting the teen in a neighborhood locale such as a restaurant are among the best ways to obtain this rich understanding of an adolescent's world.

5. Encourage youths to voice their concerns and their complaints about anything and everything.

6. Encourage the expression of hopes, dreams, competencies, and strengths. Therapists highlight these expressions and enlarge upon them. Understanding adolescent development is indispensable to effective therapy. This knowledge base guides a therapist's exploration of core topics such as how does the teen define him- or herself now, and who do they want to be or to become.

7. Comorbidity or co-occurring problems are the norm in clinical samples of adolescents. Depression and anxiety, including sequelae from past trauma, are common in substance-abusing teens. Therefore, therapists must be knowledgeable about these complex symptom presentations, and possess skill in a variety of interventions to address these linked but distinct problems. Referral to psychiatrists for psychiatric evaluations and medications, when necessary, is part of the MDFT protocol.

Parent and Parenting Module: Build the Foundation (Engagement)

1. Change in each module proceeds in steps. The first step with the parents is the assessment of current and past stress and burden (e.g., "I know it is difficult

for you to deal with your son, considering what he's been into. You have been through a lot.") Therapists routinely highlight how well parents have done given difficult circumstances.

2. Encourage parents to detail all previous efforts to address the problems with the adolescent, including treatment failures and success, their own parenting efforts, and other family members' attempts. This discussion should be multifaceted—it seeks facts, perceptions, emotional reactions, and recounting of behavior change attempts relative to what the parent and the family have been through. Competencies and strengths are important to draw out and use as a support-providing antidote to stress and pessimism, and as a behavioral platform for new change attempts.

3. Enhance and strengthen feelings of love and commitment. We use various means to resuscitate a strong emotional connection between parent and adolescent. Generally, a number of negative events have transpired that leave all family members pessimistic about change. Parents feeling defeated, inept, embarrassed, perplexed, and certainly distant—not in a mood to try to reach out to their teen, in addition to adolescent arrests, intoxication, drug- or alcohol-influenced fights or accidents—can create a deep mood of despair. In these clinical situations, emotional distance in family relationships is common. At first we use methods that are more emotionally than cognitively or behaviorally based to close this relationship gap and increase a parent's motivation to try again. We may ask parents to reflect on and talk about successful and pleasurable experiences with their child: When were things better in the family? When did your child seem more influenced by what you said to him or her? We may invoke emotions and memories from many years ago, asking a parent about the hopes and dreams they had at one time for their child. Sharing and discussing family photos at various points in their history is one way to facilitate travel on an emotional and therapeutic pathway with a parent. This is a journey that has the intention of softening some of their currently hardened perceptions and feelings about their son or daughter. Facilitating a remembrance of a time of love and parental commitment and connection, even though it might be at a very different life stage for the parent or teen, is a relationship and commitment resuscitation project. It is a powerful way to influence a parent to take that all-important step toward committing to trying new ways of relating to and parenting their adolescent.

4. Discuss the parent's childhood, the parenting they received, and the family life they experienced. These topics are not covered in order to begin in-depth psychotherapy about a parent's past. Rather, covering this background gives a therapist clues about what is in a parent's heart and mind about her- or himself at present—their conceptions about their role and an indication of how their current feelings and behavior could be understood. As with all areas of exploration, there are strengths that will be revealed. Focus and build on them.

5. Communicate to parents that this program is for them too. Just as the therapist communicates advocacy to the teen (about school and juvenile justice problems, for example), the same kind of advocacy message is given to the parents. The stress and burden of the parent is a therapeutic target in and of itself, a means by which we motivate the parent to try anew in the parenting realm, as well as a

prognostic sign about how changes in the parenting realm are going (i.e., continued stress and feelings of burden = problems in the progress to change parenting practices).

6. Motivational work with the parents is as important as motivational work with the teen. Parents are told that "You are a powerful medicine," to help their son or daughter improve and redirect his or her life. Parents of clinically referred teens come to therapy as disbelievers about the possibilities of parental influence with adolescents. Focusing on the process of becoming influential in the life of one's adolescent takes time, it improves gradually, and as is the case in any classic mutual feedback system, it involves the teen's reciprocation and positive response to the parent's increased receptivity and attempts to relate differently. When an adolescent is helped to listen more calmly and respectfully to what a parent has to say, those actions on the teen's part (which themselves are part of the cycle of change) encourage the parent to produce more effective and heartfelt communication and sharing (versus lecturing, for example).

7. Motivational tactics. With parents, one of our standard ways of motivating them to try again with their teen is to engage in the "no regrets" conversation. Here we discuss with parents how it would be unfortunate, after all they have been through, to look back at some point and conclude that they did not do everything they absolutely could to help straighten out the life course of their son or daughter. The intention is to raise questions, gently, in the parents' mind about how much they have done and how much they still might do to reach out to and participate in the comprehensive efforts to change the course of their child's development.

Parent Relationship/Family Interaction Module: **Build the Foundation (Engagement)**

1. Welcome youth and family to the program. It is important to explain the MDFT treatment program and orient them to what is required in the treatment, the format and nature of the meetings, confidentiality issues, and how contacts with school and court are part of what will help create a better situation for their child.

2. Develop a temporal orientation. Orienting the treatment around the time parameters of the treatment program helps the family and therapist organize their efforts according to limits—limits within which help is available. Time limits of therapy are used as additional definers of treatment opportunity and as motivators to take advantage of the possibilities to attend to the adolescent's difficulties.

3. Assess family interactions. What happened in the past? What went wrong up to now? Is there conflict? How do they problem-solve? How do they talk to each other? Is it superficial, or do they talk about important issues? Who talks to whom? How often do they talk to each other? How and how often do they communicate warmth and love?

4. Assess family history and family story. The therapist is looking for themes of strength as well as past problems, including significant family and relationship events such as neglect or abuse. These topics need to be addressed and worked on in Stage 2.

5. Even in the first stage, the therapist works to improve how the family talks and responds to each other. More complex topics and problem-solving happens

in Stage 2, but in the beginning of treatment, family sessions focus on eliciting the family and individual history, defining the content themes to be worked on, establishing which topics are most urgent to address, and shaping family interactions in straightforward and non-stress-inducing ways.

6. Extensive focus is given to the affective component of the parent-adolescent relationship. A therapist's intention is to help the relationship progress so that it more frequently embodies ingredients such as empathy, compassion, commitment, connectedness, and love.

Extrafamilial Module

The therapist will deal with the most accessible areas first, which helps to engage the family. Although some extrafamilial interventions are more specific to some stages, (e.g., needs assessment and establishing a working relationship with outside agencies are more often used in Stage 1), extrafamilial work is done throughout the three stages.

1. *School.* In the school realm, the therapist begins by obtaining the adolescent's records to identify his or her needs (e.g., are they in the appropriate placement?). A school meeting is immediately scheduled to introduce the MDFT program and establish a collaborative relationship with teachers, counselors, and other school officials. The therapist facilitates placement in the best possible school/educational situation and monitors it closely to make adjustments as necessary. Parents are taught how to assess school problems and interact with various systems to obtain the best services for their child. At the end of treatment, the youth should be stable in the most appropriate educational system.

2. *Court.* In collaborating with the juvenile justice system, as in working with the school, the therapist begins by obtaining the youth's records. The therapist's primary goal is to advocate for the adolescent. This is accomplished by attending court appearances and by establishing a good working relationship with the probation officer and other court officials. This is important given that these individuals are influential over the disposition of a case (i.e., recommending for or against placement). Once again, the parents are involved and are taught how to advocate for their child within this system.

3. *Recreational Services for Youth.* The therapist helps the adolescent become involved with prosocial, recreational activities, such as sports, art, music, or community service.

4. *Social Services/Support for Family.* The therapist begins by assessing needs in the areas of financial assistance (e.g., Department of Children and Families), immigration, housing, food, health care, mental health care (e.g., psychiatric or more-intensive services for any family member), disability, and social support for the family. With the assessment complete, the therapist helps and guides the family in obtaining any necessary services.

Stage 2 and 3: Work the Themes/Request Change

Stage 1 interventions are carried through and administered as necessary in Stages 2 and 3.

Adolescent Module

1. Prepare the adolescent to talk about him- or herself with the parents. Employing significant planning, the therapist organizes sessions to have adolescents tell parents about their everyday world, how they think about and make sense of what is happening with them, and, over time, what they think is needed to improve their situation relative to their drug use and in other domains of their lives.

2. Facilitate self-examination. Help teens examine the positives and negatives about their drug use, drug selling, high-risk sexual behaviors, and other aspects of their everyday life that are problematic. If the adolescent is still using drugs and engaging in delinquent behaviors, help him or her talk about the positive aspects of that involvement (e.g., pleasure, esteem, money), as well as the negatives (e.g., being arrested, beaten up or injured in fights, failing in school, being fired, disappointing or causing shame to parents). If the adolescent is drug-free, this is a chance to allow him or her to talk about how he or she misses the drugs or the lifestyle, money, and so forth.

3. Examine barriers to and ambivalence about change. Sometimes a teen may say that he or she has considered any number of self-changes and has even made self-change attempts. Any inclinations about change and previous unsuccessful attempts to change should be explored in detail, as should the perceived impediments to stopping drug use, doing better in school, getting along better with parents, and so on.

4. Help the adolescent to articulate hopes and dreams for the immediate and the long term. Among other things, therapy is about the creation of concrete, short-term alternatives to the adolescent's current life. When these alternatives are achieved (e.g., being released from juvenile detention or probation, improving in and staying in school, succeeding in a job, having better relationships at home and with friends), they can have long-term implications. Discussions about the adolescent's life course, identity and self issues, plans, hopes, and dreams for his or her own future (e.g., who I have been, who I am now, and who I want to be) are all core aspects of the therapeutic focus with the teen.

5. Become more behavioral and solution-focused over time. Discuss with the adolescent how he or she is going to get to where he or she wants to be. Help him or her to imagine alternatives, new aspects of life; make a plan and take steps to realize the plan, a little bit at a time.

6. Help youth form a new and more effective way of communicating with parents, teachers, and other adults.

7. Directly address drug abuse and other problems (e.g., delinquency, high-risk sex, school failure). Help the adolescent deal with the truth, as best he or she knows it, and about his or her behaviors and thoughts about it. Help him or her explore the risks, consequences, and health implications of drug abuse and other difficulties (e.g., "Your actions hurt others, hurt people you care about" or, "What was going on with you when you did that?").

8. If the teen is depressed and is on medications, work with the psychiatrist. Regardless of medication, launch the depression module.

    a. Educate the parent and teen about depression.

    b. Have youth keep a daily activity log. Use it in therapy sessions.

    c. Have youth keep an automatic thought log. Use it in therapy sessions.

    d. Regular consultation with the psychiatrist if youth is on medications.

9. Refer the teen to sex education and HIV prevention programs to address his or her high-risk behavior. Discuss his or her experience in therapy sessions.

10. Use the drug screen in treatment. Use both positive and negative results in the session. Allow him or her to talk about all the details regarding his or her relapse or abstinence.

11. Improve functioning in areas that get him or her in trouble: anger management, impulse control, negative thoughts, self-esteem, and hopelessness. (If the adolescent needs extra assistance with anger management and impulse control, refer him or her to anger management classes. If referred to anger management class, discuss the experience in therapy.)

12. Overall: Help the adolescents see that, as long as their current situation and problems continue, they will have difficulty achieving the things they say they want. Once this dysynchrony is developed, the therapist helps the teens—with the family's help, and in the context of the new alignments and circumstances produced via extrafamilial interventions, to create new experiences and concrete options (pathways) away from an antisocial and drug-using lifestyle and toward more positive, adaptive, and non-self-harming alternatives.

Parent and Parenting Module

1. Emphasize self-care. (e.g., "You need to take care of yourself.") The therapist develops a link between doing all that is possible for one's child, achieving positive parenting outcomes, and taking care of oneself as an individual apart from one's function as a parent. Focusing on a parent's needs is important in and of itself, and it is a foundation upon which parenting practices are more effectively examined and changed.

2. Help parents assess or inventory their own life and what they want for themselves. Assess parental level of functioning and support—do they need any extra psychiatric services? If so, make the appropriate referral and follow-up.

3. Instill hope in parents (e.g., things can change, he or she can change, power of parental influence). Develop positive expectations by bringing the small changes that happen with the teen early on to the attention of parent. Small measures of success, even a teen's increased openness and honesty about his or her circumstances, can be a breath of fresh air for the parent. These small changes in the teen's attitude and behavior, useful as they are to the adolescent, are also useful in facilitating a new openness or receptivity in the parents toward their child. New perceptions and emotional receptivity are steps in the parental change process.

4. Address interparent conflict: Motivational/Inspirational. Help parents work as a team. Teamwork is very important in parenting. Help parents realize that they must put aside their differences and come together for their child. Be encourag-

ing and positive, and always stress what's at stake—the health, well-being, and future of the teen.

5. Address interparent conflict: Behavioral. Help parents work out a plan for how they will work as a team to parent the child. Problem-solve and collaborate with parents. Take an experimental framework (e.g., "We will try it, and if it doesn't work we will try something else.")

6. Prepare the parent to hear the adolescent tell his or her story without losing control (e.g., "If you want to have influence on your adolescent you have to know him or her. You may hear some things that are difficult and that you may not like. It is very important that you are able to hear about his or her world.")

7. Help parents examine their own behaviors, including drug use or other high-risk behaviors. Encourage change in relevant areas. The ideal situation is that the parent will seek treatment for serious drug or mental health problems. It is very powerful for the adolescent to see their parents make these types of changes.

8. Encourage strong anti-drug and pro-school stances. Even if the parent has used or uses illegal substances, their non-drug use stance with the adolescent is crucial.

9. Employ psychoeducation about parenting adolescents. At times the therapist needs to advise parents, respectfully of course, but in very direct terms, about how to handle a situation. Some parents need more assistance than others with their parenting practices. Therapists use their knowledge about normative adolescent development, normative adolescent-parent relationships, and normative parenting of adolescents.

10. Empower parents. Help them be parental. Help them have influence and authority.

11. Encourage age-appropriate parenting skills, including the following sequence: parents explain their own behavior to the teen (setting a context of change, respecting, and using to the developmental level of the teen [i.e., inclusion and participation versus authoritarian stance]), monitoring, limit setting, consequences, and follow-through. Help parents start with something small that they know they can follow through with and have success. It matters less how important the limit set is, than whether the parent succeeds. It is essential for the adolescent to see his or her parent in this role. Monitoring involves knowing who the adolescent is with and where he or she is most of the time. Limit setting entails setting age-appropriate limits and house rules. Consequences refer to determining age-appropriate consequences for breaking rules, as well as rewards for following rules. Be sure the parents can live with the consequences, and remind them to follow through when applying both positive and negative consequences. As important as consequences, rewards cannot be forgotten. Even a parent's mindset about rewards can shift a negative expectational set.

12. Assist parents in establishing extra support that will help them be successful with parenting their adolescent.

13. Help parents be emotionally available to their child.

14. Reinforce small steps, small changes, and small accomplishments. Use each attempt and outcome, as minor as it might seem, as a step in the right direction; a motivational force and the foundation for even larger changes.

Parent Relationship/Family Interaction Module

1. Help the family understand how important it is for them to establish a positive, supportive relationship.

2. Bring relationship conflict out in the open. Put it on the table so the family can begin dealing with it.

3. Help the family resolve conflicts. Help them establish effective ways to problem solve. Improve conflict resolution skills, and help them learn to express themselves without fighting.

4. Encourage age-appropriate negotiation between the adolescent and parent. Work together to set certain limits and consequences.

5. Help the family find ways to have positive interactions.

6. Help the adolescent to tell his or her story to the parents. Have the adolescent tell parents about his or her world while keeping the parents from interrupting, disagreeing, diverting, or judging. Help parents listen actively, respond in constructive ways, including expressing remorse or regret or apologizing (if appropriate), and explaining their own stress and burden. A positive, emotional sharing—but not a platitudinous, lecturing, or moralizing dialogue—is the process objective.

7. If the adolescent experienced past hurts, betrayal, neglect, or abuse, facilitate a discussion about the past. Help him or her communicate his or her experience and feelings to the parent. Help parents respond in a constructive way, including apologizing (if appropriate) and explaining their stress and burden. Dialogue is the key.

8. Facilitate parent-adolescent discussion about the love, worry, and concern behind parents' efforts to set limits and/or house rules, follow-through, and so forth. Help parents to communicate and the youth to understand that the rules and consequences in place are based on parental love and commitment.

9. Help the family talk about important issues by first increasing communication between family members. Have them start with something small so that they can experience positive interactions. Have them work on the important issues that are impacting their relationships.

10. Focus on the affective component of their relationship. Support and enhance family communication of warmth and love. Help family members recognize how important they are to each other (e.g., acknowledge their positive qualities).

Stage 3: All Modules. Seal the Changes. Exit

1. Seal changes. Make all changes overt. Acknowledge the progress and changes accomplished. Acknowledge what is good. Our exit is their new beginning.

2. Help the family assess their own progress and discuss how normal bumps in the road will be handled in the context of their new lives, relationships, perceptions, experiences, and skills. No therapy should strive for perfection; it is in the therapist's best interest, for him- or herself and for the clients, to accept what might be considered "rough around the edges" outcomes.

3. Help the family members create a narrative about the nature of the changes that have occurred—specifying, for example, the key ingredients of the family's

and teen's success. Talk directly about ending treatment, do not avoid the subject. Explore each family member's thoughts and feelings about ending the treatment, and get their feedback about what you did and what the program was like.

Clinical Guidelines

The preceding list indicates the core interventions according to target and domain of intervention and stage of treatment. The following list covers clinical skill and interventions that are used throughout treatment. While hardly MDFT-unique interventions, they are nonetheless fundamental to making therapy work.

1. Check in frequently about the client's understanding of what the therapist is talking about (e.g., "Do you know what I mean? Do you know what it means? Do you know why I am focusing on this right now? Is it clear to you where we're headed with this?")

2. Gently ask leading questions. Using a supportive tone, use the Socratic questioning technique. These might be questions that a therapist might know the answer to, but, as per the Socratic method, the point is to lead the client to an area of focus and to facilitate a process of inquiry and discovery. The destination might be to increase the amount of time a client spends focusing on an important topic or area of their functioning, or it might be more bottom-line-oriented—to make a point with the parent or teen. These can be simple questions; they can be posed not to obtain information necessarily, but to help the client realize something important.

3. Constantly check in about behavior in the different locales in which outcome is expected, and fundamentally, where problems have evidenced themselves (e.g., at home and school). Ask questions such as, "How is it going? Are the changes holding? Are there problems? What has to be done to keep the changes happening and to recapture the outcomes that have been slipping?"

4. Provide a solid, predictable, and consistent therapeutic relationship, and use clinical skills that encourage and enable the experience and expression of thoughts and feelings.

5. Work individual and relationship change with different people and different subsystems simultaneously. While therapy with individuals may work with a person in multiple realms of their functioning, the leap to working with potentially several people during the same treatment on multiple fronts, some of which are common between family members and some of which are more individual in nature, can be daunting. So, therapists stay organized by remembering that there are four "corners" of each case that they must work. Within those four corners—adolescent, parent, family interaction, and the extrafamilial—there may be multiple topics and issues, and the strategies and methods may be diverse, but the most complex and challenging work involves the intersection of work in one of those corners with work in the others. The next guideline outlines some practical examples of this therapeutic intention—an intention having to do with therapeutic multiplicity—within MDFT.

6. Prepare participants individually for upcoming, likely-to-be-difficult, conversations. This overall guideline relates to the MDFT approach that emphasizes

how work on different issues and with different people is woven together like a tapestry that over time shows more emotional and behavioral complexity, as well as better relationship and behavioral outcomes. Work with the adolescent has focus and intended outcome unto itself, but it also represents the elucidation of content, issues, or sometimes proof of change that is brought to the parent in joint sessions ("See how well he is doing? Now that he is thinking so clearly about things, and more able to express himself constructively, it is important for your son to talk to you about these things that have been going wrong in his life.") Similarly, individual meetings with the parent(s) are useful to provide support and to address parental stress and burden. These meetings also serve as a place in which issues and methods for relating to their child in new ways can be contemplated, discussed, and rehearsed. This work prepares the parents to bring their new changes and insights to the next conversations with their son or daughter.

7. Setting up and working enactment in sessions is one of the more difficult skills to master in all of family therapy. At the same time, it remains a critical clinical skill to acquire, since enactment provides a unique opportunity to learn about family relationships, understand different aspects of individuals, and promote direct and immediate changes in family relationships. This is accomplished by facilitating, monitoring, guiding, encouraging, and shaping the small transactions between parents and teens as they occur in sessions.

8. Use the phone frequently between sessions with the parent, youth, and extrafamilial members. Once thought of as primarily an appointment reminder procedure, the telephone is now an indispensable part of our work. More than reminding clients about upcoming appointments, phone work builds continuity between sessions, reminds clients about important things that have happened in face-to-face sessions, and allows therapists to check in about process. Additionally, the phone provides an opportunity for ongoing intervention assessment, feedback retrieval and recalibrations, and new input on the therapist's part. We aim for change efforts to be as continuous as possible. A weekly (single session/contact) approach to therapy can handicap one's efforts to promote continuous effort and change attempts. The telephone provides another way for a therapist to get information, on a daily basis if needed, about change attempts, reactions to change attempts, and new developments in the case. Since MDFT works closely with school and juvenile justice professionals, and since events can break quickly in each system of influence in the teen's natural ecology, having access to information about events in the everyday social environment and the events themselves is instrumental to the MDFT way of working. The goal is to bring new or revised interventions vis-à-vis these connected and important ecologies into treatment as quickly as possible.

9. Use current events, particularly crises of any proportion, to resuscitate motivation, renew focus, and mobilize action. Therapists remain calm through crises—but not unconcerned or unfeeling. They teach family members about the importance of responding directly and quickly to crises, particularly those that pertain to outside sources of influence or input, such as court violations, school suspensions, relapses in drug use, or affiliation with former drug-using or delinquent peers. It is in relation to these events that significant progress to change can be

made. They provide real-life forums for new behaviors to be exercised. Although what a therapist defines as productive sessions week after week may be foundational to, or even predict ultimate changes, when changes that were planned in sessions are actualized in everyday life a new stage in the change process has occurred. The crises and ups and downs that come during the course of any given treatment episode are a normal part of the change process. More importantly, crises provide opportunity and context to work out, in real-world settings with real-world consequences, the intentions discussed in more formal therapy sessions.

10. Read client feedback and shift focus, when necessary, to respond to the client's needs and concerns.

11. Work in close emotional proximity.

12. Show warmth and compassion. Be friendly.

13. Help youth and parents talk about (i.e., stay with or go to) emotions of sadness, pain, and sensitivity, instead of focusing on anger and acting out.

14. Be supportive and nonjudgmental (e.g., "I understand what you are going through."). Communicate unconditional positive regard.

15. Initiate change in the most accessible focal area, since building motivation about and concrete encouragement to change is vital. A positive set of expectations, and beginning results of renewed effort to address current problems, helps family members consider that all of their hard work will be worth it.

16. Without overdoing it and while keeping encouragement linked to real positive outcomes, change attempts, or even attitudinal or perceptual shifts (intentions to change), reinforce small steps, changes, and accomplishments.

SPECIAL CONSIDERATIONS IN THE TREATMENT OF ADOLESCENT SUBSTANCE ABUSE

The Use of Drug Screens in MDFT

MDFT has a protocol that integrates the drug urine screening procedure and the results of the drug screen directly into the therapeutic context of parent-teen sessions (see Liddle, 2002b). Results from weekly urinalyses are shared overtly with both the adolescent and the family, creating an atmosphere of openness and honesty about drug use from the beginning of therapy. Using the results of the drug screen is a therapeutic procedure or method, but at the same time, its use is designed to be therapeutic—facilitative of an interpersonal and intrapersonal process that addresses drugs and the context of drugs, including individual perceptions and family reactions and interactions around drug taking.

The MDFT therapist, as a part of the ongoing relationship with the teen, will often say, "So, tell me what the (drug screen) results are going to be . . ." prior to conducting the urine screen. This interaction is significant because it offers the adolescent a chance to be honest about his or her drug use and builds a relationship based on openness and integrity, rather than secrecy and dishonesty. This context shift sets the stage for a teen's honest communication with parents and others. When the teen produces a drug-free urinalysis, this outcome creates a context for adolescents and parents to begin to communicate differently. Parents may rediscover hope and believe that their lives may begin to be less disrupted by drug use and its consequences. With the therapist's help, family agreements about restrictions and privileges, as well as shifts in emotional interactions, occur. Utilizing the urinalysis in this family session reduces negativity in family relationships, a core target in family-based work, and facilitates trust and agreements between family members.

When teens do not want to complete the drug test, it may be a sign that their drug use persists. The therapist may ask, "Are you afraid of what the results might be?" With a positive urinalysis, the therapist will discuss the consequences from a nonpunitive framework: "What we're doing isn't working and we're not helping you enough. What do we have to do to avoid continued use?" This process begins by eliciting the critical details of the social context of use, as well as the teen's intrapersonal functioning prior to and after drug use. Dirty urine tests facilitate the functional analysis of drug use and abuse. Important questions are asked, such as what happened; when did the teen use; what time and place; how much and what did the teen use; how many times; what were his or her thoughts and feelings before, during, and after using; which friends were present; and, most importantly, how could the use episode have been prevented? These details help the therapist determine next steps. Typically, new parental monitoring structures need to be put in place, and the therapist and teen should refocus on their work as well (i.e., triggers and urges to use, skills, peers, alternatives to drug-using lifestyle, taking care of oneself). Brief residential stabilization is used if the drug use reaches dangerous levels or has become so stable as to be unalterable in the current therapeutic attempts. Using drug screens with teens in strong denial is a powerful tool, as it provides concrete grounds for discussing restrictions and promotes the adolescent's understanding of the consequences of use.

The therapist arranges opportunities for the teen to tell his or her parents themselves that he or she has used drugs and have produced a dirty urine test. In keeping with the agreement made early in therapy that secrets are not a part of the drug recovery process, the adolescent is reminded that the parents will be told the urinalysis results, and that this is an opportunity to be honest with them. When the adolescent tells the parent that the urine test was dirty, this honesty creates openings for new relationships with the parents and with him- or herself. Parents are frequently focused on drugs as the only cause of their adolescent's problems, and see abstinence as equivalent to a return to a normal life for themselves. A clean urinalysis resuscitates hope and relieves some of the intense fear surrounding drug use. While parents frequently want the problem fixed, therapists help parents to understand that, given the nature of the adolescent's problems, recovery from serious drug use can be a rollercoaster ride, not a problem-free steady state once progress occurs. When an adolescent stops or drastically reduces his or her drug use and then relapses, parents' hopelessness is ignited again. The parents worry that history will endlessly repeat itself. The therapist's work is to shift the parents' fear to a developmental perspective of their adolescent, where they understand that the teen has several areas of impairment that need attention, and that the development of a drug-free, more-adaptive lifestyle takes time, and is dependent on a number of areas of progress coming together (individual outcomes, parent outcomes, family changes, school improvement, juvenile justice involvement decreased or stabilized). Therapists help the family to not panic in response to crises or relapses; the events of the crisis are always used as information about what has to happen next and as opportunities to rework the changes that have already begun.

Using the results of the urinalysis in sessions can be significant in the life of the teen and the parents. It allows for new and honest interactions, emotional reconnections, trust-building, and a focus on the mobilization of the family system as a whole to address and combat continued drug use. Consistent with our ecological-developmental focus, clinicians use the drug screen results with parents and teens to build toward the overall improvement of individual and family functioning and extrafamilial relationships.

Decision-Making for Individual or Joint Sessions

MDFT is a therapy of subsystems. Treatment consists of working with parts (subsystems) to larger wholes (systems) and then from wholes (family unit) back down to smaller units (individuals). Working in this way requires guidelines for how to constitute any given session or piece of therapeutic work. Session composition is not random or at the discretion of the family or extrafamilial others, although sometimes this is the case. When therapists are new to MDFT, one of their main questions is, "When is it appropriate to meet with the adolescent alone, the parent alone, or with the parent and the adolescent together?" Clinicians want to know about the inclusion of extrafamilial people in treatment as well. There is a broad-level answer to these many questions that is always the same—composition of sessions depends on the goals of that particular piece of therapeutic work, the stage of treatment, and the goals of that particular session. Goals may exist in one or more categories. For example, there may be strategic goals at any given point that dictate or suggest who should be present for all or part of a session. The first session, for example, from a strategic and information-gathering point of view, suggests that all family members and even important people outside of the family be present, at least for a large part of the session. Later in treatment, individual meetings with parents and the teen may be needed because of estrangement or high conflict. The individual sessions are information-acquiring but are also preparation for joint sessions (working parts to a larger whole). Session composition (i.e., who attends) may be dictated by therapeutic needs pertaining to certain kinds of therapeutically essential information. Individual sessions are often required to uncover aspects of relationships or circumstances that may be impossible to learn about in joint interviews. Therapeutic goals about working a particular relationship theme in vivo, via enactment for instance, may be another compelling rationale for decisions about session composition.

If decisions about session composition flow from therapeutic goals, it should be emphasized that not all goals are set a priori. For instance, some goals are at smaller operational levels than an objective such as *increase of parental competence.* Some therapeutic goals are set and existing goals are adjusted on the basis of feedback that one reads from the family and extrafamilial others. Therapeutic feedback from any and all parts of the therapeutic system and environment is sought and used constantly to answer the following core questions: How is this therapy going? What have I accomplished in terms of addressing and successfully attending to MDFT's core areas of work—the four domains of focus? (For example, do I know the teen's hopes and dreams? Do I know the parents' burdens? What am I working on extrafamilially—in the natural environment of the teen and family?) What are we working on and is this content and focus meaningful? Are we getting results? Progressing reasonably?

Thus, while core pieces of work in MDFT, such as engagement of the teen and working on parent issues (e.g., parenting practices, the shaping of the parent-teen relationship through the interpersonally and behaviorally oriented technique of enactment) may dictate session composition and participation because of the obvious nature of their work; other aspects of therapy, such as working a given therapy theme, for example, may require feedback to be read before session composition can be determined or decided. Having a clear sense about the core aspects of what one has to focus on in MDFT, working in the four domains of adolescent, parent, the teen-parent relationship, and the extrafamilial, largely, but not completely, indicates who will be involved in any given session. A therapist's realization that his relationship with the adolescent is slipping after a rough session or negative outside-of-therapy event (e.g., a tense court hearing where a decision went against the adolescent), must use this insight (i.e., reading of feedback) to right the therapeutic course. An individual meeting, in the clinic, in the home, at school, or at a fast food restaurant is needed, and it is in the therapist's best interest to act quickly in relation to feedback of this type. Decisions about session composition are important and they can be confusing. However, once one readjusts the decision-making lens to put therapeutic goals first, and to determine those goals on the basis of the generic aspects of the MDFT therapy, as well as the reading of idiosyncratic and temporal feedback, session composition decision making becomes much easier. The therapist's assessments of multiple domains of functioning provide the answer to where he or she needs to go and what needs to be focused on. From these questions derive the more simple questions—who do I work with, and when.

Therapist Assistant Duties

Some versions of MDFT have included a therapist assistant or case manager as part of the therapeutic system. The therapist assistant (TA) works closely with the therapist to ensure that the assessment of case management needs and the delivery of services coordinate with the clinical work. The therapist and therapist assistant assess families for social service needs, the nonfulfillment of which creates therapeutic barriers. A case management plan is developed and the therapist assistant, in close collaboration with the therapist, attempts to meet its objectives.

Therapist assistants work with systems outside the family. For an overwhelmed parent, help in negotiating complex bureaucracies or in obtaining needed adjunct services is therapeutic. Clients often need help to obtain services (e.g., housing, medical care, and coverage) or transportation to job training or self-help programs. TAs are involved in all of the extrafamilial systems, including school, where they (1) monitor the client's attendance and parental receipt and signatures on all school reports and forms, (2) compile monthly attendance and in-school behavior records, and (3) attend school meetings and conferences and team meetings. TAs also maintain active contacts with schools and/or alternative education programs and monitor contact and progress with tutors. With regard to job placements, TAs make referrals to appropriate agencies and are also responsible for assisting the client (parent or adolescent) with his or her appointments at job agencies, vocational rehabilitation, and/or interviews. Prosocial activities is another area where TAs contribute by (1) taking clients to 12-Step meetings, (2) facilitating parental access to support groups/12-Step meetings, (3) evaluating the appropriateness of recreational activities in terms of content, staff competence, cost, and attendance requirements for activities, and (4) accompanying the client to activities as necessary. If a family is in need of core social services, like health/ mental health care, food banks, and financial services, the TA will facilitate access to all services available, make referrals to and appointments with appropriate services, take clients to apply for and obtain services, and follow-up with service providers regularly. The TAs are used extensively when working with the court system. They make referrals to appropriate programs, maintain contact with the juvenile probation officer, conduct daily check-ins with clients regarding the conditions of probation, attend court hearings, and visit the clients in detention as necessary. For the duration of treatment there is ongoing contact (i.e., nightly and weekend check-ins by phone) between the TA and clients to monitor progress.

RESEARCH EVIDENCE SUPPORTING THE EFFECTIVENESS OF MDFT

Multidimensional Family Therapy has been developed and tested in federally funded research projects since 1985. This research program has provided evidence for the efficacy and effectiveness of MDFT for adolescent substance abuse. The studies have been conducted at sites across the United States (including Philadelphia, Miami, St. Louis, Bloomington, Illinois, and several communities in the San Francisco Bay area), among diverse samples of adolescents (African American, Hispanic/Latino, and White youth between the ages of 11 and 18) in urban, suburban, and rural settings, with various socioeconomic backgrounds. International studies of MDFT, including a European multisite trial of MDFT in five countries, are funded and currently underway. In MDFT studies, all research participants met diagnostic criteria for adolescent substance abuse disorder as well as other serious problems (e.g., delinquency and depression). The following section will review the significant findings from four types of studies: (1) randomized controlled trials, (2) process or mechanisms of action studies, (3) economic analyses, and (4) transportation or technology transfer studies.

Randomized Controlled Trials

Six randomized controlled trials have tested MDFT against a variety of comparison treatments for adolescent drug abuse. MDFT has demonstrated more favorable outcomes than several other state-of-the-art interventions, including family group therapy, peer group treatment, individual cognitive-behavioral therapy (CBT), and comprehensive residential treatment (Liddle et al., 2001; Liddle, 2002a; Liddle

& Dakof, 2002; Liddle, Rowe, Dakof, Ungaro, & Henderson, 2004; Rowe, Liddle, Dakof, & Henderson, 2004). MDFT studies have included samples of teens with serious drug abuse (i.e., heavy marijuana users, with alcohol, cocaine, and other drug use) and delinquency problems. Here is a summary of some noteworthy findings from the MDFT clinical trials:

Substance use is significantly reduced in MDFT to a greater extent than all comparison treatments investigated in five controlled clinical trials (between 41 percent and 82 percent reduction from intake to discharge) (Liddle et al., 2001; Liddle, 2002b; Liddle, Dakof et al., 2004; Rowe, Liddle, Dakof, & Henderson, 2004; Rowe, Liddle, Dakof, Henderson, Gonzalez et al., 2004). Additionally, substance-abuse-related problems (e.g., antisocial, delinquent, externalizing behaviors) are significantly reduced in MDFT to a greater extent than comparison treatments (Liddle, 2002b; Rowe, Liddle, Dakof, & Henderson, 2004; Hogue, Liddle, Becker, & Johnson-Leckrone, 2002; Liddle et al., 2001; Liddle, Rowe et al., 2004).

Youth receiving MDFT often abstain from drug use. During the treatment process and at the 12-month follow-up, youth receiving MDFT had higher rates of abstinence from substance use than comparison treatment. MDFT studies (Liddle, 2002b; Rowe, Liddle, Dakof, & Henderson, 2004) have indicated the majority of youth receiving MDFT report abstinence from all illegal substances at 12 months post-intake (64 percent and 93 percent respectively). MDFT demonstrated durability of obtained change (Liddle et al., 2001; Liddle, Rowe et al., 2004) whereas comparison treatments reported lower abstinence rates (44 percent for CBT and 67 percent for peer group treatment).

Treatment gains are enhanced in MDFT after treatment discharge; MDFT clients continue to decrease substance use after discharge up to 12-month follow-up (58 percent reduction of marijuana use at 12 months; 56 percent abstinent of all substances and 64 percent abstinent or using only once per month; Liddle, 2002a; Liddle & Dakof, 2002; Rowe, Liddle, Dakof, Henderson, Gonzalez et al., 2004).

School functioning improves more dramatically in MDFT than comparison treatments. For example, MDFT clients return to school and receive passing grades at higher rates (43 percent in MDFT versus 17 percent in family group therapy and 7 percent in peer group therapy; Liddle et al., 2001; Rowe, Liddle, Dakof, & Henderson, 2004). Overall, MDFT improves school bonding and school performance, including grades improvements and decreases in disruptive behaviors (Hogue et al., 2002; Liddle et al., 2001; Liddle, Rowe et al., 2004).

Family functioning and interaction improves to a greater extent in MDFT than family group therapy or peer group therapy using observational measures, and these improvements are maintained up to 12-month follow-up (Liddle et al., 2001; Liddle, Rowe et al., 2004). MDFT improves family functioning, including reductions of family conflict and increases in family cohesion (Diamond & Liddle, 1996; Hogue et al., 2002; Liddle et al., 2001; Liddle, Rowe et al., 2004).

Preventive effects. In addition to successfully treating adolescents drug abuse, MDFT has worked effectively as a community-based drug prevention program (Hogue et al., 2002) and has successfully treated younger adolescents who are initiating drug use (Liddle, Rowe et al., 2004; Rowe, Liddle, Dakof, & Henderson, 2004).

Psychiatric symptoms show greater reductions during treatment in MDFT than comparison treatments (Liddle et al., 2001; Liddle, 2002a; Rowe, Liddle, Dakof, & Henderson, 2004; Rowe, Liddle, Dakof, Henderson, Gonzalez et al., 2004). MDFT demonstrated 30 to 85 percent within-treatment reductions in behavior problems, including delinquent acts and other mental health problems such as anxiety and depression (Liddle, Rowe et al., 2004).

Effectiveness with comorbidity. In comparison with individual CBT treatment, MDFT had superior outcomes for drug-abusing teens with co-occurring problems (i.e., externalizing symptoms and family conflict; Henderson, Greenbaum, Dakof, Rowe, & Liddle, 2004).

MDFT decreases externalizing and internalizing symptoms. Youth receiving MDFT decrease their externalizing behaviors more rapidly from intake to discharge according to both self- and parent reports. These gains are maintained through the 12-month follow-up. Youth decrease their internalizing symptoms (e.g., general mental distress) more rapidly through the 12-month follow-up.

Delinquent behavior and association with delinquent peers decreases with youth receiving MDFT, whereas youth receiving peer group treatment reported increases in delinquency and affiliation with delinquent peers; these changes are maintained through a 12-month follow-up (Hogue et al., 2002; Liddle et al., 2001; Liddle, Rowe et al., 2004). Additionally, objective records obtained from youths' Department of Juvenile Justice records indicate that youth receiving MDFT are less likely to be arrested or placed on probation, as well as having fewer findings of wrongdoing during the study period (Rowe, Liddle, Dakof, & Henderson, 2004). MDFT transportation studies have also shown that association with delinquent peers decreases more rapidly after therapists have received training in MDFT (Liddle, Rowe et al., 2004; Rowe, Liddle, Dakof, & Henderson, 2004; Rowe, Liddle, Dakof, Henderson, Gonzalez et al., 2004).

Studies on the Therapeutic Process and Mechanisms of Change in MDFT

Studies have specified the within-treatment process of improving family interactions (Diamond & Liddle, 1996; Diamond et al., 1999), demonstrated how therapists successfully build therapeutic relationships with teens and parents (Diamond et al., 1999; Shelef, Diamond G. M., Diamond G. S., & Liddle, in press), and showed that adolescents are more likely to complete treatment when therapists have stronger relationships with their parents, and that stronger therapeutic relationships with adolescents predict greater decreases in their drug use (Shelef et al., in press). MDFT process studies have shown that parents' skills are improved during therapy and that these changes are linked to reductions in adolescents' symptoms (Schmidt, Liddle, & Dakof, 1996), and that a connection exists between systematically addressing important cultural themes and increasing teens' participation in treatment (Jackson-Gilfort, Liddle, Tejeda, & Dakof, 2001). The approach is exploring adaptations of MDFT to the needs and issues of adolescent girls (Dakof, 2000). Finally, MDFT interventions that focused on changing the family produced changes in drug use and emotional and behavioral problems (Hogue, Liddle, Dauber, & Samuolis, 2004), and in a related study of mechanisms of action, the quality of the therapeutic alliances between therapist and adolescent and therapist and parent was found to predict treatment completion or dropout (Robbins et al., in press).

Economic Analyses

The average weekly costs of treatment are significantly less for MDFT ($164) than community-based outpatient treatment ($365; French et al., 2003). An intensive version of MDFT designed as an alternative to residential treatment provides superior clinical outcomes at significantly less cost (average weekly costs of $384 versus $1,068; Liddle & Dakof, 2002). More extensive cost benefit studies are underway.

Transportation or Technology Transfer Studies

MDFT transported successfully into a representative hospital-based day treatment program for adolescent drug abusers (Liddle et al., 2002). There were several important outcomes, including the following: (1) *Clients' outcomes were significantly better after staff were trained in MDFT*—clients showed a 25 percent decrease in drug use during treatment prior to MDFT training, compared to an average of 50 percent improvement in reduction following the MDFT training (Liddle et al., 2002; Rowe, Liddle, Dakof, Henderson, Gonzalez et al., 2004); (2) *treatment gains were sustained;* following withdrawal of all MDFT clinical and research staff, clients improved at similar rates to those achieved while therapists were closely monitored by MDFT trainers (Rowe, Liddle, Dakof, Henderson, Gonzalez et al., 2004); (3) *therapists successfully delivered the MDFT according to protocol* following training, with a 36 percent increase in the number of weekly individual therapy sessions, a 150 percent increase in the number of weekly family sessions, a 390 percent increase in contact with juvenile probation officers, and a 1,400 percent increase in school contacts following training (Liddle et al., 2002; Rowe, Liddle, Dakof, Henderson, Gonzalez et al., 2004); (4) *therapists broadened their treatment focus* after MDFT training, addressing more MDFT content themes and focusing more on the adolescents' thoughts and feelings about themselves and important extrafamilial systems (Rowe, Liddle, Dakof, Henderson, Gonzalez et al., 2004); (5) *after training in MDFT and withdrawal of all MDFT clinical and research staff, therapists continued to deliver MDFT according to protocol* (Rowe, Liddle, Dakof, Henderson, Gonzalez et al., 2004); and (6) *program or treatment system level factors improved dramatically,* including adolescents' perceptions of increased program organization and clarity in program expectations.

—————————— **Case Study** ——————————

Willie is a 15-year-old Caucasian male who was referred to treatment by his 52-year-old single mother, Marge, due to his polydrug abuse and repeated school failures. Upon entry into treatment, Willie was using, alternately, cannabis, cocaine, Xanax, and Ecstasy on a daily basis. He expressed no motivation to stop doing drugs ("I love getting high, it calms me down") and had no desire to be in treatment. At 11 Willie began to use drugs. He smoked cannabis on a weekly basis. At 12 and 13 he began to take prescription drugs (Xanax), lacing the cannabis with cocaine, and increasing his drug use to two to three times a week. By age 14 to 15 he had progressed to daily drug use, using either cocaine alone or cannabis laced with cocaine (three to four times per week), and Xanax or Ecstasy with alcohol on occasion.

Willie had been using drugs steadily for several years, and although his mother believed he was using more than just cannabis, she was in denial and did not want to confront him about his drug problems. Although she was not pleased with Willie's marijuana use, given her own substantial substance abuse history, initially she was not concerned. It was only when she realized the magnitude and frequency of Willie's drug use, including the associated problem behaviors, that she became alarmed and sought help.

Formulation. We see drug abuse as developmental derailment. In this MDFT case both mother and son were struggling with their destructive substance abuse. Marge's own substance use was critical and affected her son profoundly. Although no longer using illicit drugs, Marge's extensive alcohol abuse prevented her from properly supervising Willie. He made his own decisions, had no guidance or responsibilities, and considered himself an adult. Due to Marge's lack of monitoring, Willie was taking care of himself in some ways but was using drugs and was involved with drug-using friends. When he experienced difficulties in school, there was no one to help, so he had given up and started skipping classes, which led to two consecutive school year failures. At home, the mother's absences disrupted family life and made parenting attempts impossible. There was no other significant adult figure in the client's life to care for him or be a positive role model. Since the mother-son relationship was so poor, they never discussed meaningful issues related to past hurts. Marge's own history of sexual abuse and drug use made it difficult for her to function to the best of her abilities. She had never processed her traumatic experiences, never been properly parented herself, and never received any kind of social or financial support. In working with Willie, the therapist (Elda Kanzki) was able to identify two major themes that seemed to have negatively impacted his dreams and hopes for a better life: (1) Feelings of failure associated with academics and (2) the conflict and anger he harbored towards his mother. His resentment of Marge was obvious; the adolescent repeatedly told the therapist how his mother "always talks crap" and how "she'll say things and make promises, but she doesn't follow through."

Goals. A crucial goal in therapy was to help Willie and Marge improve their relationship to facilitate open communication about salient issues (i.e., substance abuse, parental neglect, and academic failure)—an important part of the relationship transformation and healing process. One of the primary goals in working with the adolescent was to transform his drug-using lifestyle into a more developmentally normal one. Other goals included teaching Willie anger management skills, changing his involvement with drug-using peer groups, improving school functioning, providing a safe environment for him to express himself, generating hope, and facilitating self-examination. In working with Marge individually, one major goal was to motivate her to seek treatment for her alcohol abuse and psychiatric problems. Since she was not monitoring Willie, interventions to improve her parenting skills and help her to view herself as her son's medicine (an important positive source of influence) were vital.

MDFT Interventions

Adolescent Domain

During the first session, Willie was difficult to engage and angry for having been forced to undergo the program by his mother. As part of a typical initial assessment procedure, the therapist asked Willie to write down three goals he had for his future. Although reticent, he did specify goals, stating that he wanted (1) to begin playing football again, (2) to help his mother around the house, and (3) to improve in school. The therapist generated hope by having the adolescent express his aspirations and dreams.

For the next session Elda went to Willie's school, where she met with him for lunch, thus engaging him in his own environment. She observed first-hand the difficulties he was facing. She immediately noticed how being the oldest kid in his class bothered him. When Elda inquired about his classmates, Willie responded with, "Oh, these stupid bunch of stupid kids"—he was embarrassed and angry about being in a class with younger teens. Observing something that was so troubling for Willie and also being in the environment in which Willie revealed and spoke about this problem was a great advantage. Thus, improving his school situation became a therapeutic goal and facilitated the therapeutic alliance. Elda related that from this conversation forward she was able to broach other sensitive topics, such as his drug use and the relationship with his mother.

In individual sessions Elda facilitated discussions about anger and Willie was taught new ways to manage his emotions. She also prepared him for sessions with his mom. The therapist coached Willie on how to express his angry feelings in a constructive way, and Marge was asked to understand the reasons (i.e., Willie's experiences and conclusions about them) for Willie's angry mode. By continuing to explore school difficulties and his peer network, Elda sought to help Marge understand the world her son lived in.

In exploring Willie's relationship with his mother, core relational themes of neglect and abandonment were discussed, as Elda helped Willie process strong feelings of disappointment and frustration. In one poignant exchange, Willie tearfully shared his disappointment with the lack of trustworthiness shown by the people in his life (friends and especially his mother). As the therapist continued to gently probe, Willie expressed how much his mother's drinking bothered him. The therapist instilled hope by stating that they would focus on this together in therapy and that she would help him relay his feelings to his mother.

Reaching this point (i.e., discussion of hopes and dreams, the painful issues of abandonment, and his mother's alcohol and past drug use), involved a multifaceted process. This sequence, a typical one in MDFT, involved several steps whereby Elda guided the adolescent, creating links for him that fostered understanding into the reasons for his drug use and present situation. First, the therapist helped the adolescent to reflect on how having failed the eighth grade twice was a major disappointment for him, but that he suppressed it through drug use. Next, she addressed the subject of drugs, to talk about why he was using and then to connect his drug use to the chaos that his life had become. Progress on this front then allowed for a discussion about his relationship with his mother. Those discussions seemed to elicit a loving response from Willie. He may have been angry with his mother, and justifiably so, but he concluded that he wanted and needed her in his life.

Parental Domain

The mother's own drug use and recovery, past traumas (sexual abuse and abandonment), guilt with regard to neglecting her son, her own stress and burden, the mother-son relationship, and parenting practices were explored in depth. In particular, psychoeducation with this mother regarding her parenting practices was important, given the manner in which her parents had abused her; she had never had proper parenting role models. During the initial evaluation Elda assessed parenting strengths and weaknesses. According to his mother, Willie disobeyed her rules, he was truant, and he exhibited emotional and at times violent outbursts. Despite her son's disconnection, Marge's attitudes about her son were generally positive ("He's got a good heart, he's fair and caring and only hurts himself . . . he's a good boy"), and this served as a protective factor and an important foundation to use in building relationships and creating change. However, Marge's overly permissive parenting style and lack of emotional connection diminished any positive parenting outcomes at the outset.

The therapist explored ways for Marge to improve existing parenting skills and adopt new parenting behaviors. New parental skill acquisition was accomplished via the use of Parent Reconnection Interventions (PRI) (Liddle et al., 1998), which facilitated in bridging the emotional distance between Marge and Willie. The following PRIs were used extensively by the therapist: (1) Enhancing feelings of parental commitment and love, (2) validating parents' past efforts, (3) acknowledging parents' stress and burden, (4) generating hope via the therapist as an ally, and (5) by helping parents understand that their influence is crucial. Elda began by allowing Marge to discuss her own issues—she acknowledged her stress and burden by validating her personal struggles with drugs and life's difficulties.

The therapist then moved into another significant area; that of enhancing feelings of parental commitment and love. With Elda's guidance Marge was able to remember how things had been between her and her son—she felt the desire to recapture some of the "good times" they once shared as mother and son. Marge realized, with Elda's help, that it was important to have realistic expectations about some of this optimism; however, the positive expectations were cast in developmentally appropriate terms. The next step was to help Marge understand how necessary it was to (1) express her fears and concerns regarding his drug use, (2) inform him about her commitment and love for him, and (3) understand that she was the medicine for Willie. We address these themes in all parental domain work—the notion that the parent must develop a sense of potential personal efficacy and influence about their teen. Parents are told that they have a position of unique and special influence and the treatment program will help them regain that position and the positive outcomes that go with it.

Parents are not maximally effective if their own personal functioning is compromised in any way. Thus, Elda focused on Marge's recovery as well. Marge was asked to reflect on the reasons for her drinking, and how it affected her and her family. Treatment for alcoholism was discussed, and she was strongly encouraged to seek help. By the end of therapy, Marge had been attending daily Alcoholics Anonymous (AA) meetings and had remained abstinent for 8 days. She began to see a psychiatrist for treatment of depression, anxiety, and her past trauma. Her actions were meaningful and demonstrated to Willie her sincerity and commitment to dealing with their problems. Elda strongly supported Marge's efforts to help her understand the importance of what she was doing and of the message she was sending her son: "I think the bigger message with you stopping drinking is that you're saying to Willie, 'Not only do I want to save you and make you stop doing these things, but I'm willing to realize my *own* part in how you're turning out.' That's powerful, Marge!" With Elda's help, Marge concluded that if she was going to ask her son not to use drugs (and this is a critical task/outcome in every case), then she would have to remain abstinent and monitor him. It was at this point that Marge was able to commit to the reality that her son was not doing well emotionally or developmentally, was in pain, and needed her support. Thus, helping Marge face Willie's emotional turmoil was a first step. Next, Marge had to address how her lack of self-care was a factor in Willie's outcomes. Furthermore, in order to improve her parenting and thus have a chance of influencing Willie's downward spiral, she would need to take care of herself, and specifically change her drinking behaviors—then she would be in a position to help Willie. As stated earlier, Marge began attending AA meetings daily, committed to a sponsor, began short-term psychiatric treatment, and became more attentive to personal self-care needs (she lost 19 pounds over the course of treatment).

In addition to practicing self-care, Marge's parenting practices changed radically. She began to seriously monitor her son, constantly questioning him about his comings and goings, calling his teachers every single day to check on his attendance, and visiting the school on several occasions to meet with his teachers. This was tremendous for Willie because he had *never* seen his mother care about him like this before. During a family session he told his mother, "You know, I can't believe you're going to the school, that you're doing all that." For the first time in his life he was convinced that his mother was changing. Consequently, Willie began attending school again, but it took drastic measures—from the mother first, her apology and acknowledgment of past mistakes, and her regular involvement with his school and persistent effort in supervising him.

Family Domain

Here the crux of work in therapy was to help Willie and his mom reconnect. Marge's relationship with her son was worked on extensively—how she would like it to improve and what her hopes and dreams were for him. This change in the family interaction was accomplished via enactment (wherein the adolescent and his mother, facilitated by the therapist, were able to talk about past hurts and recommit to their relationship), and the work done in individual sessions with Willie and Marge. Willie and his mother were coached on how to express their feelings to one another so they could communicate how they wanted things to be different. With the therapist's help, Marge was able to tell her son that she would do anything to help make things better for him and them as a family. She also shared with him the reasons she was so adamant that he not use drugs (i.e., because of her love for him and because of the destructive force drugs had been in her life). Similarly, Willie was coached in talking to his mom about difficult subjects: Willie's reasons for using drugs and associating with drug-using friends, and his mother's drinking.

Once the mother opened up to her son, the therapist was able to gradually coach her in tackling even more delicate issues (feelings of guilt and neglect of her son). The therapist worked with the mother to prepare her for the apology—a powerful moment in therapy in which Marge expressed her remorse for actions in the past and all the pain she had caused her son. With the therapist's guidance she was able to reaffirm her love, investment, and commitment to her son, and effectively communicate her strong desire to consistently be there for him.

At the midway point of treatment, the therapist conducted an appraisal of what they had accomplished thus far and the work that still needed to be done. It was noted that after just a few sessions, the mother-son relationship had begun to show positive change. Marge and Willie were starting to communicate in new ways, and their experience of the other had changed as well. Marge recounted an incident where they had both initially responded in their typical hostile way, but then decided, together and quite deliberately, to utilize the new methods of communication they had learned. The result was that mother and son apologized to each other. Later they told Elda, individually and then in a joint session, how each had felt encouraged by this event and its new kind of outcome. At the same time, however, there were still areas needing significant improvement. The mother reported that immediately after this progress, and similar episodes in other interactions, she realized that Willie had stolen money from her. The therapist reminded her that it would not be easy for Willie, but to remember they made great strides in a short period of time. The therapist stressed the importance of discussing this incident with him in the forthcoming joint session.

Willie continued to test positive for drug use on his urinalysis screens. Although positive changes had been occurring at school (attending classes, improvement in grades), and in the mother-son relationship (better communication), he was still using drugs. With Elda's coaching, Marge expressed her concerns to Willie. In particular, Marge thought that Willie might not be able to stop using on his own. Marge decided that Willie needed to demonstrate to her that he could and would abstain. If not, they would come to a decision together that he would enter a hospital inpatient adolescent detoxification unit. Indeed, this is what occurred, Willie's drug use continued and they mutually agreed that he needed to be admitted. Several sessions took place while Willie was in a hospital inpatient adolescent detoxification unit. This service works in collaboration with the outpatient MDFT clinic, and in cases where the youth is not able to make significant enough progress in stopping or significantly diminishing his or her drug use, we employ this short-term (i.e., up to several weeks) program.

Extrafamilial Domain

In the extrafamilial realm the work focused primarily on Marge, as Elda guided her to gain knowledge about and then maneuver within different systems. Two areas were identified as primary focuses of assessment and intervention: (1) Understanding her adolescent's school situation, and (2) organizing prosocial community activities for him. The first step was encouraging the mother to take a proactive role in her son's school. The therapist coached her in how to navigate the often complex school system—its functioning, and ways she could become involved to help her son succeed. Her involvement in and of itself was therapeutic and important in that Willie finally saw his mother as his ally. Marge's intervention was consistent throughout the course of treatment and was effective, as Willie began attending classes regularly again. In one instance, with Elda's coaching, the mother single-handedly worked with the principal of the school and had her son transferred from a class he was having trouble in to a more appropriate one. This was powerful because for the first time ever this adolescent was seeing his mother clean and sober and advocating for him. Willie had doubted that his mother loved him, but through her actions she demonstrated to him her commitment to change. Another area focused on the extrafamilial domain was encouraging Marge to recognize the importance of enrolling her son in prosocial activities (e.g., Willie's interest in joining the football team).

By the end of treatment, both Marge and Willie had stopped using alcohol and drugs. During the final session—the launching of the family—mother and son were helped in negotiating house rules and establishing a contract regarding Marge's drinking. The therapist facilitated communication to help them recognize and express the many positive changes they had both made during the course of treatment. Marge told her son how proud she was of him regarding his improved performance in school (he earned his first "A"), and his staying clean and not wanting to use anymore. Willie expressed to his mother that he noticed how proud she was of him, of the choices he had been making, and acknowledged her abstinence and its positive effect on her health. By the end of the session, mother and son were learning to appreciate one another and committed themselves to building upon the positive changes they had made.

SUMMARY

Multidimensional family therapy is a family-focused, developmentally based substance abuse treatment for adolescents. MDFT operates from ten therapeutic principles designed to guide a therapist's overall mindset toward change. The therapist works to facilitate change at different system levels, in different domains of functioning, and with different people—inside and outside of the family—to end drug use and related problems, thus returning the youth and family to a normative developmental trajectory.

MDFT is administered in three stages. *Stage 1* includes a comprehensive assessment of problem areas and pockets of untapped or underutilized strength. Strong therapeutic relationships are established with all family members and influential persons such as school or juvenile justice personnel. The themes, focal areas, and goals of therapy are established in the first stage. *Stage 2* is the working phase of treatment, where significant change attempts are made within and across the interlocking subsystems (e.g., individual, family, peers, school) assessed at the outset of treatment. *Stage 3* seals the changes that have been made and prepares the teen and family for their next stage of development, using the knowledge, experience, and skills gained in the treatment. Each stage includes work in each of the four MDFT assessment and intervention domains—the adolescent, parent, the family interaction system, and the extrafamilial social system.

MDFT is a research-supported treatment, having been developed and refined over 2 decades in federally funded research. MDFT studies have found this treatment approach to be an effective and flexible clinical approach. MDFT is a treatment system that has been tested in different versions, depending on the goals of the study, characteristics of the clinical sample (e.g., level of impairment, extent of co-occurring problems, level of juvenile justice involvement), and treatment setting (e.g., outpatient clinic, drug court, day treatment program). MDFT has achieved superior clinical outcomes in comparison to several state-of-the-art, widely used treatments. The treatment engages teens and families and motivates them to complete therapy. MDFT has a lower cost than standard outpatient or residential treatment, and it has demonstrated success in treating a range of teens and families (e.g., different ethnicities, gender, ages, and severity of problems). We have developed an extensive, empirically based knowledge about how MDFT works, and have been able to successfully adapt the MDFT protocol to existing non-research treatment programs. MDFT serves as one of the most promising interventions for adolescent drug abuse and related problem behaviors in a new generation of evidence-based, multicomponent, and theory-derived treatments. Given what we know now about how research-supported therapies can influence treatment systems, provider practice, and policies that govern such practices (Liddle & Frank, in press), the next set of developmental tasks for the evidence-based therapies in this volume offer steep challenges but many exciting research and clinical practice opportunities as well.

Additional background, clinical papers, the MDFT treatment manual, and the process and outcome articles of the MDFT approach can be downloaded at www.miami.edu/ctrada.

REFERENCES

Brannigan, R., Schackman, B. R., Falco, M., & Millman, R. B. (2004). The quality of highly regarded adolescent substance abuse treatment programs: Results of an in-depth national survey. *Archives of Pediatrics and Adolescent Medicine, 158,* 904–909.

Dakof, G. A. (2000). Understanding gender differences in adolescent drug abuse: Issues of comorbidity and family functioning. *Journal of Psychoactive Drugs, 32,* 25–32.

Diamond, G., & Liddle, H. A. (1996). Resolving a therapeutic impasse between parents and adolescents in Multidimensional Family Therapy. *Journal of Consulting and Clinical Psychology, 64,* 481–488.

Diamond, G. S., & Liddle, H. A. (1999). Transforming negative parent-adolescent interactions: From impasse to dialogue. *Family Process, 38,* 5–26.

Diamond, G. M., Liddle, H. A., Hogue, A., & Dakof, G. A. (1999). Alliance-building interventions with adolescents in family therapy: A process study. *Psychotherapy: Theory, Research, Practice, and Training, 36,* 355–368.

Drug Strategies. (2003). *Treating Teens: A Guide to Adolescent Drug Programs.* Washington, DC: Author.

French, M. T., Roebuck, M. C., Dennis, M., Godley, S., Liddle, H. A., & Tims, F. (2003). Outpatient marijuana treatment for adolescents: Economic evaluation of a multisite field experiment. *Evaluation Review, 27,* 421–459.

Hawkins, J. D., Catalano, R. F., & Miller, J. Y. (1992). Risk and protective factors for alcohol and other drug problems in adolescence and early adulthood: Implications for substance abuse prevention. *Psychological Bulletin, 112,* 64–105.

Henderson, C. E., Greenbaum, P., Dakof, G. A., Rowe, C. L., & Liddle, H. A. (2004, May). Latent growth mixture modeling with intervention trials: An example from a randomized controlled trial of adolescent substance abuse treatment. In D. Feaster (Chair), *Advanced applications of general growth mixture modeling.* Symposium conducted at the annual conference of the Society for Prevention Research, Quebec City, Canada.

Hogue, A., Liddle, H. A., Becker, D., & Johnson-Leckrone, J. (2002). Family-based prevention counseling for high-risk young adolescents: Immediate outcomes. *Journal of Community Psychology, 30,* 1–22.

Hogue, A., Liddle, H. A., Dauber, S., & Samuolis, J. (2004). Linking session focus to treatment outcome in evidence-based treatments for adolescent substance abuse. *Psychotherapy: Theory, Research, Practice, Training, 41,* 83–96.

Jackson-Gilfort, A., Liddle, H. A., Tejeda, M. J., & Dakof, G. A. (2001). Facilitating engagement of African American male adolescents in family therapy: A cultural theme process study. *Journal of Black Psychology, 27,* 321–340.

Kazdin, A. E. (1994). Methodology, design, and evaluation in psychotherapy research. In A. E. Bergin & L. S. Garfield (Eds.), *Handbook of psychotherapy and behavior change* (pp. 19–71). New York: John Wiley and Sons.

Liddle, H. A. (1999). Theory development in a family-based therapy for adolescent drug abuse. *Journal of Clinical Child Psychology, 28,* 521–532.

Liddle, H. A. (2002a). Advances in family-based therapy for adolescent substance abuse: Findings from the multidimensional family therapy research program. In L. S. Harris (Ed.), *Problems of drug dependence 2001: Proceedings of the 63rd annual scientific meeting* (NIDA Research Monograph No. 182, pp. 113–115). Bethesda, MD: NIDA.

Liddle, H. A. (2002b). *Multidimensional Family Therapy for Adolescent Cannabis Users, Cannabis Youth Treatment (CYT) Series, Volume 5.* Rockville, MD: Center for Substance Abuse Treatment, Substance Abuse and Mental Health Services Administration.

Liddle, H. A. (2004). Family-based therapies for adolescent alcohol and drug use: Research contributions and future research needs. *Addiction, 99,* (Suppl. 2), 76–92.

Liddle, H. A., & Dakof, G. A. (2002). A randomized controlled trial of intensive outpatient, family based therapy versus residential drug treatment for comorbid adolescent drug abusers. *Drug and Alcohol Dependence, 66,* S2-S202(#385), S103.

Liddle, H. A., Dakof, G. A., & Diamond, G. (1991). Adolescent substance abuse: Multidimensional family therapy in action. In E. Kaufman and P. Kaufmann (Eds.), *Family therapy of drug and alcohol abuse* (2nd ed., pp. 120–171). Needham Hts., MA: Allyn and Bacon.

Liddle, H. A., Dakof, G. A., Parker, K., Diamond, G. S., Barrett, K., & Tejada, M. (2001). Multidimensional family therapy for adolescent substance abuse: Results of a randomized clinical trial. *American Journal of Drug and Alcohol Abuse, 27,* 651–687.

Liddle, H. A., Dakof, G. A., Rowe, C., Henderson, C., Colon, L., Kanzki, E., Marchena, J., Alberga,

L., & Gonzalez, J. C. (2004, August). Is an in-home alternative to residential treatment viable? In H. Liddle (Chair), *Family-based treatment for adolescent drug abuse: New findings.* Symposium conducted at the annual conference of the American Psychological Association, Honolulu, Hawaii.

Liddle, H. A., & Frank, A. (in press). The road ahead: Building on accomplishments and facing challenges to advance the science and practice of adolescent substance abuse treatment. In H. A. Liddle & C. L. Rowe (Eds.), *Treating adolescent substance abuse: State of the science.* London: Cambridge University Press.

Liddle, H. A., Rowe, C., Dakof, G., & Lyke, J. (1998). Translating parenting research into clinical interventions for families of adolescents (Special issue). *Clinical Child Psychology and Psychiatry, 3,* 419–443.

Liddle, H. A., Rowe, C. L., Dakof, G. A., Ungaro, R. A., & Henderson, C. (2004). Early intervention for adolescent substance abuse: Pretreatment to posttreatment outcomes of a randomized controlled trial comparing multidimensional family therapy and peer group treatment. *Journal of Psychoactive Drugs, 36,* 2–37.

Liddle, H. A., Rowe, C., Diamond, G. M., Sessa, F. M., Schmidt, S., & Ettinger, D. (2000). Towards a developmental family therapy: The clinical utility of research on adolescence. *Journal of Marital and Family Therapy, 26,* 485–499.

Liddle, H. A., Rowe, C. L., Quille, T. J., Dakof, G. A., Mills, D. S., Sakran, E., & Biaggi, H. (2002). Transporting a research-based adolescent drug treatment into practice. *Journal of Substance Abuse Treatment, 22,* 231–243.

Minuchin, S. (1974). *Families and family therapy.* Cambridge, MA: Harvard University Press.

National Institute on Drug Abuse (2001). *Effective drug abuse treatment approach.* Retrieved December 10, 2004, from http://www.nida.nih.gov/BTDP/Effective/Liddle.html

Newcomb, M. D., & Bentler, P. M. (1989). Substance use and abuse among children and teenagers. *American Psychologist, 22,* 242–248.

Office of Juvenile Justice and Delinquency Prevention (1999). *Strengthening America's families: Effective family programs for prevention of delinquency.* Retrieved December 10, 2004, from http://www.strengtheningfamilies.org/html/programs_1999/10_MDFT.html

Rigter, H., Van Gageldonk, A., & Ketelaars, T. (2005). *Treatment and other interventions targeting drug use and addiction: State of the art 2004.* Utrecht: National Drug Monitor (of the Netherlands).

Robbins, M., Liddle, H. A., Turner, C., Dakof, G., Alexander, J., & Kogan, S. (in press). Adolescent and parent therapeutic alliances as predictors of dropout in Multidimensional family therapy. *Journal of Family Psychology.*

Rowe, C. L., Liddle, H. A., Dakof, G. A., & Henderson, C. E. (2004, June). Early intervention for teen substance abuse: A randomized controlled trial of Multidimensional Family Therapy with young adolescents referred for drug treatment. In M. White & M. Yucell (Chairs), *Risky business among adolescents: Prevention and treatment.* Symposium conducted at the annual conference of the College on Problems of Drug Dependence, San Juan, Puerto Rico.

Rowe, C. L., Liddle, H. A., Dakof, G. A., Henderson, C., Gonzalez, A., & Mills, D. S. (2004, August). Adapting and implementing MDFT in practice: Impact and sustainability. In H. Liddle (Chair), *Family-based treatment for adolescent drug abuse: New findings.* Symposium conducted at the annual conference of the American Psychological Association, Honolulu, Hawaii.

Schmidt, S. E., Liddle, H. A., & Dakof, G. A. (1996). Changes in parenting practices and adolescent drug abuse during multidimensional family therapy. *Journal of Family Psychology, 10,* 12–27.

Shelef, K., Diamond, G. M., Diamond, G. S., & Liddle, H. A. (in press). Adolescent and parent alliance and treatment outcome in multidimensional family therapy. *Journal of Consulting and Clinical Psychology.*

Substance Abuse and Mental Health Services Administration (2004). *Multidimensional Family Therapy certified as a Model Program.* Retrieved December 10, 2004, from http://www.modelprograms.samhsa.gov/

United States Department of Health and Human Services (2002). *Best Practices Initiative for Adolescent Drug Abuse.* Retrieved December 10, 2004, from http://phs.os.dhhs.gov/ophs/BestPractice/mdft_miami.htm

CHAPTER 7

Functional Family Therapy for Externalizing Disorders in Adolescents

Thomas L. Sexton and James F. Alexander

The field of family therapy has evolved considerably in the last two decades. The founding constructs of systemic thinking and the centrality of relationships developed into an early set of theoretical models (e.g., Structural Family Therapy, Strategic Family Therapy). In turn, the early models evolved into the current group of evidence-based change models, designed for use with some of the most difficult clinical problems faced by family therapists and psychologists.

Functional Family Therapy (FFT) is one of the best examples of the current evidence-based family intervention models. FFT evolved from a long developmental history, through increasingly widespread dissemination in contexts representing extensive diversity, with well-developed quality assurance and improvement methods to ensure accountability and fidelity to the model. Like any other good therapeutic model, FFT is built upon many of the common therapeutic principles of its predecessors, more generic common factors of good therapy, and extensive clinical experience. However, FFT goes well beyond these common factors, through the use of a systematic, relationally focused, research-based approach to the complex of the mechanisms and processes of therapeutic change.

FFT is designed to address complex clinical problems, often seen as the most difficult to address: externalizing behavior disorders of youth who also often present with a myriad of comorbid conditions. Externalizing behavior disorders are frequently encountered in clinical practice. In fact, the most common clinical referrals among adolescents are for the broad range of externalizing behavior disorders, which include school problems, drug use and abuse, violence, delinquency, and oppositional defiant and conduct disorders (Kazdin & Weisz, 2003). The scope of these specific problem behaviors extends well beyond the youth, and includes significant impact on family, peers, institutions (such as school), and numerous other elements in the community. This impact results in significant economic, community, and personal safety issues. FFT is one of the few systematic, family-based models (or any treatment philosophy, for that matter) with significant evidence of success with this difficult clinical population; this evidence spans 3 decades (Alexander & Parsons, 1973; Barnoski, 2003), and includes a rich history of clinically based change mechanisms research (e.g., Parsons & Alexander 1973).

In the last decade FFT has been designated as a "model program" and an evidence-based program in numerous independent reviews (Alverado, Kendall, Beesley, & Lee-Cavaness, 2000; Elliott, 1998; U.S. Public Health Service, 2001). As a result, FFT has been implemented as the primary intervention model in over 120 community sites in more than 26 states between 1998 and 2004. In those community FFT sites, approximately 750 therapists work with approximately 20,000 families each year, using Functional Family Therapy. In addition, each clinical contact (roughly 200,000 per year) is tracked for quality assurance to maximize positive outcomes for these high-risk youth and their families. The organizations, therapists, and clients at these replication sites represent a very diverse cultural, community, and ethnic group. To date, FFT has been used in agencies that primarily serve clients who are Chinese Americans, African Americans, White/Caucasian, Vietnamese, Jamaican, Cuban, and Central American families, among others. FFT is now consistently provided in six different languages. The agencies in which FFT has been replicated range from community not-for-profit youth development agencies, to drug and alcohol groups, to traditional mental health centers. The therapists at these sites are as diverse as the clients they serve in regard to gender, age, and ethnic origin. At these sites, FFT is delivered both as an in-home service and as a traditional outpatient program in mental health, juvenile justice, school, and community-based organizations.

For clinicians providing services in these diverse contexts the utility of FFT is not in its research support or in its national designations, but is in its basic philosophy, the core elements of intervention, and the effect of our clinical procedures with respect to positive versus negative outcomes for families. Clinicians want to know how and why the decisions and interventions we undertake (or choose not to undertake) influence families positively or adversely. Clinicians want and need to know how to use their unique strengths and styles to make productive and therapeutically valuable clinical changes within the complex relationships of family therapy. FFT addresses this basic clinical—actually, basic human—need by embracing seemingly diverse principles, which at times can even seem incompatible. In other publications we have coined this process of embracing diversity in principles as "savoring the dialectic" (Alexander & Sexton, 2002; Sexton & Alexander, 2003), which is intended to suggest that the therapy is complex, requiring both structure and flexibility, creativity and scientific guidance; a nomothetic and ideographic focus—all within the same model, all within the same treatment process.

While having a strong basis in process research coupled with demonstrated and sustainable outcomes obtained through manualized and systematic treatment, training, and supervision protocols, the heart of FFT is a relationally focused model. This relational focus is responsive to the uniqueness of clients and to the individuality and creativity of the therapist. In each phase of FFT, specific relationally based change mechanisms guide the therapist in helping the family. However, this guidance is not constrained by specific behaviors or curriculum topics. Instead, it is based on relational goals (e.g., create a positive and balanced alliance, establish hope) and a relationally based philosophy (e.g., respectfulness for all family members). Thus, while they are research based, these change mechanisms and the behaviors (techniques) designed to accomplish them must be creatively implemented within a relational context in a way that matches the client for successful therapy to occur. As such, FFT is a good example of ways in which an evidence-based therapeutic model can also be attentive to the transactional process (if not the art) of therapy as a unique and individual encounter between a skilled therapist and a family struggling to find solutions. This unique encounter requires the creativity and skill of the therapist in applying the FFT model in a way that fits the family.

Our goal in this chapter is to elucidate the core theoretical principles and clinical procedures that represent Functional Family Therapy. To do so we begin with a brief history of FFT and its developmental trajectory, an overview of its theoretical principles, a detailed review of the phases and goals that make up the clinical model, and a brief overview of the research. In addition, we present a case study that illustrates the way in which FFT "savors the dialectic" between systematic and creative practice, between directing and guiding the family, between science and art. Our attempt is to add to the recent articulations of the FFT model (Alexander & Sexton, 2002; Sexton & Alexander, 2002; Sexton & Alexander, 2003; Sexton & Alexander, 2004) by focusing in on the clinical application of the model.

THE EVOLUTION OF FUNCTIONAL FAMILY THERAPY

The evolution of FFT has been a dynamic one—deductively emerging from an integrated view of psychological theory, inductively informed by empirical evidence produced by process and outcome studies, and shaped more directly from clinical need and the clinical experience in meeting that need, in numerous and diverse contexts.

The initial idea for FFT arose during a time when there were few clinical resources for those clinicians who worked with problem youth, and even fewer that seemed to offer hope of effective intervention. At that time (and even today), these families were often seen by the helping professions as treatment resistant—lacking motivation, desire, or readiness for change. In the early days of FFT, initial steps in extant treatment models often required problem and/or high-risk youth and families to be "motivated" as a prerequisite for change. Our early clinical experience, however, showed that it was helpful for therapists to take the responsibility to engage the families—to give them hope by quickly reducing the negativity and blame within the family, to provide a road map for change that matched who they were, and to provide them with the tools they needed to navigate changes and overcome roadblocks in the future. We viewed motivation as an early treatment goal rather than a required client characteristic. Thus, we adopted a strategy that, rather than managing families from the outside with services and external controls, engaged, motivated, and taught families to develop their strength from the inside. Furthermore, rather than being treatment resistant, our clinical experience suggested that if we were culturally (both narrowly and broadly defined) sensitive—if we kept the goal of enhancing their ability to make future changes, if we focused not only on stopping the maladaptive behavior but on developing the unique strengths of the family—families engaged in therapy and completed therapy, and made significant improvement in family functioning.

Early on it was also clear that there was a need for comprehensive theoretical models of clinical change that could guide practice in a way that incorporated the growing literature on process and outcome research and helped identify successful change mechanisms and successful programs. Few, if any, of the available theoretical models were process and relationally focused while at the same time being empirically driven. In fact, during the 1970s and 1980s a schism was developing between the evolving popular clinical models (both systemically based and individually focused) and empirical scrutiny. In trying to bridge this gap, the early theoretical articulations of FFT relied heavily on the work of early systems theorists (e.g., early Mental Research Institute [MRI] constructs) as well as specific behavioral technologies, such as communication training. As the model evolved, attribution and information-processing theories were integrated to help explain some of the mechanisms of meaning and emotion often manifested as blaming and negativity in family interactional patterns (Alexander & Parsons, 1982; Alexander, Waldron, Barton, & Mas, 1989). More recently, social constructionist and social influence ideas have informed FFT through a focus on meaning and its role in the constructed nature of problems, in interrupting family negativity, and in organizing therapeutic themes (Sexton & Alexander, 2002; Sexton & Alexander, 2003). The result is a theoretical model that extends beyond the boundaries of any single theory or discipline classification. While integrative in its history, the FFT clinical change model continues as a systematic and programmatic therapeutic path that clearly articulates phases of intervention, phase goals, mechanisms of change, therapist skills, and desired outcomes. Each of these, in turn, emphasizes the centrality of remaining relationally focused and responsive to the youth and their family.

Because helping youth, families, and the communities in which they live has always been a bottom-line issue with FFT, we also developed the model around the value and necessity of rigorous evaluation and clinical accountability. Popularity of theory and political philosophy is, of course, an ever present issue in our field. FFT believes that we must actually *help* people—the largest number of people we can help—and that we must access this through actual outcomes, rather than compelling arguments, charismatic leaders, or exciting case examples. So for us, even the case study presented is intended merely to exemplify, rather than prove or validate in any way, the process, outcome, or value of FFT to youth, families, or the community. As such, FFT has always been informed by the findings of scientific inquiry, and has always sought to systematically study both the outcomes and processes of our work. Process studies have helped to inform the specific clinical mechanisms included in the model and, as such, have impacted the evolution of the model; see the early work on characteristics of therapists (Alexander, Barton, Schiavo, & Parsons, 1976), including therapist gender and its interaction with family gender roles (Newberry, Alexander, & Turner, 1991). Outcome studies, in turn, suggested that when done with adherence to FFT principles and prescribed techniques, FFT was applicable across an even wider client population over diverse settings, with real therapists in local communities (Barnoski, 2003; Sexton, Mease, & Hollimon, 2003). The ongoing research efforts support the model by systematic investigations into important questions relevant for practice.

Finally, our work always has (and will continue) been driven by a social justice perspective and a passion to help troubled youth that includes, but goes beyond, issues of therapeutic efficacy. For us, FFT is a serious responsibility; failure for the families we see represents so much more than an unwanted statistical outcome. Instead, treatment dropout and unsuccessful change attempts with seriously at-risk youth are often associated with continued or exacerbated drug use, violence, crime, and tremendous unhappiness. It is because of this ever-present responsibility that we have valued careful description and monitoring, as well as research into clinical process, accountability with respect to outcomes, and careful attention to responsible dissemination.

THE FUNCTIONAL FAMILY THERAPY TREATMENT MODEL

FFT has evolved into a model that is both structured and protocol driven, while at the same time is creative, intuitive, and appreciative of the complex interactions of therapeutic change. The manualized clinical procedures represent a map that provides the critical and major process stages through which successful therapy progresses. As a map, the clinical procedures prescribe an initial set of process goals (engagement and motivation), along with specific targets of family interaction to target during the critical, initial stages of therapy. This phase is followed by a middle set of goals (competency building), which involve a different set of process goals and specific family interaction targets that are consistent with these goals. Finally, the map guides therapists to establish and strengthen community (multiple-system) links, which maintain and enhance the positive changes experienced by youth and families at both individual (e.g., drug cessation & refusal skill) and relational (e.g., conflict resolution) levels. The core principles reflected in this map provide the therapist with consistent and theoretically sound ways to describe clients, their problems, and the change process. These theoretical principles are the boundaries of a treatment model that underlie the clinical procedures and provide a basis of making the many clinical decisions that are a normal part of good family therapy.

Despite its designation as an evidence-based model, FFT is in many ways similar to the early, systemically based family therapy approaches. FFT emphasizes the therapeutic nature of the interaction between the family and the therapist as *the* linchpin for change. From our perspective, the therapeutic encounter is a transaction. The transaction is one in which family members tell their story, and the therapist responds in a personal and purposeful way, taking every opportunity to purposefully respond in ways that meet the phase-based relational goals of the model. It is within this encounter that the therapist has the opportunity to influence the family in a way that, first, changes the way the family feels and perceives each other, and then how it approaches problem behavior patterns, and, finally, how it acts.

Because of the complexity of the therapeutic transaction, we are well aware that no model can anticipate and direct the therapist through each individual clinical decision. Thus, we believe that it is the creativity and skill of the therapist that is critical in understanding each clinical decision point in terms of the core principles of FFT, in making a clinical decision in the moment that will promote the phase-specific goals, and doing so in a way that matches the style, values, culture, and relational processes of the family—even when (actually, especially when) the style and values of individual family members differ from one another. In fact, it is because of the FFT commitment to respecting and integrating the perspectives of *all* family members that we are so successful in reducing intrafamily negativity, blame, and lack of bonding that represent critical risk and protective factors in high-risk families. In this manner, while the goals in the initial stages of FFT remain the same for all families, the way in which they are attained must be unique, and dependent on the nature of the family as well as the persona and style of each therapist. In fact, we have found that the diverse pathways to meeting the goals of each phase of FFT are only limited by the ability of the therapist to understand the philosophy and processes of FFT intervention, and by their creativity in finding unique and individualized ways to respond and yet adhere to the phase-specific goals of FFT intervention.

Thus, as a dialectic, creativity and therapeutic structure are different sides of the same coin. FFT savors this dialectic by embracing two seemingly incompatible forces: being systematic and structured while *at the same time* being relational and clinically responsive. The FFT clinical model and accompanying treatment manual (Sexton & Alexander, 2004) provide a map that details the specific goals and strategies of each phase of change. In the case of FFT, the structure provided by the theoretical principles and the map of the protocol provide the structure within which the therapist provides the unique and creative application to a uniquely organized client.

A Systematic, Intentional, and Phasic Change Map

In the therapy room (or home) many important processes are unfolding, often at the same time, creating a challenging and emotionally charged atmosphere. The challenge for the therapist is to be responsive to these emerging processes and the emotions they trigger, while being anchored in the FFT principles and clinical map, in order to navigate the complex emotional, behavioral, and relational process in a way that increases the probability that concrete and important positive relational changes can occur. One of the great strengths of FFT is that its clinical protocol is, at its core, the rudder the therapist needs to help navigate the difficult waters of the negative and often blaming relational interchanges among the family members.

FFT unfolds through three sequential phases: Engagement and Motivation, Behavior Change, and Generalization. Each of the three phases of FFT has specific therapeutic goals, and neccesitates therapist skills that, when used competently, maximize the likelihood of successful accomplishment of these goals. Each phase of the model involves focused assessment and intervention components that are organized in a coherent manner. At the same time, accomplishing the goals of each phase must be done in unique and creative ways that match the strengths of the therapists and family (see Figure 7.1).

Engagement and Motivation Phase

FFT begins with the first contact between the therapist and family, as the therapist initially attempts to involve the family in the immediate activities of the session

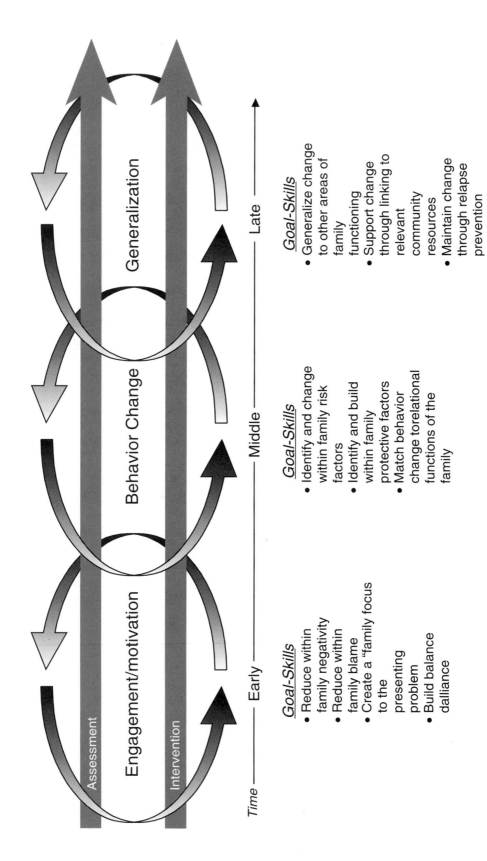

Figure 7.1 The FFT Clinical Model

(during an initial phone call), such that they become interested in taking part in and accepting of therapy (engagement). In an active and engaging way FFT therapists immediately focus on the specific goals of the phase: reducing intra-family member negativity and blame while trying to develop a family focus on the problems presented by the family, and developing alliances (both from therapist to family and from family member to family member). These are accomplished by developing and retaining a relational focus (rather than a youth focus), diverting and interrupting negativity, asking strength-based questions and pointing to positive process, and, most effectively, by actively reframing and creating a sense of balanced alliance with all family members. The desired outcome of these early interactions is that the family develops motivation by experiencing a sense of support for their current emotions and concerns, a sense of hope that the problem can change, and a belief that the therapist and the therapy can help promote those changes. When negativity and blaming is reduced hope can emerge, and therapists can demonstrate that they are capable and competent to be a helpful influence. Reduction of blaming and negativity also creates more positive interactions among family members, which contribute to a sense of hope. The outcome is an alliance that develops wherein each family member believes that the therapist supports and understands his or her position, beliefs, and values. The engagement and motivation phase is successful when the family members begin to believe that while everyone in the family has a different and unique contribution to the primary concerns, everyone shares in the emotional struggle that is occurring—when the family comes to trust in the therapist, and when they believe that the therapist has an understanding of their unique position.

Reframing is the primary intervention strategy used to accomplish the goals of the engagement and motivation phase of FFT. Reframing was initially made popular by early family therapists, and has become one of the most universal therapeutic techniques across all family therapies. In most intervention models reframing is viewed as an intervention *event,* in which the therapist delivers an alternative frame of reference to the client in hopes that the client will buy or accept the new interpretation and will ultimately change. Within FFT, reframing has a much-expanded and richer interpersonal meaning; it is an ongoing relational process, involving validation of the client-presented perspective—a reattribution involving possible alternative motivations or contextual contributions, a determination of the impact on the family, and a reformation of the theme that incorporates client feedback. Thus, in FFT we view reframing as a relational *process* between the therapist and family, with the goal of reducing negativity and blame in a way that develops alliance, refocuses the responsibility to include the speaker, and reduces the attributional and emotional focus on others as the source of problems.

FFT therapists view the blaming and negative statements family members offer in early sessions as a reframing opportunity for the therapist. Unattended, these statements generally set off a process of defensive responding and counter-blaming. For FFT therapists, the emergence of negativity and blame leads the FFT therapist to move toward the negativity or blame by first acknowledging or validating the position, statement, emotion, or primary meaning of the speaker. The *validation* supports and engages the client and demonstrates understanding and respect.

Validation is followed by a *reattribution statement,* which presents an alternative theme or perspective. The reattribution statement can take many forms, including offering an alternative explanation for the cause of the problem behavior, a metaphor that implies an alternative construct of the problem, or even using humor, to imply that "all is not what it seems." The alternative meaning or theme must be plausible and (hopefully) believable to one or more family members, such that it fits them. Changing the meaning of behavior through reframing helps reattribute an emotion, behavior, or intent of another to a more benign attribution.

As a relational process, reframing statements by the therapist are followed by an assessment of their impact, by listening to family members' responses, and by incorporating changes or alternative ideas into the next validation and reframing statement by the therapist. In this way, reframing is a constant loop of therapist and family member interactions that build together toward the therapeutic goal. The therapist and client are actually constructing a mutually agreed-upon and jointly acceptable alternative explanation for an emotional set of events or series of behaviors. Because it is jointly constructed, it is "real" and relevant to family member(s) and the therapist. Over time, the reframing process helps to organize and to provide a therapeutic thread to the engagement and motivation phase, through the development of a theme that explains the problems of the family and thus organizes behavior change efforts.

Consider some examples. Many of the families we work with have struggled with one or more major problems, the result of which are very strong emotions that are expressed in unproductive ways. Using reframing, it is possible to change the *meaning* of an event, a behavior, or the others' intention. For example, it is possible to reframe anger as the hurt that the individual feels in response to the trouble in the family, with the angry person being willing to be the emotional barometer for the sake of the whole family. It is possible to reframe the rebelliousness of an adolescent (oftentimes seen as disrespectful behavior by parents) as independence. Many of the families we work with feel hopeless. It is possible to respond in ways that challenge the family to focus attention on alternative solutions. For example, it is possible to reframe the anger and frustration of parents to the challenge of needing to manage their own emotions, so that they can help teach their child new ways of negotiating alternative behaviors. In this way the reframe moves the focus of attention from the child (being irresponsible) to the parent (managing emotions and teaching), in a way that builds individual responsibility and leads to behavior change. Oftentimes families feel they are alone and isolated in their positions. Reframing can also *link* family members together and develop a joint family definition of the struggles experienced. A family-focused problem definition is one in which everyone in the family has some responsibility and, thus, some part in the problem. However, no family member takes the blame for the state of affairs in the family. Helping the family members move to a position that reduces blame while retaining a sense of responsibility for one's own actions is a difficult but attainable goal, that can be reached through respect for all family members, creating a balanced alliance, and the use of sensitive reframing.

In each of the above examples the reattribution was helpful because it changed the focus of the behavior from being directed to another person to inside the speaker. Thus, the blame inherent in anger is now redefined as hurt, and even sacrifice, which removes negative emotions while retaining behavioral responsibility. The cognitive sets, or problem definitions, that family members bring to therapy are the meanings that contribute to the emotional intensity that is often behind the anger, blaming, and negativity seen in the interpersonal interactions between family members. These cognitive sets may exist in emotional ("it hurts and I am angry"), behavioral ("stay away from me"), or cognitive terms ("you are just trying to hurt me," "why does he or she intentionally do this?"). Focusing on changing meaning through reframing and retaining a relational, nonblaming focus significantly increases the reduction in negativity.

The engagement and motivation phase also has a phase-specific assessment component. While intervening to reduce blame and negativity, create a family focus, and develop alliance, the FFT therapist also observes the specific risk factors to be mediated and the potential protective factors that might be addressed in this family. Unlike other forms of family therapy (e. g., Structural Family Therapy), there is no enactment or assessment phase. Instead, assessment is an ongoing process based on in-the-room clinical observation. Figure 7.1 illustrates the way in which both assessment and intervention are threads that concurrently go through the engagement and motivation phase. This requires the FFT therapist to multitask; systematically intervening to change the family process (i.e., doing reframing) while simultaneously listening for and observing risk and protective factors that will become the focus of the behavior change phase.

The goals of early FFT sessions are clear—however; what therapists see and experience in the room is quite different. Few families come in asking for help with blame or negativity, seeking help in creating a family focus to the problems they are experiencing. Instead, they act in ways that reflect what their problems have come to mean to them (e.g., angry, accusing, quiet, seemingly uninvolved). As a result, the primary issues presented by the parents may be the youth's drug use, violent behavior, or other symptoms of externalizing behavior disorders. For the youth it may be overinvolvement, control, or a lack of understanding on the part of the parents. The challenge for the FFT therapist is to focus less on the *content* of the specific presenting problems or diagnostic categories, and instead to focus on the family *processes* through which these specific behaviors occur. Thus, the FFT therapist looks for common relational processes (e.g., blame, negativity, a lack of family focus) regardless of the specific problem behavior. In each case the FFT therapist focuses attention on the unique ways in which this family expresses these processes. As such, each engagement and motivation session of FFT has the same goals and desired outcomes. FFT is also individual and unique to each family, so the content of reframing (e. g., the exact nature and focus of a reframe) and other initial FFT interventions will look, by definition, different for each unique family.

Behavior Change Phase

As goals of engagement and motivation are reached, the FFT therapist refocuses the therapeutic goals toward changing specific behavioral skills of family members, thereby increasing their ability to more competently perform the myriad of tasks (e. g., communication, parenting, supervision, problem solving) that contribute to successful family functioning. Led by the risk and protective/resiliency factor literature, the *behavior change* phase is accomplished by identifying the factors that contribute to the specific problem behavior for which the family was referred, and helping change these in a way that matches the relational dynamics that underlie the dysfunctional patterns that have characterized the youth's behavior.

The emphasis in this phase is on building protective family skills that will improve the ratio of risk/protective factors that put the family and adolescent at risk. The desired outcomes of this phase are the competent performance of the primary activities associated with risk factors known to contribute to the problems of externalizing disordered youth: parenting, rewards and punishments, communication between adolescent and parent, and the negotiation of limits and rules in a way that matches the relational capabilities of the particular family, that is developmentally appropriate, and that is possible for this family with these abilities in this context. They also include the strengthening of protective factors, primarily family bonding, interpersonal validation, problem solving, and adaptive conflict management, that support youth resilience—even in the face of negative, community-based (e.g., peer) pressures.

As in the engagement motivation phase, the risk and protective factors that become targets of this phase of FFT are common regardless of the initial presentation of the family. This concept is grounded in the extensive literature on risk and protective factors for externalizing disordered adolescents that has evolved over the last decade. In family sessions, FFT therapists must listen to the unique content of the family struggle and translate that struggle into the core risk and protective factors evident in the family relational processes. Behavior change targets are then focused on these common risk and protective factors.

While the targets of a behavior change plan are the risk factors common in many families of at-risk adolescents, the way in which those changes are made must be uniquely crafted to fit the relational functioning of the individual family in treatment. Thus, there are not single interventions or curriculum for the FFT therapist to follow. Instead, the therapist understands the principles of successful communication, the principles of negotiation and problem solving, and the principles for successful conflict management. In the session, FFT therapists model, direct, teach, or redirect within-session family behaviors to create specific changes in behavior based upon these principles. Homework, directives, and other technical aids are used to help build the likelihood of successful change. The overall goal is to increase competent performance—for example, of communication—but in a way that matches rather than changes the underlying relational motivation of that particular parent and adolescent. Thus, in one family the implementation of communication change might take the form of close and connected negotiation of changes, so that both parents feel connected and part of a collaborative relationship with one another. In another family, with a different relational profile, the same communication changes would look more disconnected and distanced, with information exchanged via notes instead of conversation.

There is an assessment component to the behavior change phase. In behavior change assessment is focused on identification (of risk and protective factors), on identifying barriers to change, and on determining the unique way of implementing a behavior change strategy and determining the manner in which behavior change intervention can match the relational functions of the problem behavior (see the following section on relational functions). Like the engagement and motivation phase, assessment is ongoing, and occurs simultaneously while the therapist models, suggests, and helps build family competencies.

Generalization Phase

The final phase of FFT aims to generalize, maintain, and support the changes the family has made during behavior change. Once again, it is the therapist who refocuses the therapeutic conversation from within family changes to the ways in which the family will respond to other similar and future struggles (thereby generalizing the learned positive coping behaviors), and how the family interacts with the systems around them (e.g., schools, community, extended family). Generalization takes place both within the family and between the family and its environment. As the generalization phase begins the therapist helps the family generalize changes that have occurred in the behavior change and engagement/ motivation phase to other areas of family functioning that have not been specifically addressed. Then, the therapist works to help the family maintain change by helping families overcome the natural "roller coaster" of change. Maintenance of change occurs through using relapse prevention techniques to normalize the normal problems that occur in the future, while helping family members have confidence that their newly acquired skills will work in different situations over time. Finally, the goal of supporting change is usually accomplished by integrating the necessary community resources to support the family, and working to limit the negative effects of community forces and systems that will prevent the maintenance of positive change. In general, long-term change is accomplished when the family is helped to use its own skills to obtain these changes with the guidance of the therapist. The desired outcomes of the generalization stage are to stabilize the emotional and cognitive shifts made by the family in engagement and motivation and the specific behavior changes made to alter risk and enhance protective factors. This is done by having the family develop a sense of mastery regarding their ability to address future and different (generalized) situations.

One of the biggest difficulties with the generalization phase is motivation. For the family, things are better; negativity and blame is lower, they are working together better, and some of the skills they have developed in the behavior change phase are in place. As a result, families often consider themselves "done" with therapy. However, much like the process that occurs when antibiotics have helped a bacterial infection, despite this feeling of improvement, there is more to do, there will be more problems, and there will be more struggles. Ensuring that the family will maintain its hard-fought gains when challenged needs to be systematically addressed. As with antibiotics, if the medication is not completed (despite the fact that the feeling of sickness is gone) the infection will come back stronger and more treatment-resistant than before. Thus, developing and maintaining a motivation to continue with treatment is an important challenge in this phase. Reframing is a valuable tool in this task.

The assessment component of generalization focuses on a number of specific areas. First, it is important for the FFT therapist to identify the barriers that may stand in the way of the family continuing the changes made in the behavior change phase. Second, it is critical that the therapist identify potential community resources that may aid in supporting family change. Finally, the therapist must determine the fit between unique family processes and community resources—making a match between the two.

Core Principles of Therapeutic Change

The three phases of the FFT model represent a directional, purposeful, yet relationally based map of the therapeutic process. However, no protocol can provide answers to the clinical decisions that clinicians need to make—in the room—when working with difficult families. In fact, many of the complaints about protocol- and manual-driven treatments are based in the very real belief that "it just isn't that simple." Our experience is that the successful application of the FFT phases requires moment-by-moment creativity on the part of the therapist. In order to maximize the therapeutic outcomes, this creativity is not intuitive, or "anything goes," but instead is based upon four clearly articulated and theoretically integrated principles that guide these immediate, within-the-room clinical decisions. In therapy, core principles are not the immediate basis of decision-making, but instead exist in the background as the foundation for the required creativity and intuitive judgment that must guide the therapist in the room.

Relationally Based Motivation

There is no question that motivation to change is a critical part of successful therapy. Motivation often is viewed as a static construct—that is, a condition (incentive) that exists within that client that moves them to change. In fact, a number of change models (e.g., "stages of change" models) suggest that early assessment should focus on assessing clients' readiness or stage of change; this often leads community practitioners to choose or at least prefer clients who are ready for change. In our clinical experience it is not uncommon to work with family members who, on the surface, appear to lack motivation to change, or who first present as unwilling to even begin the change process. Examples include parents who do not want their child to remain in the home, stepparent figures who want this particular youth to leave for "the sake of the younger kids," and youth who hope to become pregnant, in order to leave the home and live with their boyfriend. We think that it is perhaps misleading to suggest that our youth and families are "not motivated" or even "anti-motivated." FFT views most clients coming to therapy as motivated to some sort of action. Unfortunately, they are motivated to maintain or engage in actions that do not produce a successful resolution of the concern!

FFT defines therapeutic motivation (an incentive to change or to act) as a relational process (alliance) that is both intrapersonal (within the client), interpersonal (between family members), and therapeutic (between therapist and each family member). Family members become motivated to change within the early stage of FFT because of the development of alliance (rather than fear or guilt). *Within-family alliance* is demonstrated by family members overcoming their negativity and working together toward the same end, with agreement on how to proceed within a positive emotional bond. *Family-to-therapist alliance* reflects the process of working together between family members and the therapist. It is increasingly clear from process research that in successful family therapy, alliance needs to be balanced. Balanced alliance occurs when the therapist has the same level of working alliance with parents and youth regardless of the overall level of alliance (Robbins, Turner, & Alexander, 2004).

Relational Focus on Clinical Problems

FFT focuses on one of the most difficult clinical populations encountered by family therapists: externalizing disorders in adolescents. The specific behaviors include conduct problems, drug abuse and use, violence, family conflict, and school behavior problems, among others. Successful therapy cannot be done without a clear conceptual model of the origin and functionality of clinical problems. A successful family therapist must wade through the myriad of content and focus on the core issues that may help the family. What becomes complex with acting-out youth is that the serious behaviors they present at referral represent a multitude of the clinical syndromes that must ultimately change. Thinking beyond specific behaviors of a youth, with a clearly articulated model of the etiology of his or her clinical problems, is critical, because it becomes the basis upon which change targets are identified and change mechanisms are utilized.

As a family-relational clinical intervention we adopt a "families first" principle in the focus of our interventions and understanding of the presenting problems of youth. FFT views specific, presenting clinical problems (clinical syndromes) as relational problems—as specific behaviors embedded within enduring patterns of behaviors that are the foundation for stable and enduring relational functions within family relationships. Figure 7.2 depicts the way in which FFT helps to focus our etiological model on the actual interaction in the room and helps the clinician conceptualize the presenting problems. This model is much like the proverbial tip of the iceberg notion. The clinical symptoms for which the adolescent was referred for treatment, that are most apparent to many, are on the tip. Like the iceberg, there is much below the surface that is, in many ways, even more important. Specific problem behaviors are, however, only the manifestations of the relational system of the family. While not as easily apparent, family behavior patterns are relational sequences of behaviors, central to the character of the family, that forms the basis of their daily life. Some of these patterns are quite effective in accomplishing the tasks of the family (e.g., parenting, communicating, supporting) and may protect the family and its members from the manifestation of specific behavior problems. Other patterns put individuals or the family as a whole at risk for individual symptoms of mental health, such as drug abuse/use, relational conflict, and externalizing behavior disorders.

These stable patterns of interaction between the youth and family are represented by the internal experiences of the individual in those relationships, and are referred to as *relational functions* (Alexander & Parsons, 1982; Alexander, Pugh, Parsons, & Sexton, 2000; Alexander & Sexton, 2002). Functions are the relational outcomes of stable relational patterns. From the perspective of an individual, the relationship patterns of which they are a part drift into the background. It is the

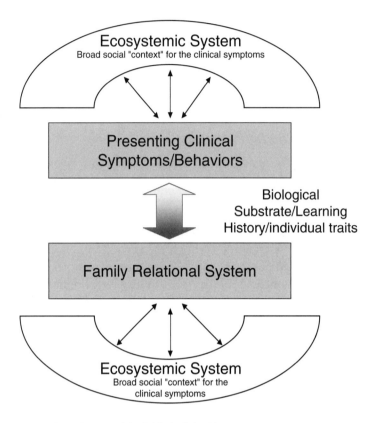

Figure 7.2   FFT Etiological Model of Clinical Problems

experience of these stable patterns (e.g., how they feel, what they mean, and their symbolic interpretation) that is most predominant, or in the foreground. Thus, from this perspective, relational functions represent the *outcomes* of patterned behavioral sequences, not specific behaviors in and of themselves.

FFT has identified two main dimensions of relational functions used to understand the internalized experience, or functional outcomes, of the redundant and common relational patterns within the family (or "relational space"): Relational connection (or interdependency), and relationship hierarchy. High degrees of relatedness are experienced as a sense of interconnectedness, psychological intensity in regard to the relationship, emotional contact, and/or enmeshment. Low degrees of relatedness are characterized by feelings of autonomy, distance, independence, and a low degree of psychological intensity. From our perspective, high and low degrees of relatedness are not different ends of a continuum. Instead, they represent two dimensions, both of which are evident to some degree in the experience of a relationship. Midpointing is the experience of a relationship represented by both high connectedness (autonomy) and distance (independence). Relational hierarchy is a measure of relational control and influence. Relational control also ranges from high to low, with symmetrical being an experience of balanced influence in the relationship.

Relational functions are difficult to identify. The concept of equifinality would suggest that there might be very different family relational patterns (e.g., constant bickering versus warmth and cooperation) that have the same relational outcome (e.g., a high degree of interconnectedness). In contrast, very similar interactional sequences (warm communication and intimacy behaviors) can produce entirely different relational outcomes (e.g., they will enhance contact in one relationship, and can increase distance in another relationship). From the FFT perspective, there is nothing wrong (or to be changed) with respect to any of these experiences (e.g., having a sense of control, receiving attention, having a sense of belonging). Each has its strengths and its weaknesses.

Respect and Strength-Based Belief in People

At its very core, FFT is built on respect and appreciation of the individuality and diversity of the families with which we work. While this may be a principle that any clinician would be hard-pressed to oppose, we find that respect is difficult to maintain amidst the many problem-focused constructs of current-day mental health, and culturally based beliefs about individual and (particularly) family behavior. Our goal is to view both the individual and families we work with as complex combinations of strengths and challenges. Much like the half-full/half-empty glass metaphor, we try to view families beyond the traditional characterizations of symptoms, diagnoses, or behaviors for which the client has been referred. While important, these views can lead the therapist to miss the "half-full" aspects of the families, and overlook the strengths and resources that have successfully served to help them cope with the very difficult contexts in which they live. Admittedly, some, if not many, of the strengths in families and youth are not realized, or even apparent. In FFT we work to see the glass as neither half empty or half full; instead, we simply work to see what is in the glass, even if the strengths are more difficult to see on the surface. For us this is a matter of respect.

"Matching" in FFT, is a way to negotiate the dialectic between the theoretical and clinical goals of a systematic intervention model while at the same time maintaining the respect for the individual differences inherent in each uniquely organized family. FFT therapists attempt to achieve the phase goals of the model in a way that fits with the family members' relational needs, problem definition, abilities, and resources. Matching to the client allows FFT to respect, value, and work within the important cultural, racial, religious, and gender-based values of the client. Matching to the unique structure of the family helps therapists avoid imposing their own value systems, social agenda, and interpersonal needs on the youth and family. Contingent clinical decisions are guided by the principle of matching therapeutic activities to the phase and to the client.

The principle of matching also speaks to the goals of treatment. The focus of FFT is on significant yet obtainable behavioral changes that will have a lasting impact on the family, but that are also ones that are responsive to their needs, values, and capacities, rather than being imposed from the outside. In that regard, FFT seeks to pursue obtainable outcomes that fit the style of the family rather than to mold families into someone else's version of "healthy," or to reconstruct the "personality" of the family or individuals therein. Treatment goals are individualized and tailored for each family and the circumstances in which they live.

Thus, in regard to the dynamics of the family, FFT believes that the common, repetitive, and highly entrenched behavioral sequences apparent in families that lead to consistent relational outcomes (functions) can only be understood from an ideographic perspective. Relationship functions are reflected in patterns of behavior that maintain, albeit often in painful ways, the relationships between family members. FFT therapists do not attempt to change the core relational experiences of the family members any more than they would consider changing such major factors as culture, parental gender identity, or spiritual beliefs. FFT does, however, insist on changing the means by which they are attained (e.g., drugs, violence, coercion, gang membership); that is, FFT changes the expression of these components when they damage others. For example, parents who control via violence learn to control via nurturance and guidance. A so-called "one-up" pattern of parenting is unacceptable if it involves physical and/or emotional abuse, but it is generally applauded if it involves authoritative parenting, child-sensitive resource allocation, and nurturing. In other words, FFT does not attempt to change the hierarchy of abusive parents, only the patterns of behavior that serve that relational function ("one-up"). In a similar manner, FFT does not attempt to force an enmeshed parent to change his or her relational function of contact/closeness; instead, FFT helps that parent replace enabling behaviors with appropriate nurturance that is contingent upon prosocial (not dysfunctional) youth behavior.

SCIENTIFIC FOUNDATIONS OF FUNCTIONAL FAMILY THERAPY

Functional Family Therapy is based on a long-term, systematic, and independently replicated series of outcome and process research studies spanning over 3 decades. These results have led the Center for Substance Abuse Prevention (CSAP, 1999) and the Office of Juvenile Justice and Delinquency Prevention (OJJDP) to identify FFT as a model program for both substance abuse and delinquency prevention (Alverado, Kendall, Beesley, & Lee-Cavaness, 2000). Similarly, the Center for the Study and Prevention of Violence (CSPV) designated FFT as one of the 10 (out of over 1,000 programs reviewed) "Blueprint" programs (Elliott, 1998). The surgeon general's report (U.S. Public Health Service, 2001) identified FFT as one of only four level 1 programs for successfully intervening with conduct-disordered, violent, and multiproblem at-risk adolescents. Finally, FFT is an evidence-based intervention model that meets any and all of the current benchmarks of empirically validated treatments (Sexton & Alexander, 2001).

The FFT clinical outcome studies have relied on a core outcome measure relevant to the population of interest; the likelihood that a youth will again enter the juvenile justice system (a common outcome in externalizing behavior-disordered youth). The cumulative data suggest that FFT is effective on two critical fronts. First, the results indicated that FFT was successful in engaging and retaining families in treatment, a difficult task with this population. Engagement rates in FFT studies range from 78 percent (Sexton, Ostrom, Bonomo, & Alexander, 2000) to 89.8 percent (Barnoski, 2003). This outcome is fairly dramatic given the traditionally high rates of dropout (50 to 75 percent) in most treatment programs (Kazdin, 1997). Second, FFT reduces recidivism between 26 percent and 73 percent with status-offending, moderate, and seriously delinquent youth, as compared to both no treatment and juvenile court probation services (Alexander et al., 2000). In a recent community-based clinical trial using community-based therapists working in community service delivery systems with very high risk youth, FFT resulted in a 38 percent (statistically significant) reduction in felony crime and a 50 percent reduction in violent crime as compared to a randomly selected control group (Barnoski, 2003) when FFT was done as it was designed. These data emphasize that FFT is effective in reducing serious reoffense rates of at-risk adolescents, but only when FFT is delivered as the model was intended to be delivered (e.g., in a competent fashion according to the national FFT dissemination protocol).

These positive outcomes of FFT remain relatively stable, even at followup times as long as 5 years (Gordon, Arbuthnot, Gustafson, & McGreen, 1988), and the positive impact also affects siblings of the identified adolescent (Klein, Alexander, & Parsons, 1977). In addition, it appears that FFT not only results in significantly lower recidivism rates, but if the adolescent recidivated at all, he or she committed significantly fewer severe crimes, even when pretreatment crime history was factored into the analysis (Sexton et al., 2000). For a complete review of the outcome studies of FFT consult Alexander et al., 2002; Alexander & Sexton, 2002 and Sexton & Alexander, 2002.

FFT has also proven to be a cost-effective intervention. Sexton and Alexander (2000) found FFT to be significantly more effective in reducing recidivism: $5,000 per case less costly than an equivalent juvenile detention intervention, and $12,000 less expensive than residential treatment of a similar course. In the most comprehensive investigation of the economic outcomes of family-based interventions to date, the state of Washington found that FFT had among the highest cost savings when compared to other juvenile offender programs. The cost of implementing the program was approximately $2,500 per family, with a cost savings (taxpayer and crime victim cost) of $13,908 per youth (Aos & Barnoski, 1998).

The model is built on a long history of process studies aimed at understanding therapeutic change mechanisms. What is unique about this line of research is that it has systematically verified many of the theoretically identified change mechanisms of the model that have been the source of input service to improve the model. For example, Alexander, Barton, Schiavo, and Parsons (1976) found that the ratio of negative to supportive statements made by family members was significantly higher in cases that dropped out of therapy than among cases that completed treatment. In turn, premature termination predicted recidivism in adolescents. Robbins, Alexander, Newell, and Turner (1996) confirmed that levels of family member negativity could successfully predict program dropouts, but this negativity was not as much a result of initial rates (first segment of session one) as it was the inability of therapists to prevent a strong escalation of negativity as the session continued. Newberry, Alexander, and Turner (1991) found that in the engagement and motivation phase, therapist supportiveness (which includes reframes and strength-based questions) increased the likelihood of a positive response and thus the reduction of negativity by family members, whereas structuring behaviors (teaching behaviors, suggesting behavior changes, establishing ground rules) led to an increase in negativity. Negativity reduction is a primary objective of the engagement and motivation phase; thus, studies such as these are critical in that they provide evidence for the theoretical constructs and mechanisms of change proposed by FFT.

Case Study

We chose Jordie and his family as a case illustration of FFT because it represents the dynamic unfolding of FFT in an actual clinical setting with a youth with multiple problems. The case also illustrates the ways in which the core principles of FFT can bridge the gap between cultures and ethnic differences between therapists and families, and the degree to which the FFT therapist must both follow a systematic model and be creative. Jordie was a 15-year-old male client referred to a forensic psychiatric treatment group in a major European city. The senior author of this chapter (Sexton) worked with Jordie in 9 family sessions over a 6-month period while training the therapists at the center to use FFT in their practice.

Jordie is Colombian. He was adopted by Dutch parents at the age of 6 months. At the time of the referral and first FFT session Jordie was in the process of being removed from his home and being placed in residential care. Jordie had been expelled from school 3 years before and had become a chronic runaway and a frequent offender, in constant contact with the police (theft, fighting, and habitual drug use). In fact, both he and his parents referred to him as a "street kid." FFT was considered the final option before residential placement. During the initial assessment period at the Forensic Psychiatric Center Jordie had been diagnosed with ADHD; the psychiatric staff was considering a diagnosis of Bipolar Disorder. Jordie lived with his two adoptive parents. His mother was a homemaker; his father was a truck driver, whose job often took him away from home. Hours before the session Jordie decided he would not attend. He did not want to talk with an American that he didn't know. The parents became hesitant—both indicated that they had done all they could do and that residential care was required. The intake counselor at the mental health center encouraged the family to attend, but Jordie made it clear he was not going to participate. This case began with many initial potential challenges, not atypical of many of the cases seen in FFT practice.

At the outset of FFT a number of practical decisions need to be made by the therapist. For example, FFT can be delivered in homes or in offices; it can be weekly or more often; it must include the family but not always all siblings (e.g., if they are very young). Decisions of this type are viewed akin to other therapeutic interventions in FFT, made according to the guiding principles of FFT and made because the outcome promotes the phase goals of the model. For example, in the case of Jordie, it was determined that he be seen in a clinic setting. The therapist made this decision because, as a street kid, the likelihood that Jordie would be home at the time of a visit was unlikely. Sessions in the office had a formal feel to them that helped point out the important nature of the task. Jordie had a younger brother (4 years old). He was not asked to come to the session because of his age. Unlike other family therapies, FFT does not always involve younger siblings who are not major players in the problem cycle. Finally, during the first session it became apparent that waiting until the next week for a second session would not help promote change in the family. Thus, as noted before, the therapist schedules a second appointment within 2 days of the first.

Engagement and Motivation Phase. The first two sessions of FFT were conducted in the first week of FFT treatment. Going into the session, the FFT therapist's primary aim was to engage the family in treatment and build motivation to change. To accomplish this task the FFT model identifies four early session process goals: identify and reduce the within-family negativity and blame, create a family focus for the presenting problem, and build therapist-to-family alliance as well as family-to-family alliance, all through the use of reframing. In addition, a systematic assessment was necessary to understand the way in which the presenting symptoms were represented in central family-relational patterns that were held together by the relational functions (relational outcomes) for each family member. The FFT therapist was not of the same cultural background as the family, so care had to be taken to adjust both the style and the manner of intervention to match to the family in a culturally sensitive and competent manner. Thus, the specific pathway to the model-prescribed goals was not apparent, and needed to emerge within the room as the therapist began to understand the family and its unique organization, values, and beliefs.

After a brief introduction, the session quickly moved to a focus on family engagement. Jordie came to the session wearing traditional Colombian clothes. The therapist took this opportunity to ask about the clothes and engaged Jordie in a brief exchange about his coat. It turns out that the coat is one of his prized possessions and, according to Jordie, makes him unique among other street kids because it identifies him as Colombian rather than of North African descent (the Netherlands has a significant Turkish, Moroccan, and Sudanese population). The exchange was a brief but purposeful attempt to engage Jordie on his terms. In a similar manner the therapist asked both parents about their English-speaking ability; where they learned the language, and some of the difficulties inherent in the challenge of talking about their family in a second language. The therapist talked about his struggle learning Dutch. Again, these interactions were a brief (1 to 2 minutes) but purposeful engagement strategy intended to identify potential barriers and "put them on the table," with the goal of engagement.

In FFT, engagement is seen as a process that occurs throughout a session, rather than the outcome of a single event. As a result, "getting to know the family" type questions and building rapport, which are common parts of other models, happen as an outcome of talking directly about the serious concern at issue. In this case the therapist quickly moved from these brief engagement discussions to a focus on the family and its presenting problems by asking, "I have been told that all of you were very reluctant to come today, that you are considering having Jordie live somewhere else. Can you help me understand what goes on between the three of you that ends up in this level of discouragement?" The initial therapist question, while subtle, represents an important core principle of FFT: problems are relational ones within families. The question directly identifies the issues known to the therapist, in nonblaming ways, while casting them within a family focus.

As is common in an FFT session, the parents responded with their perception of the presenting clinical issue; for the father, the problem was that Jordie didn't follow the simple rules. For the mother, the issue was the violent fights between her and her son that resulted because he "explodes like a volcano" whenever she asks him to do anything. Jordie said nothing. From an FFT perspective, these statements represent the problem definitions of the parents. Problem definitions are the ways in which the individual understands and attributes the struggles they are experiencing. The FFT therapist attempts to hear not the content, but the attributional element (who is blamed) and the corresponding emotional and behavioral outcomes (what they feel and do about this attribution). In this case, both parents attributed the problems to Jordie (blaming) but in ways that at that time did not include high levels of negativity (emotional and behavior).

Early in therapy the target of the FFT therapist is refocusing the attributions from blame on Jordie to trying to identify a part in the problem of the parents. Thus, the response to these opening blaming statements is to talk to the speaker about his or her part in the problem, building a more complex, family-focused definition. The therapist's first response was to the first parent that spoke—the father. Using reframing, the therapist first acknowledged the father's attention to detail and the fact that despite his clear discouragement he had not given up. Yet the struggle for him was understanding why a smart and resourceful young man was unable to follow rules that were simple, and that, as a father, his apparent anger also contained a component of hurt. Through a series of interchanges the therapist tried to introduce the theme of hurt behind the anger into the conversation. In a similar way the therapist and mother talked of the hurt behind her anger, a hurt that, despite the fact that it comes out in explosions, is one that comes from a mother who has invested much in her child and is devastated at being unable to "reach him." When his mother talked of exploding Jordie laughed. His view was that his mother yelled, and that when people yell at him he becomes "crazy." The therapist, reframing again, began with an acknowledgement of his assertiveness, a style necessary on the street, where he is the man among his peers. The reframe was focused on his difficulty in hearing his mother as a parent, and her anger as pain and not knowing what else to do to reach him. For him the struggle seemed to be the transition between his street side and his home side. Jordie's response was to begin to cry. In the minutes that followed he cried through his statement that he had lost one mother (his biological mother in Colombia) and he was not going to lose another, that his parents see him as a "bad" guy, but inside he is a boy with a heart. He spoke of other kids on the street who speak of their mothers in derogatory terms, but although he loves his mother, he sometimes gets caught up in the escalation between them.

One challenge for the therapist was to link these reframed perspectives together. In any therapy session there are many different themes that may "fit." Themes are developed through a clearly articulated process, reframing, that requires creativity and responsiveness on the part of the therapist. The goal is not to find the right theme but instead one that fits, for the therapist and for the family. In this case, what emerged from the conversation was that this is a family that, despite their attempts to stay together, has lost something. In every-day interactions they lose the core desire of each—not to give up, not to let go, and not to let go of all the work that each has done to overcome the challenges he or she faced (e.g., adoption, delinquency). Their desire gets lost in the everyday events, the explosions, that often over-shadow their ultimate goal. Each has their own part, each contributes, but each gets lost.

The intent of these early reframing interventions is not to take away the responsibility of the bad behavior from Jordie or any other family member, but to expand the problem to include everyone. In addition, the goal was to build alliance between the therapist and each family member. For the parents, the therapist was sensitive and understanding in framing the meaning of their behavior and emotion to a cause (theme) that, while not always helpful, is understandable and guided by good intention. The nonblaming and supportive way of discussing their part in the problem helps build alliance, and creates a purposeful yet safe environment where important issues are directly discussed in supportive ways. In addition, if the parents and adolescents view the therapist as taking a family focus, and not letting the problem be defined as being only about them, the probability of their further engagement and motivation will increase. In the end, the alternative theme developed through reframing links all the family members together in a way in which each has responsibility for some part but where no one is blamed.

In a written format it is difficult to portray the highly personal, interactive, and evolving way in which reframing happens in an FFT session. As noted above, reframing is not an interpretation or positive connotation the therapist gives to the family. Instead, reframing is a relational process, in which the therapist offers a theme hint, the family responds with their interpretation, and the therapist uses the response to change and expand the theme. In the end, this process results in a new problem definition that is nonblaming, nonnegative, and family focused. For the therapist, this process feels very much like going in circles. What the therapist offers must be shaped and focused throughout the conversation with the family. The result is that things are said more than once—the process must, however, be focused. Each response by the family requires the therapist to determine how a response to this statement can promote the process goals of the phase. Thus, FFT is focused and purposeful, yet individualized and interpersonal; it is directive, yet interactive; it is direct, yet respectful.

It is also difficult in a written format to express the significant challenges encountered in overcoming the cultural barriers between the therapist and the family. While there was a racial similarity (therapist and parents were Caucasian) the cultural differences were vast. In the Dutch culture public expression of pain and struggle are not common, typical prototypes of parenting are different from American culture (tolerant yet firm), and the early independence of youth is common. The challenge for the therapist in this case was to try to understand the family from the inside out, rather than by imposing expectations and values on the youth's and the parent's behavior from the outside. To overcome these barriers, the therapist purposefully adopted a style of questioning, trying to learn, and trying to understand the differences. In addition, the therapist openly discussed the differences and his lack of knowledge. At the same time, the therapist retained the role of directing the conversation in a way that accomplished the goals of the initial phase of FFT. This stance created a "working together" atmosphere in the room.

While the conversation focused on reframing and the relational process, the therapist simultaneously gathered information about the common relational pattern or sequence between the family members in which the delinquent behavior was embedded. In FFT, assessment is not a specific phase of treatment but is rather an ongoing process through therapy. In addition, the therapist began to hypothesize about the relational functions or outcomes of these patterns for each family member. Clearly, the central pattern was one of escalation between Jordie and his mother. Occasionally father would step in to support either mother (Jordie has to follow the simple rules) or Jordie (we need to be patient and understand him). This pattern was central to their interaction regardless of the specific content issue (e.g., staying out too late). What emerged was an assessment of relational functions that hypothesized the pattern between Jordie and his mother to be midpointing from Jordie's side (both contact and psychological distance), and more psychological distance (or independence) from his mother's perspective. Our assessment hypothesized father as psychologically independent (distant) from both his wife and his son. It is important to note that these relational assessments are not diagnostic. Relational functions are not the targets of change in FFT, but instead serve as descriptive and early indications of potential ways in which behavior changes can be made that match to the family. It is also important to note that the relational assessment comes from clinical observation. What goes on in the room is reframing, rather than questioning and detective work to identify the functions. In the end, the goal, as noted above, is to change the means of achieving these outcomes, not the outcomes themselves.

The engagement and motivation phase took three sessions of intensive discussion, where the focus was on the relational process between the family members, not on the specifics of behavior change, the behavioral goals of therapy, or quick solutions. After the initial encounter, the subsequent session began by the therapist restating the theme and throughout the discussion adding details to the theme. The primary therapist response to the issues raised by each family member was reframing: first acknowledging, and then refocusing the attribution, the meaning of the emotion, or linking of the family members together. Throughout the three sessions, the alliance grew (between therapist and family and among the family) as blame was reduced. Furthermore, a theme emerged that redefined the problem: an understanding of the relational functions was gained, and the therapist moved to behavior change.

Behavior Change Phase. The behavior change phase is initiated by the therapist, based on an assessment of the degree to which the goals of engagement and motivation have been accomplished. In this case, blame and negativity were significantly reduced, alliance was high, and a family-focused theme as problem redefinition, shared by therapist and family, had emerged. To successfully move into behavior change, the therapist must have identified specific behavior change targets and made a relational assessment (see the previous section). The targets of behavior change are those specific behavioral competencies that, if adopted by the family, would serve a protective function for the family. In the case of externalizing behavior-disordered adolescents, these tend to be related to the broad areas of communication, problem solving and/or negotiating, conflict management, and parenting. Like the earlier engagement and motivation phase, behavior change requires a high level of creativity on the part of the therapist. The therapist must identify relevant targets and construct a way of implementing those new behavior change competencies within the unique family system.

With Jordie and his family the initial focus of behavior change was on the escalating interaction that occurs when Jordie comes home. As noted earlier, this is a salient area for the family, in that it is the most identifiable area of struggle between them. The therapist noted that two specific competencies might be helpful. First, it seemed that helping the family find a different way of negotiating the limits of being out and coming home, and the process of conflict management when he came home late, were two fruitful areas. These were acceptable to the family because they were logical, given the organizing theme developed in the engagement and motivation phase. In the fourth session, the family came in upset about a recent incident in which Jordie had been late, not let them know, and when he came home the typical volcano explosion occurred between mother and son. Father stepped in to lecture son about rules and help mom become more patient. From the therapist's perspective, this pattern represented a common relational pattern in this family. Rather than focus on reframing, the therapist focused the conversation on teaching a skill and helping the family enhance their ability to solve this situation. The therapist said, "I think this is a common struggle between the three of you. I want to ask you to try something different in your discussion of this event. First, it seems that when you are late it is an opportunity for you and your parents to negotiate a time to come home so that they are not worried and scared. In addition, negotiation might help you find a different way to identify a common set of rules that might serve as a basis of what you can expect to occur. So, here are the steps in negotiating . . ." What followed was a teaching-focused discussion of how negotiating might take place: specific requests that are concrete and specific, presented as a set of alternatives, followed by a joint discussion of one alternative and a contract indicating what the agreed-upon choices were.

It is important to note that the negotiated agreement is much less important than helping the family follow a *process* of negotiating that helps develop and build a competency. Thus, it is not uncommon for the therapist to serve as a teacher, coach, and a director of relational processes, rather than a mediator and a problem solver for the family in this phase. In this regard, the goal is not to help find the middle or come up with an acceptable agreement to both sides. Instead, the desired outcome is to have the family know how to negotiate in the future. In addition, the introduction of behavior change requires in-session practice, using the struggles the family brings in as the content through which specific skills are developed. The challenge for the therapist is to focus on the specific phase goals of competency building in ways that match the relational functions of the family. In the three behavior change sessions the therapist took the most salient presenting issue brought to the session by the family, and focused and structured the conversation to be one in which the family practiced and refined the negotiation and conflict management strategies introduced by the therapist. In the end, it took the therapist and family working together to tailor their competencies to specifically fit the family in such a way that they could successfully replicate their new skill in multiple situations. The remaining two sessions of behavior change focused on applying negotiation and conflict management skills to numerous problem situations the family raised. In each case, the therapist's goal was on helping develop a within-family process change, not on the specific outcomes of any single event. The events brought into therapy by the family represented salient experience that provided a chance to try, practice, and experience change, rather than just talk about how it might be accomplished.

Generalization Phase. As in behavior change, it is the therapist that moves the therapy session discussion into a new phase. In this case, the family had multiple successes in utilizing their skills of negotiation and conflict management, and had demonstrated their ability to use these in situations that previously would have resulted in very emotional conflicts and threats of Jordie's removal.

It should be apparent from the previous discussion that not all of the specific struggles in Jordie's family were solved in three behavior change sessions. In addition, the school and learning problems associated with his attention problems had yet to be systematically addressed. The family was, however, feeling better, and had actually cancelled a session because they were busy. The therapist was faced with a set of challenges common in FFT: generalizing the changes made in behavior change to other areas, building motivation to continue with therapy when they felt better, helping prepare the family for future problems and relapses, and identifying other services or resources that might be needed.

Session seven began with a discussion by the therapist of an additional challenge they all faced. "The good news is that you are feeling better; the bad news is that there is yet another problem you as a family have yet to face." Puzzled, the family asked about what the therapist was trying to say. "While you have had great success, there will be additional problems you will face." Jordie was quick to say, "I have really learned that the way we have been working together will not work; I know I won't do what I did before." In a similar way, the father suggested that he was now convinced that Jordie had learned and that they were now able to work things out. The subsequent discussion focused on the many ways in which the strong emotion generated by their "volcano" reaction is likely to pull them into old patterns. In the two session that followed, the family did experience additional struggles, to which the therapist responded by helping reframe their discouragement as normal and the challenge as using their newly discovered skill again. In addition, additional areas of concern arose, particularly around Jordie's drug use. Rather than imitating a new behavior change strategy, the therapist helped the family generalize the same negotiation skill to this different area of concern. For the therapist, the primary concern was on helping the family generalize existing skills rather than on returning to behavior change, and systematically helping the family learn and practice relapse prevention. The goal was to empower the family to use their skills on their own to solve current and future problems.

It was also important to help the family support the changes they had made by utilizing outside resources. The therapist began a conversation about Jordie's school and learning struggles. Because of the between-family member alliance developed through the earlier phases, the family took this as a common and joint problem to be solved by all. The parents quickly moved to utilize the resources of the mental health center to access a psychiatric consultation, which resulted in a medication for Jordie's attention-deficit problems. The psychiatric consultation revealed that the earlier concerns about Bipolar Disorder were not as apparent, and that no further treatment was required. In addition, the family identified a contained classroom (operated by the mental health center), and Jordie enrolled. The goal was to empower the family to support the changes they had made by accessing relevant community resources. In FFT it is important for the therapist to help the family access these resources on their own, rather than by arranging and thus doing the task for the family.

At 6 months a followup appointment took place between the therapist and the family. Jordie had been arrested once for a minor curfew violation. While discouraging, this represented a minor violation, given Jordie's history. In addition, the mother and Jordie had experienced a few explosions. After fighting extensively the family was able to again use the skills learned in FFT to overcome these problems. More importantly, the family had successfully managed their discouragement by utilizing the conflict management skills learned in behavior change. Jordie was, however, successfully meeting the requirements of the special school program, he was coming home close to ontime, and he was maintaining medication. His drug use was much less frequent. Most impressive is that the family had not again threatened or asked to have Jordie removed from the home.

FFT with Jordie and his family resulted in significant, lasting, and obtainable changes in the family. Their initial blaming and negativity turned to within-family alliance. This alliance allowed them to work together, using both enhanced and newly developed behavioral skills or competencies. They were able to stick with therapy, and even thought they felt better and to generalize these skills to other areas, gain the confidence to keep at it when additional problems arise, and identify and use the available and relevant resources in the community to support what they had done. From an FFT perspective, the lasting family relational changes are the most enduring and empowering changes that therapy can make.

CONCLUSION

It is difficult to convey the dynamic, relational, and creative process of a family therapy model in written words. Any family therapist knows that the richness of the relational processes in the room can only be captured by experiencing the immediacy and intensity of the moment, and by understanding the complex clinical decisions that must get made hundreds of times in every therapy session. On the one hand, the realism of therapy, which is intimately understood by therapists, makes it difficult to accept the systematic and ordered clinical intervention models, particularly those approaches that tout their manualized format. On the other hand, those that have experienced the relational complexity of family therapy know that it is difficult to get lost.

FFT attempts to capture both phenomena. FFT attempts to "savor the dialectic" between being creative and flexible yet systematic and directional, between incorporating the lessons of science and by appreciating that these lessons must be conducted in unique ways that match individual families, between being highly adherent to the protocol and at the same time highly creative in the application of the model. In doing so we think FFT is a unique model of family therapy that can transcend the current struggles inherent in most evidence-based models.

REFERENCES

Alexander, J. F., Barton, C., Schiavo, R. S., & Parsons, B. V. (1976). Behavioral intervention with families of delinquents: Therapist characteristics and outcome. *Journal of Consulting and Clinical Psychology, 44,* 656–664.

Alexander, J. F., & Parsons, B. V. (1973). Short-term behavioral intervention with delinquent families: Impact on family process and recidivism. *Journal of Abnormal Psychology, 81,* 219–225.

Alexander, J. F., & Parsons, B. V. (1982). *Functional Family Therapy: Principles and procedures.* Carmel, CA: Brooks & Cole.

Alexander, J. F., Pugh, C. A., Parsons, B. V., & Sexton, T. L. (2000). Functional Family Therapy. In D. Elliot (Series Ed.), *Book three: Blueprints for violence prevention* (2nd ed.). Golden, CO: Venture.

Alexander, J. F., Sexton, T. L., & Robbins, M. (2002). The developmental status of family therapy in family psychology intervention science. In H. A. Liddle, D. Santisteban, R. Levant, & J. Bray (Eds.), *Family Psychology Science-Based Interventions.* Washington DC: American Psychological Association.

Alexander, J. F., Waldron, H. B., Barton, C., & Mas, C. H. (1989). Minimizing blaming attributions and behaviors in delinquent families. *Journal of Consulting and Clinical Psychology, 57,* 19–24.

Alverado, R., Kendall, K., Beesley, S., & Lee-Cavaness, C. (2000). *Strengthening America's Families.* Washington, DC: Department of Justice, Office of Juvenile Justice and Delinquency Preventions.

Aos, S., & Barnoski, R. (1998). *Watching the bottom line: Cost-effective interventions for reducing crime in Washington* (RCW 13.40.500). Olympia, WA: Washington State Institute for Public Policy.

Barnoski, R. (2003). *Outcome evaluation of Washington state's research-based programs for juvenile offenders,* Washington State Institute for Public Policy, available at: www.wsipp.wa.gov

Center for Substance Abuse Treatment. (1999). Treatment of adolescents with substance use disorders. *Treatment Improvement Protocol (TIP) Series 32.* Rockville, MD: Department of Health and Human Services.

Elliott, D. S. (Series ed.) (1998). *Blueprints for violence prevention.* University of Colorado, Center for the Study and Prevention of Violence. Boulder, CO: Blueprints Publications.

Gordon, D. A., Arbuthnot, J., Gustafson, K., & McGreen, P. (1988). Home-based behavioral systems family therapy with disadvantaged juvenile delinquents. *American Journal of Family Therapy, 16,* 243–255.

Kazdin, A. E. (1997). Practitioner review: Psychosocial treatments for conduct disorder in children. *Journal of Child Psychology and Psychiatry and Allied Disciplines 38,* 161–178.

Kazdin, A. E. (2000). *Psychotherapy for children and adolescents: Directions for research and practice.* New York: Oxford University Press.

Newberry, R. M., Alexander, J. F., & Turner, C. W. (1991). Gender as a process variable in family therapy. *Journal of Family Psychology, 5,* 158–175.

Parsons, B. V., & Alexander, J. F. (1973). Short-term family intervention: A therapy outcome study. *Journal of Consulting and Clinical Psychology, 41,* 195–201.

Robbins, M. S., Alexander, J. F., Newell, R. M., & Turner, C. W. (1996). The immediate effect of reframing on client attitude in family therapy. *Journal of Family Psychology, 10,* 28–34.

Robbins, M. S., Alexander, J. F., & Turner, C. W. (2000). Disrupting defensive family interactions in family therapy with delinquent youth. *Journal of Family Psychology, 14,* 688–701.

Sexton, T. L., & Alexander, J. F. (2000). Family-based empirically supported intervention programs. *The Counseling Psychologist.*

Sexton, T. L., & Alexander, J. F. (2001). Family based empirically supported interventions. *The Counseling Psychologist.*

Sexton, T. L., & Alexander, J. F. (2002). FBEST: Family-Based Empirically Supported Treatment Interventions. *The Counseling Psychologist 30,* 238–261.

Sexton, T. L., & Alexander, J. F. (2003). *Functional Family Therapy: A mature clinical model for working with at-risk adolescents and their families.* In T. L. Sexton, G. R. Weeks, & M. S. Robbins (Eds.), *Handbook of family therapy: The science and practice of working with families and couples.* New York: Brunner-Routledge.

Sexton, T. L., Mease, A. L., & Hollimon, A. S. (March 2003). *Models and mechanisms of change in couple and family therapy.* Paper presented at the American Counseling Association. Anaheim, CA.

Sexton, T. L., Ostrom, N., Bonomo, J., & Alexander, J. F. (2000, November). *Functional Family Therapy in a multicultural, multiethnic urban setting.* Paper presented at the annual conference of the American Association of Marriage and Family Therapy. Denver, CO.

U.S. Public Health Service. (2001). *Youth violence: A report of the surgeon general.* Washington, DC: Author.

PART II
Problems in Adults

CHAPTER 8

Psychoeducational Multifamily Groups for Families with Persons with Severe Mental Illness

William R. McFarlane

SCHIZOPHRENIA AND THE FAMILY

The nature of professional-family relationships has varied over time, according to the assumed etiology or causation of mental illness. When deinstitutionalized consumers went home to their unprepared families and to inadequate community resources, many of them suffered relapses and continuing disability. In keeping with the prevailing assumptions about families at that time, these relapses were taken as evidence that the home environment was countertherapeutic. Families found themselves in a painful situation; they not only had to experience their loved one suffering from mental illness, they were in fact blamed for its occurrence.

For most families, the guilt and confusion that occurred from being blamed by professionals and, sometimes, relatives or neighbors induced conflict within the family and usually demoralized its members. That result was particularly destructive, because it often led to breaches in family relationships and to the consumer severing ties to the family, or vice versa. Some of the homelessness that has had so many destructive effects on consumers can be traced to the rejection of the family by professionals, many of whom still expect families to provide social and economic support, housing, guidance, and control. Families in many ways were the victims of a double bind, rather than its source.

As the 1990s became the decade of the brain, professional attention turned away from the family pathology models of mental illness toward neurodevelopmental models of mental illness. With this advent of advanced research into the brain, the onus for causing mental illness began to be removed from families. From what we now know about the brain and mental illness, we recognize that attributions of psychotic disorders to family interaction are not based on scientific evidence.

The Role of Brain Abnormalities in Schizophrenia

Modern research has made it clear that alterations in brain function are consistently associated with schizophrenia. It will be important that the reader have a working knowledge of a multilevel, empirically derived model of brain function and dysfunction, because it is highly useful in guiding family and patient education and in promoting adaptation to community life and rehabilitation. This is termed the biosocial model, because it assumes reciprocal influences of the social environment on the brain and dysfunction of the brain on the social environment.

A picture is emerging from hundreds of studies using functional and anatomic scanning techniques, metabolic studies, and microscopic examination of brain tissue and cells. Physical and biochemical abnormalities correlate with symptoms and functional difficulties. Specifically, the functional axis, composed of the midbrain, thalamus, and limbic, superior temporal, and prefrontal cortices is disordered—in many patients it is reduced in volume but not severely damaged, with secondary effects on the parietal-occipital/sensory cortical areas. A key concept is that the *midbrain* is impaired in its ability to adjust appropriately the activation of the higher brain structures and the rest of the nervous system, resulting in an inability to screen out sensory stimuli and a tendency for all sensory information to be experienced as excessive, inappropriately generalized, and overwhelming. A *limbic* structure of great importance is the hippocampus, which mediates all short-term memory registration and many crucial components of attention. The defects there lead to a partial disability in verbal memory, in directing and focusing attention appropriately, and in ignoring distracting stimuli when necessary. As arousal increases in response to external or internal sources of stimulation, attention deteriorates. As attention deteriorates, arousal increases reactively, leading to a downward spiral that ends in hyperarousal in the entire limbic system, with resulting extreme states of primitive emotion, increasingly heightened sensory sensitivity, and severely limited attentional capacity.

The *prefrontal cortex,* normally the seat of most higher cognitive functions, has been found to be less active than normal, especially when the subject is challenged to do complex and frustrating mental tasks. Recent work has shown that the prefrontal area is less active in proportion to the degree of negative symptoms, verbal task demands, and cognitive impairments, and in the presence of delusions, hallucinations, and stereotyped ideas. The left *superior temporal* area tends to be overactive in association with thought disorder, negative symptoms, and verbal tasks, even while having reduced physical volume. However, it is less active in the presence of delusions and hallucinations.

The neurotransmitters involved in this axis—dopamine, serotonin, noradrenalin, glutamate, gamma-aminobutyric acid (GABA), and some neuropeptides—tend to be abnormal in complex ways that are the subject of active research. Dopamine in excess appears to mediate psychosis and, when decreased, mediates the deficit state, while excess serotonin may be serving as an antipsychotic in reaction to excessive dopamine activity, but may be deficient in some patients and in some receptor subsystems. Increasingly, the glutamate neurotransmitter system is seen as less active than normal, with widespread effects on mental functioning. The antipsychotic drugs act by down-regulating dopamine in the limbic and serotonin in the prefrontal cortex. However, this is a partial and, in some areas of research, a confusing picture. It is surely to be revised and expanded in the near future.

Biological Effects on Psychological Functioning

The net effect of these abnormalities is that the person with schizophrenia has great difficulty managing external and internal stresses, with the result that he or she experiences a nearly paralyzing sensitivity to stimulation. That has the effect of significant interference with attention, memory, and ignoring distraction. In addition, the loss of cortical volume means that there are fundamental cognitive deficits that, though varying widely among persons with the disorder, markedly impair crucial human abilities in the social, occupational, and intellectual spheres. One of the most basic insights gained in the last two decades of research is that schizophrenia is a disorder of the capacity to tolerate, defend against, and manage sensory stimulation, emotional responses to negative social interaction, and the complex cognitive demands and stresses of everyday life.

These biological abnormalities exert a major influence on the psychic state and psychological capacities of the person with schizophrenia. During periods of heightened activation and/or psychosis, arousal dyscontrol leads to pervasive anxiety and tension, often described as a sense of impending doom. This can become fearfulness, then terror, then suspiciousness, and can end in delusional thinking and fixed delusional beliefs. Sufferers complain of difficulties focusing their attention. They say that minor distractions seem larger, more intense, and pressing than when they were well. Everyday experience becomes subject to hundreds of extraneous stimuli, which cannot be ignored, but which also cannot be processed, integrated, and used to guide adaptive behavior. Perception is altered, leading to distorted and often very intense visual sensations and louder, hard-to-ignore auditory experiences. These can lead to frank hallucinations. Thinking becomes more fragmented, and is less under conscious control. As arousal increases, attention deteriorates, and anxiety and arousal rise further, often with psychosis as the result. This process can only be interrupted by medication or by unusually supportive social support and isolation from stimuli, or, preferably, both combined.

In the aftermath of a psychotic episode, as negative symptoms predominate, there is less conscious thought altogether. It remains at a more rudimentary, concrete level, without affective meaning or expression. Motivation diminishes and *le grand indifference* becomes the substitute for desire and concern. Capacities for problem solving, sequencing of behavior and action, planning, and even self-care are increasingly impaired. Emotional interaction becomes bland or anxiety-provoking, and engendering of fearfulness or suspiciousness. The ability to recognize emotional states in others is lost, reducing the appropriateness of emotional responses. All these cognitive deficits result in a significant loss of social skills and in difficulties in working. The result is social withdrawal and cognitive disability that can become as enduring as it is pervasive. As stresses impose themselves, the process can begin again, traversing prodromal symptoms, mild then severe psychotic experiences, agitation, and loss of behavioral control, and then on again into the deficit state. Recent evidence strongly points to increasing negative symptoms, disability, and reduced responsiveness to antipsychotic treatment with each episode, and probably with each day spent in a psychotic state.

What cannot be forgotten in our increased understanding of the linkages between biology and psychology is that the psychotic experience also occurs to an individual human being, whose unique personality and prior experience will also influence how much control he or she gains over the illness. In particular, outcome will be influenced by the person's desire to regain sanity and stability and his or her resilience in the attempt to retain and rebuild social relationships and a career.

The less that psychotic symptoms and experiences totally replace the personality and erode intellectual abilities, the greater the chance that the process of recovery will not be undone. Even more important influences to recovery, however, are the ability and willingness to participate in drug and other therapies, and the influence of the immediate environment—social and physical.

Quality of Life and Experienced Burden

The mere existence of mental illness within the family results in changes in structure, and challenges normal functioning and patterns of interaction in many ways. Burdens cited by families, both objective and subjective, include interference with social and leisure activities and daily routine, deterioration of one's own health and mental health—including symptoms such as insomnia, headaches, irritability, and depression—confusion, learned helplessness, and difficulty in communicating with the person with the illness. Tensions inevitably arise from unpredictable behavior, continuing hostility based on symptomatic suspiciousness, and the associated need for supervision. These tensions increase the tendency toward patient relapse and social and vocational dysfunction. As symptoms in the ill person become more pronounced and persistent, family burden increases. Families seem to have the greatest difficulty with negative symptoms, particularly if the person had functioned relatively well prior to onset of illness.

Such responses are complicated by loss, mourning the person who existed before the illness struck, and of what he or she might have become. Burden is partly a function of the number and density of social supports available. An inverse relationship has been observed between (1) satisfaction with the total social network and the degree of burden experienced and (2) network density and burden. Burden is further complicated if family members, including the individual with schizophrenia, deny or fail to accept the illness among family members. Without resources and support, both professional and personal, the intensity of this interaction can contribute to the experience that families describe of being drawn into a bottomless sinkhole.

Expressed Emotion

Research on expressed emotion, initially conducted in Great Britain during the 1950s, focused on the clinical observation that the family atmosphere of some people suffering from schizophrenia was characterized by overstimulation, dominance, overprotection, rejection, criticism, and contradictory messages—language familiar from earlier case studies on mother-child relationships, parenting, and schizophrenia. Data was collected through a lengthy series of semistructured interviews. Since the original work, expressed emotion has typically been measured by a dichotomous summary variable, reflecting either high or low expressed emotion (i.e., presence or absence of criticism and/or overinvolvement) as expressed by relatives concerning the ill family member. The initial findings in Great Britain, and subsequent replication in the United States, suggested that high levels of negative emotion were strongly associated with the exacerbation or relapse of symptoms. This work has been replicated many times over and in many cultures. In an extensive meta-analysis, Bebbington and Kuipers (1994) cite overwhelming evidence, among 25 studies representing 1,346 patients in 12 different countries, for a predictive relationship between high levels of expressed emotion and relapse of schizophrenia.

In some families, it appears that emotional overinvolvement (EOI) by relatives may impede functional progress, especially when greater interpersonal and physical distance between patient and relative is required. While dependency-inducing interaction was considered ubiquitous in families of schizophrenic patients in psychodynamic and family-systems theories of etiology, the experience of the clinicians who have worked within a psychoeducational framework is that this kind of interaction is markedly rare, *after families are reassured and supported in dealing with the illness.* Only one third of families rated high on emotional overinvolvement, and it is usually a reaction to serious symptomatology and functional disability in the patient, or secondary to isolation and relationship difficulties that are nearly inevitable in certain family constellations (e.g., single mothers living with, and caring for, male adult mentally ill children). Further, much overinvolvement can be more reasonably seen as compensation for major deficits in the social and vocational domains. Subsequent research has all but proven that criticism also is elicited in interaction with ill members who manifest high levels of hostility, even though it does not reach the level of clinical symptoms. At present, the most rigorous conclusion is that symptoms elicit expressed emotion, which in turn elicits more symptoms and, eventually, relapse. The principal intervening variables are family members' level of understanding of the nature of the illness, social support, and effective coping methods.

Stigma

For a person labeled with a mental disability, stigma can be associated with a withdrawal of social support, demoralization, and loss of self-esteem, and can have far-reaching effects on daily functioning, particularly in school and the workplace. With the availability of new medications and concomitant emphases on improved functioning and rehabilitation, stigma becomes a more important focal point for intervention. Stigma has a strong, continuing impact on well-being, even though proper diagnoses and treatment have improved symptoms and levels of functioning over time. Research has shown (1) that family members do not automatically feel stigmatized, but often withdraw as if they have been stigmatized, and (2) that friends and more-distant relatives do tend to avoid them because of stigma. Thus, many families may be isolated and stigmatized, and may feel so as well, in combinations that may be complex and variable. In many ways, family responses parallel those of the person with illness. They include withdrawal and isolation on the part of family members, which in turn are associated with a decrease in social network size and emotional support, increased burden, and decreased quality of life. Self-imposed stigma and labeling change family identity and contribute to lowered self-efficacy and increased burden. In some recent studies, relatives tried to conceal their family member's illness from friends, while in an older survey, very little concealment or shame was reported. The difference appears to relate to chronicity. This fits with clinical experience, in which relatives of younger patients may feel more shame and personal stigma than those of older patients. However, stigma on the part of friends and more distant relatives may play a role in the shrinking-network phenomenon. Stigma experienced by family members is associated with overinvolvement with the patient, but only in the presence of a smaller social network. From these and other studies it appears that experienced stigma is not universal among family members, but it may be important as a factor in shaping the social network, on the one hand, and relationships and interaction within the family, on the other.

Social Networks, Social Support, and Families

Family members of the most severely ill patients are isolated, preoccupied with, and burdened by, the ill member of the family. Brown, Birley, & Wing, (1972) noted that 90 percent of the families with high expressed emotion were small and socially isolated. Isolation of family members correlates with emotional overinvolvement and with their own experiences and sense of having been stigmatized by friends, neighbors, and relatives. Family network size diminishes with length of illness. Families report having withdrawn from their own social circles, and vice versa. The evidence across several severe and chronic illnesses indicates that ongoing access to social contact and support prevents the deterioration of such conditions and improves their course. Social support buffers the impact of adverse life events and improves the quality of life of mentally ill adults living in the community. Subjective burden experienced by relatives is related to severity of stressors, social support, and coping capabilities, while successful community tenure and coping capabilities were in themselves shown to be a function of affirming social support, of the density of the social network, and of participation in a support group.

Implications for an Optimal Environment

The psychoeducational approach of Carol Anderson and her colleagues at the University of Pittsburgh advanced treatment outcomes by linking a biological understanding of schizophrenia with a design for the social and physical environment that specifically compensates for many of the disorder's vulnerabilities and deficits (Anderson, Reiss, & Hogarty, 1986). This has proven to be an especially acceptable approach for families and patients, while proving itself to be a powerful means of fostering adaptation to community life and guiding rehabilitation. Newer treatment methods induce longer periods between episodes; negative symptoms decrease slowly but steadily, and functional capacities and some degree of mental liveliness and ability to work and study return over time. Several clinical strategies have emerged as critical to achieving that outcome.

- To compensate for difficulty in regulating arousal, the people closest to the susceptible person need to create a relatively quiet, calm, and emotionally warm environment.
- They can attempt to protect against sudden intrusions, confrontational conversations, arousing entertainment, and simultaneous and multiple kinds of sensory input.
- To help with information-processing difficulties, conversations should be shorter, less complex, and focused on everyday topics.

- Complexity in the environment and stressful life events will overwhelm cognitive capacities; these need to be protected against and buffered as much as possible.

- The optimal emotional tone is in the middle range; not intense, and especially not negative, but also not overly distant, cold, or rigid.

- To compensate for delusions, family and friends are encouraged to change the subject and not dwell on delusional ideas, but rather focus on less-stressful topics.

- Sensory overload can be avoided by these same means, and also by, for example, reducing background noise, keeping light levels moderate, and having only one conversation going at a time.

- Negative symptoms can moderate with time, but not under conditions of high stress; rehabilitation should be carried out in small, careful steps, using reductions in negative and positive symptoms as indicators of safety and success.

- There is a biological and psychological relapse recovery process that cannot be accelerated without risking another relapse, or at least stalling progress toward functional recovery; slow, careful, and steady rehabilitation can achieve remarkable degrees of functional improvement without relapse.

- Time is on the side of recovery, rather than an enemy that leads inevitably toward deterioration.

- Stresses and demands should be taken seriously, and steps toward recovery paced, to keep stress below the threshold for symptom exacerbation.

Experience has shown that different families can use and understand different parts of this overall strategy, generally needing assistance and ongoing problem solving to put them into practice. Although the knowledge requirements for each family seem to be unique, the overriding message is universal, essential, and powerful in its therapeutic impact: this is a complex, serious, and ultimately biologically based disorder that can be ameliorated by those who know and care about the person affected, when their effort is combined with optimal drug therapy and psychosocial rehabilitation.

THE ROOTS OF FAMILY PSYCHOEDUCATION AND MULTIFAMILY GROUPS

Family psychoeducation is a method for working with families, other caregivers, and friends who are providing support to persons with severe mental illness. Based on a family-consumer-professional partnership, it combines providing clear, accurate information about mental illness with training in problem solving, communication skills, coping skills, and developing social supports. The goals are both to markedly improve outcomes and quality of life for the person affected by illness and to reduce family stress and strain. It builds on and combines the complementary expertise and experience of family members, consumers, and professionals to develop coping skills that lay the foundation for mastery and recovery. Family psychoeducation has been found to improve outcomes in schizophrenia and bipolar disorder to the same degree as medication in a large number of research studies. For that reason, it should be applied as widely as medication in severe mental illness, when there is a family member available. This approach is particularly beneficial in the early years of the course of a mental illness, when improvements can have a dramatic and long-term effect, and while family members are still involved and open to participation. As well, consumers who experience frequent hospitalizations or prolonged unemployment and families who are especially exasperated and confused about the illness benefit substantially and often dramatically.

Family psychoeducation originated from several sources in the late 1970s. Perhaps the leading influence was the growing realization that conventional family therapy, in which family dysfunction is assumed and becomes the target of intervention for the alleviation of symptoms, proved to be at least ineffective and perhaps damaging to patient and family well-being. As efforts to develop and apply family therapy to schizophrenia and other psychotic disorders waned, awareness grew, especially among family members themselves and their rapidly growing advocacy organizations, that living with an illness such as schizophrenia is difficult and confusing for patients and families alike. It became increasingly clear that, under these circumstances, a well-functioning family has to possess the available knowledge about the illness itself and the coping skills specific to a particular disorder—skills that are counterintuitive and only nascent in most families. It is unrealistic to expect families to understand such a mystifying condition and to know what to do about it on their own. Given that perspective, the most adaptive family was increasingly seen to be the one that has access to information, with the implication that the treatment system is a crucial source of that information. As to coping skills, many families develop methods of dealing with positive (psychotic) and negative (functional and cognitive deficits, such as flattened affect, loss of energy and apathy) symptoms, functional disabilities, and the desperation of their ill relatives through painful trial and error. These successes, however, are rare. A critical need is that families have access to each other to learn of other families' successes and failures, and to establish a repertoire of coping strategies that are closely tailored to the disorder and to the individual person. Further, family members and significant others often provide emotional and instrumental support, case management functions, financial assistance, advocacy, and housing to their relative with mental illness. Doing so can be rewarding, but poses considerable burdens. Family members often find that access to needed resources and information is lacking.

Even with this new perspective, it took over 10 years for interest and effort in involving families in the treatment of schizophrenia to be revived, and then it emerged with an entirely different ideology. Investigators began to recognize the crucial, supportive role families played in outcome after an acute episode of schizophrenia, and endeavored to engage families collaboratively, sharing illness information, suggesting behaviors that promote recuperation, and teaching coping strategies that reduce their sense of burden. The group of interventions that emerged became known as family psychoeducation. The approach recognizes that schizophrenia is a brain disorder that is usually only partially remediable by medication, and that families can have a significant effect on their relative's recovery. Thus, the psychoeducational approach shifted away from attempting to get families to change their disturbed communication patterns, toward educating and persuading families that how they behave toward the patient can facilitate or impede recovery by compensating for deficits and sensitivities specific to the various psychotic disorders. For example, a family might interfere with recuperation if, in their natural enthusiasm to promote and support progress, they create unreasonable demands and expectations; but the same family could have a dramatically positive effect on recovery by gradually increasing expectations and supporting an incremental return of functioning.

Research conducted over the last decade has supported the development of evidence-based practice guidelines for addressing family members' needs for information, clinical guidance, and ongoing support. This research has demonstrated that meeting the needs of family members also dramatically improves patient outcomes, while improving family well-being. Several models have evolved to address the needs of family members: individual family consultation; professionally-led family psychoeducation (Falloon, Boyd, & McGill, 1984; Anderson, Reiss, & Hogarty, 1986), in single-family and multifamily group formats (McFarlane, 2002); various forms of more traditional family therapies (Marsh, 2001); and a range of professionally led models of short-term family education (Amenson, 1998), sometimes referred to as therapeutic education. There are also family-led information and support classes or groups such as those of the National Alliance for the Mentally Ill (NAMI; Pickett-Schenk, Cook, & Laris, 2000). Of these models, family psychoeducation has a deep enough research and dissemination base to be considered an evidenced-based practice. The descriptor "psychoeducation" can be misleading; family psychoeducation includes many cognitive, behavioral, and supportive therapeutic elements, often utilizes a consultative framework, and shares key characteristics with some types of family therapy.

Professionally led psychoeducational models are offered as part of a treatment plan for the consumer, and are usually diagnosis-specific. The models differ significantly in format (e.g., multiple-family, single-family, relatives-only, combined), structure (involvement/exclusion of consumer), duration and intensity of treatment, and setting (hospital/clinic, home). They place variable emphasis on didactic, emotional, cognitive-behavioral, clinical, rehabilitative, and systemic techniques. Most have focused first on consumer outcomes, although family understanding and well-being are assumed to be necessary to achieve those outcomes. All focus on family resiliency and strengths. Several models have been developed to address the needs and concerns of families of persons with mental illness, including: behavioral family management, family psychoeducation, psychoeducational multifamily groups, relatives' groups, family consultation, and professionally led models of short-term family education (therapeutic education).

Although the existing models of family intervention may appear to have substantial differences, a significant consensus about critical elements of this kind of treatment emerged in 1999, under the encouragement of the leaders of the World Schizophrenia Fellowship (1998). Leff, Falloon, and McFarlane developed the original consensus, which was then refined and ratified by many recognized clinical researchers working in this field. The process involved selection of the key components, developing a consensus based first on empirical evidence, and then on a consensus as to what each component actually represented. The resulting consensus regarding elements of family intervention that are critical to achieving the empirically validated outcomes reported can be summarized as follows.

Goals for Working with Families

To achieve the best possible outcome for the individual with mental illness, through treatment and management that involves collaboration among professionals, families, and patients.

To alleviate suffering among the members of the family by supporting them in their efforts to foster their loved one's recovery.

Principles for Working with Families

The models of treatment that are supported with demonstrated effectiveness require clinicians working with families to:

- Coordinate all elements of treatment and rehabilitation to ensure that everyone is working toward the same goals in a collaborative, supportive relationship
- Pay attention to the social as well as the clinical needs of the patient
- Provide optimum medication management
- Listen to families and treat them as equal partners in treatment planning and delivery
- Explore family members' expectations for the treatment program and for the patient
- Assess the family's strengths and limitations in their ability to support the patient
- Help resolve family conflict through sensitive response to emotional distress
- Address feelings of loss
- Provide relevant information for patient and family at appropriate times
- Provide an explicit crisis plan and a professional response
- Help improve communication among family members
- Provide training for the family in structured problem-solving techniques
- Encourage the family to expand their social support networks, for example, participation in multifamily groups and/or family support organizations, such as the National Alliance for the Mentally Ill
- Be flexible in meeting the needs of the family
- Provide the family with easy access to a professional, if needed, if the work with the family ceases

COMMON ELEMENTS OF ALL EMPIRICALLY VALIDATED FAMILY PSYCHOEDUCATIONAL APPROACHES

All evidence-based family intervention models share similar core components. These components are necessary to achieve the results described in the literature, and which justify the effort expended. As we will note in the section on research and outcomes, it appears that models that incorporate all of these elements succeed, while those that do not include them have little or no clinical results. The partial exception is family-delivered education-only programs, which have been shown to improve family well-being by reducing sense of burden and improving understanding and ability to cope. The core elements include joining with family and patient, education, problem-solving, interactional change, and multifamily contact. In this section, these basic methods are described in detail, to give the reader a sense of how each is conducted and how they relate to the issues, clinical and family-based, that the overall process addresses. Again, this is the approach that has garnered the most empirical support for efficacy and has been proven effective in many contexts, in the United States and internationally.

The psychoeducational model consists of four stages that roughly correspond to the phases of an episode of schizophrenia, from the acute phase through the slow recuperative and rehabilitation phases. This framework is based on the approach developed by Anderson and her colleagues (Anderson, Reiss, & Hogarty, 1986).

Joining

This stage refers to a way of working with families that is characterized by collaboration in attempting to understand and relate to the family. The joining phase is typically three to five sessions, and is the same in both single- and multifamily formats. The goals of this phase are the following:

- Establish a working alliance with both the family members and the consumer
- Acquaint oneself with any family issues and problems that might contribute to stress, either for the consumer or for the family
- Determine the prodromal signs of relapse and the precipitants specific to the ill member of the family
- Learn the family's strengths, social support, and resources for dealing with the illness
- Instill hope and an orientation toward recovery
- Create a contract with mutual and attainable goals

Joining, in its most general sense, continues throughout the treatment, since it is always the responsibility of the clinician to remain an available resource for the family, as well as to be their advocate in dealing with any other clinical or rehabilitation service necessitated by the illness of their relative. To foster this relationship, the clinician has the following responsibilities:

- Demonstrates genuine concern for the consumer
- Acknowledges the family's loss and grants them sufficient time and support to mourn
- Is available to the family and consumer outside of the formal sessions
- Avoids treating the family as a patient or blaming them in any way

- Helps to focus on the present crisis
- Serves as a source of information about the illness

Educational and Training Workshop

After joining is completed among all families, they are invited to attend workshop sessions conducted in a formal, classroom-like atmosphere. Biological, psychological, and social information about schizophrenia (or other disorders, as the case may be) and its management are presented through a variety of formats, such as videotapes, slide presentations, lectures, discussion, and question and answer periods. In some situations, the education is done in single-family format and can be done in the family's home. Information about the way in which the clinician and the family will continue to work together is also presented. Typically six to eight hours in length, the workshop is attended by several families at a time. The opportunity to interact with other families in similar situations greatly enhances the power of this portion of the intervention. The families are also introduced to the guidelines for management of the illness. These consist of a set of behavioral instructions for family members that integrate the biological, psychological, and social aspects of the disorder with recommended responses, those that help maintain a home environment that minimizes relapse-inducing stress.

Community Reentry

Regularly biweekly scheduled meetings focus on planning and implementing strategies to cope with the vicissitudes of a person recovering from an acute episode. Major content areas include the effects and side effects of medication, common issues about taking medication as prescribed, helping the consumer avoid the use of street drugs and/or alcohol, lowering of expectations during the period of negative symptoms, and an increase in tolerance for these symptoms. Two special techniques are introduced to participating members as supports to the efforts to follow family guidelines: formal problem solving, and communications skills training (Falloon, 1984). The application of either one of these techniques characterizes each session. Further, each session follows a prescribed, task-oriented format or paradigm, designed to enhance family coping effectiveness and to strengthen the alliance among family member, consumer, and the clinician. The reentry and rehabilitation phases are addressed using formal problem-solving methods and communication skills training. The problem-solving method is described more fully in the section on multifamily groups. The principal difference is that in single-family sessions, the participants and the recipients of ideas are the same, so that family members most commonly develop new approaches to their problems by brainstorming among themselves.

Communication Skills Training

Communication skills training (Falloon & Boyd, 1984) is a set of skills developed to address the cognitive difficulties often experienced by consumers with severe mental illnesses, especially those with a psychotic phase. The core goal is to teach family members and the consumer new methods of interacting that acknowledge and hopefully counteract the effects of mental illness on the consumer's information-processing abilities and marked sensitivity to negative emotion and stimulation. The key skills include: communication of positive and negative feelings for specific positive or negative behavior, and attentive listening behavior when discussing problems of other important family issues. The approach involves rehearsing communication skills in the session, modeling by the clinician, repeated rehearsal, and finally, homework to assist generalizing the skills learned to other contexts.

Social and Vocational Rehabilitation

Approximately 9 to 18 months following an acute episode, most consumers begin to demonstrate signs of a return to spontaneity and active engagement with those around them. This is usually the sign that the negative symptoms are diminishing; the consumer can now be offered more challenges toward achieving his or her own goals. The focus of this phase deals specifically with the rehabilitative needs of the consumer, addressing the two areas of functioning in which there are the most common deficits: social skills, and the ability to get and maintain employment. The sessions are used to role-play situations that are likely to cause stress for the consumer if entered into unprepared. Family members are actively used to assist in various aspects of this training endeavor. Additionally, the family is assisted in rebuilding its own network of family and friends, which has usually been weakened as a consequence of the illness. Regular sessions are conducted on a once- or twice-monthly basis, although more contact may be necessary at particularly stressful times.

PSYCHOEDUCATIONAL MULTIFAMILY GROUPS

The Multifamily Group as a Therapeutic Social Network

The psychoeducational multiple family group (PMFG) is a treatment approach that brings together aspects of family psychoeducation, family behavioral, and multiple-family approaches. As such, it is a second-generation treatment model that incorporates the advantages of each of its sources, diminishes their negative features, and leads to a number of synergistic effects that enhance efficacy. Building on the single-family psychoeducational family approach of Anderson, Reiss, and Hogarty, (1986) and the single-family behavioral management approach of Falloon and his colleagues, the model reflects contemporary understanding of schizophrenia and other severe mental illnesses, from biological, psychological, and social perspectives. The assumption is that an effective treatment should address as many known aspects of the illness as possible, at all relevant system levels.

Families attempting to cope with a relative who has schizophrenia or another severe mental illness are likely to experience a variety of stresses, which make this experience quite difficult to manage. These processes include social isolation, stigmatization, and increased financial and psychological burden. Multiple family groups address these issues directly, by increasing the size and richness of the social support network, by connecting the family to other families like themselves, by providing a forum for mutual aid, and by providing an opportunity to hear the experiences of others who have had similar experiences and have found workable solutions.

Many clinicians have observed that specific characteristics of the multiple family group have therapeutic effects on a number of social and clinical management problems commonly encountered in schizophrenia and other severe mental illnesses. A critical goal of all family psychoeducational and behavioral models is to reduce family-expressed emotion, and thereby to reduce the risk of psychotic relapse. The PMFG approach goes beyond this focus on expressed emotion to address social isolation, stress, and stigma as experienced by families and consumers alike. That appears to be key to better overall outcomes, because families attempting to cope with mental illness inevitably experience a variety of stresses, which secondarily put them at risk of manifesting exasperation and discouragement, as natural reactions.

Multiple family groups address these issues directly by the following:

- Increasing the size and complexity of the social network
- Reducing relatives' sense of stigma and shame
- Bringing a given family into regular contact with other families like themselves
- Providing a forum for mutual aid
- Sharing burdens and reducing the sense of burden
- Expanding the range of possible problem solutions
- Providing an opportunity to hear the experiences of others who have had similar experiences and found workable solutions
- Building hope through mutual example and experience

In addition, PMFGs reiterate and reinforce the information learned in educational and skills training workshops. Coupled with formal problem solving, the group experience serves to enhance the family's available coping skills for the many problems encountered in the course of the consumer's recovery.

Overview of the PMFG Method

The general character of the approach can be summarized as consisting of three components, roughly corresponding to the phases of the group. In the first phase, the content of the model follows that described previously, with its emphasis on joining with each family in a single-family format to build a collaborative alliance with family members, conducting an educational workshop, and focusing on preventing relapse for a year or so after discharge from an acute hospitalization or during a period of outpatient treatment. Unlike the single-family psychoeducational approach, the format for treatment after the workshop is a multifamily group. The second phase involves moving beyond stability to gradual increases in consumers' community functioning, a process that uses PMFG-based problem solving as the primary means for accomplishing social and vocational rehabilitation. This occurs, roughly, during the second year of the PMFG. The third phase consists of deliberate efforts to mold the group into a social network that can persist for an extended period and satisfy family and consumer needs for social contact, support, and ongoing clinical monitoring. This format is also an efficient context in which to continue psychopharmacologic treatment and routine case management. Expansion of the families' social networks occurs through problem solving, direct emotional support, and out-of-group socializing, all involving members of different families in the group. The multifamily group treatment approach is briefly described subsequently, and is detailed in the volume that constitutes the treatment manual for this approach—*Multifamily Groups in the Treatment of Severe Psychiatric Disorders* (McFarlane, 2002).

Joining

The intervention begins with a minimum of three single-family engagement sessions, in which one of the group leaders meets with each individual family. These are accompanied by separate meetings with the ill member of the family. The choice of including the consumer is partly a matter of clinical stability and partly a matter of choice by consumer and family members. For both philosophical and practical reasons, treatment plans are based on the consumer's and family's stated goals and desires. Joining should occur within 48 hours after an admission to a hospital or very soon after a crisis; it can occur at any time that a consumer or family could benefit from this approach. Joining can occur as outpatient care, with equal success as a way to take the next step in treatment, particularly vocational rehabilitation, community, and social connections. The coleaders of the PMFGs divide the responsibility for joining with half of the families who will make up the group. The timing of the joining sessions should occur before the planned date of the educational workshop. Schedule extra sessions if more than three weeks will pass before the workshop.

The clinician should quickly become identified as a resource to the family in navigating the mental health system. This is an active process of demonstrating commitment to the consumer and the family. This may occur by assisting with a concrete task, such as completing an application, placing a referral or call, or getting information regarding treatment concerns. Often, if clinicians are experiencing consumer or family absences, premature endings or problems, an ineffective joining can be identified. The goals are to establish rapport, be a liaison, and build a collaborative alliance of complementary expertise and strengths.

Each joining session begins with and ends with socialization, which helps to decrease the family's anxiety, cement relationships, and provide a source of information and interests outside the illness. The clinician is open and forthcoming about who he or she is as a person, at the same time taking an interest in each family member apart from their involvement with the illness. One way this principle is realized in joining is through the socializing built into each session; that is continued in the multiple family groups. During joining sessions, and throughout all the stages of treatment the clinician needs to be confident in what he or she knows about the illness, and also respectful of what the family knows and has experienced first hand. If the clinician does not know the answer to a question, he or she acknowledges ignorance, and assures the consumer and his or her supporters that the information will be sought out. Most caregivers have felt blamed and criticized by the traditional assessment questions that search for failure and pathology. In this model, the clinician emphasizes empowering family members with information and coping skills, and supporting their knowledge about and use of resources.

Whenever relevant during the joining stage, the clinician shares information about schizophrenia (or other severe mental illness) and the process and effectiveness of family-inclusive treatment. As soon as possible, the clinician explains that schizophrenia is an illness of the brain, not one that is caused by the family or the consumer. It is also helpful to emphasize that families will be able to reduce relapses and crises using the information they will learn in the treatment program. Families also need the opportunity to express their feelings of loss, frustration, anger, despair, hopelessness, and guilt. The clinician validates the expression of these feelings and may gently probe for them. When left unexpressed they can form a barrier to a family's finding the energy to learn new ways to manage. Whenever a crisis occurs during this period, for either consumer or family, the clinician deals with it as soon as possible. The clinician can use a crisis as an opportunity to demonstrate willingness to help, especially in concrete ways. From the first meeting the clinician is active in guiding the conversation. There are tasks to be completed in each of the joining sessions, so the clinician needs to be directive and structure the sessions. The structure of the sessions is reassuring; it lets people know what to expect and helps the consumers and families to feel less anxious. Within the structure, the clinician also answers questions and gives advice. Sometimes family members may quarrel or monopolize discussions, or make repetitive complaints. This kind of communication can be interrupted and redirected by acknowledging the person's frustration and concern about the illness. The clinician keeps his or her manner positive, informal, and collegial.

During the first joining sessions the present crisis is reviewed, with particular attention to the early warning signs, how the family has coped, and who or what has been helpful for interventions in the past. This first session is also used to begin the process of delineating each consumer's prodromal symptoms or personal early warning signs. The clinician guides the family through a review of the prior weeks, with emphasis on any changes in the consumer's behavior, thoughts, or feelings during that time. In most cases, there are idiosyncratic behaviors that precede the more common prodromal symptoms, (i.e., poor sleep, anorexia, pacing-restless behaviors, and irritability). These become even more important in the future to assist in preventing relapse. The other tasks for the first or second session are to review how family members have coped and to identify who or what interventions have or have not been helpful. If there is any particular assistance to be provided at the time, and it seems appropriate, the clinician should feel free to offer it.

The second joining session is focused on the impact of the illness on each member of the family. In some cases, this session may be best done in separate sessions, especially if the consumer does not accept that he or she has an illness or problem. Family members may verbalize their feelings of loss, despair, grief, and frustration about coping with the demands of the illness. The leader can offer support, validation, and recognition of these normal human reactions. It is also during this session that the clinician wants to learn about the family's social network, extended supports, and other resources. A genogram, including key friends and neighbors, might also be done during this session. The clinician will also want to learn what the family's experiences have been during past acute episodes, and what has been their experience of the mental health system. During subsequent sessions attention is directed to other areas of personal strength, such as work, hobbies, school, and institutional connections that may offer support. If the consumer is scheduled for discharge from the hospital, the clinician helps the supporters and family plan for this. In the last joining session, a discussion about the goals of treatment should occur. Short-term goals are generally identified as goals to stabilize symptoms; long-term goals usually focus on increasing vocational, academic, and social skill development, all with the eventual goal of recovery.

The clinician prepares the family for the educational workshop, where they will meet the other group members for the first time. It is wise to review the structure and goals for the regular meetings of the multifamily group that will follow. The clinician briefly describes how the group proceeds and what other participants have gained from these groups in regard to new and workable solutions to difficult problems of illness management. The clinician inquires about the participant's experience with groups and what concerns they might have (e.g., confidentiality, shyness, and feeling pressured to speak in groups or the workshop). Participants are assured that they need contribute only as much as they wish. The clinician should feel free to schedule additional sessions as needed to ensure that a good connection and sharing of information has occurred.

Education for Families: A Workshop Format

When five to eight families have completed the engagement process, the clinicians, usually including the consumers' psychiatrist, conduct an educational workshop. The biomedical aspects of the disorder are discussed, after which the clinicians present and discuss guidelines for the family management of both clinical and everyday problems in managing the illness in the family context.

Education is one of the four essential components of family psychoeducation, along with joining, problem solving, and social network expansion. Education consists of sharing information with family, other caretakers, and consumers themselves about the underlying biological and social processes of schizophrenia. The goal is to relieve families of their guilt and anxiety, while the information itself provides the foundation for subsequent treatment and rehabilitation. When families do not have information about the illness, they tend to adopt the beliefs of their own families, culture, or community. While they may have the best interests of the person with illness in mind, their actions may actually interfere with recovery, since many of the most effective interpersonal and rehabilitative approaches are counterintuitive. Therefore, providing concerned families the information and guidance that they need is crucial in promoting recovery and rehabilitation. The message for families is: *Schizophrenia is a very difficult illness for families to live with, but it will become easier if we to learn how to manage it.* It is especially important that families understand that they did not cause the illness. Another critical aspect of family education is that it gives families hope that they will be able to alter the course of illness. As the educational process continues with families, they see increasing evidence of their own effectiveness. As the consumers improve, they join in the process as partners. They become interested in the information and in achieving their own rehabilitative goals.

The key content areas include the following:

- The seriousness of the disorder
- The role of stress in precipitating episodes
- Early signs of relapse
- Symptoms, especially the negative variety
- The basics of brain function and dysfunction in schizophrenia (or other mental illnesses)
- How psychiatric medications affect brain function and cause side effects
- How severe mental illness in one member affects entire families
- Effective coping strategies and illness-management techniques
- The causes and general prognosis of the illness
- The psychoeducational treatment process itself

Psychoeducation is an opportunity for families to begin learning to cope with, and improve the outcome of, schizophrenia and other major mental illnesses. However, those solutions must fit the family's individual history and style. The challenge for clinicians is to adapt the educational process for each participant, and tailor it as much as possible to the actual participants. The presentations should be empathic as well as informative. Clinicians should use group leadership skills to elicit comments and experiences from the audience, in a manner that invites, but does not obligate, participants to respond. The leaders present in an open, collegial manner, encouraging families to comfortably ask questions. Families will discover that their experiences and problems are similar. The workshop should be organized in a classroom format, which tends to promote a more neutral atmosphere. If necessary, discussions can also be continued, either after the workshop or during a meeting of the multifamily group.

Family Guidelines

The Family Guidelines are based on the specific effects of schizophrenia on consumers and families; they were originally developed by Anderson and her colleagues (Anderson, Reiss, & Hogarty, 1986). Each person present at the workshop should have a copy of the Family Guidelines that they can refer to as the clinicians review them, one by one. This will not be the first time families have heard about the guidelines, but it is first time they will be fully discussed. Clinicians take turns reading a guideline, connecting it to the biological information discussed previously, and asking family members for their reactions, questions, and experiences.

Here's a list of things everyone can do to help make things run more smoothly:

1. *Go slow.* Recovery takes time. Rest is important. Things will get better in their own time.

2. *Keep it cool.* Enthusiasm is normal. Tone it down. Disagreement is normal. Tone it down, too.

3. *Give each other space.* Time out is important for everyone. It's okay to reach out. It's okay to say "no."

4. *Set limits.* Everyone needs to know what the rules are. A few good rules keep things clear.

5. *Ignore what you can't change.* Let some things slide. Don't ignore violence.

6. *Keep it simple.* Say what you have to say clearly, calmly, and positively.

7. *Follow doctor's orders.* Take medications as they are prescribed. Take only medications that are prescribed.

8. *Carry on business as usual.* Reestablish family routines as quickly as possible. Stay in touch with family and friends.

9. *No street drugs or alcohol.* They make symptoms worse, can cause relapse, and prevent recovery.

10. *Pick up on early signs.* Note changes. Consult with your family.

11. *Solve problems step by step.* Make changes gradually. Work on one thing at a time.

12. *Lower expectations—temporarily.* Use a personal yardstick. Compare this month to last month rather than last year or next year.

The workshop should end on a positive note. The clinicians should make sure that families feel their optimism about this approach. It is helpful to give examples of how life improves for the consumer and family with this process. The clinicians should outline the format for multifamily groups, emphasizing the problem-solving method and its usefulness for families and consumers. The agenda for the first two meetings is presented, and any questions about the multifamily group are addressed. Group members should know how to contact the clinicians in case they have questions or crises between sessions. The group cofacilitators should remind families that improvement will occur very slowly and to be patient: "Slow and steady wins the race" should be a theme. Finally, family members should be invited to talk about their reactions to the workshop.

Process and Techniques for PMFGs

The Format of the First and Second Sessions

The first meeting of the ongoing psychoeducational multifamily group follows the workshop by one or two weeks; its format includes a biweekly meeting schedule, 1 1/2 hour session length, leadership by two clinicians, and participation by five to eight consumers and their families. In most instances, the decision to have a given consumer attend is based upon his or her mental status and susceptibility to the stimulation such a group may engender. If the consumer wants to attend, that weights the decision in favor of inclusion. The format of the sessions is closely controlled by the clinician, following a standard paradigm. From this point forward, consumers are strongly encouraged to attend and to actively participate.

The task of the clinicians, particularly at the beginning, is to adopt a businesslike tone and approach that promotes a calm, supportive, and accepting group climate, oriented toward learning new coping skills and engendering hope.

During the first two multifamily group sessions, the goal is to quickly establish a partnership among all participants. The initial sessions are intended to build group identity and a sense of mutual shared interest, before going on to discuss clinical and rehabilitation issues. This approach promotes interfamily and interpersonal social support. Many previous approaches to multiple family therapy emphasized expressing feelings, and often promoted negative emotional interactions among group members. These spontaneous initial interactions can spark conflict between family members, disagreement between families about the purpose of the group, and anger or confrontation with the leaders. People with schizophrenia and other serious mental illnesses often become overwhelmed, and subsequently retire from the group before they achieve any benefits. Since successful outcomes depend on at least one member of each family participating in the group for 1 to 2 years, it is important to avoid dropouts. Solving problems in the group depends on ideas being shared and accepted across family boundaries, so it is best to proceed slowly and take the time to develop trust and empathy.

People need an opportunity to get to know one another apart from the illness. The first and second group sessions are designed to help the participants and cofacilitators learn about each other and bond as a group. People in PMFGs are encouraged to also talk about topics unrelated to the illness, such as their personal likes, dislikes, and daily activities. The first two sessions are especially important in this regard. To succeed, the coleaders act as a good host or hostess, one who makes introductions, points out common interests, and guides conversations to more personal subjects, such as personal histories, leisure activities, work, and hobbies. As well, the leaders act as role models; they should be prepared to share a personal story of their own. The facilitators guide the conversation to topics of general interest, such as where people live, where they were born and grew up, what kind of work people do (both inside and outside the home), hobbies, and so on. The guiding principles for this session are validation and positive reinforcement.

The second group session focuses more on how the mental illness has changed the lives of the people in the group. The cofacilitators should state clearly that the theme of the evening is "how mental illness has changed our lives." This session is intended to quickly develop a sense of a common experience: of having a major mental illness or having a relative with a disorder. The mood of this session is usually less lighthearted than the previous session, but it is the basis for the emergence of a strong group identity and of a sense of relief. The leaders begin with socializing, encouraging participation by modeling, pointing out connections between people and topics, and asking questions. After socializing, the clinicians proceed to the topic for this meeting. The leaders share as much as possible about their own professional and personal experiences, sharing a story about a friend or family member with mental illness, or talking about how they became interested in their work. Some individuals may find it difficult to talk about their experiences. People can say as much or as little as they wish. Point out any similarities among group member's experiences. This group meeting may be the first time some families realize that they are not alone. Compared to the first meeting, the mood of this meeting is often sad, and there may be anger and frustration expressed as well. In closing, the leaders also remind group members that during future meetings everyone will be working on solving problems like the ones expressed in this meeting, and that similar issues have been successfully dealt with in previous groups. It is important to be optimistic and send people home with the sense that the group can help them. There should be ten minutes or so to socialize before concluding the group.

The Problem-Solving Process

The problem-solving portion of the psychoeducational multifamily group is the essence of the process. Many individuals and families have expressed dissatisfaction with groups in general, due to high levels of emotion and low levels of perceived relevance or helpfulness. The problem-solving aspect of the PMFG responds to those concerns. It is in this portion of the group that patients, families, and clinicians begin to make clear gains against the ravages of the illness, in a planned and methodical manner. The goal of the multifamily group is not just to have the group's help to solve these problems. Rather, it is to provide individuals and families with an ongoing means to manage the symptoms of the illness beyond the group itself.

The multifamily group's primary working method is to help each family and consumer to apply the family guidelines to their specific problems and circumstances. This work proceeds in phases, whose timing is linked to the clinical condition of the consumers. The actual procedure uses a multifamily, group-based problem-solving method adapted from the single-family version by Falloon, Boyd, & McGill (1983). Families are taught to use this method in the multifamily group, as a group function. It is the core of the multifamily group approach, one that is acceptable to families, remarkably effective, and nicely tuned to the low-intensity and deliberate style that is essential to working with the specific sensitivities of people with psychotic disorders.

To facilitate community reentry, the multifamily group maintains stability by systematically applying the group problem-solving method, case-by-case, to difficulties in implementing the family guidelines and fostering recovery. The subsequent rehabilitation phase should be initiated by consumers who have achieved clinical stability by successfully completing this community reentry phase. As stability increases, the multifamily group functions in a role unique among psychosocial rehabilitation models; it operates as an auxiliary to the in vivo social and vocational rehabilitation effort being conducted by the clinical team. The central emphasis during this phase is the involvement of both group and family members in helping each consumer to begin a gradual, step-by-step resumption of responsibility and socializing. The clinicians continue to use problem solving and brainstorming in the PMFG to identify and find jobs and social contacts with the consumers and to find new ways to enrich their social lives. This process prepares the way for the consumer to go on to work on recovery, which occupies much of the third phase.

Each session of the PMFG begins and ends with a period of purely social chat, facilitated by the leaders. The purpose is to give the consumers and even some families the opportunity to recapture and practice any social skills they may have lost due to their long isolation and exposure to high levels of stress. Following the socializing, the clinicians specifically inquire as to the status of each family, offering advice based on the family guidelines or direct assistance, when it can be done readily. A single problem that has been identified by any one family is then selected, and the group as a whole participates in problem solving. This problem is the focus of an entire session, during which all members of the group contribute suggestions and ideas. The affected family then reviews the relative advantages and disadvantages, with some input from other families and clinicians. Typically, the most attractive of the proposed solutions is reformulated as an appropriate task for trying at home, and is assigned to the family. This step is then followed by another final period of socializing. This group format continues for most of the duration of the work, but is sometimes interspersed with visiting speakers, problem solving focused on generic issues facing several families and/or consumers, and celebrations of steps toward recovery, holidays, and birthdays.

PMFG Techniques for Problem Solving

This six-step approach helps breaks down problems into a manageable form, so that a solution can be implemented in stages, usually with more success. One of the clinicians leads the group through the six steps. The other ensures group participation, monitors the overall process, and suggests additional solutions. After a recorder is chosen, the clinicians follow each step of the problem-solving group format.

Defining the Problem

Defining the problem, while sometimes viewed as a rather simple process, is often the most difficult step in the PMFG process. If the problem is not properly defined, individuals, families, and clinicians become frustrated, and may be convinced that the problem cannot be solved. Common difficulties that groups experience in this aspect of the process are choosing a problem that is too large or too general, defining the problem in an unacceptable way for a participant, and defining the problem as the person with the problem.

> **TIP:** Most issues presented by the group members are perceived as not solvable. These are often longstanding problems that have resisted all attempts to make them better. Group members seldom have much hope that things will get dramatically better. With this in mind, facilitators should approach problem solving based on the Family Guidelines: go slow; keep things cool; set limits; keep it simple, and solve problems step-by-step. When things do indeed change, facilitators must help group members recognize the benefits of the PMFG process in resolving these issues.

The problem-solving process begins in the "go-around." The leaders address each issue presented individually, avoiding the temptation to combine similar concerns of group members. After each person has had an opportunity to "check in" about their perceptions of difficulties with the illness, the facilitators review the issues presented, to determine which will be the focus of the group's efforts. Once a problem has been defined in a way that is acceptable to each member of the family, the clinician asks the recorder to write it down and read it back to the group. The clinicians need to consider carefully any report of actual or potential exacerbation of symptoms. Areas of particular significance are safety, incorporating the Family Guidelines, issues concerning medications and substance use, life events, and disagreement among family members as to how to assist the ill member. In order to decide which problem to work on, the clinicians ask detailed questions to clarify the problem (e.g., "What is the current undesired situation?"; "When was the problem first noticed?"; "When does it occur? How often? In what situations?"), focusing on behavioral aspects as much as possible. Check in with the individual who raised this issue to be sure that the group truly understands their perception of the issue, including, "What will things look like when they are better?" The scale of problems, at least in the first few months of the group, is also a factor in selecting the problem. For instance, longstanding or previously intractable problems should only be addressed if they can be broken down into more solvable subproblems. Leaders may choose to select simpler problems early in the group, so that the members learn the method, gain trust in each other, and achieve a few successes.

TIP: In the discussion of which issue to address, it is important to stress to the group that the goal is to teach a problem-definition/problem-solving skill, and that, with practice, group members will refine that skill. It is also important to say something like, "Although the problem chosen may not be the problem of a particular individual or family, it is likely that this problem has been of concern to other members or will be experienced over the course of the group." It is also important to say that, "Over the course of the group everyone's issues will be addressed."

TIP: Group members benefit from hearing facilitators discuss the issues presented. Listening to the facilitators "thinking out loud" helps the group members learn how to simplify, clarify, and prioritize concerns.

Generating Possible Solutions

The group members are then asked to offer whatever solutions they think may be helpful. The leaders should stress that it is important to resist evaluating or discussing solutions, since doing so dramatically reduces the number of solutions presented. After all solutions have been presented, facilitators invite group members to share their thoughts on the efficacy of each solution. Each solution is addressed individually, noting the pros and cons after each solution. This allows the group to become active in thinking about possible solutions, even when there are multiple solutions available.

> **TIP:** It is often helpful to say to the group, "It has been our experience that it is difficult to resist the invitation to discuss proposed solutions. However, we have found that doing so means that some solutions are left unspoken. Therefore, we will help the group delay evaluating solutions until after all have been generated." This reminds the group that other groups and individuals have had similar experiences. It also sets the stage for the facilitators to intervene when members find it difficult to resist responding immediately to proposals.

Choosing the Best Solution

When all solutions have been evaluated, facilitators review the list, stressing those with the most positive and fewest negative responses. The whole solution list is then presented to the individuals who provided the issue originally. They are asked which of the solutions they would like to test out for themselves and for the group over the next two weeks. It is important to stress that testing solutions is for the benefit of both the individual and the group, as everyone is looking for things that work.

Implementing the Chosen Solution

Once a solution has been selected, a very detailed, behaviorally oriented plan is developed. Each step is discussed and a person is assigned responsibility for completion of each step. The greater the detail, the better. Some groups offer solutions to all group members to try, asking that the group be informed of their efforts, successes, or lack of success, thus increasing the repertoire of knowledge of the group.

Reviewing Implementation

The individual is reminded that the facilitators may call during the coming week to check on his or her progress and to offer assistance. The individual is also asked to report at the next group meeting how successful he or she was and any obstacles that were encountered.

> **TIP:** Some groups find that time is a factor and decide to streamline or eliminate the evaluation process. They simply move to presenting the solutions to the individual for their review and selection. There is some loss involved here, since valid information as to the efficacy, or lack thereof, of certain solutions may not be presented.

Fitting Family Psychoeducation to the Culture of the Consumer and Family

Working with families requires that the clinician adapt the approach to the culture and unique characteristics of the consumer and his or her family. In a sense, each family is a microculture that needs to be understood and addressed respectfully and with empathy. Doing so when one is from another culture presents another barrier to effectiveness, and adds to the number of considerations that one needs to incorporate into the work. On one hand, there are many ways to offend family members, when one does not know the proper and acceptable ways of interacting that are within a given culture. On the other hand, clinical experience (now on a global basis), has shown unequivocally that mental illness usually overrides cultural factors in determining families' perceived need for help, guidance, and support. Mental illness, in an important sense, creates its own culture, which family psychoeducation is designed to address for consumer and family alike. The result is a general rule: families will usually accept the offer of help and the opportunity to participate actively in the treatment and recovery of their ill member, if the clinician can adapt his or her approach to the culture of the family. One can do so either by being a member of that culture or actively seeking assistance and guidance in learning the key ways of respecting that culture's social norms and mores.

Family psychoeducation (FPE) has been applied in the United States and in many other countries successfully, following this general guideline. For instance, in Falloon's study in Los Angeles, the majority of the families were African Americans living in Watts (Falloon, Boyd et al., 1985). In McFarlane's (McFarlane, Lukens et al., 1995) large multisite study in New York, about 40 percent of the sample was African American, most living in Harlem. Later implementation throughout New York State showed that sensitive application of the multifamily group version of FPE was not only acceptable, but was valued by a wide range of consumers and families with varied cultural and ethnic backgrounds. Lopez, Kopelowicz, and Canive have recently adapted the multifamily group approach described here to a sizable population of Mexican Americans in Los Angeles and have found that it required little change, because it is designed to include the family's and consumer's input throughout the treatment process. They found that many of its design features matched the needs of people of Hispanic origin living in southern California. However, the therapists leading these groups are themselves Hispanic, and the groups are conducted in Spanish. There have been large-scale and very successful applications of these methods in China, Norway, Denmark, Spain, Hungary, Romania, Italy, Netherlands, Germany, Japan, England, Australia and New Zealand, and among immigrant groups (for instance, Vietnamese refugees in Melbourne, Australia). Implementation of family psychoeducation is much more extensive outside the United States than inside.

In summary, there seems to be no cultural group for which an adaptation done with creativity, sensitivity, and flexibility, and in the spirit of collaboration, understanding, and respect has not been successful. The key is to assure that either the clinicians themselves or supervisors and/or consultants are familiar with the expectations of members of a given cultural group for professionals and advisors. In particular, clinicians need to tailor the socializing aspect of the joining sessions to the specific cultural contexts of the participants.

Further, clinicians need to take the opportunity (starting with the socializing) to use their observation skills to begin to identify roles, values, and norms within the family that could later be used to enhance communication and maximize the impact of the intervention. Linked to the need to understand the cultural context of the participants is the need to acknowledge variation in communication styles. For example, there are variations in power hierarchies and turn-taking behaviors during conversation that may not appear to be normal to the clinician, but are normal for the specific cultural context of the family. Acknowledging these variations and tailoring interventions to these realities is one of the tasks requiring creativity and flexibility of clinicians. Obviously, the issue of language preferences will have to be addressed.

Case Study

Samantha is a 38-year-old woman who has schizoaffective disorder. Although she has had an illness since her teens, she has worked hard to manage her illness. Her parents are in their mid-60s and attend a multifamily group regularly with her. She lives alone with her cat and works part-time (every morning for 4 hours) in the mailroom of a large insurance company, a job she secured through problem solving in the group and the assistance of a supported employment specialist, one of the coleaders of the group. The bus stop to work is within easy walking distance of her apartment. She likes the routine of working every day, and has become quite efficient at her job, which does not vary too much from day to day. One challenge for Samantha is that the company sometimes has bulk mailings that need to go out quickly, which means there is increased pressure and tension at the worksite. Samantha found it difficult to switch her pace and tasks at these times. The problem solving in the group proceeded along the following lines.

Step 1: What is the problem?

What can Samantha do to feel less overwhelmed at work when there are bulk mailings that need to go out quickly?

Step 2: List all possible solutions.

The group generated the following solutions:

1. Quit.
2. Talk to the supervisor.
3. Set limits for yourself.
4. Take more frequent breaks.
5. Go to the gym to relieve tension.
6. Get a massage—reward yourself for good efforts.
7. Reduce your hours at those times.
8. Scream into a pillow.
9. Practice stress-reduction techniques before and after work.
10. Balance your life with a variety of activities.
11. Clean your apartment.
12. Seek out peer/mentor support.

Step 3: Discuss each possible solution.

The advantages of each suggestion were discussed first, then the disadvantages. Samantha decided she did not like number 8 (scream into a pillow), so it was eliminated.

Step 4: Choose the best solution or combination of solutions.
Samantha chose the following solutions, and her parents agreed that they were good ones to try.

1. Talk to your supervisor.
2. Practice stress-reduction techniques before and after work.
3. Balance your life.

Step 5: Plan how to carry out the best solution.
With the practitioners' help, Samantha and her family formed a plan during the MFG:

1. Talk with supervisor tomorrow.
   - Identify a good time to talk (break time?)
   - Approach the supervisor first thing in the morning to request a meeting time
2. Try to go slow.
3. Use stress reduction techniques.
   - Identify 2 techniques to try
   - Identify what techniques you will try and how often (e.g., put them on a calendar)

Step 6: Review implementation.
At the next MFG, Samantha was asked how she had done with the action plan. She reported that she had been hesitant to talk with her supervisor, so she had not approached him during the previous 2 weeks. She had been successful in identifying and trying one stress reduction technique, which she liked (listening to classical music with her headset). She also had tried some self-talk in order to *go slow.* When the practitioners questioned her about whether she would like more outside support in approaching her supervisor she said yes. Her parents volunteered that they did not want to appear as though they were taking control of this situation when they found out that she had felt uncomfortable approaching her supervisor. A discussion ensued about when the family should offer more help and how to do that without appearing controlling. The practitioners volunteered that they wished they had called her during the 2-week period when there was no MFG, which demonstrated to Samantha and her parents that the practitioners were in partnership with them. The practitioners offered to continue the problem-solving process with Samantha and her family outside of the MFG.

MODIFICATIONS FOR BIPOLAR DISORDER

As should be clear to the reader, the biosocial model of treatment assumes that the influence of biological and family processes is bidirectional. For that reason, the psychoeducational multifamily group model must be modified in several important ways for bipolar disorder. Also, it remains structured in ways that are quite similar, so that the skills developed in treating schizophrenia can readily be applied in bipolar disorder as well as in other major psychiatric illnesses. Much progress has been made by several clinical research groups to propose, develop, and test models that use the family intervention strategies for schizophrenia in those other disorders. David Miklowitz, Michael Goldstein, and their colleagues have modified the family behavioral model of Falloon and Liberman to address the complexities of bipolar disorder and have recently published evidence for the model's efficacy (Miklowitz & Goldstein, 1997; Miklowitz, Simoneau et al., 2000). Our group, in this case led by David Moltz and Margaret Newmark, has developed a variant of the multifamily group model specifically for Bipolar Disorder, which is described briefly here (Moltz & Newmark, 2002). This model was first implemented at a municipal mental health center in the South Bronx of New York City and later at a community mental health center in coastal Maine. It has been effective in these and several other settings in the United States, although it has yet to be tested empirically. Anderson and her associates compared a family process multifamily group to a psychoeducational multifamily group for treating inpatients with affective disorders. One of the few significant differences between the groups was that those attending the psychoeducational group reported greater satisfaction than those attending the process group. Therefore, whether the psychoeducational format had measurable clinical advantages, it was more valued by family members (Anderson, Griffin et al., 1986).

The process of joining is similar. Usually, initial joining sessions are held separately for the individual and the family, especially if the engagement is occurring during a manic episode. If the individual is stable, some sessions may be held jointly, because many bipolar patients are able to participate fully. The content of the joining sessions is modified to reflect the specific impact of bipolar illness on the family. It includes an extensive discussion of the history of symptoms and course of illness, identifying precipitants and prodromal signs, emphasis on differing attitudes and attributions about both the symptoms (especially of mania) and the person's native personality and emotional expression. A key element to discuss and assess is the individual's interepisode functioning; that is, how is the family's life between episodes? After several sessions with the family and the individual meeting separately, they are seen together for one or more conjoint sessions, facilitated by the two therapists who will lead the multifamily group.

The structure and format of the bipolar family workshop are similar to the schizophrenia workshop except that the affected individual is routinely included. The content is determined by the characteristics of the illness and may include the following:

- Symptoms of manic and depressed episodes
- Differences from normal emotional highs and lows
- The issue of will power
- The question of the "real" personality

- The impact of acute episodes on the family
- The long term impact of the illness on the family
- Theories of etiology of the illness
- Short- and long-term treatment strategies

The structure of the multifamily group meetings is essentially the same as the schizophrenia model. The problem-solving approach is generic, and seems to be useful and applicable across several disorders. Because it emphasizes rational rather than emotional processes, it is particularly well-suited as a counterpoint to the often-exaggerated emotional responses common to the mood disorders and even among family members, owing to the strong genetic influences that operate specifically in these disorders. It is all but routine that first degree relatives of a person with bipolar disorder also have a mood, anxiety, or substance abuse disorder, often untreated. Expressed emotion tends to reverberate, often as negativity, leading to escalations of emotional process that sometimes trigger manic episodes, and routinely produce serious family conflicts. The businesslike problem-solving approach provides a powerful antidote to these interactions, both through the structure of the proceedings themselves and through the leavening influence of several other families, by providing support, diffusing negativity, and encouraging restraint and conformity with the standards of community public behavior.

Bipolar disorder imposes specific challenges to group formation and maintenance, particularly to group formation and process. Because of the inherent diagnostic ambiguity of the mood, relative to psychotic disorders, there is a strong tendency to downplay problems and impute the effects of symptoms to personality, manipulation, voluntary hostility, or retribution. While these can be operating, especially in marital relationships, it is remarkable how much the behaviors that are imputed to these negative motivations and characteristics can diminish with good treatment. Problem solving and guidelines stress nonreactivity, patience, and a longer-term perspective when symptoms drive particularly provocative behavior on the part of the persons with the condition. Maintaining group structure is a particular challenge, simply because bipolar patients and many of their close relatives tend to be talkative, amusing, digressive, and sometimes forceful in their speech and behavior, putting a strain on the leaders' intent to stay on schedule during group sessions. Coexisting conditions, especially substance abuse, are all but universal when considering key relatives and spouses. It is common that relatives or spouses are suffering from substance abuse, sometimes arriving at group sessions intoxicated. This only exacerbates the tendency to digress and for some emotional interactions to escalate. For that reason, the leaders extend extra effort to maintain a positive, warm, but not intense emotional tone during the groups. Novice leaders will discover that family members can tolerate a fair amount of intensity, but will also appreciate the opportunity to address serious problems in a safe and organized manner and context. They will also tend to assist in reining in group members who become too activated.

From PMFG experience to date, in general, affected individuals have reported that they were less angry over time, they had less debilitating episodes when they did occur, they were better able to manage symptoms and episodes, they experienced fewer hospitalizations, and that they were more able to appreciate their family's experience. From their own perspective, family members reported increased confidence in their ability to cope with the illness, increased confidence in the individual's ability to manage the illness over time, and benefits from the group, even if the affected individual did not attend. Leaders have reported that it took about two years to master the techniques, learning to see their role more as consultant than therapist, about the family's and individual's experience of illness and their efforts to cope with it, and the awareness that each person's struggle with illness is different.

ADAPTATIONS

As will be shown in the subsequent sections on empirical outcomes in the major psychiatric disorders, the key to better outcome is family involvement in treatment on a routine basis and for an extended period, using the basic framework of joining, education, and problem solving. If the clinician is in a setting in which multifamily groups are impossible to develop, many of the advantages and outcomes of family intervention can be achieved by working with the patient and family in a single-family format. In this case, the single-family approaches described in the works of Anderson and Falloon apply, and will still achieve major improvements in clinical and functional outcomes and in family relationships. For families in which there is a minimum of negativity and the patient is responding well to treatment, the family consultation model developed by Wynne may well suffice, providing single-family sessions, after engagement and education, that are held on an ad hoc basis, to address family interactional problems as they arise (Wynne, 1994). The major differences in outcomes in the short run are observed between involving the family and not; only over the long-term and across large numbers of families will the differences between multi- and single-family formats be observed. Further, the benefits of groups are probably as much for the clinician as for the family, in that groups tend to be much less burdensome over time for the therapists, and much more gratifying as well.

RESEARCH EVIDENCE SUPPORTING FAMILY PSYCHOEDUCATION AND MULTIFAMILY GROUPS

A large number of controlled and comparative clinical trials have demonstrated markedly decreased relapse and rehospitalization rates among patients whose families received psychoeducation, compared to those who received standard individual services—20 to 50 percent over 2 years. At least eight literature reviews have been published in the past decade, all finding a large and significant effect for this model of intervention (Dixon et al., 2001; McFarlane, Dixon, Lukens, & Lucksted, 2003). Since 1978, there has been a steady stream of rigorous validations of the positive effects of this approach on relapse in schizophrenic, mood, and other severe disorders. Overall, the relapse rate for patients provided with family psychoeducation has hovered around 15 percent per year, compared to a consistent 30 to 40 percent for individual therapy and medication or medication alone. It is important to note that medication is not a variable in these studies; the design of family psychoeducational approaches has medication adherence, and its value in promoting recovery, as a central element. McFarlane and colleagues have consistently shown that when a very similar version of family psychoeducation is compared to a multifamily group version, multifamily groups lead to lower relapse rates and higher employment than single-family sessions (McFarlane, Lukens et al., 1995). The simplest explanation is that enhanced social support, inherent only in the multifamily format, reduces vulnerability to relapse, probably by reducing family anxiety and distress (Dyck, Hendryx, Short, Voss, & McFarlane, 2002).

Because of the compelling evidence, the Schizophrenia Patient Outcomes Research Team (PORT) project included family psychoeducation in its set of treatment first-rank recommendations. Other best practice standards have also recommended that families receive education and support programs. In addition, an expert panel that included clinicians from various disciplines, families, patients, and researchers emphasized the importance of engaging families in the treatment and rehabilitation process (Coursey & Curtis, 2000). Recent reports have added the strong validation of the effects in a variety of international and cultural contexts, including efficacy demonstrated in China, Spain, Scandinavia, and Great Britain.

In addition, these and other studies have demonstrated significant effects on other areas of functioning. Several of the previously mentioned models, particularly the American versions—those of Falloon, Anderson and McFarlane—all include major components designed to achieve functional recovery, and the studies have documented progress in those same domains. Other effects have been shown for improved family member well-being (Cuijpers, 1999), substantially increased employment rates (Anderson, Reiss, & Hogarty, 1986; McFarlane & Lukens, 1995), decreased deficit symptoms, (Dyck, Short et al., 2000), improved social functioning (Montero, Asencio & Falloon, 2001), decreased family medical illnesses (Dyck, Short et al., 2002), and reduced costs of care (Cardin & McGill, 1985).

Most studies have evaluated family psychoeducation for schizophrenia or schizoaffective disorder only. However, several controlled studies do support the effects of family interventions for other psychiatric disorders, including dual diagnosis of schizophrenia and substance abuse, bipolar disorder (Miklowitz, 1997), major depression (Keitner, Drury et al., 2002), mood disorders in children (Fristad, Gavazzi & Soldano, 1998), Obsessive-Compulsive Disorder (Van Noppen, 1999) and many other disorders.

Family psychoeducation has a solid research base, and a consensus has fully developed among leaders in the field regarding its marked efficacy and essential components and techniques. What remains is for a widespread acceptance of the power of empirically tested treatments to improve outcomes, lives, and futures for a vast population of people with severe mental illnesses. Given the historical tendency for therapists to dismiss treatment research as a guide to practice, the application of these new biosocial treatments may be slow in coming. What will speed the process is therapists discovering, which adopters of this approach nearly universally do, that this treatment leads to dramatically more gratification and enjoyment in the practice of treatment than currently used approaches. Work with severe mental illness, if it includes the family and groups of families, provides a strong sense that what one is offering, and one's efforts, are finally consistent with the best traditions of medicine, social science, and humane social and psychological work.

REFERENCES

Amenson, C. (1998). *Schizophrenia: A family education curriculum.* Pasadena, CA: Pacific Clinics Institute.

Anderson, C., Reiss, D., & Hogarty, G. (1986). *Schizophrenia and the family: A practitioner's guide to psychoeducation and management.* New York: Guilford.

Anderson, C. M., Griffin, S., Rossi, A., Pagonis, I., Holder, D. P., & Treiber, R. (1986). A comparative study of the impact of education vs. process groups for families of patients with affective disorders. *Family Process, 25,* 185–205.

Bebbington, P., & Kuipers, L. (1994). The predictive utility of expressed emotion in schizophrenia: An aggregate analysis. *Psychological Medicine, 24,* 707–718.

Brown, G. W., Birley, J. L. T., & Wing, J. K. (1972). Influence of family life on the course of schizophrenic disorders: A replication. *British Journal of Psychiatry, 121,* 241–258.

Cardin, V. A., McGill, C. W., & Falloon, I. R. H. (1985). An economic analysis: Costs, benefits, and effectiveness. In I. R. H. Falloon (Ed.), *Family management of schizophrenia: A study of clinical, social, family, and economic benefits* (pp. 115–123). Baltimore: Johns Hopkins University Press.

Coursey, R., Curtis, L., & Marsh, D. (2000). Competencies for direct service staff members who work with adults with severe mental illness in outpatient public mental health managed care systems. *Psychiatric Rehabilitation Journal, 23,* 370–377.

Cuijpers, P. (1999). The effects of family interventions on relatives' burden: a meta-analysis. *Journal of Mental Health, 8,* 275–285.

Dixon, L., McFarlane, W. R., Lefley, H., Lucksted, A., Cohen, M., Falloon, I., et al. (2001). Evidence-based practices for services to families of people with psychiatric disabilities. *Psychiatric Services, 52,* 903–910.

Dyck, D. G., Hendryx, M. S., Short, R. A., Voss, W. D., & McFarlane, W. R. (2002). Service use among patients with schizophrenia in psychoeducational multiple-family group treatment. *Psychiatric Services, 53,* 749–754.

Dyck, D. G., Short, R. A., Hendryx, M. S., Norell, D., Myers, M., Patterson, T., et al. (2000). Management of negative symptoms among patients with schizophrenia attending multiple-family groups. *Psychiatric Services, 51,* 513–519.

Falloon, I., Boyd, J., & McGill, C. (1984). *Family care of schizophrenia.* New York: Guilford.

Falloon, I., Boyd, J., McGill, C., Williamson, M., Razani, J., Moss, H., et al. (1985). Family management in the prevention of morbidity of schizophrenia. *Archives of General Psychiatry, 42,* 887–896.

Falloon, I. R. H. (1984). *Family Management of Mental Illness: A Study of Clinical Social and Family Benefits.* Baltimore: Johns Hopkins University Press.

Fellowship, W. S (1998). *Families as partners in care: A document developed to launch a strategy for the implementation of programs of family education, training, and support.* Toronto: World Schizophrenia Fellowship.

Fristad, M. A., Gavazzi, S. M., & Soldano, K. W. (1998). Multi-family psychoeducation groups for childhood mood disorders: A program description and preliminary efficacy data. *Contemporary Family Therapy, 20,* 385–402.

Keitner, G. I., Drury, L. M., Ryan, C. E., Miller, I. W., Norman, W. H., & Solomon, D. A. (2002). Multifamily Group Treatment for Depressive Disorder. In W. R. McFarlane (Ed.), *Multifamily groups in the treatment of severe psychiatric disorders* (pp. 318–349). New York: Guilford.

Marsh, D. (2001). *A family-focused approach to serious mental illness: Empirically supported interventions.* Sarasota, FL: Professional Resource Press.

McFarlane, W. R. (2002). *Multifamily groups in the treatment of severe psychiatric disorders.* New York: Guilford.

McFarlane, W. R., Dixon, L., Lukens, E., & Lucksted, A. (2003). Family psychoeducation and schizophrenia: A review of the literature. *Journal of Marital & Family Therapy, 29,* 223–245.

McFarlane, W. R., Lukens, E., Link, B., Dushay, R., Deakins, S. A., Newmark, M., et al. (1995). Multiple-family groups and psychoeducation in the treatment of schizophrenia. *Archives of General Psychiatry, 52,* 679–687.

Miklowitz, D., Simoneau, T., George, E., Richards, J., Kalbag, A., Sachs-Ericsson, N., et al. (2000). Family-focused treatment of bipolar disorder: One-year effects of a psychoeducational program in conjunction with pharmacotherapy. *Biological Psychiatry, 48,* 582–592.

Miklowitz, D. J., & Goldstein, M. J. (1997). *Bipolar Disorder: A family-focused treatment approach.* New York: Guilford.

Moltz, D., & Newmark, M. (2002). Multifamily groups for bipolar illness. In W. R. McFarlane (Ed.), *Multifamily groups in the treatment of severe psychiatric disorders* (pp. 293–317). New York: Guilford.

Montero, I., Asencio, A., Hernandez, I., Masanet, M. J., Lacruz, M., Bellver, F., et al. (2001). Two strategies for family intervention in schizophrenia: A randomized trial in a Mediterranean environment. *Schizophrenia Bulletin, 27,* 661–670.

Pickett-Schenk, S., Cook, J., & Laris, A. (2000). Journey of Hope program outcomes. *Community Mental Health Journal, 36,* 413–424.

Van Noppen, B. (1999). Multi-family behavioral treatment (MFBT) for OCD. *Crisis Intervention And Time-Limited Treatment, 5,* 3–24.

Wynne, L. C. (1994). The rationale for consultation with the families of schizophrenic patients. *Acta Psychiatrica Scandinavica, Supplementum, 90*(384), 125–132.

CHAPTER 9

Optimizing Couple and Parenting Interventions to Address Adult Depression

Maya Gupta, Steven R. H. Beach, and James C. Coyne

In the *Diagnostic and Statistical Manual for Mental Disorders* (*DSM-IVTR;* American Psychiatric Association, 2000), depression is treated in a largely decontextualized manner. Family therapists and others interested in this book, however, are likely accustomed to encountering depression in its broader, interpersonal context—as an issue that very much affects family members of the depressed individual, who is in turn very much affected by their reactions as well. The purpose of our chapter is to examine how couple and parenting treatments for depression can be uniquely helpful in addressing the harmful interaction between depression and couple/family distress, a topic on which there is a substantial body of research. At the same time, we discuss the issue of how these treatments may be most effectively disseminated to the potentially large populations where they could be useful, a topic that has been less extensively covered.

A DESCRIPTION OF DEPRESSION

Making a formal diagnosis of Major Depressive Disorder (MDD) requires establishment of the presence of a major depressive episode: at least two weeks of depressed mood, anhedonia (loss of interest or pleasure in activities), marked change in weight or appetite, insomnia or hypersomnia, visible psychomotor agitation or retardation, fatigue or loss of energy, indecisiveness, difficulty concentrating, feelings of worthlessness or guilt, or thoughts of death/suicide (American Psychiatric Association, 2000). Either depressed mood or anhedonia, along with four other symptoms, must be present to qualify for the diagnosis. Major depression may occur as a single episode, but it is not uncommon for it to take the form of a recurrent illness.

The symptoms of dysthymia are similar to those of Major Depressive Disorder. While only two symptoms from the set are required, they must be present for the majority of at least 2 years, considerably longer than what is required for a diagnosis of Major Depressive Disorder. It is possible for patients to be dually diagnosed with both Major Depressive Disorder and dysthymia if they are currently in a major depressive episode and also have at least a 2 year history of dysthymic symptoms.

When we use the term *depression* in this chapter, we refer principally to Major Depressive Disorder, as screening processes for inclusion in the studies we review have usually been designed to select for this diagnosis when constructing their depressed groups. However, owing to the conceptual overlap and diagnostic co-morbidity of Major Depressive Disorder and dysthymia, it is important to acknowledge that our discussion likely includes a considerable population of dysthymic individuals as well.

Clinicians also routinely encounter subclinical dysphoria—patterns of negative affect, adjustment reactions with mixed or depressed mood, or other depressive symptomatology that fails to attain diagnostic thresholds but that nonetheless is clinically significant in the extent to which it interferes with patient functioning. Critics of the *DSM*'s categorical approach to diagnostic classification have argued that qualitative distinctions between subclinical and clinical syndromes are largely arbitrary. This argument has been taken up with particular fervor in the area of depression (Beutler, Clarkin, & Bongar, 2000); statistically, individuals presenting with subclinical dysphoria are indeed at higher risk for developing Major Depressive Disorder in future (Horwath, Johnson, Klerman, & Weissman, 1992) and their first-degree relatives are also more likely to have MDD (though less likely than first-degree relatives of individuals with MDD; Lewinsohn, Klein, Durbin, Seeley, & Rohde, 2003). Other clinicians and researchers contend that sufficient distinguishing characteristics are observable to warrant a firm division between clinical and subclinical depressive presentations (Coyne, 1994; Santor & Coyne, 2001). As the debate continues, recent research suggests that for depression the answer may be both: that a continuum does exist but that certain subtypes of depressive syndrome patterns may be qualitatively distinct (Beach & Amir, 2003, but see also Ruscio & Ruscio, 2000). Supporting the hypothesis of a difference between subclinical and clinical levels of depression, it appears that the strength of the association between couple or family distress and depressive symptoms may be greater for major depression than for subclinical dysphoria (Whisman, 2001).

We do not exclude studies focusing on subclinical dysphoria from consideration in the current chapter. However, we do advise readers against making hasty assumptions regarding the extent to which treatment studies on major depression can be extrapolated to the treatment of subclinical dysphoria. The key unresolved issue concerns the need for treatment and the potential for differential effects of treatment. Although we have some confidence that major depression is a recurrent, episodic condition with long-term consequences for individual and family adjustment, with formal treatment clearly indicated, we are less confident that the same is true of subsyndromal depression. Some unknown but substantial proportion of persons with subsyndromal depression may improve with very simple supportive interventions, or even just the passage of time and no formal intervention at all. Few treatment studies have examined depression at the subclinical level, but what data are available seem to indicate that rate of improvement in the absence of formal intervention is sufficiently high to make a demonstration of the benefits of treatment difficult to demonstrate (Barrett et al., 1999; Williams et al., 2000; Bruce et al., 2004), suggesting caution in advocating treatment. At a minimum, family psychologists should adhere to the commonsense practice of advocating minimal intervention when minimal intervention achieves as good an outcome as more heroic efforts.

A COUPLES/FAMILY DESCRIPTION OF DEPRESSION

We begin our discussion of depression's couple/family context with another caution: In this area of research, as in most others, studies on married and heterosexual couples have far outnumbered studies on unmarried and/or same-sex couples. Therefore, it is not clear whether there are important differences in these populations' presentation or response to couple and family treatment for depression. Furthermore, most studies have only examined couples and families in which the female partner is depressed; although depression remains more common among women than among men, the increasing rate of depression in men highlights a need to promote research on gender-based differences in depression and the ways these may be linked to couple/family processes.

Despite these limitations in the literature, the association of couple and/or parenting difficulties with depression is well-documented. In one study, two-thirds of a group of depressed outpatients and one-half of a group of depressed inpatients met standard research criteria for marital distress (Coyne, Thompson, & Palmer, 2002). Whisman (2001) reviewed research on both clinically and subclinically depressed individuals and consistently found that those in poor-quality marriages displayed more depressive symptoms and were at greater risk for diagnosable depression. Parenting problems are also commonly reported by depressed women (Weissman & Paykel, 1974) and appear to be more prevalent in this population than among nondepressed mothers (Lovejoy, Gracyk, O'Hare, & Neuman, 2000). Levels of hostility between depressed mothers and their children may even be higher than levels of hostility between depressed women and their husbands (Downey & Coyne, 1990), highlighting the fact that depressed individuals often find themselves in coercive family environments (Hops et al., 1987). In addition, the upsetting nature of the family environment is often a presenting problem for depressed patients and a source of concern for them.

Of course, cross-sectional data provide no information about causality, and it is of interest to know whether depression is a product of relational conflict or vice versa. Longitudinal studies, though not able to provide us with definitive indications of causality, have helped to address this question by demonstrating that marital dissatisfaction predicts future depressive episodes among couples not currently depressed (Whisman & Bruce, 1999) as well as future depressive symptoms, controlling for previous depressive symptoms (Beach, Katz, Kim, & Brody, 2003). Distressed relationships between parents and children also predict maintenance of parental depressive symptoms (Keitner, Miller, & Ryan, 1994; Jones, Beach, & Forehand, 2001).

On the other hand, depression may also produce difficulties in primary relationships. For example, elevated depressive symptoms are associated with increased distress a year later (Beach & O'Leary, 1993) and are also predictive of poorer quality support for the partner (Davila, 2001). Finally, suggesting the potential for depression to become self-sustaining within family systems, longitudinal data suggest that maternal depression can fuel parent-child relationship difficulties and erode children's social support systems in a manner that leads to child mental health problems, including childhood depression (McCarty & McMahon, 2003). Likewise, maternal depression predicts increased parenting stress, which in turn is associated with greater maternal depression, illustrating the potential for a stress-generation cycle involving depression and parenting that can become self-maintaining (Jones et al., 2001).

The notion that couple and parenting difficulties cause depression may be the more intuitive of the two potential paths of association. Marriage and parenthood are important roles for many people, and strong attachments are formed within spousal and parent-child relationships. Those who attribute parent-child conflict to their own failures as parents may suffer a blow to self-esteem sufficient to precipitate depression (Teti & Gelfand, 1991), and this link might easily be hypothesized for partner relationships as well. Likewise, humiliating life events appear to be powerful factors in the etiology of depression in women (Brown, Harris, & Hepworth, 1995; Brown & Moran, 1997), and feelings of humiliation specific to partner infidelity and threats of divorce have been linked to major depressive episodes in women (Cano & O'Leary, 2000). Extending this work, Kendler, Hettema, Butera, Gardner, & Prescott (2003) identified the combination of humiliation and loss—with partner-initiated separation as a key example—as particularly predictive of major depressive episodes.[1] Additionally, severe and persistent couple and family conflict, contributing to the deterioration of a component of the primary social support network, can foster loneliness and isolation and place individuals at risk for depression.

Accordingly, there is considerable evidence of bidirectional influence between marital and parenting processes on the one hand and depressive symptoms and episodes of depression on the other. Hammen's (1991) Stress Generation theory can provide a framework for understanding this bidirectional relationship. In Stress Generation theory it is posited that depressed individuals can generate stress in their interpersonal environments in a variety of ways, but this interpersonal stress can also exacerbate depressive symptoms. Illustrating the potential for a vicious cycle to develop between depressive symptoms and marital difficulties, Davila, Bradbury, Cohan, and Tochluk (1997) found that persons with more symptoms of depression were more negative in their supportive behavior toward the spouse and in their expectations regarding partner support. In turn, these negative behaviors and expectations were related to marital stress. Finally, complet-

---

[1] Lest we treat parenting stress and partner stress as overly discrete categories, it is also important to acknowledge the potential for these to influence one another and thereby exacerbate family problems. Parent-child conflict can give rise to partner conflict as the overall level of household tension rises, particularly if there are disagreements between partners as to parenting practices. Reciprocally, conflict between partners, producing a climate of negative affect and inconsistency in parenting practices, has been demonstrated to associate with child externalizing disorders (Emery, 1982) and internalizing problems (Downey & Coyne, 1990).

ing the vicious cycle, level of marital stress predicted subsequent depressive symptoms (controlling for earlier symptoms). In a similar line of reasoning, Joiner (2000) highlights the propensity for depressed persons to seek negative feedback, to engage in excessive reassurance seeking, to avoid conflict and so withdraw, and to elicit changes in their partners' views of them. In each case, the behavior resulting from the individual's depression carries the potential to generate increased interpersonal stress or to shift the response of others in a negative direction. Joiner suggests that this increased interpersonal negativity, in turn, accounts for much of the maintenance of depressive symptoms.

JUSTIFICATION FOR INTERVENING AT THE COUPLE/FAMILY LEVEL

For couples and families where couple/parenting distress has produced depression, one might anticipate that individual treatment would have limited value in correcting the interpersonal disturbance, even if it were successful in alleviating the ongoing episode of depression. Conversely, if a focus on relationship problems or parenting problems helps prompt recovery from the episode of depression, one might suspect that intervening in the relational problems should produce improvement in both depressive symptoms and relationship problems. This hypothesis was tested by O'Leary, Riso, and Beach (1990) in the context of marital difficulties. They found that when depression preceded the marital conflict, both marital and individual therapy were helpful in alleviating the depressive episode. Additionally, participants in both individual and couples treatment groups reported gains in marital satisfaction. In contrast, when the onset of the current depressive episode followed the onset of marital discord, marital therapy equated with individual therapy in relieving depressive symptoms, but was far superior in relieving marital difficulties. Not only did individual therapy in these cases fail to relieve the interpersonal problems associated with the depressive episode, it was associated with worsening of marital discord. Thus, it cannot be assumed that individually focused interventions will alleviate interpersonal problems in all cases, in particular those in which relationship problems precede depression. At a minimum, this observation suggests the importance of providing marital interventions in these cases.

Though not as clearly documented in the parenting literature, the vicious cycle between depressed and nondepressed members of the relationship also appears to exist in relationships between depressed parents and their children, as tendencies toward poor communication patterns coupled with harsh and/or inconsistent discipline among depressed parents (for reviews see Downey & Coyne, 1990; Cummings, DeArth-Pendley, & Du Rocher Schudlich, 2001; Gelfand & Teti, 1990) may lead to child behavior problems that contribute to further deterioration in family functioning. Thus, although a primary intervention via traditional individual treatments may be indicated in many cases, couple/family treatment represents an important potential adjunct to treatment as a means of breaking vicious cycles, facilitating family members' coping with the depressed person's illness, and promoting an optimal supportive milieu for the depressed person's recovery.

WHAT WE KNOW: CLEARLY ESTABLISHED GUIDELINES FOR COUPLE AND PARENTING INTERVENTION WITH DEPRESSED INDIVIDUALS

Two empirically based treatments for couple distress and two approaches to the treatment of parent-child conflict have been implemented for use with depression. Following, we briefly present those treatments that have demonstrated empirical support in their adapted formats. However, we refer the reader to the original therapy manuals for greater detail on the implementation of these treatments.

Couple Interventions

Behavioral Marital Therapy (BMT) for Depression

Behavioral marital therapy (BMT) for depression (Beach, Sandeen, & O'Leary, 1990) is a relatively brief treatment based in social learning theory, behavioral exchange theory, and cognitive theory. First-line interventions address rebuilding of pleasant interactions and shared activities for the couple. The resultant improvement in the overall marital climate may serve as a direct catalyst for symptom reduction in the depressed partner, as well as leading to a decrease in the nondepressed partner's expression of negative affect and thereby potentially buffering the depressed partner. Other core treatment components include communication skills and problem-solving skills, both of which facilitate expression and resolution of problems in a manner designed to reduce stressful couple interactions and thus impede the vicious cycle of stress generation in depressed couples.

BMT has been demonstrated to be efficacious in three randomized clinical trials to date (Beach & O'Leary, 1992; Emanuels-Zuurveen & Emmelkamp, 1996, Jacobson, Dobson, Fruzzetti, Schmaling, & Salusky, 1991), with similar results. Jacobson et al. randomly assigned 60 married, depressed women to one of three conditions: BMT, individual cognitive-behavioral therapy (CT), or a treatment combining BMT and CT. Couples were not selected for the presence of marital discord and so could be divided into those who were more and less maritally distressed. Beach and O'Leary randomly assigned 45 couples in which the wife was depressed to one of three conditions: BMT, individual CT, or a 15-week waiting list condition. To be included in the study, both partners had to score in the discordant range of the Dyadic Adjustment Scale (DAS) and report ongoing marital discord. Finally, Emanuels-Zuurveen and Emmelkamp assigned 27 depressed outpatients to either individual cognitive/behavioral therapy or communication-focused marital therapy. The sample for this study included both depressed husbands ($n = 13$) as well as depressed wives ($n = 14$). Consistent across the three studies, behavioral marital therapy and individual therapy yielded equivalent outcomes when the dependent variable was depressive symptoms, and a better outcome in marital therapy than in individual therapy when the dependent variable was marital functioning. In addition, BMT was found to be significantly better than wait-list control in the Beach and O'Leary study.

Two of the studies reviewed indicate that the effect of marital therapy on depression is mediated by changes in marital adjustment. Beach and O'Leary (1992) found that post-therapy marital satisfaction fully accounted for the effect of marital therapy on depression. Likewise, Jacobson et al. (1991) found that changes in marital adjustment and depression covaried for depressed individuals who received marital therapy, but not for those who received cognitive therapy. Therefore, it appears that marital therapy influences depressive symptomatology either by enhancing marital satisfaction or by producing changes in the marital environment associated with enhanced satisfaction.

Interpersonal Psychotherapy for Depression-Conjoint Marital (IPT-CM)

Interpersonal psychotherapy for depression (IPT; Klerman, Weissman, Rounsaville, & Chevron, 1984) is an individual therapy focusing on depressed patients' maladaptive interpersonal environments. Role disputes, role transitions, grief upon role loss, and interpersonal deficits are the four targeted components of this environment. IPT-CM (Foley, Rounsaville, Weissman, Sholomskas, & Chevron, 1989) represents an attempt to involve the spouse of the depressed patient in the treatment process, incorporating communication skills techniques but preserving IPT's attention to role renegotiation—here in the context of the couple's relationship—as a primary area of change. Important IPT techniques include explanation of the "sick role," a process of educating the couple about the debilitating nature of depression and thereby promoting acceptance of the depressed partner. A unique aspect of IPT-CM is its deliberate distinction between individual problems and relationship problems, which is more implicit than explicit in BMT. Based on careful assessment of the depressed individual's interactions with the partner, treatment progresses to renegotiating partners' clashing expectations of marital roles, establishing new roles, and allowing expression of grief as old roles (however problematic they may have been) are left behind.

IPT-CM was subjected to a clinical trial by its authors (Foley et al., 1989). Eighteen depressed outpatients were randomly assigned to either IPT or IPT-CM. Consistent with the findings of the three previously mentioned studies comparing behavioral marital therapy with an individual approach, participants in both treatments exhibited a significant reduction in depressive symptoms, but there were no significant differences between treatment groups. Both interventions also produced equal enhancement of general interpersonal functioning. However, participants receiving IPT-CM reported marginally higher marital satisfaction scores on the Locke-Wallace Short Marital Adjustment Test and scored significantly higher on one subscale of the DAS at session 16.

Parenting Interventions

For parenting problems related to oppositional behavior and Attention-Deficit/Hyperactivity Disorder (ADHD), several closely related forms of behaviorally grounded parenting skills programs, known variously as parent-child interaction therapy, parent training, and behavioral family intervention, all of which focus on improving the quality of the parent-child relationship as well as implementing effective discipline strategies, have been examined in relation to their effect on parental depression (Bagner & Eyberg, 2003; Dadds & McHugh, 1992; Forehand, Wells, & Griest, 1980; Sanders & McFarland, 2000; Webster-Stratton, 1994).

These trials have all demonstrated improvement in depression and couple or parenting problems as a result of treatment. In the Sanders and McFarland trial, in which mothers were selected for the presence of major depression or dysthymia, an enhanced intervention that added a module targeting mothers' mood-related cognitions and coping skills was also tested. Although both the standard and enhanced interventions produced reductions in depression and in child behavior problems, these were better maintained at follow-up for the enhanced condition.

Given the prominence of parent-child disputes among the concerns of depressed parents (Weissman & Paykel, 1974), it seems likely that parent training could also be an important point of intervention with depressed patients, particularly in cases in which the child has a diagnosable disorder that could respond to effective parent training. One reason that parent training might have been under-investigated as an intervention for parents with a diagnosis of depression is that depressed parents seem to do somewhat less well in parent training than do other parents. For example, depressed mothers have greater difficulty learning parenting skills (Dumas, Gibson, & Albin, 1989) and are more prone to drop out of treatment prematurely (McMahon, Forehand, Griest, & Wells, 1981). Accordingly, one obstacle to the use of parent training may be providing it in a way that allows it to be successful with a depressed population. However, the research by Sanders and McFarland (2000) indicates that parent training, itself an efficacious form of therapy for child-management problems, can be provided to depressed persons in a safe and efficacious manner and may have beneficial effects, both with regard to child outcomes as well as with regard to parental depression. As that study suggests, it will be useful to consider ways to enhance parent training to make it easier to consume for depressed parents, and perhaps to enhance its long-term effects on depressive symptoms. Combinations with various elements of cognitive therapy may be useful in this regard.

Conclusions and Recommendations

General Conclusions

What conclusions can be drawn about the use of couple and parenting treatments for depression based on the studies reviewed above? First, it is clear that efficacious forms of couple therapy and parenting interventions can be safely and usefully applied to a depressed population while performing at least as well as individual therapies in ameliorating depression. At the same time, we know that getting over a depressive episode through traditional individual treatments for depression will help some, but not all, patients recover from couple and family discord, and that in cases in which the relationship problems are longer standing than the current depressive episode, recovery from depression may be associated with a decrease in relationship satisfaction (O'Leary et al., 1990).

BMT emerges as a specific and efficacious treatment for couple discord in a depressed population, having been demonstrated to produce significant change in marital distress while outperforming a control group and/or an alternative intervention in terms of producing change in marital satisfaction. Currently, BMT for depression is the only procedure that could be formally designated "efficacious" for the treatment of family problems in this population, insofar as one remains focused on direct support from outcome studies. However, IPT-CM also provides a promising avenue for intervention pending further documentation in clinical trials, and several of the parenting interventions described previously may also, in time, meet criteria for designation as empirically supported treatments for parenting problems in the context of depression—once they have been replicated. More broadly, at present we have no reason to assume that BMT will turn out to be the only efficacious conjoint treatment for depression. As evidence-based practitioners, we recommend the use of empirically supported treatments wherever possible, but it is important to recognize that failure of otherwise efficacious treatments for marital, parenting, or family problems to demonstrate efficacy in the context of depression may simply reflect insufficient experimental attention rather than any inherent weakness of the approach.

Implications for Clinical Decision-Making

Given the current data, we can also formulate some clinical guidelines regarding the use of couple or parenting interventions for depressed patients as an initial or an adjunct treatment for depression. First, when depressed individuals report no or mild couple distress and little parenting difficulty, spouses or other family members often may be involved as helpful adjuncts to therapy (Emanuels-Zuurveen & Emmelkamp, 1997). The family psychoeducational model may be a useful framework in such cases (McFarlane et al., 2003), and may focus on strengthening support processes within the family (but see Clarkin et al., 1990, for a negative outcome with a psychoeducational framework). Conversely, when depressed individuals report substantial difficulties in couple and/or parenting relationships, and indicate that the current episode of depression followed the onset of the relationship problems, an initial approach that focuses on systemic problems (e.g., couple therapy or enhanced parent training) may produce positive outcomes and provide benefits that are greater than those obtained from an individual focus (Beach & O'Leary, 1992; O'Leary et al., 1990). When depressed individuals report substantial relationship problems, but these emerged only after the onset of the depressive episode, an initial focus on either the individual and his or her symptoms of depression or an initial focus on the relational problems may be appropriate and useful. However, there is unlikely to be a unique benefit to an initial focus on relationships relative to an initial individual focus. In such cases, it may be appropriate to treat the individual while carefully monitoring changes in couple or parenting relationships. If the relationships change in response to individual treatment, no further treatment may be required. However, if relational problems do not respond to individual treatment it may be necessary to provide direct attention to these problems at a later stage of therapy.

An additional consideration in clinical decision-making is suggested by Ilardi & Craighead's (1994) observation that individual cognitive therapy for depression yields substantial (but not full) treatment response within the first several weeks of treatment for those who are going to respond. A similar pattern has been noted for marital therapy for depression (Beach et al., 1990). This suggests that when patients do not show any change in depressive symptoms within the first 4 to 6 weeks of treatment, regardless of the initial approach being used, it may be appropriate to refer them for treatment using one of the other empirically supported treatments for depression. Although it has been less well examined in the context of parent-child problems, it seems quite likely that similar guidelines apply.

WHAT WE THINK WE KNOW: ADDITIONAL CONSIDERATIONS FOR WORKING WITH DEPRESSED COUPLES AND FAMILIES

The use of empirically based, efficacious treatments in clinical practice represents a tremendous step forward for the field of psychotherapy. Accordingly, family practitioners are fortunate to be able to draw from an efficacy literature supporting at least two areas of family intervention for depression: couples and parenting approaches. At the same time, data from randomized clinical trials (RCTs) have certain limitations that render them incomplete in terms of providing guidelines to clinicians. Because efficacy studies are designed to search for results in the absence of confounding factors, variables representing important real-world differences among patients—such as patient preferences and limitations that influence their decisions about the types of treatment they will select—are not well modeled in controlled trials. Patient attitudes toward treatment are, however, a critical element of any psychotherapy, and appear to be associated with treatment outcome (Addis & Jacobson, 1996). This issue becomes especially important when one considers that researchers conducting efficacy studies do not, for the most part, need to be concerned about whether they are reaching the full population of interest: Willing participants come to them, drawn by free or reduced-cost treatment, and a sample comprised of participants with desired characteristics can be selected, because there are typically more respondents than can be accommodated in the study. Furthermore, unless samples are very large it is not possible to examine the role of particular participant characteristics (e.g., family education/literacy level, attachment style) that might interact with particular intervention strategies. Notably, an apparent match or mismatch between patients' self-generated reasons for their depression and the theoretical model underlying the type of treatment they received (behavioral activation or cognitive therapy) was also found to be associated with treatment outcome in Addis and Jacobson's work. Traditional RCTs with moderate sample sizes provide very weak tests of these possible treatment-by-patient interaction effects.

Accordingly, at present, RCTs—while furnishing valuable information concerning basic treatment efficacy—provide little guidance either for therapists or for potential consumers with regard to treatment matching. The purpose of the following section is to identify several scenarios in which, based on our clinical experience, it may be advisable to tailor one's approach to optimize the benefits of empirically supported interventions. At the same time, these suggestions may also be viewed as hypotheses about patient-treatment matching in need of further direct empirical examination. Because the literature is somewhat larger for marital interventions, many of our caveats pertain primarily to marital dyads.

Separation and Divorce

In couples with very low levels of commitment, whether from a nondepressed partner's frustration or a depressed partner's tendency toward withdrawal and escape, higher dropout rates and poorer overall outcome are likely to occur (Beach & Broderick, 1983). Although couples seeking marital therapy may often have doubts about their ability to work things out, they are often willing to make an explicit commitment to work on their relationship and begin to make things as good as they can be (see Fincham, Fernandez, & Humphreys, 1993). Couples in which either or both partners, explicitly or implicitly, are unwilling to make a commitment to work on improving the relationship or to remaining in the relationship are less than optimal candidates for standard couple therapy for depression. In the absence of both partners being able to make such a commitment, it is unlikely that the dyad will be able to complete couple assignments or experience the benefits of joint couple activities. Accordingly, it may be more useful to offer such couples individual therapy for one or both members of the dyad. Indeed, in cases where couples are seriously leaning toward separation or divorce, it may be against both partners' best interests for the therapist to attempt to forge ahead with couple therapy or any therapy targeted at salvaging the relationship (Klerman et al., 1984).

Suicidality

With one exception, outcome studies to date have uniformly excluded actively suicidal participants, though not those with passive suicidal ideation. Consequently, the results of these studies may not be extrapolated with confidence to actively suicidal populations. Nonetheless, this is an important subpopulation of depressed patients, and one that requires attention clinically. In one study of a small group of couples in which one partner was actively suicidal (O'Leary, Sandeen, & Beach, 1987), BMT proved difficult to implement, because the immediate needs of the suicidal partner tended to overshadow attention to BMT components. By comparison, participants assigned to individual CT showed better treatment gains. Although the small sample size used in this study renders any conclusions rather tentative pending replication, for the moment it appears safer to channel actively suicidal patients into individual therapy—at least until they are sufficiently stabilized that marital activities can emerge as a sustained focus of clinical attention.

Inpatient Populations

The percentage of couples who are maritally discordant is likely to be higher in outpatient populations than inpatient populations. However, when marital dissatisfaction is present among inpatient populations, it is present to a striking degree, typically in the form of an erosion of positive affect resulting from depressed patients' passivity and inactivity. As a result, conjoint work with severely depressed inpatients may require increased emphasis on rebuilding positive interactions, as opposed to managing conflictual interactions. However, owing to the brevity of the modal length of stay in inpatient facilities, interventions may also be constrained by time. Therapists may be limited to one or perhaps two meetings with the depressed patient and partner, in which it may be most fruitful to make highly specific recommendations concerning rebuilding of support (e.g., shared activities, pleasant behavioral exchanges). These should be supplemented by referrals, or if possible the therapist may wish to see the couple for aftercare.

Mutual Acknowledgment of the Problem

Clinical observation suggests that couples in which both partners agree on the presence of difficulties in their relationship may be better suited for couple therapy than couples in which one partner denies any problems. Agreement about the existence of a problem may prove a more crucial factor in predicting treatment success than the severity of the problem itself. Additionally, while some disagreement about the source of problems (the "his fault/her fault" phenomenon) is to be expected in distressed couples, particular challenges may be expected from those couples in which each partner presents an entirely different rationale for the problem, without willingness to entertain the other's viewpoint. If these disagreements appear sufficiently resistant to change, especially when they concern a focal issue such as depression, it may be more useful to consider individual treatment approaches. Alternatively, approaches to couple therapy that rely less on couple agreement, such as Integrative Behavioral Couple Therapy (IBCT; Jacobson & Christensen, 1996), may provide a better fit for such couples than does traditional BMT.

Refusal of One Partner to Attend

Partners may present for therapy on their own and report that they are concerned about relationship issues, but that their partners are opposed to coming in, either because they view therapy as an accusation that they are performing poorly as a spouse, or are leery of what will occur in couple therapy (Coyne & Benazon, 2001). Experience suggests that in this scenario the partner presenting alone is likely to be a female, depressed partner. When confronted with this situation, therapists may attempt to invite the unwilling partner in to help in a limited fashion. Devising a method of conveying clearly that the unwilling partner will not be blamed for the partner's depression, but that she or he may be a valuable asset in the depressed partner's recovery and may stand to derive personal benefit from treatment involvement as well, may serve to draw in the unwilling partner to a point where some approximation of conjoint therapy is possible. This may be facilitated by adopting a interpersonal psychotherapy (IPT) model in which the granting of a limited "sick role" to the depressed partner lifts blame by placing responsibility within the disease entity (while still affirming the importance of the depressed partner's effort in combating the illness). As Coyne and Benazon (2001) suggest, this approach can also shift the nondepressed partner's focus away from the burden of managing the depressed partner and toward self-care and self-fulfillment, which stands to improve relationship satisfaction and hence couple functioning as well.

Alternatively, it may be possible to embark upon an approach to treatment of the relationship that focuses on the individual, using either IPT or a self-control-focused marital therapy (Halford, 1998). Our sense is that this is a very common phenomenon: Confronted with a situation in which a depressed individual with concerns about couple and family problems cannot or prefers not to bring the spouse to treatment, the therapist proceeds to treat the individual, but with both patient and therapist cognizant that interpersonal problems drove the help-seeking. Both the empirical literature on outcome of IPT (Klerman et al., 1984) and the emerging literature on self-control-focused marital therapy (Halford, 1998) suggest it is possible to make gains with regard to symptoms alleviation and perhaps with regard to relationship improvement using these approaches.

In an illustration of an individual focus to deal with a relational problem, Watzlawick and Coyne (1980) describe in detail a case in which a severely depressed stroke victim refused treatment, but encouraged his wife and family to go, with all well aware that the man was the focus of treatment. The five-session treatment focused on interdicting the wife's well-meant but self-defeating efforts to encourage and cajole the man to shed some of his invalid status and reclaim some basic functioning. Watzlawick and Coyne articulated some of the most general ethical and practical issues involved in treating a couple or family in the absence of a key family member. Namely, all but the most inert or ineffective psychotherapy affects persons who are not in attendance. The issue is not whether others are affected without their consent, but rather how therapy can proceed humanely and effectively, taking their likely response into consideration. Furthermore, there is no special ethical quandary posed by one person seeking individual treatment because of concern about his or her effect on another. Strategizing about or simply guessing the response of other people is part of the grist of most individual therapy.

WHAT WE'D LIKE TO KNOW: HOW TO OPTIMIZE FUTURE INTERVENTIONS THROUGH A PUBLIC HEALTH PERSPECTIVE ON TREATMENT DISSEMINATION

Several of the considerations outlined previously highlight the challenges of adapting techniques from empirically supported therapies to diverse clinical scenarios. By drawing from a combination of research implications and clinical experience, we feel that it is possible for the astute clinician to devise effective intervention strategies in the majority of cases of couple/family depression that appear in the clinic. However, we have not yet addressed what, if anything, can be done to serve the considerable proportion of cases that never present to clinics.

For example, traditional approaches to couple therapy assume that both partners are willing to participate in treatment. Given concerns about husbands' involvement in therapy in many subcultural groups, a considerable proportion of couples may be unlikely to take advantage of traditional couple therapy formats, or to remain in formal marital treatment even if they can initially be brought on board. Likewise, in some households parents may be reluctant to present for treatment in conventional psychotherapy settings because of apprehensions about being seen as a bad or ineffective parent, and/or beliefs that parenting is a family concern that should not be disclosed to others. We have addressed the issue of one partner seeking help in the context of the other partner's refusal. However, we have not considered how to reach populations where both partners are apprehensive about presenting for treatment, or where a potential patient desirous of help does not take the initiative to contact a therapist in the face of a partner's or family member's opposition.

Further, the very characteristics of couples and families may present a unique challenge to the effectiveness of marital and parenting interventions for depression. Particularly when conjoint formats are required, parents' need to find and pay for childcare for other children in the family in order to attend evening sessions, or to coordinate schedules to attend sessions jointly, may render it quite difficult for couples and families to attend a formal treatment program. If they do attend, it may not be frequently and consistently enough to complete treatment. Problematically, most evidence-based interventions are structured and tested in a weekly, building-block format, where missed sessions or lengthy gaps between sessions could conceivably result in significant loss of treatment gains.

Thus, two issues that are poorly resolved by RCTs are the questions of how to attract patients to therapy and how long to keep patients in therapy. Typically, RCTs have a set "dose" (number of sessions) that is delivered to all participants. The dose is often set at the high end to make sure that every patient receives enough. From the standpoint of an efficacy trial this is simply prudent, but from the standpoint of effectiveness the issue may appear quite different. That is, clinicians may be more interested in whether the treatment can be made widely enough available that it can reach into the populations where it is needed. Also, once available, can the longer, RCT-supported approach to treatment be marketed in communities that may already be wary of psychological services? A longer clinic-based treatment will be less affordable for many communities and will be less desirable to some consumers for reasons of cost, time, and repeated travel. Likewise, one may wonder whether patients who do attempt a lengthy treatment will continue for the full number of sessions or drop out prematurely. Finally, if amendments are required to make a treatment more palatable for a given community, does the treatment remain useful, or has it been altered beyond recognition?

How important are these universal questions of effectiveness when considering the application of couple and parenting interventions for the treatment of depression? We are prepared to argue that for this documented, high-prevalence problem, affecting a broad range of populations, clinician attention to issues such as dissemination and palatability across various subpopulations is vital if available efficacy-based treatments are to be put into useful service. The sheer number of couples and families that could benefit from couple/parenting treatment for depression renders it important to consider the possibility of alternatives to the traditional 10 to 20-session, clinic-housed format of established psychotherapy interventions.

How might evidence-based clinicians, committed to preserving therapy forms that have been shown to work well in controlled research settings, go about filling in the gaps between these settings and the world in which they practice? If depression can justifiably be considered an epidemic, an epidemiological perspective may lend insight into how to improve treatment effectiveness and reach. In public health models, the need to manage illness on a population-wide scale is approached with a multipronged, multitiered intervention system. This system fosters treatment dissemination through whatever mechanisms are available in the community, reducing burden on traditional care providers and allowing more people to be treated. The addition of a triage system allows the most costly, intensive interventions to be conserved for recipients with higher levels of need, while those at lower risk receive streamlined versions of treatment. Reduced-form treatments represent a way to offer something to those who do not need full-scale interventions, and who would be crowded out by higher-risk individuals and potentially denied access to services altogether if only full-scale interventions were offered. Supporting the possibility that less intensive forms of intervention might be effective, Rotheram-Borus & Duan (2003) suggest, "Dissemination of efficacious interventions into real-world settings may be hampered by inclusion of many activities, techniques, and strategies that go far beyond their underlying theories" (p. 519). That is, if therapies as tested in RCTs contain detrimentally superfluous elements, stripping away these components may not only be possible, it may actually improve effectiveness.

Promise for Couple/Parenting Interventions Based on Public Health Models

Moving from the realm of possibility into the arena of pragmatics, several templates are available for the application of public health models to the treatment of couple and parenting problems.

Parenting Interventions

The most well-defined example of a public health approach to parenting interventions is the "Triple P" Positive Parenting Program (Sanders, 1992). The program has been widely implemented in Australia and New Zealand, where geographic separation and vast rural areas render it difficult for the portion of the population not living in the few urban centers to reach sophisticated mental health care networks. Five levels of involvement in the program are available, incorporating flexibility within each level. Level One, a nationwide campaign directed by regional program coordinators in cooperation with the media, utilizes a variety of media outlets to disseminate general preventive information about healthy parenting, introduce families unfamiliar with psychological services to the concept of interventions for child behavior problems, and inform those who may need additional help of ways to become involved at more structured levels of the program. Level Two, delivered through school personnel and primary care providers who have been trained in Triple P, offers one to two brief consultation sessions regarding specific parenting problems, in conjunction with supplemental tip sheets and videos. Because most families already have contact with schools and medical care, housing a version of Triple P in these institutions maximizes its availability. Additionally, parents have traditionally turned to teachers and doctors for advice on child behavior problems, so they may be more open to the treatment program if it is delivered through these familiar channels. Level Three increases the number of sessions to three or four and incorporates active skills training for management of particular problems. Level Four, an 8 to 10-session treatment that can be delivered in individual, group, or self-guided form, most closely approximates a standard parenting intervention. Choice of modality may be determined by patient preference as well as by individual family factors (level of motivation for self-directed treatment, difficulty reaching a Triple P center, need for more individualized attention, perceived benefit of the parents receiving group feedback from other parents). Finally, Level 5 is designed for parents who have not achieved sufficient gains via Level 4 participation or for whom other factors—couple distress and parental depression figuring prominently among them—have complicated treatment. Three three-session modules are available and may be combined according to the clinician's judgment: additional skills practice; partner communication, relationship enhancement, and problem-solving training; and a cognitive-behaviorally based introduction to the management of depression.

Couple Interventions

To date, several public health-based systems for ameliorating couple distress have been proposed, each less elaborate than the Triple P system but promising in their design nevertheless:

PREP. The Prevention and Relationship Enhancement Program (PREP), a prevention-oriented version of behavioral couple therapy, has been adapted to multiple formats to maximize effectiveness in dissemination. A popular self-help book, *Fighting for Your Marriage* (Markman, Stanley, & Blumberg, 1994), explains skills and sets up practice exercises for couples to pursue one chapter (or session) at a time. Versions of this book dealing with specific topics pertinent to African American couples, Jewish couples, and empty nesters have also been published. A videotape series is also available for couples who may prefer this medium, as is an audiotape series that may be ideal for commuters and others "on the go" who have already embraced the books-on-tape market. A fourth option combines tape instruction with workbooks that offer more individualized application and practice. For those requiring a higher level of directive support in pursuing the program, PREP is offered as a 6 to 12-hour educational workshop, which may be offered as a one-day, weekend, or multisession course to suit couples' varying schedules and tastes. Workshops are offered in the United States as well as in 27 other countries, and training is readily available for professionals wishing to become PREP leaders. A slightly higher level of support involves small group mentoring, where the educational workshop approach is combined with opportunities for leaders to provide a certain amount of individual attention to couples. Mental health professionals who are trained as PREP leaders may also advertise that they offer PREP in the context of private therapy for individual couples, allowing couples with more complex problems (e.g., partner depression) to receive the maximum amount of individualized attention. A Christian-based version of PREP has also been developed, in order to reach an audience for whom religion and spirituality are important components of marriage. Capitalizing on the fact that churches have traditionally been a trusted resource for premarital and marital guidance, efforts to disseminate the Christian PREP program by training clergy as program leaders are currently undergoing evaluation. Initial evidence suggests that clergy are as effective at delivering PREP interventions as are other group leaders trained in the approach (Stanley et al., 2001).

Fincham and Beach (2002). In developing a proposed forgiveness-based intervention for individuals who have experienced transgressions in their relationships,

Fincham and Beach adopted a public health model in order to respond to a population that is both too large to be accommodated by traditional mental health treatment and unlikely to seek such treatment even if available. As with Triple P and PREP, the proposal for the Fincham and Beach program incorporates extensive use of the Internet and printed self-help materials, which would allow it to be followed largely on a self-directed basis where feasible and/or necessary. Minor support would be available in the form of periodic check-in; conversely, individuals requiring more support could be identified via this check-in process and referred for more intensive treatment. The proposed program also incorporates a role for paraprofessional providers, in order to make more intensive services more readily available to those who do seek them.

Using the Internet. One might also imagine that use of the Internet would be a good way to reach a wider audience. Because it is a structured approach with a strong didactic component, it would seem particularly likely that traditional behavioral marital and parenting technologies might be delivered in an Internet-based format. Some initial tests of this approach are underway (Banawan & Beach, manuscript in preparation). Ideally in such an approach, rather than simply providing electronic access to written materials, the program would be interactive, storing responses and providing a degree of individualized guidance to each participant. Such accommodation to individual preferences seems quite within the reach of current technology. Likewise, although currently in its preliminary stages of development, it is conceivable that e-mail or real-time conferencing could serve as an adjunct or alternate to telephone or face-to-face check-ins for those who require them. Such advances would expand the range of options for those who cannot meet face-to-face with a clinician or for whom this is not necessary. Of course, it is quite possible that such approaches would face effectiveness obstacles of their own. For example, access to Internet services may not be possible for some high-risk populations. Alternatively, Internet delivery may prove less likely to attract and maintain the involvement of those most in need of services. In that case, the apparent reach of the Internet might prove more illusion than reality. Nonetheless, a greater attempt to explore this delivery system seems warranted at the current time.

Moving Forward

As these examples suggest, there is clear potential for couple and parenting treatments for depression to be adapted to a public health format. Short of designing complex systems of tiered treatments, clinicians can still adopt a public health perspective to facilitate dissemination and palatability and thereby increase their ranges beyond the patient bases they already serve. Through an emphasis on identifying differing levels of risk or need and providing varying services to meet these needs, combined with the use of nontraditional formats (e.g., paraprofessional service providers, workshops, self-guided materials, phone, television, and Internet) and capitalization upon emerging technology, it should theoretically be possible to expand an umbrella wide enough to provide some form of treatment to anyone, anywhere.

As we attempt to build effective interventions upon the foundation provided by efficacy studies, it is likely that we will need to dramatically expand the variables we consider as well. For example, consideration of efficiency, cost effectiveness, patient preference, clinical judgment, and how to manage patients for whom different levels of treatment are indicated at different points in time may become more central. Of course, in some circumstances where not all levels of care may be available (such as in remote areas), assignment to lower-intensity levels may occur by necessity. Such situations preclude involvement of either patient preference or objective determinations of optimal treatment level. Where greater freedom of choice is available and is incorporated into the system, however, some participants may self-select a low level of intervention as a tentative first sampling of the program, and may find that this turns out to be ineffective. So that such participants do not get discouraged and conclude that the entire program is of no use for them, they need to be made aware that a treatment failure may indicate that a higher level of involvement is necessary. There must then be a user-friendly way for these people to connect with more advanced services, so as not to lose them at this juncture. As in Triple P, it may be advisable to target the entire population with the lowest level of an intervention (e.g., a television program) and incorporate into that intervention messages about the availability of other levels of service. This allows those who need more treatment or who perceive their problems as being more severe to self-select into a more intensive form of treatment. Alternatively, universal screening may be conducted, using screening questionnaires in general practice settings. This method takes advantage of the fact that contact is already established between most families and some form of general health provider, and also permits some flexibility in the assessment process. Unfortunately, the ability to screen effectively for psychopathology through primary care has not yet been demonstrated, as noted by Palmer and Coyne (2003).

Self-selection is likely to present far thornier problems at the other end of the spectrum, where, with a widely popular program, couples and parents may clamor for the maximum levels of treatment in excess of available supply. This situation could very well occur when targeting an intervention exclusively for a population with comorbid depression and couple/parenting distress, who represent the most severely impaired group identified in the Triple P program, and for whom the most intense level of Triple P intervention is already reserved. If advanced clinical judgment is necessary to determine which treatment applicants are functioning well enough that they can be adequately served through less intense levels of intervention, it is possible that this assessment procedure alone could demand substantial system resources, particularly the type of resources that are in shortest supply (i.e., experienced clinicians). As a partial solution to this problem, program developers have begun to advocate the establishment of sound, objective assignment rules that can be employed by other professionals already involved in the program, without the need for extensive training. While initially time-consuming and costly to develop such an assessment system, it could pay for itself by subsequently distributing the assessment workload among the program.

However, this goal should not overshadow the importance of preserving patient preference and limitations in treatment selection; even the most carefully structured system of assessment and treatment assignment will break down if participants drop out upon finding that they have been placed into a treatment where their needs and wishes are not adequately accommodated. Harmonizing treatment assignment with patient preference and limitations may take the form of first determining which of the available interventions are feasible, given the life circumstances and preferences of a particular couple or family, and then in a second stage relying on actuarial prediction to guide recommendations about which of the available and acceptable options might result in the best outcome. This process could occur through interactive media, some form of human consultation, or a combination of both.

CONCLUSION

In this chapter, we provided evidence of the considerable comorbidity between adult depression and couple/parenting distress, explicated the logical relationship between these problems, and thereby demonstrated a case for intervening in depression at the couple/family level. After referring the reader to empirically supported treatment packages that can be used in this area by clinicians with considerable confidence in their efficacy, we addressed pragmatic complications associated with moving from efficacy to effectiveness and maintaining accessibility and palatability in the context of the potentially large population that stands to benefit from these services. We encountered many unanswered questions but also much promise. It is clear that couple and parenting interventions have a place in the treatment of depression. It may be equally true that they have a place in a public health approach to depression.

REFERENCES

Addis, M. E., & Jacobson, N. S. (1996). Reasons for depression and the process and outcome of cognitive-behavioral psychotherapies. *Journal of Consulting and Clinical Psychology, 64,* 1417–1424.

American Psychiatric Association. (2000). *Diagnostic and statistical manual of mental disorders* (4th ed., Text Revision). Washington, DC: Author.

Bagner, D. M., & Eyberg, S. M. (2003). Father involvement in parent training: When does it matter? *Journal of Clinical Child and Adolescent Psychology, 32,* 599–605.

Banawan, S., & Beach, S. R. H. (2004). *On internet trials and tribulations: The use of the internet to deliver traditional behavioral marital therapy.* Manuscript in preparation.

Barrett, J. E., Williams, J. W., Oxman, T. E., Katon, W., Frank, E., Hegel, M. T., et al. (1999). The treatment effectiveness project. A comparison of the effectiveness of paroxetine, problem-solving therapy, and placebo in the treatment of minor depression and dysthymia in primary care patients: Background and research plan. *General Hospital Psychiatry, 21,* 260–273.

Beach, S. R. H., & Amir, N. (2003). Is depression taxonic, dimensional, or both? *Journal of Abnormal Psychology, 112,* 228–236.

Beach, S. R. H., & Broderick, J. E. (1983). Commitment: A variable in women's response to marital therapy. *American Journal of Family Therapy, 11,* 16–24.

Beach, S. R. H., Katz, J., Kim, S., & Brody, G. H. (2003). Prospective effects of marital satisfaction on depressive symptoms in established marriages: A dyadic model. *Journal of Social and Personal Relationships, 20,* 355–371.

Beach, S. R. H., & O'Leary, K. D. (1992). Treating depression in the context of marital discord: Outcome and predictors of response for marital therapy versus cognitive therapy. *Behavior Therapy, 23,* 507–528.

Beach, S. R. H., & O'Leary, K. D. (1993). Dysphoria and marital discord: Are dysphoric individuals at risk for marital maladjustment? *Journal of Marital and Family Therapy, 19,* 355–368.

Beach, S. R. H., Sandeen, E. E., & O'Leary, K. D. (1990). *Depression in marriage.* New York: Guilford.

Beutler, L. E., Clarkin, J. F., & Bongar, B. (2000). *Guidelines for the systematic treatment of the depressed patient.* New York: Oxford University Press.

Brown, G. W., Harris, T. O., & Hepworth, C. (1995). Loss, humiliation and entrapment among women developing depression: A patient and non-patient comparison. *Psychological Medicine, 25,* 7–21.

Brown, G. W., & Moran, P. M. (1997). Single mothers, poverty and depression. *Psychological Medicine, 27,* 21–33.

Bruce, M. L., Ten Have, T. R., Reynolds, C. F., Katz, I. I., Schulberg, H. C., Mulsant, B. H., et al. (2004). Reducing suicidal ideation and depressive symptoms in depressed older primary care patients: A randomized controlled trial. *JAMA: Journal of the American Medical Association, 291,* 1081–1091.

Cano, A., & O'Leary, K. D. (2000). Infidelity and separations precipitate major depressive episodes and symptoms of nonspecific depression and anxiety. *Journal of Consulting and Clinical Psychology, 68,* 774–781.

Clarkin, J. F., Glick, I. D., Haas, G. L., Spencer, J. H., Lewis, A. B., Peyser, J., et al. (1990). A randomized clinical trial of inpatient family intervention, V: Results for affective disorders. *Journal of Affective Disorders, 18,* 17–28.

Coyne, J. C. (1976). Toward an interactional description of depression. *Psychiatry, 39,* 28–40.

Coyne, J. C. (1994). Self-reported distress: Analog or ersatz depression? *Psychological Bulletin, 116,* 29–45.

Coyne, J. C., & Benazon, N. R. (2001). Not Agent Blue: Effects of marital functioning on depression and implications for treatment. In S. R. H. Beach (Ed.), *Marital and family processes in depression; A scientific foundation for clinical practice* (pp. 25–43). Washington, DC: American Psychological Association.

Coyne, J. C., Thompson, R., & Palmer, S. C. (2002). Marital quality, coping with conflict, marital complaints, and affection in couples with a depressed wife. *Journal of Family Psychology, 16,* 26–37.

Cummings, E. M., DeArth-Pendley, G., Du Rocher Schudlich, T., Smith, D. A. (2001). Parental depression and family functioning: Toward a process-oriented model of children's adjustment. In S. R. H. Beach (Ed.), *Marital and family processes in depression: A scientific foundation for clinical practice* pp. 89–110. Washington, DC: American Psychological Association.

Dadds, M. R., & McHugh, T. A. (1992). Social support and treatment outcome in behavioral family therapy for child conduct problems. *Journal of Consulting and Clinical Psychology, 60,* 252–259.

Davila, J. (2001). Paths to unhappiness: The overlapping courses of depression and romantic dysfunction. In S. R. H. Beach (Ed.), *Marital and family processes in depression: A scientific foundation for clinical practice* pp. 71–87. Washington, DC: American Psychological Association Press.

Davila, J., Bradbury, T. N., Cohan, C. L., & Tochluk, S. (1997). Marital functioning and depressive symptoms: Evidence for a stress generation model. *Journal of Personality and Social Psychology, 73,* 849–861.

Downey, G., & Coyne, J. C. (1990). Children of depressed parents: An integrative review. *Psychological Bulletin, 108,* 50–76.

Dumas, J. E., Gibson, J. A., & Albin, J. B. (1989). Behavioral correlates of maternal depressive symptomatology in conduct-disorder children. *Journal of Consulting and Clinical Psychology, 57,* 516–521.

Emanuels-Zuurveen, L., & Emmelkamp, P. M. G. (1996). Individual behavioural-cognitive therapy versus marital therapy for depression in maritally distressed couples. *British Journal of Psychiatry, 169,* 181–188.

Emanuels-Zuurveen, L. & Emmelkamp, P. M. G. (1997). Spouse-aided therapy with depressed patients. *Behavior Modification, 21,* 62–77.

Emery, R. E. (1982). Interparental conflict and the children of discord and divorce. *Psychological Bulletin, 92,* 310–330.

Fincham, F. D., & Beach, S. R. H. (2002). Forgiveness: Toward a public health approach to intervention. In J. H. Harvey & A. Wenzel (Eds.), *A clinician's guide to maintaining and enhancing close relationships* (pp. 277–300). Mahwah, NJ: Lawrence Erlbaum.

Fincham, F. D., Fernandes, L. O. L., & Humphreys, K. (1993). *Communicating in relationships: A guide for couples and professionals.* Champaign, IL: Research Press.

Foley, S. H., Rounsaville, B. J., Weissman, M. M., Sholomskas, D., & Chevron, E. (1989). Individual versus conjoint interpersonal psychotherapy for depressed patients with marital disputes. *International Journal of Family Psychiatry, 10,* 29–42.

Forehand, R., Wells, K. C., & Griest, D. L. (1980). An examination of the social validity of a parent training program. *Behavior Therapy, 11,* 488–502.

Gelfand, D. M., & Teti, D. M. (1990). The effects of maternal depression on children. *Clinical Psychology Review, 10,* 329–353.

Halford, W. K. (1998). The ongoing evolution of behavioral couples therapy: Retrospect and prospect. *Clinical Psychology Review, 18,* 613–634.

Hammen, C. (1991). *Depression runs in families: The social context of risk and resilience in children of depressed mothers.* New York: Springer-Verlag.

Hops, H., Biglan, A., Sherman, L., Arthur, J., Friedman, L., & Osteen, V. (1987). Home observation of family interactions of depressed women. *Journal of Consulting and Clinical Psychology, 55,* 341–346.

Horwath, E., Johnson, J., Klerman, G. L., & Weissman, M. M. (1992). Depressive symptoms as relative and attributable risk factors for first-onset major depression. *Archives of General Psychiatry, 49,* 817–823.

Ilardi, S. S. & Craighead, W. E. (1994). The role of nonspecific factors in cognitive-behavior therapy for depression. *Clinical Psychology: Science & Practice, 1,* 138–156.

Jacobson, N. S., & Christensen, A. (1996). *Acceptance and change in couple therapy: A therapist's guide for transforming relationships.* New York: Norton.

Jacobson, N. S., Dobson, K., Fruzzetti, A. E., Schmaling, K. B., & Salusky, S. (1991). Marital therapy as a treatment for depression. *Journal of Consulting and Clinical Psychology, 59,* 547–557.

Joiner, T. E. (2000). Depression's vicious scree: Self-propagating and erosive processes in depression chronicity. *Clinical Psychology: Science and Practice, 7,* 203–218.

Jones, D. J., Beach, S. R. H., & Forehand, R. (2001). Stress generation in intact community families: Depressive symptoms, perceived family relationship stress, and implications for adolescent adjustment. *Journal of Social and Personal Relationships, 18,* 443–462.

Keitner, G. I., Miller, I. W., & Ryan, C. E. (1994). Family functioning in severe depressive disorders.

In L. Grunhaus & J. F. Greden (Eds.), *Progress in Psychiatry: No. 44. Severe depressive disorders* (pp. 89–110). Washington, DC: American Psychiatric Association.

Kendler, K. S., Hettema, J. M., Butera, F., Gardner, C. O., & Prescott, C. A. (2003). Life event dimensions of loss, humiliation, entrapment, and danger in the prediction of onsets of major depression and generalized anxiety. *Archives of General Psychiatry, 60,* 789–796.

Klerman, G. L., Weissman, M. M., Rounsaville, B. J., & Chevron, E. S. (1984). *Interpersonal psychotherapy of depression.* New York: Basic Books.

Lewinsohn, P. M., Klein, D. N., Durbin, E. C., Seeley, J. R., & Rohde, P. (2003). Family study of subthreshold depressive symptoms: Risk factor for MDD? *Journal of Affective Disorders, 77,* 149–157.

Lovejoy, M. C., Gracyk, P. A., O'Hare, E., & Neuman, G. (2000). Maternal depression and parenting behavior: A meta-analytic review. *Clinical Psychology Review, 20,* 561–592.

Markman, H., Stanley, S., & Blumberg, S. L. (1994). *Fighting for your marriage.* San Francisco: Jossey-Bass.

McCarty, C. A., & McMahon, R. J. (2003). Mediators of the relation between maternal depressive symptoms and child internalizing and disruptive behavior disorders. *Journal of Family Psychology, 17,* 545–556.

McFarlane, W. R., Dixon, L., Lukens, E., & Lucksted, A. (2003). Family education and schizophrenia: A review of the literature. *Journal of Marital and Family Therapy, 29,* 223–245.

McMahon, R. J., Forehand, R., Griest, D. L., & Wells, K. C. (1981). Who drops out of therapy during parent training. *Behavioral Counseling Quarterly, 1,* 79–85.

O'Leary, K. D., Riso, L., & Beach, S. R. H. (1990). Beliefs about the marital discord/depression link: Implications for outcome and treatment matching. *Behavior Therapy, 21,* 413–422.

O'Leary, K. D., Sandeen, E., & Beach, S. R. H. (1987, November). *Treatment of suicidal, maritally discordant clients by marital therapy or cognitive therapy.* Paper presented at the 21st annual meeting of the Association for Advancement of Behavior Therapy, Boston.

Palmer, S. C., & Coyne, J. C. (2003). Screening for depression in medical care: Pitfalls, alternatives, and revised priorities. *Journal of Psychosomatic Research, 54,* 279–287.

Rotheram-Borus, M. J., & Duan, N. (2003). Next generation of preventive interventions. *Journal of the American Academy of Child and Adolescent Psychiatry, 42,* 518–526.

Ruscio, J., & Ruscio, A. M. (2000). Informing the continuity controversy: A taxometric analysis of depression. *Journal of Abnormal Psychology, 109,* 473–487.

Sanders, M. R. (1992). *Every parent: A positive approach to children's behaviour.* Sydney, Australia: Addison Wesley.

Sanders, M. R., & McFarland, M. (2000). Treatment of depressed mothers with disruptive children: A controlled evaluation of cognitive behavioral family intervention. *Behavior Therapy, 31,* 89–112.

Santor, D. A., & Coyne, J. C. (2001). Evaluating the continuity of symptomatology between depressed and nondepressed individuals. *Journal of Abnormal Psychology, 110,* 216–225.

Stanley, S. M., Markman, H. J., Prado, L. M., Olmos-Gallo, P. A., Tonelli, L., St. Peters, M., et al. (2001). Community-based premarital prevention: Clergy and lay leaders on the front lines. *Family Relations: Interdisciplinary Journal of Applied Family Studies, 50,* 67–76.

Teti, D. M., & Gelfand, D. M. (1991). Behavioral competence among mothers of infants in the first year: The mediational role of maternal self-efficacy. *Child Development, 62,* 918–929.

Watzlawick, P., & Coyne, J. C. (1980). Depression following stroke: Brief, problem-focused family treatment. *Family Process, 19,* 13–18.

Webster-Stratton, C. (1994). Advancing video tape parent training: A comparison study. *Journal of Consulting and Clinical Psychology, 62,* 583–593.

Weissman, M. M., & Paykel, E. S. (1974). *The depressed woman: A study of social relationships.* Chicago: University of Chicago Press.

Whisman, M. A. (2001). The association between depression and marital dissatisfaction. In S. R. H. Beach (Ed.), *Marital and family processes in depression: A scientific foundation for clinical practice* (pp. 3–24). Washington, DC: American Psychological Association.

Whisman, M. A., & Bruce, M. L. (1999). Marital distress and incidence of major depressive episode in a community sample. *Journal of Abnormal Psychology, 108,* 674–678.

Williams, J. W., Barrett, J., Oxman, T., Frank, E., Katon, W., & Sullivan, M., et al. (2000). Treatment of dysthymia and minor depression in primary care: A randomized controlled trial in older adults. *JAMA: Journal of the American Medical Association, 284,* 1519–1526.

CHAPTER 10

Couples Therapy for Alcoholism and Drug Abuse

Gary R. Birchler, William Fals-Stewart, and Timothy J. O'Farrell

BRIEF INTRODUCTION TO COUPLE-BASED TREATMENT FOR SUBSTANCE USE DISORDERS

Although alcoholism and drug abuse have been viewed historically as individual problems best treated on an individual basis, a large and growing body of empirical literature suggests the family often plays a crucial role in the lives of alcoholics and drug abusers (Stanton & Heath, 1997). In turn, clinical applications of marital and family therapy to the treatment of alcoholism and drug abuse have increased considerably over the last 3 decades. In fact, the Joint Commission on Accreditation of Health Care Organizations (JCAHO) standard for accrediting substance abuse treatment programs in the United States now requires that an adult family member who lives with an identified substance-abusing patient be included at least in the initial assessment (Brown, O'Farrell, Maisto, Boies, & Suchinsky, 1997).

Enthusiasm for understanding the role family members may play in the development, maintenance, and treatment of alcoholism and drug abuse has not been limited to the research community. In the lay press, the sheer volume of texts which have appeared on the topics of codependency, adult children of alcoholics, addictive personality, enabling, and so forth is staggering. For example, an Internet search of a large online book retailer revealed that over 250 books were available presently for purchase on the topic of codependency alone. Moreover, self-help support groups for family members of alcoholics and drugs abusers (e.g., Alanon) are available in virtually every community.

Because relationship problems and substance use disorders so frequently co-occur, it would be very difficult to find clinicians who specialize in the treatment of adult substance use disorders or relationship problems who have not had to address both sets of issues concurrently for many clients seeking help. The purpose of the present chapter is to provide an overview of a behaviorally oriented, couple-based treatment for substance use that would be useful to both specialists in either the treatment of alcoholism and drug abuse or the treatment of marital/relationship distress. Our goal is to provide an integrated conceptualization of substance use problems and dyadic relationships that is grounded in the empirical literature that has evolved over the last 30 years, and thus is an alternative to the psychology of family and addiction that has dominated the popular press for much of the late twentieth century.

ALCOHOLISM AND DRUG ABUSE: A RELATIONSHIP-BASED CONCEPTUALIZATION

Defining Alcohol and Drug Use Disorders

Before examining the interrelationship of substance abuse and relationship functioning, it is important to provide contemporary diagnostic definitions of alcoholism and drug addiction. There are actually several different definitional frameworks for these disorders that have appeared in the literature. The most widely used is the psychiatric diagnostic approach, exemplified in the *Diagnostic and Statistical Manual of Mental Disorders* (*DSM-IV;* American Psychiatric Association, 1994). In *DSM-IV,* the diagnosis of alcohol or psychoactive substance use disorders includes two general subcategories: abuse and dependence. A cluster of cognitive, behavioral, and physiological symptoms indicating that the individual continues to use a given psychoactive substance despite significant substance-related problems marks *Substance Dependence.* To meet diagnostic criteria for dependence on a psychoactive substance, an individual must display at least three of the following seven symptoms: (1) physical tolerance, (2) withdrawal, (3) unsuccessful attempts to stop or control substance use, (4) use of larger amounts of the substance than intended, (5) loss or reduction in important recreational, social, or occupational activities, (6) continued use of the substance despite knowledge of physical or psychological problems that are likely to have been caused or exacerbated by the substance, and (7) excessive time spent using the substance or recovering from its effects.

In contrast, the essential feature of *Substance Abuse* is a maladaptive pattern of problem use leading to significant adverse consequences. This includes one or more of the following: (1) failure to fulfill major social obligations in the context of work, school, or home, (2) recurrent substance use in situations that creates the potential for harm (e.g., drinking and driving), (3) recurrent substance-related legal problems, and (4) continued substance use despite having persistent social or interpersonal problems caused or exacerbated by the effects of the substance.

Although the *DSM-IV* definitions of alcohol and drug use disorders were claimed to be largely atheoretical by their developers, it is clear that their classifications entail both ontological and epistemological assumptions arising from a disease model. In contrast, behavioral scientists have proposed an alternative approach to the disease concept of alcoholism and drug abuse that underlies the *DSM* classifications (Adesso, 1995; Nathan, 1981). In this framework, alcohol and drug use disorders are not defined as a unitary disease, nor is it implicitly assumed that the observed substance use symptoms are the manifestation of a disease state. Symptoms are viewed as acquired habits that emerge from a combination of social, pharmacological, and behavioral factors. Emphasis is placed on environmental, affective, and cognitive antecedents and reinforcing consequences of substance use. The outgrowth of this functional conceptualization of substance use is that drinking and drug use are ruled by motivation and learning principles, as are other human behaviors.

Without question, the disease model of addiction is the dominant view held by the vast majority of treatment providers in the substance abuse treatment industry. Consequently, treatments for alcoholism and substance abuse have evolved largely from this orientation. Thus, from a practical standpoint, for any intervention for alcoholism and substance abuse (couple-based or otherwise) to be used widely in most treatment settings, it must be acceptable for clinicians and clients who define and treat these disorders from a disease perspective. However, it should be noted that the behaviorally oriented treatment approach described in this chapter and espoused by the authors broadly assumes a "problems perspective," in which problem behaviors presented by couples seeking help are modified to promote sobriety. Nonetheless, the intervention methods we espouse herein actually fit rather easily into a disease model framework if clients and treatment providers accept the premise that behavioral change is the fundamental ingredient to controlling the disease of alcoholism and drug abuse.

Prevalence of Alcohol and Drug Use Disorders and Comorbidity with Relationship Problems

Epidemiological surveys of alcohol and drug use disorders indicate that they are among the most common psychiatric disorders in the general population. The most recent national survey on the prevalence of alcohol and drug use disorders is the National Longitudinal Alcohol Epidemiologic Survey (NLAES; Grant et al., 1994), in which 42,862 noninstitutionalized respondents living in the contiguous United States, aged 18 years and older, were interviewed regarding their use of alcohol and other substances, using *DSM-IV* classification criteria. According to the NLAES, in 1994 the combined prevalence of alcohol abuse and dependence was 7.4 percent representing more than 13 million Americans; the lifetime rate was 18.2 percent, or nearly 34 million Americans.

Prevalences of *DSM-IV* drug use disorders were much lower than those reported for alcohol use disorders. Rates for 1994 abuse and dependence for most drugs were less than 1 percent, with the exception of cannabis abuse and dependence combined (1.2 percent). The prevalence of 1994 abuse or dependence on any drug was 1.5 percent. Overall, the lifetime rate of any drug abuse or dependence was 6.1 percent.

There are several lines of converging evidence that indicate substance abuse and relationship distress covary. Although individuals diagnosed with alcohol abuse or dependence are just as likely to marry as the rest of the population, they are more likely to divorce or separate. Moreover, men and women with drinking problems are more likely to divorce than individuals with any other type of psychological disorder. Several studies have found that levels of relationship distress among alcoholic and drug-abusing dyads are high (e.g., Fals-Stewart, Birchler, & O'Farrell, 1999; O'Farrell & Birchler, 1987). Relationship problems are predictive of a poor prognosis in alcohol and drug abuse treatment programs (Fals-Stewart & Birchler, 1994; Vanicelli, Gingerich, & Ryback, 1983). Finally, poor response to substance abuse treatment is predictive of ongoing marital difficulty (e.g., Billings & Moos, 1983; Finney, Moose, Cronkite, & Gamble, 1983).

The Interplay between Substance Use and Marital Adjustment

The causal connections between substance use and marital discord are complex and appear to interact reciprocally. For example, chronic drinking outside the home is correlated with reduced marital satisfaction for spouses (e.g., Dunn, Jacob, Hummon, & Seilhamer, 1987). At the same time, however, stressful marital interactions are related to increased problematic substance use and are related to relapse among alcoholics and drug abusers after treatment (Fals-Stewart & Birchler, 1994; Maisto, O'Farrell, McKay, Connors, & Pelcovitz, 1988). Thus, the relationship between substance use and marital problems is not unidirectional, with one consistently causing the other, but rather each can serve as a precursor to the other.

Viewed from a family perspective, there are several antecedent conditions and reinforcing consequences of substance use. Poor communication and problem solving, arguing, financial stressors, and nagging are common antecedents to substance use. Consequences of substance use can be positive or negative. For instance, certain behaviors by a non-substance-abusing spouse, such as avoiding conflict with the substance-abusing partner when he or she is intoxicated, are positive consequences of substance abuse and can thus inadvertently reinforce continued substance-using behavior. Partners avoiding the substance abuser or making disapproving verbal comments about his or her alcohol or drug use are among the most common negative consequences of substance abuse. Other negative effects of substance use on the family, such as psychological distress of the spouse, and social, behavioral, academic, and emotional problems among children increase stress in the family system and may therefore lead to or exacerbate substance use.

Three Common Models for the Treatment of Substance Use and Couple Distress

Although several systems of family therapy have been used with substance-abusing patients, three theoretical perspectives have come to dominate family-based conceptualizations of substance use, and thus have become the basis for the treatment strategies most often used with substance users (Gondoli & Jacob, 1990; O'Farrell, 1995). The best known of these and the most widely used is the *family disease approach,* which views alcoholism and other drug abuse as an illness of the family, suffered not only by the substance user, but also by family members. The *family systems approach* applies the principles of general systems theory to families, with particular attention paid to ways in which families maintain a dynamic balance between substance use and family functioning and whose interactional behavior is organized around alcohol or drug use. *Behavioral approaches* assume that family interactions serve to reinforce alcohol- and drug-using behavior. We will now review the treatments that have evolved from these systems in more detail, emphasizing the hallmark therapy techniques identified with each approach.

Disease Model

From this perspective, alcoholism and drug abuse are thought of or viewed as a family disease, which affects all (or nearly all) family members. Family members of substance users are viewed as suffering from the disease of codependence, which describes the process underlying the various problems observed in the families of individuals who abuse psychoactive substances. Schaef (1986) argues that codependence is a disease that parallels the addiction disease process and is marked by characteristic symptoms (e.g., external referencing, caretaking, self-centeredness, control issues, dishonesty, frozen feelings, perfectionism, fear). The hallmark of codependency is enabling, which, as the term implies, is defined as any set of behaviors that perpetuates the psychoactive substance use. These include making it easier for the alcoholic or drug abuser to engage in substance use or shielding the substance user from the negative consequences often associated with drinking or taking drugs.

Although the problem of substance abuse exists within the family, the solution, from this popular and widely used perspective, is for each family member to recognize that he or she has a disease, detach from the substance user, and to engage in his or her own program of recovery (e.g., Al-Anon, Al-Ateen, or Adult Children of Alcoholics groups). Family members are taught there is nothing they can do to help the substance user to stop using other than to cease enabling and to detach and focus on themselves so as to reduce their own emotional distress and improve their own coping.

Family Systems Model

The family systems model views the acquisition and use of alcohol or other drugs as a major organizing principle for patterns of interactional behavior within the family system. A reciprocal relationship exists between family functioning and substance use, with an individual's drug and alcohol use being best understood in the context of the entire family's functioning. According to family systems theory, substance abuse in either adults or adolescents often evolves during periods in which the individual family member is having difficulty addressing an important developmental issue (e.g., leaving the home) or when the family is facing a significant crisis (e.g., job loss, marital discord). During these periods, substance abuse can serve to (1) distract family members from their central problem or (2) slow down or stop a transition to a different developmental stage that is being resisted by the family as a whole or by one of its members (Stanton & Todd, 1982).

From the family systems perspective, substance use represents a maladaptive attempt to deal with difficulties that develop a homeostatic life of their own and regulate family transactions. The substance use itself serves an important role in the family; once the therapist understands the function of the substance use for the family, she or he can then explain how the behavior has come about and the function it serves. In turn, treatment is aimed at restructuring the interaction patterns associated with the substance use, thereby making the drinking or drug use unnecessary in the maintenance of the family system functioning.

Behavioral Model

Behavioral family therapy treatment models draw heavily upon operant and social learning theories to understand the behavior of the substance user in the family context. Substance use is viewed as a behavior learned in the context of social interactions (e.g., observing peers, parents, role models in the media) and reinforced by contingencies in the individual's environment. Thus, from a family perspective, substance use is maintained, in part, from the antecedents and consequences that are operating in the family environment. Three general reinforcement patterns are typically observed in substance-abusing families: (1) reinforcement for substance-using behavior in the form of attention or caretaking, (2) shielding the substance user from experiencing negative consequences related to his or her drinking or drug use, and (3) punishing drinking behavior (McCrady, 1986).

Following from the operant and social learning principles, treatment emphasizes contingency management designed to reward sobriety, reduce negative reinforcement of drinking or drug use, and increase prosocial behaviors that may be incompatible with substance use. The substance user and involved family members are trained in methods to increase positive interactions, improve problem solving, and enhance communication skills. Use of these newly developed skills serves to reduce the likelihood of continued drinking or drug use by the substance-using family member.

OVERVIEW OF BEHAVIORAL COUPLES THERAPY

As noted, Behavioral Couples Therapy (BCT) works directly to increase relationship factors conducive to abstinence. A behavioral approach assumes that family members can reward abstinence—and that alcoholic and drug-abusing individuals from happier, more cohesive relationships, with better communication, have a lower risk of relapse. The substance-abusing patient and the spouse are seen together in BCT, typically for 15 to 20 outpatient couple sessions over 5 to 6 months. Generally, couples are married or cohabiting for at least 1 year, without current psychosis, and one member of the couple has a current problem with alcoholism and/or drug abuse. The couple starts BCT soon after the substance user seeks help.

BCT sees the substance-abusing patient with the spouse to build support for sobriety. The therapist arranges a daily Sobriety Trust Discussion in which the substance user states his or her intent not to drink or use drugs that day (in the tradition of one day at a time adapted from Alcoholics Anonymous), and the spouse expresses support for the patient's efforts to stay abstinent. Using a series of behavioral assignments, BCT increases positive feelings, shared activities, and constructive communication, because these relationship factors are conducive to sobriety. Relapse prevention is the final activity of BCT. At the end of weekly BCT sessions, each couple completes a Continuing Recovery Plan that is reviewed at quarterly follow-up visits for an additional year or two.

ASSESSMENT AND TREATMENT STRATEGIES FOR UNDERSTANDING THIS PROBLEM

The multifaceted aspects of both substance-using behavior and relationship adjustment are targets of assessment procedures with alcoholic and drug-abusing couples. We advocate a multimethod assessment approach with these couples, typically including semistructured conjoint and individual interviews, paper-and-pencil questionnaires, and observed samples of couple problem-solving communication. Although beyond the scope of the present chapter, Fals-Stewart, Birchler, and Ellis (1999) provide a detailed description of assessment inventories and procedures often recommended with couples in which partners abuse alcohol or drugs.

We typically inform clients that the first 2 to 3 sessions are used to gather assessment information and that neither they, nor the therapist, are committing to engaging in treatment. After the assessment phase is complete, the partners and the therapist mutually determine whether the information gathered suggests that treatment would be helpful. The information garnered from the assessment is used to develop and implement a couple-specific treatment plan. Because there are clear therapeutic benefits to participating in the assessment (i.e., increased knowledge about substance use, rapport building, facilitating the contemplation of change), the discrimination between assessment and treatment is, in reality, a false dichotomy. But making this distinction serves an important purpose; for many clients, participating in an initial assessment is less threatening than committing prematurely to treatment. The assessment phase includes both an evaluation of substance use severity and dyadic adjustment.

We advocate getting a comprehensive psychosocial history from each partner. Typically, we will conduct one early interview session with each partner separately to obtain his and her personal developmental histories. In these individual sessions we usually advocate a policy of *limited confidentiality,* whereby the therapist indicates that he or she will not keep secrets that may affect the integrity of and ethical allegiance to the couple. At the therapist's discretion, personal history items may indeed be held in confidence, but not if the information will compromise the basic understanding and goals of the couple contract for relationship therapy. The most likely (and so discussed) exception to this "no secrets" policy relates to partner safety, as in the case of domestic violence or potential harm. In general, the purpose of the individual interview is fourfold: (1) to obtain a basic developmental psychosocial history so as to better understand who the partners are and what trials and tribulations may have affected their lives to date, (2) to assess their substance-abuse histories in some detail, including the non-substance-abusing partners' past experiences with, beliefs about, and current interactions with substance-abusing intimates, (3) to further probe partners' levels of commitment to the relationship, to the therapy process, and possibly explore other agendas partners may have, and (4) to provide an opportunity for the individual partners to ask the therapist any questions about the prospects and process of therapy that may be more easily addressed one-on-one. Through this individual interview procedure, one primary goal is to fully understand each partner's past and current relationship to alcohol and drug use.

Assessment of Substance Use

The assessment of substance use involves inquiries about recent types, quantities, and frequencies of substances used, whether the extent of physical dependence on alcohol or other drugs requires detoxification, what led them to seek therapy at this time, the outcomes of prior efforts to seek help, and the goals of the substance abuser and the family member (e.g., reduction of substance use, temporary or permanent abstinence). Along with alcohol and drug use severity, it is strongly recommended that assessment include an evaluation of problem areas likely influenced by substance use, including (1) medical problems, (2) legal entanglements, (3) financial difficulties, (4) psychological distress, and (5) social/family problems.

Assessment of Relationship Problems and The Seven Cs Evaluation Framework

Concurrently with assessment of substance use and abuse, various aspects of partners' dyadic adjustment are evaluated. This process includes a multimethod evaluation of partners' general satisfaction with and stability of the relationship (i.e., current or planned separations as well as any past separations) along with an assessment of each partner's psychological and personality functioning. One important conjoint assessment procedure is the observation of an in vivo sample of conflict communication provided by the couple. Note that this procedure is a hallmark of BCT and it is described in more detail subsequently, following the discussion of the 7 Cs. Finally, several studies now suggest that spousal violence is alarmingly high among both alcoholic and drug-abusing couples (O'Farrell & Murphy, 1995); thus, evaluation of family violence and fears of recurrence must be assessed.

Birchler and Fals-Stewart (2000) have developed a conceptual framework called the "7 Cs," which describes seven critical elements of a long-term intimate relationship that may well be evaluated as part of any comprehensive assessment of couple functioning.

Character Features

This dimension refers to the basic type of person and personality that one brings to the relationship. For example, if one has a sense of humor, personal integrity, honesty, loyalty, a positive upbringing and outlook on life, and is free of significant mental or physical health problems, then one would be rated more favorably for character features. On the other hand, more challenging character features related to maintaining an intimate relationship may include a pervasive, negative attitude about life, substance abuse, significant mental or physical health problems, dishonesty, untrustworthiness, and so on. In addition, some otherwise okay character features simply may not be compatible or a good mix for a given couple (i.e., one wants to go out and socialize constantly, the other is more solitary and wants to stay at home). Interestingly, relatively unfavorable character features, if compatible, do not necessarily constitute a problem for a given couple (i.e., both partners engaging together in substance abuse).

Most likely, however, significant substance abuse affects one's ability to function interpersonally. Moreover, substance abuse often coexists with other psychological or personality problems, most notably depression, anxiety, Antisocial Personality Disorder (ASPD), or conduct disorders. These problems may serve to cause substance abuse, or substance abuse may cause or exacerbate these related problems. For example, some people self-medicate with alcohol in an attempt to treat depression or anxiety disorders; others experience an increase of symptoms such as depression or anxiety as a result of substance abuse.

Cultural and Ethnic Factors

This domain refers to the developmental and contextual environments in which each partner was raised and the traditions and preferences she or he has for living life. Couples can either benefit from or be in conflict about one or many of the following factors: cultural, ethnic, racial, and religious differences; male and female gender roles and responsibilities; how to appreciate and be responsible for working; the importance of and management of money; how to handle and express anger; how to discipline children; how to celebrate birthdays and holidays, and others. Although cultural and ethnic similarities may serve to reduce relationship adjustments, too much sameness can be boring or growth inhibiting. On the other hand, differences can add diversity and excitement, but they can also make compromise and adjustment difficult.

Contract

The dimension of Contract refers to the difference between what each partner wants and what each one gets from the relationship. How close does one's experiences match his or her expectations? Contract features may be explicit and openly understood: We are going to have a baby, and you will stay at home while I work outside the home. Or, as is more likely the case in intimate relationships, contract features may be implicit and therefore more vulnerable to misunderstandings: I expect that you will help me care for the baby and we will accomplish the housework as equals. Couple contracts evolve inevitably over the relationship life cycle; most couples need to be able to revise or renegotiate their relationship contracts to maintain growth and satisfaction.

Commitment

There are two important aspects of the Commitment domain to consider. One aspect is *stability*. Relationships last longer when partners are loyal and committed to one another for the long run—for better or for worse, and they entertain little or no desire to separate despite the inevitable problems. The second important aspect of commitment is commitment to *quality*. That is, partners are willing to invest effort in the relationship, to do the work that is required to make it healthy and personally satisfying for both partners.

Some couples have commitment to stability but not to quality. They can experience long, unhappy marriages. Other couples are committed to quality and personal happiness, but they disengage at the first signs of difficulty, offering little effort to work through the inevitable problems. Couples who are committed to stability and to quality have the best chance for developing a satisfactory, long-term intimate relationship.

Caring

Caring is a broad term that incorporates several important aspects of an intimate relationship. Couples rated high in caring actively demonstrate support, understanding, and validation of their mates; they have and show appreciation for who they are as people. In addition, there is sufficient activity and compatibility in the ways in which partners demonstrate affection to one another. Greetings, touching, intimate talking, companionship activities—all are desired and expressed in compatible ways. For happy couples, individual and mutually rewarding activities are in balance, in contrast to unhappy partners, who may feel abandoned, trapped, or possessed by their respective mates' activity preferences. Finally, the couple's sex life is satisfactory, healthy, trustworthy, and active at a level satisfactory to both partners. Couples rated lower in caring have identified problems and need improvement in one or more of the caring areas of function.

Communication

Communication is the basic interaction skill that allows for a relationship to function and evolve. Couples who develop and maintain effective communication skills are much more likely to be able to address all the other concerns identified in the 7 C's framework. Effective communication occurs when both partners possess the competence and motivation to share important information with one another about their thoughts, feelings, and actions. When the messages truly intended and sent by speakers are the same exact messages that are fully understood by the listeners, effective communication results.

Conflict Resolution

In addition to basic conversation and communication skills, couples also have to be able to work effectively together to make decisions, to solve daily problems in living, and to manage the inevitable relationship conflicts that arise. Elements of accommodation, assertiveness, negotiation and compromise, emotional expression and regulation, and anger management all come into play. Some couples get into trouble by being too conflict-avoidant, and therefore important issues do not get addressed; others tend to escalate conflicts into patterns of verbal and sometimes physical abuse. Either style, if present in the extreme, can do certain damage to the relationship. Couples need to be able to resolve disagreements, or agree to disagree, without becoming disconnected or abusive.

Communication and conflict resolution behaviors can most readily be observed by having the couple provide a live sample of communication as they attempt to resolve a conflict identified by the couple, with assistance from the therapist. In the now classic BCT procedure, partners are asked to discuss a moderate-intensity conflict issue for 10 to 15 minutes while the therapist observes the interaction (ideally, the therapist goes out of the room and watches from behind a one-way mirror or via video monitoring). In this manner, the couple typically offers an opportunity for the therapist to analyze real-time behaviors related to effective or ineffective communication and problem solving. There is no good substitute for obtaining such important skill-related information. It has been demonstrated that certain behaviors observed during this type of interaction can predict the likelihood of separation and divorce several years later (Gottman, 1994).

In summary, an analysis of the 7 Cs, combined with other assessment information derived from the initial interviews and optional inventory measures, provides ample information for the therapist to understand the (dys)function of the couple and to formulate feedback and a master treatment plan.

In our treatment model, after assessment information has been gathered, the clients and therapist meet for a feedback session, which we refer to as a "round-table discussion," in which the therapist provides an overview of the assessment results, including impressions of the nature and severity of both the substance abuse and relationship problems. Partners are invited to be active participants in this discussion, sharing their impressions and providing any critical information that they deem to be missing, inaccurate, or incomplete. The goals of this feedback session are to (1) provide the partners with objective, nonjudgmental information about the couple's dyadic functioning and the negative consequences of the substance misuse and (2) increase motivation for treatment.

Substance Abuse-Focused Interventions

The first purpose of couple treatment is to establish a clear and specific agreement between the substance abuser and partner about the goal for the substance use and each partner's role in achieving that goal. It is important to discuss possible exposure to alcoholic beverages, drugs, and substance use-related situations. Using alcohol use as an example, the spouse should decide if he or she will drink alcoholic beverages in the abuser's presence, whether alcoholic beverages will be kept and served at home, whether the couple will attend social gatherings involving alcohol, and how to deal with these situations. Help partners identify particular persons, gatherings, or circumstances that are likely to be stressful. Also, address couple and family interactions related to substance use, because arguments, tensions, and negative feelings can precipitate more abusive behavior. Discuss these patterns with the couple and suggest specific coping procedures for partners to use in difficult situations.

Behavioral Contracting

Written behavioral contracts to promote abstinence have a number of common elements that make them useful. The substance use behavior goal is made explicit. Specific behaviors that each spouse can do to help achieve this goal are also detailed. The contract provides alternative behaviors to negative interactions about substance use. Finally, and quite importantly, the agreement decreases the non-abusing spouse's anxiety and need to control the substance abuser and his or her use behavior. The contract we recommend features the *Sobriety Trust Discussion.* In it, the patient reports his or her sobriety during the past 24 hours and states his or her intent not to drink or use drugs that day (in the tradition of one day at a time). The spouse expresses appreciation for the patient's efforts to stay abstinent for the past day and offers any needed support for the next 24 hours. The spouse records the performance of the Sobriety Trust Discussion on a calendar you give him or her. Both partners agree not to discuss past drinking or fears about future drinking at home, to prevent substance-related conflicts that can trigger relapse. These discussions are reserved for the therapy sessions. At the start of each BCT session, review the Sobriety Contract calendar to see how well each spouse has done his or her part. If the Sobriety Contract includes 12-step meetings, urine drug screens, or the taking of medication designed to inhibit substance use, these instances also are marked on the calendar and reviewed. The calendar provides an ongoing record of progress that the therapist rewards verbally at each session. Have the couple practice the behaviors of their Sobriety Trust Discussion in each session to highlight its importance and to let you see how they conduct it.

Attendance at Self-Help Meetings

Although there is little empirical evidence about the effectiveness of AA-type support groups (e.g., AA, Narcotics Anonymous [NA], Al-Anon), there also is little doubt in the substance abuse treatment community that such activity is probably very helpful toward maintaining sobriety. Accordingly, whenever possible, regular attendance at such meetings is recommended. We encourage at least the substance abuser to participate regularly and the partner to attend appropriate meetings if they so desire. As noted above, the attendance plan and performance records are usually a part of the Sobriety Contract established between partners engaged in BCT.

Consumption of Medication Designed to Help with Maintaining Sobriety

Antabuse (disulfiram) is a drug that produces extreme nausea and sickness when the person taking it drinks. As such, in times past it has been an option for drinkers with a goal of abstinence. Naltrexone is a medication sometimes prescribed to opiod abusers because the drug inhibits the high associated with opioids. Methadone is an opiate antagonist used to ease the symptoms of heroin or opiate withdrawal. Typically, patients who have been prescribed any of these medications have come into the programs with the prescriptions written by a supervising physician. Accordingly, our treatment programs have been willing to incorporate such medication-taking into the ongoing Sobriety Contract. In some programs, specific interaction with the prescribing physician is done for coordination purposes, but direct contact is not required so long as the drinker is willing and medically cleared to take Antabuse, Naltrexone, or Methadone, and both the patient and spouse have been fully informed and educated about the effects of the drugs. In current practice, prescribing such medications has declined because patient compliance has been a significant problem. However, when incorporated into the Sobriety Contract as a component of BCT, research has demonstrated that for patients taking these medications, compliance improves significantly, which results in better abstinence rates. Moreover, when included, the regular and routine medication-taking procedure also decreases alcohol- and drug-related arguments between the drinker and his or her spouse. The substance abuser agrees to take the appropriate drug each day while the spouse observes. The spouse, in turn, agrees to positively reinforce the patient and to record the observation on the calendar provided to them. Each spouse should view the agreement as a cooperative method for rebuilding lost trust—not as a coercive checking-up operation.

Relationship-Focused Interventions

Once the substance abuser has decided to change his or her abuse, you can focus on improving marital and family relationships. Family members often experience resentment about past abusive behavior and fear and distrust about the possible return of abusive behavior in the future. The substance abuser often experiences guilt and a desire for recognition of current improved behavior. These feelings, experienced by the substance abuser and the family, often lead to an atmosphere of tension and unhappiness in marital and family relationships. There are problems caused by substance abuse (e.g., bills, legal charges, embarrassing incidents) that still need to be resolved. There is often a backlog of other unresolved marital and family problems that the substance abuse obscured. These longstanding problems may seem to increase as abuse declines, when actually the problems are simply being recognized for the first time, now that substance abuse cannot be used to excuse them. The couple frequently lacks the communication skills and mutual positive feelings needed to resolve these problems. As a result, many marriages and families are dissolved during the first 1 to 2 years of the substance abuser's recovery. In other cases, marital and family conflicts trigger relapse and a return to drinking or drug use. Even in cases where the substance abuser has a basically sound marriage when he or she is not drinking or drugging abusively, the initiation of sobriety can produce temporary tension and role readjustments while also providing the opportunity for stabilizing and enriching the marriage and family. For these reasons, many substance abusers can benefit from assistance to improve their marital and family relationships once changes in substance abuse have begun.

Relationship Promises During Treatment

Over the course of the development of BCT, the authors have found it advantageous to ask couples to make four types of promises as regards their participation in the individualized or group BCT programs. First, couples are asked to "Attend Therapy Sessions and Do Homework as Assigned." Partners promise to renew their relationship through education and skills training. In order for change to occur, both partners must be active in working toward change. Renewing the relationship takes time, and personal dedication to the process is an important initial promise.

"No Threats of Divorce or Separation" is the second couple promise encouraged. Threatening separation or divorce can interfere greatly with relationship improvement efforts as well as feelings of commitment to the relationship. Making this promise discourages the use of threats as ammunition during arguments or as a result of overall frustration. This promise does not require a lifetime commitment or mean that separation consideration is not valid; rather, that during BCT the topic will be reserved for discussion with the therapist present to facilitate the discussion.

The third important couple promise is: "Focus on the Present, Not the Past or the Future." The objective for this promise is for partners to refrain from bringing up past problems or grievances in anger or in a manner that discourages couple cooperation and maintenance of sobriety. Although the tendency is great, there is little to gain from rehashing past problems; the nonsubstance abuser most likely becomes resentful and angry, the substance abuser becomes guilty, shameful, and resentful. This promise helps partners to focus on positive changes for the present and hope for the future.

Finally, the fourth promise is: "No Angry Touching." Each partner promises not to use or threaten his or her partner with any violence. The use of force of any kind to deal with conflict is not only ineffective, but also very destructive to the relationship. This means no pushing, shoving, hitting, and so forth. Making this promise encourages the practice of positive communication and conflict resolution skills.

Two major goals of interventions focused on the substance abuser's couple relationship are (1) to increase positive feelings, goodwill, and commitment to the relationship; and (2) to resolve conflicts, problems, and desires for change. Even though they often overlap in the course of actual therapy sessions, we will be describing procedures useful in achieving these two goals separately. The general sequence in teaching couples skills to increase positive interactions and resolve conflicts and problems is (1) therapist instruction and modeling, (2) the couple practicing under your supervision, (3) assignments for homework, and (4) review of homework with further practice.

Increasing Positive Exchanges

A series of procedures can increase a couple's awareness of benefits from the relationship and the frequency with which spouses notice, acknowledge, and initiate pleasing or caring behaviors on a daily basis. Tell the couple that caring behaviors are "behaviors showing that you care for the other person," and assign homework called "Catch Your Partner Doing Something Nice" to assist couples in noticing the daily caring behaviors in the marriage. This requires each spouse to record one caring behavior performed by the partner each day on forms you provide them. The couple reads the caring behaviors recorded during the previous week at the subsequent session. Then you model acknowledging caring behaviors ("I liked it when you ____. It made me feel ____."), noting the importance of eye contact, a smile, a sincere, pleasant tone of voice, and only positive feelings. Each spouse then practices acknowledging caring behaviors from his or her daily list from the previous week. After the couple practices the new behavior in the therapy session, assign for homework a 5-minute, daily communication session at home, in which each partner acknowledges one pleasing behavior noticed that day. As a couple begins to notice and acknowledge daily caring behaviors, each partner begins initiating more caring behaviors. In addition, many couples report that the 5-minute communication sessions result in more extensive conversations. A final assignment is that each partner gives the other a "caring day" during the coming week by performing special acts to show caring for the spouse. Encourage each partner to take risks and to act lovingly toward the spouse, rather than wait for the other to make the first move. Finally, remind spouses that at the start of therapy they agreed to act differently (e.g., more lovingly) and then assess changes in feelings, rather than wait to feel more positively toward their partner before instituting changes in their own behaviors.

Shared Rewarding Activities

Many couples have discontinued or decreased shared leisure activities because in the past the substance abuser has frequently sought enjoyment only in situations involving alcohol or drugs, and has embarrassed the partner by using. Reversing this trend is important, because participation by the couple and family in social and recreational activities improves outcomes. Planning and engaging in Shared Rewarding Activities (SRA) can be started by simply having each spouse make a separate list of possible activities. Each activity must involve both spouses, either by themselves or with their children or other adults and can be at or away from home. Before giving the couple homework of planning an SRA, model an SRA planning session illustrating solutions to common pitfalls (e.g., waiting until the last minute so that necessary preparations cannot be made, getting sidetracked on trivial practical arrangements). Finally, instruct the couple to refrain from discussing problems or conflicts during their planned SRAs.

Communication Skills Training

Inadequate communication is a major problem for substance abusers and their spouses (O'Farrell & Birchler, 1987). Inability to resolve conflicts and problems can cause abusive drinking or drugging and severe marital and family tensions to recur. We generally begin our work on training in communication skills by defining effective communication as "message intended (by speaker) equals message received (the impact on the listener)" and emphasizing the need to learn both listening and speaking skills. We introduce the notion of two types of miscommunication filters which can interfere with intent/impact: (1) situational variables (e.g., a headache, rough day, happy hour, stressful freeway driving, grouchy children, late night) and (2) relatively enduring vulnerabilities (e.g., one's negative beliefs, expectations, prejudices, biases, persistent assumptions) that serve to distort the intended or received communication. Therapists use instructions, modeling, prompting, behavioral rehearsal, and feedback to teach couples how to communicate more effectively. Learning communication skills of listening and speaking and how to use planned communication sessions are essential prerequisites for problem solving and negotiating desired behavior changes. Start this training with nonproblem areas that are positive or neutral. Move to problem areas and emotionally charged issues only after each skill has been practiced on easier topics.

Communication sessions are planned, structured discussions in which spouses talk privately, face-to-face, without distractions, and with spouses taking turns expressing their points of view, without interrupting one another. Communication sessions can be introduced for 5 minutes daily when couples first practice acknowledging caring behaviors, and in 10 to 15-minute sessions three to four times a week in later sessions, when the couple discusses current relationship problems or concerns. Discuss with the couple the time and place that they plan to have their assigned communication practice sessions. Assess the success of this plan at the next session and suggest any needed changes. Just establishing a regular communication session as a method for discussing feelings, events, and problems can be very helpful for many couples. Encourage couples to ask each other for a communication session when they want to discuss an issue or problem, keeping in mind the ground rules of behavior that characterize such a session.

Listening skills help each spouse to feel understood and supported, and to slow down couple interactions so as to prevent quick escalation of aversive exchanges.

Instruct spouses to repeat both the words and the feelings of the speaker's message and to check to see if the message they received was the message intended by their partner ("What I heard you say was. . . . Is that right?") When the listener has understood the speaker's message they change roles and the first listener then speaks. Teaching a partner to communicate support and understanding by summarizing the spouse's message and checking the accuracy of the received message before stating his or her own position is often a major accomplishment that has to be achieved gradually. Additionally, a partner's failure to separate his or her understanding the spouse's position from agreement with it is often an obstacle that must be overcome.

Speaking skills (i.e., expressing both positive and negative feelings directly) are alternatives to the blaming, hostile, and indirect responsibility-avoiding communication behaviors that characterize many substance abusers' relationships. Emphasize that when the speaker expresses feelings directly, there is a greater chance that he or she will be heard, because the speaker says these are his or her feelings, his or her point of view, and not some objective fact about the other person. The speaker takes responsibility for his or her own feelings and does not blame the other person for how he or she feels. This reduces listener defensiveness and makes it easier for the listener to receive the intended message. The use of statements beginning with "I" rather than "You" is emphasized. After presenting the rationale and instructions, model correct and incorrect ways of expressing feelings, and elicit the couple's reactions to these modeled scenes. Then, have the couple role-play a communication session in which spouses take turns being speaker and listener, with the speaker expressing feelings directly and the listener using the listening response. During this role-playing, coach the couple as they practice reflecting the direct expressions of their feelings. Assign for homework similar communication sessions, 10 to 15 minutes each, three to four times weekly. Subsequent therapy sessions involve more practice with role-playing, both during the sessions and for homework. Increase in difficulty each week the topics on which the couple practices. Help partners to gain the ability to appreciate their partner's experience and point of view, and to express understanding and empathy with their positions. Learning how to determine, through effective communication process, "what makes sense" about what their partner is saying and feeling is very helpful toward establishing a recovering relationship.

Negotiation for Requests

A fairly straightforward and very effective communication skill that we teach couples is how to make a request from one's partner. Typically, partners, especially distressed couples, tend to make complaints, criticisms, and so-called "You" statements when they want something from their partners. These behaviors reliably tend to put message receivers on the defensive, and an argument may well ensue. Teaching partners a "soft start-up" strategy along with how to ask for what they want or would prefer in a positive "I" statement is much more likely to bring success and satisfaction with the process. Many couples also benefit from direct suggestions about how to both assert their feelings and desires and how to negotiate and make compromises toward "Win-Win" versus "Lose-Lose" outcomes.

Problem-Solving Skills Training

After the couple has first learned the basic communication skills noted earlier; partners can next learn specific skills to solve problems stemming from both external stressors (e.g., job, extended family) and relationship conflicts. In solving a problem, the couple should first define the problem and list a number of possible solutions. Then, while withholding judgment regarding the preferred solution, the couple considers both positive and negative and short-term and long-term consequences of each solution. Finally, the spouses rank the solutions from most- to least-preferred and agree to implement one or more of the solutions. Using problem-solving procedures can help spouses avoid polarizing on one solution or another. It also avoids the "yes, but . . ." trap of one partner pointing out problems with the other partner's solution.

RELAPSE PREVENTION: POSTTREATMENT ACTIVITIES TO MAINTAIN THERAPY GAINS

Three methods are employed in BCT to ensure long-term maintenance of the changes in alcohol or drug abuse problems. First, plan maintenance prior to the termination of the active treatment phase. This involves helping the couple complete a Continuing Recovery Plan that specifies which of the behaviors from the previous BCT sessions they wish to continue in a planned activity program (e.g., a Sobriety Contract, including perhaps a daily Sobriety Trust Discussion, or Medication Contract, AA/NA meetings, Shared Rewarding Activities, planned couple communication sessions). Second, anticipate what high-risk situations for relapse to abusive drinking or drugging may occur after treatment. Discuss and rehearse possible coping strategies that the substance abuser, partner, and other family members can employ to prevent relapse when confronted with such situations. Third, discuss and rehearse how to cope with a lapse or potential relapse if and when it might occur. A specific couple relapse-episode plan, written and rehearsed prior to ending active treatment, can be particularly useful. Early intervention at the beginning of a lapse or relapse episode is essential: impress the couple with this point. Often, spouses wait until the substance abuse has reached dangerous levels again before acting. By then, much additional damage has been done to the couple relationship and to other aspects of the substance abuser's life.

We suggest continued contact with the couple via planned in-person and telephone follow-up sessions, at regular and then gradually increasing intervals, up to 5 years after a stable pattern of recovery has been achieved. Use this ongoing contact to monitor progress, to assess compliance with the Continuing Recovery Plan, and to evaluate the need for additional therapy sessions. You must take responsibility for scheduling and for reminding the couple about follow-up sessions, and for placing agreed-upon phone calls, so that continued contact can be maintained successfully. Tell couples that the reason for continued contact is that substance abuse is a chronic health problem that requires active, aggressive, ongoing monitoring to prevent or to quickly treat relapses for up to 5 years after an initial stable pattern of recovery has been established. The follow-up contact also provides the opportunity to deal with marital and family issues that appear after a period of recovery.

SPECIAL CONSIDERATIONS

Intimate Partner Violence

The effect of BCT on the occurrence of intimate partner violence (IPV) has been the focus of several recent investigations. The results of multiple studies suggest that IPV is a highly prevalent problem among substance-abusing patients and their partners. For example, roughly two thirds of the married or cohabiting men entering treatment for alcoholism, or their partners, report at least one episode of male-to-female physical aggression in the year prior to program entry, which is four times higher than IPV prevalence estimates from nationally representative surveys (e.g., O'Farrell, Fals-Stewart, Murphy, M., & Murphy, C. M., 2003). Recent studies have found that the likelihood of male-to-female physical aggression was nearly eight times higher on days of drinking than on days of no drinking, and was roughly three times higher on days of cocaine use than on days of no substance use, for married or cohabiting men entering alcoholism treatment (Fals-Stewart, 2003; Fals-Stewart, Golden, & Schumacher, 2003).

In a recent study, O'Farrell, Fals-Stewart, Murphy, C. M., Stephan, & Murphy, M. (2004) examined partner violence before and after BCT for 303 married or cohabiting male alcoholic patients, and used a demographically matched nonalcoholic comparison sample. In the year before BCT, 60 percent of alcoholic patients had been violent toward their female partners; five times the comparison sample rate of 12 percent. In the year after BCT, violence decreased significantly—to 24 percent of the alcoholic sample—but remained higher than the comparison group. However, among remitted alcoholics who received BCT, the violence prevalence was 12 percent, and was thus identical to the comparison sample and less than half the rate among relapsed patients (30 percent). Results for the second year after BCT yielded similar findings to those found for the first-year outcomes. Attending more scheduled BCT sessions and using BCT-targeted behaviors more during and after treatment were related to less drinking and less violence after BCT, suggesting that skills couples learn in BCT may promote both abstinence and violence reduction.

Fals-Stewart, Kashdan, O'Farrell, and Birchler (2002) examined changes in IPV among married or cohabiting drug-abusing patients and their partners. This study examined partner violence among 80 married or cohabiting drug-abusing men who were randomly assigned to receive either BCT or an equally intensive individual-based treatment. Although nearly half of the couples in each condition reported male-to-female physical aggression during the year before treatment, the number reporting violence in the year after treatment was significantly lower for BCT (17 percent) than for individual treatment (42 percent). Exploratory analyses indicated that BCT reduced violence better than individual treatment because BCT reduced drug use, drinking, and relationship problems to a greater extent than did individual treatment.

Effect of Couples Therapy on Children in the Home of Participants

During much of the last century, an extensive literature has evolved examining the functioning of Children of Alcoholics, who are collectively referred to as COAs. In general, these investigations have concluded that COAs are more likely to have psychosocial problems than are children of non-substance-dependent parents. For example, COAs experience increased somatic complaints, internalizing (e.g., anxiety, depression) and externalizing behavior problems (e.g., conduct disorder, alcohol use), lower academic achievement, and lower verbal ability. Although research on children of drug-abusing parents is far less evolved than the COA literature, available research also suggests that children of parents who abuse illicit drugs, who are often referred to as Children of Substance Abusers, or COSAs, display significant emotional and behavioral problems. Preliminary studies indicate the psychosocial functioning of COSAs may, in fact, be significantly worse than that of demographically matched COAs (e.g., Fals-Stewart, Kelley, Fincham, Golden, & Logdson, in press).

Despite the emotional and behavioral problems observed among COAs, surveys of patients entering substance abuse treatment who also have custodial children suggest that these parents are very reluctant to allow their children to engage in any type of mental health treatment (Fals-Stewart, Kelley, Fincham, & Golden, 2002). Thus, the most readily available approach to improve the psychosocial functioning of these children may be by successfully treating their parents, with the hope that positive outcomes observed in couples therapy for substance abuse (e.g., reduced substance use, improved communication, reduced conflict) would lead to improvements in their custodial children.

Kelley and Fals-Stewart (2002) reported on two completed investigations that involved a parallel replication of the same study design with alcoholic and drug-dependent male patients who were also the custodial parents of one or more school-aged child (i.e., between the ages of 6 and 16 years). In these investigations, 64 married or cohabiting men with a primary drug dependence diagnosis and 71 married or cohabiting men with a primary alcohol dependence diagnosis were randomly assigned to one of three equally intensive outpatient treatments: (1) BCT, (2) Individual-Based Treatment (IBT), or (3) Couples-based Psychoeducational Attention Control Treatment (PACT; consisting of lectures to both partners on various topics related to drug abuse, including the etiology and epidemiology of drug abuse, effects of the drugs on the body and brain, and so forth). Couples in these studies also had at least one school-aged child residing in their home. Results in the year after treatment revealed that BCT produced a greater reduction of substance use for men in these couples and more gains in relationship adjustment than did IBT or PACT. BCT also improved psychosocial functioning of the couples' children significantly more than did the individual-based treatment or the attention-control treatment, based on the Pediatric Symptom Checklist (PSC; Jellinek & Murphy, 1990) scores. Children of fathers in all three treatments showed improved functioning in the year after treatment, but children of fathers who participated in BCT improved more than did children in the other treatments. Moreover, of these three treatments, only BCT showed reduction in the number of children with clinically significant psychosocial impairment (i.e., the proportion of children who surpassed the PSC cutoff score for clinically significant impairment was lower for those children whose parents participated in BCT versus the other treatments). It is important to emphasize that the BCT intervention contained no session content directly related to parenting practices or problems with children, yet the positive effects of BCT for the couple appeared to influence children in these homes positively.

When Both Partners Use

In nearly all of the published BCT studies, an exclusion criterion for participation is couples in which both partners currently have a diagnosis of an alcohol or other substance use disorder. An implicit assumption of BCT as a treatment for substance abuse is that there is support within the dyadic and family systems for abstinence, particularly from the non-substance-abusing partner. However, among couples in which both partners abuse drugs or alcohol, the dyadic system is almost always not supportive of abstinence.

The problem faced by BCT investigators is that a significant proportion of married or cohabiting patients who enter substance abuse treatment are involved in intimate relationships with individuals who also have current problems with drugs or alcohol. This appears to be particularly true of women seeking treatment for substance abuse. Our clinical experience with partners in these couples suggests they have fairly poor outcomes. If one of the partners receives individual treatment and successfully reduces or eliminates his or her substance use, the relationships often dissolve. In most instances, however, the treatment-seeking partners fail to stop drinking or using drugs and the relationships survive. Standard BCT with these couples has also been largely ineffective because there exists little support for abstinence within the dyadic system.

Among these couples, the family system is strongly interrelated with the substance use behavior, with many of these partners forming drinking or drug use partnerships. In fact, partners in these couples often describe substance use as a central shared recreational activity (despite its negative consequences). Unless the dyad separates (which in our experience is infrequent), intervention efforts are needed to address the family and the substance use together. A variant of BCT may be a strong candidate as an approach to address these issues among such couples. However, because the implicit BCT assumption—that there is support for abstinence within the dyad—is often violated in these couples, some modification to the standard BCT approach is clearly necessary.

Motivational interviewing, developed by Miller and Rollnick (2002) and modified for use with at-risk couples by Cordova and colleagues (Cordova, Warren, & Gee, 2001; Gee, Scott, Castellani, & Cordova, 2002), is an empirically validated clinical approach designed to actively facilitate people's intrinsic motivation to change.

What makes motivational interviewing particularly compelling as a possible adaptation for BCT with dual substance-abusing couples is the substantial evidence that motivational interviewing works well as a prelude to other treatments, even treatments with very different theories of change. In addition, Cordova and colleagues have demonstrated that motivational interviewing can be adapted easily to couples work resulting in measurable and sustained improvements in relationship functioning. In sum, future research may determine whether a couples-based motivational interviewing approach can be added as a prelude to BCT for dual substance-abusing couples, to effectively ready them to work collaboratively as partners during subsequent BCT.

Human Immunodeficiency Virus (HIV) Risk Behaviors

Human Immunodeficiency Virus is the virus that causes acquired immunodeficiency syndrome (AIDS). This virus can be passed from one person to another through blood-to-blood and sexual contact. HIV is present in semen, blood, vaginal fluid, and breast milk. It is a sensitive and alarming social health problem in the United States. The Center for Disease Control and Prevention estimates that 650,000 to 900,000 U.S. residents are living with HIV infection, of whom more than 200,000 are unaware of their infection. This is an alarming statistic because of the potential for unknowingly infecting others through risky needle practices, multiple sexual partners, receiving blood from an infected person, and unprotected sex with partners other than one's spouse.

Most married or cohabiting individuals report they do not use condoms while engaging in sexual relations with their partner. Therefore, if the spouse/partner engages in risky needle practices or unprotected extramarital sexual relations, the non-substance-abusing partner is at increased indirect risk for HIV infection, because there is an exchange of potentially infected bodily fluids.

BCT is potentially a very good program through which to educate substance abusers and their partners about the very real risks of HIV infection associated with drug and alcohol abuse. Preliminary program trials that have inquired into partners' risk-related behaviors and their awareness levels have indicated that not only are these couples relatively unaware of these risks, but that the non-substance-abusing partner is particularly unaware of the range of risky behaviors engaged in by his or her partner (especially unprotected sex outside the relationship), and that he or she is fairly amenable to the educational process and has some willingness to seek HIV testing as a precaution. More research is needed to determine the full potential for BCT to be helpful to couples at risk for HIV infection.

The Effects of Gender and Culture Using BCT

There seem to be some reliable and notable, but not profound effects of gender and culture when using the BCT approach for treating substance abuse. For example, although the research conducted on female alcoholic partners is much less prevalent than the research conducted on male substance abusers, it appears that there needs to be a relatively greater focus on the relationship versus substance abuse factors when working with female substance-abusing couples. In contrast, more attention to substance abuse factors versus relationship factors seems important in the treatment of male substance-abusing couples. We believe that this effect is due to the female gender's greater interest in and responsiveness to positive as opposed to negative relationship factors as they get involved with and recover from substance abuse. This is not to say that males are unaffected by relationship factors operating during initiation in and recovery from substance abuse, but they seem relatively more susceptible to risk factors outside of the relationship. Similarly, comparing these two types of couples, female non-substance-abusing partners tend to be more invested in supportive roles in relationship than are the non-substance-abusing male partners. Otherwise, we have not found major gender effects in the work to date. Overall, BCT has been shown to be effective for both sexes as far as general treatment outcomes are concerned.

Perhaps surprisingly, we have found little in the way of discriminating cultural and ethnic factors. Our study populations have included significant proportions of Caucasian, African American, and Hispanic males, for example, with few if any cultural effects. There is a significantly greater sense of paranoia and secrecy found when working with alcoholics versus drug abusers, but this particular cultural effect is both anticipated and does not seem to be related to racial or ethnic differences.

RESEARCH EVIDENCE

Alcoholic Patients

Investigations dating back nearly 30 years have compared drinking and relationship outcomes for alcoholic patients and their partners treated with BCT to various forms of therapy that only involve the individual patient (e.g., individual counseling sessions, group therapy). Outcomes were measured at 6-months posttreatment in earlier studies and at 18 to 24 months after treatment in more recent investigations. Despite variations in assessment, differences in certain aspects of the BCT treatment methods, or use of varying types of individual-based treatments used for comparison purposes, the results of the investigations have been very consistent, revealing a pattern of less frequent drinking, fewer alcohol-related problems, happier relationships, and lower risk of marital separation for alcoholic patients who receive BCT than for patients who receive only individual-based treatment (e.g., McCrady, Stout, Noel, Abrams, & Nelson, 1991).

Drug-Abusing Patients

Although investigations examining the effects of BCT for alcoholism have been ongoing since the 1970s, research on the effects of BCT for married or cohabiting patients who abuse drugs other than alcohol has only recently been completed. The first randomized study of BCT with married or cohabiting drug-abusing clients compared BCT plus individual treatment to an equally intensive individual-based treatment for married or cohabiting male patients entering outpatient treatment (Fals-Stewart, Birchler, & O'Farrell, 1996). Clinical outcomes in the year after treatment favored the group that received BCT both in terms of drug use and relationship outcomes. Compared to patients who participated in individual-based treatment, those who received BCT had fewer days of drug use, fewer drug-related arrests and hospitalizations, and a longer time to relapse after treatment completion. Couples who received BCT also reported more positive relationship adjustment and fewer days separated due to relationship discord than couples whose partners received individual-based treatment only. Very similar results favoring BCT over individual-based counseling were observed in another randomized clinical trial that investigated married or cohabiting male patients in a methadone maintenance program (Fals-Stewart, O'Farrell, & Birchler, 2001).

Finally, although the BCT studies with alcoholic and drug-abusing patients have recruited samples that consisted largely or exclusively of married or cohabiting male patients and their non-substance-abusing female partners, Winters, Fals-Stewart, O'Farrell, Birchler, & Kelley (2002) recently conducted the first BCT that focused exclusively on female drug-abusing patients. The profile of outcome findings was very similar to those found with male substance-abusing patients, suggesting BCT may work equally well with both types of couples.

———————————————— **Case Study** ————————————————

We will briefly present an example of a couple in which both partners are recovering from substance abuse. As is not uncommon, Bill and Monica met at an AA meeting. Bill is 34 years old, divorced with no children, a currently unemployed hospital worker who has been clean and sober for about three years. His drug of choice was alcohol; however, he also used marijuana and methamphetamine occasionally in social situations. He lost his job and first marriage as a result of alcohol abuse. Monica, single and aged 31, was attending the AA meetings primarily because no NA meetings were convenient to her. She is a heroin addict who, at this point in her course of addiction, used no other drugs or alcohol, but had been using heroin heavily over the past decade. She had last used heroin about 5 months previously. She was working at the time of couple intake evaluation, yet having significant difficulty holding her job due to intermittent illnesses related to hepatitis C that she had contracted through drug use behavior. The couple had been living together in a house rented by Bill for several months; they encountered communication problems, increasing conflict about independence-dependence issues, some prescription drug-seeking behavior on the part of Monica, and their desire to prepare for marriage.

The psychosocial histories for these two Caucasian partners were not similar. Bill came from a family including a functional alcoholic father and a part-time working, occasionally depressed mother, and a younger brother. His dad had a number of jobs over the years and the family moved on a number of occasions. This lifestyle made it difficult to get connected socially as he grew up; however, he did "okay" in school, getting average grades and making a few friends. He entered the Navy within 1 year of graduation from high school in San Diego and he did quite well in the service, learning hospital administration at the seaman-and-above level. He did not experience combat and did not have significant interpersonal or disciplinary difficulties, but did acknowledge learning to drink heavily. He met his first wife while in the service; they were married for about 8 years before his chronic drinking and drifting apart ended the relationship. During this period his primary job was working at a Navy hospital as a low- to mid-level administrator. For years he would drink steadily throughout the week and more heavily on weekends, often spending excessive time with drinking buddies who did the same.

Compared to Bill, as Monica grew up in Philadelphia she had quite a different upbringing and substance use history. She never knew her father because he left home when Monica was about 1 year old. Monica described her mother as an angry or depressed and disorganized slob who paraded a number of boyfriends through the house for most of Monica's childhood and adolescent years. Monica did benefit from the structure and social friendships that she experienced in her early school years, but by junior high school the situation between her and her mother deteriorated, and Monica ran away from home at age 14. Unfortunately, living on the streets, she became sexually promiscuous and participated in heavier and heavier drug abuse. By age 21, she had held several menial jobs, but often lost them due to interpersonal conflicts, poor attendance, or lack of motivation to work. For several years she lived in and out of institutional halfway houses, crisis centers, and crash pads. Amazingly, at age 26 Monica met a boyfriend, and moved to San Diego with him to start a new life. However, within a few months that relationship failed, and she was back on the unfamiliar streets of San Diego, using heroin again. It was then she contracted hepatitis C, became very sick, and was hospitalized. The illness forced her to make yet another attempt at abstinence and recovery. It was then that she met Bill, at the AA meeting.

At the initial intake the therapists learned of the presenting problems, the couple's goals noted previously, and briefly about their substance abuse and relationship histories. It should be noted here that during the month of couple evaluation, Monica was let go from her job. The reason she was given was unreliability in attendance due to her frequent sickness. She was quite distressed by her job loss, for both personal and financial reasons. In any case, the next two sessions, including separate individual sessions, were devoted to evaluating the couple according to the 7 Cs framework. During the second conjoint session a communication sample of conflict resolution was also obtained. The couple chose to discuss the matter of sharing household tasks. The therapists learned much about the process and content of their interaction during this exercise. Process-wise, Bill seemed both focused and very gentle with Monica. He carried the topical discussion, kept them on task, and demonstrated unusual caring and listening skills, even though he was the person most concerned about this issue. Monica, for her part, seemed more childlike in her demeanor and behavior, apologizing, making excuses, and if allowed, becoming tangential and distracted. Content-wise, it was clear that Bill had the burden of keeping the household functioning, from cooking to cleanup, bill paying, and so on. Monica seemed to have neither the motivation nor the competence to function well in these areas; the couple did not reach any sort of resolution in the 10-minute discussion. Their communication style, if anything, seemed conflict avoidant. Nether had any intention of rocking the boat. Despite this, a certain sense of caring and commitment pervaded this conflict-based interaction.

We assess and actually rate the 7 Cs on a scale from 1 to 7, according to couple function on the dimension being a major problem area or a significant asset for the couple. After the three evaluation sessions were completed and the roundtable was planned, the therapists rated the couple as follows. A score of 4 is the midpoint; scores below 4 are definite areas for BCT to target; scores at 4 and above also could be areas for some attention and improvement. The goal at the end of treatment is to have all scores at 5 or above. *Character features* was scored a 3; both partners have a significant character challenge to maintain sobriety, with Monica being at significant risk for relapse. Neither had good models or good histories for developing and maintaining a long-term, intimate relationship. Both partners were now unemployed; their work histories were not very good. *Cultural and ethnic factors* was rated 5; the couple did not report any conflicts about race, religion, social preferences, money management, dealing with in-laws, and so forth. There were some gender role-related concerns to be addressed—thus the score of 5. *Contract* was rated 4; this dimension might have been rated a little higher; however, the therapists were aware that this couple was in the midst of developing and negotiating a major contract: how to maintain sobriety in the context of preparing for marriage and rehabilitating many aspects of their lives (e.g., jobs, friendships, health, mutual intimacy). *Commitment* was rated a 5; here, the score might have been rated lower, given the risk of maintaining the relationship in the face of high risk for substance abuse relapse (with severe consequences, especially in the case of Monica). However, the therapists were impressed with the sincere motivation coming from these people to "be there" for one another and to make a better life together. *Caring* was rated 6; these two seemed genuinely caring about one another. Again, given some concerns about sexual function and comfort (i.e., Monica often did not feel well or in the mood, and Bill did not want to push her in this area), the score might have been lower. But the tenderness and fondness shown by these people was impressive in their circumstance and needed some validation in the scoring. *Communication and conflict resolution* both were rated 3; although their style was conflict avoidant, it was considered so at a fault. For fear of upsetting one another, many issues were swept (and left) under the rug, and the process was vulnerable to resentments building, problems not being addressed and solved, and disengagement or conflict flare-ups. Work in these areas was considered important. In summary, at the roundtable, the agreed-upon goals for BCT were to (1) establish a Continuing Recovery Plan for both substance abusers, while supporting their efforts to obtain employment, (2) develop a healthy, interpersonal contract for this new relationship through open sharing and negotiation, and (3) learn more effective and satisfying communication and problem-solving skills to maximize collaboration and minimize anger, resentments building up, and unresolved conflicts.

The couple had planned a 1-week summer vacation before starting the treatment phase of BCT. Inexplicably, they did not show up for the first treatment session, and no one answered a check-up phone call the same day of the appointment. The next day Bill called the therapist to inform her that one day during the break Monica had overdosed on heroin while he was out looking for work. Not only did she have to be intubated for breathing purposes, but also a tracheotomy had to be performed to facilitate her breathing. Her situation was both traumatic and serious. Amazingly, both partners expressed an interest in continuing BCT, and they did appear for a first treatment session 2 weeks later.

Immediately, the task was to debrief the recent traumatic events for this couple and to institute substance-abuse-focused interventions by beginning work on dual Sobriety Contracts. Interestingly, both people had longstanding substance abuse problems, and this situation is usually an added risk factor for both partners. However, the fact that their drugs of choice and use patterns were so very different, together with the mutual respect that they had for the power of addiction, combined with their relative commitment to both maintaining sobriety (in principle at least), this situation was framed as an asset. Their collaborative set was to guard against self-deception and behaviors that would enable or condone relapse versus seducing each other into it. For example, during the ongoing preparation of their Continuing Recovery Plans, it was clear that the situational and psychological risks for Bill's relapse to alcohol abuse and Monica's relapse to heroin use were very dissimilar. For example, Bill's contract called for him to avoid social situations at nights and on the weekends with his former drinking friends, to attend AA twice weekly by himself or with another member (not including Monica), and to have a sponsor outside of the couple relationship to process his urges and to develop ongoing strategies to maintain sobriety. Monica was all in favor of his sobriety, but she was not really strong enough to help him discuss the details of his program and its related challenges. Therefore, his Sobriety Trust Discussion, nevertheless planned daily with Monica, was brief and to the point. In sharp contrast, Monica wanted and needed Bill's active participation in her program to avoid heroin relapse. She got into trouble when she was socially isolated, got depressed, and put pressure on herself to reduce internal negative psychological states and fears about the future by getting high. Her program featured increasing social contacts with Bill and other clean and sober friends, attending NA (often transported if not attended by Bill, and by keeping close contact on a daily basis with Bill about her urges and fears. Her version of the Sobriety Trust Discussion was more detailed and comprehensive regarding getting through the day, particularly since she had become unemployed.

As suggested above, the relationship-focused interventions were designed to increase both perceived and real intimacy, to increase the couple's communication and problem-solving abilities, and to work on new relationship contract elements (i.e., expectations for roles, responsibilities, and plans for the future of the relationship). Intimacy enhancement was addressed initially by instituting *Catch Your Spouse Doing Something Nice, Caring Behaviors,* and, after a few weeks, *Shared Rewarding Activities.* Together with the Sobriety Trust Discussions, these interventions helped to establish a coordinated and easy-to-follow plan for improving basic couple connection and satisfaction. By the third treatment session, the couple was introduced to the Intent-Impact Model for communication; after practicing listening and speaking skills in session they were give homework practice to further acquire these new behaviors. After 4 weeks of basic communication skills training, problem solving and conflict management skills were added to the target behaviors for intervention. This couple, being conflict avoidant to a fault, were helped to maintain their caring and empathy while learning to be more assertive and to work toward addressing important issues as they came up, versus editing their responses or avoiding the issues. Requesting positive behaviors when partner behavior change was desired was also helpful for Bill and Monica; when they did talk, they tended to make complaints negatively and feared the consequences.

The couple was seen for a total of 17 sessions (i.e., four evaluation meetings, 10 weekly meetings over 13 weeks, and three follow-up sessions over an additional 3 months). Progress was interrupted at treatment week number 6, when Monica was prescribed painkiller medication for her poorly healing trachea and she was called to task by her husband for taking more than the prescribed dosage. Over 3 weeks, when confronted gradually by both the husband and therapist, she admitted to being seduced and comforted by the medication, but Bill could tell she was quickly becoming dulled and dependent on the drug. With her agreement, he became the keeper and dispenser of the medication over the following week or two, until the pain subsided. This lapse actually was helpful to the couple, because the partners learned that their improved relationship skills (regarding closeness, collaboration on recovery plans, and better communication) had stood the test of real-life temptation. The three booster sessions were scheduled over 3 months by design to help the couple extend their BCT gains into a less structured therapy situation. Obviously, there was some slippage; however, this is expected with a brief course of treatment, and the follow-up sessions are designed to review system vulnerabilities and to make additional preventative and rehabilitative plans for action. For Bill and Monica, stress had increased as Bill's unemployment insurance was ending, Monica's supplemental security income disability was pending but not yet approved, and so it was necessary that Bill look seriously for work. This situation caused a significant change in couple contact time and his support for Monica's abstinence. The follow-up meetings served not only to reinforce skill and intimacy gains for the couple, but to help them cope with this inevitable change in the mutual support contract, as Bill, at least, returned to the workforce. As BCT ended, the couple was still carefully monitoring Monica's psychological and behavioral function, in particular, but they also were making active plans to move into a larger apartment in a better neighborhood and begin making plans for marriage. All 7 Cs were rated at 5 or better. The couple was encouraged to call for an appointment in the future if significant problems arose. At the time of this writing, no call had been received for almost 10 months, though it certainly is possible, if not likely, given the challenges posed for this young couple recovering from two essentially lifelong addictions.

CONCLUSION

This chapter outlines the background and current treatments for couples that are attempting to recover from alcohol and/or drug abuse. Basic models for conceptualizing the association and interaction between substance abuse and intimate relationships were described. The research and practice of Behavioral Couples Therapy, developed continuously over the past 3 decades, were featured, including descriptions of the essential substance-abuse-focused and relationship-focused intervention components associated with BCT. Special considerations for future work using the BCT approach also were described. The chapter concluded with a case study of a dual substance-abusing couple that benefited from BCT.

REFERENCES

Adesso, U. J. (1995). Cognitive factors in alcohol and drug use. In M. Galizio & S. A. Maisto (Eds.), *Determinants of substance abuse: Biological, psychological, and environmental factors* (pp. 179–208). New York: Plenum Press.

American Psychiatric Association. (1994). *Diagnostic and statistical manual of mental disorders* (4th ed.). Washington, DC: Author.

Billings, A. G., & Moos, R. H. (1983). Psychosocial process of recovery among alcoholics and their families: Implications for clinicians and program evaluators. *Addictive Behaviors, 8,* 205–218.

Birchler, G. R., & Fals-Stewart, W. (2000). Considerations for clients with marital dysfunction. In M. Hersen & M. Biaggio (Eds.), *Effective brief therapies: A clinician's guide* (pp. 391–410). San Diego, CA: Academic Press.

Brown, E. D., O'Farrell, T. J., Maisto, S. A., Boies, K., & Suchinsky, R. (Eds.), *Accreditation guide for substance abuse treatment programs.* Newbury Park, CA: Sage.

Cordova, J. V., Warren, L. Z., & Gee, C. B. (2001). Motivational interviewing with couples: An intervention for at-risk couples. *Journal of Marital and Family Therapy, 27,* 315–326.

Dunn, N. J., Jacob, T., Hummon, N., & Seilhamer, R. A. (1987). Marital stability in alcoholic-spouse relationships as a function of drinking pattern and location. *Journal of Abnormal Psychology, 96,* 99–107.

Fals-Stewart, W. (2003). The occurrence of interpartner violence on days of alcohol consumption: A longitudinal diary study. *Journal of Consulting and Clinical Psychology, 71,* 41–52.

Fals-Stewart, W., & Birchler, G. R. (November, 1994). *Marital functioning among substance-abusing patients in outpatient treatment.* Poster presented at the Annual Meeting of the Association for Advancement of Behavior Therapy, San Diego, California.

Fals-Stewart, W., Birchler, G. R., & Ellis, L. (1999). Procedures for evaluating the marital adjustment of drug-abusing patients and their intimate partners: A multimethod assessment procedure. *Journal of Substance Abuse Treatment, 16,* 5–16.

Fals-Stewart, W., Birchler, G. R. & O'Farrell, T. J. (1996). Behavioral couples therapy for male substance-abusing patients: Effects on relationship adjustment and drug-using behavior. *Journal of Consulting and Clinical Psychology, 64,* 959–972.

Fals-Stewart, W., Birchler, G. R., & O'Farrell, T. J. (1999). Drug-abusing patients and their partners: Dyadic adjustment, relationship stability and substance use. *Journal of Abnormal Psychology, 108,* 11–23.

Fals-Stewart, W., Golden, J., & Schumacher, J. (2003). Intimate partner violence and substance use: A longitudinal day-to-day examination. *Addictive Behaviors, 28,* 1555–1574.

Fals-Stewart, W., Kashdan, T. B., O'Farrell, T. J., & Birchler, G. R. (2002). Behavioral couples therapy for drug-abusing patients: Effects on partner violence. *Journal of Substance Abuse Treatment, 21,* 1–10.

Fals-Stewart, W., Kelley, M. L., Fincham, F. D., & Golden, J. (2002, April). *Examining barriers to involvement of children in treatment: A survey of substance-abusing parents.* Poster presented at the Conference on Human Development, Charlotte, NC.

Fals-Stewart, W., Kelley, M. L., Fincham, F. D., Golden, J., & Logsdon, T. (in press). The emotional and behavioral problems of children living with drug-abusing fathers: Comparisons with children living with alcohol-abusing and nonsubstance-abusing fathers. *Journal of Family Psychology.*

Fals-Stewart, W., O'Farrell, T. J., & Birchler, G. R. (2001). Behavioral couples therapy for male methadone maintenance patients: Effects on drug-using behavior and relationship adjustment. *Behavior Therapy, 32,* 391–411.

Finney, J. W., Moos, R. H., Cronkite, R. C., & Gamble, W. (1983). A conceptual model of the functioning of married persons with impaired partners: Spouses of alcoholic patients. *Journal of Marriage and the Family, 45,* 23–34.

Gee, C. B., Scott, R. L., Castellani, A. M., & Cordova, J. V. (2002). Predicting 2-year marital satisfaction from partners' reaction to a marriage checkup. *Journal of Marital and Family Therapy, 28,* 399–408.

Gondoli, D. M., & Jacob, T. (1990). Family treatment of alcoholism. In R. R. Watson (Ed.), *Drug and alcohol abuse prevention* (pp. 245–262). Totowa, NJ: The Humana Press.

Gottman, J. M. (1994). *What predicts divorce?* Hillsdale, NJ: Lawrence Erlbaum.

Grant, B. F., Harford, T. C., Dawson, D. A., Chou, S. P., Dufour, M., & Pickering, R. (1994). Prevalence of *DSM-IV* alcohol abuse and dependence: United States, 1992. *Alcohol, Health, and Research World, 18,* 243–247.

Jellinek, M. S., & Murphy, J. M. 1990. The recognition of psychosocial disorders in pediatric office practice: The current status of the Pediatric Symptom Checklist. *Developmental and Behavioral Pediatrics, 11,* 273–278.

Kelley, M. L., & Fals-Stewart, W. (2002). Couples- versus individual-based therapy for alcoholism and drug abuse: Effects on children's psychosocial functioning. *Journal of Consulting and Clinical Psychology, 70,* 417–427.

Maisto, S. A., O'Farrell, T. J., McKay, J., Connors, G. J., & Pelcovitz, M. A. (1988). Alcoholics' attributions of factors affecting their relapse to drinking and reasons for terminating relapse events. *Addictive Behaviors, 13,* 79–82.

McCrady, B. S. (1986). The family in the change process. In W. R. Miller & N. H. Heather (Eds.), *Treating addictive behaviors: Process of change* (pp. 305–318). New York: Plenum.

McCrady, B., Stout, R., Noel, N., Abrams, D., & Nelson, H. (1991). Comparative effectiveness of three types of spouse involved alcohol treatment: Outcomes 18 months after treatment. *British Journal of Addiction, 86,* 1415–1424.

Miller, W. R., & Rollnick, S. (2002). *Motivational interviewing: Preparing people for change* (2nd ed.). New York: Guilford.

Nathan, P. E. (1981). Prospects for a behavioral approach to the diagnosis of alcoholism. In R. E. Meyer, T. F. Babor, B. C. Glueck, J. H. Jaffe, J. E. O'Brian, & J. R. Stabenau (Eds.), *Evaluation of the alcoholic: Implications for theory, research, and treatment* (pp. 85–102). Washington, DC: National Institute on Alcohol Abuse and Alcoholism.

O'Farrell, T. J. (1995). Marital and family therapy. In R. Hester & W. Miller (Eds.), *Handbook of alcoholism treatment approaches.* (2nd ed., pp. 195–220). Boston: Allyn and Bacon.

O'Farrell, T. J., & Birchler, G. R. (1987). Marital relationships of alcoholic, conflicted, and nonconflicted couples. *Journal of Marital and Family Therapy, 13,* 259–274.

O'Farrell, T. J., Fals-Stewart, W., Murphy, M., & Murphy, C. M. (2003). Partner violence before and after individually-based alcoholism treatment for male alcoholic patients. *Journal of Consulting and Clinical Psychology, 71,* 92–102.

O'Farrell, T. J., Fals-Stewart, W., Murphy, C. M., Stephan, S. H., & Murphy, M. (2004). Partner violence before and after couples-based alcoholism treatment for male alcoholic patients: The role of treatment involvement and abstinence. *Journal of Consulting and Clinical Psychology, 72,* 202–221.

O'Farrell, T. J., & Murphy, C. M. (1995). Marital violence before and after alcoholism treatment. *Journal of Consulting and Clinical Psychology, 63,* 256–262.

Schaef, A. (1986). *Codependence misunderstood/mistreated.* New York: Harper & Row.

Stanton, M. D., & Heath, A. W. (1997). Family and marital treatment. In J. H. Lowinson, P. Ruiz, R. B. Millman, & J. G. Langrod (Eds.), *Substance abuse: A comprehensive textbook* (3rd ed., pp. 448–454). Baltimore: Williams and Wilkins.

Stanton, M. D., & Todd, T. C. (1982). *The family therapy of drug abuse and addiction.* New York: Guilford.

Vanicelli, M., Gingerich, S., & Ryback, R. (1983). Family problems related to the treatment and outcome of alcoholic patients. *British Journal of Addiction, 78,* 193–204.

Winters, J., Fals-Stewart, W., O'Farrell, T. J., Birchler, G. R., & Kelley, M. L. (2002). Behavioral couples therapy for female substance-abusing patients. Effects on substance use and relationship adjustment. *Journal of Consulting and Clinical Psychology, 70,* 344–355.

CHAPTER 11

Making Treatment Count: Client-Directed, Outcome-Informed Clinical Work with Problem Drinkers

Scott D. Miller, David Mee-Lee, William Plum, and Mark A. Hubble

"The proof of the pudding is in the eating."

—Cervantes, *Don Quixote*

The misuse of alcohol is a serious and widespread problem. Whether clinicians are interested, available evidence indicates they will encounter it on a regular basis throughout their careers. Indeed, the prevalence of abuse and its impact on the drinker, significant others, and society makes avoiding the problem impossible in any clinical, health, or medical setting. According to the Substance Abuse and Mental Health Services Administration (SAMHSA) in the Department of Health and Human Services (HHS), the latest research indicates that an estimated 22 million Americans suffered from substance dependence or abuse due to drugs, alcohol, or both (National Survey on Drug Use and Health [SAMHSA], 2002). Data from the National Institute on Alcohol Abuse and Alcoholism (NIAAA) further shows that problem drinking is associated with more than 100,000 deaths per year—the statistical equivalent of a plane crash killing 274 people every single days—and costs society an estimated $185 billion (Tenth Special Report to Congress on Alcohol and Health, 2000).

The consequences of problem drinking on the family are well established. In the January 2000 issue of the *American Journal of Public Health,* for example, researchers found that 25 percent of all U.S. children are exposed to alcohol abuse and/or dependence in the family (Grant, 2000). This dry recitation of statistics takes on a sense of urgency when the problematic use of alcohol in the home is linked with poorer school performance, increased risk of delinquency, child neglect, divorce, homelessness, and violence. With regard to the latter, available evidence indicates that as many as 80 percent of incidents of familial violence are associated with alcohol abuse (Collins & Messerschmidt, 1993; Eighth Special Report to the U.S. Congress on Alcohol and Health, 1993).

Sadly, many people who want or could benefit from professional intervention do not get the services they need or desire. For example, of the 362,000 people who recognized and sought help for a drug abuse problem in the year 2002, nearly a quarter (88,000) were unable to obtain treatment. That same year, 266,000 problem drinkers were turned away (National Survey on Drug Use and Health [SAMSHA], 2002). As is true of any large social issue, the reasons for the failure to provide services to those in need are likely many, including poor funding of treatment programs, lingering social stigma associated with problem drinking, lack of professional knowledge and skills, and confusing and often contradictory information about the components of effective care.

Whatever the cause of the disconnect, research leaves little doubt about the overall effectiveness of therapy once it is obtained. Regardless of the type of treatment, the measures of success included, the duration of the study or follow-up period, study after study, and study of studies, document improvements in physical, mental, family, and social functioning, as well as decreased problematic use of alcohol or drugs following intervention (Hubbard, Craddock, Flynn, Anderson, & Etheridge, 1997), Institute of Medicine, 1990; Project MATCH, 1997; Stanton & Shadish, 1997). The same research documents the impact of services on stability of housing and employment in addition to decreased involvement with the criminal justice system.

Taken together, the extent of the problem and the general efficacy of treatment provide astute clinicians with a tremendous opportunity—the chance to partner with problem drinkers, their families, and significant others to both arrest the damage and chart a course toward a more rewarding and productive life. In the sections that follow, the elements of a client-directed, outcome-informed approach are presented. Along the way, emphasis will be placed on documenting how this way of thinking about and working with problem drinkers facilitates better client engagement and improved treatment outcomes. We begin with history and development.

ROOTS OF THE APPROACH

"Do not become the slave of your model."

—Vincent van Gogh

As is true of the field of therapy, the history of drug and alcohol treatment has been marked by contention and debate. In 1956, for example, the American Medical Association declared the misuse of alcohol a "disease" requiring careful examination and detoxification by a physician. Controversy soon followed. Supporters of the disease model of alcoholism cited research showing a progressive loss of control characteristic of an underlying pathophysiological process (see Jellinek, 1960) or pointed to studies indicating that the problem ran in families (see Goodwin, Schulsinger, Hermansen, Guze, & Winokur, 1973). Dissenters, in turn, were quick to cite numerous, and what are now widely acknowledged, flaws in the early studies. These latter researchers noted that the majority of people with alcoholic parentage do *not* go on to abuse alcohol, thus calling any simple view of genetic transmission into serious question (Murray, Clifford, & Gurling, 1983).

Efforts to identify the elements of effective care have been similarly divisive. Historically, the most popular view among clinicians and the public has been that people can recover from alcoholism, but never be cured. For many years, the right treatment involved a hospital-based detoxification, followed by a stay in a 28-day residential facility, lifelong commitment to total abstinence from alcohol, and ongoing participation in some form of mutual help group (e.g., Alcoholic's Anonymous, Rational Recovery). Meanwhile, a smaller group of researchers, academics, and clinicians published data critical of virtually every aspect of the dominant perspective. As just one example, research consistently failed to provide any evidence of superior outcomes for traditional, long-term (and, therefore, expensive) treatment over brief, targeted intervention, or even a single session of advice-giving with a family physician (Bein, Miller, & Tonigan, 1993; Miller, & Hester, 1986; Orford & Edwards, 1977). Where detox was once thought an essential first step toward sobriety, subsequent research has found that the practice actually increased the likelihood of future episodes of medically supervised withdrawal that, in turn, enhanced the risk of impaired neurocognitive functioning (Duka, Townshend, Collier, & Stephens, 2003; Miller & Hester, 1986).

Over the last 15 years, professional discourse and practice has continued to evolve, gradually but steadily moving away from the diagnosis and program-driven treatment discussed above and toward what Mee-Lee (2001) terms "individualized, assessment-driven treatment." Rather than trying to fit people into treatments based on their diagnosis, this perspective, as the term implies, attempts to fit services to the individual, based on an ongoing assessment of that person's needs and level of functioning.

The idea of matching treatments to clients has a considerable amount of commonsense appeal and, at first blush, research support. Virtually all of the literature, for instance, shows that clients vary significantly in their response to different approaches (Duncan, Miller, & Sparks, 2004). The question, of course, is whether the variables assessed by clinicians lead to treatment matches that reliably improve outcome.

Enter Project MATCH, the largest and most statistically powerful clinical trial in the history of the field of alcohol and drug treatment (Project MATCH Research Group, 1997). Briefly, this NIAAA-organized study assessed the impact of matching people to one of three possible treatment approaches based on 21 carefully chosen variables, including severity of alcohol involvement, cognitive impairment, psychiatric severity, conceptual level, gender, meaning-seeking, motivational readiness to change, social support for drinking versus abstinence, sociopathy, and typology of alcoholism. The results were less than encouraging. *Out of 64 possible interactions tested, only one match proved significant.* Moreover, while participants in the study showed considerable and sustained improvement overall, no differences in outcome were found between the three competing approaches. The same results were observed in a follow-up study conducted 10 years after the formal initiation of Project MATCH. As researchers Tonigan, Miller, Chavez, Porter, Worth, & Westfall et al., (2003) conclude, "No support for differential treatment response was found using percent days abstinent (PDA), drinks per drinking day (DDD), and total standard drink measures in comparing cognitive behavioral (CBT), motivational enhancement (MET), and twelve step facilitation (TSF) therapies 10 years after treatment" (p. 1).

As unexpected as the results were to researchers and clinicians, they are entirely consistent with findings from the field of psychotherapy. As Wampold (2001) concludes in his review of the data, "decades of research" conducted by different researchers, using different methods on a variety of treatment populations, provides clear evidence that "the type of treatment is irrelevant, and adherence to a protocol is misguided" (p. 202). Simply put, the method does not matter. Indeed, available evidence indicates that the particular approach employed accounts for 1 percent or less of the variance in treatment outcome (Wampold, Mondin, Moody, Stich, Benson, & Ahn, 1997).

The same body of evidence showing the broad equivalence of treatment approaches provides important clues about the predictors of successful intervention (Hubble, Duncan, & Miller, 1999). To begin, research makes clear that, regardless of type or intensity of approach, *client engagement* is the single best predictor of outcome. Forgoing the customary equivocation typical of researchers, Orlinsky, Grawe, & Parks (1994) conclude:

> The quality of the patient's (*sic*) participation stands out as the most important determinant of outcome . . . these consistent process-process outcome relations, based on literally hundreds of empirical findings, can be considered *facts* established by 40-plus years of research. (p. 361)

High on the list of factors mediating the link between participation and outcome is the quality of the therapeutic relationship—in particular, the *consumer's* experience *early* in treatment (Bachelor & Horvath, 1999; Orlinsky, Grawe, & Parks, 1994). In fact, meta-analytic studies indicate "a little over half of the beneficial effects of psychotherapy . . . are linked to the quality of the alliance" (Horvath, 2001, p. 366). Similar findings have been reported in the alcohol treatment literature, where between 50 to 66 percent of the variance in outcome is attributable to qualities of the alliance between client and therapist (Miller, Wilbourne, & Hettema, 2003). Said another way, the therapeutic relationship contributes 5 to 10 times more to outcome than the particular model or approach employed (Bachelor & Horvath, 1999; Duncan, Miller, & Sparks, 2004; Wampold, 2001). Given such findings, it should come as little surprise that a post-hoc analysis of the Project MATCH data found that the therapeutic relationship was, unlike the particular treatment approach employed, a significant predictor of treatment participation, drinking behavior during treatment, and drinking at 12-month follow-up (Connors, Carroll, DiClemente, Longabaugh, & Donovan, 1997).

Another factor known to be a significant predictor of outcome is the client's subjective experience of improvement early in the treatment process (Duncan, Miller, & Sparks, 2004). In one study of more than 2,000 therapists and thousands of clients, for example, Brown, Dreis, & Nace (1999) found that treatments in which no improvement occurred by the third visit did not, on average, result in improvement over the entire course of therapy. This study further showed that clients who worsened by the third visit were twice as likely to drop out as those reporting progress. More telling, variables such as diagnosis, severity, family support, and type of therapy were "not . . . as important [in predicting eventual outcome] as knowing whether or not the treatment being provided [was] actually working" (p. 404). Similar results were found in Project Match, where all of the change in the outpatient arm of the study occurred within the first 4 weeks (Stout, Del Boca, Carbonari, Rychtarik, Litt, & Cooney, 2003).

In recent years, researchers have been using data generated *during* treatment regarding the alliance and improvement to enhance the quality and outcome of care (Howard, Moras, Brill, Martinovich, & Lutz, 1996; Johnson, 1995). In one representative study, clients whose therapists had access to outcome *and* alliance information were less likely to deteriorate, more likely to stay longer (i.e., remain engaged), and *twice as likely* to achieve a clinically significant change (Whipple, Lambert, Vermeersch, Smart, Nielsen, & Hawkins, 2003). Notably, these findings were obtained without any attempt to organize, systematize, or otherwise control the treatment process. Neither were the therapists in this study trained in any new therapeutic modalities, treatment techniques, or diagnostic procedures. Rather, the individual clinicians were completely free to engage their individual clients in the manner they saw fit. The only constant in an otherwise diverse treatment environment was the availability of formal client feedback.

Such findings, when taken in combination with the field's continuing failure to discover and systematize therapeutic process in a manner that reliably improves success, have led us to conclude that conventional approaches to assessment, diagnosis, and treatment selection are no longer viable. Moreover, a simpler path to effective, efficient, and accountable intervention exists. Instead of assuming that a therapist's a priori assessment of the client's needs, level of functioning, and severity of illness will lead to a match with the type and level of treatment most likely to lead to favorable results, ongoing feedback from consumers regarding both the process and outcome of care can be used to construct and guide service delivery as well as to inspire innovation. Rather than attempting to fit clients into fixed programming or manualized treatment approaches via "evidence-based practice," we recommend that therapists and systems of care tailor their work to individual clients through "practice-based evidence." On the basis of measurable improvements in outcome alone, practice-based evidence may be the most effective evidence-based practice identified to date. Indeed, as Lambert, Whipple, Hawkins, Vermeersch, Nielsen, & Smart (2003) point out, "those advocating the use of empirically supported psychotherapies do so on the basis of much smaller treatment effects." (p. 296)

SPECIFIC INTERVENTION STRATEGIES

> *"Absolutely anything you want to say about alcoholics is true about some of them and not true about all of them."*
>
> —Thomas McLellan

The client-directed, outcome-informed approach described in this chapter contains no fixed techniques, no invariant patterns in therapeutic process, no definitive prescriptions to produce good treatment outcome, and no causal theory regarding the concerns that bring people into treatment. Because the particular method employed or type of problem being treated is not a robust predictor of outcome across clients (~1 percent of variance), almost any type (e.g., dynamic, cognitive-behavioral, family-of-origin treatment, 12-step), mode (e.g., individual, group, family sessions), or intensity (e.g., medically supervised detoxification, residential, inpatient or outpatient setting, self-help, or any combination thereof) of service delivery has the potential to be helpful. As a result, therapists may, in principle, work in whatever manner they wish, limited only by practical and ethical considerations and their creativity.

Of course, in practice, both individual practitioners and the larger healthcare systems in which most work require structure and direction in order to operate. In this regard, operationalizing client-directed, outcome-informed work in real-world clinical settings involves the following three key procedures:

1. A highly individualized service delivery plan for each client in care.
2. Formal, ongoing feedback from clients regarding the plan, process, and outcome of treatment.
3. The integration of both the plan and feedback into an innovative and flexible continuum of care, that is, because of points 1 and 2, maximally responsive to the individual client.

As is clear, the underlying theme is making sure that the client is an integral partner, rather than a passive or compliant recipient, of a treatment program. While the procedures are, in and of themselves, not imbued with the power to ensure a positive outcome, they do serve to provide therapists and systems of care with enough structure to begin treatment and avoid organizational chaos. As will be shown, the three activities also enable therapists to meet their ethical obligations to do no harm and be good stewards of the limited treatment resources available. A detailed discussion of each of these three steps now follows.

Developing an Individualized Service Delivery Plan

The individualized service delivery plan is basically a written summary—a snapshot, so to speak—of the alliance between a particular client and therapist (or treatment system) at a given point in time. While definitions vary from researcher to researcher, most agree that an effective alliance contains three essential ingredients: (1) shared goals; (2) consensus on means, methods, or tasks of treatment; and (3) an emotional bond (Bachelor & Horvath, 1999; Bordin, 1979; Horvath & Bedi, 2002). To these three, we have added a fourth; namely, the client's frame of reference regarding the presenting problem, its causes, and potential remedies—what has been termed the client's theory of change (Duncan, Hubble, & Miller, 1997).

With regard to the client's theory, a significant amount of data indicates that congruence between a person's beliefs about the causes of his or her problems and the treatment approach results in stronger therapeutic relationships, increased duration in treatment, and improved rates of success (Duncan, Miller, & Sparks, 2004; Hubble, Duncan, & Miller, 1999). Consider a study conducted by Hester, Miller, Delaney, & Meyers (1990) comparing the effectiveness of a traditional alcohol treatment with a learning-based approach. Consistent with previous studies, no differences in outcome were found at the conclusion of treatment. At follow-up, however, participants who prior to the formal initiation of treatment believed that problems with alcohol were caused by a disease were much more likely to be sober had they received traditional (e.g., abstinence-based) treatment. In contrast, people who believed that their problematic use of alcohol was a "bad habit" did better in the learning-based (e.g., moderation management) treatment (Wolfe & Meyers, 1999).

The four parts of the alliance can be thought of as a three-legged stool (see Figure 11.1). In this analogy, each leg of the stool stands for one of the core ingredients of the therapeutic alliance. Holding everything together is the client's theory of change. Consistent with the metaphor, goals, methods, and a bond that are congruent with the client's theory are likely to keep people comfortably seated (i.e., engaged) in treatment. Similarly, any disagreement between various components works to destabilize the relationship, either making the stool uncomfortable or toppling it completely.

When the individualized service plan is considered to be *a* written reflection of the alliance between a client and therapist and not *the* game plan for expert intervention, both the document and the process leading to its creation are entirely different from traditional care. Instead of being a fixed statement of how treatment will proceed, given the client's diagnosis, severity of illness, level of functioning, and available programming, the plan becomes a living, dynamic document—a collaboratively developed synopsis of the goals, type, and level of interaction the client wants from the counselor or system of care.

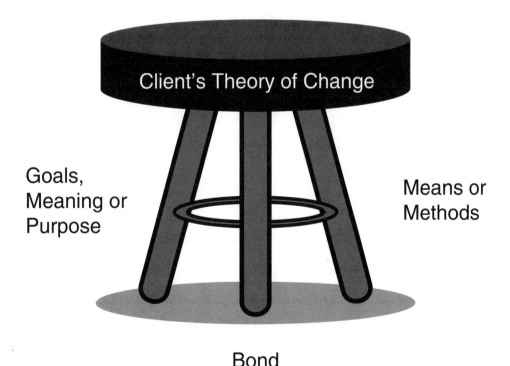

Figure 11.1   The Therapeutic Alliance

In the case of family therapy, the notion of developing an individualized service plan may, at first pass, seem incongruous. Not infrequently, for example, the person believed to have an alcohol problem is not sure or even actively denies there is a problem. Even more challenging, perhaps, are those occasions where concerned family members attend the session and the identified client is absent. An individualized service plan is, however, not the same as a service plan for a client seen individually. The question is, "Who is the client?" In the latter instance, the family is presenting for services. As such, the service plan is the written summary of the alliance between the counselor and the family members present at that visit. As is the case in individual treatment, services are aimed at fulfilling the hopes or resolving the concerns that led the family to seek assistance in the first place (e.g., fix our loved one, get our [child, parent, or others] to stop drinking). Conversely, when a person presents for services *because* of the family (e.g., my spouse or kids are nagging me, my parents don't trust me or are on my back all the time), the alliance is organized around solving the specific problems that motivated that client to seek help (e.g., help me get my spouse to stop nagging, help me get my parents to give me more freedom and independence). Developing a plan when the various family members have different views, concerns, and objectives is the focus of the case example at the conclusion of this chapter.

One structured format for developing an individualized service plan was developed by the American Society of Addiction Medicine (ASAM; Hoffmann, Halikas, Mee-Lee, & Weedman, 1991; Mee-Lee, Shulman, Fishman, Gastfriend, & Griffith, 2001). Briefly, this tool uses six dimensions for organizing client information and tracking services received, including: (1) acute intoxication and/or withdrawal potential; (2) medical conditions and complications; (3) emotional, behavioral, or cognitive conditions and complications; (4) readiness or interest in change; (5) potential for relapse or continued use; and (6) living/recovery environment. When done correctly, the multidimensional assessment criteria (MDA) not only help practitioners identify, organize, and stay focused on what clients want, but also provide suggestions for the type and level of care most likely to be congruent with their goals.

Several controlled studies have found that treatment congruent with service plans based on the MDA are associated with less morbidity, better client functioning, and more efficient service utilization than mismatched treatment (Gastfriend & Mee-Lee, 2003). Moreover, a recent survey of 450 private substance abuse treatment agencies conducted by the National Treatment Center (NTC) found that adoption of the ASAM Patient Placement Criteria was associated with program survival. Specifically, programs that had not survived 24 months after the initial survey were less likely to be ASAM adopters, and those that closed within 6 months of the initial survey had even lower adoption rates. The association between the criteria and program survival is intriguing, and the NTC study group will propose more detailed, longitudinal follow-up, including a study of the impact on treatment quality and outcomes (Clinical Trials Network Bulletin, 2004).

As an example of using the MDA to develop an individualized service plan likely to engage a client at the outset of care, consider the following two cases. The first, Tracey, is a 16-year-old female brought to the emergency room of an acute care hospital by the police. The teenager was taken into custody following an altercation with her parents that culminated in her throwing a chair. Both the police who responded and Tracey's parents, who called 911, believe that she was under the influence at the time of the incident.

When interviewed by an ER physician and a nurse from the hospital's psychiatric unit, Tracey reports that this latest episode was one of many recent clashes at home, typically starting whenever her parents—especially her father—complain about her drinking, late hours, or poor choice of friends. She freely admits to being angry with her parents, noting, in particular, that they treat her "like a toddler rather than a teenager." When asked, she says she had been drinking "some" earlier that evening, but denied using alcohol or drugs on anything more than an occasional basis. "The problem," she maintains, is her parents—"They are always on my back." Until that is resolved, she continues, "Sending me home is a bad idea."

Where intake and assessment traditionally focus on finding a placement for Tracey that fits her psychiatric diagnosis, the emphasis of the MDA is on developing a partnership with clients around the goals, type, and level of interaction desired from the counselor or system of care. To that end, using the six dimensions, the clinical information presented by Tracey, the police, and her parents were organized as follows:

1. *Acute intoxication and/or withdrawal potential:* Tracey is no longer intoxicated and denies using alcohol or other drugs in large enough quantities over a long enough period to worry about any problems with withdrawal.

2. *Biomedical conditions and complications:* During the interview in the ER, Tracey indicates that she is not taking any medications and has no complaints of a medical nature. On observation, she appears physically healthy.

3. *Emotional, behavioral, or cognitive conditions and complications:* Tracey is admittedly frustrated and angry. She confirms throwing the chair but denies being tempted to act on her feelings if separated from the parents.

4. *Interest in change (readiness):* Tracey talks openly with the physician and nurse. She views her parents as being overbearing and mistrustful and expresses interest in anything (e.g., therapy) that will "get her parents off [her] back." At the same time, however, she is clear about not wanting to go home with her parents.

5. *Relapse, continued use, or continued problem potential:* Given Tracey's statements, a reoccurrence of the fighting appears likely if she is returned home this evening.

6. *Recovery environment:* Tracey reports considerable discord at home. Her parents, who are in the waiting room at the ER, report being frustrated and angry, and ask that Tracey be admitted to the hospital.

While both the ER physician and the psychiatric nurse are initially tempted to admit Tracey to the psychiatric unit—at least for the night—a review of the MDA suggests otherwise. Yes, Tracey threw the chair when she was intoxicated. She is no longer under the influence, however, and the incident appears to be directly related to problems at home. In addition, no evidence of severe or imminently dangerous biomedical, emotional, behavioral, or cognitive problems requiring the resources of a medically managed intensive inpatient setting exists. Finally, and most important, Tracey views her parents as the problem. As such, hospitalization is more likely to evoke opposition and defiance than engagement and cooperation.

Instead, the physician and nurse use the MDA to provide a structure for conducting an open and collaborative conversation with Tracey and her parents. Everyone present agrees that a physical separation would decrease the chances of another fight. When various options are considered, the family decides to have Tracey stay overnight with a trusted relative. Sessions with the family are scheduled for the next day, in order to address the difficulties at home. As far as the Individualized Service Plan is concerned, the various agreements and MDA are written down and signed by Tracey, her parents, the nurse, and the physician. While significant challenges remain, all are engaged and anticipating the services to come by the end of the process.

In the second case, a 45-year-old man named Bob presents for services at an outpatient alcohol and drug treatment center. It does not take long to determine his goal for treatment either. Within minutes, he says, "The only reason I'm here is because of the wife. She says she's going to divorce me if I don't get the treatment." Bob then continues, "and don't give me any of that 'one day at a time,' or '90 meetings in 90 days' crap. Been there, done that. I don't have no allergy to alcohol. No sir. I got an allergy to my wife. Her nagging."

As the interview proceeds, the therapist is careful to avoid any conversation about alcohol dependence or hints that Bob needs to be in a recovery-oriented treatment program. Instead, the majority of time is spent working with Bob to determine the best way to keep his marriage, and even, if he wishes, gathering the evidence needed to show his wife that he does not have a drinking problem. In both instances, the MDA provide a structure for exploring how best to reach his goal and a written service plan. For example, Bob quickly agrees that his wife's threats about ending the marriage escalated when a recent physical turned up evidence of alcohol-related liver damage (Dimension 2): a visit to the physician that was prompted, by the way, following her complaints about his moodiness (Dimension 3) and recent absenteeism from work (Dimension 6). At the conclusion of the interview, changes in physical and emotional health (e.g., liver enzymes, general energy, decreased depression) in addition to improved work attendance were simply written into the initial individualized service plan as formal treatment objectives. His active participation in the services that followed indicates that the plan, as constructed, fit with his view of the problem and goals for therapy.

Naturally, as is true of any relationship, treatment or otherwise, plans change. Time, experience—even chance events—impact what people want, are interested in, or are willing to try or do. Given that any fracturing of consensus between the plan and the client risks disengagement, some way for monitoring the status of the alliance and progress in treatment is required. In the section that follows, we take a detailed look at methods for obtaining and incorporating client feedback in therapy.

Formal Client Feedback

As any experienced clinician knows, therapy is a complex affair, full of nuance and uncertainty. In contrast to the examples found in manuals and textbooks—where the treatment, if done in the manner described, seems to flow logically and inexorably toward the predetermined outcome—finding what works for a given client most often proceeds by trial and error. Traditionally, the frenzy of real-world clinical practice has been managed by programming—standardized packages, or treatment "tracks," to which clients are assigned and their progress assessed by their degree of compliance and movement from one level to the next. In contrast, the client-directed, outcome-informed approach to problem drinking described in this chapter begins with the experience and outcome the *client* desires, then works backwards to create the means by which they will be achieved. All along, the client is in charge, helping to fine tune or alter, continue, or end treatment via ongoing feedback.

While most therapists strive to listen and be responsive to clients, available data suggests that they are not, despite their best efforts, alert to treatment failure (Lambert et al. 2003). Moreover, a virtual mountain of evidence shows that clinical judgments regarding the alliance and progress in treatment are inferior to formal client feedback (Duncan, Miller, & Sparks, 2004).

Gathering feedback begins with finding measures of process and outcome that are valid, reliable, and feasible for the context in which the tools will be employed (Duncan & Miller, 2000). In reality, no perfect measure exists. Simple, brief, and therefore user-friendly measures, for example, are likely to be less reliable. At the same time, any gains in reliability and validity associated with a longer and more complicated measure are likely to be offset by decreases in feasibility.

In our own work and research, an effective balance for obtaining feedback regarding the client's experience of treatment process was achieved with the *Session Rating Scale* 3.0 (SRS; Miller, Duncan, & Johnson, 2000).[1] Briefly, the *SRS* is a four-item measure of the therapeutic alliance. It takes less than a minute to complete and score and is available in both written and oral forms in several different languages. In addition to being practical, the scale possesses sound psychometric qualities and has been applied in a variety of clinical settings with positive effect (e.g., outpatient, inpatient, residential, group, individual, and family therapy). Most important, studies have found the *SRS* to be a valid measure of those qualities of the therapeutic relationship noted earlier to be associated with retention in and outcome from treatment (Duncan, Miller, Reynolds, Sparks, Claud, Brown, & Johnson, 2004).

As for obtaining feedback regarding the client's experience of change, we use the Outcome Rating Scale (ORS; Miller & Duncan, 2000). Similar in structure to the SRS, the ORS is a four-item visual analog scale. Clients simply place a hash mark on a line nearest the pole that best describes their experience. The measure takes less than a minute to administer and score and is available in both written and oral forms in several languages. Research to date indicates that the scale pos-

---

[1] Individual practitioners can download copies of the SRS and ORS for free at www.talkingcure.com

sesses good psychometric qualities, with estimates of internal consistency and test-retest reliability at .74 and .66, respectively (Miller, Duncan, Brown, Sparks, & Claud, 2003). The same research shows that the ORS is a valid measure of the outcomes most likely to result from the treatment offered at the settings in which we work (i.e., change in individual, relational, and social functioning). Finally, and of critical importance when selecting an outcome tool, the ORS has been shown to be sensitive to change in those undergoing treatment while being stable in a non-treated population (Miller et al., 2003). As Vermeersch, Lambert, & Burlingame (2000) point out, many scales presently in use were not specifically designed to be sensitive to change, but rather to assess stable personality traits or a specific problematic behavior (e.g., *DSM* diagnostic categories, MAST [Michigan Alcoholism Screening Test], AUDIT [Alcohol Use Disorders Identification Test], ASI [Addiction Severity Index]).

Incorporating the outcome and process tools into treatment can be as simple as scoring and discussing results together with clients at each session, or as complex as an automated, computer-based data entry, scoring, and interpretation software program. The approach chosen will depend on the needs, aims, and resources of the user. Regardless of the method, the purpose of the scales is always explained to clients, and their active participation is solicited prior to the formal initiation of treatment.

As for the actual interpretation of the results, a single-subject case design, in which measures are hand scored and results tracked and discussed from session to session, will suffice for most practitioners. The SRS, for example, is administered at the end of each session. Scores of 36 or below are ordinarily considered cause for concern, as they fall at the 25th percentile of those who complete the measure. Because research indicates that clients frequently drop out of treatment *before* discussing problems in the alliance, a therapist would want to use the opportunity provided by the scale to open discussion about the relationship, review the individualized service plan, and remedy whatever discrepancies exist between what the client wants and is receiving (Bachelor & Horvath, 1999).

On the other hand, the ORS is typically given at or near the start of each visit. Higher rates of client dropout or poor or negative treatment outcomes are associated with an absence of improvement in the first handful of visits, when the majority of client change occurs (Duncan, Miller, & Sparks, 2004). In such instances, the MDA can provide a structure for reviewing the type and level of treatment being offered, as well as suggesting alternatives. As the MDA make abundantly clear, failure at one type or level of care does not automatically warrant an intensification of services but rather a review of the individualized service plan (Mee-Lee, Shulman, Fishman, Gastfriend, & Griffith, 2001). Nor should a client have to experience a poor outcome at a lower level of service before being admitted to a more intensive treatment option. In all instances where a client worsens in the initial stages of treatment, or is responding poorly to care by the eighth session (or measure of outcome), however, a change of therapists or treatment settings is almost always warranted, because the available research shows the client to be at significant risk for dropping out or ending treatment unsuccessfully (Duncan, Miller, & Sparks, 2004).

A special index on the ORS, known as the "clinical cutoff," can provide a check on any decisions made via the MDA about the intensity of treatment (e.g., outpatient versus inpatient, treatment versus education or supportive care). Brown et al. (1999) and Miller, Duncan, Brown, Sorrell, & Chalk (2004) found, for example, that as many as one third of clients entering treatment started with a score on the outcome tool that exceeded the clinical cutoff (a score of 25 or higher on the ORS). Such clients, it turns out, are at significant risk for worsening rather than improving over the course of treatment. Encouraging therapists to adopt a strengths-based or problem-solving approach in lieu of depth-oriented, confrontational, or other intensive treatment strategies can serve to maximize engagement while minimizing the risk of client deterioration.

In situations that include multiple participants or stakeholders (e.g., family or group therapy, court-referred clients) the same general guidelines for interpreting the scales apply. At the same time, both the kind of information sought by the measure and the manner in which it is used during treatment varies, depending on specific circumstances involved. As an example, consider the case of mandated clients. In our experience, it is common for such people to score above the clinical cutoff on the ORS (> 25). Rather than trying to convince the client that matters are actually worse than he or she might think, the client's view of the referral source's rating of him or her is plotted and used to assess change over the course of treatment (Duncan, Miller, & Sparks, 2004). In such cases, the client and therapist are technically working together to resolve the problem that the referent (e.g., court, employer, family) has with the client.

A similar procedure can be followed in family therapy when the focus of concern is on a particular person—the so-called "identified patient" (Duncan, Miller, & Sparks, 2004). Moreover, where differences of opinion exist, a graph on which each family members outcome score is plotted in a different color provides a simple yet effective structure for stimulating a manageable and inclusive discussion about who is most interested in change, what the problem is, and what needs to happen for improvement. A graph containing each member's response on the SRS can, in turn, be used to monitor engagement, providing both the family and therapist with an opportunity to reach out to anyone feeling excluded from the process. The process is virtually the same when treatment is delivered via groups—the underlying principle being utilization of the scales in a manner that increases the engagement of everyone involved.

Consider the case of Ted, a 47-year-old who presented for outpatient services after being confronted about his drinking by his wife Sharon and their three adult children. Given that Ted wanted to do anything to save his marriage, couples therapy became a part of the individualized service plan developed at the first visit. Not surprisingly, the couple's scores on the ORS and SRS differed significantly. As a result, the therapist began asking Ted and Sharon at each visit to guess how the other would rate the session and progress. Any differences were then discussed.

At one session, for example, Ted rated the alliance high while Sharon scored quite low. On inspecting the measure, it was clear to both the therapist and couple that the difference centered on a disagreement over the goals of the therapy. The content of the hour had focused almost exclusively on Ted's problematic use of alcohol. However, when asked, Sharon indicated that she was actually less concerned about the drinking than she was about the affairs her husband had when he drank. As one can imagine, discussion of this important difference changed the focus of the work in the couple's therapy significantly.

While the single-subject design previously described profits from ease and simplicity of use, it suffers in terms of precision and reliability. The broad guidelines for evaluating progress, for example, are based on data pooled over a large number of clients. Because the amount and speed of change in treatment varies depending on how an individual client scores at the first session, such suggestions are likely to underestimate the amount of change necessary for some cases (i.e., those starting treatment with a lower score on the outcome measure) while overestimating it in others (i.e., those with a higher initial score). A simple linear regression model offers a more precise method for predicting the score at the end of treatment (or at any intermediate point in treatment), based on the score at intake. Using the slope and an intercept, a regression formula can be calculated for all clients in a given sample. Once completed, the formula is used to calculate the expected outcome for any new client based on his or her intake score.

Miller et al. (2004) employed linear regression as part of a computerized feedback system employed in a large healthcare organization. Figure 11.2 depicts the outcome of treatment derived from an ORS administered at the beginning of each session of therapy with a sample client. The dotted line represents the expected

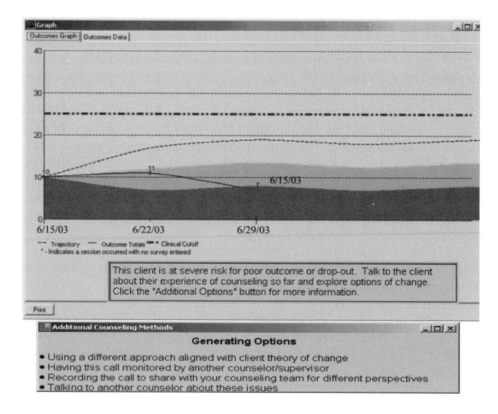

Figure 11.2   Signal Outcome Feedback Screen

trajectory of change for the clients at this clinic, whose total score is four at the initial visit. In contrast, the solid line plots the client's actual score from session to session. As can be seen, the two lines are divergent, with this client reporting significantly less progress than average. In fact, scores falling in the solid dark area represent the 10th percentile of responders. As a result, the therapist receives a "red" signal, warning of the potential for premature dropout or negative outcome should therapy continue unchanged. An option button provides suggestions, including everything from simply reviewing the matter with the client to, depending on amount of time in treatment, referring the client elsewhere. Client responses on the SRS were plotted in a similar fashion at the end of each visit. Scores falling below the 25th and 10th percentiles triggered a yellow and red signal, respectively. The program further encouraged therapists to check in with their client and to express concern about their work together. Exploring options for changing the interaction *before* ending the session is critical, as available research indicates that clients rarely report problems with the relationship until they have already decided to terminate (Bachelor & Horvath, 1999).

Prior to moving on to the next section, mention should be made of two related advantages of automated data entry and feedback. The first is the ability to compare the customer service (e.g., alliance) and effectiveness levels of different clinicians and treatment sites. Research indicates, for example, that *who* the therapist is accounts for six to nine times as much variance in outcome as *what* treatment approach is employed (Lambert, 1989; Luborsky, Crits-Christoph, McLellan, Woody, Piper, Liberman, Imber, & Pilkonis, 1986; Luborsky, McLellan, Diguer, Woody, & Seligman, 1997; Wampold, 2001). Being able to compare therapists not only allows for the identification of therapists in need of training or supervision, but also identifies those with reliably superior results—an obvious benefit to both payers and consumers (Lambert, Whipple, Bishop, Vermeersch, Gray, & Finch, 2002).

To illustrate, consider data on 22 therapists reported by Miller et al. (2004) in Figure 11.3. In this sample, a therapist is statistically above average at a 70 percent confidence interval when the bottom end of his or her range falls above the average effect size for the agency as a whole. A number of research projects currently underway are attempting to identify any differences in practice between the effective and ineffective providers that might serve to inform therapy in the future (Johnson & Miller, manuscript in preparation). Of perhaps greater importance, while having documented tremendous improvements in cases at risk for a negative or null outcome, Lambert (personal communication, 2003)[2] has not found that the overall effectiveness of individual therapists improves with time and feedback. If confirmed, such findings, when taken in combination with the weak historical link between training and outcome in therapy (Lambert & Ogles, 2004),

---

[2] In an-email to the first author, dated July 3, 2003, Lambert said: "The question is—have therapists learned anything from having gotten feedback? Or, do the gains disappear when feedback disappears? About the same question. We found that there is little improvement from year to year even though therapists have gotten feedback on half their cases for over 3 years. It appears to us that therapists do not learn how to detect failing cases. Remember that in our studies the feedback has no effect on cases who are progressing as expected—only the signal alarm cases profit from feedback."

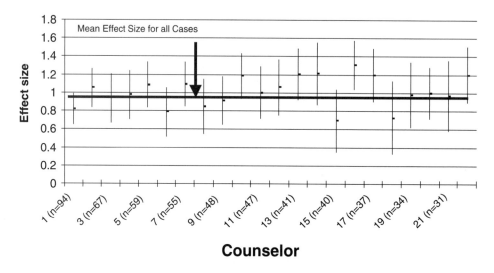

Counselor's Outcomes
(n=30 or more cases)

Figure 11.3   Comparison of effect sizes of 22 therapists in a single agency

further underscores the need to spend less time and resources training clinicians in new treatment approaches and more in helping them solicit and use formal client feedback to guide services.

In a similar way, automatic data entry and feedback can be used to provide real-time quality and outcome assurance for traditionally underrepresented and underserved client groups (e.g., diagnostic, low-income, ethnocultural). Much has been written of late, for example, regarding the importance of cultural competence in clinical work with clients from different ethnic groups. As Clarkin & Levy (2004) point out, however, "Unfortunately, the clinical wisdom offered for maximizing treatment benefits is seldom studied and remains largely untested" (p. 204). In fact, the mix of culturally sensitive stereotypes swirling inside the therapist's interpretive head may actually diminish connecting with a particular client. In contrast, Duncan & Miller (2000) describe a step-by-step process, starting with the selection of the measures used, through data gathering and norm derivation, to insure that feedback is representative of and generalizable to the particular client being treated. As was the case with therapists and settings, such data can be used to identify effective practices, settings, and clinicians, as well as quality improvement opportunities for different client groups.

Integrating the Plan and Feedback into a Flexible Continuum of Care

Historically, treatment was synonymous with completing a program of predetermined length and fixed number of steps or modules. Problem drinkers were sent to rehab for whatever length of time third party payers would cover. While its origins are now long forgotten, the once popular 28-day stay in residential treatment was not a product of science but rather a result of limits on reimbursement imposed by insurers (Institute of Medicine, 1990). Unfortunately, the evidence indicates that programming often took precedence over client preference in such settings and, in turn, had a negative impact on client engagement and retention.

If a key to effective services exists, it is, in a word, flexibility. As a result, when client-directed and outcome-informed, treatment contains no fixed program content, length of stay, or levels of care. Instead, a continuum of possibilities is made available to the client that includes everything from community resources, natural alliances with the family and significant others, to formal treatment and care within healthcare institutions. Literally everything is on the table. Along the way, the MDA and formal client feedback provide a structure for collaborating with the client in the development, continuation, modification, or termination of contact. As the old saying from Alcoholics Anonymous goes, "The question is not *if* we should help but instead *when* and *how.*"

Borrowing an example from business, a truly flexible continuum of care offers all the benefits associated with large discount chains such as Target and Wal-Mart—where a wide number of products are available in one place and at a good price—with the individual attention and customer service typically reserved for fashionable boutiques. When the setting and resources are, by definition, limited in scope (e.g., private practice, rural settings), practitioners serve their clients best by following another standard business practice: outsourcing. Even under the most optimal conditions, no provider or system of care can be all things to all people. When formal client feedback indicates that the partnership with a particular therapist or treatment center is not working, a network of informal yet organized contacts in the local community ensures continuity of care across a virtually limitless continuum of possibilities (e.g., church, service and support groups, volunteer organizations, community leaders, local healers, contacts via e-mail or the Internet).

RESEARCH EVIDENCE SUPPORTING CLIENT-DIRECTED, OUTCOME-INFORMED CLINICAL WORK

> *"Frothy eloquence neither convinces or satisfies me . . . you've got to show me."*
> —William Duncan Vandiver

A number of empirical studies, including one meta-analysis, now exist that document significant improvement in retention rates and outcome from therapies that incorporate formal, ongoing client feedback regarding both the process and outcome of treatment (Lambert, Whipple, Smart, Vermeersch, Nielsen, & Hawkins, 2001; Lambert et al., 2002; Whipple et al., 2003; Lambert et al., 2003). In one study of several thousand cases conducted by the first author of this chapter (Miller et al., 2004), use of process and outcome feedback effectively doubled the average effect size of clinical services (from .4 to .86) and significantly lowered dropout rates (see Figure 11.4). With regard to the latter, clients of therapists who failed to obtain feedback regarding the alliance were twice as likely to drop out of treatment and three to four times more likely to have a negative or null outcome. Notably, retention and success rates in this study improved the moment that formal feedback

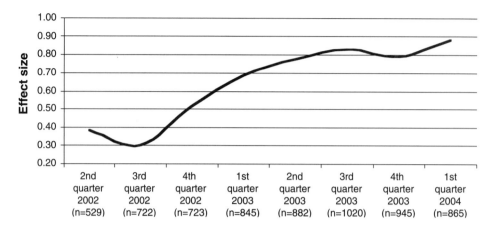

Figure 11.4   Improvement in effect size following feedback

became available to clinicians, without any attempt to organize, systematize, or otherwise control treatment process or training in any new diagnostic or treatment procedures. Similar to the study by Whipple et al. (2003), formal client feedback was the only constant in an otherwise diverse treatment environment.

Because this particular chapter is focused on the treatment of problem drinking, it is also important to note that improved outcomes were observed whether the clients were seeking help for a mental health concern, alcohol or substance problem, or a combination of the two. Indeed, if anything, those being treated exclusively for problems related to their use of alcohol fared better. Specifically, the average client in the study was better off than approximately 70 percent of people without the benefit of formal treatment (ES = .80), while those treated for drug and alcohol problems were better off than 86% (ES = 1.13).

In summary, the results of Miller et al. (2004) and other studies previously cited are compelling enough for Lambert et al. (2004) to argue that clinicians begin "routinely and formally to monitor patient response" (p. 288). Clearly, the treatment effects associated with so-called empirically supported psychotherapies are much smaller (Feedback ES = .39 versus Average ES difference = .20, p. 296). And yet, more research remains to be done. Most studies to date have focused on services delivered to adults in outpatient settings or via the telephone. Projects aimed at determining the degree to which the approach applies across modes of service delivery (e.g., inpatient, residential, group), consumer groups (e.g., children, adolescents, elderly, mandated versus voluntary), and on specific treatment issues (e.g., substance abuse, psychosis) are currently underway.

 Case Study

". . . personal perspective . . . is the only kind of history that exists."

—Joyce Carol Oates

Heather is a 21-year-old female who agreed to meet with a counselor for an assessment after being confronted by her parents about using alcohol and cocaine.

Over the preceding year, this once outgoing young adult had dropped out of college, become pregnant following unprotected sex with a stranger while she was intoxicated, began dealing drugs, and spent $20,000 feeding her growing habit. In addition to losing many of her close friends, Heather had recently come under surveillance of the local police. When word spread that a bust was imminent, a former college friend who had a contact within the police department tipped Heather's parents.

Although Heather readily acknowledged using alcohol and drugs, she initially refused to obtain help, insisting instead that she could quit on her own. Exasperated and concerned, her parents eventually issued Heather an ultimatum. She could either come home at once and get substance abuse counseling, or continue living with her two drug-dealing roommates, and face whatever personal and legal consequences followed alone. They further informed her that choosing the latter alternative would result in their contacting the police to share what they knew about their daughter. Thankfully, Heather chose to enter treatment, showing up for her first appointment with her parents.

Briefly, the agency where Heather sought treatment is the second largest provider of substance abuse services in her home state, encompassing a broad continuum of care that includes medical detoxification, residential, intensive outpatient, and individual and family outpatient services. In any given year, this center serves approximately 6000 culturally and economically diverse clients, ranging in age from 15 to 80. From 1997 to 2004, the agency underwent a radical transformation, shifting from a fixed-length, diagnosis-driven, and one-size-fits-all treatment program to a state-of-the-art, client-directed, outcome-informed service delivery system. Once suffering from poor staff morale, high client attrition rates, and nearing economic collapse, the agency now enjoys a large economic surplus, high rates of client retention and satisfaction, and a highly engaged and motivated staff. Outcome and alliance data gathered at the treatment center using the ORS and SRS since summer 2002 compare favorably with data reported by Miller et al. (2004).

Typically, the initial contact with clients at the agency where Heather sought care is limited to the person with the identified drug or alcohol problem. The reason for this policy is that clients are often guarded about sharing information when the family is present—particularly in cases involving abuse or neglect. In this instance, however, Heather's parents asked to be present during the first part of the initial session. Heather agreed, and the meeting began with the administration of the ORS.

Next, the therapist scored the instrument. Importantly, everyone fell below the clinical cutoff of 25, with Heather at a total score of 16 and her parents rating somewhat lower (Mother = 12; Father = 10). As such, each family member scored more like people who are in treatment and looking for a change. These results, as well as the philosophy of client-directed, outcome-informed work, were then explained to the family.

Therapist: Thank you for taking the time to fill out the forms.

Heather: That's okay.

Parents: We're just glad you're here.

Therapist: Well, thank you, and, let me just start by repeating a bit of what I told you on the phone. At the center, we are really dedicated to helping people get what they want from treatment. And this is one of the forms that will help with that.

Father: Uh huh, okay.

Therapist: Here's how it works. Basically, the research says that if we're going to be helpful, we should see signs of that sooner rather than later.

Heather: (*nodding*).

Therapist: Now, that doesn't mean that the minute things start improving, we're going to say, "Get out!"

Heather: (*laughing*).

Mother: Good.

Therapist: No, it just means that everyone's feedback is essential. It will tell us if our work together is on the right track, or whether we need to change something about it, or, if we're not helping—that happens sometimes—when we need to consider making a referral to some one or some place else in order to help you get what you want.

Heather and Parents: (*nod*).

Therapist: Does that make sense to you?

Heather and Parents: (*nodding*). Yes.

Therapist: And so, let me show you what these scores look like. Um, basically this just kind of gives us a snapshot of how things are overall in your lives and family.

Heather and Parents: (*leaning forward to view graph*).

Therapist: . . . this graph tells us how things are overall in your life. And, uh, if a score falls below this dotted line.

Heather: Uh huh.

Therapist: Then it means that the scores are more like people who are in therapy and who are saying that there are some things they'd like to change or feel better about.

Mother: Looks like we're all feeling that way . . . that something needs to change.

Therapist: Yes . . . it does . . . and we'll be working to get the scores above that line.

Father: That could take a long while. This is a pretty serious situ—

Heather: (*interrupting*). Dad!

Therapist: Well . . . as long as there is measurable change, and you want to continue, we can continue to work together as long as you like . . . but this will just help us stay on track. And you can see, you're pretty much in agreement here . . . with each of you saying that you're feeling like there are things that need to change in your lives.

Everyone expressed agreement with the therapist's last statement, and a lively discussion followed. About midway through the visit, a natural break in the conversation occurred and the therapist asked to speak with Heather alone. Heather's parents agreed, and left the interviewing room. It was during this time that Heather disclosed her pregnancy, indicating further that she wanted this information to be kept confidential for the present.

As the end of the interview neared, Heather's parents were invited back into the room. The therapist then used the six dimensions of the MDA to both organize the information presented and initiate a dialogue about the type and level of service desired.

Therapist: We have a lot of choices when it comes to services. And so, uh, we've found it helpful, when trying to figure out where to go and what to do, to look at everything you've talked about in terms of six different areas.

Heather: Uh huh.

Parents: (*nodding*).

Therapist: Here are the six areas, and I'll just read them just like they are written. The first is "acute intoxication or withdrawal potential." That means, you know, are you high now or have you been using enough that we need to be concerned. And, Heather, you said earlier that you haven't used for over a week. Is that right?

Heather: Yeah.

Therapist: And so, that means that we don't need to send you like to detox so that you could be monitored by a doctor and such.

Heather: Uh huh.

Therapist: The second is, "biomedical conditions." Heather indicates that she is in good health.

Parents: (*nodding*).

Heather: Mmm huh.

Dimension 2 of the MDA is actually the appropriate area for recording important biological and health-related data, such as pregnancy. While documented in the medical record, this information, given Heather's wishes, was not shared with her parents. The discussion continued uninterrupted:

Therapist: Okay. Emotional, behavioral, cognitive disorders or conditions. We talked about this, and the main reason you're here is because of the alcohol and drugs, right?

Heather: Yes.

Therapist: And all of you said that no one has ever been in counseling before for any other kind of problem?

Heather and Parents: (*nodding*).

Therapist: Again . . . that basically tells us that we can focus on the alcohol and drugs . . . because before all this, you were doing really well . . . you've been a good student, you've always had a lot of friends.

Father: Right.

Therapist: The next area is "interest in or readiness for change." And if I've understood this correctly, you're saying, Heather, that you're ready.

Heather: Yeah.

Therapist: And mostly, you're concerned about your relationship with your, how this all has affected your relationship with your parents?

Heather: Yeah . . . 'cause I think I can quit on my own . . . but they don't think so . . . and so, I don't want to lose them . . . and I know how concerned they . . . we've got to get back to where we were before . . . able to talk. Like I said, my Mom and Dad have always been my best friends . . . and this has really screwed it all up.

Father: We want that, too.

Therapist: Okay. Getting close here. . . . "Dimension 5: Continued use, relapse, continued Problem Potential." You said you're still having cravings.

Heather: (*nodding*).

Therapist: So . . . this is an issue . . . and this is also where your Mom and Dad fit in because you said, that you don't think . . . that. . . . You know you need their help to deal with that . . . so, at a minimum, in terms of services, we do want to have everyone involved in some way.

Heather and Parents: (*nodding*).

Father: Like family sessions or something.

Therapist: Exactly, right . . . and that fits really well with the next area, "recovery environment." You're planning to stay at home. Everyone agrees that there won't be any contact with your old roommates . . . and that as long as there is no drug or alcohol use, your parents will help pay your bills . . . and so it makes sense that we work together in some family sessions . . . to get things back on track. Does that sound right?

Heather and her parents agreed, and the interview concluded with a plan for intensive outpatient services and weekly family sessions. As discussed, the focus of the individual work would be on her use of alcohol and drugs—initially, dealing with her cravings for cocaine. At the same time, meetings with the family would center on restoring relationships via improved communication. Just prior to ending the visit, the therapist asked everyone to complete the SRS. From the scores, all appeared to be satisfied with the therapist, the interview, and the plan for services.

In the weeks that followed, Heather and her parents followed through with the service plan that was developed in the first meeting. Each person's scores on the ORS improved gradually and steadily, indicating that the combination of intensive outpatient services and family sessions were working. Scores on the SRS remained high throughout. And, while one might wonder what the therapist actually did in the sessions that led to such scores, it is important to remember that from a client-directed, outcome-informed point of view, the particular therapeutic approach employed is irrelevant. Rather, a plan for services that fits with the client's subjective experience of the alliance and improvement early in the treatment process is critical to success.

By the fourth week, communication had improved enough for Heather to feel comfortable telling her parents about the pregnancy. She did so at home. According to the family, this was a major milestone. Indeed, the discussion had gone so well that the family had been able to come to an agreement about what to do prior to their session that week. The pregnancy would be ended. In fact, an appointment for an abortion had already been made.

Scores on the ORS confirmed the family's view of progress. Everyone had passed the clinical cutoff (> 25) and the scores even appeared to be leveling off. While historically seen as problematic, such plateauing is actually quite common, and can be used to guide decisions regarding treatment intensity. Research suggests, on the one hand, that the probability of change is maximized by meeting clients on a more regular basis in the beginning of treatment, when the slope of change is steep. On the other hand, change is best maintained by spacing visits as the rate of change decreases (see Howard et al., 1996). In any event, when this research and the family's results on the ORS were discussed, all agreed to less intensive services. Heather would leave the intensive outpatient program but continue her work in weekly sessions with an individual counselor. At the same time, the family would continue to meet as a group on a monthly basis.

In a family session 6 months later, Heather reported that she had used alcohol on a couple of occasions in the company of friends. At this point, she was working full time and still living at home. There had been no contact with her drug-dealing roommates, and no further use of cocaine. What's more, Heather's parents were aware she had been drinking. Everyone agreed, however, that communication continued to be good. In fact, Heather had approached her parents prior to drinking, to discuss having a beer with friends after seeing a movie. According to her parents, Heather had continued to keep reasonable hours and had not returned home intoxicated.

When the therapist expressed concern, fearing this would lead to a relapse to cocaine abuse, or simply increased drinking, Heather's father responded, "It's not like we think she has to be a 'teetotaler' or something," and then added, "we just don't want her to get hurt, and to be responsible." And, in truth, abstinence from alcohol had never been one of Heather's or her parent's goals for treatment. All felt that the services they had received had been helpful. "The key is that we're talking again," Heather's mother concluded, "We're all confident that will continue." The session concluded with a brief review of the six dimensions of the MDA and the SRS. Within weeks, the family discussed ending ongoing treatment, opting for sessions in the future on an "as needed" basis. At last report, Heather had rented an apartment near her parents' home. She was working full time, planning on returning to school, and had no further problems with alcohol or cocaine.

CONCLUSION

"Data talks, bullshit walks."

—Geraldo Rivera

More than any previous time in the history of the field, policymakers and payers are stridently insisting that to be paid, therapists and the systems of care in which they operate must deliver the goods. Consumers are also demanding results. Indeed, while stigma, lack of knowledge, and concerns about the length of treatment are frequently offered as explanations, a significantly larger number of potential consumers identify low confidence in the outcome of services as *the* major deterrent to seeking care (76 percent versus 53 percent, 47 percent, and 59 percent respectively [APA, 1998]).

In an attempt to provide effective and efficient services, the field of alcohol and drug treatment has embraced the notion of evidence-based practice. Briefly, the idea behind this perspective is that specific techniques or approaches, once identified and delivered in reliable and consistent fashion, will work to enhance success. Of course, we believe the data indicate otherwise. What's more, in this chapter, we have presented a much simpler method for insuring effective, efficient, and accountable treatment services. Instead of attempting to match clients to treatments via evidence-based practice, the client-directed, outcome-informed perspective uses practice-based evidence to tailor services to the individual client.

In closing, imagine a treatment system in which clients are full and complete partners in their care, where their voice is used to structure and direct treatment. Gone and gladly forgotten will be the countless hours devoted to the generation of histories, interview protocols, and treatment programming. Notes and documentation will report events in the treatment that bear directly on outcome. Gone, too, will be the attitude that therapists know what is best for their clients. When it is more important to know whether change is occurring in any given circumstance, theories of therapy and the many diagnostic labels they have sponsored become distractions. Therapists will no longer be evaluated on how well they "talk the talk," at best a dubious standard for competence, but by how well they "walk the walk." For those reared on the belief that change, should it occur at all, is an internal and arcane experience, long in coming and perhaps unmeasurable, the client's input from one session to the next may feel disconcerting, even suspect. And yet, failing to respond to the demands of payers, policymakers, and consumers is sure to court exclusion. As the American psychotherapist, Carl Rogers, once said, "the facts are always friendly." Better to know what is working or not, in the here and now, than mere failure down the road.

REFERENCES

American Psychological Association. (1998). *Communicating the value of psychology to the public.* Washington, D.C.: Author.

Bachelor, A., & Horvath, A. (1999). The therapeutic relationship. In M. A. Hubble, B. L. Duncan, & S. D. Miller (Eds.), *The heart and soul of change: What works in therapy* (pp. 113–178). Washington, DC: American Psychological Association Press.

Bein, T. H., Miller, W. R., & Tonigan, J. S. (1993). Brief interventions for alcohol problems: A review. *Addiction, 88,* 315–336.

Bordin, E. S. (1979). The generalizability of the psychoanalytic concept of the working alliance. *Psychotherapy, 16,* 252–260.

Brown, J., Dreis, S., & Nace, D. K. (1999). What really makes a difference in psychotherapy outcome? Why does managed care want to know? In M. A. Hubble, B. L. Duncan, and S. D. Miller (Eds.), *The heart and soul of change: What works in therapy* (pp. 389–406). Washington, DC: American Psychological Association Press.

Clarkin, J. F., & Levy, K. N. (2004). The influence of client variables on psychotherapy. In M. J. Lambert (Ed.), *The handbook of psychotherapy and behavior change* (pp. 194–226). (5th ed.). New York: Wiley.

Clinical Trials Network Bulletin. (March 10, 2004). Treatment matching interest group. Volume 04–05, 4.

Collins, J. J., & Messerschmidt, M. A. (1993). Epidemiology of alcohol-related violence. *Alcohol Health and Research World, 17,* 93–100. Washington, DC: United States Department of Health and Human Services, National Institute on Alcohol Abuse and Alcoholism.

Connors, G. J., Carroll, K. M., DiClemente, C. C., Longabaugh, R., & Donovan, D. M. (1997). The therapeutic alliance and its relationship to alcoholism treatment participation and outcome. *Journal of Consulting and Clinical Psychology, 65,* 588–598.

Duka, T., Townshend, J. M., Collier, K., & Stephens, D. N. (2003). Impairment in cognitive functions after multiple detoxifications in alcoholic inpatients. *Alcoholism: Clinical and Experimental Research, 27,* 1563–1573.

Duncan, B. L., Hubble, M. A., & Miller, S. D. (1997). *Psychotherapy with impossible cases.* New York: Norton.

Duncan, B. L., & Miller, S. D. (2000). *The heroic client: Principles of client-directed, outcome-informed therapy.* San Francisco: Jossey-Bass.

Duncan, B. L., Miller, S. D., Reynolds, L., Sparks, J., Claud, D., Brown, J., & Johnson, L. D. (2004). The session rating scale: Psychometric properties of a "working" alliance scale. *Journal of Brief Therapy, 3,* 3–11.

Duncan, B. L., Miller, S. D., & Sparks, J. (2004). *The heroic client: Principles of client-directed, outcome-informed therapy* (revised). San Francisco: Jossey-Bass.

Eighth Special Report to U.S. Congress on Alcohol and Health From the Secretary of Health and Human Services (1993). Rockville, MD: U.S. Department of Health and Human Services.

Gastfriend, D. R., & Mee-Lee, D. (2003). The ASAM Patient Placement Criteria: Context, Concepts and Continuing Development in Addiction Treatment Matching—Research Foundations of the American Society of Addiction Medicine (ASAM) Criteria. *Journal of Addictive Diseases, 22,* Supplement no. 1, 2, 1–8.

Goodwin, D. W., Schulsinger, F., Hermansen, L., Guze, S. B., & Winokur, G. (1973). Alcohol problems in adoptees raised apart from alcoholic biological parents. *Archives of General Psychiatry, 28,* 238–243.

Grant, B. F. (2000). Estimates of U.S. children exposed to alcohol abuse and dependence in the family. *American Journal of Public Health, 90,* 112–115.

Hester, R., Miller, W., Delaney, H., & Meyers, R. (1990, November). *Effectiveness of the community reinforcement approach.* Paper presented at the 24th annual meeting of the Association for the Advancement of Behavior Therapy. San Francisco, CA.

Hoffmann, N. G., Halikas, J. A., Mee-Lee, D., & Weedman, R. D. (1991). *Patient placement criteria for the treatment of psychoactive substance use disorders.* Washington, DC: American Society of Addiction Medicine.

Horvath, A. O. (2001). The alliance. *Psychotherapy, 38,* 365–372.

Horvath, A. O., & Bedi, R. P. (2002). The alliance. In J. C. Norcross (Ed.), *Psychotherapy relationships that work* (pp. 37–69). New York: Oxford University Press.

Howard, K. I., Moras, K., Brill, P. L., Martinovich, Z., & Lutz, W. (1996). Evaluation of psychotherapy: Efficacy, effectiveness, and patient progress. *American Psychologist, 51,* 1059–1065.

Hubbard, R. L., Craddock, S. G., Flynn, P. M., Anderson, J., & Etheridge, R. M. (1997). Overview of 1-year follow-up outcomes in the Drug Abuse Treatment Outcome Study (DATOS). *Psychology of Addictive Behaviors, 11,* 261–278.

Hubble, M. A., Duncan, B. L., & Miller, S. D. (1999). Directing attention to what works. In M. A. Hubble, B. L. Duncan, & S. D. Miller (Eds.), *The heart and soul of change: What works in therapy* (pp. 407–448). Washington, DC: American Psychological Association Press.

Institute of Medicine. (1990). *Broadening the base of treatment for alcohol problems.* Washington, DC: National Academies Press.

Jellinek, E. M. (1960). *The disease concept of alcoholism.* New Haven, CT: Hillhouse Press.

Johnson, L. D. (1995). *Psychotherapy in the age of accountability.* New York: Norton.

Johnson, L. D., & Miller, S. D. *Qualities of effective mental health clinics.* Manuscript in preparation.

Lambert, M. J. (1989). The individual therapist's contribution to psychotherapy process and outcome. *Clinical Psychology Review, 9,* 469–485.

Lambert, M., & Ogles, B. (2004). The efficacy and effectiveness of psychotherapy. In M. J. Lambert (Ed.), *Bergin and Garfield's handbook of psychotherapy and behavior change* (5th ed., pp. 139–193). New York: Wiley.

Lambert, M. J., Whipple, J. L., Bishop, M. J., Vermeersch, D. A., Gray, G. V., & Finch, E. (2002). Comparison of empirically derived and rationally derived methods for identifying clients at risk for treatment failure. *Clinical Psychology and Psychotherapy, 9,* 149–164.

Lambert, M. J., Whipple, J. L., Hawkins, E. J., Vermeersch, D. A., Nielsen, S. L., & Smart, D. W. (2003). Is it time for clinicians routinely to track patient outcome? A meta-analysis. *Clinical Psychology, 10,* 288–301.

Lambert, M. J., Whipple, J. L., Smart, D. W., Vermeersch, D. A., Nielsen, S. L., & Hawkins, E. J. (2001). The effects of providing therapists with feedback on patient progress during psychotherapy: Are outcomes enhanced? *Psychotherapy Research, 11,* 49–68.

Luborsky, L., Crits-Cristoph, P., McLellan, T., Woody, G., Piper, W., Liberman, B., Imber, S., & Pilkonis, P. (1986). Do therapists vary much in their success? Findings from four outcome studies. *American Journal of Orthopsychiatry, 56,* 501–512.

Luborsky, L., McLellan, A. T., Diguer, L., Woody, G., & Seligman, D. A. (1997). The psychotherapist matters: Comparison of outcome scores across twenty-two therapists and seven patient samples. *Clinical Psychology, 4,* 53–65.

Mee-Lee, D. (2001). Persons with addictive disorders, system failures, and managed care. In E. Clarke

Ross (Ed.), *Managed behavioral health care handbook* (pp. 225–266). Gaithersburg, MD: Aspen Publishers.

Mee-Lee, D., Shulman, G. D., Fishman, M., Gastfriend, D. R., & Griffith, J. H. (Eds.). (2001). *ASAM Patient Placement Criteria for the Treatment of Substance-Related Disorders* (2nd ed. revised) Chevy Chase, MD: American Society of Addiction Medicine.

Miller, S. D., & Duncan, B. L. (2000). *The Outcome Rating Scale.* Chicago: Authors.

Miller, S. D., Duncan, B. L., Brown, J., Sorrell, R., & Chalk, M. B. (2004). Using outcome to inform and improve treatment outcomes. *Journal of Brief Therapy.*

Miller, S. D., Duncan, B. L., Brown, J., Sparks, J., & Claud, D. (2003). The outcome rating scale: A preliminary study of the reliability, validity, and feasibility of a brief visual analog measure. *Journal of Brief Therapy, 2,* 91–100.

Miller, S. D., Duncan, B. L., & Johnson, L. D. (2000). *The Session Rating Scale 3.0.* Chicago: Authors.

Miller, W., & Hester, R. (1986). Inpatient alcoholism treatment: Who benefits? *American Psychologist, 41,* 794–805.

Miller, W. R., Wilbourne, P. L., & Hettema, J. E. (2002). What works? A summary of alcohol treatment outcome research. In R. K. Hester & W. R. Miller (Eds.), *Handbook of alcoholism treatment approaches: Effective alternatives* (pp. 13–63). New York: Allyn & Bacon.

Murray, R. M., Clifford, C. A., & Gurling, H. M. D. (1983). Twin and adoption studies: How good is the evidence for a genetic role? In M. Galanter (Ed.), *Recent developments in alcoholism* (pp. 25–48). New York: Plenum.

National Survey on Drug Use and Health. (2002). Substance Abuse and Mental Health Services Administration (SAMHSA). Retrieved at www.DrugAbuseStatistics.samhsa.gov

Orford, J., & Edwards, G. (1977). *Alcoholism: A comparison of treatment and advice, with a study of the influence of marriage.* Oxford: Oxford University Press.

Orlinsky, D. E., Grawe, K., & Parks, B. K. (1994). Process and outcome in psychotherapy–noch einmal. In A. E. Bergin & S. L. Garfield (Eds.), *Handbook of psychotherapy and behavior change* (4th ed., pp. 270–378). New York: Wiley.

Project MATCH Research Group. (1997). Matching alcoholism treatments to client heterogeneity: Project MATCH posttreatment drinking outcomes. *Journal of Studies on Alcohol, 58,* 7–29.

Stanton, M. D., & Shadish, W. R. (1997). Outcome, attrition, and family-couples treatment for drug abuse: A meta-analysis and review of the controlled, comparative studies. *Psychological Bulletin, 122,* 170–191.

Stout, R., Del Boca, F., Carbonari, J., Rychtarik, R., Litt, M. D., & Cooney, N. L. (2003). Primary treatment outcomes and matching effects: Outpatient arm. In T. F. Babor & F. K. Del Boca (Eds.), *Treatment matching in alcoholism* (pp. 105–134). Cambridge, England: Cambridge University Press.

Tenth Special Report to U.S. Congress on Alcohol and Health From the Secretary of Health and Human Services. (2000). Rockville, MD: U.S. Department of Health and Human Services.

Tonigan, Miller, Chavez, Porter, Worth, & Westfall, et al., (2003). Project Match 10-year treatment outcome: Preliminary findings based on the Albuquerque Clinical Research Unit. Accessed at http://casaa-0031.unm.edu/crbposters/project%20match%2010-year%20treatment%20outcome.pdf

Vermeersch, D. A., Lambert, M. J., & Burlingame, G. M. (2000). Outcome questionnaire: Item sensitivity to change. *Journal of Personality Assessment, 74,* 242–261.

Wampold, B. E. (2001). *The great psychotherapy debate: Models, methods, and findings.* Hillsdale, NJ: Lawrence Erlbaum.

Wampold, B. E., Mondin, G. W., Moody, M., Stich, F., Benson, K., & Ahn, H. (1997). A meta-analysis of outcome studies comparing bona fide psychotherapies: Empirically, "all must have prizes." *Psychological Bulletin, 122,* 203–215.

Whipple, J. L., Lambert, M. J., Vermeersch, D. A., Smart, D. W., Nielsen, S. L., & Hawkins, E. J. (2003). Improving the effects of psychotherapy: The use of early identification of treatment and problem-solving strategies in routine practice. *Journal of Counseling Psychology, 50,* 59–68.

Wolfe, B. L., & Meyers, R. J. (1999). Cost-effective alcohol treatment: The community reinforcement approach. *Cognitive and Behavioral Practice, 6,* 105–109.

CHAPTER 12

Family Therapy: Working with Traumatized Families

Michael Barnes and Charles R. Figley

Trauma and its sequelae have become a major focus in the counseling community since the tragic terrorist assaults of September 11, 2001. Training opportunities and traumatology institutes have begun to emerge throughout the United States and the world at large, to ensure that professionals are trained to deal with terrorism and a wide variety of natural and man-made disasters. While the focus on trauma has been positive in terms of awakening society to the very real threat of traumatic events, it has failed to bring to light the reality that trauma has always been a very real and somewhat normal part of life as we know it.

Given the statistics associated with traumatic events, it is unlikely that anyone will escape the direct consequences of a traumatic event or be otherwise closely associated with a trauma victim. The National Center for Posttraumatic Stress Disorder (http:www.ncptsd.org/facts/general/fs_epidemiological.htm) reports that 61 percent of men and 51 percent of women report having experienced at least one traumatic event in their lives, with 10 percent of men and 6 percent of women having experienced four or more such events. Of these trauma victims, 8 percent will actually receive a diagnosis of Posttraumatic Stress Disorder (PTSD; American Psychiatric Association, 2000).

The variability associated with the nature of traumatic events is considerable. In the year 2000 alone the number of violent crimes reported in the United States was remarkable, with 15,527 murders, 90,186 forcible rapes, 407,842 robberies, and 910,744 aggravated assaults having been reported (http://www.disastercenter.com/crime/uscrime.htm). Barnes (2005) reports that 700,000 children are victims of abuse and neglect, 140,000 children are treated in emergency rooms for falls from bikes, 200,000 for falls from playground equipment, and another 320,000 for injuries sustained in automobile accidents. Thousands more will be forced to deal with the diagnosis of some form of cancer. Given the nature of these traumatic events, while it is important for therapists to have the skills needed to assist victims of terrorist attacks, it is far more likely that a therapist will be faced with clients who are suffering from the same traumatic events that have been present for generations.

While the phenomenal growth in the availability of training in the treatment of traumatic stress has been valuable, its primary shortcoming has been the continued focus on attending to the primary trauma victim. Unfortunately, trauma does not happen in isolation, and those who love and care for traumatized individuals may experience their own secondary traumatic stress reaction. Figley (1995) defines secondary traumatic stress as tension experienced as a result of the demands of living with and caring for someone with Posttraumatic Stress Disorder. Therefore, spouses, parents, children, and siblings who must deal with the sudden traumatization of someone they love; cope with the physical, emotional, and behavioral changes that follow the trauma; and who must face their own uncertainty and personal vulnerability are clearly candidates for this secondary traumatization (Barnes, 1998, 2005).

While traumatization may be a primarily linear process resulting from an individual's experience of a traumatizing event, the maintenance of traumatic stress symptoms is a systemic process that results from the interactional dance between the primary victim and those who interact with him or her on a daily basis. For this reason, family therapy should be included as a primary treatment methodology shortly following the traumatic event.

PRIMARY RESPONSE TO TRAUMA

Although a major interest in traumatic stress studies has emerged in the past 25 years, the concept of trauma and the study of individual reactions to traumatic events is by no means a new endeavor. The concept of trauma as the response to some type of physical event or altercation stems originally from ancient Greek verbs that meant to pierce, exhaust, or wear out. These verbs were also used to signify some type of wound or injury (Benyakar, Kutz, Dasberg, & Stern, 1989). Figley (1988) reports that as early as 1900 BC, the Kunus Papyrus, an Egyptian medical text, referred to human reactions to traumatic events and Trimble (1985) discussed references to PTSD-like symptoms from such nonprofessional literature as Shakespeare's *King Henry IV,* Samuel Pepys' diary entry after the great London fire of 1666, and an entry in Charles Dickens' diary after his involvement in a serious train accident in 1865.

Up until and throughout the 1970s, researchers and clinicians from a wide variety of therapeutic specialties continued to work on individuals' responses to specific types of traumatic events. At that time, traumatic stress was discussed in terms of the psychosocial stressors that were directly experienced by the victim (Figley, 1988). Examples include rape trauma syndrome, battered wife syndrome, post-Vietnam syndrome, and so forth. It was not until the publication of the *Diagnostic and Statistical Manual of Mental Disorders, Volume III (DSM-III)* (American Psychiatric Association, 1980), that a singular definition of posttraumatic stress response patterns was identified.

PTSD is a disorder that results when an individual is subjected to a traumatic event that is so horrifying that the prevailing experience is one of intense fear, horror, or helplessness. Figley (1995) proposes that these traumatic events are "outside the range of usual human experience that would be markedly distressing to almost anyone" (p. xv), while the *DSM-IV-TR* (American Psychiatric Association, 2000) defines them as (1) an actual or threat of death or serious injury; (2) a threat to one's physical integrity; (3) witnessing an event that involves death, injury, or a threat to the physical integrity of another person; or (4) learning about the unexpected or violent death, serious harm, or threat of death or injury experienced by a family member or other close associate. Generally, a diagnosis of PTSD is made based on the client's exhibition of symptoms from three primary symptom categories: (1) persistent experiencing of the stressor, (2) persistent avoidance of reminders of the event and numbing of general responsiveness, and (3) persistent symptoms of arousal (American Psychiatric Association, 2000).

THE TRAUMATIZED FAMILY

Figley (1988; 1989) notes that nuclear families are affected by trauma in at least four separate ways: (1) Families experience simultaneous effects, as when trauma is experienced by all family members simultaneously, as in the case of an auto wreck, a fire, or a disaster in which everyone was there when it happened; (2) families experience vicarious effects, as when a trauma strikes one or some family members and other family members are affected secondarily, without direct contact with them; (3) families experience a "chiasmal effect" through direct contact with the traumatized member, which is another secondary traumatic stress effect; (4) intrafamily trauma is a direct result of a family member being victimized by another family member, the perpetrator.

Later, Figley (1995) proposed, "people can be traumatized either directly or indirectly" (p. 4). Secondary trauma occurs when the victim is traumatized through the process of learning about the primary trauma that has been experienced by a loved one or by the secondary victim's frequent interactions with a primary trauma victim and their presentation of primary trauma symptoms. Therefore, while the symptoms associated with primary and secondary trauma are remarkably similar, there is one fundamental difference. When the primary trauma victim experiences symptoms that are directly associated with some aspect of the traumatic event, "the secondary trauma victim experiences symptoms that are associated with the primary trauma victim" (Barnes, 1998, p. 77). Please see Table 12.1 for a comprehensive comparison of symptoms for both primary and secondary trauma victims.

This discussion is not intended to imply that all families that deal with a traumatic event will develop significant primary or secondary posttraumatic stress symptoms. In most cases, families and other interpersonal networks are powerful systems for promoting recovery following traumatic experiences. Figley (1989) identified several characteristics that differentiated families that tend to effectively cope with stressful traumatic events from those that do not. In general, effective families are able to quickly accept their responsibility for dealing with the situation and mobilize their energy and resources for action. They tend to shift their focus away from any one family member and recognize that it is a problem that the entire family must face together. They move quickly from a blaming stance to a solution-oriented, problem-solving focus, and family members exhibit increased tolerance and patience for one another. Individual family members tend to clearly identify and express emotions associated with the traumatic event and verbalize their commitment to one another throughout the recovery process. These effective families quickly recognize the need to access their own individual and interpersonal resources, as well as those outside the family. They tend to reach out without difficulty and with little sense of embarrassment. Finally, highly effective

Table 12.1   *DSM-IV* PTSD Symptom Comparisons: Individual versus Interpersonal Relationships

Individual	Interpersonal Relationships
Criterion A:	
The person has been exposed to a traumatic event in which both of the following have been present:	*One or more member of the system was/were exposed to a traumatic event in which both of the following have been present:*
(1) the person has experienced, witnessed, or been confronted with an event or events that involve actual or threatened death or serious injury, or a threat to the physical integrity of self or others	(1) All of or some of the stimuli noted to the left, plus the system is exposed to knowledge of the event which has activated a systemic response to assist.
(2) the person's response involved intense fear, helplessness, or horror. Note: In children, it may be expressed instead by disorganized or agitated behavior.	(2) The system is exposed to all or some of the reactions noted to the left which is associated with the necessary methods of coping. Note: Once parents link a child's behavior with traumatic stimulus they initiate strategies for coping.
Criterion B: The traumatic event is persistently reexperienced in one (or more) of the following ways:	
(1) Recurrent and intrusive distressing recollections of the event, including images, thoughts, or perceptions. Note: In young children, repetitive play may occur in which themes or aspects of the trauma are expressed.	(1) Increased demand for support and potential conflict due to the distressing recollections symptoms noted to the left.
(2) Recurrent, distressing dreams of the event. Note: In children, there may be frightening dreams without recognizable content.	(2) Increased demand for support and potential conflict due to the sleep disruptions symptoms noted to the left.
(3) Acting or feeling as if the traumatic event were recurring (includes a sense of reliving the experience, illusions, hallucinations, and dissociative flashback episodes, including those that occur upon awakening or when intoxicated). Note: In young children, trauma-specific re-enactment may occur.	(3) Increased demand for time, energy, problem solving, and support in response to the traumatic memory-inducing symptoms noted to the left.
(4) Intense psychological distress at exposure to internal or external cues that symbolize or resemble an aspect of the traumatic event.	(4) Increased demand for time, energy, problem solving, and support in response to the traumatic distress symptoms noted to the left when exposed to reminders of the trauma.
(5) Physiological reactivity upon exposure to internal or external cues that symbolize or resemble an aspect of the traumatic event.	(5) Increased demand for time, energy, problem solving, and support in response to the traumatic reactivity when reminded of the trauma.
Criterion C: Persistent avoidance of stimuli associated with the trauma and numbing of general responsiveness (not present before the trauma), as indicated by three (or more) of the following:	
(1) Efforts to avoid thoughts, feelings, or conversations associated with the trauma.	(1) Increased demand for time, energy, problem solving, and support in response to the traumatized person's reminder avoidance efforts.
(2) Efforts to avoid activities, places, or people that arouse recollections of the trauma.	(2) Increased demand for time, energy, problem solving, and support in response to the traumatized person's reminder avoidance efforts.

Table 12.1   *(Continued)*

(3) Inability to recall an important aspect of the trauma.	(3) Increased demand for time, energy, problem solving, and support in response to the traumatized person's inability to recall an important aspect of the trauma.
(4) Markedly diminished interest or participation in significant activities.	(4) Increased demand for time, energy, problem solving, and support in response to the traumatized person's withdrawal for significant activities.
(5) Feeling of detachment or estrangement from others.	(5) Increased demand for time, energy, problem solving, and support in response to the traumatized person's feeling of detachment or estrangement from others.
(6) Restricted range of affect (e.g., unable to have loving feelings).	(6) Increased demand for time, energy, problem solving, and support in response to the traumatized person's restricted range of affect (e.g., unable to have loving feelings).
(7) Sense of a foreshortened future (e.g., does not expect to have a career, marriage, children, or a normal lifespan).	(7) Increased demand for time, energy, problem solving, and support in response to the traumatized person's sense of a foreshortened future (e.g., does not expect to have a career, marriage, children, or a normal lifespan).

Criterion D: Persistent symptoms of increased arousal (not present before the trauma), as indicated by two (or more) of the following:

(1) Difficulty falling or staying asleep.	(1) Increased interaction due to difficulty falling or staying asleep.
(2) Irritability or outbursts of anger.	(2) Increased interpersonal conflict due to irritability or outbursts of anger.
(3) Difficulty concentrating.	(3) Disruption of interpersonal relationship due to difficulty concentrating.
(4) Hypervigilance.	(4) Disruption and increased interpersonal conflict due to hypervigilance.
(5) Exaggerated startle response.	(5) Disruption and increased interpersonal conflict due to exaggerated startle response.

Criterion E: Duration of the disturbance (symptoms in Criteria B, C, and D) is more than one month.

Criterion F: The disturbance causes clinically significant distress or impairment in social, occupational, or other important areas of functioning.

Specify if:
   * Acute: If duration of symptoms is less than 3 months.
   * Chronic: If duration of symptoms is 3 months or more.

Specify if:
With Delayed Onset: If onset of symptoms is at least 6 months after the stressor.

families are able to deal effectively with significant emotion without resorting to impulsive violence or dependence on alcohol or other drugs.

AXIOMS ASSOCIATED WITH ASSESSING SYSTEMIC FAMILY PATTERNS

From a family therapist perspective, it is imperative to understand that the family members associated with a traumatized individual(s) may experience a significant disturbance in individual and systemic functioning, which may begin almost immediately following the traumatic events. Barnes (2005) reviewed the literature related to trauma response patterns of family members following traumatic events, accidents, and illness. He proposes axioms to be considered when assessing the individual and systemic patterns in families presenting for family therapy.

Individual Reactions

As was identified in Table 12.1 previously, family members will report having experienced emotional, cognitive, and behavioral symptoms that are similar to those reported by the primary trauma victim (Barnes, 2005). Barnes reports that the symptoms of secondary trauma reported in the literature include: intrusive thoughts, nightmares, flashbacks, feelings of detachment and estrangement from others, restricted affect, avoidance of activities that remind them of the traumatic event, sleep disturbances, hypervigilance, and fatigue. Clearly, individuals, couples, and families may present to therapy with a wide variety of presenting problems that may or may not be initially presented as being associated with a traumatic event and its posttraumatic sequelae. Often, presenting problems will focus on the behavior of other family members or marital or couples issues that are consistent with secondary trauma, rather than the primary posttraumatic symptoms of the trauma victim. This is often seen following an automobile accident or successful resolution of a life-threatening illness, such as cancer or a cardiac condition. In these cases, family members seek therapy to resolve their own symptoms, but fail to recognize the connection between their symptoms and the past traumatic event. A complete assessment of past traumatic events, including accidents and medical problems, is important to identify individual issues that often underlie the presenting systemic problems.

Altered Family Worldview

Barnes, Todahl, and Barnes (2002) studied the impact of traumatic injuries and intensive care treatment on the families of injured children. In this study, treatment experts supported the contention that family members frequently experience a change in worldview associated with personal vulnerability, safety, and control. Catherall (1998) proposes that all human systems develop their own unique and idiosyncratic interpretations of reality within their own world. It is through this reality filter that families develop unique attitudes, beliefs, values, rituals, and ways of operating and behaving that become reinforced through interfamily and extrafamily interactions. Following a traumatic event, families commonly experience a shift in attitudes and beliefs that represent a need to focus on safety issues, as they relate to the self and others. Catherall (1998) contends that safety issues are "expressed in the family's world view in the form of suspicious, distrustful attributions concerning the motivations of others, but it can also be seen in various symptoms of family members (i.e., fearfulness, phobias, and other anxiety reactions)." (p. 203)

Centrality of Family Members' Perceptions Associated with the Traumatic Event

Family members' perceptions of the amount of stress caused by the traumatizing event will have a greater impact on their interactional patterns, coping mechanisms, and the amount of emotional sequelae experienced, than the life stressors that may be observable to others (Barnes, 2005). In this respect, it is clearly the case that family therapists must take the time to investigate each family member's understanding of what actually happened during and after the traumatic event, to gain an understanding of each family member's reality orientation associated with the impact of the event on his or her life, and an understanding of what options or resources he or she believes have been available in order to deal with the crisis situation. Whether the event is perceived to be traumatic to others is not as important to the traumatized families as whether they have experienced the event for themselves as traumatic.

Shaw and Halliday (1992) propose that families will possess either a mastery frame of reference or a fatalistic frame of reference concerning the crisis situation. A family with a mastery orientation will maintain the perception that they have the resources, or access to the resources, that will enable them to have some control over the traumatic event. This often leads to solution-oriented thinking geared toward dealing with the crisis. Figley (1988) proposes that ultimately, families that are able to recognize the strengths they have developed through their struggles following the traumatic event are better able to recover from their experience of secondary trauma. A fatalistic frame of reference will maintain a perception that the family does not have access to resources to deal with the trauma, and will promote behavior that will enable the family to passively live with or be controlled by the crisis situation. Manne, Duhamel, & Redd (2000) propose that mothers of children who have been diagnosed with cancer experience greater PTSD symptoms when they feel inhibited in expressing cancer-related thoughts and feelings. This perceived lack of freedom to express thoughts and feelings make it difficult for family members to find meaning or to obtain advice and coping assistance from others. Clearly, the family members' constraining beliefs that restrict alternative views about the crisis (Shaw & Halliday, 1992) may play as significant a role in the development of primary and secondary traumatic stress, as the traumatic event itself.

Structural/Organizational Changes Resulting in a Systemic Traumatic Stress Response

Multiple stressors resulting from the immediate needs of a spouse, parents, siblings, and the traumatized family member(s) may result in a systemic traumatic stress reaction among family members. Barnes et al. (2002) report that a traumatizing event may result in immediate stressors that can impact the lives of all family members for days, weeks, months, or years. This wound to the family system may impact much more than the family's life routines and may be observable through disruptions in the family members' stable patterns associated with communication, discipline, and emotional support. Failure on the part of the family to deal with these disruptions in family interactional patterns may ultimately result in increased arguments, resentments, and attention-seeking interactions between family members. If systemic stressors continue to go unattended, noticeable patterns of triangulation and blaming may become common family dynamics.

In families where a child is the primary trauma victim, the mother/child relationship often becomes closer than the father/child relationship (Hoekstra-Weebers, Jaspers, Kamps, & Klip, 1998). This relationship therefore places the mother in a position as guardian, where she is compelled to manage the child's care and ensure that the child is protected. The impact of these additional responsibilities and their influence on her ability to cope with day-to-day stressors is believed to influence the quality of all family relationships. Marital conflicts may arise due to the triangulation that results when one parent becomes overinvolved and the other "shuts down" and maintains an emotional distance. In both cases, the attempted coping mechanism assists both individuals in avoiding confronting their own feelings about the traumatic event, and prevents the partners from receiving much-needed social support (Wade, Borawski, Taylor, Drotar, Yeates, & Stancin, 2001).

Given the previous discussion of family members' tendency to utilize hypervigilance and control as ways to deal with increased anxiety and feelings of vulnerability, it is common for families to bond with the traumatized family member, while altering role patterns with their spouse and the other children. Koch (1985) and Madan-Swain, Sexson, Brown, and Ragab (1993) each support the contention that the primary trauma victim and at least one other family member may develop a bond following the traumatic event, which serves to isolate the other family members from the individuals involved in the special relationship. During these times, older children are often required to take on parental roles in the family, and frequently assume the role of emotional caretaker for the adults/parents by hiding their own feelings and fears. Other children often act out in an attempt to express their anger and to gain parental attention. This posttraumatic reorganization around the needs and limitations of the primary trauma victim may assist family members to avoid feelings of anxiety and vulnerability, but it does not ensure that the traumatized individual is protected from posttraumatic disability. In reality, enmeshed overinvolvement often results in even lower levels of functioning for the traumatized individual. Families who are able to openly and honestly face the reality of the traumatic event are better able to make appropriate adjustments in power structure, role relationships, and relationship rules in response to traumatic stress (Zarski, DePompei, & Zook, 1988). Paradoxically, family members whose primary coping mechanisms include the suppression or denial of painful affect often experience increased levels of anxiety and psychological distress (Wade et al., 2001).

FAMILY THERAPY AND THE TRAUMATIZED FAMILY

This broadening of the trauma experience to include the secondary traumatization of family members is significant in that it moves the treatment of trauma from the individual to the family system context (Figley, 1989). This shift is also significant in that it challenges the family therapist to move beyond the systemic concept of circular causality, to acknowledge that traumatic events can directly impact all individuals within a family system. It is critical that all therapists who work with trauma victims and their families understand the parallel processes of both individual and systemic stress reactions that may occur and remain present for years following a traumatic event. Brooks (1991) suggests that a systemic focus can be maintained that will address the interactional patterns of the traumatized family while also acknowledging the extraordinary experiences of the primary trauma victim. From the standpoint of secondary traumatization, the family members' extraordinary experiences must also be acknowledged.

When we consider the axioms presented above, it is easy to see that individuals and families can present to therapy with a wide variety of emotional, cognitive, behavioral, and interactional problems that are related to their attempts to cope with the fear, helplessness and terror associated with a traumatic event. Some individuals will enter therapy with the awareness that they are dealing with individual and systemic response patterns that have resulted from their attempts to cope with a traumatic event, while others will come to therapy with no such awareness. It is the responsibility of the therapist to assess the client's presenting problems and to recognize when symptoms are related to past or present traumatic events. As therapists, we have worked with traumatized individuals in a variety of clinical settings that include: hospital intensive care units, community mental health centers, veterans centers, and academic counseling centers. We have come to recognize the signs and symptoms of traumatic stress and have come to believe that expanding the treatment to include the larger family system empowers each family member to better understand the traumatic event, the coping strategies that each used to mitigate painful feelings, and to understand how the family system response served to prevent family members from resolving the traumatic symptoms.

We believe that whether we are working with an individual or a family in therapy, that the steps for resolving the trauma symptoms are similar. The therapeutic model of family therapy that we utilize is an integration of Figley's (1989) Empowerment Model and Minuchin's (1974) Structural Family Therapy. Figley's model begins with the establishment of a strong therapeutic alliance, while encouraging individual family members to reexperience the traumatic event, to identify and contemplate their emotional and cognitive responses to the event, and to then work together to make sense of the incident and its impact on them as a family. Whether we are working with individual clients, couples, or families in therapy, we believe that it is imperative to expand the client(s) view of the trauma from the individual to the context of the individual in relationship with others. Once a trauma has been identified as an influence on the presenting problem that has brought the client(s) to therapy, it is our preference to include as many family members as possible in the therapy sessions.

While at first it may seem odd to integrate the cognitive process in Figley's model and the focus on structural reorganization in the structural model, Minuchin and Fishman (1981) propose that "any change in family structure will change the family's world view, and any change in world view will be followed by change in the family's structure" (p. 207). Therefore, the model allows the therapist to work with the family on multiple issues at the same time. From our perspective, Figley's five-phase model serves as the roadmap that guides the therapeutic process, from the initial stages of developing a therapeutic relationship to the final stages of developing a family healing theory. The structural model serves as a lens, through which the therapist sees the family's posttraumatic reorganization and how they utilize their homeostatic patterns to avoid feelings, memories, and the threat of further traumatization. The therapist uses structural interventions as the family moves through Figley's treatment phases to interrupt dysfunctional interactional patterns, to maintain order and safety in the session, and to enable family members to experience and understand the traumatic event in new ways that allow for alternative solutions.

Safety

When working with trauma as a primary issue, safety must be understood in individual and systemic terms. From an individual perspective, the therapist must be able to identify individual symptoms, such as hyperarousal, intrusive thoughts and memories, constricted affect, dissociation, and regression that occurs when individuals become vulnerable and overwhelmed. The ability to control the pace of the therapy session and to lead the family through the recovery process is a critical skill for the family therapist. Individual family members must begin to recognize the difference between feeling safe and being safe, and it is the therapist's job to create a therapeutic environment in which family members can make a gradual shift from "unpredictable danger to reliable safety both in their environment and within themselves" (Baranowsky, Gentry, & Schultz, 2003, p. 19).

System level safety requires the therapist to understand the functionality of the homeostatic maintenance activities that families initiate to keep members safe and to avoid feelings of great anxiety, fear, horror, and so on. The enmeshment, triangulation, overprotectiveness, boundary adjustments, and role changes are all failed solutions. When asked to speak openly and honestly about each member's reaction to the traumatic event, one would expect to be able to observe the family's homeostatic dance to maintain the roles, rules, and relationships that have evolved in the posttraumatic period. It is for this reason that Structural Family Therapy is utilized as a theoretical roadmap for identifying here-and-now changes in family organization that will promote a sense of order, safety, and control. Minuchin (1974) states that the "therapist joins the family with the goal of changing family organization in such a way that the family members experience change" (p. 13). Structural interventions are useful throughout the therapeutic process to promote active change that will facilitate individual family members' experience of safety and to risk investigating and trying new solutions to the presenting issues.

Figley's Empowerment Model

As the family members come to accept the reality that the issues that brought them to treatment may have been symptomatic of the underlying primary, secondary, and systemic traumatic stress, the focus of therapy can move to resolving the trauma. Family members must begin to recognize that the thoughts, feelings, and behaviors that evolved following the terrifying event were normal and that they served a valuable role in the survival of the family. The therapist must expect and accept that these adaptive symptoms were useful and that they will continue to function throughout the early part of this therapeutic process. This will be especially true as long as the family members are struggling to experience the therapeutic environment and therapeutic process as individually and systemically safe. Often, family members will have to deal with painful, frustrating, and/or frightening issues that are associated with the secondary trauma symptoms before they can deal directly with the traumatic event. Family members may have to share their resentment at how much time parents spend away from the family when focusing on the needs of the traumatized member. Spouses may have to tell their partners how angry they are at having to deal with so much of the trauma alone. Children may have to share resentment at having to take over parental responsibility, or one spouse may have to share how much it hurts to be rejected by the enmeshed relationship between a traumatized child and the other parent. Once individual feelings and resentments are expressed and resolved, the issues of safety and trust will be maximized, and it will provide a more fertile environment in which family healing can take place.

1. Building a Commitment to the Therapeutic Objectives

The initial phase of this model calls for the therapist to work with the family to build a commitment to the therapeutic objectives. As is the case in most therapeutic models, the primary focus of this phase is to build a sound therapeutic alliance and to spend sufficient time in joining with the family members. Colapinto (1991) refers to joining as the attention to simple "rules of etiquette, such as making friendly contact with all family members, confirmation of family members' expressions of concern, sadness, anger, fear, even rejection of therapy and maintenance of the rules that govern distance and hierarchies within the family system" (p. 437). When one considers the altered worldviews, concerns about safety and trust, and closing of system boundaries that occur following a traumatic event, joining with a traumatized family must be approached patiently. Care must be taken not to retraumatize the family by pushing too quickly to investigate the specifics of the traumatic event. It is very important to let "the family know that the therapist understands them and is working with and for them. Only under this protection can the family have the security to explore alternatives, try the unusual, and change" (Minuchin & Fishman, 1981, pp. 31–32).

Like Minuchin and Fishman (1981), Figley believes that it is important in this early phase for the therapist to be seen as an expert who is competent in working with these types of difficult trauma cases. Key to this expert status is the therapist's ability to manage the session and the behaviors within the session. As was stated before, the therapist's ability to pace and lead throughout the session is recognized by the family members as a sign of competence and often leads to a greater sense of safety. Also, at this same time, it is imperative that the therapist is able to demonstrate a nonanxious presence (Baranowsky et al., 2003) as the family shares painful feelings and chaotic, disruptive interactional patterns emerge.

Ultimately, it is the task of the therapist to initiate a discussion with each of the family members to elicit the major sources of traumatic and posttraumatic stress that brought them to therapy. In most cases, the family members will be able to clearly identify these stressors. In other cases, family members will disagree with one another about what the primary sources of stress are. It is critical at this point in therapy that clients experience the treatment environment as a safe place to speak their minds. Each client must be given the right to speak without being interrupted. Care must be taken on the part of the therapist to recognize individuals who begin to dissociate or regress during the discussion of stressors, or during periods of disagreement or conflict between the family members. This discussion is an opportunity to begin to assess family organizational issues, but also time for intervening on trauma symptoms and defensive avoidance. Blocking interruptions and unbalancing power differentials may be necessary interventions in order to maintain an environment in which all family members can share. Once the stressors have been identified, the therapist moves the discussion to identifying the coping mechanisms that the family members used to deal with the stressor prior to entering therapy. Again, this may be an opportunity for family members to disagree or to become anxious, angry, or controlling. As the therapist attends to each family member's comments, trust and a sense of safety begin to develop. Next, the topic of discussion will focus on attainable goals for therapy. Each family member should be given the opportunity to share how he or she would like the family and the posttraumatic symptoms to be changed when therapy is finished. As individuals share their beliefs, it is important for the therapist to normalize the family's symptoms and response patterns. Family members are usually quite relieved to hear that their experience is not out of the norm when compared with others who have been through similar situations. The therapist must present an optimistic stance when discussing the family's chances for achieving the goals identified earlier. Care must be taken throughout this initial phase of treatment to calibrate the optimism to fit the situation. "Too much optimism too early may trivialize and minimize the family's ordeal: too little too late may have no impact at all" (Figley, 1989, p. 73).

2. Framing the Problem

The second stage of the model is a time for framing the problem. "Memory management is the key ingredient in recovery from post-traumatic stress disorder" (Figley, 1989, p. 78). Therefore, it is the task of the therapist to assist the family in recalling important bits of information about the traumatic event and to then "help them manage, restructure, and reframe this information" (p. 78). The primary task in this second phase is to allow each family member to tell his or her story without interruption and without the need to edit or defend his or her position. This is a time to promote the discussion of individual perceptions associated with the traumatic event and to talk about the negative disruption that has been experienced since. This is a time for promoting new rules of communication, understanding, acceptance, and identification of trauma-related consequences; an opportunity for social support; and a shift in attention from the primary victim/patient to a family focus. The goal of this stage of therapy is to begin to identify the building blocks for a healing theory—a statement of what, how, and why this terrible thing happened (Figley, 1989). It must be noted that this may be a difficult stage for the family members. As each shares his or her story, it may be received by the other family members as attacking, blaming, and painful. Even if family members do not agree with the speaker's experience of the traumatizing event, the therapist must not allow the others to interrupt. It is important for the family members to understand that all aspects of the family experience of the trauma must be placed on the table, where they can be dealt with in an open and honest fashion. Therefore, the therapist must be prepared to quickly intervene on interruptions and other types of disruptive behaviors.

As the therapist introduces the focused task for this phase, it is important to clearly identify the guidelines that will make the task effective and healing. First and foremost, the family members should be instructed to tell their whole story. From their perspective, what happened? What did they do during and following the most upsetting moments of the event? What were they feeling at the time of the event and how are they feeling since? Each family member, even smaller children (age 6 and above) should be included in the storytelling process. Each should be asked to share without editing to protect others. Clearly, with each story being told, the therapist must recognize that family members are engaging in an activity that in the past was not supported within the family system. To speak openly about the family secrets associated with the event may open the door for significant hurt, anger, and resentment.

Within this discussion it is important for the therapist to promote new rules of communication. Allowing everyone in the family an opportunity to speak about anything in front of everyone else in the family, including a stranger (the therapist), often violates the family's unwritten rules of silence. As these rules are broken, the therapist must be open for anxiety reactions on the part of family members. Children may begin to act out to reduce the stress and anxiety; adults may attempt to censure other family members or attempt to argue points being made by various family members. Structural issues associated with hierarchy and parental authority should be monitored and maintained. Supporting parents to manage childrens' behavior issues creates a message to the children that the parents are strong enough and safe enough to risk experiencing painful feelings and reexperiencing painful emotions.

Family members must be helped to conceptualize their trauma-related problems through a lens of empathy, understanding, and acceptance of others among the family members. Family members need to be encouraged to accept the need to hear the views of everyone so that they can both account for why they acted as they did and are acting now. As this understanding and acceptance grows, the family members can begin to work more closely as a team.

Family members must be encouraged to stop victimizing and blaming other family members. One of the goals of this therapy is to enable family members to purge these feelings and, in the end, implicitly or explicitly communicate forgiveness. This expression of forgiveness begins a process of shifting family interactions from a victim frame to interactional patterns in which individuals accept responsibility for their actions, feelings, and so on. It also facilitates a shift from an individual's use of hypervigilance and control as a means of soothing and individual survival to a focus on family system survival.

3. Reframing the Problem

While phase 2 was the most demanding for the clients, phase 3 requires the most creativity. Family members must be able to think outside of the box in order to understand their symptoms and coping strategies through the eyes of their fellow family members. It is the ultimate task of this phase of treatment to assemble these reframed views into various, compatible components of a healing theory. While some families may achieve the level of openness and understanding needed to begin this process within a few months of starting therapy, many families remain stuck in old patterns and struggle for many months to be open enough to see their situation differently.

After each family member has had the opportunity to tell his or her recollection of the traumatic event, and the following individual and family reactions to the trauma, the primary task of the third stage is to assist the family in reframing the problem. In this stage, the therapist assists the family members in reaching some consensus about their views of the traumatic experience and in beginning to identify new frames through which the family can begin to conceptualize new, more manageable, and functional coping behaviors. In this stage, family members are urged to discuss the aspects of each family member's recollections that appear important to them. Frequently, comments center around family members' amazement at how differently each individual remembered the details associated with the traumatic event. This is a time for caring debate, confrontation, and consensus building between family members. Again, the therapist must be prepared to intervene quickly to maintain order and safety in the therapeutic environment. Family members are challenged to consider an array of perceptions about their predicament that includes a view that is more tolerable and adaptable for their family functioning. Once the family members can begin to perceive the circumstances associated with the trauma differently, they can begin to understand a different worldview, which allows for the identification of new and more solution-focused coping strategies. It is hoped that families will begin to see beyond the negative and recognize the positive challenges that were presented to them through this terrible circumstance.

Throughout this phase there are two primary issues for reframing. Initially, family members must begin to reframe their traumatic experiences. It is imperative that family members are given the opportunity to process their memories regarding the sequence of actions, and who did what, when. It is through this process of open discussion and trust building that a seed of doubt is planted, related to what actually happened. Once family members can doubt their memory of what happened, they can also begin to investigate alternative realities related to the symptoms that they have developed. Once family members can quit blaming themselves or others for the traumatic event, they can begin to look at their own response patterns through a different lens. Individuals can begin to recognize that their response to the traumatic event and attempts to deal with the residual feelings of fear, anger, and anxiety are in actuality very similar to most other trauma victims.

4. Developing a Healing Theory

In the fourth stage of the model, individual family members are challenged to develop their own healing theories. A healing theory is defined as a set of principles or hypotheses that enables the individual to understand the events impacting on his or her life, why he or she reacted in the way that he or she did, and how he or she might better deal with a similar future event (Figley, 1989). This theory emerges for each individual as family members simultaneously support one another, as they continue to openly communicate about the traumatic event. Ultimately, it is a time when family members are assisted in the process of stating the new meaning that has begun to emerge associated with the traumatic event and everyone's specific response patterns. This individual sharing becomes a therapeutic conversation, with an ongoing process culminating in a cocreated family healing theory. Throughout this process families are empowered to take control of their lives and their futures. Family members are given more control over the sessions, while the therapist assumes a position of participant observer or objective consultant, who serves to clarify and encourage. "Specifically, family members are encouraged to help other family members in (1) clarifying insights, (2) correcting distortions, (3) substituting new interpretations, (4) answering victim questions, and (5) constructing a family healing theory" (Figley, 1989, p. 98).

In the process of developing the healing theory, each individual and, ultimately, the family as a whole must answer five victim questions. In answering these questions, family members are encouraged to work cooperatively and to show signs of insight and acceptance of the current crisis, and optimism about handling this and future challenges. As each family member discloses his or her theory, other family members frequently ask for clarification or justification. In the end, the family settles on a consensus view about the event and its impact on the family. The first question is, what happened? This question assists the family members to fully grasp specifically what took place at the time of the traumatic event and immediately following. The second question is, why did it happen? This question is more difficult to answer and the answer tends to be very personal for each individual. Often issues of faith or religion come into play in answering this question. The third question is, why did we act as we did during the event? Often, the individual's view of the way he or she reacted to a traumatic event is as troubling as the event itself. Frequently, individuals' reactions during a traumatic event make sense only on reflection, months or years later. Family members must not only understand and accept their own actions during the traumatic event; they must also accept their fellow family members' reactions. Once again, in hindsight, family members may gain a better understanding of how the response patterns of other family members were tied to a significant need for safety and survival. The fourth question is, why have we reacted as we have since the traumatic event? Individuals are often perplexed at their actions and feelings following the event. It is important to educate the family members about the immediate and long-term psychosocial process of recovering from traumatic stress. It is imperative that we assure clients that their actions were completely normal and predictable reactions to an abnormal and unpredictable set of events. The final question is, what if something like this happens again? The answer that is developed builds on the answers to the other victim questions. Often families will ruminate over the possibility of a similar event happening again. Even when the chances are unlikely, it is reassuring for the family members to discuss the contingencies and reach a general consensus about the handling of future catastrophes. Ultimately, "having such a plan is one more sign that they are no longer traumatized, they have recovered from the catastrophe, and they are in control" (Figley, 1989, p. 108).

In the development of a family healing theory, the family members consider all of the answers to the victim questions, as well as the many insights and new perspectives that have emerged among the family members. It is the challenge of the family members to come together to collaborate on an answer for each question that each can agree upon as being true and consistent with their family's experience of the traumatic event. This is a process that may take some time to evolve, and it is important for the therapist to be patient in allowing the family to create this new understanding.

5. *Closure and Preparedness*

Once the family is able to articulate its healing theory, they are ready to begin the process of closure and preparedness. In this final phase of treatment it is important for family members to recognize that they have reached the goals that they had established in the initial phases of treatment. At this time it is important for the therapist to ensure that the family members experience a genuine sense of accomplishment for their recovery efforts. A discussion should be carried out that focuses on the family members' readiness to deal with future stressful events, and to provide an opportunity for family members to outline newly established rules and roles that have been identified to successfully deal with future traumatic events. Ultimately, the need for both intrafamilial and extrafamilial social support should be discussed, and family members should be able to articulate whom they will turn to in future times of need.

CONCLUSION

As the nation continues to attend to the war on terror, the mental health community continues to prepare for a variety of manmade and natural traumatic events. While this increased attention to traumatic stress has been positive in many respects, it has failed to maintain the perspective that trauma has always been a normal part of human experience and that the traumatic victimization of one family member continues to traumatize entire family systems. As was said earlier in this chapter, while traumatization may be a primarily linear process resulting from an individual's traumatic experience, the maintenance of traumatic stress symptoms is a systemic process that results from the interactional dance between the primary and secondary trauma victims. This ongoing focus on the primary trauma victim has prevented therapists, counselors, psychologists, and others from recognizing and treating the systemic changes that serve to protect family members from the painful feelings associated with the traumatic event. It is precisely for this reason that family therapists must become more active in the treatment of traumatized individuals and their loved ones in the family context.

Posttraumatic Stress Disorders result when an individual's experience of an event results in intense feelings of fear, horror, and helplessness. Primary traumatization occurs when the victim either experiences or witnesses an event that is lifethreatening in nature. Secondary traumatization occurs when the victim learns about the traumatization of someone that they love. In either event, the resulting symptoms are nearly identical. It is imperative that the family therapist understands and has the skills to intervene on both the individual and systemic symptoms that follow traumatic events. Respect must be shown for each family's presenting problems, whether they are individual concerns, such as intrusive thoughts, depression, restricted affect, or feeling of detachment and estrangement from others, or traditionally systemic difficulties, such as marital problems, boundary issues, disrupted parenting styles, and difficulty with children's behaviors.

From a family therapy perspective, the integration of Structural Family Therapy and Figley's Empowerment Model is significant because both have been found to be effective in assisting families to identify and change the response patterns that have commonly been attributed to traumatized families. The Structural Family Therapy model allows the family to begin the process of reorganization that will create the safety and trust needed to begin working on the painful trauma memories. Figley's model encourages family members to experience and discuss their painful effect, to acknowledge and share their perceptions of the event and the consequences that they have experienced. It urges families to break the rules of silence and resume the process of family social support. It also addresses the significant issue of family perception of stressors, allowing family members to create new perceptions and new solutions to their problems. Together, the family co-constructs a healing theory of understanding about the traumatic causes and consequences for them in the present and in the future. This process is empowering, because it shifts the power from forces beyond their control—the traumatic events—to themselves and their love for one another. The power of family relationships cannot be underestimated.

Finally, it is important to appreciate the positive consequences of exposure to traumatic events. Trauma not only is a humbling experience that renders its witnesses victims, but can also inspire these same people to spring back and achieve far more than they ever imagined. Just as 9-11 shocked a city and a nation into action, the action was first to bind together in selfless attention to those in greatest need. And since that horrific date considerable soul-searching, debriefing, postevent analysis, and rebuilding has taken place. In the process we are a stronger and more humble nation, better prepared to prevent and respond to similar attacks. So too, in a family there is this reparative instinct, this need to understand, to bind, and to prepare. Family therapists can play a vital role in helping systems, nation and family, to bind and prepare.

REFERENCES

American Psychiatric Association. (1980). *Diagnostic and Statistical Manual of Mental Disorders* (3rd ed.). Washington, DC: Author.

American Psychiatric Association. (2000). *Diagnostic and Statistical Manual of Mental Disorders* (4th ed., Text Revision). Washington, DC: Author.

Baranowsky, A. B., Gentry, J. E., & Schultz, D. F. (2003). *Trauma practice: Tools for stabilization and recovery.* Toronto, Ontario: Traumatology Institute.

Barnes, M. F. (1998). Treating burnout in families following childhood trauma. In C. R. Figley (Ed.),

Burnout in families: Secondary traumatic stress in everyday life (pp. 177–185). Boca Raton, FL: CRC Press.

Barnes, M. F. (2005). When a child is traumatized or physically injured: The secondary trauma of parents. In D. R. Catherall (Ed.), *Specific stressors: Interventions with couples and families* (pp. 77–94). New York: Brunner-Routledge.

Barnes, M. F., Todahl, J. L., & Barnes, A. (2002). Family secondary trauma on the pediatric critical care unit. *Journal of Trauma Practice, 1,* 5–29.

Benyakar, M., Kutz, I., Dasberg, H., & Stern, M. J. (1989). The collapse of a structure: A structural approach to trauma. *Journal of Traumatic Stress, 2,* 431–449.

Brooks, G. R. (1991). Therapy pitfalls with Vietnam veteran families: Linearity, contextual naiveté, and gender role blindness. *Journal of Family Psychology, 4,* 446–461.

Catherall, D. R. (1998). Treating traumatized families. In C. R. Figley (Ed.), *Burnout in families: Secondary traumatic stress in everyday life* (pp. 187–215). Boca Raton, FL: CRC Press.

Colapinto, J. (1991). Structural Family Therapy. In A. S. Gurman and D. P. Kniskern (Eds.), *Handbook of family therapy* (revised ed., pp. 417–443). New York: Brunner/Mazel.

Figley, C. R. (1988). Treating traumatic stress in family therapy. *Journal of Traumatic Stress,1,* 1.

Figley, C. R. (1989). *Helping traumatized families.* San Francisco: Jossey-Bass.

Figley, C. R. (1995). Compassion fatigue as secondary traumatic stress disorder: An overview. In C. R. Figley (Ed.), *Compassion fatigue: Secondary traumatic stress disorder in treating the traumatized* (pp. 1–20). New York: Brunner/Mazel.

Hoekstra-Weebers, J. E., Jaspers, J. P. C., Kamps, W. A., & Klip, E. C. (1998). Marital dissatisfaction, psychological distress, and the coping of parents of pediatric cancer patients. *Journal of Marriage and the Family, 60,* 1012–1021.

Koch, A. (1985). "If only it could be me": The families of pediatric cancer patients. *Family Relations, 34,* 63–70.

Madan-Swain, A., Sexson, S. B., Brown, R. T., & Ragab, A. (1993). Family adaptation and coping among siblings of cancer patients, their brothers and sisters, and nonclinical controls. *The American Journal of Family Therapy, 21,* 60–70.

Manne, S., Duhamel, K., & Redd, W. (2000). Association of psychological vulnerability factors to post-traumatic stress symptomatology in mothers of pediatric cancer survivors. *Psycho-Oncology, 9,* 372–384.

Minuchin, S. (1974). *Families and family therapy.* Cambridge, MA: Harvard University Press.

Minuchin, S., & Fishman, H. C. (1981). *Family therapy techniques.* Cambridge, MA: Harvard University Press.

Shaw, M. C., & Halliday, P. H. (1992). The family, crisis and chronic illness: An evolutionary model. *Journal of Advanced Nursing, 17,* 537–543.

Trimble, M. R. (1985). Post-traumatic stress: History of a concept. In C. R. Figley (Ed.), *Trauma and its wake: The study and treatment of Posttraumatic Stress Disorder* (pp. 5–14). New York: Brunner/Mazel.

Wade, S. L., Borawski, E. A., Taylor, H. G., Drotar, D., Yeates, K. O., & Stancin, T. (2001). The relationship of caregiver coping to family outcomes during the initial year following pediatric traumatic injury. *Journal of Consulting and Clinical Psychology, 69,* 406–415.

Zarski, J. J., DePompei, R., & Zook, A. (1988). Traumatic head injury: Dimensions of family responsivity. *Journal of Head Trauma Rehabilitation, 3,* 31–41.

PART III

Couple Relationship Difficulties

CHAPTER 13

Integrative Behavioral Couple Therapy

Brian Baucom, Andrew Christensen, and Jean C. Yi

All couples face difficulties during the course of their relationships. The difficulties can be intense or mild, long-term or short-term, and can stem from numerous causes. Some sources of distress are easily resolved, while others cannot be resolved regardless of the time and effort invested in attempting to do so. Couples need the ability to work through obstacles when disagreements can be resolved and to accept differences when they cannot. Integrative Behavioral Couple Therapy (IBCT) is a behaviorally based treatment designed to help couples use and foster acceptance to work through problems and increase satisfaction.

CENTRAL IDEAS BEHIND INTEGRATIVE BEHAVIORAL COUPLE THERAPY

IBCT has its roots in traditional behavioral couple therapy (TBCT). TBCT is a skills-based treatment that seeks to improve satisfaction through the use of deliberate change strategies. TBCT views an individual's satisfaction with a relationship to be determined by the ratio of positive to negative reinforcers in his or her relationship. Dissatisfied spouses are thought to engage in positive interactions less often overall, and are more likely to respond to a negative behavior from their partner with a negative behavior of their own. Cognitive aspects are also incorporated into the TBCT theory of satisfaction. People compare the perceived benefits and costs of their current relationship with the perceived benefits and costs of alternative relationships. When the cost-to-benefit ratio in the current relationship is greater than in an alternative one, an individual will stay in the current relationship, even if it is unsatisfying. The major focus of TBCT interventions is to help partners maximize the benefits of their relationship by increasing positive interactions, while simultaneously minimizing the costs by decreasing negative interactions.

TBCT uses rule-governed change strategies to help partners alter the way that they interact with one another. In these strategies, an individual deliberately changes his or her behavior by complying with a rule or guideline, such as a rule to speak in a certain way to the partner. Although the new behavior occurs initially through deliberate efforts to change, TBCT assumes that the new behavior will be reinforced and will therefore occur habitually after training and practice (Skinner, 1966). TBCT therapists use two classes of rule-governed interventions to help couples create change in their relationships: behavior exchange (BE) and communication and problem skills training (CPT). BE is the rubric for a variety of techniques in which the therapist directs the couple to increase positive activities. Although BE can directly create rapid, positive changes in a couple's behavior outside of the session, its focus is on positive behaviors that are not a source of controversy between the partners; BE is usually not intended to help couples work through longstanding problems.

CPT is intended to provide couples with a universally beneficial set of skills that they can use to work through problems anytime that they are encountered. Couples are trained in CPT through didactic instruction, modeling, and monitored rehearsal. Two separate but related sets of skills are taught in CPT. Communication training (CT) focuses on expressing thoughts and feelings, conveying understanding, and providing emotional support. The skills taught in CT can be helpful for any type of discussion—from a routine "how was your day" interaction to an emotional discussion of a complex and emotionally laden issue. In contrast to CT, problem-solving training (PST) is intended exclusively for helping couples come to specific solutions for problems. Research has shown that BE and CPT work more effectively when used together than when either was given without the other, and that the combination of BE and CPT was able to help a sizable percentage of couples (Jacobson, 1984).

Research also showed that five factors discriminated couples that responded well to TBCT from those who did not. The couples that responded positively to TBCT were younger, more committed to their relationship, more emotionally engaged, more egalitarian, and had similar ideas of what their ideal relationship would look like (Jacobson, Follette, & Pagel, 1986). Christensen and Jacobson (1998) interpreted these factors as indications of an ability and willingness to change.

Thus, results showed that TBCT was effective for couples that entered therapy with a set of characteristics indicating the ability and willingness to adjust their relationships to fit each other's needs, but was not as effective for those who did not. Researchers were faced with the challenge of making behaviorally based couples therapies more effective for a wider variety of couples, especially for the couples that did not respond well to TBCT. In response to this challenge, researchers created numerous different solutions. Some researchers sought to stay close to the framework and theory of TBCT, but to improve upon it by incorporating additional factors, such as cognitions and emotions, into the case conceptualization and treatment techniques. These researchers went on to found the field of Cognitive Behavioral Couples Therapy (CBCT; Baucom & Epstein, 1990).

In CBCT, marital distress is seen as the result of inappropriate information processing, stemming from distorted interpretations of relationship events and/or unreasonable expectations of how a relationship should work. A major goal of the CBCT therapist is to help spouses alter their information processing errors and extreme standards, assuming that once partners alter their information processing errors and relationship standards, positive changes in behaviors will result (Baucom & Epstein, 1990). Detailed information about the specific techniques used for addressing cognitions, emotions, and behaviors in CBCT is beyond the scope of this chapter (see Baucom & Epstein, 1990, for a detailed description of CBCT techniques).

Findings from numerous studies indicate that CBCT successfully improves reported levels of relationship satisfaction for many couples, and that the levels of improvement are similar to but not superior to those produced by TBCT (Baucom & Lester, 1986; Baucom, Sayers, & Sher, 1990; Baucom, Shoham, Mueser, Daiuto, & Stickle, 1998; Halford, Sanders, & Behrens, 1993). However, there are several limitations of CBCT that are important to note. First, CBCT largely ignores broader patterns and core themes of couples' relationships, instead opting to focus on discrete and specific behaviors and cognitions. Second, CBCT largely ignores the contribution of environmental factors to relationship distress. Third, an overwhelming focus of CBCT is on reducing negative behaviors, while much less attention is given to increasing positive behaviors.

Epstein and Baucom (2002) have continued the evolution of CBCT by incorporating elements of additional theoretical approaches in creating Enhanced Cognitive Behavioral Therapy (ECBCT). ECBCT utilizes a systems approach in combining elements from CBCT, emotionally focused couples therapy, and insight-oriented couples therapy to address the limitations of previous versions of CBCT and to provide a much broader perspective on relationship functioning. In addition to emphasizing the role of cognitions and discrete behaviors, ECBCT also addresses broader patterns and core themes, the developmental stage of the relationship, the role of the environment, and the role of the individual in its adaptation model of couple functioning. Due to the recentness of the development of ECBCT, there is currently no empirical evidence available for its effectiveness.

In creating Integrative Behavioral Couples Therapy (IBCT), Christensen and Jacobson (1998) based their treatment around a fundamentally different understanding of relationship distress than the one underlying TBCT. Both TBCT and IBCT assume that all couples are going to have problems at some point in time. Conflict is thought to be normal and inevitable, and is not assumed necessarily to be the source of enduring distress. TBCT assumes that couples become distressed because they lack the skills to work through these problems, and that it is possible to improve almost all relationships by improving skills. In contrast, IBCT suggests that a lack of skills plays only a limited role in dissatisfaction. Rather, it is the origins of the problems, such as differences between the partners, and the associated vulnerabilities of each partner, that cause couple distress. IBCT suggests that it is not possible to resolve all of the problems caused by differences between partners by creating behavioral change. Some differences between partners are not possible to alter, regardless of the amount of time and effort spent attempting to do so. However, it is possible to work with the complainant to change his or her reaction to their differences.

Early in relationships, many spouses are not only able to tolerate differences with their partners but are often excited by differences, finding themselves more attracted to their partners because of them. A common example of such a difference is seen in Amanda and Scott's relationship. Amanda is very organized and does a great deal of planning, while Scott is carefree and spontaneous. The differences between Amanda and Scott embody the things about their own person-alities that they sometimes wish were different. Scott is habitually "a day late and a dollar short," and initially appreciated Amanda's organization, business sense, and punctuality. In a like manner, Amanda wished for more excitement in her life, and Scott's spontaneity provided a sense of excitement.

As time passes, differences become less a source of attraction and more an an-noyance or threat. Continuing with our example, Amanda began to resent the fact that Scott was always late for their dates unless she called to make sure that he was leaving when he was supposed to, and Scott began to see Amanda as a "worry-wart" who always had to have things planned out in advance. Partners become less tolerant of their differences over time. Also, the differences may become a source of major emotional upset if they tap into each other's vulnerabilities. If Amanda gets anxious easily and eases that anxiety through careful planning, Scott's care-free approach may be particularly upsetting to her when it occurs around issues of anxiety. Similarly, if Scott has a history that has made him sensitive to being controlled by others, he may react with strong emotions when Amanda tries to ex-ert control over him through her planning.

Rather than being a positive source of attraction or even a tolerable annoyance, the differences that are fueled by vulnerabilities can create an emotional battle-ground. Partners try to change one another, and because of the strong emotions they feel, they usually resort to negative, coercive strategies, such as nagging, crit-icism, and angry withdrawal, to convince their partners to change. As partners be-come more intense in their efforts to change one another, each feels more justified in his or her position and takes a more extreme stance. Amanda began to insist more forcefully that Scott stick to the plan after several incidents where things did not work out well. In her mind, the reason for these disappointments was because Scott deviated from the plan that they had discussed ahead of time. Scott felt that the reason things had not gone well was because Amanda had wanted to stick to her plan—even after they both saw that it was not going to work. When Amanda "tightened the screws" on Scott to stick to their plan, he reacted by being more impulsive and less willing to agree to a plan. This polarization makes it even less likely that either partner is going to be willing to change. The conflict has now es-calated to the point where not only is the original conflict still unresolved, but both partners are interacting in harsh and unloving ways that result in further distanc-ing and less acceptance.

In addition to their overt struggles, partners begin to view each other in un-sympathetic ways, often casting their differences as deficiencies in the other. Thus, for example, Amanda may view Scott as irresponsible and reckless, and Scott may view Amanda as up-tight and controlling. Therefore, it is not simply the existence of a difference between the two partners that is the cause of relationship distress. Rather, it is also the way that spouses react to differences that causes dissatisfac-tion to occur.

In accordance with this unique conceptualization of relationship distress, the intervention strategies used in IBCT are focused as much or more on spouse's emo-tional reactions to their differences, and the conflicts over them, as they are on the differences themselves. In fact, a major goal of IBCT is to foster emotional acceptance between partners of the differences that exist between them, and which may always exist between them. When partners become more accepting they are able to appreciate their differences, and reduce the reactive conflicts between them. Amanda and Scott may differ on their level of organization, but they can see the value of the qualities that each brings to the relationship, and not fight about organization as much. Acceptance reduces the pressure partners put on each other to change, and this reduction sometimes allows for greater change. Over time, with greater acceptance, Scott may become more organized (although never in Amanda's league) and Amanda may become more spontaneous (although never in Scott's league). Also, the greater closeness and understanding that comes from the interventions to promote acceptance sometimes motivate spontaneous changes in behavior. For example, Scott may become more aware of Amanda's anxiety and take steps to see that he doesn't inadvertently increase it. However, IBCT doesn't just focus on acceptance. It also uses the change strategies of TBCT as well. The incorporation of acceptance-based intervention strategies and their integration with change-based interventions is one major feature that sets IBCT apart from TBCT and other behaviorally based interventions.

Besides its focus on acceptance, IBCT differs from other behavioral approaches in its strategy for altering relationships. IBCT emphasizes contingency-shaped rather than rule-governed change (Skinner, 1966). In rule-governed behavior, a set of rules or guidelines determines what constitutes appropriate and desirable behavior. The reinforcement for these behaviors is the sense of accomplishment gained by following the rules as well as any particular reward that is built into the rules. For example, an agreement between Amanda and Scott in TBCT might generate a set of rules that describe how Amanda should make requests of Scott (so she doesn't come across as controlling), and how Scott should respond to those requests in a timely way (so he doesn't behave irresponsibly). When each has followed through with his or her part of the agreement for one week, that person will be able to reward himself or herself by purchasing a gift of a certain amount of money. However, reinforcement is dependent on the spouse's ability to abide by the rules and to perform the reinforcing behaviors.

In contrast to rule-governed behavior strategies, contingency-shaped behavior strategies shift the context of interaction and create conditions under which new behaviors will be elicited and reinforced by natural consequences. For example, a therapist in IBCT might engage Amanda and Scott in a series of discussions about the anxiety that Amanda experiences around a particular issue, and how she tries to actively cope with that anxiety by planning and structuring her environment. These discussions would include her reactions to Scott's lack of compliance with her plans as well as Scott's reactions to her manner of speaking to him about her plans, which he experiences as controlling. If the IBCT therapist were able to create a context for these discussions, so that Amanda and Scott would avoid their usual argumentative style and instead engage in compassionate discussions, where they might experience empathy for each other's positions, or humorous discussions, where they could laugh at how extreme they can get in their polarized positions, they might gradually become more accepting of each other (i.e., each does not take the other's behavior so personally or become so emotionally reactive to it) and make small but significant changes in their behavior toward each other (e.g., Scott becomes more respectful of Amanda's need for structure and Amanda becomes more respectful of how she talks to Scott). These changes would result from the contextual shift in their interaction around the issues, rather than from a deliberate agreement to change their behaviors.

Importantly, spouses often report that contingency-shaped change feels more authentic and natural to them than does rule-governed change. IBCT suggests that the authenticity of the changes makes it more likely that couples will maintain the changes. It also makes these changes more meaningful for spouses because they know that the behaviors their partners are performing are being generated by the partners themselves, instead of by a set of rules created by the therapist.

In this section, we have distinguished IBCT from TBCT and CBCT, with which it shares a similar background. We have described its analysis of couple distress as emanating from common differences between partners, differences that are fueled emotionally by partners' vulnerabilities. Partners' understandable efforts to cope with these differences are often coercive and counterproductive, polarizing the pair in their positions. As partners get more extreme in their positions they often vilify each other for their differences, and feel stuck in their struggle.

We have also described the emphasis in IBCT on acceptance and its goal of integrating acceptance and change. Finally, we have described the primary strategy of intervention in IBCT—contingency-shaped change. Rather than focusing primarily on rule-governed strategies of deliberate change, IBCT tries to alter the context in which partners interact, in ways that will promote greater emotional acceptance and spontaneous change.

Now that we have described some of the central ideas behind IBCT, we can move to a description of the concrete ways in which IBCT therapists go about assessing couples and intervening with them.

ASSESSMENT

The aim of assessment in IBCT is to use a functional analysis of behavior to develop a case conceptualization and a treatment plan. A functional analysis of behavior is one in which a therapist seeks to understand behavior as a product of its antecedents and consequences. A functional analysis of behavior is also used in TBCT, and it is important to understand how the two versions differ.

In TBCT, a functional analysis of behavior focuses on discrete, identifiable behaviors that lead up to and follow problematic behaviors. A great deal of attention is given to sequences of events that lead to upset. In IBCT, greater emphasis is placed on the broad response patterns of the couple and on what those broad response patterns represent for the couple, as opposed to individual, molecular actions. Couples often have a laundry list of seemingly unrelated complaints that they bring in to therapy. By seeking to uncover what unites these various complaints, it is possible to identify broad patterns and core themes that play out in a relationship time and again.

For example, Amanda and Scott often argue about paying their monthly bills. The argument frequently occurs when Scott pays a bill without showing it to

Amanda first. Amanda typically asks Scott about the bill that he paid and he responds by telling her not to worry about it, because he has taken care of it. Amanda then presses Scott for details about the bill, such as when he paid it, what the amount was, and so on. Scott feels hurt that Amanda doesn't thank him for handling the bill and refuses to answer her questions. When Scott will not answer her questions Amanda gets frustrated, because they have agreed that she is in charge of managing their money, and she feels that Scott is once again changing their plan as he sees fit without consulting her. Scott also gets frustrated, feeling hurt that Amanda doesn't trust him to pay a simple bill. TBCT would key in on the specific sequence of events in the argument. For example, Scott's refusal to answer Amanda's questions about the details of the bill would be important in TBCT. While Scott's response to Amanda's questions would be important in IBCT, more emphasis would be placed on how this example illustrates their typical argument pattern, with Amanda pursuing and demanding and Scott withdrawing. IBCT would also seek to identify the underlying vulnerabilities that trigger these broad response patterns, for example, Amanda's anxiety about money and Scott's sensitivity to being influenced, or, as he experiences, being controlled.

In IBCT, the assessment phase consists of four sessions. The initial session is a conjoint session, which is then followed by an individual session for each partner. During these three sessions, the therapist seeks to answer six basic questions: how distressed is the couple; how much is each spouse committed to this relationship; what are the primary issues for each spouse; why are these issues such a problem for them; what are the couple's strengths; how can treatment help them (Christensen & Jacobson, 1998). In addition to using interviews to gather information during the first three sessions, pencil-and-paper measures are often used to assess important relationship dimensions, such as level of satisfaction, commitment level, and domestic violence. The Dyadic Adjust Scale (DAS; Spanier, 1976) is a commonly used measure of marital satisfaction and commitment; the Conflict Tactics Scale (CTS; Strauss, 1979) is a commonly used measure of domestic violence. Dimidjian, Martell, and Christensen (2002) present a list of additional measures that are useful for many IBCT therapists. The fourth session is a feedback session in which the therapist presents the couple with the case formulation as well as the treatment plan. This feedback session is intended to be a collaborative process, where the couple actively works with the therapist to make sure that the formulation and treatment plan makes sense to them and feels like a good fit.

The challenge of developing a working understanding of the broad patterns and core themes of a complicated relationship in a matter of three sessions can be a daunting task. To aid therapists in this process, there are guidelines for each of the assessment sessions. The purpose of the first conjoint session is threefold: to socialize the couple to the process of therapy and educate them on the structure of IBCT; to build rapport; and to begin gathering information about their relationship. Socializing the couple to therapy involves several steps: informing the couple of the sequence of the assessment phase (namely, that there will additionally be two individual assessment sessions followed by a feedback session); highlighting the difference between the assessment phase and the treatment phase of IBCT; and providing couples with an idea of what treatment will involve. The primary way that therapists build rapport in the first session is by making sure that both partners feel heard and supported. The information gathered in the conjoint session should include descriptions of the couple's current presenting problems as well as the history of the relationship. However, the initial session is not the time to get all of the details about the couple's presenting problems—the individual sessions are used to get a fuller picture of the presenting problems. Just enough information should be gathered about the presenting problems in the conjoint intake session to make sure that both partners feel heard and understood, and to make sure that the therapist has a good sense of what is going on in the relationship.

After gathering information about presenting problems, IBCT therapists usually shift to a focus on the couple's relationship history. Topics such as what initially attracted the partners to one another, and how the relationship worked when each member was happy, help the therapist understand the strengths in the relationship and can assist in formulating goals for therapy. In IBCT, the focus of treatment is not exclusively on reducing the level of distress felt by each partner. Rather, it is shared between distress reduction and relationship enhancement. Discussing positive aspects of the relationship may also have benefits for the spouses. Focusing exclusively on problematic aspects of the relationship can cause spouses to feel hopeless—that there is nothing that can be done to help their relationship. Maintaining an exclusively negative focus may also connote therapy as a place where only negative, painful topics will be discussed. The inclusion of positive aspects of the relationship reminds spouses that there are parts of their partners and their relationships that they liked or still enjoy, provides hope that the situation can improve, and potentially makes therapy a place that can be enjoyed.

There are three main aims for the individual assessment sessions: (1) to gather more information about the presenting problems, (2) to discuss the partner's family-of-origin experiences, or experiences in other romantic relationships, that might be relevant to the current problems, and (3) to assess the level of commitment to the relationship and the presence of any current or past violence in the relationship. It is also important to address the confidentiality of the individual sessions before any discussion begins. The therapist's responsibility is to the couple. Therefore, anything that is discussed in an individual session is assumed to be fair game to discuss during subsequent, conjoint sessions—unless the partner specifically says that he or she does not want something brought up in front of his or her partner. Requests for privacy of material revealed during an individual session are always granted. However, when the information revealed is crucial to the ongoing couple therapy (such as an affair), the therapist will ask the partner to either resolve the situation on his or her own (i.e., end the affair), or tell the spouse about the situation. In the rare case that a partner is unwilling to resolve or reveal the situation, an IBCT therapist will indicate to this partner that couple therapy cannot proceed until the partner has done so.

Additional details about the presenting problems should be gathered in the individual sessions. Oftentimes there is not enough time to fully discuss all aspects of presenting problems during the conjoint interview. There may be features of these problems that spouses are uncomfortable discussing in front of one another but may be willing to reveal to the therapist in a one-on-one setting.

Important familial relationships and past romantic relationships often provide a useful model for understanding the couple's relationship. Both the spouse's parents' relationship with one another as well as the spouse's relationship with each parent should be explored as models for the couple's relationship, as well as causes of vulnerabilities of both spouses. The culture of the families of origin should also be explored, as it is often particularly beneficial for understanding the behavior of each spouse. Additional current and past familial and romantic relationships should also be explored if they appear germane to the spouses' current relationship.

It is easy to assume that spouses are committed to improving their relationship when they come to couple therapy, but this is not always the case. The individual sessions provide a forum for discussing the commitment of each individual to the relationship. Often, the therapist has an idea of how committed an individual is to the relationship beforehand, based on the DAS. Knowing the commitment level of each individual is important information for treatment planning and goal setting.

It is an unfortunate reality that a majority of couples who seek therapy have some level of domestic violence (O'Leary, Barling, Arias, Rosenbaum, Malone, & Tyree, 1989; Simpson, Doss, Wheeler, & Christensen, unpublished manuscript). Therefore, we believe couple therapists should always assess for domestic violence, but particularly during individual sessions when partners can talk freely. We regularly give the CTS during the conjoint session and ask partners to return it at the individual session, so we have some data on violence that can serve as a basis for discussion. Even if the CTS does not indicate the presence of any current or past violence in the relationship, we recommend that the issue be raised during the individual session.

Information gathered during the conjoint and individual sessions is then synthesized into the formulation, which is the foundation upon which the acceptance-based interventions of IBCT are built. A good formulation describes the couple's major themes, each partner's vulnerabilities associated with these themes, the polarization process that has occurred in their relationship, and how their themes and polarization process are played out in common disagreements. It is often helpful to use examples from the conjoint and individual sessions to illustrate the themes, vulnerabilities, and polarization process being discussed.

It is important that the couple understands the formulation and feels that it is a good fit for their relationship. Therefore, the formulation is presented to and discussed with the couple during the feedback session. At the outset of the feedback session the therapist should remind the couple that the feedback session is intended to be a collaborative process. Spouses' comments often provide helpful information that can and should be used to alter the formulation so that it is consistent with the couple's own understanding of their relationship, while also maintaining the critical elements of the therapist's conceptualization.

The feedback session begins with a discussion of the couple's distress level. The distress level is determined from both clinical observation and questionnaire measures, such as the DAS. Next, the couple's commitment level is addressed. Like distress level, the commitment level of the couple is a combination of both clinical intuition and questionnaires. In discussing distress and commitment, the therapist should either attempt to highlight the gravity of the situation or provide the couple with hope, depending on which is most fitting for the couple. For example, in working with a couple that is moderately distressed but highly committed, it might be useful to highlight how highly committed the spouses are to one another, even though they are currently unsatisfied with the relationship, whereas in working with a couple that was highly distressed and weakly committed, the therapist might tell the spouses that they are both dissatisfied and that their relationship is in danger of falling apart if major efforts aren't made to save it. The therapist next turns to the major issues in the couple's relationship and discusses the formulation with the couple, including the major themes, the associated vulnerabilities, and the polarization process in which they have engaged. Almost every relationship has positive, redeeming elements, and an IBCT therapist also wants to discuss these strengths of the relationship during the feedback session, too. The feedback session ends with a discussion of the treatment goals and plan.

There are two major treatment goals in IBCT, both of which are intended to help couples reshape the natural contingencies of their relationships. The first is for spouses to become more understanding and accepting of each other; the second is to use that new understanding and acceptance to get spouses into a frame of mind where they can work together to create, implement, and maintain the necessary changes for their relationship. Acceptance can be thought of as a change itself, an affective-cognitive shift that often leads spontaneously to changes in behavior. However, sometimes there are specific, deliberate changes that couples are seeking that need additional attention and work. Specific treatment goals should be developed for these desired changes.

INTERVENTION TECHNIQUES AND STRATEGIES

Acceptance-Focused Strategies

IBCT uses a combination of acceptance-based and change-based intervention techniques. Acceptance-based techniques are used to provide couples with an opportunity to turn their problems into vehicles for increased intimacy, as well as to build tolerance for problems and to lessen their impact on the relationship. Intimacy-enhancing techniques include empathic joining and unified detachment; tolerance-building techniques include pointing out the positive aspects of negative behavior, enacting negative behaviors in the therapy session, faking negative behaviors outside of the session, and self-care (Christensen & Jacobson, 1998). Change-based techniques are used to directly create specific changes in behavior, and include behavior exchange, communication skills, and problem-solving skills training.

IBCT therapists normally begin intervention with acceptance-based strategies. There are some exceptions to this rule, such as when a couple comes in specifically requesting communication training. Acceptance-based interventions will often create seemingly spontaneous behavioral change in one or both of the spouses. However, couples sometimes seek specific behavioral changes that require additional work, beyond acceptance-based efforts. In these cases, it is often beneficial to use change-based techniques to achieve these specific goals.

Although a major focus of IBCT is on acceptance, it is important to bear in mind that IBCT deems some behaviors inappropriate candidates for acceptance and/or tolerance work. These behaviors include, but are not limited to, domestic violence or battering, substance abuse, and extramarital affairs. Acceptance-based strategies are not meant to maintain an unacceptable status quo. Rather, they are intended to help couples use problems to increase their sense of intimacy or to lessen the negative impact of unchangeable problems on the relationship.

Empathic joining is one of the principal techniques used to encourage acceptance in IBCT. The goal of empathic joining is to create an emotional connection between partners, even in the face of their most serious difficulties. Typically, an empathic reaction is elicited when one partner discloses deeply felt thoughts and emotions that pull the other into an emotional resonance with the disclosing partner. Most often this empathic reaction is triggered by what we call soft self-disclosures, that present the self as vulnerable. Feelings such as disappointment, or thoughts that one cannot make it without the other, would be examples. However, couples in distress frequently present hard self-disclosures that present the self as strong, tough, and able to attack and defend. Feelings such as contempt, and thoughts that one will not be manipulated by the other, are examples. Because they are attacking, these expressions usually push the other away. Therefore, in order to achieve empathic joining, the IBCT therapist must often transform hard disclosures into softer ones.

Before we discuss the ways in which a therapist might change hard disclosures into softer ones, we should note that IBCT is more interested in the function of behavior than in its topography. The goal is not to promote soft expressions for their own sake. The goal is to create closeness between partners. Often, soft disclosures help to achieve that goal—but not always. If one partner regularly expressed soft emotions that were ignored by the other, an IBCT therapist might try to get the ignored partner to make a different kind of disclosure, such as a hard disclosure. It could well be that a hard disclosure might get the other's attention and be a first step in overcoming the alienation between them.

However, in the usual case, couples in treatment have a plethora of hard disclosures; the therapist's goal is to limit the argument, attack, and defense that go with these expressions, and then elicit softer disclosures that might facilitate intimacy between the pair. As a way of reducing unproductive argument, IBCT therapists often have couples talk directly to the therapist rather than to each other. Without the provocative reactions of their partner, each member of the couple may be able to disclose feelings and thoughts to the therapist that are less inflammatory than if expressed to each other. Also, since each partner is talking to the therapist, the therapist can react to their statements in ways that might alter the client's expressions. The IBCT therapist can model empathy for each partner and reflect what they have said in ways that make it easier for the other to hear.

IBCT assumes that there are soft components, such as injury and vulnerability, to most hard disclosures; the trick is getting spouses to admit to these feelings and to share them with their partners. IBCT therapists promote soft disclosures by reframing couples' interactions, using themes from the formulation. For example, an IBCT therapist might reframe Amanda's controllingness as coming from her strong state of anxiety at the time. IBCT therapists also suggest feelings and thoughts that might be occurring in each spouse. It can be easier for spouses to agree with feelings or thoughts once they have been suggested by the therapist than it is for spouses to generate the words on their own. When Scott resists Amanda's efforts, an IBCT therapist might suggest that Scott is worried that he is going to lose his identity with Amanda. Some couples will be uncomfortable acknowledging their vulnerabilities as well as openly voicing them. Alternatively, couples may be so wrapped up in their own view of the situation that they are unable to detach from it enough to get a perspective on the role that vulnerability plays in their behavior. In these instances, therapists can sometimes encourage empathic joining by suggesting the possibility of similar vulnerabilities in both partners.

The second major acceptance strategy is unified detachment. The goal of unified detachment is very similar to one of the goals of empathic joining—to allow couples to talk about their problems without assigning blame and/or making accusations. However, the methods for achieving this end are very different. Whereas emotional heightening is encouraged in empathic joining, spouses are encouraged to intellectualize their problems when using unified detachment. When unified detachment is successful, couples are able to recognize their relationship themes as they happen, and to see how isolated events are connected by way of this theme.

There are a number of exercises that an IBCT therapist can use to promote unified detachment. One is to discuss the sequence of events surrounding a recent incident and to reframe the events, using the themes and patterns from the formulation. For example, Amanda and Scott told their therapist of an incident where Amanda had gotten very upset with Scott because he had come home very late from a business dinner without calling to tell Amanda that he was going to be later than he had anticipated. Their therapist said, "Let's act as if we are climbing up on a hill so we can see the whole picture of this interaction, but let's put on our binoculars so we can see it clearly." Then, the therapist had them describe each of the major events of the evening, detail how the actions of one triggered those of the other, and, whenever possible, relate these events back to their overarching theme of planning versus spontaneity. By using the metaphors of climbing a hill and putting on binoculars, the therapist encouraged a "from a distance" view of the interaction. Then, the therapist promoted an analytic discussion of what led to what. In so doing, Scott and Amanda were able to move away from a blaming stance when discussing this interaction, and more toward an understanding one.

Although unified detachment and empathic joining are conceptually distinct, they are often done together in practice. For example, in this example, Amanda and Scott's therapist also helped them to explore the emotions in each that were triggered by this incident. Toward the end of the session, Scott was able to see that his not calling had made Amanda feel that he didn't value her, and Amanda understood that her repeated phone calls and yelling at him when he got home made Scott feel distrusted.

Another unified detachment strategy is to give the couple's problematic pattern, as well as the roles that each partner plays in the pattern, humorous names. For example, Scott's problematic behavior might be named "flower power," Amanda's might be called "the well-oiled machine," and the pattern might be named the "palm pilot." Giving the problematic pattern a humorous name lightens the atmosphere in the therapy room when the problem is discussed, and encourages the couple to have more perspective on the problem.

Two additional, unified detachment exercises are to speak to the problem as an "it," and to have the couple imagine that the therapist is present when they have a disagreement outside of the therapy session. In speaking to the problem as an "it," the therapist will bring a fourth chair into the therapy room and designate that chair as belonging to the problem. Spouses are then asked to speak directly to the problem as an "it." Similar to using a fourth chair, imagining that the therapist is present allows couples to talk to the therapist, perhaps envisioned on a chair in their home, during outside-of-session disagreements. Both strategies can help some couples avoid the pitfalls of blame and accusation outside of the therapy setting and can keep disagreements from escalating emotionally.

As was mentioned earlier in this chapter, it is important to maintain a functional, analytic approach in IBCT. With regard to using acceptance-based interventions this means that the best intervention for a couple is the one that works. There are no hard and fast rules for when to emphasize emotional heightening strategies or unified detachment strategies. Emotional heightening would likely work well for a couple that tends to intellectualize their problems, while unified detachment would likely be more beneficial for a couple that is already highly emotional and expressive. Nor are there rules for how to maximize the effectiveness of a given intervention. Using culture to explain the behaviors of each spouse might resonate for some couples, while it might result in a lengthy treatise on the variability of behaviors within a given culture from others. The course of therapy should be guided by the functional value of the interventions for each problem for each couple.

It would be nice if all of the problems that couples face could be used as vehicles to increase intimacy in their relationships. The reality is that there are some problems that have very little hope of being useful as avenues for increased emotional closeness. Tolerance-building strategies are used to deal with these types of problems, but only after the therapist has tried to address them by using empathic joining and/or unified detachment. Like intimacy-enhancing acceptance strategies, the goal of tolerance-building exercises is to help spouses stop the endless cycle of trying to change one another. Tolerance building also helps to minimize the negative impact of problems and the amount of time needed to rebound after a destructive interaction. IBCT contains four primary methods for building tolerance: pointing out the positive aspects of negative behaviors, practicing negative behaviors during therapy sessions, faking negative behaviors outside of the therapy setting, and self-care (Christensen & Jacobson, 1998).

In pointing out the positive aspects of negative behaviors, a therapist makes use of a functional understanding of problematic behaviors to show partners how some aspect of negative behaviors serves an adaptive purpose for the relationship. The therapist still acknowledges that there are negative aspects of the behavior. This strategy should only be employed when there truly are positive aspects of problematic behaviors.

Problems can have positive aspects in many different ways. Two of the most common are being sources of initial attraction and serving to balance the relationship. As was discussed earlier, many spouses are initially excited about one another because of differences between them. Over time, the differences may become frustrating and annoying. These facts can often be used to reframe problem areas as differences that serve as both positive and negative forces in their relationship. Additionally, differences between couples often serve to create balance in the relationship. One partner's strength might be the other partner's weakness. When discussed in these terms, the differences may be able to be tolerated more effectively and be seen as less distressing.

Some problematic behaviors are extremely difficult to reframe in a positive light—the best that a therapist can hope for is to desensitize the couple to the behavior. Practicing negative behaviors during therapy sessions is the IBCT strategy for achieving desensitization. It also allows the therapist to point out the impact of the behaviors on the recipient, to discuss how the reactions of the recipient encourage the problematic behavior, and to closely monitor the situation in order to prevent damage from being done. For example, Scott finds it highly upsetting when Amanda asks during the week what they are going to do for the coming weekend. He often responds by telling her that he does not want to do anything if they are going to have to decide on it ahead of time, and then refuses to say anything further. This response both hurts Amanda's feelings and causes her to plan their weekends on her own, because Scott does not want to be involved in the planning. Scott's response to Amanda's question not only creates emotional distance between them but also causes him more frustration when Amanda plans without him. In practicing the behavior in session, an IBCT therapist would want to work with Scott to not only become less reactive to Amanda's request for planning, but also to help him see how his choice of responses can cause him more frustration in the future. Similarly, an IBCT therapist would want to work with Amanda to help her become less reactive to Scott's disinterest in planning and to see how her responses can exacerbate the situation.

IBCT assumes that regardless of the amount of effort that a couple invests in improving their relationship, mistakes are going to happen. Practicing negative behaviors in sessions also helps to prepare spouses to respond to these slipups when they occur in the future. It is important for spouses to know that occasional mistakes are not signs that all of the effort that they have invested in couple therapy has gone to waste, and that, if handled well, these mistakes need be nothing more than speed bumps in their relationship.

Faking negative behaviors outside of the therapy setting involves instructing partners to pretend to engage in a problematic behavior when they are not naturally inclined to do so. These instructions are given in front of both partners so that each is aware that some negative behavior on the part of the other might not be real. The partners are also instructed to inform one another shortly after the fact that they were faking the behavior, and to discuss what they observed the impact of their behavior on the other to be.

Having spouses fake negative behaviors when they are not feeling the associated emotional arousal provides them with an opportunity to observe their partner's distress. That experience can provide the faker with new insight into the impact of their response on the partner. That insight may result in increased tolerance for the partner's behavior. Additionally, simply going through the exercise of attempting to fake a behavior may help spouses to gain a higher level of control over their own behaviors. Realizing the situations and circumstances that typically elicit a problematic response may help spouses avoid engaging in those problematic behaviors in the future.

There are times when, regardless of the best efforts of both spouses to work together to change, problematic behaviors continue to occur and to have a detrimental impact on the relationship. In these cases, it is often possible for spouses to use self-care to lessen the impact of their partner's behaviors on themselves and to increase their tolerance for the behaviors as a result. One way to use self-care is to explore alternative methods for meeting a partner's needs. When one is unable or unwilling to meet the other's needs, it is beneficial if the needy partner can find alternatives available that at least partly satisfy the needs that the other is unable or unwilling to meet. These alternatives are beneficial in two ways. The first is that it is likely that partners will be able to be more tolerant of each other's behaviors when their needs are being at least partially met. The second is that it reinforces each partner's personal responsibility for his or her own happiness. All spouses need to remember that their partners have limitations. Sometimes the best solution is for individuals to recognize these limitations and to place the onus for meeting some of their needs on themselves, rather than on their partners. It is important to realize that alternative solutions are not meant to be permanent solutions—nor are they intended to be used to avoid particularly sensitive problem areas. Rather, they are intended to help individuals in circumstances when it is impossible for them to look to their partner to meet their needs.

Change-Focused Strategies

The change-based strategies of IBCT are the behavior exchange (BE) and communication and problem-solving training (CPT) techniques first developed for use in TBCT and briefly described earlier in this chapter. For a more detailed account of these techniques, please refer to Jacobson and Margolin (1979). The content of these strategies is similar in both IBCT and TBCT, but there are important differences in the way that the content is delivered. In TBCT, a similar set of skills is taught to every couple, based on the assumption that these skills are helpful for all couples. IBCT aims to stay closer to a functional analysis of behavior, by only teaching skills that are related to a given couple's problematic patterns. For example, if one spouse was not feeling heard by the other, the therapist might demonstrate active listening for the couple—without going into the other aspects of communication skills training. Additionally, in TBCT, there is a structured method for teaching the skills that are used for all couples that is not emphasized in IBCT. For example, TBCT teaches couples to define problems and to begin solving those problems in separate phases of problem solving. IBCT is much less concerned about whether defining the problem and attempting to solve it are separated, or whether they occur somewhat simultaneously, because potential solutions and reactions to the potential solutions help to define what the problem is really about. For more information about how TBCT strategies are used in IBCT, see Christensen and Jacobson (1998).

IBCT includes acceptance-based as well as change-based strategies because there is often a need to use each of these strategies at various points in working with a couple. In general, it is recommended that the treatment begin with empathic joining and unified detachment. This recommendation is made for several reasons. First, acceptance-based interventions strive to increase closeness and intimacy between partners, changes that may be more important than the specific behavioral changes that are part of the couples' presenting problems. Second, when the acceptance-based interventions are successful, the changes that partners were seeking when they entered therapy may happen as a natural byproduct of increased acceptance and decreased polarization. Third, acceptance-based interventions may create changes that are more natural and enduring than those created with change-based interventions.

When a couple appears to be stuck, and intimacy enhancement work is not creating the intended changes, it is recommended that the therapist consider tolerance-building interventions. After using tolerance-building interventions, it may be possible to return to intimacy enhancement strategies, and to use them more effectively now that the couple has developed more of a collaborative spirit in dealing with their problems. It is also possible to turn to change-based interventions at this point.

Research has shown that change-based interventions are successful in producing rapid change in couples that are willing and able to work together to create change, that is, they possess a strong collaborative set in their relationship. Acceptance-based strategies encourage the development of a collaborative set. Therefore, change-based interventions are more likely to be effective when they are used after a collaborative set has been developed by acceptance-based strategies.

CLINICAL SKILLS IN IBCT

There are several clinical skills that are crucial to possess when using IBCT. They include: flexibility, maintaining a focus on the formulation, the ability to uncover themes, vulnerabilities, and polarization processes, and the ability to benignly interrupt destructive interactions when they are occurring during a therapy session. These skills are needed in addition to the skills required to successfully conduct any couple therapy, such as rapport building and empathic listening.

While there may be a desire on the part of the therapist to have a sense of continuity in the topics discussed across sessions, there is a strong focus in IBCT on the salient emotion that partners bring to the session. If the plan for the current session is to continue the discussion of an issue from a previous session, it is important to follow the salient emotion even if it takes the focus of the session in a different direction than had been planned. IBCT assumes that these emotions highlight an incident or issue pertinent to the themes raised in the formulation (assuming the formulation is accurate). Furthermore, this emotion provides the energy for partners to work on this incident or issue. The IBCT therapist should be careful to make sure that one spouse is not using emotion as a strategy to dominate the focus of therapy. It is important that both spouses are attended to and that both partners' thoughts and feelings are solicited.

IBCT does not have a moral stance on divorce nor does it presume that there is any universally beneficial outcome of therapy. An IBCT therapist works with a couple to develop the most reasonable goals for therapy based on the desires of both partners. Additionally, the goals of therapy may shift over time. An IBCT therapist does not presume to know what is right for the couple, but rather takes cues from the couples as to what they want and need from therapy. In doing so, an IBCT therapist models the acceptance and empathy that he or she is nurturing in the couple to develop while at the same time tailoring therapy to best meet the needs of the couple.

Though the specific problems and the interventions used to address them change over time, it is important to maintain a focus on the formulation while these changes are occurring. Couples have a tendency to get sidetracked, and continued attention to the formulation can keep therapy on course. The importance of the formulation in IBCT cannot be stated strongly enough. It is the unifying element of all of the IBCT intervention strategies.

Due to the importance of the formulation, it is necessary to very carefully evaluate information as it is received from the couple in order to make sure that the formulation fits the couple as closely as possible. It can be tricky to decipher the complex and often contradictory information that couples present. Just as it is important to maintain flexibility in the therapy session, it is also important for the therapist to be open to the idea that his or her initial formulation may need to be altered and/or amended during the feedback session, as well as over the course of therapy.

One way to gauge the impact that the formulation is having on the couple is by paying attention to how often they describe their interactions in terms of the formulation. When couples are able to describe interactions in terms of the formulation it is a sign that it feels like a good fit to the couple, and that they are able to understand their behaviors in terms of the themes contained in the formulation. Regular use of the formulation means that partners have adopted its more benign conceptualization of their problems, and may indicate that termination is near.

--- **Case Study** ---

The following example is from a couple that was enrolled in our randomized, clinical trial comparing IBCT with TBCT. Carol and John were previously married, and had been married to each other for 15 years when they sought therapy. They are a middle-aged couple; the wife has four daughters from her previous marriage. They are both Caucasian and middle class.

Assessment and Feedback—Session 1–4

The therapist begins the first session by explaining to the couple how the next few sessions will go.

> **Therapist:** Well, I'd like to do a couple of things today. I want to find out a little bit about what brought you in now, what made you decide to call the study, and a little bit about your current problems, and to talk a little bit about them just so that I'm up to date. But then I also want to get to know a little bit more about your history as a couple. When we meet individually, I'm going to want to get to know about each of your histories as individuals.

John and Carol are experiencing distress around finances. Although this is a common source of stress for couples, the IBCT therapist looks for the repeated ways in which the couple tries to cope with this problem. John does not like to give Carol bad news, so he avoids revealing financial difficulties. In response, Carol feels distrustful of John and asks him lots of questions, which are often accusatory. These questions make him even more reluctant to volunteer negative information in the future. Toward the end of the session, the therapist sums up the escalated form of their pattern as follows:

> **Therapist:** Just from what you're saying today I have this little flash of Carol, you confronting John, and, John, you get in your pickup and leave. And that may be a pattern that we're going to have to come back to and visit.

The therapist then uses the information gathered in this session and the two individual sessions to create the formulation, which is presented to the couple during the feedback session. The early part of the session may be used to gather additional information, but the main focus is to present and discuss the therapist's formulation with the couple, and to provide the couple with an outline for treatment.

> **Therapist:** It seems to be that there are sort of two [themes] at work. One is fairly straightforward and easy to describe, but I'm going to talk about the other one in a little more poetic sense. The pretty straightforward one is distrust.

The couple agrees that their first theme is distrust. Carol feels that John has been hiding things from her and, in doing so, has led her to the conclusion that she can no longer trust him. In particular, if the issue has to do with money, then this theme becomes activated. For the next theme, the therapist uses a metaphor to describe their pattern.

> **Therapist:** The other thing I was thinking, like I said in a little more poetic sense, is what I would call the "deep well and the stormy sea." John, you're much more quiet, keeping everything inside, trying to keep on the surface of things. Looking calm, the deep well. And Carol, it's not that you're labile, because you're not, but you're willing to express your emotions and, you know, if the winds and the waves and the storms come, you'll let it be and you'll express it.

The couple also agrees with this metaphor. The therapist links the two themes together very nicely, by saying these differences in emotional responding, the deep well and the stormy sea, are not necessarily problems, *unless* the first theme of trust is at work. In fact, the therapist points out that this difference in emotional reactivity can be beneficial for them, when not in the context of distrust.

After explaining the main themes in the relationship, the therapist moves to talking about the polarization process, and how the theme operates in the midst of distress.

> **Therapist:** When the two of you are experiencing problems, that's when we talk about a term that we refer to as polarization, being at opposite poles. It seems

that there's a fairly consistent pattern with the two of you. John, it's not like you start this pattern, but I have to start somewhere in talking about this, but you don't like to be the bearer of bad news, and you want to please Carol. So you will sugarcoat things, or in some ways avoid things where there's a potential for you to get blasted; you'll avoid having to confront that. I also think you feel guilty if you have to bear bad news; you don't want to make her unhappy. That puts you more on this pole of moving away and avoiding things, and, Carol, you are on the opposite end. You want to be kept up-to-date. You want to know what's going on. I think you can face things pretty well if you know what you have to face. You want to know so you get into a pattern where you push for the details, maybe even scream and holler. As you're getting in that stance emotionally, it's bringing you further away, but you're also trying to get closer. Carol, you're demanding, and then, John, you're withdrawing more, but ultimately it brings you both further and further apart emotionally. You both feel more isolated from one another.

The couple also agrees with the description of their polarization process. The therapist then moves to explain these differences, using each partner's learning history. Then, the therapist talks about each partner's vulnerabilities from a developmental perspective.

> **Therapist:** I think with you, Carol, you came from a family that was very unreliable, and you sort of picked up on that. You felt a little bit like Cinderella. You were the one that tried to keep things manageable. All of a sudden John, who has been a rock in your life, is looking unreliable, and that's pretty hard for you to tolerate, given this history.

The therapist also ties control into this pattern, as Carol has learned that she needs to be in control of the situation, and becomes distressed when she feels as if she is not in control. Then, the therapist discusses John's history, and how it has led to his position in their dilemma.

A formulation of a couple's problems often includes the "mutual trap." Through the polarization process, the couple becomes stuck and feels trapped. Each partner can feel that no matter what they do, they cannot change their partner or the painful pattern in which they find themselves. The therapist also offers hope for the couple, discussing their strengths, which often include the very differences that cause them problems. The therapist typically ends the feedback session by discussing the broad goals and the procedures of therapy. The broad goals include reducing the polarization between the spouses, increasing mutual acceptance of their differences, and helping each to make changes that might make their relationship function more effectively. The procedures of therapy refer to the format and the focus of therapy sessions. For example, the therapist explains that each week the therapy will focus on emotionally salient incidents and issues related to the formulation. For John and Carol, that could be a positive incident where John shared some bad news with Carol and she didn't blame him for it, or a negative incident where Carol became critical and John became withdrawn. For an emotionally volatile couple, the therapist might explain that the initial format of therapy will involve each partner talking directly to the therapist rather than to each other. If one or both of the partners do not agree with the formulation, the therapist can incorporate feedback, such that the formulation then rings true for the couple.

Intervention

Empathic Joining

The couple came in to session five, the first session after feedback, discussing a fight they had about gardening during the previous week. During the discussion, the therapist talks with John about his reactions to Carol's communication style. Because of his acute sense of responsibility and his guilt about their financial problems, John is particularly sensitive when Carol questions him. These questions suggest to him that she does not trust him. For her part, Carol likes to know what is happening around her. From her life history, she was the one to always take care of things, and one of the attributes of John that she really liked was that she knew that he would always take care of things. However, with the financial situation a mess, and Carol feeling as though she should have been more involved in the finances, she is asking John more questions about everything. But, in John, that brings up feelings of inadequacy, that he is not doing well enough. These feelings of vulnerability are what the therapist is looking for in soft disclosures.

> **Therapist:** One of the things that sometimes is good to do is to talk about the feelings beneath the feelings. Not so you're always like bleeding hearts, because neither of you strike me as the kind of people that would like that. I'm not trying to get you to be touchy-feely people or something like that, but to be able to say if you're feeling like, "I'm a dud," or that "I don't know what I'm doing."

The therapist is encouraging the couple to use soft disclosures. In doing so, John reveals to Carol and the therapist that when she asks him if he has done something, in this case, gardening, he feels as if he is not the husband that she envisioned, and he feels guilty because he thinks that he is not the husband that she wants. This insight changes the tone of the interaction, as Carol now experiences John's acute sense of guilt. Further disclosures reveal Carol's anxiety, particularly about money, but also about tasks in general. She checks on John, not because she thinks that he is incapable of doing the activity, but the process of asking questions reduces her anxiety. Thus, Carol asks questions out of her own anxiety, and John feels guilty because he interprets the questions to mean that Carol thinks he is incompetent. These disclosures, over time, help the couple avoid destructive escalation in their patterning of questioning and defensive withdrawal.

Unified Detachment

In unified detachment, the therapist tries to get the spouses to distance themselves from their conflicts and to see them from a more objective stance. For example, in session 19, the therapist talks with John about his tendency to take things personally.

Therapist: So, it seems like a combination of frustration with the fact that things aren't getting accomplished. But I think that's hard. It's hard to separate yourself, John, when you've had a rough week, and then you tell Carol that you have to go out of town again. You know that disappoints her, and then she's upset because things aren't getting accomplished. I would think it would be darn near impossible to have such distance from it, to say, "That's just where Carol is at, that's not my fault." I think you take it personally.

The therapist acknowledges that it is difficult to separate oneself and try to be objective about what is occurring in the relationship, but encourages John in that direction.

Tolerance Building

Tolerance-building strategies include a number of techniques, described earlier, that serve to make the negative behaviors of one more acceptable to the other. In the following exchange, John learns that Carol can tolerate a delay in response to her questions.

John: Okay. Because I don't, when Carol starts in on something. I try to defend it when I should say, "I really don't want to talk about this right now."

Carol: I can deal with that.

Therapist: You can deal with that?

Carol: Yeah.

Therapist: Even if you're feeling really, really anxious about something? What's the likelihood of that happening. Have there been times when you have said, "But we have to deal with it right now?"

Carol: If there was something we had to deal with, it would have to be something where he felt the importance of it. Otherwise I wouldn't, I don't think, force us to talk about it. My wanting to talk about it right then wouldn't be reason enough to make us have the conversation.

Therapist: You're able to put it off.

Carol: Yeah. I can put it off.

The therapist is asking Carol if she can expose herself to her own anxiety without feeling the urge to ask John lots of questions. At this point in therapy, Carol realizes the impact of her questions on John, and is able to respect him if he says that he is tired, overwhelmed, and unable to listen to her questions. Thus, the wife is building tolerance to her husband's desire not to communicate, and to her own anxiety.

Another technique to build tolerance is to focus on the positive aspects of negative behavior. In the following example, the therapist frames each partner's reactivity to the other in terms of their desire to protect the other. The therapist also points out a similarity between them.

Therapist: See, it kind of sounds like you both are very sensitive, but you are both also wanting to protect one another. What you, Carol, just said about giving anything about not having to tell John about these phone calls sounds like, John, the kind of things you would say about Carol for so long. You would give anything to not have to tell her these things, and at some point haven't told her these things.

The Last Session

The last session is an opportunity to recap what has transpired during treatment and to help the couple think about how to deal with stressors in the future. For this couple, one of the major themes had to do with trust. The therapist checks in on that in this last session, session 25.

The couple has progressed in treatment to the point where both partners are on the path to feeling more trust in their relationship. Now, the therapist wants to make sure that the couple is able to spot the polarization process, the vulnerability factors related to the process, and to take a step back and stop the process.

> **Therapist:** Are you aware of when the two of you begin to polarize? Of how to spot that in the future?
>
> **Carol:** I have with him. I don't know if he has with me.
>
> **John:** Yeah, I know. I can tell.
>
> **Carol:** So, I think the thing is that maybe more so than one person recognizing it in the other person, is the person who is doing it recognizing that they're going south or something.
>
> **John:** Right.
>
> **Therapist:** And I wonder if you're set up a little more to polarize in situations that come up where you, Carol, are feeling anxious and, John, where you feel a little depressed and discouraged.

The therapist is pointing out the potential vulnerabilities in each partner that could set up the polarization process, such as Carol's anxiety or John's discouragement. Highlighting these patterns prepares the couples for slips and lapses that could happen in the future.

At the pretreatment assessment, John's score on the DAS was in the seriously distressed range, while Carol's was in the normal range. By the end of treatment, John's score had risen substantially, to the nondistressed range, while Carol's had risen slightly. By the two year follow-up assessment, John's score had continued to rise but Carol's had dropped somewhat.

EMPIRICAL SUPPORT FOR IBCT

IBCT has received empirical support in a number of studies to date. Wimberly (1997) randomly assigned 17 couples to either a group format of IBCT ($n = 8$) or to a waitlist control condition ($n = 9$). Results showed that the marital satisfaction of the 8 IBCT couples improved significantly more than did the marital satisfaction of the 9 waitlist control couples. In an unpublished study (cited in Christensen

& Heavey, 1999), Trapp and colleagues showed that IBCT was as effective in reducing marital distress and depression as CBCT in a study of 29 depressed and maritally distressed women.

In an initial pilot study comparing IBCT to TBCT (Jacobson, Christensen, Prince, Cordova, and Eldridge, 2000) and in a large, ongoing two-site clinical trial (Christensen, Atkins, Berns, Wheeler, Baucom, & Simpson, 2004), couples in IBCT demonstrated as much positive relationship change as couples receiving TBCT. In the ongoing clinical trial, 71 percent of IBCT couples were found either to be reliably improved or recovered (in the nondistressed range of functioning on the DAS) at the end of therapy. Similarly, 59 percent of TBCT couples were found either to be reliably improved or to be recovered at treatment termination. Response to treatment was also compared across ethnic groups in the ongoing clinical trial, and ethnic minorities were found to respond to both IBCT and TBCT in a similar manner as Caucasians (Yi, George, Atkins, Christensen, 2004). Though IBCT and TBCT produced similar amounts of change in the ongoing clinical trial, there were some important differences in how the change happened (Christensen et al., 2004). The change in satisfaction by TBCT couples was rapid early on in therapy and then plateaued, while the change in IBCT couples was slower but steady throughout the course of treatment. Preliminary follow-up results suggest that IBCT couples show significantly greater continuing improvement than TBCT couples during the 2 years post treatment. The couples in this study will be followed for 5 years after treatment termination to see if these preliminary findings hold up over the long term.

The ongoing clinical trial also examined the broader impact of IBCT and TBCT on the family. Both IBCT and TBCT were found to be related to reduced interparental conflict and improved child functioning. Furthermore, these parenting and child variables were associated with improved marital satisfaction, and the parenting variables mediated the relation between marital satisfaction and improved child adjustment (Gattis & Christensen, 2004).

The evaluation of any treatment rests upon the positive changes that it can demonstrably generate. At this point, the data suggest that IBCT is a promising treatment. Only the remaining data from the current clinical trial as well as future studies can determine if IBCT should be a routine part of our strategy for assisting distressed couples.

REFERENCES

Baucom, D., & Epstein, N. (1990). *Cognitive-behavioral marital therapy.* Philadelphia: Brunner/Mazel.

Baucom, D., & Lester, W. (1986). The usefulness of cognitive restructuring as an adjunct to behavioral marital therapy. *Behavior Therapy, 17,* 385–403.

Baucom, D., Sayers, S., & Sher, T. (1990). Supplementing behavioral marital therapy with cognitive restructuring and emotional expressiveness training. *Journal of Consulting and Clinical Psychology, 56,* 636–645.

Baucom, D., Shoham, V., Mueser, K., Daiuto, A., & Stickle, T. (1998). Empirically supported couples and family therapies for adult problems. *Journal of Consulting and Clinical Psychology, 66,* 53–88.

Christensen, A., Atkins, D., Berns, S., Wheeler, J., Baucom, D. H., & Simpson, L. (2004). Traditional versus integrative behavioral couple therapy for significantly and chronically distressed married couples. *Journal of Consulting and Clinical Psychology.*

Christensen, A., & Heavey, C. (1999). Interventions for couples. *Annual Review of Psychology, 50,* 165–190.

Christensen, A., & Jacobson, N. S. (1998). *Acceptance and change in couple therapy: A therapist's guide to transforming relationships.* New York: Norton.

Dimidjian, S., Martell, C., & Christensen, A. (2002). Integrative behavioral couple therapy. In A. Gurman & N. Jacobson (Eds.), *Clinical handbook of couple therapy* (pp. 251–277), New York: Guilford.

Epstein, N., & Baucom, D. (2002). *Enhanced cognitive-behavioral therapy for couples: A contextual approach.* Washington, DC: American Psychological Association.

Gattis, K., & Christensen, A. (2004). *Couple therapy, parenting, and child adjustment.* Unpublished dissertation, University of California, Los Angeles.

Halford, W. K., Sanders, M., & Behrens, B. (1993). A comparison of the generalization of behavioral marital therapy and enhanced behavioral marital therapy. *Journal of Consulting and Clinical Psychology, 61,* 51–60.

Jacobson, N. (1984). A component analysis of behavioral marital therapy: The relative effectiveness of behavior exchange and problem solving training. *Journal of Consulting and Clinical Psychology, 52,* 295–305.

Jacobson, N. S., Christensen, A., Prince, S. E., Cordova, J., & Eldridge, K. (2000). Integrative Behavioral Couple Therapy: An acceptance-based, promising new treatment for couple discord. *Journal of Consulting and Clinical Psychology, 68,* 351–355.

Jacobson, N. S., Follette, W., & Pagel, M. (1986). Predicting who will benefit from behavioral marital therapy. *Journal of Consulting and Clinical Psychology, 54,* 518–522.

Jacobson, N. S., & Margolin, G. (1979). *Marital therapy: Strategies based on social learning and behavior exchange principles.* New York: Brunner/Mazel.

O'Leary, K., Barling, J., Arias, I., Rosenbaum, A., Malone, J., & Tyree, A. (1989). Prevalence and stability of physical aggression between spouses: A longitudinal analysis. *Journal of Consulting and Clinical Psychology, 57,* 263–268.

Simpson, L. E., Doss, B. D., Wheeler, J., & Christensen, A. (2003). *Physical and verbal aggression among couples seeking therapy: Common couple violence or battering?* Unpublished manuscript. UCLA.

Skinner, B. (1966). Contingencies of reinforcement in the design of a culture. *Behavioral Science, 11,* 159–166.

Spanier, G. B. (1976). Measuring dyadic adjustment: New scales for assessing the quality of marriage and similar dyads. *Journal of Marriage and the Family, 38,* 15–28.

Straus, M. A. (1979). Measuring intrafamily conflict and violence: The Conflict Tactics (CT) Scales. *Journal of Marriage and Family, 41,* 75–88.

Wimberly, J. (1997). An outcome study of integrative couples therapy delivered in a group format. *Dissertation Abstracts International, 58*(12-B), 6832. University of Montana.

Yi, J., George, B., Atkins, D., & Christensen, A. (2004). *Ethnic minorities in couple therapy: How do they fare?* Unpublished manuscript. University of Washington.

CHAPTER 14

Brief Integrative Marital Therapy: An Interpersonal-Intrapsychic Approach

Alan S. Gurman

Significant cultural changes in the last half century have had an enormous impact on marriage and on the expectations and experiences of those who marry or enter other long-term, committed relationships. Reforms in divorce law, more liberal attitudes about sexuality, increased availability of contraception, and the growth of women's economic and political power have all increased the expectations of marriage to go beyond mere economic viability and reliable procreation. For most couples nowadays, marriage is also expected to be the primary source of adult intimacy, support, and companionship, and a facilitative context for personal growth. With changing expectations not only of marriage itself, but also of the permanence of marriage, the public health importance of the "health" of marriage has understandably increased. Whether through actual divorce or chronic conflict and distress, the breakdown of marital relationships exacts enormous costs.

Recurrent marital conflict and divorce are associated with a wide variety of problems in both adults and children. Divorce and marital problems are among the most stressful conditions people face. Partners in troubled relationships are more likely to suffer from anxiety, depression and suicidality, and substance abuse, and from both acute and chronic medical problems and disabilities such as impaired immunological functioning and high blood pressure, and health risk behaviors such as susceptibility to sexually transmitted diseases and accident proneness. Moreover, the children of distressed marriages are more likely to suffer from anxiety, depression, conduct problems, and impaired physical health.

Although physical and psychological health are affected by marital satisfaction and health, there are more common reasons why couples seek, or are referred for, conjoint therapy. These concerns usually involve relational matters, such as emotional disengagement and waning commitment, power struggles, problem-solving and communication difficulties, jealousy and extramarital involvements, value and role conflicts, sexual dissatisfaction, and abuse and violence. More generally, couples seek therapy because of threats to the security and stability of their relationships with the most significant attachment figures of their adult life.

PREDICTABLE PATTERNS OF MARITAL DIFFICULTY

Therapists of different theoretical orientations define the core problems of the couples they treat quite differently, ranging from relationship skill deficits to maladaptive ways of thinking and restrictive narratives, to matters of self-esteem, to unsuccessful handling of normal life cycle transitions, to unconscious displacement onto the partner of conflicts with one's family of origin, to the inhibited expression of normal adult needs, to the fear of abandonment (Gurman, 1978).

Despite such varied views of what constitutes the core of marital difficulties, in recent years marital therapists of different orientations have sought a clinically meaningful description and understanding of functional versus dysfunctional intimate relationships that rests on a solid research base (Lebow, 1999). Quite remarkably, and perhaps uniquely in the world of psychotherapy, the major findings coming from this body of (mostly cognitive, behavioral, and social psychological) research (e.g., Gottman, 1999) have been uniformly praised by and incorporated into the treatment models of a wide array of marital therapists, ranging from eclectic to cognitive-behavioral and behavioral to humanistic and experiential and even to psychodynamic, transgenerational, and feminist (Donovan, 1999; Gurman, 2002). These findings, taken as a whole, provide a theoretically and clinically rich and credible description of the typical form and shape of healthy and unhealthy marital interactions. Therapists of different orientations will make sense of such findings in their own ways, and will complement such findings with observations about functional versus dysfunctional marriages that are specific to their own perspectives. Because these data have been so widely recognized as relevant to clinical practice, a summary of the overall pattern of these findings (Gurman, 2002) is needed.

In regard to both marital satisfaction and long-term marital stability, satisfied (functional, happy) couples, compared to dissatisfied (dysfunctional, unhappy) couples, show: (1) higher rates of pleasing behavior and lower rates of displeasing behavior; (2) lower probability of reciprocating negative behavior ("If you're nasty to me, I'll be nasty to you"); and (3) better communication skills and problem-solving skills.

Poor communication and problem-solving is characterized by (3a) "harsh start-ups" of problem-focused conversations (e.g., "Hey, why are you always so damned late when we're going out together!") and poor ability to repair ruptures, especially early in couple exchanges (e.g., by the use of humor or shows of affection). These interactions show a focus on affect rather than problem solving, and tend to be accompanied by negative physiological arousal (especially in men), combined with the aroused partner's difficulty in self-soothing. This pattern may culminate in the rapid escalation of two-way aversive experiences, setting up the couple for developing a chronic pattern of emotional disengagement and withdrawal via a familiar process of escape/avoidance conditioning. In addition, (3b) distressed couples tend to become deadlocked over inherently unresolvable differences, known as "perpetual problems" (e.g., core personality or value differences), but mistakenly deal with these differences as though they were resolvable, thereby inevitably leading to feelings of frustration and resentment. Finally, (4) in unhappy couples, partners try to influence each other by using styles characterized by pain control (e.g., providing emotionally painful consequences to a partner's undesired behavior via criticism, contempt, stonewalling, and/or defensiveness) rather than by mutual reciprocity.

In the cognitive realm, unhappy couples (5) show negative attributional biases in the form of disregarding both the presence of positive partner behavior and even increases in desired partner behavior. Unhappy couples see negative partner behavior as reflecting permanent characteristics, and positive partner behavior as reflecting temporary states. In unhappy couples, negative events have longer-lasting negative effects than in happy couples. Unhappy partners tend to blame each other for their couple problems, while taking little responsibility for them, and tend to make faulty attributions about their partners' motivations and intentions. They also tend to engage in cognitive distortions such as all-or-nothing thinking, overgeneralization, jumping to conclusions, and catastrophizing and magnification. Finally, (6) unhappy couples are more likely than happy couples to have more unrealistic expectations of both marriage in general and of their actual partner.

As compelling as these findings are, they are merely descriptive, and do not themselves address the central clinical question: Why do such patterns persist? What keeps such patterns of behavior going, despite the pain they bring? To address this question, some couple therapy theorists (e.g., Scharff & Bagnini, 2002) have brought renewed attention to the unconscious levels on which marital conflict exists and persists, and others (e.g., Gurman, 2002; Snyder & Schneider, 2002) have sought to develop models of couple therapy that address both overt and covert dimensions of marriage, and both interpersonal and intrapsychic aspects of marital conflict. Indeed, the most fascinating, challenging, and rewarding aspect of doing therapy with couples is probably working to deal with couples on both levels of their relationships. Depth-oriented work with couples that lacks a significant, active behavior change thrust is likely to lead to heightened self-understanding without enhanced relationship skills, while methods that focus exclusively on surface-level events, whether in behavior or conscious thought, leave powerful unconscious elements of both marital connectedness and sensitivity untouched. Both approaches significantly limit the potential for relationship healing.

THE DEVELOPMENT OF BRIEF INTEGRATIVE MARITAL THERAPY

Brief Integrative Marital Therapy (BIMT), developed over the last 2 decades by Gurman (1981, 1992, 2002), is a therapeutic approach to the treatment of the relationship difficulties of married or otherwise committed couples that attends simultaneously and systematically to both interpersonal and intrapersonal factors. BIMT's implicit values, intervention focus, and usual techniques tend to render it a relatively brief experience (see Gurman, 2001). BIMT emphasizes clinical parsimony, and change that occurs outside therapy. BIMT rests on a foundation of general systems theory and adult developmental theory, including attachment theory, but is most pervasively influenced by applied social learning and object relations theory. In these ways, BIMT reflects the growing shift in couple therapy toward theoretical and technical integration (Gurman & Fraenkel, 2002; Lebow, 1997). These integrative developments include particular attention to both the individual and the dyadic dimensions of marital difficulties and their treatment.

BIMT emphasizes the repetitive cycles of interaction between partners, and how these cycles reciprocally include both intrapsychic process (conscious and unconscious) and overt behavior; that is, how the deep structures and the surface structures of intimate relationships operate together. In BIMT, object relations theory provides the way for mapping deep structures. Conflict is seen as arising when the implicit "rules" (unspoken agreements) of the relationship that are central to either partner's sense of self or core schema for close relationships are violated. BIMT also emphasizes what Gurman (2002) calls "implicit behavior modification," partners' unwitting reinforcement of undesired behavior in their mates, and punishment of behavior that they consciously wish for. These kinds of reinforcing and punishing contingencies occur in a circular relationship, and can be triggered internally, between the spouses, or by external events.

The core assumption in BIMT is that couple therapy can lead to change in both interaction patterns and inner representational models of intimate relationships, and that such unconscious experiencing can be changed via direct, as well as indirect, therapeutic methods. In addition to its object relations base, BIMT relies heavily on the main attribute of clinical behavior therapy approaches, functional analysis, for a more fine-grained assessment of couple problems. Functional analysis is concerned not with the form of behavior, but with its effects; that is, with the factors that maintain a problematic pattern, whether these factors be interactional, cognitive, affective, or biological. Functional analysis does not assume a priori that any particular class of events has more influence over a couple's difficulties than any other. In BIMT, behavior is behavior, and "behavior" is construed broadly to include unconscious experience. Although the content of therapy sessions varies over time in BIMT, treatment is usually organized around a small number of dominant themes, what behavior therapists call "response classes," in which the form of behavior is secondary to its relationship- and self-function, purpose, or effect.

ASSESSMENT AND TREATMENT FORMULATION

So, why do unhappy couples not communicate and problem solve better, please each other more, repair conversational ruptures, stay calm even in the face of discussing differences, and so on? Why do they escalate their conflict, reinforce the very behaviors in each other that they object to so passionately, block out from their awareness the good in their partners and highlight the bad, and attribute the most unkind motivations to each other? What are they really fighting about?

In order to understand why BIMT emphasizes particular therapeutic strategies and techniques, one must first understand how treatment goals are established. Similarly, to understand BIMT's approach to goal setting, one must appreciate the conceptual framework that directs the therapist's attention to the treatment goals that are selected. This framework is primarily shaped by the views of behavior therapists and object relations theorists.

Behavior therapy traditionally has emphasized purported skill deficits to explain marital dysfunction. Distressed couples were thought to lack certain essential relationship skills, for example communication and problem solving, which, when taught to them, would help to relieve their suffering. Still, both research and clinical observation makes clear that most partners in distressed marriages actually have problems of performance rather than missing skills. That is, they are regularly able to interact well with many people outside their marriages, but have difficulty using the skills they actually possess in intimate relationships.

The object relations perspective (Scharff & Bagnini, 2002) helps us understand *why* conflicted couples seem to lack relationship skills, and *why* they behave in such repetitive negative patterns, as summarized earlier. In this framework, the core source of marital dysfunction is both partners' failure to see themselves and each other as whole persons. Conflict-laden aspects of oneself, presumably punished or aversively conditioned earlier in life, are repudiated and split off. These aspects of self are projected onto the mate, who, in turn, accepts the projection, that is, behaves in accordance with it. This two-way pattern constitutes what is referred to as "collusion," a sort of unconscious, quid pro quo agreement that both defines and sets limits on how both partners allow themselves to be seen, and on how they allow themselves to experience themselves. The problematic aspect of this unconscious quid pro quo is not only that it is a mutually reinforcing process of projective identifications but also, and perhaps even more importantly, that there is an implicit agreement not to talk about or challenge the unstated agreement. The collusion is a joint, shared avoidance that involves both intrapsychic and interpersonal defenses against various fears, for example, merger, attack, or abandonment. Collusion is a bilateral process in which partners seek to maintain a consistent, if maladaptive, sense of self. It represents attempted solutions to individual and dyadic problems. When such collusion is rigid, partners have great difficulty seeing each other as real contemporary people, and tend to adopt very polarized psychological roles, limiting their capacity to adapt to new circumstances in marriage, whether generated by changes internal to the couple relationship or external to it.

In order to get beyond the relational limitations imposed by such rigid, projectively based collusion, couples must be able to engage in effective "containing" and "holding." Containing is an individual process in which the partner is able to allow painful feelings and thoughts into consciousness, without the need to project them onto the mate. Holding is a dyadic process in which the listener/recipient can identify with the speaker's feelings (i.e., empathically hear them as belonging to the speaker), whether they are about the speaker or the listener, without experiencing intolerable anxiety (i.e., he or she is able to contain any discomfort associated with the speaker's behavior). If the recipient is unable to identify with the speaker and contain his or her own feelings, he or she is more likely to enact reciprocal, problematic behavior. This may lead to the commonly seen escalation process in couple conflict, in which partners unyieldingly push their own point of view, do not acknowledge their partners' feelings and may even denigrate them, and so on. These couples are stuck in the same fight, often on the same topic, over and over—they spin their wheels until there is no traction left, and feel as though they are just going in circles. Alternatively, when anxiety about intimate relating is just too high for either or both partners, they may get caught up in the well-known pursuer-distancer dance. Alternatively, passionate conflict over rigidly held positions in marriage can also lead to a chronic state of mutual disengagement.

In BIMT, then, the presence of apparently poor social skills in intimate relationships more often than not is seen as reflecting the more basic, unspoken rule of limited intimacy. Stated otherwise, using existing social skills increases the potential for intimacy, while not using such skills helps to maintain relational distance. The unfortunate protective function of what may appear to be skill deficits requires that the therapy include explicit attention to the mutually avoidant defensive function of such presumed deficits in order to challenge the joint defenses in the very service of which the apparent deficits exist. That is, apparent skill deficits are likely to characterize a distressed marriage as long as the partners cannot be relatively, nondefensively themselves in open dialogue.

Unfortunately, in chronically distressed marriages, partners unwittingly (and wittingly, as well) tend to reinforce and extinguish behavior in their mates that is allowed and disallowed, respectively, according to their own conscious and (especially) unconscious expectations of a marital partner. They do likewise in response to the behavior of their mates that is allowed and disallowed, according to unspoken rules of how they need to see themselves. This implicit behavior modification takes several predictable forms, each of which may provide cues to the therapist about useful points at which, and about useful patterns about which, to intervene. Thus, in couple relationships, these mutual processes of reinforcement and punishment occur in such a way that (1) each partner reinforces behavior of the partner that is consistent with that person's mate ideal; (2) each partner reinforces behavior of the partner that is consistent with one's self-view; (3) each partner (covertly) reinforces his or her own behavior that is consistent with the self-view that is required; (4) each partner punishes and/or extinguishes (e.g., via avoidance, denial) behavior in the partner that is inconsistent with that partner's mate ideal; (5) each partner punishes and/or extinguishes behavior in the partner that is inconsistent with that person's required self-view; and (6) each partner (covertly) punishes and/or extinguishes his or her own behavior that is inconsistent with his or her required self-view. In addition, partners in chronically conflicted relationships (7) regularly reinforce the very behaviors in their mates that they complain about.

Carrying Out the Assessment

The assessment process in BIMT is almost entirely carried out via traditional clinical interviews. Paper and pencil self-report inventories and the like are almost never used. The therapist has the responsibility for creating a clinical formulation that includes data from not only patient self-reports and the therapist's direct observations in the interview, but also from the therapist's conceptual understanding of the recursive interplay between the interpersonal and the intrapersonal, and between the conscious and the unconscious forces in couple relationships.

Assessment is almost always done in conjoint interviews, although on occasion, for unavoidable, pragmatic reasons such as a clinic's service policies, individual interviews may occur. Since the central theory of change in BIMT requires parallel individual and interactional emphases, the active, change-oriented phase of BIMT is always carried out conjointly. Early individual sessions, when they occur, are limited to establishing a tentative working alliance with a patient in order to increase the chances of the reluctant partner's eventual participation.

In BIMT, no variables or factors are viewed a priori as being inherently more important than others for assessment purposes. The core assessment method in BIMT is the functional analytic approach of behavior therapists, but with a twist. The functional analytic method usually focuses on rather discrete patient behaviors. In BIMT, the functional approach (see the following) is applied to both highly specific couple behaviors and to broader classes of couple behavior, roughly equivalent to what Christensen, Jacobson, & Babcock (1995) call "derivative events" (i.e., specific interactions) versus "controlling themes" (i.e., pervasive, significant patterns). Unlike this distinction within behavioral couple therapy, the central controlling themes in BIMT regularly also include both the individual and dyadic motivations that are implicit and out of the partners' awareness, and therefore unrecognized by them as playing pivotal roles in the maintenance of the problems for which they seek help. It is this attribute of BIMT that renders it a "depth-behavioral approach" (Gurman, 2002).

The functional analytic approach, which emphasizes case-specific formulation rather than the application of a standardized or manualized treatment, is seen as the ultimate expression of respect for patients, in that, while certainly incorporating universal principles of behavior maintenance and behavior change, it fundamentally emphasizes the uniqueness of each couple and of each member of the couple. In this very important way, then, the functional analytic foundation of BIMT is flexible and inherently responsive to differences between couples based on ethnic, racial, class, religious, and gender differences. Although the cultural context in which marital problems occur is almost always interesting to consider, it does not necessarily follow that culture-level factors are causally relevant, that is, problem maintaining, in the given case. Moreover, even when significant cultural determinants of marital problems are at work, and even when they are undeniably so, they are not necessarily able to be influenced via the vehicle of psychotherapy. In the first case, the cultural dimensions of a couple's life might not be addressed at all, after the assessment, since they are not seen as part of current problem-maintaining patterns. In the second case, they might likewise receive minimal attention after the initial assessment, since they have been seen as being outside the realm of likely therapeutic influence. Cultural factors in couple distress are not seen in BIMT as inherently any more or less important than any other set of possibly relevant factors (e.g., individual psychopathology, poor relationship skills, maladaptive cognitive processes, unconscious strivings). Problematic behavior patterns are targeted not because of their form, but because of their function in the couple's dysfunction. Thus, the therapist's sensitivity to and awareness of cultural differences among couples can serve as a basis for generating useful hypotheses about problem-maintaining factors, as can any body of knowledge that helps to organize complex information about general behavioral tendencies in a particular group of people (e.g., the symptom pattern of a given patient diagnostic group; Hayes & Toarmino, 1995). But the functional analytic emphasis of BIMT requires that any potential problem-maintaining variable be considered salient only if it matters in this particular case.

BIMT assessment is largely present-oriented, for three reasons. A large proportion of couples come to therapists in crisis, and one or both partners are often eager to flee the "enforced togetherness" (Brewster & Montie, 1987) of conjoint therapy. As a result, the rapid development of a working therapeutic alliance (also see the following) is essential if the couple is to return to treatment. Conversations in early meetings that focus on the present are usually experienced by patients as more tuned in to their perceptions and their pain. Second, present-focused conversations generally allow more useful therapist mappings of the problem-maintaining patterns of the couple via the appearance of real-time enactments (whether prompted by the therapist or not) of recurrent, interactional difficulties. Finally, while some history-taking is a standard part of the BIMT approach (see following), historically oriented conversations tend to occur in the longer midphase of BIMT. *The core assumptions of the change process in BIMT, that couple therapy can lead to change in both interactional patterns and inner representational models, and that such changes often occur via direct behavior change efforts,* reinforce a decidedly present-time emphasis.

Another general characteristic of the assessment phase of BIMT is that there is no sharp distinction between an assessment phase and an intervention phase. Indeed, at least by standards of traditional individual therapy, potentially change-inducing interventions may occur quite early, even in the first session (Gurman, 1992). Naturally, this is more likely to occur when BIMT is practiced by a more experienced therapist. Even in opening conjoint sessions, more experienced therapists may construct probes, prescribe tasks, offer interpretive reframings, pose challenges, ask anticollusive questions, and so forth, as varied means of both assessing central problem-maintaining dynamics, and of testing a couple's capacity for change.

Universal Areas of Couple Assessment: The Seven C's

While the elements of a comprehensive couple assessment are presented here, all these areas do not require equal emphasis. In most cases, a few areas will stand out as especially pertinent to the therapist's understanding of the nature and maintenance of the problem(s) at hand, and others will quickly be revealed to be of little or no functional significance. Moreover, while in most cases the therapist might need two to four sessions to have a strong sense of understanding the couple in each of these areas (except with the most severely disengaged, enraged, or disorganized couples), a reasonably experienced couple therapist should be able to form at least tentative impressions in most of these areas (Budman & Gurman, 1988) after one or two sessions.

BIMT therapists routinely take stock of couple patterns, problems, and possibilities in seven areas which, taken together, constitute a comprehensive mapping of the content areas in which functionally relevant factors in the maintenance of couples problems may be identified. These areas certainly do not all require clinical attention after the early assessment, but serve as a guide for generating case-specific treatment formulations. *Conflict* includes the couple's visible communication and problem-solving skills, and their ability to collaborate and compromise. It also necessarily includes the presenting problem(s) and attempted solutions to these problems. *Commitment* refers to the partners' intent to stay in or leave the relationship, as well as to patterns that may threaten commitment (e.g., affairs, other secrets) or strengthen it (social support, positivity of the couple's history). *Connectedness* is the couple's sense of "we-ness," and involves their basic degree of compatibility, the security of their attachment, their capacity for mutual acceptance, and their sexual expression. *Character* refers to therapeutically relevant aspects of each partner's personality style and individual psychopathology, as well as to individual strengths and emotional resilience. *Context* refers to the broader cultural, developmental, familial, and physical (i.e., biological, medical) forces that may both affect and be affected by couple functioning and dynamics. Included here are such factors as various external stressors (i.e., nondyadic) and life cycle obstacles or impediments. Context importantly also includes answers to the central opening clinical question—"Why now" (Budman & Gurman, 1988) is this couple presenting for treatment? *Causality and Change* involves the partners' "theories" of both the origins and maintenance of their problems (with particular emphasis on the degree to which each partner can acknowledge his or her own contributions to problem maintenance), treatment goals (noting also discrepancies between partners regarding goals), and any significant differences between partners in terms of their readiness for change. Finally, *Countertransference* expresses itself in couple therapy primarily in terms of ongoing (versus occasional) side-taking by the therapist (e.g., speaking too much for one partner, finding it much more difficult to empathize with one partner than the other), and, even earlier, by obvious difficulty forming a therapeutic alliance with either partner, or less commonly, with both partners.

Focal-Functional Assessment

Certain overriding goals are important for all couples in BIMT; for example, more accurate self-perception, more accurate perception of one's partner, and resolution of presenting problems. In addition to the universal or molar areas of assessment previously described, a more fine-grained, molecular assessment of the couple's most salient problem-relevant patterns is, of course, necessary. To this end, BIMT calls upon both an object relations understanding of the couple's core conflictual issues, and a social learning theory-oriented assessment of these core issues.

The molecular aspect of BIMT assessment emphasizes what behavior therapists call functional analysis, or behavioral analysis. Functional analysis is concerned not with the topography, or form, of behavior, but with its effects, roughly equivalent to its purposes. Functional analysis is a method of connecting assessment and treatment planning, including technique selection. The goals of functional analysis are to identify behaviors, or patterns of behavior, of clinical concern, to identify the conditions that maintain these patterns, to select appropriate interventions, and to monitor the progress of treatment.

The function of a behavior, or behavior pattern, is assessed by identifying the factors that control or maintain the pattern. This typically calls for a description of the behavior (pattern), including its frequency, the conditions, settings, or context(s) in which it occurs, and the (overt and covert) consequences of its occurrence. That is, the (overt and covert) antecedents to (discriminative stimuli) and consequences (positive or negative reinforcement, punishment) of the behavior are tracked. When a functional analyst is asked "Why" someone does something, she or he provisionally finds the answer in the particular pattern of antecedents and consequences attendant to the behavior. Historical facts or experiences are relevant in a functional analysis to the degree that they establish learned behavior or patterns that continue into the present and are clinically relevant to the problems for which change is sought (as one former colleague put it, "If it doesn't matter now, it doesn't matter").

Typically, couples identify very particular or even singular triggering situations (e.g., a recent argument), as though those situations or events constitute the problem. While occasionally this is appropriate, it is much more likely that the therapist needs to be cognizant of the recurring pattern that is problematic, the latest (or almost any chosen) instance of which is probably merely an illustration. The patterns, or themes (Christensen et al., 1995) are technically referred to as functional classes, or more commonly, response classes. That is, various behaviors are considered to be members of a larger functional class, in that apparently different behaviors share the same function (purpose, effect). Response classes are not determined by the similarity of the content or form of particular behaviors or events. The practical implication of thinking in terms of response classes is that, because the behaviors that make up the class are functionally equivalent, changing one particularly frequent or salient component of the response class may lead to parallel change in other topographically different behaviors within the class, thus fostering generalization. Moreover, tracking the function of apparently different behaviors may help the therapist identify a functional theme that the couple fails to see, instead of seeing each problematic event or interaction as though it were a separate problem unto itself.

To facilitate a reasonably coherent experience of therapy, and to have a relatively clear thematic focus, it is essential that the therapist think in terms of such response classes. In most cases, the marital problem will be in a "hot" area, one in which the partners are less likely to respond to change with comfort. Even when a couple's early presentation makes it chaotically appear that there is an endless list of difficulties, but no central, unifying theme, there *is* a theme. It is the therapist's responsibility to make thematic sense out of apparent chaos. Kanfer and Saslow (1969) set forth a widely influential description of "behavioral diagnosis;" that is, functional analysis. Their analytic model went beyond the standard A(ntecedents)—B(ehavior)—C(onsequences) behavioral assessment model, to include variables about the state of the organism, recast as S(timulus)—O(rganism)—R(esponse)—C(onsequences). Consideration of the "O" factor includes, for example, hunger, or arousal. It also includes what Kanfer and Saslow call a "motivational analysis." These four elements make up the functional assessment, and when a plan for Intervention (I) is added, a clinically relevant (i.e., change-oriented) functional analysis (S-O-R-C-I) is available. While behavior therapists almost universally regard the notion of unconscious motives as a useless construct, in BIMT it is seen that it is just such unconscious motives that may provide useful clues to what is most distressing to a couple. And, at the beginning of therapy, it is often only by the use of reasonable therapist inferences and hypotheses about such unspoken, and unspeakable, motives that sense can be made of the underlying pattern of the partners' varied complaints and concerns.

Thus, one may say that to identify the central couple collusions, the BIMT therapist must look for the ways in which the S-O-R-C analysis—including a motivational analysis of unconscious factors—of the marital partners intersect and mutually affect one another. BIMT's view that the relevant contingencies to couple conflict exist within the partners as well as between them is what renders it an interpersonal-intrapsychic approach.

It is essential in BIMT to help partners modify not only the overt behavior about which they complain, but also the patterns of reciprocal projective identification around their thematically central concerns. Since the circular process of mutual projective identification, or collusion, is an inferred one (supported, of course, by overt interaction), it cannot be observed directly. Nonetheless, there are a number of behavioral patterns that signify its active and pernicious presence. Mutual projective identification is manifest in many forms, usually with several present in the interaction of a particular couple, for example, (1) partners consistently fail to see salient aspects of each other's behavior or personality that are readily perceptible to a third person (e.g., therapist); (2) partners often fail to see changes in each other that are perceptible to a third party who is familiar with them; (3) partners behave in ways that protect them from behaving in a manner inconsistent with their preferred view of themselves in the relationship; (4) partners unconsciously often reinforce in the other's behavior the very behavior or characteristics about which they complain; (5) partners largely fail to see, or at least acknowledge, their own contribution to the problems at hand; (6) partners agree that one or the other of them is the problem, usually by virtue of that person's purported personality pathology or psychiatric diagnosis; (7) partners argue over whose personality pathology accounts for their problems; or (8) partners exaggerate their differences and minimize their similarities, appearing at first blush to be totally opposite from each other.

Goal Setting

BIMT seeks change in both individuals as well as in their interaction, more accurate self-perception, and more accurate perception of one's partner, as well as resolution of what the couple define as their presenting problem. The form these changes take varies, of course, as defined by the functional analysis. The functional analysis is inherently responsive to individual differences, and thus incorporates whatever factors are deemed relevant, whether their origins or present source are intrapsychic (cognitive or affective, conscious and unconscious), dyadic, larger family systems, sociocultural (e.g., race, ethnicity, class, gender) or biological/physiological. It is not necessary, nor usually appropriate, to attempt to address all identifiable areas of couple discord, or all aspects of spouses' individual conflicts that impinge on the couple relationship. As a well-done functional analysis usually reveals, disharmony is usually determined and characterized by a few major issues.

Just as ultimate treatment goals vary, so do early treatment goals. Some couples in crisis require containment, structuring, and even practical advice at the outset. Only after the crisis has become muted can they fully engage in cooperative exploration of their relationship, and of themselves as individuals within that relationship. Even when the immediate stimulus to the couple's crisis is an external event (e.g., job loss, family of origin conflict, recovery from illness), the BIMT therapist tries to formulate the working relationship models within each partner, without necessarily voicing these inferences and hypotheses. Other couples, with basically flexible styles of interaction and a more robust degree of self-acceptance when facing situational problems, may be helped with rather direct, concrete, problem-solving guidance. The couple's view of their presenting problem must, of course, be taken seriously. Still, even when externally generated problems comprise the couple's initial problem presentation, it is appropriate for the therapist to include in his or her formulation how the current dilemma or stressor fits within the internal relationship schema of each partner. The great majority of couples who seek therapy, however, present difficulties that are much more complex in both their origins and their maintenance, and thus require a therapist's intervention at multiple levels of experience, using a rather broad array of techniques, as will be discussed.

PRINCIPLES OF INTERVENTION AND THERAPEUTIC TECHNIQUES

Three general principles guide the interventive activities of the BIMT therapist: the interruption and modification of collusive processes; the linking of individual experience and relational experience; and the creation of therapeutic tasks.

Interruption and Modification of Collusive Processes

The ways in which therapists can interrupt and block collusive processes as they occur in the immediacy of the conjoint sessions are limitless, and probably are constrained in their variety only by the therapist's clinical creativity and technical mastery. Some general guidelines can be set forth regarding what it is that the therapist should do, that is, the therapeutic strategy, as distinct from how to do it—the therapeutic technique (which will be discussed subsequently). In-session interruption and modification of collusive processes is facilitated by: (1) encouraging each partner to differentiate between the experiential impact of the partner's behavior and the intent attributed to the latter's behavior; (2) interrupting partner behavior that is aimed at reducing anxiety in the other spouse, especially when that partner is behaving in ways that are historically contrary to the couple's collusive interactional contract; (3) focusing each partner's attention on concrete evidence in the behavior of the other partner that denies similarly anachronistic perceptions of that partner; and (4) encouraging each partner to acknowledge directly his or her own behavioral changes that are incompatible with the maladaptive ways in which he or she has tended to see himself or herself and to be seen by the partner.

Blocking Interventions

Here, I present some illustrative techniques for interrupting and modifying in-session collusive processes. The aim of blocking techniques is to block, interrupt, or divert couple enactments of habitual, unconscious contracts in response to observable in-session behavior. Thus, blocking techniques are used reactively and responsively, rather than proactively. Their use and the timing of their use cannot be predicted, anticipated, or planned. They are called upon by the therapist in the natural, emerging flow of the therapeutic conversation. Blocking interventions are explicitly process oriented.

Two blocking interventions often used in BIMT are central in the practice of other influential couple therapy approaches, but are used with a rather different intent. *Cognitive restructuring,* common in both individual cognitive behavior therapy and cognitive behavioral couple therapy, challenges partners' automatic thoughts about and overt reactions to their mate's behavior. Such negative overgeneralizations, common in repetitive couple conflict, prevent each partner from seeing his or her mate as a whole person, and prevent the misperceived partner from being seen more holistically, as well. These selectively inattentive attributions usually reflect underlying projective elements. *Shifting affective gears* is nearly identical to Emotionally Focused Marital Therapy's (see Woodley & Johnson, this volume) method of moving couples from "hard" to "soft" feelings, and Integrative Behavioral Couple Therapy's (see Baucom, Yi, & Christenson, this volume) emphasis on enhancing partners' mutual acceptance as well as changing discrete behavior. Shifting affective gears calls for a refocusing of one partner's negative feelings, for example, anger, and focus on the undesirable behavior of the other partner, to a focus on that partner's internal feelings—for example of sadness or loneliness. Such a shift interrupts (blocks) recurrent, negative interactions, thus allowing opportunities for new behavior to replace old, destructive behavior. In the BIMT view, the shift also reveals the truth exposed by the shift itself, that is, that the expression of destructive and pain-inducing feelings really is an indirect cover for, or defense against, the direct expression of feelings involving vulnerability. Moreover, BIMT emphasizes that the attacking partner's avoidance of shows of vulnerability reflects not only his or her own anxiety, but also the anxiety of the attacked partner about the attacking partner's expression of vulnerability. Containment and holding are both essential to the development of stable intimacy. When the attacking partner shifts focus to softer feelings, the therapist must not only support this frightening movement, but also must block any behavior by the attacked partner that can switch the attacking partner back into a negative, defensive mode.

Two other blocking interventions are unique to BIMT: *Containment Coaching* and *Anticollusive Questioning.* Containment Coaching involves the use of the principles of behavioral self-control for the purpose of containing disturbing internal states (thus blocking maladaptive projection, which, if not blocked, may then stimulate defensive counterprojection in the mate, followed by further mutual escalation, withdrawal, and so forth). In Containment Coaching, in a moment of escalating argumentation, each partner is coached to say "Stop!" (or something equivalent) aloud (and eventually, silently), and to reflect, also aloud, on what he or she is trying to achieve in the interaction at that moment. Individual self-control or self-regulation training thus focuses on altering one's response to the partner's undesired behavior, changing one's approach to trying to persuade one's partner to change, and so on. It may also include self-soothing elements, to allow more genuine and less defensive engagement with the partner. Anticollusive Questioning (1) points to partners' inferred, hence unspoken, wishes and fears that help to maintain problematic patterns; (2) directs partners' attention to problem-maintaining behavior that is outside their conscious awareness; (3) hints at the un-witting (unconscious) ways in which the couple cooperates to appear to be working toward change, yet maintaining the status quo; and (4) identifies self-contradictions between partners' overt behavior and their stated preferences and desires. These sorts of questions may be asked in a somewhat rhetorical tone, left only to plant a seed for later questions, and requiring no direct patient response—or, they may be asked with the explicit expectation that the partner(s) consider and address the matter, theme, or issue raised by the therapist's question at the time it is presented. As with all blocking techniques, these anti-collusive questions are al-ways asked in immediate response to what a partner (or partners) does or says in the session. Blocking, anti-collusive questions force attention on the problem-maintaining elements of the couple's relational patterns, and, in so doing, both in-vite the partner to disengage from relationally destructive behavior at the moment, and to reflect on the unconscious purposes of the broader pattern of which this present behavior is but a therapeutically convenient example. There is no formal limit on the number or types of blocking, anti-collusive questions that could be asked, but there are a number of recurrent problematic marital themes for which the following illustrative questions seem often to be appropriate. These questions are typically preceded by a therapist's segue, such as, "You know, when you say (or do) that, I wonder . . .

- could it be that you fear that you two are really too similar rather than too different?
- how do you protect each other from even worse pain?
- can you imagine anything negative that might happen if your couple prob-lems just disappeared? (or, "if your partner suddenly started to behave ex-actly the way you say you wish she or he would?")
- if, despite your complaining about (X) in (your partner) right now, might there be times when you actually (like, admire) X?
- even though you often complain about (X in your partner's behavior), do you ever find that sometimes you do X yourself?
- are there sometimes moments when (your partner) is behaving in some way you've really wanted to see more of, and yet you don't 'stroke' him or her for it?
- what stops you from accepting what (your partner) is giving you, especially since it seems to be just what you're asking for?
- where did you first learn to be uncomfortable with (whatever the partner is repeatedly complaining about in the other partner) in yourself?
- what do you do to get him or her to behave in ways that, ironically, bother you so much?
- when you think of some things you could do differently to help solve the

problem, how do you stop yourself from doing these things? What do you say to yourself?

- what would it be like if you were married to a (man, woman) who was virtually identical to yourself psychologically?

- how can you help (him or her) help you to change whatever *you* want to change in yourself?

- how do you think you would feel if the two of you were to switch (psychological) roles for a while?

- what can you do to help (him or her) to do (less or more) of what you'd like to see different in your relationship?

Anti-collusive questions such as these cannot be used in a rote, staged fashion. They must organically and thematically fit, and be woven into the conversational flow of the session. When appropriately tuned to the affective and substantive context of the session, they appear quite intuitive and empathic to the bilateral fears of the couple. When the therapist is well tuned to the couple's maladaptive, collusive contract, evocative questions such as these do, in fact, arise intuitively.

Linking Individual Experience and Relational Experience

The types of anti-collusive blocking actions just described are seen in BIMT as facilitating change by directly modifying each partner's self-experiencing and experiencing of his or her mate. In general, such therapist-generated experiences in the session should precede, rather than follow, the offering of a cognitive explanation (i.e., interpretations of the underlying dynamic struggles addressed by the therapist's actions). More often than not, prior explanations are counterproductive, in that they may impose so much safe structure that they minimize the level of anxiety or discomfort that the therapist's actions are designed to expose the partners to in the first place. Thus, the potential for experiencing, rather than talking about, new ways of being with oneself and one's partner may be constrained.

The BIMT therapist values cognitive awareness as well as behavioral change. In BIMT, the development of insight, and the use of interpretation to foster such insight, is seen as but one of many potentially useful therapist interventions. Specifically, and in contrast to its role in traditional, insight-oriented psychoanalytic therapies, it is but one helpful means of fostering therapeutic exposure, which in turn allows for the development of more adaptive and flexible interactions.

In couple therapy, interpretation is intended to expose partners to their hidden feelings (or impulses, etc.) about themselves as well as to their hidden feelings about their mates. Whatever their origins, such feelings are hidden in the present, and so, in BIMT, most therapist interpretations are present-oriented rather than historically or genetically focused. Even when an interpretation is focused on one partner's experience from an individual historical perspective (e.g., regarding one's family of origin), its implications for the current marital relationship must be identified, or at least struggled with.

The use of exposure-enhancing therapist interpretations requires a solid therapist-partner alliance as a buffer against anxiety. What cannot be overlooked in the process of couple therapy, however, is that therapist interpretations that expose one partner also require an adequate partner-to-partner alliance and an atmosphere of reasonable empathy and safety, lest a therapist's interpretations be used by the second partner as a weapon against the first partner. For this reason, such individually focused interpretations usually are less common early in therapy than later on.

Thus, there are three main purposes to interpretation in BIMT: first, by naming the previously expressed feeling, in order to contain the "bad stuff" that would otherwise be projected onto one's partner; second, by thus accepting (by exposure) the projected material as being in oneself, to decrease blame and increase acceptance of the partner; and third, by therapeutically derailing repetitive, redundant interactions from persisting in the moment, shifting the couple's interaction to allow new relational possibilities, including, prominently, the partner's empathy. Insight in BIMT is not sought so much for its truth value (although the BIMT therapist rarely offers an interpretation which he does not believe), but for shifting couple interactions that are maintained, in part, by existing implicit partner theories of what constitutes the couple's dysfunctionality.

Creating Therapeutic Tasks: Instigative Interventions

Therapeutic tasks refer to the general category of what, in BIMT, are called *instigative interventions*. In contrast to blocking interventions, these interventions typically do not arise out of the immediate, natural flow of a therapy session. Rather, in contrast to the more process-oriented blocking interventions, instigative interventions are more goal-oriented and directive, and are "strategic" in Stanton's (1981) sense that "the clinician *initiates* what happens during treatment and *designs* a particular approach for each problem" (p. 361, emphasis added). Thus, instigative interventions are usually more planned by the therapist, even (and often) to the point of being designed outside the therapy sessions. While the BIMT therapist obviously plans such interventions in a way that is responsive to the treatment needs of each couple as the therapist assesses them, they typically are not set forth in immediate response to the couple's behavior, and are generally experienced as being "brought into" the therapy session. The other major difference from blocking interventions is that blocking interventions are used to interrupt and draw attention to, and increase awareness of, maladaptive couple patterns, while instigative interventions are designed to initiate or prompt or model healthier interactions. That is, instigative interventions focus on promoting change in a positive direction.

Out-of-session tasks vary from exploring the consequences of new marital behavior, to reflecting on particular themes identified during therapy sessions, to pinpointing concrete desires for change in one's partner or in oneself. Tasks may be as loosely constructed as asking a couple to "think about how you yourself contribute to the problems that bother you most in your relationship." Paradoxical techniques, though used sparingly in BIMT, may also foster BIMT goals (Gurman, 1981) for valid psychodynamic reasons.

Other Instigative Interventions

Many other out-of-session tasks commonly used by couple therapists also qualify as both instigative and anti-collusive. Coming from the behavioral tradition, for example, encouraging the use of positive reinforcement for change is a deceptively simple technique. This intervention, which calls for the therapist to coach and encourage partners to positively reinforce (via concrete simple acknowledgement, expression of thanks, and so on) the appearance of behavior they have been asking to see more of, by definition is intended to increase the partner's desired behavior. In addition, following through on this principle, especially when partners reciprocate, often has the more subtle effect of inhibiting their tendency to engage in projective identification. As discussed earlier, partners in sustained marital conflict often identify as unwanted, behavior in their mate that stimulates anxiety about their own impulses, needs, and desires. Direct therapist instruction to positively reinforce desired changes in partners' behavior implicitly requires that each partner attend to and acknowledge aspects of their mate that are characteristically minimized or discounted. The couple is put in a win-win situation by the therapist's encouragement of reinforcing desired change. If, on the one hand, the couple follows through as suggested, they strengthen valued elements of their relationship. On the other hand, a lack of follow-through by the couple, even after it is clear in-session that they understand the rationale for the therapist's idea, may signify the intensity of their stuck, projective process. The therapist could then redirect attention to the unspoken motivations and attributions of each partner that drive them, behaviorally speaking, to continue to emphasize negative perceptions of each other. Such a formulation does not universally explain couples' noncompliance with suggested prosocial behavioral reinforcement approaches, but it provides a conceptual framework that is often very useful in helping the therapist and the couple make sense of their anxieties about change. Once thus identified, such anxieties themselves, again following a functional analytic approach, can then be addressed.

The Sequencing of Interventions

Just as the sequencing of ultimate and mediating treatment goals varies from couple to couple, as earlier noted, so does the sequencing of different types of therapeutic interventions vary across couples. Indeed, in BIMT, there is a fluid interplay of depth-oriented and behavior change-oriented therapist intervention, and how much of each occurs in any given phase of therapy is more a matter of emphasis than of exclusion. At times, the BIMT therapist may push for highly specific behavioral changes in session or out of session, in order to unblock long-term and rigid interactional obstacles to intimacy, while at other times, she or he may "go deep," and work to address painful, individual vulnerabilities in order for the couple to establish enough of a sense of safety to be willing to make visible changes outside the therapy, that is, without the therapist present.

Still, some guidelines can be offered about therapist decision making in the choice, and especially the timing and sequencing, of different types of interventions in BIMT. BIMT conceives of three levels of therapist intervention into the object relational (OR) realm of couple dynamics and interaction. At Level 1, *Inadvertent OR Intervention,* the therapist is using any therapeutic method with which he or she is familiar, without any intention to produce change in the object representational inner world of the marriage. As explained subsequently, many common couple therapy interventions, such as communication and problem-solving training, unwittingly facilitate object relational changes. Inadvertent OR Interventions are common among what in BIMT are called Instigative Interventions.

At Level 2, *Implicit OR Interventions,* the therapist may use the very same kinds of interventions as in Level 1, but does so with full awareness of the likely inner representational meaning of the interventions, for example, by wondering, "How might use of this particular technique unbalance the couple's particular collusive 'agreement' to avoid exposure and closeness?" Level 2 interventions also include variations on the use of Anticollusive Questioning, discussed earlier, in hinting at the functional significance of partners' unconscious strivings, including projective identification, but without explicitly identifying or labeling them.

At Level 3, *Explicit OR Interventions,* the therapist explicitly and directly interprets unconscious experience and its role in the marital dynamics. Accessing the feelings that underlie maladaptive overt behaviors, such as angry criticism, and interpreting its defensive function, is a common example of a Level 3 intervention. Level 3 interventions tend to be more thematic than incident- or event-focused, as they point to recurrent couple patterns, as illustrated by the content of a particular therapeutic moment and interaction.

BIMT therapists always *prefer* to begin therapy with a significant use of Level 3 interventions, but clinical reality does not always allow this. Since Level 3 interventions emphasize functionally relevant themes in the couple's conflict, they include more of the controlling factors in the couple's tension, or put another way, they emphasize a larger sampling of the various functionally related ways in which different content plays out in the couple's central problems. Moreover, thematic interventions that help the couple improve their understanding of the unconscious dimensions of their relationship inherently attend to both overt and covert factors in the couple interaction. In these ways, helpful Level 3 interventions are more likely to generalize to the couple's life outside therapy.

What, then, should influence the therapist's decision as to whether Level 3 interventions are appropriate early in therapy? The guide is to be found, once again, in the functional analysis. Not the functional assessment of what maintains the couple's core problems, but the "I," or Intervention component of the full functional analysis. The therapist's predictions about how the partners may respond to Level 3 interventions, combined with sensitivity to their reactions to such interventions, are the key. Essentially, the cues the therapist must stay aware of involve the couple's openness to Level 3 interventions. Openness is influenced by the couple's general psychological-mindedness, but especially by their level of comfort at dealing with non-surface level aspects of their relationship. There are no absolute guidelines as to who these "open" couples are. "Difficult" couples—those marked by intense hostility, individual vulnerability, and chronic marital tension—might seem at first to be too easily dysregulated by many Level 3 interventions, but this is not automatically the case. The moderating factor in such cases can be the quality of the therapist-patient alliance, or more specifically, whether strong alliances can be established early in therapy. If not, then more alliance-building is needed in order for the therapist to provide an adequate level of holding for the couple's anxiety. Interestingly, but not surprisingly, while many couples find therapist empathy and support to be key to being adequately held, others find a therapist's structuring, for example, via behavioral exchanges, or offering of directives, to serve the same therapeutic function. Alternatively, couples who appear very open to simple behavioral exchanges early in therapy may be so because they are fundamentally well connected, flexible, and open to each other's influence. It is also possible that they are open to focusing on discrete changes out of a shared avoidance of dealing with deeper issues. Once again, what matters is not the form of the (therapist's or couple's) behavior, but its function.

Varied Pathways to Therapeutic Couple Exposure

BIMT regularly calls upon the therapeutic tasks and techniques associated with both traditional and integrative behavioral couple therapies (see Baucom, et al., this volume). In BIMT, these strategies are used to aid the process of helping partners reintegrate denied aspects of themselves and their mates, that is, behavioral interventions are used to facilitate object-relational ends.

Marital partners in conflict must be exposed to aspects of themselves and their mates that are blocked from awareness. These self-aspects are blocked from awareness because of the anxiety they evoke. The required exposure can be accomplished in couple therapy in a manner roughly analogous to that used in behavioral treatments for anxiety and phobic disorders, such as systematic desensitization and anxiety management training. These are specific, common technical operations that illustrate the learning theory principle of exposure or, more specifically, the contact with, and prevention of escape or avoidance from, anxiety-eliciting stimuli.

The use of exposure in couple therapy differs from its usual use in individual behavior therapy in two ways. First, setting up a formal and explicitly negotiated hierarchy of anxiety-eliciting stimuli in couple therapy is practically unmanageable because of the complexity, thematic multidimensionality, and reciprocal interactivity of problematic couple patterns. The second difference from the usual use of exposure treatments in behavior therapy is that the anxiety-eliciting stimuli of clinical concern are events and experiences that occur within the partner-patient, not outside the patient, as in the exposure treatment of, say, a height phobia. Therapeutic couple exposure is more akin to the treatment of agoraphobia, in which the private, cognitive, and physiological anxiety-eliciting cues constitute the treatment targets. At the same time, therapists need to keep in mind that not all marital avoidant behavior is irrational or unwarranted. The partners in chronically distressed marriages almost always display what behavior therapists would call genuinely aversive consequences. Marital partners and therapists alike must deal differently with real versus imagined responses to their behavior. Ultimately, for a marital partner to be open to exposing his or her vulnerabilities, there must be good reason for the partner to be seen as a "safe, real person" (Dicks, 1967, p. 43).

Application of the kinds of principles, strategies, and techniques for interrupting and modifying dysfunctional, collusive couple behavior in-session, described earlier, creates opportunities for therapeutic exposure to warded-off aspects of the self and the other. Less obviously, but equally powerfully, commonplace behavioral couple therapy interventions also create such relational learning opportunities. Indeed, it is a practical premise of BIMT that behavioral marital therapy, and Integrative Behavioral Couple Therapy in particular, in large measure *is* exposure therapy. While a variety of behavioral interventions are used, such as behavioral exchange, the traditional, defining methods of communication and problem-solving training constitute the foundation and core of BIMT's behavioral techniques. Such techniques can facilitate the process of helping partners reintegrate repudiated aspects of themselves and their mates, that is, they can serve as a means of enabling partners to emerge as whole persons in intimate relationships.

It must be emphasized that in BIMT, rather than quickly attempting to control the dance of projective identification and do away with unpleasant feelings, the therapist often will welcome its real-time enactment in the session. The BIMT therapist may even work to intensify the split-off feelings in the partner in whom they originated, in order to gain access to underlying fears and vulnerabilities, as a step that precedes encouraging the couple to "find a different way to get, say, or do what you need or want right now." This intensification process aim in BIMT is analogous in the individual behavior therapy exposure treatment of agoraphobia, to arranging exposure experiences in which the patient is required to experience, not avoid (for example, by distraction), reasonably high levels of anxiety.

In IBCT, the focus is exclusively on each partner's acceptance of the other partner. In the BIMT framework, each partner must also come to accept in themselves what they have denied in themselves and projected onto their mates. Accepting undesired behavior in one's mate is an important step toward acceptance of oneself, but it is not equivalent to doing so. Both expressions of acceptance are required for lasting change.

The Healing Role of Communication and Problem-Solving Intervention

In BIMT, familiar communication and problem-solving enhancement methods are seen as offering very direct, partial antidotes to unconscious collusion. That is, the use of these techniques requires that the couple partners (1) speak only for themselves, not for their mate; (2) assume responsibility for their own thoughts and feelings; (3) systematically track their own affective and cognitive experience; (4) focus on current intrapersonal and interpersonal events; (5) desist from the idealized, defensive stance that their mate should be able to know what they want without having to be asked; and (6) attend to their own contributions to displeasing couple patterns.

Such traditional BMT techniques, on aggregate, counter collusion and promote relationally healthy integration of the self in several important ways: (1) BMT techniques emphasize self-differentiation, for example, even by intermittent encouragement by the therapist for partners to state their views and feelings from a time-honored, if not a bit overworked, "I-position;" (2) BMT techniques emphasize self-change, and in so doing, counter predictable partner-blaming (projective identification). Inner awareness is promoted in place of outer (and other) attack; (3) BMT techniques lower partners' needs to escape and avoid aversive arousal, and thus increase intimate, safer engagement; (4) BMT techniques shift awareness from the unconscious reinforcement of avoidant behavior (in self and partner) to the conscious reinforcement of desired behavior; (5) the empathic emphasis contained in communication skill coaching directly increases acceptance of one's partner. Moreover, when such empathic relating is focused on a partner's exposing of the vulnerabilities that motivate his or her undesired behavior, the partner's enhanced acceptance includes acceptance of the bad, or of the unchangeable, in the mate, plus acceptance of disavowed parts of the self along similar thematic lines. In brief, empathy neutralizes projective identification; and (6) while improving overt communication, communication skill training techniques also counter-collusively decrease each partner's fantasy of who her or his mate should be, and increase the reality of who the mate actually is. Poor communication is more often than not both a symptom of collusion *and* a maintainer of collusion. Poor communication reflects an implicit rule of limited intimacy through shared avoidance of self-disclosure and self-exposure. Improved communication allows real differences to be revealed. Private fantasies about the idealized partner may be a natural part of early romantic attraction, but engagement with the real partner is essential for genuine, long-term intimacy.

SPECIAL ISSUES IN THE PRACTICE OF BIMT

Four general treatment issues that need to be considered in any type of couple therapy are of particular importance in BIMT. These issues are (1) the role of the therapist and the central mechanisms of change; (2) the creation of therapeutic alliances; (3) the place of individual treatment; (4) couple therapy and the larger family; and (5) termination.

The Therapist's Role and Mechanisms of Change

The BIMT therapist has three central roles: she or he inculcates systemic awareness and thinking; she or he teaches and coaches relationship skills; and she or he challenges dysfunctional relationship rules or contracts.

The *inculcation of systemic awareness* may occur implicitly or explicitly. This style of intervention fundamentally involves enhancing a couple's capacity for doing their own functional analysis. It often involves the modeling of context questions, such as, "What were you doing, Bob, just before Sue told you how anxious she was feeling," or "Sue, what was the first thing you saw Bob do after you told him how anxious you were?" By modeling the basic principles of functional analytic inquiry by her or his own questions, reflections, and observations in sessions, the therapist helps the partners become more sensitive to the recurrent circular processes in their relationship that maintain their primary problems, including intrapsychic events and cues. In effect, the BIMT therapist conversationally models and encourages the couple to become curious about the discriminative stimuli that set the occasion for, or become circularly involved in, problematic interaction patterns. Thus, they become more adept at being able to problem solve in ways that are meaningful to them. This kind of systemic or functional analytic sensitivity training directly fosters the development of a more multicausal, "both-and" couple perspective, which may help to counter the common, and always problematic, single-factor, "either-or" style of thinking in which distressed couples regularly engage in their mutual, projective dance.

The BIMT therapist's second major role involves the *teaching, and elicitation, via modeling and feedback, of facilitative relationship skills,* especially those focusing on communication and problem solving. The use of such skill training in BIMT has already been discussed.

Finally, in BIMT the therapist plays the all-important role of *challenging the couple's maladaptive relationship rules,* especially those that are centrally linked, that is, functionally related, to their core thematic problem. The therapist must be particularly attuned to the implicit, out-of-awareness rules that govern pertinent and persistent marital patterns. The therapist's role in BIMT in this regard, is, in effect, to violate the couple's dysfunctional rules in a safe environment that prevents avoidance of or escape from exposure to both old fears and new possibilities about one's self and one's partner, and therefore increases the opportunity for new and more satisfying relational learning. Often, such a therapeutic violation of the couple's rules involves asking the unaskable or saying the unsayable. At times in BIMT, this violation may require a therapist to rather forcefully express what one or both partners may be thinking or feeling, but not directly saying, based on a finely nuanced understanding of each partner. In this third role of challenging dysfunctional relationship rules by eliciting and interpreting unexpressed feelings, the BIMT therapist significantly serves as a model of how the partners can provide effective holding for each other.

In all of this, the therapist's overriding role is to facilitate the partners' experiencing of each other *and* themselves as whole persons, and to do so in a safe, yet challenging, environment, that works against their repetitive joint avoidances, thus leading to more genuine encounters and improved communication and problem solving. The therapist closely tracks the alliances with each partner, and between her- or himself and the couple as a couple, but focuses on the partner-partner alliance, because that is viewed as the central healing relationship in BIMT. In BIMT, the most powerful transferences are seen as occurring between the marital partners, and it is there that the therapeutic attention must be focused. The "corrective emotional experience" in BIMT is to be found within the couple-as-patient, where one of the most corrective types of experience is learning to discriminate the real, current partner from the misperceived, past inner partner.

Therapeutic Alliances

BIMT conceives of three alliances that must be fostered from the very outset of treatment. *Therapist-partner alliances* require attention in the very first session. Each partner should feel that something of personal value has been achieved, though how this occurs varies from person to person. Some people feel an alliance emerging when offered empathy and warmth, while others require insight, beginning directives for behavior change, or reassurance about the viability of their marriage. Consistent with the emphasis on the functional analysis of problems, BIMT requires that the therapist quickly discern what is functionally relevant to each partner in terms of establishing a therapist-partner alliance that is likely to increase the chances that he or she will continue in therapy. One size or approach does not fit everybody, and the therapist must also be prepared to offer different bases for an alliance even within the same couple. The *therapist-couple alliance* refers to the therapist's need to speak to both partners at once, as it were, even when overtly addressing only one of them. This second alliance is best established by speaking empathically to the mutually contingent manner in which the partners collude to keep aspects of themselves and of each other out of awareness. In the early phase of therapy, the therapist's aim here is to offer a tentative acknowledgment and attribution of the dominant ways in which the couple's overt struggles reflect the growth-oriented purposiveness of their initial attraction and later commitment. Finally, the *partner-partner alliance* is often strengthened by the therapist's acknowledging that while the partners show stylistic and/or behavioral differences in how they deal with conflict, similar relationship strivings lie behind such patterns.

The most common, and most dangerous therapist error in BIMT, as in any couple therapy, is nonstrategic side-taking, that is, side-taking, particularly of a recurrent nature, that is born of the clinician's failure to appreciate the anxiety and pain behind the negative behavior of either partner. While the therapist can and should use her or his own countertransference reactions as important guides to what is most distressing and fearful for the marital partners, again the focus must remain on the partner-partner relationship. The therapist's self-awareness should emphasize an understanding of what it is in the *couple's* relationship that draws side-taking inclinations out of the therapist.

This side-taking error is particularly dangerous, of course, very early in therapy. It is at that time that the partners are likely to be most entrenched in their split, rigidly projected, negative views of each other, increasing the possibility that the therapist will be unwittingly taken in by one partner whose characteristics or (mis-) attributions about the mate strike an uncomfortable chord in the therapist. Such unfortunate, though nearly inevitable, problematic countertransference reactions, if they are not recurrent, can be more easily repaired later in therapy.

The Structure of Therapy and the Place of Individual Treatment

In the ideal practice of BIMT, all treatment sessions would include both couple partners, since it is emphasized that the core healing components of BIMT lie within that relationship. Consequently, the BIMT therapist is very reluctant to see partners individually, and almost never sees one partner alone for the initial interview. When partners are seen alone, the BIMT therapist maintains particular awareness of any interactions that might carry significant implications for the alliances already established in the three-way conjoint meetings, and is especially attuned to any interactions that might disturb the husband-wife alliance. Relatedly, except in genuine crises or emergencies, partners are never seen alone when one partner fails to appear for a therapy session, whether due to a marital argument, a disinterest in continuing therapy, acute illness, unexpected work conflicts—or even bad weather or traffic conditions!

As noted earlier, partners are not separated during the initial assessment phase. During the active intervention phase of therapy, the only time the therapist initiates individual sessions with the partners is when conjoint sessions regularly have become unmanageable, to the point of being counterproductive, rather than merely unproductive, as some sessions inevitably are in any course of therapy. This occasion typically involves couples in which both partners have great difficulty self-regulating their anger or dramatic expressions of emotional turmoil, who are not reliably able to be soothed and calmed by the therapist, and/or who persistently engage in mutual blaming, to the virtual exclusion of seeing their own role in the couple's difficulties. Often, a focused, short-term series of individual sessions with each partner may allow a more cooperative and less inflammatory ambiance to be established when conjoint sessions are resumed.

Although BIMT values thematic consistency and a clear therapeutic focus (or foci), the therapist does not usually impose a topical agenda on therapy sessions. Quite the contrary, just as couples are seen as the major healing agents, they are also given the responsibility for deciding what is addressed in therapy. Also, because the BIMT therapist is sensitive to the factors that bias most couple therapy toward brevity, it is not assumed that a couple will wish to address the same secondary, derivative problem from session to session. Indeed, couples regularly are unaware of how seemingly different problems-of-the-day are connected thematically. It is the therapist's responsibility to foster such understanding. Thus, in BIMT, couples are routinely asked at the beginning of the session, "What would you like to focus on today?" This deceptively simple inquiry implies (1) that the couple is in charge of knowing what matters to them; (2) that all therapy sessions must have a focus, purpose, or goal; and (3) that their needs, sensibilities, and struggles are not static, but shift through time.

Despite BIMT's unabashedly interpersonal emphasis, it is commonplace in couple therapy for individual issues to intermittently rise to the fore. These may be centrally and transparently linked to the major couple problem theme, as when an emotionally distancing wife talks about the abuse that took place in her family when she was a child. Or, such an individual issue may at first seem more tangential to the relational focus, as when one partner expresses anxiety about stresses or conflicts in the workplace. When people are in couple therapy, they know they are in couple therapy. Nothing that is brought up for the therapist to hear about is brought up randomly, or without meaning. Almost always, this meaning, unclear though it may be at first to the therapist, involves the couple's relationship, the process of the couple therapy, and so forth. When partners themselves are not able to see such connections, it falls to the therapist to facilitate such understanding.

There are two common situations in which such individual factors arise. The first occurs when one partner has a diagnosable, and probably diagnosed, psychiatric disorder of a largely symptomatic nature, such as depression or anxiety. The second situation occurs when an important aspect of one partner's contribution to the couple problem reflects significant psychopathology, largely of an interpersonal nature, as in cases of personality disorders. In both situations, BIMT focuses on the functional relationships between an individual's symptoms or personality characteristics and central, problematic couple themes. BIMT looks upon nomothetic descriptions of psychiatric disorders as a useful source of hypotheses about a given individual, not as a set of facts. To be of practical use, these hypotheses require verification in the individual case, and once verified, must be functionally relevant to the central relational problems. If not, they probably fall outside the purview of BIMT, which insists on maintaining a clear treatment focus.

Some sessions in BIMT may look, to an outside observer, like individual therapy being done in the presence of a partner. The guiding principle in BIMT is that the implications of such individually oriented conversations for the couple's relationship must be made explicit, at the latest, before the end of the session. It is especially valuable if this individual material can be coherently connected to the central theme(s) of the joint therapy. Not everything that affects a couple's comfort and satisfaction in their relationship is about, or derives from, that relationship. And so, with its simultaneous interpersonal and intrapersonal awareness, BIMT respects the relevance of individual issues in the couple's life, but insists that since this is couple therapy, virtually everything that is discussed is discussed in a relational light. It is not an error to do some individual therapy within couple therapy. It is an error to do so without connecting such individual conversation to the marital relationship, and it is an error to do so if the treatment emphasis becomes the therapist-partner relationship(s) rather than the partner-partner relationship.

Individual Therapy during Couple Therapy

As noted, a fair amount of "individual therapy" may occur in BIMT; at the same time, BIMT therapists are extremely hesitant to schedule actual individual sessions. Carrying on a parallel, true individual therapy with a marital partner who is being seen by the therapist in conjoint couple therapy is never an option in BIMT. Moreover, concurrent individual psychotherapy done by other therapists during the course of BIMT is generally not favored—though, admittedly, it often cannot be avoided. Unless such therapies are clearly focused on discrete symptoms, such as phobias or compulsions, there is a great likelihood that the couple's relationship will become a prime topic for discussion, especially during a period of marital crisis. Therein lies the risk of either a duplication of similar therapeutic efforts and approaches or, more worrisome, therapeutic aims and interventions that are contradictory. More broadly, such parallel, concurrent individual therapies often dilute the patient's therapeutic energy and focus away from the focused couple therapy, and may weaken rather than strengthen the therapeutic alliance between the marital partners that needs to be sustained for effective work.

Couple Therapy and the Larger Family

Marriages do not exist in a vacuum. The children of distressed marriages are more likely to suffer from anxiety, depression, conduct problems, and impaired physical health (Gottman, 1994). Likewise, the illnesses or other problems of children may create significant stress for couples. While a systemically sensitive couple therapist will keep her or his ears open for child problems, in BIMT there is no automatic focus on the couple's children, or on the parent-child relationship. These areas of family life are addressed in BIMT when they are functionally relevant to the couple's problems, for example, the couple regularly fights about parenting differences, or a child is evidently caught up in a scapegoated role in the parental conflict. Likewise, the BIMT clinician pays ongoing attention to other dimensions of family life, such as historically salient family of origin issues, and real-time, present extended family matters, when either the initial functional analysis, or later revisions of the functional analysis, reveal the functional relevance of such aspects of the couple's difficulties. Since a clinically useful functional analysis is not merely descriptive of a problem and what maintains a problem, but necessarily includes a plan for intervention, that is, change, the form of BIMT intervention in wider family issues may vary widely for pragmatic reasons. Thus, family-oriented discussion of how one partner's childhood experiences help to make sense of his or her present relationship vulnerabilities may be called on to increase his or her spouse's empathy when he or she behaves in ways that are distressing. Alternatively, with the very same couple, the therapist might decide to give the husband an out-of-therapy task involving his family of origin, designed to enhance his differentiation from his family. Indeed, both types of family-sensitive interventions might, and probably would, be used in the same course of therapy. Such intervention decisions flow naturally from an adequate, functionally relevant case formulation, in which family-level factors are certainly possible candidates for intervention, but are not necessarily candidates for intervention.

Termination

Because the primary attachment and transference in BIMT is between the marital partners, the ending of therapy is usually relatively uneventful. Couples often stop therapy when their central symptoms or problems have been resolved, or at least abated. As much as the therapist may hope to engage with the couple at multiple levels of intervention, there may not be enough time available to do so. As a result, with the anticipation that termination may always be not far away, the BIMT therapist seeks to intervene at multiple levels of experience in an active style that evokes, exposes, and modifies problematic, projectively induced and sustained patterns.

In BIMT, contact with the couple is not infrequently on a brief, intermittent basis, with couples returning to the therapist about similar or different issues than when they were initially seen. One of the hallmarks of effective and practical brief therapy, including couple therapy, is the development of a therapist-patient (couple) relationship not unlike that of a primary care physician, to whom the patient returns as life demands and changes require. Thus, BIMT does not usually view termination as final.

The BIMT therapist again takes advantage of all opportunities to reinforce his or her central therapeutic messages about relationship change. First, in the knowledge that one never fully casts off projected aspects of oneself, the therapist may inquire, supportively rather than confrontatively, whether "there is anything problematic about the ways you used to be with your partner that you sometimes feel an urge to return to, even though you mostly don't." This question is not posed paradoxically, but as an expression of a genuine therapist acceptance of the understandable ambivalence with which people typically engage in meaningful change. Relatedly, in the termination session, the BIMT therapist will not only ask the partners to review what changes have occurred, but will also ask, and if necessary, push, the partners to acknowledge both their own contribution to the positive changes that have occurred and those of their mate.

THE EFFICACY OF BIMT

The efficacy and effectiveness of BIMT have not been tested to date in controlled clinical trials or in self-report survey research. Still, there is good reason to expect that such studies would yield a positive empirical picture for BIMT. First, BIMT regularly incorporates most of the therapeutic interventions that research by students of Behavioral Marital Therapy and Integrative Behavioral Couple Therapy (see Baucom, et al., this volume) have shown to make a difference clinically, such as communication and problem-solving training, behavioral exchange, and acceptance training. While behavioral methods emphasize acceptance of the *partner*, BIMT places an equal emphasis on the acceptance of *self*. Moreover, BIMT also regularly includes a number of the core strategies and techniques of Emotionally Focused Couple Therapy (see Woodley & Johnson, this volume), for example, the softening of harsh emotions, and connecting interpersonal and intrapersonal experience. BIMT also includes attention to unconscious psychodynamic forces in marital tensions, as does the Affective Reconstruction Approach of Snyder (2002), which has shown very positive treatment effects at rather long follow-up periods, and BIMT pays attention to such factors more consistently during the course of therapy than does Snyder's approach. Finally, BIMT is the only marital therapy approach that articulates both the theoretical and technical integration of ideas and strategies from other demonstratively effective methods of working with distressed couples.

Case Study

A course of brief (10 session) therapy with Sara and Bob illustrates the way in which BIMT therapists operate at multiple levels of experience in marital difficulty, addressing current, external situational matters, multigenerational patterns, unconscious collaboration in problem maintenance, and individual personality styles. Work with Sara and Bob also illustrates the flexible use of therapist interventions designed to promote change in different domains of the couple's experience.

Bob came to the clinic alone at first, identifying his main problem as being depressed and pessimistic about the viability of his marriage to Sara, to whom he had been married for 9 years, and with whom he had two children, ages 5 and 2. While Sara was supportive of his desire to get help for his depression, Bob's initial solo appearance exemplified the couple's central marital conflict; Bob was the relationship initiator, and relatedly the "complainer," and Sara was the relationship reactor, rarely explicitly expressing her needs or dissatisfactions.

The external stimulus for Bob's initial appearance was career related. An outgoing, successful young insurance company executive, Bob was actively being recruited by a larger firm in another city. He saw this job change opportunity as being likely to open exciting and rewarding career possibilities, and he needed to make a decision about it within the next few months. Sara, a part-time nurse, was less of a risk-taker, describing herself in the first three-way session as more of a "homebody type." Taking care of others in both her professional and private lives was a core part of her identity. But now, the idea of taking care of Bob by moving was more than even she could tolerate, especially given her close connections to her nearby family of origin.

Bob saw himself in "a kind of competition" with Sara's family for her attention, and had seen himself in this position long before the new job possibility arose.

When he would raise this issue, Sara would counter that he "should have known better than to think about moving, since I've always been close to my family." Indeed, Sara's stance on this matter was hardly news to Bob. While representing a perfectly real life-transition decision that the couple had to make, moving also signified Bob's longstanding concern about the emotional distance in the marriage that Sara seemed to prefer. In addition to her family of origin relationships, she also was devoted to her young children, regularly placing their needs, interests, and welfare ahead of those of her husband, the marriage, or indeed, herself, rationalizing that "there will be plenty of time for us (later), but the kids need us now."

This pattern of "putting our marriage in second place," as Bob described the problem, was now taking on another form, as well. Bob's recent success at work had earned him an all-expense-paid trip for two to Hawaii in January (a most welcomed prize in wintry Wisconsin). He saw this trip as a chance to "recharge" the marriage by "having some 'alone time' without the kids." He also saw it as a sort of yardstick as to whether Sara "really wants to be involved in this relationship." Sara was very hesitant about going on this trip, for two reasons. First, she had a "flying phobia" (though the couple had taken several flights together during their marriage), and second, she was very concerned that "it might be very upsetting for the kids for us to be away from them for six days" (though this idea had never been tested, and though there were relatives, including similar-aged cousins, with whom they were very familiar and comfortable, living nearby, and with whom they could stay). While Sara's travel- and child-related anxieties seemed clearly enough to be functionally involved in her pattern of avoiding marital closeness, they were also quite real in their own right, and needed to be respected as such.

As for his part in the marital distance, Bob was, of course, hardly uninvolved. A significant aspect of his outgoing style was a kind of overbearing neediness, in Sara's eyes, which she saw as a sort of off-putting dependency. During their courtship, Sara had seen his gregariousness as showing self-confidence, which attracted her to him, because it offered the possibility of her being taken care of by someone else, without having to ask very much. She had grown up in a family of seven children, in which the parents were preoccupied with their careers and inaccessible to the needs of their children. Sara learned to take care of herself, not in a mutually supportive, interdependent way, as marriage requires, but in an isolative, conflict-avoiding way. Bob, though overtly quite different from Sara, was struggling with the very same conflicts and fears. Raised in a family with a chronically depressed mother and an alcoholic, intermittently abusive, father, Bob had decided long ago that when he had a family, he would never treat them the way he had been treated. He would foster family relationships, between husband and wife and between parent and child, at any personal cost. Sara struggled with her attachment fears by protecting herself from further hurts by not exposing her needs, but was sad and self-contained. Bob struggled with his attachment fears by seeking contact with and reaching out to those who mattered to him, but often reaching out in a way that felt smothering to Sara.

Bob and Sara were in a mutually reinforcing cycle of pursuing-distancing. When she would begin to express her needs, which he said he wanted her to do, Bob would subtly, but perceptibly to her, not support her, by turning away and becoming uncharacteristically quiet, which she interpreted as disinterest. At times, upon therapist inquiry, he would acknowledge that while he wanted her to be more expressive ("real") with him, because this would mean "she really cares," he would feel afraid as she spoke, fearing his needs would be forgotten. When he reconnected conversationally, she would retreat into a passive listening style that she said was "respectful," but which he experienced as "uninvolved." They could take turns expressing their needs and wishes, but doing so usually had the tone of "me," then "you," with little sense of "we."

The overriding treatment goal, as described by the therapist and agreed to by the couple, was "to increase your sense of being more of a 'we' in a way that feels safe, so that each of you still knows who *you* are in the process." The therapist's interventions to this end took very specific forms focused on both the in-session process and out-of-session patterns. To decrease the couple's cautious turn-taking style, in which conflict (at the overt level at least) was avoided by passive rather than active listening, the therapist created the idea that Sara and Bob needed to learn to get comfortable with having "balanced conversation." Not balanced as in "I go, then you go," but as in being more immediately verbally responsive; for example, allowing interruptions, shortening the speaker's "floor time" paired with invitations (from both the speaker and the therapist) for responses by the partner, encouraging more direct eye-to-eye contact, and less speaking to or through the therapist. These conversational shifts occurred in the context of whatever subject matter the couple brought to the session to focus on. They were not based on structured or planned exercises or formats. The intent was to block, in vivo, each partner's recurrent ways of avoiding genuine dyadic exchange, fueled by the fear of neglect (Bob) and reprisal (Sara). The main antidote to each partner's anxiety about less cautious exchange was the therapist's close tracking and acknowledging of each partner's discomfort, as they allowed the therapist to guide them in "new ways of speaking, where you can *both* be *heard,* without being *hurt.*" The therapist's empathic tracking facilitated for Bob and Sara a capacity to stay "in tune with yourself even while you're tuning in to each other." Each partner's being able to acknowledge his or her discomfort aloud also helped to contain anxiety, reducing the internally driven (and externally reinforced) need to escape (that is, by nonverbally withdrawing) and to unwittingly punish the partner for his or her expressiveness. The main process component of the therapist's intervention, then, could be seen as a kind of systemically sensitive, bilateral, simultaneous exposure therapy, wherein increasing what he referred to in-session as "the conversational flow" opened up previously warded-off exposure to both unacceptable aspects of self and feared aspects of the partner.

In addition, out-of-session exposure tasks, designed to challenge the couple's rigidities, were also created. For example, Sara's "flying phobia" was addressed by the therapist's direct coaching in the principles of relaxation training and other relatively easily learned behavioral self-control skills (for example, rational disputation and "reality checking" via common cognitive behavior therapy methods). These were presented to Sara as "some ways to take care of yourself and the relationship at the same time." On Bob's side, the therapist suggested that he also use common rational restructuring techniques when he became unduly anxious about the (more) apparent (than real) urgency for making his job-change decision, and, as a former successful athlete, renew his involvement in anxiety-reducing (cardio-vascular) exercise. For both Sara and Bob, then, these out-of-session, self-soothing, and self-care activity ideas were offered not only in an effort to merely reduce each partner's anxiety, but also, and more significantly, to remove obstacles to closer and safer couple encounters, and to counter aspects of each partner's externalizing defenses ("Airplanes make me afraid," or "Employers pressure me").

A few weeks before therapy came to a close, Bob and Sara had returned from the Hawaii trip (which she managed with minimal anxiety, bolstered by their children being well taken care of and happy to stay with relatives), and had jointly agreed to not move away (with Bob more confident than before that other good career-enhancing opportunities would come along). Even over the course of a relatively brief treatment, Bob and Sara had each become more accepting of aspects of their own individual experience that had previously been avoided, and more accepting of the needs and anxieties of their partner. Although they both agreed that there were other areas of their relationship that deserved therapeutic attention, they felt sufficiently closer, and sufficiently safely closer, at that point to "try to do some of the work on our own," and so therapy concluded, with an open door to return at any time.

REFERENCES

Brewster, F., & Montie, K. A. (1987). Double life: What do family therapists really do in private practice? *The Family Networker,* 33–35.

Budman, S. H., & Gurman, A. S. (1988). *Theory and practice of brief therapy.* New York: Guilford.

Christensen, A., Jacobson, N. S., & Babcock, J. C. (1995). Integrative behavioral couple therapy. In N. S. Jacobson & A. S. Gurman (Eds.), *Clinical handbook of couple therapy* (2nd ed., pp. 31–64). New York: Guilford.

Donovan, J. (Ed.). (1999). *Short-term couple therapy.* New York: Guilford.

Gottman, J. (1994). *Why marriages succeed or fail.* New York: Simon and Schuster.

Gottman, J. (1999). *The marriage clinic: A scientifically based marital therapy.* New York: W. W. Norton.

Gurman, A. S. (1978). Contemporary marital therapies: A critique and comparative analysis of psychoanalytic, behavioral and systems theory approaches. In T. Paolino & B. McCrady (Eds.), *Marriage and marital therapy* (pp. 445–566). New York: Brunner/Mazel.

Gurman, A. S. (1981). Integrative marital therapy: Toward the development of an interpersonal approach. In S. H. Budman (Ed.), *Forms of brief therapy* (pp. 415–462). New York: Guilford.

Gurman, A. S. (1992). Integrative marital therapy: A time-sensitive model for working with couples. In S. H. Budman, M. Hoyt, & S. Friedman (Eds.), *The first session in brief therapy* (pp. 186–203). New York: Guilford.

Gurman, A. S. (2001). Brief therapy and family/couple therapy: An essential redundancy. *Clinical Psychology: Science and Practice, 8,* 51–65.

Gurman, A. S. (2002). Brief integrative marital therapy: A depth-behavioral approach. In A. S. Gurman & N. S. Jacobson (Eds.), *Clinical handbook of couple therapy* (3rd ed., pp. 180–220). New York: Guilford.

Gurman, A. S., & Fraenkel, P. (2002). The history of couple therapy: A millennial review. *Family Process, 41,* 199–260.

Hayes, S. C., & Toarmino, D. C. (1995). If behavioral principles are generally applicable, why is it necessary to understand cultural diversity? *The Behavior Therapist,* 21–23.

Johnson, S. M., & Denton, W. (2002). Emotionally focused couple therapy: Creating secure connections. In A. S. Gurman & N. S. Jacobson (Eds.), *Clinical handbook of couple therapy* (3rd ed., pp. 221–250). New York: Guilford.

Kanfer, F. H., & Saslow, G. (1969). Behavioral diagnosis. In C. M. Franks (Ed.), *Behavior therapy: Appraisal and status* (pp. 417–444). New York: Pergamon.

Lebow, J. L. (1997). The integrative revolution in couple and family therapy. *Journal of Marital and Family Therapy, 20,* 127–138.

Lebow, J. L. (1999). Building a science of couple relationships: Comments on two articles by Gottman and Levenson. *Family Process, 38,* 167–173.

Lebow, J. L., & Gurman, A. S. (1995). Research assessing couple and family therapy. *Annual Review of Psychology, 46,* 27–57.

Scharff, J. S., & Bagnini, C. (2002). Object relations couple therapy. In A. S. Gurman & N. S. Jacobson (Eds.), *Clinical handbook of couple therapy* (3rd ed., pp. 59–85). New York: Guilford.

Snyder, D. K., & Schneider, W. J. (2002). Affective reconstruction: A pluralistic, developmental approach. (pp. 151–179). In A. S. Gurman & N. S. Jacobson (Eds.), *Clinical handbook of couple therapy.* (3rd ed., pp. 151–179). New York: Guilford.

Stanton, M. D. (1981). Strategic approaches to family therapy. In A. S. Gurman & D. P. Kniskern (Eds.), *Handbook of family therapy* (pp. 361–402). New York: Brunner/Mazel.

CHAPTER 15

Creating Secure Connections: Emotionally Focused Couples Therapy

Scott R. Woolley and Susan M. Johnson

INTRODUCTION

The creation of a secure, long lasting romantic relationship is universally desired. Indeed, various forms of marriage or community sanctioned, committed relationships are found in virtually all cultures. However, in recent decades, industrialized countries have experienced unprecedented rates of marital breakup. Although the divorce rate seems to have stabilized, it has done so at extraordinarily high levels that are historically unprecedented (Pinsof, 2002).

Relationship discord, divorce, and other forms of relationship breakup are generally highly distressing for both adults and children. A substantial body of research has documented the impact of relationship distress and termination. Children whose parents do not remain together, for example, are more likely to experience poverty, violence, abuse, depression, serious mental health problems, academic problems, and long-term instability in their own adult romantic relationships. Adults who experience relationship breakup are more likely to acquire infectious diseases, have accidents, abuse drugs and alcohol, have financial problems, be depressed, develop serious mental illnesses, be unsatisfied with their lives, and die sooner. Similar problems are reported in those whose relationships are characterized by high degrees of conflict and distress (Amato & Booth, 1997; Kiecolt-Glaser, Malarkey, Cacioppo, & Glaser, 1994).

There is strong evidence that couple relationship distress is characterized by powerful negative emotions and responses that include criticism, hostility, anger, anxiety, jealousy, distancing, and defensiveness (Gottman, 1994). Reciprocal negative response patterns, such as criticize/demand followed by distancing/defense, evoke and maintain negative emotions, so that safe emotional engagement becomes more and more difficult. Recent research suggests that it is not so much the occurrence of conflict that distinguishes distressed marriages that end in divorce. Instead, decreases in affectional expression, positive emotional engagement, and partner responsiveness seem to predict relationship dissolution (Roberts & Greenberg, 2002).

The effective treatment of couple relationship distress has proved challenging.

Indeed, there are still only a small number of tested and proven approaches, the best validated being emotionally focused couples therapy (EFT) and behavioral marital therapy. Research on EFT is very positive. It indicates that between 70 and 73 percent of treated couples recover from distress, and 90 percent of treated couples are able to significantly improve their relationship when compared to untreated couples (Johnson, Hunsley, Greenberg, & Schindler, 1999). A 2-year follow-up on relationship distress in the parents of chronically ill children, a population at high risk for divorce, suggest that EFT has less of a problem with relapse than does behavioral therapy, and that some couples, even if faced with stressful events, continue to improve in the 2 years following termination from therapy (Cloutier, Manion, Walker, & Johnson, 2002).

EFT ROOTS AND ASSUMPTIONS

EFT is an integration of experiential, humanistic, and family systems approaches to treatment, and is firmly rooted in attachment theory. From the experiential, humanistic, and systemic philosophies, EFT has derived the following assumptions:

1. Even when people and relationships are highly distressed, they can heal, grow, and improve. The best therapeutic stance is a nonpathologizing one. Acceptance and validation of client experience is essential as a first step in the change process.

2. A collaborative, therapeutic relationship is a necessary part of the healing process.

3. People's inner and outer relational realities define each other. The manner in which emotions are constructed and expressed shapes habitual ways of engaging with significant others; engagement patterns, in turn, shape key emotional responses. Self-reinforcing feedback loops of emotional responses constitute the basic drama of intimate relationships. In fact, each key emotion has a distinctive dramatic plot. EFT is then a systemic therapy, but one that includes the inner realities of partners as part of the relational system.

4. Emotion is the primary organizing factor in relationship-defining interactions with loved ones. It is the music of the dance between intimates. Working with emotion is most often the best, most efficient, and often the only way to transform close relationships. Emotions tell us and our partners what matters most and what our needs are. They are a compass that directs us to what matters most. Emotions are compelling; they move and motivate us, and communicate to others.

5. Growth, healing, and change occur through new, corrective relationship experiences. The de-escalation of conflict can occur in many ways, but the creation of safe emotional engagement and a more secure bond requires new, corrective emotional experiences.

6. Attachment theory offers the couple therapist a map to the terrain of couple and family relationships. Adult love is best viewed as an attachment bond (Johnson, 2003a & 2003b).

From an EFT perspective, problematic responses are understood through a focus on context and interaction patterns. Indeed, responses cannot be understood without understanding the relational context in which they occur. All behavior is assumed to have a communication function, and assessment focuses on identifying negative, repetitive interaction patterns and relationship strategies, rather than personality traits. Both partners are assumed to contribute to and be victimized by destructive, negative patterns of interaction. Determining who is at fault or who is pathological is not a part of EFT. Instead, the focus is on interrupting destructive patterns and on creating safe, nurturing interactional events and cycles that redefine the relationship as safe and secure (Johnson, 2004a).

EFT is firmly rooted in attachment theory, which serves as a theory of love. From an attachment perspective, seeking and maintaining secure relationships is a primary motivating force that is active throughout life (Bowlby, 1988). Indeed, isolation and loss of connection are seen as inherently traumatizing (which is why solitary confinement is used as a torture technique). In attachment theory, as in many feminist approaches, secure interdependence is seen as necessary for true autonomy, not the antithesis of autonomy. From an attachment perspective, there is no such thing as too much dependency—only effective or ineffective dependency. Ineffective dependency produces anxious clinging and desperate coerciveness or depression and isolation, rather than autonomy. Research has found that those who have a sense of felt security with attachment figures also have a more coherent, positive, and articulated sense of self.

Secure couple relationships involve powerful emotional bonds where each partner is accessible and responsive to the needs of the other. These types of safe, committed, intimate relationships offer a secure base from which to explore the world (intellectually, emotionally, and physically). They can also provide a safe haven from the storms and traumas of life, and an optimal environment for healing when injuries occur. Secure bonds are the natural antidote to the traumas and terrors life inflicts (Johnson, 2002).

Behaviors that attempt to create safety, closeness, and security in intimate relationships are called *attachment strategies,* since they are designed to create and strengthen attachment bonds (Bowlby, 1988). Fear, hurt, and uncertainty activate attachment needs and lead people to engage in attachment strategies. Effective attachment strategies, such as asking in a clear, open way for comfort and reassurance, evoke emotional responsiveness in others, and optimally lead to a secure, safe relationship, in which the answer to the key questions, "Can I depend on you? Will you respond to me when I need you—when I am vulnerable?" is positive. Less effective attachment strategies often have the opposite effect. For example, complaining, nagging, or even yelling are most often attempts to call up greater accessibility and responsiveness in a partner, even though they usually have the opposite effect. These responses are also often reactions to feeling shut out or abandoned. Withdrawal or placating is often an attempt to contain an interaction so that it does not get out of control or become destructive—although again, these strategies usually have the opposite effect. Withdrawal can also be an attempt to avoid rejection or it can be a possible confirmation that the self is unlovable. Accessibility and responsiveness are the touchstones of a positive, secure bond.

Attachment theory views the sense of self as being ongoingly defined in inter-actions with significant others. Working models of the self and the other are shaped and reshaped by our interactions with loved ones. These models are not just cognitive schemas, but involve goals, beliefs, expectations, and strategies that are infused with emotion. Securely attached people see themselves as worthy of love and care, and as basically competent and agentic people. They believe others will be responsive when needed, and can better tolerate difference and distance in others when necessary. More insecurely attached people often have serious ques-tions about whether they are worthy of love, whether they can obtain love and security in relationships, and whether others can be trusted to be responsive and nurturing. They tend, then, to either avoid close connection and depending on others, or to anxiously push for this connection. EFT views the drama of marital distress through the lens of attachment deprivation, loss, rejection, and abandon-ment, and assumes that there is a universal need to be valued by and connected to key others that crosses cultures and continents. Once attachment anxieties and needs are addressed and partners can form a more secure bond, they are able to access and use communication and problem-solving skills, and to open the door to the compassion and caring that elude them in the heat of the drama of distress.

TREATMENT IN EFT

Mechanisms of Change

The primary process of change in EFT involves identifying the negative cycles of interaction, accessing the emotions that are both a response to and organizers of these cycles, and reprocessing these emotions to create new responses that shape secure bonding events and new cycles of trust and security. This is very different than cognitive restructuring, problem solving, or skill building. In EFT, it is as-sumed that once emotional bonding events occur and the interactional cycle has become secure and supportive, couples essentially have, or can help each other generate, the skills and insights needed to solve their own problems. It is emotional experiencing and reprocessing that is seen as a key component in changing nega-tive cycles and creating a safe connection.

In EFT, the therapist is an active agent and plays a central role in creating change. For example, the therapist actively works to create strong therapeutic re-lationships with both members of the couple, which assists in conflict de-escalation and helps create the security needed for strong emotional experiencing. The ther-apist helps the couple identify their negative cycle and access the emotions that underlie it, and then actively helps the couple develop new ways of interacting that lead to powerful bonding events and new, safe cycles of interaction.

The Three Stages and Nine Steps of Change

In EFT, there are three stages in the change process: de-escalation of negative cycles, restructuring interactional positions toward secure connection, and con-solidation and integration. There are nine interactive steps within these stages (see Table 15.1 for an overview). These steps are not rigidly sequential but are flexibly

Table 15.1.   The Three Stages and Nine Steps of EFT

Stage 1: Assessment and Cycle De-escalation
 1. Create an alliance and identify the conflict issues in their core struggle.
 2. Identify the negative interaction cycle, and each partner's position in that cycle.
 3. Access unacknowledged primary emotions underlying interactional positions.
 4. Reframe the problem in terms of underlying emotions, attachment needs, and the negative cycle.

Stage 2: Changing Interactional Positions and Creating Bonding Events
 5. Promote identification with disowned needs and aspects of self, and integrate these into relationship interactions.
 6. Promote acceptance of the other partner's experiences, aspects of self, and new interaction patterns.
 7. Facilitate the expression of needs and wants to restructure the interaction, and create emotional engagement.

Stage 3: Consolidation and Integration
 8. Facilitate the emergence of new solutions to problematic interactions and old relationship issues.
 9. Consolidate new positions and new cycles of attachment behaviors.

interactive and additive, so that often an EFT therapist is working on multiple steps at the same time.

Stage 1—De-escalation. The de-escalation stage involves helping the couple stop fighting, criticizing, attacking, and defending. The first step is to create an alliance and to identify what they typically struggle with or fight about—the themes and moves in their drama of distress. It is essential that each partner feels completely heard and understood by the therapist, in order to start building the essential therapeutic bonds of safety and security.

The second step is for the therapist to identify the cycle, at least in its basic form—the action tendencies the couple is caught in. This cycle usually involves a pursue/blame/criticize/coerce—withdraw/placate/defend/distance pattern. In this step, the therapist can also begin to identify the overt reactive emotions that are associated with each position. For example, the therapist may say to the wife, "So, when you both get home and you start on dinner and he starts watching television, you get irritated and try to get him to help. However, because you are irritated, your attempts to get him to help often come out as complaints or criticisms." Then to the husband the therapist might comment, "You hear her complaining about you and you hang back. You say that you will be there in just a moment in order to get her to settle down, but inside, you also feel irritated, because it seems that she is not willing to even let you rest for a bit after work." Then the therapist says to the wife, "When he doesn't come after he says he will, you get angry, like your needs don't matter, and eventually you come in and let him have it. At that point [to the husband] you feel attacked and either defend yourself, you attack back, or you just try to ignore her. You turn away and kind of shut down. Either way [to the wife], that is just more upsetting to you, and you either attack some more or you leave, and the two of you are cold with each other for the rest of the evening. Is that how it goes?" The therapist then places this dance in an attachment frame; "This leaves you both feeling alone and unsupported," and frames the dance as having a life of its own, victimizing both partners.

The third step is to access and make explicit the unacknowledged attachment emotions that underlie and drive the cycle. In the prior example, this might involve accessing emotions, such as the wife's hurt and sadness over his distance, her sense of feeling disrespected and used, her fear of abandonment, and her loneliness. It might also involve accessing the husband's hurts, his fears of her anger, and his own loneliness and sense of inadequacy or failure. The safety and accurate empathy and validation offered by the therapist encourages even the most inexpressive, withdrawn partners to begin to access and explore underlying emotions. Empathic reflection and gentle, evocative questioning structures the session and reassures partners that they will not be blamed or pathologized. The therapist uses vivid but simple nonpathologizing words, such as speaking of how a partner shuts down to stop the fights, to try to smooth out the ride with the partner, as well as to limit the exchange of painful messages; but, in the process, she or he shuts the other partner out and so evokes anger in that partner. In EFT, clients tell us that they feel seen, understood, and supported, and so can risk opening up in a session and discovering their underlying emotions. Blocks to emotional experience are also specified, validated, and explored.

In the fourth step, the final step in Stage 1—De-escalation, the therapist systematically reframes the problem in terms of the cycle the couple is caught in, their underlying emotions that are driving the cycle, and their attachment needs and fears. For example, the therapist might reframe the conflict over household tasks in the following manner: "If I am getting this right, what is actually happening here is that you are caught in this cycle, where you [to the wife] want him more engaged, not only in helping around the house, but also just in talking and sharing. But, you end up feeling used, hurt, abandoned, and afraid, because he seems so indifferent to you. However, it doesn't feel safe enough to talk about those feelings, so instead you get angry and you criticize him—you push to get a response in hopes that he will listen and will engage with you.

"On your end of this cycle [to the husband], you end up being afraid of her anger and criticism and you feel hurt when she attacks you. In response, your first response tends to be to tell her what you think she wants to hear, to placate her, to try to get her to settle down so it will be safer. But then, because of your own hurts and fears, you stay away and don't follow through on promises, and so she feels even more hurt and angry—and that comes out in the form of more criticism. You have gotten used to just shutting down and avoiding her anger and the message that she is disappointed with you."

Then to both of them the therapist might say, "So you are both caught in this cycle where you [to the wife] pursue and attack in various forms, and you [to the husband] placate, occasionally attack back, and ultimately withdraw. However, underneath, you both end up feeling deeply hurt and afraid that the other person will leave you. You both care deeply about each other but you don't talk about it, because this cycle with the hurt and fear and anger gets in the way."

The process of identifying the conflict issues, the cycle and the emotions that underlie the cycle, and then reframing the marital problem in terms of this cycle and the emotions that underlie it, is usually very effective in de-escalating conflicts and creating more hope, safety, and collaboration. When done successfully, the cycle becomes the enemy, not the other spouse.

Stage 2—Changing interactional position and creating new bonding events. The first step in changing interactional positions is promoting the articulation of disowned attachment fears, needs, and desires, and working to integrate them into the interactions of the couple in ways that begin to create new responses (Step 5). For example, the husband in the couple described might begin to access and confide his sense of helplessness and failure. Process research on EFT indicates that partners who allow themselves to deeply feel their own emotional experience change the most in therapy. Often, partners are so caught in the experience of secondary reactive emotions such as anger, frustration, and resentment, that they do not identify with their deeper primary emotions, such as loneliness, hurt, and fear, and their needs for safety and connection. Helping clients access and identify with their own disowned needs and emotions is often done through repeatedly emphasizing, using each partner's own language, the primary emotions and needs that underlie the issues being processed in the session. It is critical for the therapist to create as safe an environment as possible for these emotional expressions, which are often very difficult for clients to engage with and express. It is also critical for the therapist to repeatedly heighten and validate these primary emotional expressions as being real and important. This step lays the foundation for the key change events, withdrawer reengagement and blamer softening (Johnson & Denton, 2002), which are key shifts in the development of new interactional positions and in helping the couple reengage in a safe and secure manner.

The next step in changing interactional positions is promoting acceptance of the other partner's primary emotional experiences and needs (Step 6). In this step, partners see each other in a new light. For example, a withdrawing husband, who may have seen his wife as being angry and critical, begins to see her loneliness and fear of abandonment. A wife who may have seen her distant husband as purposely shutting her out may instead see him as being frozen in his fear of not being able to respond adequately or to keep their conflict from getting out of control.

It is critical that in this step the other spouse is seen as *being* different, not just *acting* different. In order for this shift to occur, spouses must both see real emotional expression, and be supported as they begin to trust this new perception and see their spouse as being different. As new emotional needs and desires are expressed by one partner, it is quite common for the other spouse to not believe them or have a hard time accepting them. Often, new emotional expressions need to be highlighted and repeated for the other spouse to trust them. It is also very important for the therapist to validate the listening partner's reactions to new emotional expressions. For example, saying "You are not used to hearing this from him. You are used to seeing him as being distant and cut-off. You are not used to seeing him as feeling scared, and as desiring to come close. This is like seeing a whole different side of him, and it is hard to trust that it is real or will stay. It is going to take some time to trust this new side of him. Is that it?" This kind of support helps the listening spouse see new emotional responses as being real, and validates how different they might appear from what has previously been seen. As with the other steps, it is common for this step to evolve over several sessions, with the primary emotional expressions of attachment fears and longings by both spouses—along with the reactions of both to new expressions by the other—being repeatedly being highlighted and validated.

The final step in changing interactional positions involves facilitating the expression of needs and wants directly between partners, so as to restructure the interaction and create emotional engagement (Step 7). In this step, the therapist is working to create emotional engagement through creating enactments where the couple shares primary emotional experiences, needs, and desires directly with each other. More explicitly, the therapist is first working to help a less engaged spouse become fully open and engaged, and a critical spouse to soften and reach for comfort and connection in a way that pulls the partner towards him or her. This last move, called a softening, is a critical change event in EFT, and is associated with successful outcomes (Bradley & Furrow, 2004). This step, in which both spouses are reciprocally engaged and responsive, involves creating new and powerful bonding events that redefine the partner as a safe attachment figure who can be trusted. These events create new, positive cycles of trusting, caring, and engagement that become as self-reinforcing as the old negative cycles were (Johnson, 2004a). This Stage 2 change event is also one of the more difficult tasks in EFT, and is a place that therapists can get stuck. Consequently, it will be described in some detail.

In order for the critical partner to soften, the less engaged partner must already be reengaged in the relationship and be relatively accessible and responsive. This reengagement involves having the less engaged partner assert his or her needs and having those needs and desires validated and supported. If the previously less engaged partner is not reengaged, the critical partner will find it too dangerous to soften and reach for the other partner, or will reach for the partner and find the partner not there—which can easily then be wounding, and reinforce old, negative perceptions of the other. Reengagement occurs through highlighting the needs and desires that have been accessed in previous steps and encouraging their direct and open expression to the other spouse. It is very important that these expressions reflect primary, core attachment needs around issues of safety and connection, not instrumental or less central desires. For example, a formerly distancing spouse may say, "I want to be connected with you. I want a safe relationship with you where I don't run away, and so I need you to stop being so critical of me. I really do care for you and need you, and I want to connect with you and learn to really be there." This type of expression of core attachment desires, done in a tender and soft manner, is important in facilitating enough safety for the blaming partner to then reach and engage.

Once the critical, pursuing spouse can see the formerly distancing spouse as being present and engaged and desiring contact, it is time for the therapist to work to directly facilitate a softening. To do this, the therapist accesses primary attachment needs in the critical spouse and encourages their expression to the other partner. This might look something like the following with a newly engaged husband and a formerly critical wife:

Therapist: I get the idea that you are feeling confused right now to see him opening up like this. Is this a little hard to grasp?

Wife: Yes, yes, I don't know why he can't be like this all the time.

Therapist: Yes, so often he has been distant. But now he is engaged—he is really here. Do you know what you need from him right now?

Wife: I don't know.

Therapist: What is happening right now for you? What is going on inside of you?

Wife: Well, I am still angry, maybe—he has been gone for so long and it has been so hard to get him to open up.

Therapist: Yes, you are angry that he hasn't been there for you and it has been so painful for you. (*She nods. Therapist continues in an intense, soft voice.*) It is very painful, very painful to have been alone in this relationship for so long (*She nods and weeps*).

Therapist (to the husband): Can you see her pain, how difficult it has been for her to feel alone in this relationship all these years?

Husband: Yes, I see that it has been difficult for her. It has been difficult for both of us, but I didn't see her pain like I see it now.

Therapist: Yes, you didn't see her pain, just her anger, but what is it like to see her pain now?

Husband: It is difficult, I want to help, I want to comfort.

Therapist: Can you tell her that? Talk to her and tell her about that.

Husband (turning to his wife): I really want to comfort you, I want to be there for you like I haven't been in the past. Please let me in, give me a chance.

Therapist (to the wife): Can you hear him? Can you hear him ask for you to risk it and give him a chance?

Wife: Yes, but it, it is very scary—I'm not sure if I can.

Therapist: Yes, yes, it is scary. Can you tell him it is scary to risk opening up to him?

Wife (to the husband): It is scary to open up to you again and trust you (*in a soft and scared voice*).

Husband: I know, I haven't been there for you, but I want to be there. Please give me a chance. See that I am different.

Wife: I want to, but it is hard. If I do, I don't want you to leave me again—to shut me out in the cold.

Therapist: So if you risk you have to know he'll respond—you don't want him to leave you, it is scary that he could again, but can you see him right now—how much he wants to support you (*pointing to the husband*). Can you ask him for support and comfort right now?

Wife (to the husband): I need your support. Don't leave me. This is scary, but I need you. I just want you to hold me. (*Husband leans over and embraces the wife. Therapists backs away and is silent*).

To some degree, every softening is a little different—but there is a general pattern. The process steps in this pattern have been identified and validated in research studies and involve the following sequence of events. When there is a female blamer and a male withdrawer, the following sequence occurs.

1. She expands her experience and accesses specific attachment fears, sometimes shame (as in, "I am weak—should not need this"), and the longing for contact and comfort. Emotions tell us what we need.

2. She engages her partner in a different way. Fear organizes a more affiliative stance. She articulates emotional needs, and so changes her stance in the dance. New emotions prime new responses and actions.

3. Her partner sees her differently, as afraid rather than dangerous, and is pulled toward her by her expressions of vulnerability.

4. She risks and reaches and he comforts. She sees him differently. A new, compelling cycle is initiated—an antidote to negative interactions—a redefinition of the relationship as a secure bond.

5. They exhibit more open communication. This then leads into more flexible problem solving and resilient coping. The couple can then go on to resolve issues and problems (Stage 3 of EFT).

6. There are shifts in both partner's sense of self. Both can comfort and be comforted. Both are defined as "lovable" and entitled to caring.

Stage 3—Consolidation and integration. The final phase in EFT involves helping couples find new solutions to old problems (Step 8) and consolidate their new interaction cycles and integrate them into their everyday lives (Step 9). Once a couple has reengaged and has replaced old cycles with cycles of intimacy, safety, and engagement, it can be helpful to revisit old issues. Sometimes these are no longer issues, because the underlying attachment issues that fueled them have been resolved. For example, a couple who used to fight about whether or not to have children may now feel secure enough to welcome a child into their relationship, or a couple who used to fight about where to go on vacation may now work together on it, since vacation may no longer represent escaping the relationship.

However, it is common for longstanding, difficult issues to need some type of resolution. The job of the therapist is to facilitate the discussion and to highlight new ways of interacting around the problems. Often, in the new atmosphere of trust, new solutions emerge to old problems. For example, a couple who have fought over how to deal with in-laws may come to an agreement on structuring time and supporting each other when visiting each other's family. In some cases, couples will learn to agree to disagree, which is a solution that would have been intolerable when the relational bond was weak, but can now be a comfortable solution and can help an issue become relatively insignificant.

In the final step of EFT, the therapist helps the couple consolidate and integrate their gains into their everyday lives. This involves highlighting the changes they have made, processing how different their relationship is, and getting them to talk about how they will continue to strengthen their relationship through connecting and supporting each other's primary attachment needs for security, support, safety, and love. The therapist focuses on and highlights moves and moments of bonding and connection, so that they recognize them and focus on how they are going to keep these moments of connection alive. Often, this involves outlining regular times for connection or small rituals that help them create this connection. For example, one couple would come home and drink cocoa with each other at the kitchen table every night and talk about what happened to each of them during the day. Another couple developed "snuggle times" where they would snuggle on the couch and talk about their day or problems or successes, and they would regularly ask each other for "snuggle time."

PRIMARY PROCESSES AND INTERVENTIONS IN EFT

The EFT therapist works both intrapsychically (with a focus on emotion), and interpersonally (with a focus on response patterns). It is critical for an EFT therapist to create a strong therapeutic alliance, to be comfortable with intense emotions, and to be able to access, shape, and expand emotional expression. It is also essential for the EFT therapist to be able to track and shape ongoing interactional processes. There are a number of interventions used by EFT therapists to accomplish these tasks (see Table 15.2 for an overview). They are explained briefly here and in more depth elsewhere (Johnson & Denton, 2002; Johnson, in press).

Creating and Maintaining a Therapeutic Alliance

Creating and maintaining the therapeutic alliance is critical to all other interventions in EFT. It is the base on which all other interventions rest. The goal is for the therapist to establish the trust and safety with each client that will enable the client to have the security in therapy to risk being vulnerable, experiencing strong emotion, and exploring new ways of interacting. To establish and maintain a strong alliance, the EFT therapist works hard to empathically attune to each client and to create an atmosphere of acceptance and safety. The therapist has to validate each partner's role in the system, and the choices and coping mechanisms they have felt compelled to make, without invalidating or blaming the other spouse. The therapist attempts to be present, genuine, and transparent, and to actively monitor the connection with each partner.

Empathic attunement is central to the implementation of EFT. Empathy has been described as the active use of imagination to momentarily inhabit another's

Table 15.2   Primary EFT Interventions

Exploring, Expanding, and Reformulating Emotions
  1. Reflecting emotional experience.
  2. Validation.
  3. Evocative responding.
  4. Heightening.
  5. Empathic conjecture.

Restructuring Interactions
  1. Tracking, reflecting, and replaying interactions.
  2. Reframing in the context of the cycle and attachment processes.
  3. Restructuring and shaping interactions.

world. An EFT therapist is constantly working to empathically attune to clients' experiences of themselves and their relationships, and to communicate that understanding to the clients in such a way that they know the therapist is connected to and understands their experiences. The therapist processes experience *with* each client, and *discovers* new elements of this experience with each client.

Apart from creating and maintaining the alliance, the two central tasks for the EFT therapist are to access, shape, and expand emotion, and to restructure interventions to create a more secure bond between partners.

Task One: To Access, Shape, and Expand Emotion

Accessing, shaping, and expanding emotional experience is at the heart of the EFT change process. There are at least five core interventions used in EFT to access, shape, and expand emotional experience: reflection, validation, evocative responding, heightening, and interpretation or conjecture. Each is described briefly here.

Reflecting Emotional Experience

Reflecting emotional experience is not simply paraphrasing, but rather requires an intense focus by the therapist to accurately read, understand, and communicate back to the client the client's emotional process. If done well, the client feels seen and understood. For example, a therapist might say, "So what I think you are saying is that it is intensely painful, very very difficult for you when your husband simply turns away from you and shuts you out. Is that is it?" The main function of reflection is to track emotional processes, build and strengthen the therapeutic alliance, and clarify emotional responses that underlie interactional positions. Reflection also structures and focuses a session, since the therapist reflects certain elements and bypasses others. A good reflection also helps to order and organize experience so that it can be grasped more fully.

Validation

Validating the perceptions, experiences, and emotions of both members of the couple supports each member of the couple. It also helps partners explore how they construct their experiences. Validation of a hostile response might look something like this: "It is very scary to reach for him when he has not been there in the past—very scary. Part of you just wants to refuse—to tell him to go to hell—that hell will freeze over before you risk again—part of you might even want to know you can hurt him—is that it?" The main function of validation is to legitimize emotions and experiences, and help partners own their own response, as well as building the alliance.

Evocative Responding

The Latin word *evocare* means "to call." Evocative responding involves focusing on and calling up the unclear or emerging or bypassed aspects of a client's experience. The therapist works to expand the experience through open questions about specific stimuli, bodily responses, associated desires and meanings, and action tendencies. For example, the therapist might say, "When you say that, something changed in your eyes. What is happening to you right now? What is that in your eyes?" Or, "So when you see her open like this, part of you wants to reach out and connect, but part of you really wants to run and hide. Is that it?" Evocative responding develops and expands the elements of the client's experience to help reorganize the experience. It also can help formulate unclear or marginalized elements of experience for the first time, and encourages exploration and engagement.

Heightening

Heightening involves using repetition, images, metaphors, or enactments to focus on or intensify emotion, experience, meaning, or interaction. For example, it might sound like, "So could you turn to her and tell her about how inadequate you feel about being able to meet her needs." Or, "I hear you saying that this is very painful, it hurts a great deal, it is so painful that you just want to run so you don't get hurt any more, so you don't have to feel the intense pain again. It is that painful that you just want to run." The main function of heightening is to highlight key experiences that organize responses, or to help formulate new experiences that reorganize the interaction. Heightening helps to distill a partner's experience to its core elements, and to have clients engage with, rather than discuss or reflect on, experience from a distance.

Empathic Conjecture or Interpretation

Empathic conjecture involves making inferences about the emotional experience of the clients—to expand and clarify the experience so that the client can create new levels of meaning. The goal is not to create insight per se, but rather to facilitate more intense experiencing, which helps create new meanings. The therapist goes one step ahead, one step further than the client. For example, "I get the idea somehow that underneath that anger this is very difficult for you, it is very, very painful—is that what is happening when you get angry?" Or, "It seems that whenever you attack her, what is happening underneath is that you are feeling very unloved and afraid that she is going to leave you or reject you. Is that right?" The main functions of empathic conjecture are to clarify and formulate new meanings, especially regarding interactional positions and definitions of self.

Task Two: Restructuring Interventions

There are essentially three types of interventions used in EFT to restructure the relationship and create emotional engagement. They are: tracking, reflecting, and replaying interaction; reframing problems and symptoms in the context of the cycle and attachment processes; and restructuring and reshaping interactions.

Tracking, Reflecting, and Replaying Interactions

Here, the therapist focuses on both the emotions of the clients and their behavioral interaction processes, and reflects and replays them to the couple. For example, "So what just happened here? It seems that you dropped your anger and reached out to him. It is that right? And then you, Bob, it seems that you were still focused on her anger and you missed her attempt to connect. Is that right? Is that what happened?" The main functions are to slow down and clarify the interactional dance and to replay important interactional sequences in order to intensify them.

Reframing in the Context of the Cycle and Attachment Processes

Reframing in the context of the cycle can be a powerful way of helping the couple experience themselves and each other differently. For example, "You freeze because she matters to you so much, not because you don't care. But Sally, that is not the way you experience it. You don't see it as caring when he freezes up." Reframing in the context of the cycle and attachment processes helps shift the meaning of specific responses, and helps to develop a more positive perception of the partner.

Restructuring and Shaping Interactions

This is done through enacting present positions so that they can be seen and owned, enacting new behaviors based upon new emotional responses, and structuring specific responses to build change events. The therapist might say, for example, "Can you tell him 'I am shutting you out so that you can't hurt me anymore'?" Or, "Could you turn and tell her how much you really want to connect with her in a safe way?" Or, "Could you ask him for what you need right now?" The primary function is to expand and clarify negative interaction patterns and structure new interactions which lead to new emotional experiences of the other.

The manner in which these interventions are offered to clients is crucial. The acronym RISSSC is used to describe the therapists nonverbal manner that potentiates EFT interventions (Johnson, 2004a). At key moments the therapist often *R*epeats client's phrases or images; the therapist uses *I*mages whenever possible, since they evoke physiological responses and enhance engagement in an evolving experience; the therapist tends to speak *S*oftly, *S*lowly, and in *S*imple language at key times in therapy. The therapist also notes and returns to each *C*lient's specific phrases and ways of expressing him- or herself.

SPECIAL ISSUES IN EFT

Diversity

Attachment needs and longings, primary emotions and the interactive cycles that characterize couple relationships are seen as universal in EFT, but how they are expressed is often culturally defined and can be very different. Contextual issues are key in EFT, and therapists must include issues of social class, cultural oppression, and cultural differences. Although research on EFT has been done primarily with white North Americans, EFT has been used effectively with African Americans, Latino, Asian, Middle Eastern, cross-cultural, and same-gender couples living in North America. Additionally, EFT trainers have found that Native American therapists, and therapists in Australia, England, Finland, India, Israel, Hong Kong, and Taiwan have enthusiastically embraced EFT and believe it works well with the couples they treat.

A key factor in using EFT with diverse populations is in understanding the practices and language of love and safety in the couple's culture or cultures. In some cultures, the direct labeling of emotions such as fear and vulnerability may not be appropriate. Instead of saying, "You get afraid and then you run" the therapist may say, "It is very unpleasant for you when your wife does this, very unpleasant—you just want to leave or ignore her—is that right?" Therapists may need to ask specific questions and make adjustments in typical procedures based on the cultural meanings and practices around marriage, couple identities and roles, sexuality, and relationships with in-laws and children. For example, in cultures where a husband's mother is traditionally heavily involved in the couple relationship, her role in the cycle can be described, the emotions related to her role can be accessed and expressed (in a culturally safe manner), and de-escalation and reengagement can involve the mother and her role, even if she never enters therapy. The basic skills of attending, genuine empathy, and working with emotion, and the ability to identify patterns, are powerful in understanding and creating safety, and in working with couples from diverse cultural backgrounds. Ignoring cultural practices, processes, and differences can make therapy unsafe and make it impossible to develop and maintain a therapeutic relationship, rendering the effective use of EFT impossible.

Contraindications

The main contraindications in EFT are conditions that would make it impossible to create trust. Typically, these are ongoing physical violence, serious, active addictions, or ongoing affairs. In order to effectively do EFT, violence needs to be contained or stopped, so there can be enough safety to start to produce trust. The same is true in most cases for serious, active addictions and ongoing affairs, both of which tend to result in serious continued deception, betrayal, and instability.

Attachment Injuries

An attachment injury is a specific type of betrayal, abandonment, or violation of trust that creates an impasse in the process of relationship repair (Johnson, Makinen & Millikin, 2001). They can be viewed as relationship traumas, which call into question basic attachment assumptions about the relationship and the intentions of the other partner. The betrayal most often occurs at a crucial moment of need—when someone is vulnerable and needs the connection with the other. The injury then defines the relationship as insecure for the injured party. For example, it is common for an attachment injury to occur if a woman has a miscarriage or goes into labor and her husband is not there or does not make an effort to be there.

Sometimes there is a single injury and sometimes there are multiple injuries that have occurred over a period of years. The degree of injury often depends on how the injured partner interprets the event and how the other spouse responds to expressions of hurt by the injured spouse. If the injuring spouse denies, minimizes, or dismisses the injury, it compounds the injury. Attachment injuries are best understood in terms of their attachment significance, not their content. In one couple, both had affairs, but only one construed this as an attachment injury. The wife was very upset at how much her husband was working, and told him that if he didn't work less she was going to have an affair. He kept working late, so she told him who she was going to have the affair with; he kept working, so she went ahead and had the affair, and told him all about it. He then went and had an affair himself, but he did it secretly. She broke off her affair because she felt guilty, and it wasn't working to get her husband away from work, and then found out about his affair. She also learned that he was with his lover on a day when she was robbed when going to her car, and thus he wasn't with her. She had a deep attachment injury as a result of his affair, whereas he did not have an attachment injury from her affair.

Once an attachment injury has occurred, there can be flashbacks at moments of risk or emotional engagement so that the relationship is defined as dangerous and the injury blocks close engagement. In many ways, attachment injuries parallel the symptoms of Posttraumatic Stress Disorder, including excessive rumination and hypervigilance. Because attachment injuries leave an indelible imprint they cannot be left behind, but must be dealt with. Seven steps are identified in the EFT literature in healing an attachment injury.

1. The injured partner articulates injury and its impact in detail.

2. The injured partner integrates the narrative and emotion and accesses attachment fears and longings associated with the injury event.

3. The other partner understands the significance of the event and acknowledges the partner's pain and suffering.

4. The injured partner moves toward a more integrated articulation of the injury, and ties it to the attachment bond.

5. The other partner acknowledges responsibility, and empathically engages.

6. The injured partner asks for reparative comfort and caring.

7. There is a bonding event or events, which are an antidote to the traumatic experience, and the relationship is redefined as a potential safe haven.

Like the steps of EFT, the steps of healing an attachment injury are often not followed in a linear, sequential manner, but each step is important to bring about a full resolution of the injury. The steps, along with detailed explanations of how to help couples through each task are found in Johnson, Makinen, & Millikin (2000) and in Johnson (2004a).

EFT with Trauma Survivors

Many people who come for couple therapy are trauma survivors, either from childhood traumas or recent adulthood traumas. A traumatic response follows exposure to an extreme stressor, and usually involves intense fear, pain, helplessness, or horror. It is especially severe if the stressor is of human design because it is a violation of the human connection. The trauma literature tells us (van der Kolk, Perry, & Herman, 1991) that the best predictors of the effects of trauma are whether a person can seek and obtain comfort in the arms of another, rather than the specifics of the trauma history itself.

Trauma symptoms usually involve difficulties in regulating emotions. For example, survivors often oscillate between hypervigilance or angry outbursts and frozen numbness or depression. Flashbacks, regression, and internal disorganization are not uncommon, and sexuality and associated intimacy is often a problem.

From an EFT perspective, the natural antidote to trauma is a safe, secure, connected relationship (Johnson, 2002). Often, therapists try to provide that for clients. However, therapists are often not available when clients need them most. Partners who are engaged and responsive can provide a safe haven. In a distressed relationship, however, the partner is perceived as being dangerous. It is not uncommon for trauma survivors to seek contact with their partner, only to find that that contact is too scary to maintain, and then push away, often leaving the partner confused and hurt. The lack of a safe haven perpetuates the effects of trauma, and the effects of trauma perpetuate relationship distress.

There are several ways in which therapy with a couple that has a trauma survivor is different from regular EFT. There is generally more distress and, often, highly intense cycles of distance, defensiveness, and distrust. Violence and substance abuse are also more likely. There is a need to offer psychoeducational information regarding trauma and the effects of trauma on relationship cycles. The therapeutic alliance is always more fragile, and has to be constantly monitored—and the therapist must be particularly collaborative and transparent. Emotional storms and crises must be expected, and emotion must be contained as well as heightened. Defenses are validated but not undermined. Validation allows survivors to slowly evaluate their need for their defenses, and either continue to use them or let them go. Shame often overrides positive cues, such as expressions of caring in trauma survivors, especially sexual abuse survivors, so working with shame responses is critical. The destination of therapy may also be more idiosyncratic and specific to the couple. For example, instead of working toward a frequent, spontaneous sexual life, a couple may instead focus on developing a safe, cuddling connection, and carefully structure and limit more involved sexual intimacy. The need to coordinate with other therapists is critical, and safety is everything. Risks must then be "sliced thin," and clients supported at each step.

Dealing with Impasses

Impasses in EFT generally occur in getting the couple to de-escalate, or, in Stage 2 change events, getting the withdrawer to reengage, or especially in getting the blaming partner to soften. There are a number of interventions that can help, including making the impasse explicit, accepting clients inability to risk, "slicing risks thinner," and using stories and disquisitions to reflect the in-session process.

Making the Impasse Explicit

Here, the therapist reflects and heightens both the emotions and the interactional elements of an impasse. As the impasse is repeatedly processed, different elements come forth that can help in breaking up the impasse. The change comes from experiencing fully and owning a response that threatens the relationship, and how compelling and legitimate these responses are. So, when a client is able to say, "I can't—I will not let you in—I will shut you out—even though I know it terrifies you and pushes you away," this is the beginning for this client letting his or her spouse in.

"Slicing Risks Thinner"

Here, the therapist works to identify, in as much detail as possible, the very core emotions and interactional strategies and cycles that are related to the impasse. This is often done through detailed, empathic conjecture around each person's position in the cycle, and tying it to action tendencies and interactions. Like making the impasse explicit, slicing it thinner brings about change through helping the couple fully experience what is happening around the impasse for each of them, and how that translates into actions and patterns. If a partner cannot turn and share new emotions with his or her spouse, the therapist will ask him or her to tell the spouse that it is too hard to share these emotions—thus beginning the process of sharing.

Disquisitions

A disquisition is a story that is told that vividly reflects the negative pattern and the drama the couple is caught in, but in an indirect manner, that does not elicit resistance or defensiveness. The story can involve fantasy, or other clients (real or imagined), or a story from some other source. The therapist attempts to capture the couple's essential attachment drama, but in a totally unchallenging manner. This intervention is described in Johnson (2004a).

Family Therapy and EFT

There is a family version of Emotionally Focused Therapy, and its effectiveness has been tested (Johnson, Maddeaux, & Blouin, 1998). Attachment security is viewed as an inner resource that allows people to cope with the trials of parenting more effectively (Simpson, Rholes, Campbell, Wilson, & Tran, 2002). We assume, then, that when partners can create a secure bond this promotes secure bonding between parents and children and positive parenting behaviors, so that the family can become a safe haven that promotes the growth of all members.

EFT RESEARCH

EFT has a strong empirical base. There are now five process studies, 11 outcome studies, a meta-analysis, and a 2-year follow-up study (Clothier, Manion, Walker, & Johnson, 2002) supporting the validity and effectiveness of EFT. The focus of EFT is also consistent with John Gottman's and other researchers' groundbreaking research on the nature of marital distress and satisfaction (Gottman, 1994); the theory of close relationships used in EFT, namely attachment theory, has a substantial and ever-growing research base (Cassidy & Shaver, 1999; Johnson & Whiffen, 2003).

Process Research

A unique aspect of EFT is that it is informed by process research, research that is designed to investigate and identify change processes and interventions that are relevant and useful to clinicians. For example, Bradley and Furrow (2004) studied softenings, and identified close linkages between therapist interventions and successful softenings, stressing the importance of interventions such as evocative responding and heightening. There has also been research that shows that clients who have the deepest emotional experiences in session have the greatest satisfaction with therapy, and have the best outcomes (summarized in Johnson, Hunsley, Greenberg, & Schindler, 1999). People often wonder whether EFT can be effective with traditional, inexpressive men. Research on predictors of success in EFT has indicated that the degree of traditionality does not impact effectiveness, and that older men, described as inexpressive by their spouse, do well in EFT. In this research, the initial degree of distress predicted only 4 percent of the variance in outcome 3 months after the end of therapy, suggesting that initial distress level is not a major factor in EFT outcomes. The faith of the female partner—that her spouse still cared for her—and the quality of the alliance were the best predictors of success in EFT in this study.

Outcome Research

EFT has demonstrated greater effects than other approaches that have been tested (Johnson et al., 1999; Johnson, 2003c), and a generally large effect size. The finding that 70 to 73 percent of couples recover from distress in 10 to 12 sessions of EFT, and that 90 percent improve significantly, is extremely positive. The main way in which research studies differ from general practice is that treatment is shorter in research studies (in clinical practice EFT is usually implemented in 15 to 20 sessions), due to regular clinical supervision and support.

EFT is also used in clinical practice with many different kinds of couples; couples dealing with depression and anxiety disorders such as Posttraumatic Stress Disorder (PTSD) for example, same-sex couples, minority and cross-cultural couples, and low socioeconomic couples. Ongoing studies include the effectiveness of EFT with maritally distressed breast cancer patients and with trauma survivors.

--------------------------------- **Case Study** ---------------------------------

In order to give the reader a brief snapshot of a key change event in EFT, a sketch of key client statements follows. The client, Sam, was a clinically depressed and highly intellectual older man who had suddenly announced to his wife of 28 years that he no longer wished to be married to her. She became intensely distressed and he very reluctantly agreed to come for couple therapy. The couple completed the de-escalation phase of EFT with Sam, the husband, agreeing to work on the relationship, and his wife, Ellen, battling her anxiety and exploring her "mistakes" in the marriage. She articulated these as her becoming stuck in a critical and demanding stance. He was able to articulate how distant and placating he had become over the years, generally telling his wife "what she wanted to hear, and staying at work more and more." They were now able to see the cycle they had become caught in—they had become "friends"—but the issue of commitment was not resolved. This crisis also occurred at a transition point; all the children had finally left home, and Sam had encountered a major career disappointment. As he put it, "Just as I came up empty—had nothing to give—she wanted more and more of me. And it brought everything to a head." The key statements of the moves and moments in the withdrawer reengagement in Stage 2 of EFT follow:

"I was feeling just so numb, detached. Given up. But now we are friendly, more open. I think I have realized that it was all about being judged. So I did shut her out. But now, I am still not sure what I want—that is just who she is—will it change—really?

"I am coming back to life—but unsure—the pressure is still there—it's overwhelming. Not sure if it would not be better to just be friends and separate.

"I will never be enough for her needs—never. (*To her.*) I will never make it with you. I will fail all the tests (*He weeps, but then becomes more abstract and reflective.*) I am constricted—diminished—small—it's discouraging.

"I am caught—part of me wants to leave—part of me to stay.

"Well—here it is. Maybe I am tired of feeling powerless—dancing to your tune—proving I am okay—never accepted—never enough—never safe enough to ask if I need comfort. I am angry.

"I'm on guard for the 'not acceptable' message—so, saying 'I can leave' is a way out—an escape—it feels better—like I have some control.

"I'm afraid—so I shut down—I'm risk aversive. I never felt accepted—so I gave up—hopeless. So, when I lost all my career hopes—well—I found I was alone anyway—so why not be alone.

"I hurt—don't test and criticize me—I won't be tested—You can't drive this train anymore—I'm lonely, and I want some safety and some comfort—and to be able to be me—I'm tired—so afraid to be vulnerable with you—do I even want it? I am so afraid—if I let myself need you—

"I need your listening and comfort—not advice—no more judgments. It's hard to even let myself need that—but I want your acceptance—I need those moments of caring—I want us to be close and safe together again. Don't want to be alone and telling you what you want to hear—I want you to just come and be with me—"

In eight sessions, Sam moves from numb depression, to engaging his pain at being tested and found wanting, to despair and hopelessness, and then into anger and threats to leave. He then moves into his fear and his aloneness. He is then able to stay engaged with his own emotions and to assert his emotional needs with his wife. As he does so, he becomes more available and responsive to his wife, who is then able to also move in new ways in their mutual dance. Sam's depression also lifts as he redefines his part in this attachment drama. The therapist continually tracked and reflected the interactional dance and tracked emotional responses, helping each client to distill and develop their emotional experience. The therapist heightened and deepened Sam's emotional responses and supported Ellen to hear and process Sam's move into anger and despair. As she said, and as attachment theory predicts, "I would rather have your anger than nothing—than this empty separateness." The therapist's reframe of Sam's threats to leave as his only escape from despair and fear was crucial. Even more crucial were the enactments the therapist structured to shape new kinds of interaction; for example, "So, can you tell her, please, 'I am tired of dancing to your tune—trying to please you and being a disappointment.'" "Can you tell her?" Or, "Can you tell her—'I am afraid to feel—to let myself need you—your comfort—your acceptance—to trust you and put myself in your hands—I am afraid.'" Once harnessed, the power of emotion and the power of attachment longings enabled this couple, step by step, to create a new openness and safety in their relationship.

The field of couple therapy is changing (Johnson, 2003c). Every day we understand more about the essential nature of marital distress and the nature of adult love, and we learn more and more about how to harness the power of emotion to create change. The journey from distress to deep and lasting bonds of connection then becomes more possible for all of us.

REFERENCES

Amato, P. R., & Booth, A. (1997). *A generation at risk: Growing up in an era of family upheaval.* Cambridge, MA: Harvard University Press.

Bowlby, J. (1988). *A secure base.* New York: Basic Books.

Bradley, B., & Furrow, J. (2004). Softenings—A process study. *Journal of Marital and Family Therapy, 30,* 233–246.

Cassidy, J., & Shaver, P. (1999). *Handbook of attachment.* New York: Guilford.

Gottman, J. M. (2004). *What predicts divorce: The relationship between marital processes and marital outcomes.* Hillsdale, NJ: Lawrence Erlbaum Associates.

Johnson, S., Hunsley, J., Greenberg, L., & Schindler, D. (1999). Emotionally focused couples therapy: Status & challenges. *Clinical Psychology: Science & Practice, 6,* 67–79.

Johnson, S. M. (2002). *Emotionally focused couple therapy with trauma survivors: Strengthening attachment bonds.* New York: Guilford.

Johnson, S. M. (2003a). Attachment theory: A guide for couples therapy. In S. M. Johnson & V. Whiffen (Eds.), *Attachment processes in couple and family therapy* (pp. 103–123). New York: Guilford.

Johnson, S. M. (2003b). Changing attachment relationships. In S. M. Johnson and V. Whiffen (Eds.), *Attachment processes in couple and family therapy* (pp. 3–17). New York: Guilford.

Johnson, S. M. (2003c). The revolution in couple therapy: A practitioner scientist perspective. *Journal of Marital and Family Therapy, 29,* 365–385.

Johnson, S. M. (2004a). *The practice of emotionally focused marital therapy: Creating connection* (2nd ed). New York: Brunner/Routledge.

Johnson, S. M. (in press). Emotion and the repair of close relationships. In W. Pinsof & J. Lebow (Eds.), *Family psychology: The art of the science*

Johnson, S. M., & Denton, W. (2002). Emotionally focused couples therapy: Creating connection. In A. S. Gurman (Ed.), *The clinical handbook of couple therapy* (3rd ed., pp. 221–250). New York: Guilford.

Johnson, S. M., Makinen, & Millikin, J. (2001). Attachment injuries in couples relationships: A new perspective on impasses in couple therapy. *Journal of Marital and Family Therapy, 27,* 145–156.

Johnson, S. M., Maddeaux, C., & Blouin, J. (1998). Emotionally focused family therapy for bulimia: Changing attachment patterns. *Psychotherapy, 35,* 238–247.

Johnson, S. M., & Whiffen, V. (Eds.). (2003). *Attachment processes in couple and family therapy.* New York: Guilford.

Kiecolt-Glaser, J. K., Malarkey, W. B., Cacioppo, J. T., & Glaser, R. (1994). Stressful personal relationships: Immune and endocrine function. In R. Glaser & J. K. Kiecolt-Glaser (Eds.), *Handbook of human stress and immunity* (pp. 321–339). San Diego, CA: Academic Press.

Pinsof, W. M. (2002). The death of "Till death do us part": The transformation of pair-bonding in the 20th century. *Family Process, 41,* 135–157.

Roberts, L., & Greenberg, D. R. (2002). Observational windows to intimacy processes in marriage. In P. Noller & J. Feeney (Eds.), *Understanding marriage* (pp. 118–149). Cambridge: Cambridge University Press.

Simpson, J. A., Rholes, W. S., Campbell, L., Wilson, C., & Tran, S. (2002). Adult attachment, the transition to parenthood and marital well-being. In P. Noller & J. A. Feeney (Eds.), *Understanding marriage* (pp. 385–410). Cambridge: Cambridge University Press.

Van der Kolk, B., Perry, C., & Herman, J. (1991). Childhood origins of self-destructive behavior. *American Journal of Psychiatry, 148,* 1665–16671.

CHAPTER 16

Domestic Violence-Focused Couples Treatment

Sandra M. Stith, Eric E. McCollum, Karen H. Rosen, Lisa D. Locke, and
Peter D. Goldberg

Intimate partner violence is an all-too-common phenomenon. Recent Department of Justice statistics indicate that the incidence of intimate partner violence is about 1 million cases per year for women and 150,000 cases per year for men (Rennison & Welchans, 2000). In addition to the more obvious physical consequences of abuse, those who experience intimate partner violence are at much greater risk of psychological problems, including depression, anxiety, and Posttraumatic Stress Disorder. Intimate partner violence has also been shown to have profound and long-lasting negative emotional and behavioral effects on children who witness parental violence (Jaffe, Wolfe, & Wilson, 1990). Children who have observed violence between their parents have been found to assault their siblings and their parents, to commit violent crimes outside the family, and to assault their own intimate partners more than children who have not witnessed violence between parents. Furthermore, children in families in which there is partner abuse are also more likely to be hit themselves.

Historically, intimate partner violence has been viewed as a private, family matter. It is now viewed as a societal problem as well as a crime subject to legal punishment. This shift in perspective has changed the way intimate partner violence is handled in communities. Whereas legal authorities were once reluctant to intervene in private family matters, offenders now are often faced with mandatory jail time or mandatory treatment. Two clear messages emerge: the aggressor must be held accountable, and the victim must be protected. Based on these two primary concerns, treatment programs for intimate partner violence have traditionally provided separate treatment for males and females. Since men are most frequently identified as offenders and women are most frequently identified as victims, treatment programs for interpersonal violence have generally been provided to men in men's groups. While support groups for female victims have been offered, the main focus of treatment has been on male offenders.

The purpose of this chapter is to provide therapists with a rationale and tools to consider other treatment approaches, including conjoint couples therapy, for some violent partners. There is increasing consensus in the field that all offenders do not need the same treatment. The treatment program described here, Domestic Violence-

Focused Couples Treatment (DVFCT) is limited to one subtype of offender—the family-only offender—who is most likely to benefit from couples therapy.

The treatment model described in this chapter was developed in an effort to address the diversity of individuals assessed as violent and the couple dynamics present in many cases. DVFCT is intended for a specific group of couples in ongoing relationships where mild-to-moderate violence has occurred and both partners want to end the violence in their relationships. We incorporated strategies into the model to decrease the risk of violence, to assure that the victim can speak candidly, and to hold the primary aggressor accountable for violence.

The goals of DVFCT are straightforward. Our primary objective in working with couples is to end violence of all kinds between partners. A secondary objective is to help couples improve the quality of their relationship, whether they stay together or separate. Even if they divorce, many couples will need to work together as parents, and having a less conflictual relationship will benefit both adults and children. We do not see divorce as a failure of our program, nor do we necessarily see couples staying together as success. Rather, we judge our success on the elimination of violence.

OUTCOME RESULTS

In January 1997, we received funding from the National Institutes of Mental Health (NIMH) to develop and pilot test a manualized treatment program for couples who choose to stay together after mild-to-moderate, male-perpetrated domestic violence. We compared three groups of couples; those completing individual couple therapy, multicouple therapy, and a no-treatment comparison group.

Initial findings from this project are encouraging. The attrition rate for the couples treatment condition was 27 percent lower than that found in other studies of domestic violence treatment (Edleson & Tolman, 1992). Male violence recidivism rates 6 months after treatment were significantly lower for the multicouple group (25 percent) than for the comparison group (66 percent). In contrast, men in the individual couple condition were not significantly less likely to recidivate (43 percent) than those in the comparison group. Likewise, marital satisfaction increased significantly, and both marital aggression and acceptance of wife battering decreased significantly among individuals who participated in multicouple group therapy—but not among those who participated in individual couple therapy or the comparison group.

At the 2-year assessment, among treated couples (individual couple and multicouple group treatment combined), only one woman reported that her male partner had been violent since the 6-month follow-up, a 6 percent recidivism rate. In contrast, half the women in the comparison group who were contacted reported a subsequent violent incident (50 percent recidivism). Thus, based on the women we were able to contact, men who completed treatment were less likely to recidivate at the 2-year follow-up than those in the comparison group.

RATIONALE FOR VARIATIONS IN TREATMENT

The literature describes negative effects from men's treatment groups for some men. The potential for negative male bonding and victim blaming has been described in the literature (Edleson & Tolman, 1992). Sometimes, group members support each other's negative attitudes about women, or implicitly or explicitly support a man's use of abusive behavior. In our work with couples, women have reported that it was not uncommon for men to use techniques, such as time-out, abusively when women were not also taught the technique.

Furthermore, male batterers are a heterogeneous group (Stuart & Holtzworth-Munroe, 1995). Three subtypes of batterers have been identified—family only, dysphoric/borderline, and generally violent/antisocial. Some authors propose that tailoring treatment to each subtype of violent men might improve treatment outcome. Stuart and Holtzworth-Munroe (1995) hypothesize that family-only batterers are likely to be the least violent of the groups, and that their violence may be associated with problems such as insecure attachment patterns, mild social skills deficits, and low levels of impulsivity. They further hypothesize that this type of batterer may be the most appropriate for couples treatment.

In addition to treating subgroups of offenders differently, there is reason to include female partners in treatment, even when the male partner is the primary aggressor. Both men and women are often violent in relationships. Despite the much lower probability of physical injury resulting from attacks by women, assaults by women are serious. If reciprocal violence is taking place in relationships, treating men without treating women is not likely to stop the violence. In fact, research has shown that cessation of partner violence by one partner is highly dependent on whether the other partner also stops hitting (Feld & Straus, 1989; Gelles & Straus, 1988).

Moreover, while men's treatment groups address men's role in intimate partner violence, they do not address any underlying relationship dynamics that may impact each partner's decision to remain in the relationship despite the violence, or that may play a part in maintaining the violence. Finally, many women who have been abused remain with their abusive partners, or return to them after leaving a woman's shelter or otherwise separating from them. Failing to provide services to both parties in an ongoing relationship may inadvertently disadvantage the female partner who chooses to stay.

Considerable controversy continues to surround the use of any treatment program that involves both partners in the treatment of interpersonal violence. Some providers are concerned that offering conjoint treatment suggests that the victim is equally responsible for the abuse. Also, a serious concern regarding conjoint treatment is the potential for violence to escalate, thereby increasing the danger for the victim. Finally, when couples are seen together the abused spouse may be reluctant to speak freely for fear of retaliatory abuse. In our program, these concerns are addressed by careful assessment, individual interviews, gender-specific pretreatment, and regular individual check-ins throughout treatment.

ASSESSMENT OF APPROPRIATENESS FOR CONJOINT TREATMENT

Disguised Presentation

Although partner violence is a pervasive problem, family members often hide it from their therapists. O'Leary, Vivian, and Malone (1992) found that only 6 percent of women seeking counseling indicated on their intake form that marital violence was a significant problem in their relationship. However, when asked to complete a standardized assessment instrument, 53 percent indicated that their husbands had physically assaulted them. Clients have various reasons for not reporting the presence of violence in their relationships. They may not see violence as the primary problem that brought them to therapy. They may be embarrassed to admit to being in a violent relationship, or the abused partner may fear retribution from the abuser if she or he talks with the therapist about the abuse. Every client is different, and will have his or her own reasons for not reporting or for underreporting violence, but all therapists working with couples need to be able to assess this all-too-common problem.

Assessment Procedures

The first step in assessing partner violence is to determine if any form of aggression is occurring in the relationship. This assessment should take place with every couple being seen, and it includes both an oral interview and a written assessment instrument. It is vital that interviews regarding potential interpersonal violence be conducted with each individual separately. When each partner is asked privately about his or her own and the partner's violence, the clinician needs to be able to consider each person's story and the degree of consensus between stories.

Each partner should complete assessment instruments in different rooms, so that he or she can feel safe to report accurately on his or her experiences and so that he or she will not be endangered by the responses. The most widely used instrument is the Conflict Tactics Scale (CTS; see Straus, 1979, for actual instrument) which contains 18 items, and asks respondents about their own and their partner's behavior. Straus, Hamby, Boney-McCoy, and Sugarman (1996) developed a revised version of the CTS that contains 78 items and is more comprehensive than the original CTS in assessing psychological, physical, and sexual abuse. Both forms of the CTS are appropriate for both offenders and victims.

Eligibility and Exclusion Criteria for Conjoint Treatment

To be eligible for conjoint treatment, therapists should require that both partners (when interviewed privately) voluntarily choose to participate in a conjoint treatment program. Both partners must want to end the violence in their relationship and must want to improve their relationship.

Clients should be excluded from conjoint treatment if they have ever used severe violence in their relationship, which includes any use or threatened use of handguns, violence that results in an injury to their partner that involved hospitalization, or violence that could result in such an injury. We have accepted some clients that had experienced severe violence more than 2 years in the past, and who had successfully completed a batterer intervention program with no evidence of physical violence since completing the program. We also exclude clients who have a pattern of violence outside the home (strangers, friends, etc.) within the past 2 years, current problems with alcohol or other drugs, who are unwilling to remove handguns from their immediate access, and/or individuals who refuse to sign a no-violence contract before beginning treatment. If therapists decide to exclude clients from a treatment program, it is important for therapists to recommend participation in a program designed to treat offenders and victims separately.

GENDER-SPECIFIC PRETREATMENT GROUP

Preparation for conjoint treatment is essential, and in our program it consists of a required 6-week anger management program. Couples are separated into gender-specific groups, with both a male and female facilitator in each group. Each weekly session lasts 2 hours. Both the men's and women's groups learn the same information, and both sets of facilitators are continuously in communication regarding the agenda of the sessions, issues that arise in session, and any safety concerns. The format of the group is psychoeducational, with group discussions and interactions. This type of group is appropriate for either male-to-female, female-to-male, or mutually perpetrated domestic violence. The 6-week anger management portion of the treatment follows a specific agenda that covers a wide range of issues and topics pertinent to couples that experience mild-to-moderate domestic violence. Each participant receives a copy of *On the level: Foundations for violence-free living,* written by David Matthews (1995a), and the facilitators receive training using the facilitator's guide for this program, *Foundations for violence-free living: A step-by-step guide to facilitating men's domestic abuse groups* (1995b). While we have adapted ideas from these books to meet our own needs, these books serve as a foundation and guide. The 6-week program is structured as in Table 16.1.

There are many goals for the 6-week, gender-specific groups. Of utmost importance are developing safety plans and beginning to develop time-out plans. Even though the formal topic of safety plans and time-out are not addressed until the third week, the safety of participants is the top priority and comes before anything else. Each couple must sign a no-violence contract before they begin any treatment. If a safety issue arises, the group will revise the psychoeducational information and focus on that topic. Sometimes, this revised focus has lasted an entire session. The use of two facilitators in each gender-specific group offers the built-in luxury of a facilitator pulling out an individual (or couple) to work intensely on safety concerns. De-escalation techniques can be employed, safety plans and time-out plans developed, and so forth, depending on the need of the individual and/or couple.

Within the group sessions, there is a focus on accountability and taking responsibility for individual behavior. The group also provides a forum to increase the comfort level of individuals to speak about the violence that has occurred in their relationships, as well as a further screening regarding the appropriateness of individual couples to participate in the 12-week conjoint program. We have excluded some couples from the conjoint portion of the program when we found that the primary aggressor was unable to accept responsibility for his or her behavior, and/or if we felt that the couple would not be safe working conjointly to end violence and enhance their relationship. We found through interviews with our female participants that they gain a sense of empowerment and balance by participating in a group with other women before beginning couples treatment.

The first session of an anger management program should focus on joining and

Table 16.1

Week	Content
Week One—Introduction to Domestic Violence	• Purpose of group • Guidelines of group • Group rules and principles • Introduction of participants' exercise • Definition of domestic violence and anger • Differences between domestic violence and anger • Types of abuse • Characteristics of a batterer • Pattern of abuse/cycle of violence
Week Two—Types of Abuse	• Physical • Emotional • Sexual • Verbal • Intimidation • Male Privilege • Social Isolation • Religious • Child Abuse • Power and Control Issues
Week Three—Control Strategies, Time-Out, Safety Plans	• Control Strategies • Types of Control • Power and Control Wheel • Equality Wheel • Time-Out Planning • Safety Planning
Week Four—Escalations Signals, and Conflict/Response Styles	• Escalation signals • Escalation ladder • Conflict escalation • Conflict styles • Response styles
Week Five—Alcohol and Drug Use	• Alcohol/drug use and anger/domestic violence • Defining problem drinking and drug use • Screening usage in my own life • Planning for the future
Week Six—Conflict Resolution and Accountability	• Conflict resolution skills • Becoming accountable for my own actions

on an introduction to domestic violence. Participants are directed to engage in a ritual to facilitate getting to know one another. In our program, this ritual diverges from the traditional model of participants introducing themselves, by having the group divide into pairs and interview each other. The pairs are given a list of four questions to ask each other, and then they introduce their partner to the rest of the group. The questions have a solution-focused slant. We ask what they hope to gain in the first 6 weeks, and for a personal strength. This joining ritual typically lasts 20 to 30 minutes. The remainder of the session focuses on introducing guiding principles (which include the concept that each individual is responsible for his or her own behavior, violence of any kind is never acceptable, etc.), defining the various types of domestic violence, reviewing the characteristics of someone who uses violence, defining anger, and identifying the pattern of abuse. Subsequent sessions support and build upon earlier sessions, providing more information on the topics mentioned earlier as well as introducing other topics, such as power and control.

Building awareness is another major focus for a gender-specific program. Each group is led through exercises designed to increase their awareness of their own escalation signals, anger triggers, conflict styles, response to anger styles, as well as identifying their own ways of appropriately and inappropriately displaying their anger. As the group progresses and each person becomes more aware, each person begins to take ownership of his or her anger and make plans to change his or her behaviors. Again, the focus is on individual responsibility; how the individual can change, not how the partners can change.

Since many violent couples also struggle with substance abuse issues, one of the 6 weeks should be specifically focused on substance abuse. A nonconfrontational, motivational interviewing approach to this discussion appears to work well. In our program, brief information is presented about the relationship between substance use and abuse and violence. Each group member is then asked to evaluate privately—through a structured exercise—the advantages and disadvantages of substance use in their lives and relationships. No direct suggestions or requirements for substance abuse treatment are given at this point, but participants are asked to write down what changes, if any, they would like to make in their use of substances in the next 6 months. These plans are sealed in envelopes and given back to the participants, unread by the leaders, at the end of the full 18 weeks of treatment. In contrast to confrontational approaches, which may in fact increase substance use, motivational interviewing has been found to result in less substance use and more frequent initiation of substance abuse treatment.

The group dynamics of each gender-specific group grows over time. It is this dynamic that makes this type of format powerful. In the beginning, the groups bond together and begin to share a commonality with each other. As the group progresses and the bonding builds, participants begin to challenge one another. This is a compelling experience, since the confrontation is coming from other group members who have similar experiences, have gained each other's respect, and have built camaraderie together. The group members are able to have open discussions and to encourage others to become accountable and responsible for their own behaviors. This then sets the stage for continued challenges in the individual couple or multicouple format of the remaining 12 weeks.

INDIVIDUAL COUPLE OR MULTICOUPLE TREATMENT

Theoretical Basis of Conjoint Treatment

In understanding how therapists use theoretical models, Wile (1993) differentiates between therapists' "primary pictures" and their "secondary pictures." Primary pictures are the constellation of assumptions and approaches that guide our work most of the time. They are our preferred views of people and the nature of problems, and the accompanying set of techniques that flow from them. Secondary pictures are the assumptions and approaches that we turn to when we are constrained from using our primary pictures. Thus, a therapist who generally prefers a collaborative and nondirective stance as her or his primary picture may turn to a more directive and authoritative stance when a couple's angry interchanges make it impossible to maintain the collaborative position. Secondary pictures are typically used only until the constraint is resolved, at which point the therapist will return to his or her primary picture to direct therapy. In DVFCT, our primary picture is de Shazer and Berg's Solution-Focused Brief Therapy (SFBT) approach (de Shazer, 1985, 1988; Berg & Miller, 1992). When constraints arise—primarily the threat of a recurrence of violence—we turn to a set of adjunctive tools to help resolve the constraint and allow a return to the SFBT approach.

Solution-Focused Brief Therapy—the Primary Picture

While detailed descriptions of this model and its assumptions exist elsewhere, the following five broad components comprise a theoretical foundation for conjoint work with violent couples. These components are derived from the definition of SFBT currently being developed by the Solution-Focused Brief Therapy Association.

The appreciative stance. The appreciative stance is a basic belief and orienting posture in interactions with clients, and is based on the presupposition that clients bring not only problems but also large measures of competence, resources, and strength when they come to treatment. These areas of competence are often obscured by clients' and other service providers' focus on problems and broad labels (for example, "batterer" or "victim") that do not leave room for more complex understandings. Using the presupposition of strength as a lens, therapists should then observe, ask questions, and gather data to begin to develop a picture that includes the areas of success and competence already occurring in clients' lives. Finally, therapists should try to reflect this vision of clients back to them in language that they find both familiar and believable. While the specific techniques of SFBT (for example, the miracle question, scaling, looking for exceptions) can be used from within a variety of theoretical approaches, adopting the appreciative stance is key to truly using SFBT. Without the appreciative stance, therapists will lose confidence in the search for strengths, as problem descriptions and broad labels reassert themselves.

Descriptions of solutions. In contrast to approaches that emphasize a detailed understanding and description of the problem and its interactional context, a tenet of SFBT is that generating more complex and elaborated descriptions of the absence of the problem is useful in treatment. Often, couples' goals for treatment are appropriate, but vague—"we'll be happy together," or, "we'll get along"—while their complaints are well-developed and specific—"when we talk about money problems, he gets mad and just walks away. If I follow him and try to make him finish the conversation he'll get madder and that's when he hits me. If I don't follow him, we never talk about it again."

Creating a specific and detailed picture of the desired outcome has several advantages. First, it gives clients a concrete picture of the goals they are working toward, allowing them to envision the intermediate steps and strategies they will need to reach that goal. Further, it allows them to observe the ways in which parts of their preferred outcome already exist in their lives. This not only gives clients hope, it helps the therapist join with their existing competencies, typically a different experience for clients who primarily interact with professionals around their deficits—violence, danger to their children, and so forth.

Changing static descriptions to fluid descriptions. A third tenet of SFBT is that life is a constant process of change—although our descriptions of it often remain static. Helping clients shift their static descriptions of problem states ("we're unhappy") to more fluid descriptions ("sometimes we get along pretty well, and other times we fight") both reflects reality and creates a path to explore the areas of success and competence that exist in their lives. Seeing that there are already areas of solution helps clients (and therapists) have hope about change, and build on already-existing pockets of solutions—rather than feeling that solutions must be created anew.

Client goals structure treatment. A fourth tenet of SFBT is that clients' goals for treatment remain in the forefront, and structure treatment. This is particularly important with violent couples, since any number of goals have typically been imposed on clients by the time they come to therapy. The legal system may have imposed the goals of managing anger on the perpetrator. The batterer's intervention program may have imposed the goal of ending the use of male privilege. Finally, the victim's support group may have imposed the goal of leaving the batterer on the victim. None of these are bad or necessarily inappropriate goals. However, when they are experienced as imposed from the outside, without the consent of the clients, they are hard to truly accept. When using a program to treat these couples, therapists should begin by trying to find what goals the couple actually wants to work toward, and use these to structure therapy. Since one of the inclusion criteria should be that both partners pledge to end violence in the relationship and both want to remain together, therapists can work with stated goals that do not necessarily focus on violence per se.

Many paths to a solution. Finally, in contrast to approaches that prescribe a certain set of steps that must occur in order for clients to solve their problems, SFBT adopts a more flexible approach. In this view, there are many avenues clients can take to solve their problems, and none should be rejected out of hand because they do not fit the therapist's view of a correct solution. Sometimes imposing a path to a solution is not only ineffective, it can be harmful. There is data to suggest, for instance, that forcing people to debrief after traumatic experiences can be retraumatizing if the person does not feel it will be helpful to him or her (Rose, Bisson & Wessely, 2004). It is important to help clients develop and refine their own paths to a solution, based on amplifying pieces of the solution that are already present.

In summary, SFBT techniques are primarily linguistic and cognitive. They aim to use language carefully, to change thinking, with a resulting change in behavior and with a focus on the present, and (especially) on the future. This is in contrast to approaches that have as their goal eliciting and resolving emotional conflicts, or changing the client's understanding of his or her past experiences. The therapist approaches clients with the conviction that there are strengths and capacities in the client that can serve as a foundation for solutions. This approach helps the

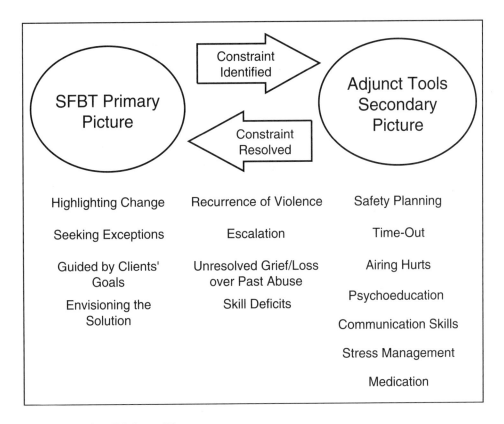

Figure 16.1   SFBT Primary Picture

client develop a picture of the future without the problem, and asks questions and makes responses in a way that generates more complex and fluid descriptions of life, rather than static, one-dimensional descriptions.

Shifting to the Secondary Picture

The secondary picture of treatment comes into view when constraints arise that prevent therapists from continuing with an SFBT orientation. The primary constraint in this work is the recurrence, or the risk of recurrence, of violence. The other common constraint is that victims of violence are often unable to move to solution finding until they feel their partner understands the depth of suffering he or she has caused through violence. Thus, at times, therapists must become more directive and instructive than the SFBT model describes in order to assure that therapy participants are safe and understood. Figure 16.1 illustrates the relationship between primary and secondary pictures and the resolution of constraints.

TREATMENT STRUCTURE

Minimizing Risk

Safety is a primary concern for therapists, who should seek to minimize risk to both partners. Couples treatment is not appropriate for all couples, even some couples who both say they want couples treatment. Beyond inclusion and exclusion criteria, the structure of each session provides a second line of defense. In our program, each session begins and ends with an individual meeting with each partner. This provides a time for each to report privately about the prior week and for each to debrief after the conjoint session, to make sure no one is leaving therapy angry and in danger of becoming violent.

First Conjoint Session

The treatment program can be offered to individual couples or to multicouple groups. Regardless of the format, it is preferable to use cotherapists to deliver the treatment. Using cotherapists allows each member of the couple to be seen individually without requiring partners to wait while the therapist speaks with his or her partner. One cotherapist is also able to take a couple or individual out of the group and provide individual work, when needed. The first session should begin with the cotherapists meeting with the couple or the group of couples. The cotherapists welcome all participants to the session, introduce themselves, and review the format of the sessions. The cotherapists need to avoid discussion of difficult issues while they begin the conjoint portion of the program. One of the cotherapists has been working with the men (or man) previously and one has been working with the women (or female partner) but the other partner(s) may not have had an opportunity to get to know the other therapist. If the couple is seen as part of a multicouple group, the therapists work with the group to develop group rules, which should include issues like: Information that is shared within the group is confidential; everyone speaks for themselves and not for their partners; the group begins on time; no one should be coerced into speaking, if they are not comfortable; no one can participate in the group under the influence of drugs and/or alcohol. The therapists should also explain that each session will begin and end with separate conversations with each participant. Next, the cotherapist that has not met with the man (or men) will meet with the men and the other therapist will meet with the woman (or women).

Meeting with the female partner (or women's group). When meeting with women, the therapist gives them an opportunity to share their thoughts about participating in the conjoint portion of the program and/or to ask any questions. The therapist reminds the women that they developed a safety plan in the gender-specific group, and encourages them to use the plan if necessary. Sometimes it is necessary to caution the women that although couples counseling can be an effective way of stopping violence and helping couples get along better, it is not a sure-fire cure. They still need to be prepared to take steps to assure their safety to the best of their abilities. During this first session the therapist also asks the women if they feel safe discussing difficult issues in the session and if they have fears about the treatment program. The therapist also asks about any ongoing abuse in the relationship, and about any hopeful signs. This information will be helpful in planning the rest of the session. Finally, the therapist should compliment them for their willingness to participate in the program and for their determination to do whatever they can to ensure that if they remain in the relationship, it becomes a healthy, supportive, nonviolent relationship.

Meeting with the male partner (or men's group). The therapist who has not met with the man (or men) should welcome the men to treatment and give them an opportunity to share their thoughts about participating in the program and/or to ask any questions. They should be complimented for attending couples counseling and for their willingness to address violence. They should be asked what it says about them—that they are able to face the violence, and participate in a treatment program designed to end violence and enhance relationships. One male client, when interviewed by a project researcher about his experience in our program, talked specifically about his appreciation that the therapists complimented him on his courage for coming to therapy:

> I like the way they acknowledge right up front, they said, "I know it took a lot of courage for you to come here." I appreciate that . . . I like the way they acknowledge—because it does. It takes a lot to go in there and start talking to people that you don't know about something you're having a problem with.

The men should be asked about fears regarding couples treatment, ongoing abuse, and about the hopeful signs they have noted. This information will help therapists guide the rest of the session.

Therapists' check-in. After meeting with the male and female separately (or men's and women's groups), the therapists should meet briefly to plan the rest of the session. If they hear about ongoing violence, or if they become concerned about anything they hear in the pregroup meeting, they may choose to revise the plan for the conjoint session. They may continue meeting with the men and women separately or may change the focus of the conjoint session.

Conjoint meeting. Both therapists should meet with the couple (or multicouple group) for most of the rest of the session to continue the joining process, and to help the clients begin to think about strengths and resources they bring to the session. The content of this meeting will include instruction about the negotiated time-out, and recognition of presession change.

Negotiated time-out. Although time-out is a common component of most batterer intervention programs, feedback we received from both victims and offenders suggested that time-out as traditionally taught is often ineffective and, even worse, can be used as a form of control. Therefore, we developed a negotiated time-out procedure, a variation of the traditional de-escalation tool, which we present to both partners concurrently (Rosen, Matheson, Stith, McCollum, & Locke, 2003).

The essential components of negotiated time-out are very similar to what is traditionally taught. They include: recognizing internal cues that anger is escalating; deciding that time-out is needed, since anger is escalating past the safety zone; using an agreed-upon gesture, such as a "T" symbol, and saying, in a calm voice, "I am going to take a time-out;" acknowledging the time-out by the partner; going to separate, agreed-upon locations; participating in calming activities; and reconnecting to continue the discussion when calm. A key difference is that both partners develop a plan together with the help of their therapist, and leave the session with an agreement about when and how they will use time-out. This negotiation process may take a significant portion of the first or second couples session.

Both partners must be motivated to use this tool, since many clients, particularly women, are opposed to using time-out. Therapists can motivate clients by beginning a discussion of how the time-out procedure is currently used in their relationship, asking both partners to discuss their concerns about the procedure. Listening to their concerns and affirming their efforts to use time-out often helps soften resistance. Therapists should then explain that couples will be taught to use this tool in a way with which they are both comfortable, and in a way that will empower them to be in charge of their conflict resolution process. The couples are asked to set aside some of their concerns and to try the technique. They are assured that if they are not satisfied with their initial attempts to use it, the technique will be revised until they are satisfied.

After therapists explain the components of the process, they should ask each partner to describe how he or she knows when he or she is becoming angry, or what signs indicate that his or her efforts to deal with a conflict are becoming unproductive and unsafe. The therapist is very active during the negotiation process, making sure that both partners feel heard and contribute to the decision-making process. Couples should be encouraged to practice the technique in session and between sessions, and subsequent sessions are used to revisit and revise the process as needed. We have found that this process increases the likelihood that both partners will follow the plan they developed; additionally, it empowers the woman, who, up until that point, may have felt left out of the process; and, it provides the content around which the couple can strengthen negotiation skills.

Recognizing presession change. A specific intervention aimed at joining, highlighting strengths, and setting the stage for a therapy that focuses on solutions rather than problems, is called recognizing presession change (Weiner-Davis, de Shazer, and Gingerich, 1987). It is based on the assumption that change is always happening, and that part of the work in therapy is finding out what changes have occurred. To do this, therapists should ask clients what has changed since they became involved in the gender-specific pretreatment program, and to anticipate and ask about changes that have occurred since they found out that they would begin couples treatment. If therapists do not ask about change, it is often not noted by clients or therapists. A way to ask this question is as follows:

> I know that you are just beginning to work together on your relationship, but research shows us that many couples already start to make some positive changes before they even begin couples therapy. Therapists miss knowing about those changes because we forget to ask. It's certainly important for us to talk about problems, but we'd like to begin by asking what positive changes you've noticed in your relationship since you began working separately on your problems.

This question is not asked to simply create a catalog of changes. If clients are able to recognize positive changes in their relationship, it is important for the therapist to comment on these changes. For example:

> You know, as I listen to you talk about all the things you've changed since you began the pretreatment program, I am encouraged that you do have the ability to solve this problem. It also lets

me know that you want things to be different, and that you're willing to put some effort into making a change.

The therapists highlight changes, compliment clients, and begin to direct them toward looking at the part they played in making the changes happen. This intervention can be used with individual couples or with multicouple groups.

When clients are unable to identify changes, therapists may ask them how they have coped with such a difficult predicament. This gives them a chance to talk about strengths without having the therapist disqualify their view of the situation as having no positive aspects right now. Therapists should compliment them for their ability to cope with the problem and for their commitment to continuing to work on improving the relationship.

Postsession meeting with each partner. At the end of each session one therapist should meet with the male partner (or the men's group) and one with the female partner (or women's group) to determine if everyone feels safe leaving the session. This will also be a time for clients to process any angry feelings. The postsession meeting can serve as something of a mini time-out, a time for each individual to reflect on his or her emotional state and vulnerability to violence or relationship conflict. If anyone is especially angry, the therapist can acknowledge the anger, let the client ventilate, and then help the client plan how to deal with his or her feelings. Questions to ask might include the following:

> How do you usually manage to cool off when you are upset with your partner? What will be the signs you will see that tell you your anger is under control? What will make you feel good about dealing with the things you are feeling now?

The clients can also be advised not to discuss further the issues that were brought up in the session until they meet again for therapy, or until at least a day or two has passed. In addition to discussing angry or difficult feelings, we ask each partner to complete a short questionnaire about his or her perception of the helpfulness of the session and his or her feelings of immediate safety. Four scaling questions assess the extent to which the clients are convinced that they or their partner will not be physically or psychologically abusive during the following week. If either partner expresses significant fear that physical or psychological abuse will occur, the therapist discusses the situation in more detail with that client. If they are afraid that they are in immediate danger (e.g., "I just don't want to go home with him while he's in this mood"), the therapist may suggest that the couple leave the session separately, and have an agreed-upon cooling-off period of several hours or more. The clients may need to put their safety plan into action and not return home until the fearful partner is convinced it is safe to go home. It is always best to have the more fearful partner leave first, so that she or he doesn't fear the other one will wait for her or him in the parking lot. If the fear is not immediate, but is still strong (e.g., "Things feel pretty unpredictable at home; I just don't know where he's at some of the time"), each partner can be reminded of his or her contract for no violence and the use of time-out. In addition, the woman's safety plan can be reviewed with her, and any additional resources she might need can be suggested (women's shelter, police, and hotline numbers). The man can also be asked to review his plan to make his home safe. If either partner expresses fear about safety at the end of the session, the therapists consult with one another and make a risk management plan before letting the clients leave.

TROUBLESHOOTING AFTER THE FIRST SESSION

Couples Minimize Violence

While this treatment emphasizes amplifying strengths and avoiding shaming clients, it is important for each partner to recognize verbal and physical abuse, and to know that they do not have to live with violence in his or her life. It is often helpful, if violent behavior is minimized, for the therapist to label the behavior as violent or abusive. If the client's life was endangered, this should be pointed out. For example, if the male client minimizes the abuse, the therapist may comment, "Since I know how much you care about_____, it must have been very frightening to you to realize how much you hurt her," or, "how you could have really hurt her." Helping clients recognize the violence occurring in their lives is a first step toward helping them end the violence. This work is often most effective when done separately, so that one partner does not feel shamed in front of the other partner.

STRATEGIES USED IN SUBSEQUENT SESSIONS

Developing a Vision of a Healthy, Violence-Free Relationship

Developing a clear vision of a healthy, violence-free relationship helps clients clarify what specific changes they want to see in their relationship, and moves attention away from past mistakes and blaming. There are a number of ways to help clients develop their vision of a violence-free relationship. If clients have difficulty thinking about their own relationship, it may help for the therapist to ask the question from a third person perspective. For example, we ask clients, "When you think about a healthy relationship, what are building blocks?" We have also found it helpful to ask, more directly, "What kind of a marriage do you want to have with Jane?" We help clients be as specific, concrete, and behavioral in their descriptions as they can. Many clients will begin by reporting an internal, emotional change, such as "I'd be happy." If this happens, we may ask the client, "If I were there, or if I videotaped the two of you, what would I see you doing that would tell me you were happy?"

By using solution-focused language, the therapist can also help clients anticipate the signs that tell them they are moving toward their vision of a healthy, violence-free relationship, as well as establish the fact that achieving their goal is a process that will take time to accomplish. Therapists might ask them to pay attention to what their new, nonviolent relationship will look like, so they will notice when a part of this relationship seems to be evident: "What are the signs that you are making progress toward the relationship that you and Jane would like to have?" "What kinds of steps would you like to take first?" "After the first indication that progress is being made, what would happen next?"

Lack of trust is often a roadblock to moving toward couples' visions of healthy, violence-free relationships. Violent partners may have promised to stop being violent a number of times before and, justifiably, victims may be wary. It is important for both partners to recognize that developing trust is a process, and that wariness is normal. The therapist may ask, "What will be the signs that Jane has begun to feel confident that the violence will not recur?" "Jane, how will you know when you are beginning to feel safe?" Developing trust and reestablishing safety are key components of making couples' visions a reality.

Teaching and Practicing Communication Skills

Often couples lack the skills to communicate with each other effectively. When this seems to be the case, therapists should set aside a session or two for communication skill enhancement. Concepts to cover include sending clear I-messages, empathic listening, and responding in a way that shows the speaker was heard and the message accepted without judgment. Then, couples may be asked to choose an issue to discuss that is not laden with too much intensity. Couples take turns practicing sending clear I-messages, listening empathically, and responding in a way that lets their partner know they heard and understood what was said. In a group setting, group members and cotherapists coach couples and give feedback, based on their perspective of messages sent and responses given. In the individual couple treatment, the cotherapists give the clients feedback about their experience.

Metadialogue

Cotherapists sometimes use metadialogue (dialogue with one another in the presence of the couple or group) to de-escalate intensity, comment on the process, challenge gender role stereotypes, shift the focus from problems to strengths, model conflict resolution skills, or to introduce difficult material without directly challenging either partner (Tucker, Stith, Howell, McCollum, & Rosen, 2000). Clients are asked to listen to what the cotherapists say without responding immediately, or at all. The metadialogue invites couples to step outside their constricted view of themselves and to consider other ways of seeing the situation. By adopting a respectful, not-knowing stance that does not foreclose reality through the therapists' pronouncement of "what is," therapists can reflect about "what might be" from a solution-focused lens, thus inviting couples to see from different angles. During a metadialogue, cotherapists can present competing views without directly endorsing any of them. For example, a concern about a woman's safety, and empathy for the pain she has experienced, can be juxtaposed to a wish to support the man, as he struggles to accept responsibility for his past acts of violence and struggles to prevent future ones.

Addressing Pain and Anger from a Solution-Focused Perspective

Early in our work with couples who had experienced domestic violence, we found that many victims had a very hard time considering exceptions, a vision of the future, or even the possibility of change. What seemed to be getting in their way was the conviction that their partner had never really acknowledged the depth of pain his or her abuse had caused them. Underlying that conviction was a strong sense of anger at not feeling heard. Dealing with negative emotions may, at first, seem like a dilemma from the perspective of SFBT, given that model's focus on the future, exceptions to the problem, and areas of strength and competence in the clients' lives. However, de Shazer and Isebaert (2003) have recently written about the importance of "honoring the problem" in solution-focused practice. Just because we are solution-focused does not mean we are problem-phobic. Without acknowledging the impact that the problem has had in the couple relationship, therapists risk clients feeling misunderstood and dismissed. Thus, it is essential to set aside time, if needed, for the victim to describe to the partner the anguish experienced as a result of this abuse. Even if both partners have assaulted one another, usually women's aggression toward men does not instill the same sense of threat and trauma as does men's aggression toward women. Often the women's discussion of the abuse and its effect will not be simply an intellectual description of what she has gone through, but a sharing of the affect associated with it. This can be a difficult experience for the male. The therapist must support him if he is to be emotionally present during the woman's presentation. He should be helped to listen and acknowledge what she says, without beginning to deny the impact of his actions or defend himself for what he has done. Following such talks, it is also very important to check in with the male to make sure that he has not simply hidden his anger at what his partner said, thereby risking retaliation later. It is also vital to help the man deal with his growing realization that he has hurt a person whom he purports to love.

As the woman grows more convinced that her partner has understood the effect of his acts, the therapist can gently guide the couple toward a more future-oriented view. Questions that make this transition include, "What will you see your partner doing in the next week that will tell you that he now really understands the effect the abuse had on you?" "If your partner continues to work hard at understanding the effect his violence has had on you, what do you think you will be seeing in your relationship 6 months from now? What positive changes will there be?" These questions begin to help the couple define the state of resolution or understanding, and shift their focus now to the future. However, trying to move to this discussion before the woman feels understood and acknowledged will likely have the effect of simply alienating her from treatment.

Dealing with Relapse

While the process of identifying and strengthening aspects of the relationship that are violence-free or that otherwise meet clients' goals seems straightforward, temporary returns to problem behavior will often accompany a general trend toward improvement. Therapists need to be ready to help clients deal with relapses, to be patient with the therapeutic process, and to help clients avoid making a relapse a catastrophe.

There are two types of relapse: one is a return to problematic couple behavior that does not include violence, and the other is the recurrence of violence. If the couple reports a return to problematic but nonviolent patterns, therapists should first try to gauge the clients' reactions to the relapse and then empathize with and validate their discouragement if that is prominent. While therapists may see such a relapse as temporary and normal, it can be quite discouraging for clients, who view a relapse as evidence that there is no hope they will be able to change. The second step is to help the clients realistically gauge the extent of their relapse. Couples often use "all or nothing" language to describe the recurrence of problems. For example, a couple might say that they've had a bad week and that nothing went well. However, as the therapist begins to get a clear, behavioral description of what happened, he or she may discover that the clients had a 20-minute argument on their way to the session after 6 days of managing their conflicts in healthy ways, which may be quite a positive change for a couple that has been fighting daily. It is important to point out the long period of success the clients had and to normalize the recurrence of problems. This discussion may help the therapist gauge how realistic the couple's goal is. For instance, if a couple thinks that success means they will have no conflict whatsoever, therapists may need to discuss the inevitability of conflict in relationships and emphasize that the important factor is how conflict is managed. Finally, strength-based change questions are essential. For example, therapists may ask clients scaling questions, judging how they see the past week overall, including the relapse, compared to where they were when they began therapy. Another approach to a relapse is to ask clients to tell how they limited the extent of the relapse. "How did you limit the argument to 20 minutes?" "How did you avoid fighting earlier in the week?" And, of course, therapists should also ask how couples managed to keep violence out of their conflict. Finally, couples can be asked what they have learned from this relapse that will help them in facing such situations in the future.

When violence is part of a relapse, or when either partner feels threatened with violence during a relapse, therapists need to take a different stance. Safety becomes the primary concern at this point. It is best to talk with each partner alone and to confer briefly with a cotherapist to decide if a conjoint session should take place at all. Procedures for assuring safety, described earlier, should be used with the partners individually. Violence is never minimized. Therapists may need to review and refine the time-out plan that the couple developed once clients describe where they got off track.

TROUBLESHOOTING THROUGHOUT THE TREATMENT PROCESS

Primary Aggressor May be Frustrated about Partner's Lack of Trust

The primary aggressor may become frustrated that his or her partner still does not trust the changes that have been made. Clients who have been physically abused should be encouraged to avoid premature trust in their partner's changes with respect to violence. The primary aggressor needs to be reminded that, although it may be normal to want the partner to rush to forgiveness, the onus is on him (we use him because the primary aggressor is usually the man) to demonstrate long-term change before expecting his partner to trust him. Many of the males in our treatment program believed that since they had learned to control their anger and had become nonviolent, through anger management tools, their partners should trust them. However, since trust does not often come easily, the disappointment may lead to more anger and resentment for both partners. Therapists should normalize both the tendency not to regain trust quickly and the tendency to become frustrated, and they should add that long-term change will be the foundation for a stronger relationship. The man is also encouraged to extend his understanding and sensitivity, particularly towards his partner's experience (Jenkins, 1990). The therapist may ask, "Do you have a sense of what makes it so hard for Jane to trust that you mean it this time?" Or, it can be stated that experience has taught that demanding trust prematurely does not work. The man can be asked, "How will you resist the urge to demand her trust prematurely?" or, "How can you show her that you are prepared to be patient?" If appropriate, therapists may ask the woman, in her partner's presence, "Do you think Jack understands what makes it hard for you to trust him?"

Couples May Decide to Separate

Sometimes, although initially believing that couples therapy would preserve the relationship, either partner may decide that change is too slow or that he or she may never feel secure that violence will not recur. These couples should be encouraged to continue counseling to process separation issues, especially if there are children involved. However, if they decide to end the relationship, they should be given referrals to other resources to help them deal with the issues that will emerge. If they are able to separate without violence, stalking, psychological abuse, and so forth, they should be affirmed for their accomplishment.

One Partner Stomps Out of the Session

One partner may leave angrily in the middle of a session. If this occurs, therapists should reframe this behavior, noting that while stomping out of a session is not the best way to take a time-out, it is a way of de-escalating conflict and thus keeping violence from occurring. The partner who remains in the room should be helped to consider safety and how to respond to the partner. If the female partner is left behind and is afraid for her safety, help her activate her safety plan. If she is frustrated but not frightened, help her to consider the progress made and the reality of the ups and downs of making changes. It is often helpful for the therapist to contact the partner who left the session before the next session to thank him or her for choosing to de-escalate and to encourage him or her to return to the next session.

Honeymoon Period

There may be cause for concern when a couple seems to be in a honeymoon period, where they experience a renewed sense of closeness and a sense that nothing can go wrong. Of course, this is a good thing; therapists should punctuate how they are making this important change, and check with both partners individually to make sure both see the change. However, if their optimism is in stark contrast with their earlier presentation, or seems primarily based on total absence of conflict, therapists may decide to normalize a relapse (a relapse should not be interpreted as a recurrence of abuse) by saying that change sometimes occurs by taking two steps forward and one step back. Telling them that it would not be unusual for them to experience periods of disharmony and frustration serves to prevent their viewing these periods as signs of failure. It might also be helpful to discuss what they think a step back might look like, and how they can keep their angry feelings from getting out of control—in effect, hope for the best and plan for the worst. If the couple does get discouraged because they have had a fight, remind them that that is a normal part of the process.

Termination

The final session should be a celebration. One technique that is often helpful is to ask each couple to write an affirmation letter to themselves and to their partner about their resolve to stay on track and their commitment to the relationship. The letters can be placed in sealed envelopes and given to the therapist, who will mail them to the couples in 6 months to remind them about their commitment to change and about their thoughts at this time.

Another ritual, which has been well received in the group format, begins by having the therapist ask group members in advance to prepare for the final session by thinking about how their relationship was when they first came to group; about what was going better for them as a couple, a family, and as individuals now; and what they would like to see continue or see more of in their partners in the future. Since the couples, by the end of treatment, have developed good and supportive relationships with each other, they are also asked to think about the other couples and what positive changes they have seen in them. In the final session they share their thoughts with the rest of the group. This exercise often provides profound affirmation and hope.

Alumni Group/Ongoing Couples Treatment

Clearly, not all issues that couples bring to treatment will be resolved in 12 weeks of conjoint sessions. In response to the requests of our first group cohort of clients, we have initiated an "Alumni Group"—a multicouple group that meets every 2 to 3 weeks to provide those who have finished the 18-week program with ongoing support. The group is open to couples who have completed either the individual or group treatment modality, and is open-ended. Couples may join at any time and leave as they see fit. The alumni group focuses on helping couples continue to use and refine the skills they learned during the more intensive treatment. It is also a chance for couples with some months of successful, violence-free living to coach couples who have just completed the 18-week treatment. This benefits both parties—the newly completed couples are able to gain from the experience and wisdom of the more senior couples, and the more senior couples are able to solidify their gains by sharing with others what they have learned.

It often happens that issues identified during the 18-week program go beyond the bounds of what can be addressed in this format. Issues such as parenting difficulties, strained relations with families of origin, and past abuse histories and their effects on the current relationship are only a few examples of such issues. Once the couple has managed to stop the violence in their relationship, therapists may need to refer them for more traditional marital therapy to work on these issues and to increase the quality of their relationship. One male participant remarked, as he and his wife embarked on marital therapy to deal with a variety of longstanding problems in their relationship, "You helped us make our home a safe home. Now, we need to make it a happy one."

―――――――――――――――――――― **Case Study** ――――――――――――――

Lucia and Mark were referred for therapy by the court system. During an altercation, Lucia had become enraged; Mark initially tried to physically restrain her but eventually chose to call the police. Lucia was arrested and released after a few hours.

Mark was 40 years old, Caucasian, and college educated. He was 6' tall, with a stocky build and blond hair. He was shy, friendly, and quiet. Lucia was 27 years old, of Brazilian descent, with a high school education. She was 5'8" tall, heavyset, with black hair. She spoke and understood English sufficiently well to participate in the group, although at times she requested that conversations be slowed down so she could participate more actively. She was friendly, direct, and outspoken. Neither identified drugs or alcohol as an issue in their relationship.

The couple had been married for 6 years and had three small children, ages 1, 3, and 5. Mark worked full-time in the military and Lucia stayed home and raised the children. Both were committed to finding a solution to their anger and violence. In spite of their very intense fights, it was apparent during sessions that they both cared deeply for each other and were committed to the marriage.

During the intake, the couple completed the CTS2 and provided important information about their relationship and how violence was affecting them. Mark identified five incidents where *he* yelled, pushed, or slapped his partner as a result of their conflict. He identified six incidents where *she* yelled, pushed, or slapped him. Lucia identified 31 incidents where *she* yelled, threw objects, pushed, slapped, punched, choked, or slammed him against the wall. She reported 13 incidents where *he* had insulted, twisted her arm, pushed, punched, or slammed her against the wall. Both reported to have done something to their partner that resulted in the partner having to get emergency medical care one time. Mark expressed a need to understand what was happening with his wife when she was angry; he wanted to learn how to communicate with her better. He expressed some reservations about being in a multicouple group. He felt awkward about talking in front of others about his problems. He was afraid to find out that *he* may be the cause of the problems. Lucia expressed a wish to learn how to deal with her anger and wished that her husband would stop being afraid of her; she wanted him to say what he thought and to not worry so much.

Mark and Lucia were one of three couples that completed an 18-week group to which they were assigned. Both Mark and Lucia participated in six gender-specific anger management sessions preceding multicouple group sessions. In spite of difficulties (fear, shyness around strangers, shame at their violent behavior) normally experienced in the early stages of groups, both Mark and Lucia were active participants in their gender-specific groups; both identified their own styles of abuse and understood their personal contribution to the violence in their home.

Their openness to the process was helpful to others in the groups, and served as a catalyst for self-reflection while limiting the more familiar styles of blaming one's partner for one's anger.

Lucia had trouble understanding the safety plan, since she was not afraid of Mark and was unwilling to call 911 after having been arrested. She expressed concern about her treatment by the police and about her upcoming court appearance. Eventually she agreed to contact a sister who lived nearby and to consider 911 as an option if the violence recurred. During these sessions she continued to express fear of her ability to control her anger and concern about how long she stays resentful. During the 6-week gender-specific group, both Mark and Lucia discussed the possibility that Lucia may be depressed and may be suffering from premenstrual syndrome (PMS). The cotherapists encouraged her to consult a physician. After consulting a doctor Lucia decided not to take any medication, since the couple was interested in having another child. By the end of the 6-week women's group, Lucia believed she was able to identify anger earlier and was able to take steps to mitigate it most of the time. She found the time-out periods helpful, but admitted to having a very hard time when Mark called a time-out.

Mark and Lucia did not attend the first week of the 12-week couples group. The therapists contacted the couple and were informed that the couple's reluctance to come to group had been caused by Lucia's court appearance; she felt ashamed by having to appear in court and angry at what she felt was her partner's betrayal by calling the police. Mark felt guilty and responsible for Lucia's anger. After some discussion over the phone the couple was able to identify that they still felt very committed to their marriage and to each other and identified the intensity of their emotions as confusing them and contributing to a sense of hopelessness. Upon their return the couple was distant, quiet, and reluctant to work out a viable, negotiated time-out contract. As Mark and Lucia observed the other couples identify in concrete terms what they envisioned for their marriages, and what they were already doing toward meeting these visions, they began to open up. Mark and Lucia observed the other couples using new communication skills (such as "I" statements, or reflective listening) to express their needs and their frustrations without anger derailing their objectives. After several sessions, Lucia and Mark were able to describe their vision for their relationship. Lucia described how she often felt protected and cared for by Mark; she felt he was a great father to their children and she was very attracted to him. Mark expressed a deep love and attraction for Lucia; he felt she was a very sensitive and caring wife and mother. Both said they wanted more of these good feelings in their marriage.

The couple was willing to discuss specific incidents that highlighted their communication patterns; Mark would agree to do an activity with Lucia and their children, then, without warning or consultation, he would change the plans, and leave her alone with the children while they waited for him. After some time he would reappear and want to continue with the original plans. This pattern illustrated both his need to feel independent and in control, and his need to have her near him. Mark's actions triggered her anger around feeling abandoned and discounted in decision making. For Lucia, being left alone without prior warning elicited many strong emotions around abandonment, unpredictability, and feeling controlled.

She recognized these as familiar patterns from her childhood with an alcoholic father, whom she loved very much, but who was unpredictable and often disappeared from her life for days. The couple identified times when similar situations were resolved without serious conflict, and what each had done differently at those times.

These sessions were significant for Mark because he was able to identify how his actions impacted Lucia, since he had not been aware that he was being controlling and disrespectful, and that this was triggering a lot of anger in Lucia. For Mark, being in control meant not talking about his needs and/or negotiating them. He just did what he wanted. Lucia was able to see that the anger she was experiencing was understandable, and that expressing her feelings earlier in the process was necessary for her to avoid building up resentment that eventually led to her feeling out of control.

The couples were helped to identify their patterns of psychological abuse and were encouraged to identify times when they were able to handle disagreements in positive ways. Most of the couples tended to focus on one moment during the week when things went badly; through the group discussion, the couples began to recognize that several days during the week they were able to handle daily conflicts and stress very well. Mark and Lucia needed more practice with communication skills around the real-life problems they were experiencing, since they were still experiencing rapid escalation and at times were reluctant to use time-out. Until Mark and Lucia had more practice at handling their intense emotional responses to conflict, they were reluctant to recognize the times when they dealt with conflict successfully.

As the sessions progressed, the couples were able to be more specific with each other about their visions for their relationship. Lucia expressed her wish that Mark would feel free to be open with her and to let her in on what he was thinking—this was important for her—to feel more connected and intimate with him. Both talked about their distancing and pursuing patterns and how these resembled conflicts in their families of origin. These sessions coincided with visits from both Lucia's and Mark's mothers. Lucia described the tensions and distance between them, and how she felt abandoned by Mark when conflicts arose between Lucia and the two visiting mothers. During these sessions Lucia's reactions shifted from rage to deep sadness, and Mark's shifted from avoidance to frustration with himself at finding it difficult to express his affection and love to Lucia in ways that she could accept as genuine. During the next weeks the couple continued to have emotionally charged conflicts, but were able to use time-outs and then reconnect in more effective ways. Lucia identified what she would like to see Mark do differently for her in order to feel that Mark was really there for her. Mark made efforts to get close to Lucia, but Lucia said she did not notice—Mark found this very frustrating.

During these last sessions the therapists used metadialogue to bring out into the open the apparent inconsistencies between what Lucia was saying she needed, and how Mark was interpreting what Lucia said. During these sessions, the other couples were able to contribute to the discussion, and Mark found it helpful to have the other male members of the group identify what they understood Lucia wanted and where Mark was missing the point. Lucia, by feeling understood, was willing to more calmly express her needs, both to Mark and to the other couples.

Everyone recognized that Lucia was having to deal with cultural and language difficulties in addition to the conflicts that all the couples were confronting. This shift in Lucia made it less threatening for Mark to approach her, and it was also identified as an area Mark needed to continue to work on after group was over.

During the final session, Mark and Lucia reported that they felt happy with the efforts each had made to keep their anger at manageable levels. Lucia felt relief at being able to understand that she had legitimate reasons for getting angry and that Mark was being helpful by listening to her and trying to understand what she was saying to him. They announced that they were being transferred because of Mark's job and that they were both happy with this move.

When completing the CTS2 again, during the final session, Mark reported that each shoved and yelled at the other once during the 18 weeks of treatment. Lucia reported that both insulted the other three times; she threw things at him two times and he threw things at her once. She destroyed something of his and both shouted at the other once. Both Mark and Lucia returned and completed a number of follow-up tests 3 months after treatment ended. At that time both reported that there had been no incidents of physical violence during the previous 3 months.

REFERENCES

Aldarondo, E., & Straus, M. A. (1994). Screening for physical violence in couple therapy: Methodological, practical, and ethical considerations. *Family Process, 33,* 425–439.

Berg, I. K., & Miller, S. D. (1992). *Working with the problem drinker: A solution-focused approach.* New York: Norton.

de Shazer, S. (1985). *Keys to solution in brief therapy.* New York: Norton.

de Shazer, S. (1988). *Clues: Investigating solutions in brief therapy.* New York: Norton.

de Shazer, S., & Isebaert, L. (2003). A solution-focused approach to the treatment of problematic drinking. *Journal of Family Psychotherapy, 14*(4), 43–52.

Edleson, J. L., & Tolman, R. M. (1992). *Intervention for men who batter: An ecological approach.* Newbury Park, CA: Sage.

Feld, S. L., & Straus, M. A. (1989). Escalation and desistance of wife assault in marriage. *Criminology, 27,* 141–161.

Gelles, R. J., & Straus, M. A. (1988). *Intimate violence.* New York: Simon and Schuster.

Jaffe, P. G., Wolfe, D., & Wilson, S. (1990). *Children of battered women.* Newbury Park, CA: Sage.

Jenkins, A. (1990). *Invitations to responsibility: The therapeutic engagement of men who are violent and abusive.* Adelaide, Australia: Dulwich Center.

Matthews, D. (1995a). *On the level: Foundations for violence free living.* St. Paul, MN: Amherst H. Wilder Foundation.

Matthews, D. (1995b). *On the level: foundations for violence free living: A step-by-step guide to facilitating men's domestic abuse groups.* St. Paul, MN: Amherst H. Wilder Foundation.

O'Leary, K. D., Vivian, D., & Malone, J. (1992). Assessment of physical aggression against women in marriage: The need for multimodal assessment. *Behavioral Assessment, 14,* 5–14.

Rennison, C. M., & Welchans, S. (2000). *Intimate Partner Violence.* Washington, DC: Bureau of Justice Statistics.

Rose, S., Bisson, J., & Wessely, S. (2004) Psychological debriefing for preventing Posttraumatic Stress Disorder (PTSD; Cochrane Review). *Cochrane Library, 1.* Retrieved April 14, 2004, from http://www.cochrane.org/cochrane/revabstr/AB000560.htm

Rosen, K. H., Matheson, J. L., Stith, S. M., McCollum, E. E., & Locke, L. D. (2003). Negotiated time-out: A de-escalation tool for couples. *Journal of Marital and Family Therapy, 29,* 291–298.

Saunders, D. G., Lynch, A. B., Grayson, M., & Linz, D. (1987). The inventory of beliefs about wife beating: The construction and initial validation of a measure of beliefs and attitudes. *Violence and Victims, 2,* 39–57.

Schumm, W. R., Nichols, C. W., Schectman, K. L., & Grigsby, C. C. (1983). Characteristics of responses to the Kansas Marital Satisfaction Scale by a sample of 84 married mothers. *Psychological Reports, 53,* 567–572.

Straus, M. A. (1979). Measuring intrafamily conflict and violence: The conflict tactics (CT) scale. *Journal of Marriage and the Family, 41,* 75–88.

Straus, M. A., Hamby, S. L., Boney-McCoy, S., & Sugarman, D. B. (1996). The Revised Conflict Tactics Scales (CTS2): Development and preliminary psychometric data. *Journal of Family Issues, 17,* 283–316.

Stuart, G. L., & Holzworth-Munroe, A. (1995). Identifying subtypes of maritally violent men: Descriptive dimensions, correlates and causes of violence, and treatment implications. In S. M. Stith & M. A. Straus (Eds.), *Understanding partner violence: Prevalence, causes, consequences, and solutions* (pp. 162–172). Minneapolis, MN: National Council on Family Relations.

Tucker, N. L., Stith, S. M., Howell, L. W., McCollum, E. E., & Rosen, K. H. (2000). Meta-dialogues in domestic violence focused couples treatment. *Journal of Systemic Therapies, 19,* 56–72.

Weiner-Davis, M., de Shazer, S., & Gingerich, W. J. (1987). Building on pretreatment change to construct the therapeutic solution: An exploratory study. *Journal of Marital and Family Therapy, 13,* 359–363.

Wile, D. B. (1993). *After the fight: Using your disagreements to build a stronger relationship.* New York: Guilford.

CHAPTER 17

Treating Affair Couples: An Integrative Approach

Donald H. Baucom, Kristina C. Gordon, and Douglas K. Snyder

INTRODUCTION TO TREATING AFFAIRS

Extramarital Affairs as Interpersonal Trauma

Affairs appear to be relatively frequent occurrences in marriages in the United States. In recent studies with large representative samples, approximately 22 to 25 percent of men and 11 to 15 percent of women indicate that they have engaged in extramarital sex on at least one occasion (Lauman, Gagnon, Michael, & Michaels, 1994). In any given year, it is estimated that, on average, between 1.5 percent and 4 percent of married individuals will engage in extramarital sex, with about twice as many men as women reporting extramarital sex in the past year (e.g., Laumann et al., 1994; Wiederman, 1997). Even more significant for understanding marital disruption, 40 percent of divorced women and 44 percent of divorced men reported more than one sexual contact during the course of their marriages (Janus & Janus, 1993). However, despite the prevalence of this problem, many therapists do not have an adequate way to conceptualize infidelity or know how to develop a treatment plan for this problem (Whisman, Dixon, & Johnson, 1997). Thus, the purpose of this chapter is to outline an integrative approach to helping couples recover from an affair that integrates treatment strategies from trauma interventions, forgiveness interventions, cognitive-behavioral couple therapy, and insight-oriented couple therapy.

Both clinical observations and empirical investigations agree that the discovery of an affair can have an overwhelming and devastating impact on a couple. (Throughout this discussion, the term "participating partner" is used to describe the person having the affair, and "injured partner" is the term used to describe the person not having the affair, while recognizing that both partners may be injured considerably by what has occurred.) Clinicians report that for the injured partner, intense emotions often vacillate between rage toward the participating partner and more inward feelings of shame, depression, overwhelming powerlessness, victimization, and abandonment (Abrahm Spring, 1996; Brown, 1991; Gordon, Baucom, & Snyder, 2004; Lusterman, 1998; Pittman, 1989; Reibstein & Richards, 1993). Taken as a whole, many of these emotional, cognitive, and behavioral responses parallel the criteria for Posttraumatic Stress Disorder. Therefore, conceptualizing the response to an affair as a reaction to an interpersonally traumatic event aids in the formulation of these difficult cases and the conduct of treatment (Glass & Wright, 1997; Gordon & Baucom, 1998).

Literature on traumatic responses suggests that people are most likely to become emotionally traumatized when an event violates basic assumptions about how the world and people operate (Janoff-Bulman, 1989). Several important couple assumptions may be violated by an affair (e.g., assumptions that partners can be trusted, assumptions that the relationship is a safe place to be). The trauma literature also suggests that when these basic beliefs are violated, the injured person can lose a great deal of predictability for the future, and thus experiences a loss of control. Thus, an extramarital affair is not merely another very negative event; instead, the violation of basic assumptions such as trust and predictability means that the injured person often experiences the shattering of core beliefs essential to emotional security. Common statements reflecting such turmoil include, "I don't know you; you aren't the person I thought you were, and our relationship isn't what I thought it was," or, "This just makes no sense; I can't understand how you could do this; I thought I could trust you." Given this unpredictability and lack of trust, the injured person typically cannot move forward with the relationship, even if the affair has ended. As long as injured partners do not have a clear sense of why the affair occurred, they cannot trust their partners not to hurt them again; instead, the participating partners are likely to be seen as malicious people, whose very faces or voices may serve as stimuli for painful emotions such as anxiety, confusion, anger, depression, and shame. Unfortunately, the participating partner often is dealing with his or her own feelings of guilt, shame, anger, or depression, and, thus, often responds to the injured partner's strong expressions of emotions with withdrawal, justification, or retaliation.

An Integrated Approach to Treating Affairs

Trauma and Forgiveness-Based Approaches

Given the conceptualization of affairs as an interpersonal trauma, there is considerable potential benefit in borrowing from the literature on both the traumatic response and interpersonal forgiveness when considering how to conceptualize and organize an effective treatment. Treatments that arise from trauma theories generally assist clients in focusing more clearly on the trauma, expose them to the memories of the trauma, and help them to reconstruct their basic schemas about how the world operates and to regain a new sense of control over their outcomes (Calhoun & Resnick, 1993). Interestingly, these themes are echoed in newly developed forgiveness-based interventions, which are therapeutic approaches beginning to gain greater attention in mainstream psychological literature. Studies have emerged recently indicating that forgiveness-based interventions aimed at helping the individual cognitively reframe the interpersonal betrayal and gain a greater understanding of why the trauma occurred are effective in increasing participants' levels of forgiveness and in improving their levels of both individual and dyadic psychological functioning (Freedman & Enright, 1996; McCullough, Worthington, & Rachal, 1997; Worthington, in press).

Similar to the trauma-based approaches, in most theories of forgiveness the primary focus of the process is on developing a changed understanding of why the betrayal occurred and reconstructing a new meaning for the event (Enright & the Human Development Study Group, 1991; Gordon & Baucom, 1998). Despite some differences, most theories of forgiveness are fairly consistent in their definitions of the end state of forgiveness, indicating three common elements: (1) gaining a more balanced view of the offender and the event, (2) decreasing negative affect toward the offender, potentially along with increased compassion, and (3) giving up the right to punish the offender further.

There are at least two major benefits in combining trauma and forgiveness-based perspectives on extramarital affairs. First, the trauma approach offers a thoughtful explanation for why the cognitive-restructuring that appears ubiquitous in forgiveness theories is necessary; individuals need, and are motivated, to reconstruct their assumptive networks after they have been disrupted. Basic assumptions are necessary to allow an individual to move through life on a daily basis in an efficient manner, without questioning every encounter. Second, because an affair is an interpersonal trauma, the forgiveness literature offers additional guidance on how the dyad can rebuild their relationship, or move beyond bitterness, through (1) the development of empathy or compassion for each other, and (2) enacting behaviors designed to rebalance their relationships.

To date, both the trauma and forgiveness literatures have primarily emphasized interventions targeting individuals. Left largely unaddressed are how best to conceptualize the recovery process and what specific interventions to pursue when dealing with interpersonal trauma from a couple perspective. To this end, it is useful to turn to two empirically supported couple therapy approaches: cognitive-behavioral couple therapy and insight-oriented couple therapy.

Integrating Cognitive-Behavioral and Insight-Oriented Approaches

Several years ago, the current authors were reflecting on couples we had found particularly difficult to work with clinically, and what we believed were essential elements of change that had somehow been missing in treatment. We were struck by our common perception that a critical component of couple therapy that had been largely neglected in controlled clinical trials involved partners' capacity to recover from relationship injury. We also recognized an important distinction between minor hurts and disappointments that occur almost daily, as an inherent aspect of intimate relationships, versus major betrayals that disrupt the fundamental trust and emotional attachment that serves as the foundation of a couple's relationship, and the importance of forgiveness in a restorative process, from such injuries. As a result, we decided to collaborate in developing a couple-based treatment specifically targeting relationship trauma and investigating critical mechanisms in the forgiveness process. Extramarital affairs emerged as the vehicle for examining recovery from relationship injury, both because of their prevalence and their devastating impact on individual and relationship functioning for most couples experiencing this event.

Our collective efforts to design a treatment for couples struggling to recover from an affair emphasized integration of couple therapies previously shown to be efficacious in addressing a broad spectrum of relationship difficulties. Cognitive-behavioral couple therapy (CBCT) builds on skills-based interventions of behavioral couple therapy, targeting couple communication and behavior-exchange by directing partners' attention to explanations they construct for each other's behavior and to expectations and standards they hold for their own relationship and for relationships in general (Epstein & Baucom, 2002). Previous work by Baucom and colleagues (Baucom & Lester, 1986; Baucom, Sayers, & Sher, 1990) and by Halford, Sanders, and Behrens (1993) have shown that approximately 55 to 70 percent of couples treated for relationship distress using CBCT show improvement, with approximately 40 to 50 percent no longer distressed at the end of therapy.

The structured, directed strategies offered within cognitive-behavioral interventions provide focus and direction to couples at a time when they are particularly needed. Before couples can explore the meaning of an affair for their relationship or reestablish trust and intimacy, they first need assistance in containing the emotional turmoil and destructive exchanges that often characterize initial responses to the disclosure or discovery of an affair. Partners frequently need assistance in communicating feelings in a constructive manner and reaching intermediate decisions about how to set boundaries regarding involvement with the outside affair person, how much information to share with children or extended family, and how to interact with each other. Moreover, in exploring the factors that placed their relationship at risk for an affair, couples frequently need to improve their ability to negotiate basic changes in how they interact and manage daily challenges of their relationship. Cognitive-behavioral couple therapy is particularly well suited to these therapeutic objectives. However, CBCT's general focus on the present and the future also leaves important gaps in dealing with such couples. Many couples report that they cannot merely move forward and put the affair behind them; they need some way to process the trauma that has occurred and some way to make sense of the past.

Insight-oriented couple therapy (IOCT) offers therapeutic strategies designed specifically to help partners understand current relationship struggles from the perspective of partners' developmental histories. In IOCT, previous relationships, their affective components, and strategies for emotional gratification and anxiety containment are reconstructed, with a focus on identifying, for each partner, consistencies in their interpersonal conflicts and coping styles across relationships (Snyder, 1999). In addition, ways in which previous coping strategies vital to prior relationships represent distortions or inappropriate solutions for emotional intimacy and satisfaction in the current relationship are articulated. In a previous controlled trial of IOCT, 73 percent of couples showed significant improvement and 40 percent were no longer distressed at the end of treatment (Snyder & Wills, 1989). Moreover, in a 4-year follow-up of couples in this study, only 3 percent of couples receiving IOCT were divorced—compared to 38 percent of couples receiving traditional behavioral couple therapy (Snyder, Wills, & Grady-Fletcher, 1991).

Hence, insight-oriented strategies in couple therapy offer the potential of helping partners to gain a better understanding of both their own and each other's developmental histories, the role that their respective pasts have played throughout their marriage, and how individual and relationship dynamics influenced by their pasts may have served as potential risk factors contributing to the participating partner's extramarital affair. Not only do insight-oriented strategies yield crucial information about why an affair occurred, which enables the partners to develop more realistic attributions about the affair, but these revelations of vulnerability also help the partners develop more empathy and compassion for each other. Furthermore, as will be demonstrated, as this increased understanding and insight occur, this understanding is placed within a cognitive-behavioral framework of developing a well-balanced set of attributions for the event, along with a focus on what changes are needed in the relationship for the future.

Couple interventions for extramarital affairs also require a significantly greater focus on affect than often has been the case in cognitive-behavioral interventions. Again, this results from the phenomenon under consideration. Given that an extramarital affair can be considered as an interpersonal trauma, the overwhelming emotions incurred in experiencing any trauma are often present. Thus, the therapist usually must attend to the regulation of the short-term emotional upheaval that is characteristic of early stages of trauma. Similarly, even if the couple is not overtly expressing negative affect, they may still be experiencing hurt, anger, and unexpressed anxiety about their future. Unless these emotions are addressed fully, there is the potential of long-term resentment and hostility resulting from the affair that can continue to interfere with individual and relationship functioning. Additionally, as will be shown, the therapist needs to promote a greater atmosphere of empathy between the partners as both of them examine their individual histories and their personal vulnerabilities, as well as the impact of these issues upon their relationship. Thus, an effective couple intervention for extramarital affairs might draw upon cognitive-behavioral interventions integrated with insight-oriented approaches to provide a treatment strategy that balances the past, present, and future with an increased emphasis on affect and developmental factors.

Overview of Current Model

Gordon and Baucom (1998) developed a stage model of forgiveness that parallels a response to trauma, including three major stages in the forgiveness process: (1) dealing with the impact, (2) a search for meaning, or understanding of why the affair occurred, and (3) recovery, or moving forward. The treatment described here builds on this model of forgiveness and integrates cognitive-behavioral, insight-oriented, forgiveness-based, and trauma-based approaches to relationship difficulties. The treatment model includes three phases of treatment, each of which is directly tied to a stage from the authors' forgiveness model.

Given that the first stage of dealing with an affair involves addressing the impact of the event, the treatment components for Stage 1 of the therapy are primarily cognitive-behavioral, and directly target problems that arise from the immediate impact of the affair, such as emotional dysregulation, depression, the need to express feelings of anger and hurt, and "damage control" where necessary. Next, because the goal of the second stage is helping the couple explore both proximal and distal factors that contributed to the participating partner's decision to engage in the affair, treatment strategies in Stage 2 of the therapy are more insight oriented and incorporate cognitive restructuring strategies, particularly with regard to attributions for the affair. Finally, in Stage 3, the couple is encouraged to (1) address the issue of forgiveness, (2) consolidate what they have learned about each other, (3) reexamine their relationship, and (4) decide how or whether they wish to continue their relationship in the future. At this time, the couple begins work on either improving their relationship in the here and now, or initiating termination procedures.

Although designed and presented to couples as a three-stage intervention, the amount of time allocated to each stage necessarily varies as a function of specific needs dictated by aspects of partners' individual and relationship functioning. For example, affairs that have occurred and become known months or even years earlier sometimes require less attention to boundary setting or self care, comprising a portion of Stage 1 interventions. Similarly, in higher-functioning couples who have successfully explored the impact and meaning of the affair in Stages 1 and 2, decisions about how to move on, addressed in Stage 3, may already have been largely resolved by the time those issues are introduced explicitly in treatment.

Couples' initial preferences for addressing various aspects of the affair also vary. For example, some couples assert their determination to remain in their relationship before resolving the initial turmoil or reaching a deeper understanding of how the affair came about; in such cases, we typically affirm their positive aspirations for their relationship, but indicate our intent to revisit this decision once they have achieved a deeper understanding of all the contributing factors to the affair and the meaning these have for each of them. Occasionally, one partner has so much anger that it interferes with an ability to commit to the recovery process we advocate in this treatment; with such couples, we work to resolve immediate crises and to reach intermediate decisions about how to get through the next few days or weeks, until achieving an equilibrium permitting more informed consideration of whether to pursue couple therapy as a means for dealing with the affair conjointly and reaching more enduring decisions about the relationship. Some couples want to delve immediately into why the affair occurred, before developing a shared understanding of the impact the affair has had on their relationship or on partners' willingness to engage collaboratively in a therapeutic process; for these couples, we emphasize that exploring the diverse, complicated factors typically involved in an affair first requires a basic level of trust in each other's understanding of what has happened, and that at least a few sessions facilitating such an understanding are a prerequisite to exploring contributing factors in an effective manner. In our experience, once the three-stage model and its rationale are carefully explained to couples at the outset of treatment, couples usually agree to an initial course of therapy based on this formulation.

The components and challenges of each stage of treatment are subsequently described in further detail. Following this description, we present initial findings regarding the treatment's effectiveness and a brief clinical case study exemplifying key components of this intervention.

STAGE 1: ADDRESSING THE IMPACT OF AN AFFAIR

Assessment

The first stage of the treatment encompasses assessment and management of the affair's impact. Using common assessment strategies for couples (Epstein & Baucom, 2002), basic aspects of couple functioning relevant to all couples should be assessed (e.g., satisfaction, communication skills, and commitment level). Furthermore, a conjoint session focused on gathering information about the couple's relationship history should be conducted, with specific attention paid to events and experiences leading up to the affair. In addition, the therapist should gather information about what is known about the affair, how the affair came to light, and how the couple is currently dealing with the impact of the affair, looking at both strengths and weaknesses in the couple's current functioning.

In addition, individual assessment sessions, one for each partner, are beneficial. During the conjoint session, it is important to set the stage for confidentiality in the individual sessions. This requirement is necessary in order to allow each partner, during the individual sessions, to air his or her genuine feelings about the situation and individual goals regarding the couple therapy. Because the emotional climate often is highly charged during conjoint sessions following the discovery of an affair, individual sessions are helpful to allow each person a safer, less volatile environment for talking with the therapist. Also, many partners are more open and honest when the other partner is not present, because they do not have to be concerned about the partner's response.

However, this increased honesty during the individual sessions can at times lead to complications. If, during an individual session, information arises that has major implications for the progress of therapy, such as the fact that the affair is still ongoing, or that one of the partners is planning to end the relationship, then the therapist should work with the client to plan how best to address these issues with the other partner. Many therapists are unclear about what information can be held confidentially and what should be shared with the other partner. There is no need that all details revealed by one partner during an individual session be shared with the other partner. What is important is that one partner not share information with the therapist that is contrary to what the other partner is being told in conjoint sessions that would affect the treatment (e.g., commitments to monogamy, or commitment to working on the relationship). If one person is not willing to share appropriate information with his or her partner, then she or he should be urged to reconsider whether to engage in couple therapy at this time, or the therapist might make the decision to terminate treatment.

In addition to additional information about the status of the affair and commitment to the current relationship, the focus of the individual session is to obtain an individual history for each partner, paying particular attention to aspects of his or her development that may have impacted actions surrounding the affair. Examples of these issues may be patterns in past relationships, beliefs about marriage, parental history and attitudes toward marriages, or any strong needs or desires that seem to be particularly urgent for the client.

If the couple contacts the therapist soon after an affair has become known, typically they will be in a state of crisis. Consequently, it is important to conduct the initial assessment quickly, not spending an hour a week over several weeks. Extended assessment sessions or several sessions in one week can be appropriate, so that the couple and therapist can focus on the therapeutic process.

Therapeutic Components of Stage 1

After completing the assessment, the therapist should have a good understanding of how the couple is functioning. The therapist should then provide the couple (1) the therapist's conceptualization of what led up to the affair, (2) a summary of what problems the couple is currently facing in their relationship, and why they are experiencing these problems, and (3) a treatment strategy. Then, the couple should be given an explanation of the stages of the recovery process and the response to trauma conceptualization described in the introduction. For example,

> **Therapist:** We see the recovery process from an affair as having three stages. First, there is an impact stage; then there is a "meaning/understanding" stage; and then there is a "moving-on" stage. I'll explain these stages in more detail in a minute. Research on people who are recovering from a traumatic event, such as earthquakes, muggings, and so on, suggest that most people go through these stages when they are trying to put their lives back together. We think events like affairs or major betrayals in close relationships are also very upsetting and traumatic, and we believe that people go through similar stages of recovery. Does this make sense to you so far?

> **Jim:** Yes—this all does feel traumatic to me—but Nancy doesn't understand. She keeps saying "Let's get over it and move on." But I can't move on. I'm stuck.

> **Therapist:** Exactly. We think it's next to impossible to really move on until you move through these stages. After an affair occurs, most people are mostly trying to figure out what has happened to them, and are often reeling from the impact. To go back to the example of a trauma from a natural disaster, you could think of this phase as being similar to what persons feel after experiencing an earthquake. Their whole world has literally been shaken up and their foundation feels very unstable and insecure. This is a very emotional stage, and the emotions can change daily, hourly, or by the minute. These emotions are very tied to what you're thinking. Until you are able to reconstruct that foundation, make some sense of what has happened and why, and feel secure again, it's hard to let go of those painful feelings and thoughts.

In addition to assessment and feedback, the first stage of therapy has five basic components: (1) boundary setting, (2) self-care techniques, (3) time-out and venting techniques, (4) emotional expressiveness skills and discussion of the impact of the affair, and (5) coping with flashbacks.

Boundary Setting

When a couple feels out of control and in crisis, providing healthy boundaries can help to create some sense of normality and predictability. Because their own relationship has become dysregulated, setting boundaries or limits on how the partners interact with each other can be very helpful. Second, the injured partner often is greatly distressed about the outside person who had an affair with the participating partner. This intrusion of a third party into their lives is a major factor creating anxiety and a lack of safety. Therefore, setting strong and clear boundaries on interactions with the outside, third person is very important.

First, the couple's own relationship must be targeted, to create a sense of safety in the relationship and to minimize further negative effects on the couple. A major problem confronting many couples dealing with the impact of the affair is the fact that the negative emotions engendered by the betrayal may flood into many aspects of their functioning. Even areas within the marriage that were not problematic prior to the affair are likely to be affected by the increase in negativity in the marriage. For example, a couple who once prided themselves on their ability to parent well together may find themselves arguing bitterly in front of their children. Given that the couple is likely to experience a high level of conflict, and that this conflict often occurs at a much higher frequency than normal, they are likely to need immediate assistance from the therapist in setting limits on their negative interactions. For some couples, this involves making agreements about when, how often, and what aspects of the affair they will discuss. Otherwise, some couples report that they spend hours each day discussing the affair, often repeating the same conversations, typically resulting in negative, hurtful interactions. At times, the injured partner becomes dangerous, either to him- or herself or to the participating partner. We have worked with couples in which an injured partner who has never been violent becomes physically abusive once an affair is revealed. In such instances, appropriate boundaries might involve separating the two partners and having them reside in separate locations, with interactions occurring only in safe settings.

Using directed problem-solving or decision-making strategies (Epstein & Baucom, 2002), the therapist should help the couple to develop their own limits and boundaries for this problematic stage. It is important to emphasize that some of these solutions might be temporary ones, primarily designed for damage control. The participating partner may have to agree to some behaviors that would not be typical in marriage in the long term, but which are needed in the short term to help the injured partner regain a sense of control or safety and to demonstrate the participating partner's remorse for the affair. For example, if a common cause of arguments is a wife's anxiety regarding her husband's whereabouts, then her husband may agree to be zealous in checking in with his wife until some trust or security has been reestablished.

Second, in order for the injured partner to feel safe enough to engage in the therapeutic process, it is important for the participating partner to set strong boundaries on interactions with the outside third party. This is most easily obtained if the participating partner agrees to end the relationship with the third person, with no further contact. However, this absolute termination is sometimes difficult to create—for a variety of reasons. Some participating partners are unwilling to terminate all interaction with the outside person when the affair is discovered; sometimes logistics makes it impractical to have no interactions, at least immediately (e.g., the participating partner and third person work together); and at times, the outside person continues to contact the participating partner, despite being told not to do so. Because rebuilding trust is a crucial part of the therapeutic process, the therapist encourages the participating partner to be honest in stating what boundaries he or she is willing to set with the outside person at present and how that will be carried out, along with agreements for how the injured partner will be informed of contact with the outside person. Thus, the partners likely need to discuss various forms of communication, including face-to-face interactions, telephone and email contacts, letters, and so on, including a clarification of whether the participating partner can initiate any of these types of contact and how to respond if the other person initiates contact. Also, the content of acceptable conversations (e.g., to clarify that the relationship must end, to communicate needed information if the person is a work colleague) must be agreed upon. It is important to explain to the couple that more contact with the outside person will likely lead to more negative interactions between the partners, greater distress for the injured person, and greater difficulty in moving forward as a couple. That is, there are natural, predictable consequences for continuing the other relationship and interacting with the outside person.

For example, Jim had difficulty extricating himself from his extramarital relationship with Tammy, even though he had promised to reconcile with his wife, Ann. However, he enjoyed his discussions with Tammy and felt he could not bear to lose them, so he continued to meet with her for lunch, rationalizing that it was just platonic. Very quickly, Ann discovered these lunches, which had a devastating impact on the already shaky process of rebuilding their marriage. Then, when Jim attempted to sever all ties with Tammy, Tammy felt used, "led on," and retaliated by telling his office staff about their affair. In therapy, Jim later ruefully wished that he had made a clean break with Tammy from the beginning.

It's not unusual for some participating partners to believe initially that they can suspend sexual aspects of an affair relationship but still retain a deep friendship or emotional components of that relationship without costs or further risk. We challenge such beliefs by noting two factors that render them unrealistic: (1) First, once an affair relationship has developed, it is extremely difficult to maintain interactions without strong emotional and sexual feelings being continually stirred up that lead to renewal of the sexual relationship; and (2) second, even if such interactions were possible for both the participating and outside partner, such interactions compose a significant threat to the injured partner and almost always preclude working toward recovery from the affair.

Self-Care Guidelines

As noted earlier, the emotional sequelae of affairs often involve feelings of anxiety, depression, shame, and lowered self-esteem. Unfortunately, these feelings occur at a time when people are least equipped to deal with them; in fact, both partners may become involved in a vicious cycle wherein these feelings make them less effective in their interactions with their partners, which in turn makes them more depressed or anxious. Consequently, another major target for this stage of therapy involves helping both partners to take better care of themselves, in order to have more emotional resources to use as they work through the aftermath of the affair.

The current treatment offers basic self-care guidelines that encompass three areas: (1) physical care, including such aspects as eating well, sleep, decreased caffeine, and exercise; (2) social support, with careful attention paid to what is appropriate to disclose to others and what is not; and (3) spiritual support, such as meditation, prayer, and talking with spiritual counselors if consistent with the partner's belief system. These guidelines typically are presented in individual sessions with each partner, which allow the therapist to express support for each partner, talk with him or her about the upcoming sessions, and develop a plan for attempting to manage his or her emotions during the painful discussions to come and in his or her interactions outside of therapy.

It is in these sessions that the therapist might best be able to discuss with the participating partner the particular emotions of guilt, anger, shame, and ambivalence that they may be feeling, and to examine how best to address these issues in the conjoint sessions. At this stage in the therapy, when the injured partner's anger and hurt are likely to be at their highest levels, the participating partner's own anger and ambivalence may not be effectively heard by the injured partner, and may cause more polarization between the partners. These issues are best addressed and supported in individual sessions in the initial stage of therapy, and then addressed in conjoint sessions during the second stage of therapy as the participating partner begins to examine his or her reasons for the affair. However, injured partners are more likely to be able to hear the participating partner's feelings of remorse, shame, and guilt early in the therapy, because these feelings provide evidence that the participating partner is aware of the magnitude of his or her actions and that the affair is having a similarly negative impact on the participating partner.

On occasion, in these individual sessions one or both partners may express such strong doubts or uncertainty about their wish to salvage their relationship that they are uncertain whether to commit to an initial course of conjoint therapy. In cases of strong ambivalence, where a decision to end their relationship has *not* been made, we sometimes recommend concurrent individual therapy with another therapist—to explore these feelings while also working in conjoint therapy to contain the initial turmoil resulting from the affair, and to reestablish equilibrium in daily routines. Alternatively, when individuals have reached a decision to end their relationship but have not yet found a way of informing their partner, we work with them to explore their reservations about sharing this decision, and help them explore ways of doing so within the relative safety of conjoint couple sessions.

Time-Out and Venting Techniques

In light of the increased likelihood of negative interactions between the partners at this stage in the process, most couples need a strategy that allows them to disengage when the level of emotion becomes too high. Time-out strategies are introduced in the individual sessions, and the partners are instructed on how to recognize when one needs to be called and how to do so effectively. Partners are encouraged to agree ahead of time on a mutually acceptable way to call the time-out and on a specified length of time before they return to the discussion at hand. In addition, instead of using time-outs to fume and plan a counterattack, the partners are instructed in how to use the time-outs constructively—for example, to vent their tension through nonaggressive physical exercise, or to calm themselves through relaxation strategies.

Discussing the Impact of the Affair

A common need for the injured partner in this situation is to express to the participating partner how she or he has been hurt or angered by the affair. It is likely that this need serves both a punitive and a protective function. By its punitive qualities this discussion serves as a way to communicate that what happened was wrong, and to ensure that the participating partner also feels as much discomfort as possible, as a result of his or her actions. In this sense, expressing hurt and anger hopefully ensures that infidelity will not happen again, which in turn protects the person from additional harm in the future. However, despite the injured partner's need to express such feelings, these interactions between partners are often rancorous, and complicated by feelings of anger and guilt on the part of the participating partner. Often, the participating partner also has feelings of bitterness about an earlier hurt or betrayal in the marriage, which interferes with his or her ability to sympathize with the injured partner's feelings of betrayal. As a result, the injured partner is not likely to feel heard, and may increase demands or comments, precipitating a negative interaction cycle between the partners.

The current treatment seeks to interrupt this cycle through three means. First, the couple is taught to use appropriate emotional expressiveness skills, for both speaker and listener, to help the injured person be more effective in communicating feelings, and the participating partner to be more effective in demonstrating that she or he is listening (Epstein & Baucom, 2002). Second, the couple is given a careful conceptualization of why this step is necessary. The participating partner must understand that his or her own perspective of the affair will most likely not be effectively understood by the injured partner unless the injured partner is first able to experience that the participating partner truly understands and is remorseful for the effect of his or her actions on the injured person and the relationship. Participating partners are reassured that they will have a chance to address their own issues in the second stage of therapy, when they are more likely to be heard. If the initial feelings of anger are not addressed effectively the couple is unlikely to reach a successful resolution of the process.

Finally, the injured partner is encouraged to write a letter exploring his or her feelings and reactions to the affair, which is first given to the therapist. After feedback from the therapist, the letter is then revised and read to the participating partner. This process allows injured partners to explore their reactions in a calmer manner, and then enables them to take time to express their feelings in ways that are not attacking or abusive and are likely to be heard by the participating partner. Consequently, the participating partner often hears vulnerable emotions and reactions that she or he did not know existed. With support in the session from the therapist, the participating partner can be coached in responding supportively and empathically to these vulnerable emotions, thus providing the couple with a more positive exchange regarding these painful emotions than they are likely to accomplish on their own. We have written more extensively regarding the theoretical rationale and benefits of written disclosure when working with relationship trauma elsewhere (Snyder, Gordon, & Baucom, 2004). Following is an excerpt from a letter that Sam wrote to Amanda during the early phase of couple therapy, after learning about her affair:

> Amanda, since you told me about the affair, I've been feeling really miserable. I've had so many different thoughts going on in my head that it is hard to describe the way I was feeling. It was almost as if everything that I knew was suddenly untrue. I still don't understand how you could do this.

I can't sleep at night. Each time I see you I feel out of place somehow. I'm not sure how to act around you and I feel like I always have to be careful about what I say so that you don't get upset even more. I think back to how things used to be, when we first started dating, and can't believe that we are going through this now. I don't know what you think of me anymore and I don't know when you stopped feeling excited about us. I don't know where I stand with you and I get really frustrated by this. Sometimes I feel like just saying to hell with all this, but the thought of not being with you seems just as bad.

When I met you, you were like a gift. You seemed to appreciate and respect me, and you never took advantage of me or lied to me. I always felt lucky to be with you. Now, I'm not sure what to think anymore. Sometimes I tell myself that I should have known better and that I was just stupid. I don't know if I can ever completely trust you again, and this is unbelievably painful to think about.

Amanda, I don't know what is in our future, but I am scared when I think about us getting a divorce. I truly want to make things better between us and I'm not sure how. I don't want to lose you. But I also don't want to ever go through this again, so if you don't think you can be happy with only me, please tell me now. Love, Sam

Coping with "Flashbacks"

A final, but critical component in Stage 1 is the explanation of "flashback" phenomena and the development of a plan for how to cope with them. As noted earlier, the reaction to an affair strongly parallels the traumatic response; thus, not surprisingly, both partners also are likely to encounter reexperiencing phenomena as well. For example, a wife may discover an unexplained number on a telephone bill, which may then remind her of the unexplained telephone calls during the affair, and trigger a flood of affect related to her husband's affair. If the husband is not aware of this sequence of events, his wife's emotions may appear inexplicable, which in turn may cause him to question the progress they may be making in recovering from the affair. By explaining and normalizing this process to the couple, they may be less likely to misattribute these interactions to lack of progress. Instead, they have a better conceptualization of what is happening, and they are given the opportunity to problem-solve on what each person needs to do to cope with the situation effectively. In working with couples, we explain the concept of a flashback in this context, and how to address such experiences.

> **Therapist:** When one person has had an affair it tends to make the other person extremely sensitive and reactive to things that directly or even indirectly remind them of the traumatic event. That is why a strange number on the phone bill or being at a restaurant where your partner ate with the other person can so easily set you off. What we think may be happening is that the person has started to associate certain experiences, memories, objects, and so on, with the traumatic event. This kind of association happens to us every day. Have you ever smelled something and then immediately were reminded of a past experience? Like smelling chalk dust and immediately thinking of elementary school? This association is what may be going on when people experience a strong emotional reaction to small things. "Innocent" objects or smells or sounds may immediately remind them of the affair. Add to this that people tend to be on edge, anyway, after a traumatic event has happened, and it is not surprising that you can easily find yourself reacting strongly to

otherwise small things. We call these kinds of experiences "flashbacks." Does this make sense in terms of what you are describing has been happening?

We often provide a handout with the following guidelines for addressing flashbacks.

1. If you notice that you are responding to your partner in a panicky, worried, accusatory, or angry manner, then this is a signal that you need to step back and evaluate the situation.
2. If you decide that this is a realistic reaction, given the immediate circumstances, then you should express these feelings to your partner and then work to find a more acceptable solution to this problem.
3. If you decide that this reaction is most likely not based on what has just happened, but is more a reaction to a memory of the affair, you should let your partner know what is happening (e.g., "driving by that motel just triggered memories of your affair"), using good communication skills.
4. You should take care not to express these feelings in such a way that your partner is put on the defensive. Your partner should also be careful to avoid responding defensively to these conversations.
5. Both of you may wish to problem-solve on the event that triggered the flashback—for example, your partner may try not to perform that behavior, or she or he may develop a supportive way to approach that behavior to make it less scary.
6. Both of you need to *balance* the amount that you discuss these flashbacks. If they are happening very often, then you should try to find additional ways to deal with your emotion, so you and your partner do not become worn out with too many of these painful, emotional exchanges.
7. However, it is appropriate that both of you talk about these feelings and flashbacks, as long as it is not being done to the point of exhaustion.
8. When these discussions occur, they are more likely to be successful if both of you use good communication skills. You should avoid attacking the participating partner if you want to have a successful discussion; similarly, your partner should avoid being defensive and should use his or her listening skills.

STAGE 2: CONTEXT

Therapeutic Components

Exploration of the Factors Contributing to the Affair

After the emotional chaos or emotional distance from Stage 1 has been addressed, the second stage of the treatment focuses on helping the couple explore and understand the context of the affair. This is a crucial part of the therapy and typically occupies the greatest amount of time. Given that basic assumptions about both partners and their relationship have been disrupted by the affair, they cannot move forward until they have a more complete and thoughtful understanding of why the affair occurred. Such an explanation sets the stage for helping the couple decide whether they want to maintain their relationship, what needs to change, or if they should move forward by ending their relationship.

First, the couple must understand the logic behind this exploration of why the affair occurred. The therapist is asking them to address and reexperience very painful feelings and memories. If the affair has ended, often the participating partner wants to put it behind him or her and move on, declaring; "Why go back and dig up all that dirt when it is over, in the past?" The therapist can explain that going back and discussing the affair and the context in which it occurred can have several benefits. Specifically, the increased understanding can:

1. Help the injured partner to change some of his or her initially inaccurate explanations of why this event occurred—for example, the affair did not happen because she or he was a bad spouse, unattractive, or boring.

2. Help the injured partner to realize more clearly the participating partner's intentions about the affair—that is, the participating partner did not maliciously intend to hurt the injured partner, but did make very bad decisions that caused him or her pain (unless the affair was done out of spite, in which case there is a need to look at why the participating partner felt the need for this revenge).

3. Help the injured partner to understand why this event happened, which makes it feel less like something frightening that came "out of the blue." This understanding may also have the result of decreasing the injured partner's sense of anxiety about the relationship, and help to set the stage for rebuilding trust.

4. Help both partners realize areas of weakness that can be improved, so that they can reduce the likelihood of this event happening again.

5. Help both partners realize their own individual areas of weakness or defensiveness that may be preventing them from getting important needs met within the relationship.

6. Help both partners realize how their behaviors hurt each other, and motivate them to change or inhibit these behaviors, out of empathy for each other.

7. Promote greater resiliency within the relationship by increasing the understanding of and empathy for each partner's imperfections and susceptibility to engaging in hurtful behavior.

8. Increase empathy and compassion for the participating partner, thus reducing some of the negative emotions, such as anger and hurt in the injured person.

After the couple understands the reasons for exploring the bases for the affair, then the focus of the therapy turns toward examining the different factors that may have influenced the participating partner's decision to have the affair. These factors include: (1) aspects of the relationship, such as difficulty communicating with or finding time for each other; (2) external issues, such as job stress, financial difficulties, or in-laws; (3) issues specific to the participating partner, such as his or her beliefs about marriage, or his or her social development history; and (4) issues specific to the injured partner, such as his or her developmental history, or his or her relationship skills. This last point is likely to be most problematic for the couple, given that it may appear to be blaming the victim. At this point, the couple needs to understand an important distinction between contributing to the context of the affair versus responsibility for engaging in the affair. In this treatment, the participating partners are always held responsible for their choices to have the affair, but it is important to understand the context within which they made that decision.

It also is important that the injured partners be able to look at how they may have contributed to the context of the affair or the dilemma that the participating partners attempted to "solve." For example, the injured partner might have "looked the other way" out of fear of conflict, when it was clear that there were problems in the relationship—or the injured partner might have been preoccupied with his or her own problems, and was unable or unwilling to attend to the other partner's needs. Furthermore, as noted earlier, often participating partners may themselves feel bitter about hurts that the injured partners may have caused. In these instances, it may be beneficial to explore these problems as well. Using this example, the participating partner may have felt hurt and rejected by his or her partner's preoccupation, and as a result may need to come to a better understanding of that preoccupation. In other words, participating partners may need to engage their own forgiveness process.

In any case, although the injured partner is not responsible for the participating partner's decision to have an affair, it is important that the injured partner becomes aware of the result of his or her own actions in the relationship, and how their own actions can cause the relationship and the other partner to become more vulnerable to problems. Such a perspective is crucial as the couple begins contemplating what to change if they want to stay together and improve their relationship. This knowledge, while painful, may help the injured partner regain a sense of control in the relationship. Identifying weak points in their relationship allows the couple to pinpoint danger signals, which in turn allows both partners to feel safe, thus reducing the need for constant hypervigilance. In addition, it is also important to acknowledge the developmental factors contributing to the injured partner's response to the affair. For example, the injured partner's response to the affair may be stronger if she or he has experienced previous betrayals. His or her response may also be affected by general expectations for relationships. To give an extreme example, the response to the affair may be surprisingly calm if the injured partner expects his or her partner to have an affair, believing "that's what men (or women) do."

These sessions exploring the context of the affair typically are conducted in two ways. Depending on the couple's level of skill and their motivation to listen to and understand each other, these sessions may take the form of structured discussions between the partners, as they attempt to understand the many factors that contributed to the affair. The therapist intervenes as necessary to highlight certain points, reinterpret distorted cognitions, or draw parallels or inferences from their developmental histories that the couple is not able to do themselves. However, if the couple's communications skills are weak, if either partner is acutely defensive, or if they are having difficulty understanding each other's positions, then the therapist may structure the sessions so that they are more similar to individual therapy sessions with one partner, while the other partner listens and occasionally is asked to summarize his or her understanding of what is being expressed.

In both types of sessions, the therapist also is attempting to promote empathy between the partners, by helping the listening partner draw parallels between what the other partner is describing and his or her own similar experiences, or by encouraging them to use their imagination and put themselves in their partners' place as best they can. McCullough et al.'s (1997) findings demonstrate that empathy is an important mediating factor in people's ability to forgive and move beyond interpersonal betrayals. Thus, treatment pays particular attention to using the information the couple has gained about each other and their acknowledgment of vulnerability to promote an atmosphere of mutual caring and support.

In addition, the therapist also looks for patterns and similarities between what the partners have reported in their individual histories and the problems they are reporting in their relationship. It is in these aspects of the therapy, the promotion of empathy and the developmental exploration, that the treatment borrows most heavily from insight-oriented approaches. Understanding how past needs and wishes influence an individual's choices in the present is a critical element to understanding why the individual chose to have an affair, or how the injured partner has responded to this event. Often, the decision to choose an affair as a possible solution to present problems is influenced by strategies that have worked in the past, or by developmental needs that were not met in the past. For example, a woman who was repeatedly rejected sexually in early adolescence and young adulthood, and consequently sees herself as unlovable and undesirable, may be particularly vulnerable to choosing a sexual affair to solve her feelings of rejection and abandonment in her marriage. Helping her and her husband to see that pattern and to understand the reasons behind it may serve both to increase empathy between the spouses, by changing her husband's attributions about why the affair occurred, and to increase her ability to choose new behaviors to meet her needs. Directing both members of the couple to explore these influences helps them gain a deeper understanding of each other's vulnerabilities, and may help promote a greater level of empathy and compassion between them.

Problem-Solving or Cognitive Restructuring on Problematic Issues in the Relationship

Throughout the sessions, the need to make changes in numerous aspects of the relationship and in themselves as individuals may become evident to the couple, and they may then naturally begin to engage in problem solving. However, it is also beneficial to build in specific, problem-solving sessions for two reasons. First, over time, the couple may become frustrated with daily difficulties that are separate from the affair or that may have contributed to the affair and are still ongoing; therefore, they often need structured time in the sessions to address these current relationship difficulties and to arrive at a good resolution. As a result, the therapist needs to balance the work of therapy between focusing on the affair and focusing on ongoing relationship difficulties. Second, giving the couple opportunities to work on these issues and the opportunity to have small successes together may make them feel more hopeful about the relationship, and the ensuing positive feelings may help promote additional exploration sessions. In addition, the couple also may require cognitive restructuring as well as behavioral changes. Often, the therapist may observe that one or both of the partners hold problematic cognitions about their relationship or relationships in general. In these instances, the therapist should bring these thoughts or interpretations to the couple's attention and help them explore the effects of holding these cognitions on their relationships. For a more complete description of these interventions, see Epstein and Baucom (2002).

STAGE 3: MOVING ON

Therapeutic Components

Summary and Formulation of the Affair

The therapist's first task in this stage is to help the couple to put the pieces of information they have gleaned in Stage 2 together into a coherent story that explains how the affair came about. This task is critical, because understanding how the affair came about is central to developing a new set of assumptions about each person and the relationship. For example, the injured partner might conclude, after a careful discussion of the factors involved in the participating partner's decision to have an affair, that the participating partner has a deep sense of insecurity about his or her appeal and attractiveness to other people, and needs to be frequently reassured by members of the opposite gender how desirable he or she is. In such an instance, the injured partner might have appropriate concern that affairs or other inappropriate behavior to seek reassurance might recur unless the participating partner develops a greater sense of self-assurance and belief in him- or herself interpersonally.

This task of putting together what they have been discussing in Stage 2 can be accomplished in several ways. First, the therapist can explain to the couple that this is the next task, and ask each partner to prepare for the next session by trying to "put it all together," including a focus on the (1) relationship issues, (2) environmental issues, (3) individual issues related to the participating partner, and (4) individual issues related to the injured partner that contributed to the context within which the affair occurred. The couple and therapist then discuss their fullest understanding at the next session. As an alternative, each partner can be asked to write a letter for the next session (similar to the task in Stage 1 described earlier) in which each person describes, now in a fuller and less angry manner, what he or she understands to be these relevant factors. Below is an excerpt from a letter that Janis wrote to Tom about his affair as they began Stage 3 of therapy:

> Dear Tom, as I write this letter I can't help but think how I feel so much different writing this one compared to the first letter I wrote you when we started this counseling. I think about all that we

have been through in therapy and I am thankful that we are still together. I am thankful that we understand each other better, and I am thankful for your willingness to make changes and to help me change.

Being with you is the most important thing in my life. I could never imagine losing you, and I think that when I started to feel that you were unhappy in our marriage, I didn't know how to handle it and actually ended up making the situation worse. Things were so wonderful in the beginning and over time things just seemed to change. I now know that there were all sorts of things that put our relationship at risk, and I also know that I contributed to these circumstances. Before, I blamed you entirely for the affair and thought that everything we were going through was your fault. This is hard for me to say, but I was also at fault for the problems in our relationship that led to your affair. I realize now that although I saw that you were unhappy, I didn't make any attempt to change. Instead, I avoided the problems and consumed myself with the very things that were making you unhappy. I now recognize that I wasn't the greatest communicator and that I could have made myself more emotionally available to you when you needed me. I never want you to feel that you can't come to me for support, and I will do my best to make this easier for you than it was before this all happened.

Tom, you have always been my inspiration, and I love you more than words can express. I know you didn't intend to hurt me. I know that we still have some work ahead of us, but I am willing to continue what we have started so far in therapy. We have learned so much from each other, and I am excited to keep working to make our marriage stronger. I am sorry for my own part in our problems, and I never again want to come so close to losing you. Love, Janis

As a result of such issues arising from the discussion of the affair, the therapist and the couple discuss what aspects of their relationship may need additional attention, and how this can be accomplished in order to help them avoid future betrayals. In this respect, the therapy begins to move from a focus on the past to a focus on the present and future of the relationship. At this point, the interventions are likely to resemble the frequently used strategies employed in cognitive-behavioral couple therapy, in which the couple focuses on their current and future relationship (Epstein & Baucom, 2002).

Discussion of Forgiveness

Although the entire process outlined in this treatment is based on the authors' model of forgiveness, and thus can be conceptualized as a process of working toward forgiveness, this concept is not introduced to the couple until near the end of the treatment. Addressing forgiveness early in treatment often is not effective, due to the excessively negative atmosphere between the couple. However, we find that the introduction of this concept at a later point in the treatment, when the anger has subsided and the couple's understanding of what led to the betrayal is clearer, is more likely to have a successful outcome. In addition, we have found that when the couple is introduced to the authors' three-stage model of forgiveness, they are able to recognize that they have largely completed the work of the first two stages, which can motivate them to continue the process and consider forgiving as an appropriate and possible choice.

Four basic aspects of forgiveness are discussed with the couple: (1) a description of the forgiveness model, (2) common beliefs about forgiveness, (3) consequences of forgiving or not forgiving, and (4) addressing blocks to forgiving, and "moving on." The authors' three-stage forgiveness model is presented to the couple and then the therapist draws parallels between this process and the work that the couple has just completed. Discussion then centers on the couple's reactions to this model and their own particular beliefs about forgiveness. For example, couples often report difficulty with forgiveness out of mistaken beliefs that forgiving their partner is "weak," or is equivalent to saying that what happened is acceptable or excusable. Gently addressing this belief by presenting couples with the definition of forgiveness described earlier, and exploring whether one may forgive and yet also appropriately hold the partner responsible for his or her behaviors, may result in the couple developing a new conceptualization of forgiveness that feels more possible for them to achieve.

For example, Manuel, an Hispanic male, was struggling to come to terms with his wife Anna's affair. To complicate matters further, his parents subscribed to Latino concepts regarding the importance of machismo. To them, any forgiveness of Anna's affair was unmanly and weak; they believed he should cut her off immediately and refuse to forgive her. In sessions, Manuel struggled with the concept of forgiveness as weak versus forgiveness as a position of strength and of benefit to himself. Ultimately, he decided that because he did not have to forgive Anna, and because Anna was genuinely repentant, his choice to forgive her and to do the difficult work of understanding and rebuilding their relationship was a strong decision, and not unmanly. They then problem-solved on how they would present a united front to Manuel's family regarding their relationship.

However, if these discussions do not help the couple feel more open to forgiveness, then the therapist may wish to help the couple evaluate the consequences of not forgiving. Recent research has indicated that continuous anger and bitterness can have detrimental effects on individuals' physical and emotional health (Huang, 1990), on their relationships with their children, and on future relationships (Ashleman, 1997; Holeman, 1994). It is critical that these issues are discussed with the couple in a balanced way; the therapist should avoid communicating to the couple that they should or must always forgive. In some situations, particularly in abusive relationships, forgiveness may not be appropriate, particularly if the behaviors are likely to reoccur, or if the injured partner is likely to be continually reinjured. In these cases, forgiveness before the injury is rectified or stopped may be premature or inappropriate. Furthermore, in some cases, the person may not be ready to forgive. In such a case, the therapist must examine what function the anger and negative affect are serving for the couple, and then, based on what was discovered, appropriately address these blocks to their "moving on."

Exploration of Factors Affecting Their Decision to Continue Their Relationship

As noted earlier, in this final stage of treatment couples are encouraged to use what they have learned about each other to decide whether their relationship is a healthy one for them or not. In other words, forgiveness does not require reconciliation. Thus, couples who have successfully negotiated the forgiveness process still may make appropriate decisions to dissolve their relationship based on their new understandings of themselves, and thus ideally be able to separate without intense anger and resentment toward each other. To this end, couples are encouraged to ask themselves separately and then to discuss together within the sessions a series of questions that the therapist designs to help them evaluate their relationship. Typically, these questions relate to whether either member of the couple has shown the desire or the ability to make the needed changes in their relationship in order to ensure that the betrayal would not happen again. Questions that the therapist can have the clients consider include the following:

1. Is the participating partner willing and able to make individual changes needed to decrease high risk factors or situations?

2. Is the injured partner willing and able to make individual changes needed to move forward in the relationship, including taking gradual, appropriate risks to develop new trust in the partner and their relationship?

3. Are both partners willing to make environmental changes that are needed to decrease the risk of an affair or to deal with the outside person—including job changes, moving to other locations, and so forth?

4. Are both partners willing to make changes in their relationships as needed, including:

   a) Behaviors specifically contributing to higher risks for an affair, or necessary for recovering from this previous affair?

   b) General improvements for strengthening the relationship as identified and discussed earlier in the therapy?

For example, both Alan and Maria were clear that Alan's problem with alcohol abuse was a clear risk factor for the occurrence of an affair and was a major reason for his past extramarital involvement. Consequently, in this section of treatment, Maria and Alan both struggled with whether Alan would be able to reduce his alcohol use and create a sense of safety for Maria. Maria realized that she needed to see Alan make this change before she could feel secure in recommitting to their relationship. Alan desperately wanted his marriage to survive, and he began to realize that the negative impact of his drinking also extended beyond his marriage into his work, so he agreed to enter a treatment program for alcoholism.

Other times, when reaching the end of Stage 2, partners may conclude that critical factors contributing to the affair cannot be resolved, and may determine that the best decision for them is to end this relationship and move on separately. For example, a participating partner may come to recognize that a key factor contributing to the affair was an enduring inability or unwillingness of the injured partner to devote time or emotional energy to their relationship, rather than to their work or to the pursuit of individual activities. Alternatively, an injured partner may discover that despite the participating partner's contentions otherwise, their partner demonstrates a lifelong inability to commit to difficult decisions in either work or relationships that require him or her to forgo gratification of more selfish wishes or needs. In either event, when either partner concludes, after careful consideration of all the relevant information, that continuing the relationship is not in his or her best interests, we work to help them dissolve the relationship in a manner that is least hurtful to both of them and to others they care for, as described below.

Problem-Solving or Cognitive Restructuring on Problematic Issues in the Relationship or on Issues Relating to the Decision to Separate

If the couple decides to recommit to each other, then the remainder of treatment focuses on (1) problematic issues in the relationship that may have helped to create the context for the affair (e.g., a lack of emotional intimacy) and would need to be addressed to decrease the likelihood that an affair would recur in the future, and (2) positive ways to enhance the relationship. Likewise, the treatment must address problems that resulted from the affair, such as rebuilding trust (see the following), physical intimacy, or more general, ongoing issues in the relationship that may or may not be directly related to the affair (e.g., power and control issues, communication problems, or difficulty finding time together). In terms of physical intimacy, our observations indicate that there is wide variability in couple functioning on this issue after an affair. Whereas many couples' sexual relationship is seriously compromised following discovery or disclosure of an affair, other couples report increased frequency and quality of their sexual relations. Hence, it is critical that therapists assess individual and couple dynamics related to sexual functioning both prior to and following an extramarital affair, and intervene in these processes accordingly. Common cognitive-behavioral techniques such as skills training, homework assignments, and cognitive restructuring are used to accomplish these goals of rebuilding trust and intimacy; see Epstein and Baucom (2002) and Prager (1995) for a more complete description of these techniques.

If the couple decides to separate, then the focus of therapy moves to helping them to do so in the healthiest manner possible. The partners are encouraged to think about how they can use the information that they have learned during the treatment to maintain respect, and possibly empathy, for each other during the difficult process of separation. They are encouraged to evaluate the consequences of maintaining bitterness versus the benefits of letting go of the anger and recrimination, as appropriate. Furthermore, in addition to helping them plan how to maintain a sense of forgiveness, the therapist also helps the couple problem-solve on the many issues that arise during separation, such as childrearing, finances, and similar decisions.

SPECIAL CONSIDERATIONS IN THE TREATMENT OF AFFAIRS

Problems Encountered in Stage 1 of Treatment

Emotion Dysregulation

Difficulties in emotion regulation are common during Stage 1, particularly for the injured partner but often for the participating partner as well. Uncertainties about the future of their relationship, profound feelings of betrayal, shame, mistrust, and similar emotions all have the potential to generate unregulated anger both in and outside of sessions. It's important for the therapist to help partners recognize and understand the sources of these feelings, to help them contain their negative impact outside of sessions (using time-out and venting techniques, described earlier), and to balance their expression and moderation in sessions as a means for processing this traumatic event.

Achieving this balance of expression versus moderation of intense affect is a difficult challenge throughout therapy, but particularly so during this first stage. A core assumption of treatment communicated to both partners is that recovery from the affair requires reestablishing security, and that this security extends to emotional safety within sessions. Hence, neither partner is permitted to continue in emotionally aggressive behavior toward the other, unchecked by the therapist. At the same time, coming to understand the profound emotional impact of the affair requires an ability to both express and tolerate intense and typically uncomfortable feelings. A strategy we find useful in striving toward this balance is to monitor the level of expressed affect to discern the ability of both partners to tolerate its intensity at any given moment, to gently but firmly interrupt its expression when either the intensity or duration appears destructive or has led to negative escalations between partners, and to soften the affect by reframing the anger as an expression of deep hurt or as an emotional response to threats to the security of the relationship.

Defensiveness

Defensiveness is best addressed proactively. In an individual session with the participating partner, the therapist attempts to establish a strong rapport and therapeutic alliance, while at the same time clearly laying out expectations for the sessions to come. The more the partners understand how these sessions are important to the recovery process, and how crucial managing their defensiveness is, the more motivated they may be to engage in the strategies developed in the individual sessions to control their tendency to be defensive and to justify their behavior. The participating partner needs to understand that acknowledging his or her inappropriate behavior and taking responsibility for the affair is what will help to move the recovery process forward. As long at the person denies responsibility for the affair, then his or her partner is likely to see the participating partner as more likely to engage in an affair again, because the person accepts no responsibility and likely little remorse for such behavior.

Crises

When a couple arrives at the session in crisis, the therapist must first assess the extent of the crisis and whether its resolution is crucial to the progress of the session, or if the crisis is more attributable to the couple's general level of functioning. If the crisis is critical to the progress of the session, the therapist may spend his or her time addressing that issue; however, if the crisis is more a function of the couple's general distress level, a more effective approach would be to put the problem into the larger context of the couple's functioning and the recovery process itself; the feelings are thus acknowledged, supported, and then normalized. Then, the couple should be gently urged to continue with the treatment strategy.

It's not uncommon for couples to experience recurrent crisis moments during this first stage of treatment. Two particularly prevalent sources of distress involve (1) unexpected or mismanaged interactions involving the outside affair person, and (2) conflicting needs between the injured partner's wish to discuss the affair or obtain further information and the participating partner's wish to avoid the emotional turmoil often accompanying such discussions. Dealing with such crises therapeutically requires more than empathic listening or reframing as a normal part of the recovery process; they typically require explicit directives from the therapist about how to manage these moments on an intermediate basis to contain their negative escalation. Couples are encouraged to bring such incidents into treatment, so that they can be addressed more constructively within sessions, until partners acquire or restore both the emotional equilibrium and the communication skills essential to managing these effectively on their own.

Ambivalence

Either or both of the partners may experience ambivalence about entering therapy. For example, the injured partner may fear getting close again to the participating partner, or may have doubts about whether she or he even wants to continue a relationship with someone capable of inflicting so much emotional pain. The participating partner may still be grieving the loss of the outside affair person, and may be focusing on the positive qualities of that person that are not present in the couple's relationship. This ambivalence should be normalized for the couple as a natural occurrence arising from the affair, and the couple reminded that the goal is to help them understand what happened more clearly so that they can make a good decision about whether or not they wish to stay in the relationship.

Problems Encountered in Stage 2

Resistance to Exploring the Context of the Affair

Initially, the couple may exhibit reluctance to explore the factors contributing to the development of the affair. Consequently, it is helpful to set the stage for this phase of treatment by explaining the difference between understanding and excusing the affair, and by thoroughly describing the benefits of the increased understanding of each other and their relationship that they will gain through this process.

Lack of Empathy

Another potential difficulty in this phase of treatment is the inability of either partner to experience empathy for the other person, particularly if both partners associate empathy with excusing the behavior. Consequently, the therapist should draw a careful distinction between these concepts. In addition, before the couple begins to explore the context of the affair, it is useful to ask them questions designed to prime them to experience empathy in reaction to the other partner's experiences. For example, some questions may be designed to prompt both partners to think about times in their own lives when they have hurt others, and their own reasons for so doing, or about times in their lives when they were under a great deal of stress or difficulty and consequently made bad decisions.

Reluctance to Acknowledge Progress

In addition, often the injured partners show great reluctance to acknowledge progress in the therapy or any efforts at change on the part of the participating partner. A large part of this reluctance to acknowledge change may be due to the injured partner's need to stay angry at the participating partner. One motivation may be punishment; acknowledging the participating partner's efforts may seem to the injured partner as if she or he were relenting, or letting the participating partner off the hook. If this reason is behind the injured partner's reluctance, then the therapist should remind the injured partner that acknowledging the good qualities or efforts of the participating partner will never erase his or her inappropriate behaviors. The injured partner should understand that it is acceptable and normal to feel good about progress or change, yet still feel angry or hurt about what happened. Similarly, they also may be afraid to acknowledge change, because they feel that that would mean they would have to stay in the relationship. The therapist also should challenge this belief. Instead, the injured partner should be encouraged to note the changes occurring in the present with the understanding that this is important information about what the participating partner is able to do. However, the injured partners also should be told that, despite the changes occurring in the present, they still have the freedom to decide that they cannot live with what happened in the past and, thus, can choose to end the relationship. This permission is given in hopes that it will free the injured partners from their need to protect themselves and allow them to become more impartial observers of the changes occurring in the relationship.

Problems Encountered in Stage 3

Resistance to the Idea of Forgiveness

Resistance to forgiveness may stem from problematic beliefs about forgiveness, such as the notion that forgiveness is excusing the behavior or condoning the offense, or from hidden motives that are served by a continuation of anger and bitterness. These motives may range from the anger providing a needed sense of safety or strength to an unacknowledged desire to end the relationship, a goal that may be considerably strengthened by the anger. In cases where an individual seems particularly hostile to the concept of forgiveness, the therapist must carefully assess for such motives, which may or may not be recognized by partners themselves. This process may best be accomplished in individual sessions. Once uncovered, these additional considerations will influence how the therapist proceeds.

Difficulties with Rebuilding Trust

A second common, problematic issue in this phase is that even though a couple may successfully negotiate the forgiveness process, they still may have difficulties with trust. In this situation, the couple should be given a conceptualization that makes this difficulty comprehensible to both partners, yet also encourages the injured partner to take small, manageable, increasing risks with the participating partner in order to rebuild the relationship. Thus, trust-building is viewed as following an exposure-based paradigm. The injured partner is encouraged to identify a series of small, hierarchical steps that involve increasing levels of emotional risk-taking in the relationship (e.g., confiding something vulnerable to the partner, or not asking the partner to check in while away). This graduated, hierarchical exercise may enable the couple to gradually rebuild a sense of reliability and predictability without the injured partner taking a seemingly overwhelming risk. The therapist must be clear with the participating partner that he or she must in fact act in a reliable, predictable manner, or else she or he will cause greater damage to the relationship. For example, if the injured partner has been checking frequently on the participating partner's whereabouts, the first step may be to decrease the amount of checking, from 100 percent to 50 percent—but still do some random checks to reassure him- or herself that the participating partner is acting in a trustworthy manner. After the participating partner has demonstrated being where he or she reported being, then the injured partner may be encouraged to take a risk and decrease the checking even further.

Resistance to Forgiveness in Separation and Divorce

The decision to divorce or separate, described in Stage 3, is not always mutual— even if it is, it may still create much bitterness between the partners. At this point, it is crucial that the therapist continues to provide the couple with the "big picture," that is, the balanced view of each other and the relationship that emerged during their exploration of the context of the affair. In addition, the therapist should also continue to point out the benefits of forgiveness and the adverse consequences to themselves and to others if they continue to harbor their acrimony. It is important that the partners not end the relationship with a great deal of bitterness that either person carries forward into his or her personal life; moreover, if the couple has children, then the children's well-being is greatly enhanced if partners can end a marriage with forgiveness.

General Considerations in Responses to Affairs and Implications for Treatment

Psychopathology

As with most couple treatments, a high level of psychopathology is a poor prognostic indicator for successful recovery (Snyder & Whisman, 2003). This problem may be particularly true when the participating partner engages in affairs because she or he has antisocial or narcissistic traits and believes he or she is above social norms and mores. This belief communicates to the injured partner that the participating partner is at risk for additional affairs, particularly if she or he is not remorseful, or is inordinately defensive about the current affair. Therefore, if the injured partner continues in this relationship he or she may run the risk of being retraumatized. In this instance, an important goal of treatment may be to ensure that the injured partner becomes fully aware of this pattern of behavior and is able to make a good decision about whether to continue the relationship.

In a similar vein, a participating partner's dependence upon alcohol and/or other substances is also likely to complicate treatment. In these cases, the substance often has played a major role in the decision to become involved in the affair, and if the participating partner continues to use, the injured partner is likely to continue to feel vulnerable to an affair's recurrence. In addition, the emotional upheaval that is often engendered by engaging in couple treatment for an affair, and the painful exploration involved during treatment, can trigger greater substance use and can endanger the sobriety of the newly abstinent. Consequently, couple treatment is likely to work best if the focus is initially on the dependent partner's developing sobriety. Only when this person has developed stable skills to combat the urge to use substances should the focus of treatment turn to an affair. Injured partners are often highly supportive of this focus, given that alcohol is often causing relational disruption in addition to the affair. Nonetheless, these partners will require a great deal of support from the therapist when exercising restraint from dealing with the affair directly in couple treatment.

However, problems with emotional health are usually not limited to the participating partner. Often, the injured partner might have preexisting difficulties with affect regulation, and in these cases the treatment is likely to be less effective, or at best progress more slowly. More therapeutic effort is needed to help contain negative affect if the injured person generally struggles with regulating negative feelings; the strategies described in Stage 1 of treatment can be useful for these situations. We currently are in the process of evaluating a couple-based intervention for couples in which one person has difficulty with affect regulation (Kirby & Baucom, 2004). In addition, the impact of the betrayal may be much greater, and his or her ability to regain a healthy sense of safety or self-worth after the affair may be compromised if the injured partner had a premorbid, fragile sense of self-worth due to other abandonment or negative relationship experiences. Consequently, these individuals may be more likely to evidence greater distortions in their cognitive and affective reactions to the affair.

Comfort with Affect

The stereotypic affair couple usually presents with chaotic, emotionally charged, negative interactions; however, not all such couples engage with each other in this manner. Indeed, we have found avoidance of conflict often to be a major contributor to the couple context surrounding the affair. Not surprisingly, this same reluctance to address conflict often continues after the discovery of the affair, and may appear within the context of therapy. Such couples might easily agree to forgive each other, particularly if the affair has ended, without addressing the critical issues described in this treatment. Strategies to address this discomfort with affect are discussed earlier regarding Stage 1 interventions. However, it may also be important to address the developmental source of this problem in Stage 2 of therapy, focusing on meaning, particularly if avoidance of conflict is a major contributor to the affair. Often, these individuals have had either direct or vicarious experiences with intense emotions that had frightening or devastating outcomes. Thus, a major therapeutic task would be exploring these fears and the consequences of continued avoidance, and creating an explicitly safe environment for the expression of negative affect.

Sensitivity to Rejection

Our work also suggests that individuals with significant histories of rejection may be more vulnerable to having affairs and to extreme reactions to one's spouse having an affair. For example, if, as a result of this history, a husband holds a deep-seated belief that he is unattractive or unlovable, he may be more vulnerable to real or perceived rejections by his partner, which in turn could trigger a search for external validation from another woman. In the case of the injured partner with a history of rejection, the discovery of an affair may serve to confirm his or her underlying, negative self-schemas, which in turn would negatively impact his or her ability to recover from this event. Again, this developmental pattern may need to be addressed in Stage 2, through support and exploration, in order to help the injured person feel safe enough to move on. A referral to individual treatment may also be necessary.

Levels of Commitment

First, a higher level of commitment to the relationship may lead couples to work harder in the treatment and to be more willing to engage in emotional risk taking within the therapy. However, an initial ambivalence about the relationship is not necessarily a prognostic indicator of treatment failure. Ambivalence at the beginning of treatment does not preclude the couple's ability to try to improve and understand their relationship in order to come to a good decision about whether to continue with the marriage, and in fact is often quite understandable in light of the presenting issue. It is often helpful to frame this ambivalence as such, in order to normalize these feelings.

However, as the treatment progresses, one may find that the issue of commitment in the treatment of infidelity is related to a developmentally based fear of intimacy, or feelings of being trapped in a stable relationship. Attachment theorists describe a pattern of attachment that is characterized by approach-avoidance (Hazan & Shaver, 1987). Individuals with this pattern may need intimate relationships and seek them out, yet fear them to such an extent that they find it difficult to feel safe in long-term, intimate relationships. Affairs may then serve as a means to create a safe level of distance from their partners (Allen & Baucom, 2004). In this case, the participating partner may need adjunctive individual treatment targeted toward this issue before the couple relationship is able to recover.

Differences in Affair Patterns

Reactions to a one night stand may be quite different from the same person's reactions to the discovery of a long-term, emotional, and sexual extramarital involvement. These various types of affairs may have different implications for the continuation of the couple's relationship. In addition, empirical research by Glass and Wright (1985) found that affairs in which there is both emotional and sexual involvement are more predictive of couple dissatisfaction than either of these types alone. Affairs in which both types of involvement are present are likely to be more disruptive to the relationship and require a greater amount of time and processing for the couple to adequately address pertinent issues.

Similarly, a history of repeated affairs also may have implications for treatment. If the injured partner has been through the process several times before, the participating partner's expressions of remorse and protestations of good behavior may ring hollow. Not surprisingly, it will be more difficult for the injured partner to take the emotional risks required to rebuild trust and intimacy in the relationship. Indeed, it may be the therapist's task to help the injured partner realistically evaluate if she or he even should take those risks. They may still be able to go through the recovery process, but they may need to evaluate the potential risks and benefits of staying in a relationship with a partner who is vulnerable to engaging in extramarital affairs on a repeated basis.

Finally, in extending this model to couples for whom the affair is ongoing, interventions during the Stage 1 of treatment would be expanded to work toward a decision to end or suspend interactions with the outside person as a basis for continuing with further interventions. Oftentimes, participating partners may initially be reluctant to end an affair that has been ongoing for some time and that provides emotional as well as physical intimacy—particularly if the marital relationship is currently dominated by emotional distance or conflict. Demanding that the participating partner terminate the outside affair relationship immediately and completely may prematurely precipitate that partner's decision to end both the therapy and their marriage. At the same time, it is important that the therapist clearly communicate that any continuation of the outside relationship on either an emotional or sexual level will preclude the couple's ability to recover stability in their own relationship and evaluate whether they can restore trust and intimacy in the long term. Hence, in situations involving an ongoing affair, the therapist should work to (1) promote the participating partner's agreement to limit or suspend involvement with the outside person on an intermediate basis, (2) construct a tentative timeline for reaching a more permanent decision about whether to end the outside relationship, and (3) assist both partners in defining specific ground rules for how they will interact with each other, as well as with others outside their relationship, during the interim.

PRELIMINARY FINDINGS REGARDING TREATMENT EFFECTIVENESS

Using a replicated case-study design, we have completed an initial pilot study investigating the effectiveness of this treatment in reducing partners' initial distress and restoring relationship accord (Gordon, Baucom, & Snyder, 2004). Six couples struggling to recover from an extramarital affair participated in the study. In four couples, the wife was the injured partner and the husband was the partner participating in the affair; for the remaining two couples, these roles were reversed. The majority of injured partners entering this treatment initially showed significantly elevated levels of depression and symptoms consistent with a posttraumatic stress disorder. Concern with emotional survival and struggles to understand their betrayal dominated. Relationship distress was severe; feelings of commitment, trust, and empathy were low. Injured partners' positive assumptions about themselves, as well as their partners, were disrupted. Overall, their capacity to move beyond profound hurt to pursue a life with renewed optimism and purpose was sorely compromised. Although participating partners showed less distress than injured partners at the outset of treatment, they also demonstrated moderate elevations on measures of depression, PTSD symptomatology, and state anger. Moreover, they displayed moderately high levels of overall dissatisfaction with their marriage.

By termination, injured partners demonstrated gains in each of these areas. Most importantly, gains were greatest in those domains specifically targeted by this treatment, such as decreases in PTSD symptomatology and mastery over successive challenges of the forgiveness process. For injured partners, the treatment's effect sizes across measures of individual and relationship functioning were moderate to large (ranging from 0.86 to 1.74), and generally exceeded average effect sizes for efficacious marital therapies not specifically targeting couples struggling from an affair (Baucom, Shoham, Mueser, Daiuto, & Stickle, 1998). By comparison, although the average reduction in marital distress was modest for the participating partners, the treatment was not without impact on them. When describing the impact of treatment, participating partners expressed that the treatment was critical to (1) exploring and eventually understanding their own affair behavior in a manner that reduced likely reoccurrence, (2) tolerating their injured partners' initial negativity and subsequent flashback reactions, (3) collaborating with their partners in a vital but often uncomfortable process of examining factors contributing to the affair, and (4) deferring their own needs for immediate forgiveness until a more comprehensive process of articulating the affair's impact, exploring its causes, and evaluating the risks of reoccurrence had been completed.

Case Study

Beth and Steve entered couple therapy a few weeks after Steve disclosed a 3-week affair he had had with a colleague at work. Steve had already ended the affair, but his guilt from the affair caused him to pull back from Beth. He didn't believe he deserved her forgiveness, and the only solution he could envision was ending the marriage so that Beth could move on. Beth didn't want to end their marriage, but acknowledged that she was devastated by Steve's affair. She had never felt worthy of Steve, and had always worried that he might eventually leave her for someone else. Now her worst fears had come true, and she had trouble believing his promises to do whatever it might take to work through this.

The first month after Steve disclosed his affair was particularly difficult for them. Steve wanted to hold and comfort Beth, but his guilt and shame made it difficult for him to discuss what had happened, or why. Beth's fear of pushing Steve further away caused her to avoid bringing up his affair, but her profound sadness, difficulty in sleeping, and stiffened response to his touches conveyed clearly to Steve how deeply wounded she was. In Stage 1, Beth gradually disclosed to Steve her feelings of hurt, but also her feelings of unworthiness and her fears of losing him. Steve wrestled with his own shame, but gradually disclosed the distance he had been feeling between them, his needs for closeness he hadn't really understood, and then his inability to confront and resist the physical approaches from the other woman at work. Steve disclosed enough information about the outside relationship to help Beth be clearer about what had happened and about steps Steve had taken to end the affair and break off all further contact with the other woman.

Following Stage 1 work, the couple spent 2 months examining closely all the factors that had placed them at risk for such an affair developing. Their own relationship had become increasingly distant as each of them poured their energy into their respective careers and devoted whatever time was left to caring for their two children. Each of them had also taken on considerable responsibilities for caring for one of their aging parents. Beth had struggled with health problems that depleted her strength and her desire for lovemaking. Steve had found Beth's expressions of uncertainty about her attractiveness to him as an attack on his devotion to her rather than as a plea for reassurance and closeness.

As therapy continued, Steve struggled to develop better skills in identifying his own feelings and communicating them to Beth. As he did so, Beth not only came to understand Steve's emotions in a way she had been blocked from doing previously, but also recognized Steve's efforts in this regard as evidence of his own commitment to their marriage and to changing himself. Beth continued to struggle with longstanding issues of feeling undesirable and unworthy. Gradually, she worked toward trusting Steve's reassurances. She came to recognize that the expressions of insecurity she had previously relied on to elicit positive affirmations from her family or friends had instead caused Steve to feel inadequate and to pull away from her. Beth and Steve also came to recognize that their sense of responsibility to others—including their children and extended family—had persisted at such high levels that they had neglected even deeper feelings of responsibility to each other and to their marriage. They developed specific strategies for preserving separate time for themselves as a couple, on a weekly basis, and subsequently sustained these—even through some very difficult challenges, when members of their extended families resisted these changes. They also struggled successfully through a job change for Beth and the potential loss of Steve's job. Their ability to weather these challenges and maintain commitments to protect and nurture their marriage offered them new confidence in themselves and their relationship.

As Stage 3 of therapy began, Beth and Steve discussed their personal beliefs about forgiveness. Beth reached forgiveness toward Steve readily, and offered it to him first implicitly but then explicitly in a letter. Steve struggled with forgiving himself, but eventually recognized that his own enduring guilt was blocking the very intimacy he sought with Beth. At their therapist's suggestion, the couple crafted a ritual of forgiveness for themselves that involved going away for a weekend to their favorite retreat at a state park, where they renewed their marriage vows and pledged to support each other in moving on and building a stronger and richer relationship.

CONCLUSION

Extramarital affairs occur frequently, produce both individual and relationship turmoil, and are one of the most difficult couple problems to treat. Working effectively with couples struggling to recover from an affair requires managing initial responses to this interpersonal trauma, helping partners to come to a shared understanding of how this event occurred, implementing individual and relationship changes to reduce the potential for a future recurrence, and moving on in a manner no longer dominated either emotionally or behaviorally by the affair. Such work will benefit from an explicit framework, as described here, that incorporates interventions from multiple theoretical modalities and organizes these in a sequential and flexibly structured manner.

REFERENCES

Allen, E. S., & Baucom, D. H. (in press). Adult attachment and patterns of extradyadic involvement. *Family Process.*

Ashleman, K. (1997, April). *Forgiveness as a resiliency factor in divorced families.* Paper presented at the Biennial Meeting of the Society for Research in Child Development, Washington, DC.

Baucom, D. H., & Lester, G. W. (1986). The usefulness of cognitive restructuring as an adjunct to behavioral marital therapy. *Behavior Therapy, 17,* 385–403.

Baucom, D. H., Sayers, S. L., & Sher, T. G. (1990). Supplementing behavioral marital therapy with cognitive restructuring and emotional expressiveness training: An outcome investigation. *Journal of Consulting and Clinical Psychology, 58,* 636–645.

Baucom, D. H., Shoham, V., Mueser, K. T., Daiuto, A. D., & Stickle, T. R. (1998). Empirically supported couple and family interventions for marital distress and adult mental health problems. *Journal of Consulting and Clinical Psychology, 66,* 53–88.

Brown, E. (1991). *Patterns of infidelity and their treatment.* New York: Brunner/Mazel.

Calhoun, K. S., & Resnick, P. A. (1993). Posttraumatic Stress Disorder. In D. H. Barlow (Ed.), *Clinical handbook of psychological disorders* (pp. 48–98). New York: Guilford.

Enright, R. D., and the Human Development Study Group. (1991). The moral development of forgiveness. In W. Kurtines & J. Gewirtz (Eds.), *Handbook of moral behavior and development, 1,* 123–152. Hillsdale, NJ: Earlbaum.

Epstein, N., & Baucom, D. H. (2002). *Enhanced cognitive-behavioral therapy for couples: A contextual approach.* Washington, DC: American Psychological Association.

Freedman, S. R., & Enright, R. D. (1996). Forgiveness as an intervention goal with incest survivors. *Journal of Consulting and Clinical Psychology, 64,* 983–992.

Glass, S., & Wright, T. (1985). Sex differences in type of extramarital involvement and marital dissatisfaction. *Sex Roles, 12,* 1101–1120.

Glass, S., & Wright, T. (1997). Reconstructing marriages after the trauma of infidelity. In W. K. Halford & H. J. Markman (Eds.), *Clinical handbook of marriage and couples interventions* (pp. 471–507). Chichester, England: John Wiley & Sons.

Gordon, K. C., & Baucom, D. H. (1998). Understanding betrayals in marriage: A synthesized model of forgiveness. *Family Process, 37,* 425–450.

Gordon, K. C., Baucom, D. H., & Snyder, D. K. (2004). An integrative intervention for promoting recovery from extramarital affairs. *Journal of Marital and Family Therapy, 30,* 213–231.

Halford, K. W., Sanders, M. R., & Behrens, B. C. (1993). A comparison of the generalization of behavioral marital therapy and enhanced behavioral marital therapy. *Journal of Consulting and Clinical Psychology, 61,* 51–60.

Hazan, C., & Shaver, P. (1987). Romantic love conceptualized as an attachment process. *Journal of Personality and Social Psychology, 52(3),* 511–524.

Holeman, V. T. (1994). *The relationship between forgiveness of a perpetrator and current marital adjustment for female survivors of childhood sexual abuse.* Unpublished doctoral dissertation, Kent State University Graduate School of Education, Ohio.

Huang, S. T. (1990). *Cross-cultural and real-life validations of forgiveness in Taiwan, The Republic of China.* Unpublished doctoral dissertation, University of Wisconsin-Madison.

Janoff-Bulman, R. (1989). Assumptive worlds and the stress of traumatic events: Applications of the schema construct. *Social cognition, 7,* 113–136.

Janus, S. S., & Janus, C. L. (1993). *The Janus report on sexual behavior.* New York: John Wiley & Sons.

Kirby, J. S., & Baucom, D. H. (2004). *A couple-based intervention for emotional dysregulation.* Manuscript in preparation.

Lauman, E. O., Gagnon, J. H., Michael, R. T., & Michaels, S. (1994). *The social organization of sexuality.* Chicago: University of Chicago Press.

Lusterman, D. D. (1998). *Infidelity: A survival guide.* Oakland, CA: New Harbinger Publications.

McCullough, M. E., Worthington, E. L., & Rachal, K. C. (1997). Interpersonal forgiving in close relationships. *Journal of Personality and Social Psychology, 73,* 321–336.

Pittman, F. (1989). *Private lies: Infidelity and the betrayal of intimacy.* New York: Norton.

Prager, K. J. (1995). *The psychology of intimacy.* New York: Guilford.

Reibstein, J., & Richards, M. (1993). *Sexual arrangements: Marriage and the temptation of infidelity.* New York: Scribner's.

Snyder, D. K. (1999). Affective reconstruction in the context of a pluralistic approach to couples therapy. *Clinical Psychology: Science and Practice, 6,* 348–365.

Snyder, D. K., Gordon, K. C., & Baucom, D. H. (2004). Treating affair couples: Extending the written disclosure paradigm to relationship trauma. *Clinical Psychology: Science and Practice, 11,* 155–160.

Snyder, D. K., & Whisman, M. A. (Eds.). (2003). *Treating difficult couples: Helping clients with co-existing mental and relationship disorders.* New York: Guilford.

Snyder, D. K., & Wills, R. M. (1989). Behavioral versus insight-oriented marital therapy: Effects on individual and interspousal functioning. *Journal of Consulting and Clinical Psychology, 57,* 39–46.

Snyder, D. K., Wills, R. M., & Grady-Fletcher, A. (1991). Long-term effectiveness of behavioral versus insight-oriented marital therapy: A 4-year follow-up study. *Journal of Consulting and Clinical Psychology, 59,* 138–141.

Spring, A. J., & Spring, M. (1996). *After the affair: Healing the pain and rebuilding trust when a partner has been unfaithful.* New York: Harper Collins.

Whisman, M. A., Dixon, A. E., & Johnson, B. (1997). Therapists' perspectives of couple problems and treatment issues in the practice of couple therapy. *Journal of Family Psychology, 11,* 361–366.

Wiederman, M. W. (1997). Extramarital sex: Prevalence and correlates in a national survey. *The Journal of Sex Research, 34,* 167–174.

Worthingon, E. L. (Ed.), (in press). *Handbook of forgiveness.* New York: Brunner-Routledge.

CHAPTER 18

Couple Sex Therapy: Assessment, Treatment, and Relapse Prevention

Barry W. McCarthy and L. Elizabeth Bodnar

A fascinating paradox of couple sexuality is that when sex is functional and healthy it plays a positive, integral, but relatively small role, contributing 15 to 20 percent to marital vitality and satisfaction. However, when sexuality is dysfunctional, conflictual, or nonexistent it can play an inordinately powerful role, as much as 50 to 75 percent, robbing the marriage of vitality and even threatening its viability.

The primary functions of marital sexuality are a shared pleasure, a means to deepen and reinforce intimacy, and a tension reducer to deal with the stresses of life and marriage. A fourth, optional function, is to produce a planned, wanted child. In essence, sexuality energizes and makes special the marital bond. The most common sexual problems are sexual dysfunction (especially inhibited sexual desire), an extramarital affair, or a fertility problem (an unplanned, unwanted pregnancy, or an unexpected infertility problem). Contrary to cultural myths, sexual problems are most likely to occur in the first 2 years of marriage, and are a major cause of separation or divorce. Thus, although intimacy and sexuality are integral parts of a healthy marital bond, problematic or conflictual sex has a more powerfully negative role than the positive role of healthy sexuality. In this chapter, we will describe sex therapy with married couples, as well as sex therapy with non-married and gay couples.

In traditional marital theory and therapy, sexuality is seen as a symptom, a symbol of a more basic relationship dynamic. The traditional strategy is to deal with the basic relationship problem, with the expectation that once it is resolved, the sexual problem will take care of itself. This strategy treats sexual problems and sexual dysfunction indirectly.

Although it is true that sexuality is complex, multicausal, multidimensional, with large individual, relational, cultural, and value differences, there is an increasing consensus that for most couples, intimacy and sexuality issues need to be addressed and treated directly. This is especially true when the sexual dysfunction is primary (lifelong as opposed to acquired), global (occurring in all situations), or is caused by anxiety or psychosexual skill deficits, and is the couple's primary reason for seeking treatment. Treating sexuality with benign neglect is likely to lead to chronic and severe sexual problems. If the sexual problem has not improved after 6 months it is unlikely to spontaneously remit, and will probably require couple sex therapy.

SEXUAL FUNCTION AND DYSFUNCTION

Healthy sexual functioning involves the ability of each person to experience desire (positive anticipation of being sexual and a sense of deserving sexuality to be a positive part of life and marriage), arousal (receptivity and responsivity to sensual and sexual touch), orgasm (the voluntary experience of high arousal culminating in an orgasmic response), and satisfaction (feeling good about yourself and more bonded after the sexual experience). Sexually healthy women and men integrate intimacy, pleasuring, and eroticism into their lives and marriage.

Sexual dysfunction has been studied much more extensively than healthy sexual functioning, but the data is nowhere close to being as reliable and valid as would be scientifically desirable. Sex research has badly lagged behind other health and mental health research because of a lack of funding and political, social, and value-oriented controversies regarding the role and meaning of sexuality in the culture. The Sex in America study (Michael, Gagnon, Laumann, & Kolata, 1994) provides the best database for sexual information. A recent study by Heiman (2002) provides estimates of rates of sexual dysfunction. However, sexual dysfunction does not necessarily lead to marital dissatisfaction unless the problem involves inhibited desire, cessation of affection, and avoidance of sex and intimacy. The best estimates are that over 50 percent of married couples experience sexual dysfunction or dissatisfaction, with the numbers of unmarried people and couples experiencing sexual problems being significantly higher. The most common sexual dysfunctions by gender are the following:

MALE SEXUAL DYSFUNCTIONS

1. Premature Ejaculation—approximately 30 percent; for the majority of men it is a primary dysfunction.
2. Erectile Dysfunction—the great majority are secondary dysfunctions, highly influenced by age; approximately 10 percent of males under 35 experience erectile dysfunction, and over 50 percent by age 50.
3. Inhibited Sexual Desire—almost all are secondary dysfunctions, also influenced by age. Affects 15 percent of males over 50.
4. Ejaculatory Inhibition—a primary dysfunction for approximately 2 percent of males under 25 and an intermittent, secondary dysfunction for 15 percent of males over 50.

Although males experience lower levels of sexual dysfunction than females, when couples stop being sexual, it is typically the male's unilateral, nonverbal decision (in over 90 percent of couples). This finding is contrary to the cultural myth of males always wanting sex.

FEMALE SEXUAL DYSFUNCTION

1. Inhibited Sexual Desire—affects approximately 33 percent of women, with more than half being secondary dysfunction.

2. Non-Orgasmic Response During Couple Sex—affects approximately 25 percent of women, the majority as a secondary dysfunction. Approximately 15 percent of women have primary nonorgasmic response during partner sex.

3. Sexual Pain (Dyspeurunia)—affects 15 percent of women; the great majority are secondary dysfunctions.

4. Female Arousal Dysfunction—a new and controversial category, affecting 15 percent of women; predominantly a secondary dysfunction.

5. Primary Non-Orgasmic Response—approximately 5 to 7 percent of women have never been orgasmic by any means.

6. Vaginismus—affects 2 percent of women and can be either a primary or secondary dysfunction.

Interestingly, the major sexual complaint—the woman not being orgasmic during intercourse—is not a sexual dysfunction. In fact, one of three women who are regularly orgasmic during couple sex never orgasm during intercourse. This is a normal variation of female sexuality, not a dysfunction.

A contradiction of the sexual dysfunction field is that although problems are categorized by individual dysfunctions, the reality is that sexuality is an interpersonal phenomenon, not an individual one. If people were only interested in predictability and efficacy of sexual function, with the goal of orgasm, they would rely on masturbation rather than couple sex. By its nature, couple sexuality is inherently variable in terms of function and satisfaction, especially with the aging of people and the aging of their marriage. The core of couple sexuality is desire, pleasure, and satisfaction. Arousal and orgasm are healthy and integral for both women and men, but are not the essence of sexual satisfaction. At heart, sexuality is about giving and receiving pleasure-oriented touching. The main functions of marital sexuality are to energize the marital bond and reinforce special feelings of being an intimate couple.

When one (or both) spouse has a sexual dysfunction it negatively impacts both people and their marital bond. This impact is multiplied if the couple falls into a self-blame / partner-blame cycle. The sense of guilt and stigma build if they avoid intimate talking and touching, consequently falling into the trap of a low-sex marriage (being sexual less than twice a month; 25 times a year) or a non-sexual marriage (being sexual less than once a month; 10 times a year). The sexual problem can control and subvert the marital bond.

The recommended therapeutic strategy is to approach the sexual dysfunction from the personal responsibility-intimate team model of understanding and change. In this model, each person is responsible for her or his own sexuality, including desire, arousal, and orgasm. It is not the spouse's responsibility to give the other person desire or orgasm. For example, people with a history of primary sexual dysfunction bring this problem into the marriage. The man with lifelong pre-mature ejaculation starts his marriage as a rapid ejaculator. However, what predis-poses or precipitates a sexual dysfunction is often not what maintains the sexual problem. The man who tries to compensate for his premature ejaculation by dis-tracting himself, or being less erotically involved, can cause erectile problems as well as desire and arousal problems for his partner. His performance for her and fixation on her orgasm can increase her self-consciousness, resulting in secondary orgasmic dysfunction. The cycle of anticipatory anxiety, tense and performance-oriented sexual encounters, and embarrassment and sexual avoidance exacerbate the problem, heightening couple dissatisfaction.

A prime concept in the personal responsibility-intimate team model is that each person assumes responsibility to understand and change sexual attitudes, behav-ior, and emotional responses. The couple then work as an intimate team to build a comfortable, functional couple sexual style. So, even if the sexual dysfunction predates the relationship, it is a couple task to build sexual comfort, skill, and con-fidence. This one-two combination of personal responsibility and being an inti-mate team is at the crux of the couple sex therapy process.

The most common, and arguably most influential, sexual problem is inhibited sexual desire. Premature ejaculation or ejaculatory inhibition usually does not lead to sexual avoidance, although erectile dysfunction often does. Female arousal and orgasm problems typically do not lead to desire or avoidance problems, al-though sexual pain problems often do. Desire problems are more prominent in fe-males, involving women of all ages. Desire problems in men are usually the result of performance problems, especially erectile dysfunction, and increase with age. As stated previously, when a couple stops being sexual it is usually the male's non-verbal, unilateral decision.

BIOPSYCHOSOCIAL APPROACH TO SEXUAL DYSFUNCTION

Since the introduction of Viagra in 1998, there has been a revolution in both the medical and public understanding of sexual problems and their treatment. Viagra (and other drugs, especially Cialis) can be valuable adjuncts in the treatment of erectile dysfunction. However, as a stand-alone intervention, drug treatments have a high risk of discontinued use and relapse, which eventually creates a de-vitalized, hopeless couple. Unrealistic expectations about Viagra, and misuse of medical interventions, have perhaps created more nonsexual marriages than any-thing in history. Medical interventions, whether Viagra, vacuum pumps, penile injections, or testosterone and estrogen supplements, need to be integrated into the couple's intimacy, pleasuring, and eroticism style or they run the risk of being iatrogenic.

Optimally, sexual problems are treated as multicausal and multidimensional, with respect for individual, couple, cultural, and value differences. Sexuality is ba-sically an interpersonal process, but the role of medical, hormonal, vascular, and neurological functioning needs to be understood and assessed in order to formu-late a comprehensive treatment plan. Anything that negatively affects physical health will also impact sexual health and functioning. However, contrary to popular myth, neither disease nor aging stop sexual functioning—although they can alter sexual function. The major negative medical impact is from side effects of prescribed medications, especially hypertensive and antidepressant medications. Particularly if the man or woman reports sexual dysfunction in all situations, including masturbation, it is imperative to have a medical assessment by either an internist or family practitioner, or ideally a sexual medicine specialist. Examples of common medical and/or physical factors negatively affecting sexual functioning are: infections (especially prostitatis) causing premature ejaculation; drug or alcohol abuse, causing dysfunction in desire and arousal; vaginal infections, causing sexual pain; lowered, or nonexistent levels of testosterone causing inhibited desire; and stress or fatigue causing inhibited sexual desire.

Identifying and treating a physical problem is often not sufficient to restore sexual function. A comprehensive approach, assessing and changing individual, couple, and psychosexual skills is typically necessary to rebuild sexual comfort and confidence.

SEX THERAPY ASSESSMENT

The sex therapy contract typically involves a couple approach. The format begins with a conjoint session to understand the couple's history and present situation, assess motivation for treatment and desire to change, explore their understanding of the sexual problem and previous attempts to resolve it, and whether a couple sex therapy contract is feasible. The ideal couple is committed to their marriage, their problem is acute or this is their first attempt to address it with professional help, their dysfunction is caused primarily by anxiety or lack of psychosexual skills, their target behavior is orgasm, and there is no hidden relationship or sexual agenda. Conversely, a difficult couple for sex therapy is very ambivalent, or threatening divorce (even contacting a divorce attorney); their problem is chronic, with several unsuccessful attempts to resolve it, their dysfunction is secondary inhibited sexual desire in the male, there are feelings of shame, guilt, and blame, and there is a major, hidden sexual or relationship agenda (e.g., affair, sexual orientation conflict, cybersex addiction).

Traditionally, therapy recommendations were to address problems in a sequential manner. For example, traditional therapy recommends that the therapist first deal with depression, alcohol abuse, sexual trauma, family of origin conflicts, and extramarital affairs. Once the primary problem is resolved, the therapist should address the sexual dysfunction. The guideline we advocate is a "both-and" approach—to address sexual issues in tandem with other issues, rather than treat sexual problems with benign neglect. Of course, this guideline will not be applicable when other problems are both acute and severe, such as one spouse's alcoholism being totally out of control, active battering or physical intimidation, an acute psychotic episode, an active extramarital affair, or high levels of chaos and alienation. For high-conflict couples who are motivated to address difficult issues, the usual guideline is the "both-and" approach of using renewed sexuality to reenergize the couple to address the difficult conflict issues at a different time and in a non-bedroom context. Ideally, couple sex therapy would address individual, relational, and sexual problems in one multidimensional therapy contract. In other cases, the couple sex therapy works cooperatively with an individual or marital therapist who is treating the other couple problems (depression, panic attacks, family of origin issues).

The next step in the assessment process is to conduct an individual sexual history with each partner. The person is encouraged to be frank and open, particularly regarding sensitive and secret material. The therapist's opening statement is, "I want you to be as honest and forthcoming as possible about your sexual history, both before you met your spouse and during the marriage. I need to know about both strengths and vulnerabilities. At the end of the session, I will ask if there is anything which is sensitive or secret that you do not want shared with your spouse, and I will not share that without your permission. However, I need to know about these difficult issues if I am to help you understand and change the sexual problem." The danger of doing a sexual history with the spouse present is that significant material will not be disclosed, and the therapy program fails because core issues were not addressed. Release of information forms are signed to allow telephone contact with past and present therapists, physicians, and, occasionally, ministers or lawyers.

The comprehensive sexual history allows the careful exploration of sexual strengths and vulnerabilities both before and during the marriage. This self-exploration/personal confrontation can be of great value to the client and the therapist. Rather than feeling shame or blaming the spouse, the client can objectively begin sorting out his or her role in the development and maintenance of the sexual dysfunction.

Typically, the sexual history session takes 45 to 90 minutes. The guideline is to ask open-ended questions, then follow up by exploring attitudes and feelings about an experience, both when it occurred and in retrospect. Usually, the clinician moves from less-anxiety-provoking material to more difficult sexual disclosures. The first question is about sex education experiences, which allows the clinician to explore general education, family structure, family approach to sexuality, and religious beliefs in childhood and at present. Developmental issues, such as body image, friendship patterns, academic and athletic experiences, and negative sexual experiences during childhood and adolescence are explored. The client is asked how old he or she was when first orgasmic and whether it was a positive or negative experience.

It is important to ask open-ended questions. An example might be, "Many people have sexual experiences with older children or adults that made them feel uncomfortable or felt abusive; what were your experiences?" If the therapist asked a yes-no question, it is too easy for the client to deny negative or shameful experiences. This format allows the person to discuss experiences, and if that is not an issue for them, to simply say no. This open-ended question format—with permission to explore the experience—is also used with issues of masturbation, same-sex encounters, and extramarital affairs. The message to the client is that all kinds of sexual experiences and feelings can be explored in a nonjudgmental manner. Was sexuality seen by the client, her or his friends, and family as something to be accepted, or as shameful, but exciting? Another useful open-ended question is, "As you think about your childhood and adolescence, what was the most sexually negative, confusing, or traumatic experience for you?"

Dating and sexual experiences after high school are explored, not with the focus on numbers and details, but on themes of self-worth and ability to cope with sexual issues. Were dating and sexual experiences positive or negative? What were the best and worst experiences? Did the person experience pregnancies or STDs, and how were they dealt with? Was there forced sex, and if so, how did the client cope with that experience? Emotionally and sexually, was young adulthood a good or a problematic period in the client's life?

In discussing how the spouse came into the client's life, the clinician wants to focus on the perceptions and feelings, not just the behavior. How did sex begin and when did sexuality feel best in the relationship? It is amazing how many people say that the best sex was in the first 6 months of the relationship. If so, the clinician needs to explore why they were unable to make the transition from the romantic love/passionate sex phase of the relationship to an intimate, interactive couple sexual style.

It is important to ascertain the state of the marital bond and how intimacy and sexuality fits into the relationship. In addition, specific questions about desire, arousal, orgasm, and satisfaction are explored, for the client and his or her perceptions about the spouse. When has sexuality been best in the marriage and when has it been worst? How motivated is the client to improve the sexual relationship? Is there ambivalence or a hidden agenda? What are the client's goals for couple sex therapy, and how realistic are they?

In completing the sexual history, the clinician asks a number of open-ended questions, the most important of which is whether there are any sensitive issues the person wants to keep secret. About 75 to 85 percent of people have at least one sensitive or secret area. Often, these are things from the past that cause embarrassment or shame, which would be therapeutic to share. With the client's permission, this material is processed as part of the couple feedback session. Some secrets render a couple sex therapy contract unviable, such as an active extramarital affair, or one spouse is gay. In this case, the client is told that the secret will not be disclosed without his or her permission, but that a different therapeutic recommendation will be made. Typically, the person gives permission to share the secret and it does promote the therapy process.

A final, open-ended question is, "As you look back on your entire life, what is the most negative, confusing, or traumatic experience you had?" Even though the clinician has spent over an hour chronologically reviewing the client's sexual history, approximately one in four people (especially males) will disclose a previously unmentioned incident. This indicates how difficult, yet how important, it is to deal with past or present sexually traumatic experiences and feelings. The last question is whether there is anything the client wants to ask the clinician. The most common question is if there is any hope for the marriage or for marital sex. Unfortunately, most couples come to therapy not when the problem is acute and they are hopeful, but when the problem is chronic and severe, and there are layers of resentment and blame. A crucial role for the therapist is to offer a new perspective and realistic hope.

This sets the stage for the couple feedback session, which is the most important component in successful sex therapy. There are three focuses in this session: (1) present an understanding of the development and maintenance of the sexual dysfunction that is acceptable to both clients, gives new information, provides motivation to change, and reinforces what each person needs to do and how to work together; (2) outline a therapeutic plan for change, with an optimistic view of success and increased awareness of individual and couple traps to monitor; and (3) introduce the first sexual exercise to engage in at home. Ideally, the couple leaves the feedback session feeling more aware and motivated to address the sexual dysfunction.

THE PROCESS OF SEX THERAPY

Although the format of therapy emphasizes couple sessions, it is not rigid and allows for individual work as necessary. The ongoing therapy sessions are semistructured, with the therapist taking an active role. Over time, the sessions become less structured, with the couple assuming more responsibility for bringing up issues and ultimately being their own therapist.

There are three phases to each session. The first is a fine-grain analysis of the attitudes, behaviors, and emotions elicited during the sexual homework exercises, exploring both the positive and problematic experiences. Second, processing what the couple is learning about their sexual style and their comfort and/or ability to deal with intimacy and sexuality issues, as well as therapeutic exploration of individual and couple traps. Finally, discussing and individualizing sexual exercises to engage in during the week. In addition to building comfort and skill, the couple is encouraged to change attitudes, confront inhibitions, deal with negative feelings, and establish practical and emotional conditions that facilitate functional, satisfying couple sexuality.

In addition to the traditional, nongenital-pleasuring exercises (sensate focus 1) and genital pleasuring exercises (sensate focus 2), there are semistructured exercises for female sexual dysfunction (self-exploration and masturbation, increasing arousal, becoming orgasmic) and male sexual dysfunction (learning ejaculatory control, arousal and erections, overcoming ejaculatory inhibition), as well as individual and couple exercises to challenge inhibited desire and build bridges to sexual desire. Other exercises involve developing a couple sexual style and preventing relapse (nondemand pleasuring, intercourse as a pleasuring experience, eroticizing marriage, special turn-ons, and sexuality and aging). Learning to utilize, process, and individualize sexual exercises is a central skill in sex therapy. Reading about and discussing sexual exercises helps change each person's attitudes and cognitions. Engaging in the exercises increases comfort and builds psychosexual skills. Processing positive as well as negative experiences results in altering feelings toward intimacy and sexuality. Rather than being a technical or mechanical approach, integrative couple sex therapy addresses the multidimensional aspects of sexual desire, arousal, orgasm, and satisfaction.

The sex therapy change process is seldom easy or problem-free. It is a gradual process, characterized by "two steps forward, one step back." The role of the therapist is to acknowledge and focus on the personal responsibility-intimate team model for change. When there are disappointments, setbacks, or failures, the therapist remains active, and urges the couple to learn from experiences and mistakes. Rather than becoming panicked or discouraged when there is a negative sexual experience, the couple is challenged to learn from the experience, thus building a resilient couple sexual style. This increases a sense of sexual self-efficacy and is a major resource for relapse prevention. A particularly helpful guideline is that change is facilitated by a 5-to-1 ratio of positive to negative reinforcement. Integral to the sexual change process is that the couple refrain from defensive or attack-counterattack behaviors. Rather, they are supportive, problem solving, and, most important, committed to being an intimate team.

A crucial component of healthy couple sexuality is developing and maintaining positive, realistic sexual expectations. The therapist attempts to provide accurate sexual information and helps to establish realistic expectations. In movies and other media, sex is portrayed in a highly unrealistic manner; both people are completely aroused before touching begins, the sex is short, intense, nonverbal, and perfect. Interestingly, marital sex is rarely portrayed. Instead, premarital sex or extramarital affairs are most commonly viewed. In reality, among happily married, sexually satisfied couples, less than 50 percent of sexual experiences involve equal desire, arousal, and orgasm. In 20 to 25 percent of encounters, sex is very good for one spouse (usually the man) and good for the other spouse. Another 15 to 20 percent of encounters are okay, but unremarkable. The most important information is that 5 to 15 percent of experiences are dissatisfying or dysfunctional. This is part of normal couple sexual variability, not a reason to panic or worry that you are a failed sexual couple. If a couple has movie-quality sex once a month, they are lucky. The prescription for vital, resilient couple sexuality is to integrate intimacy, nondemand pleasuring, and erotic scenarios and techniques with positive, realistic sexual expectations.

The process of couple sex therapy is challenging for the husband, wife, and therapist. The more chronic and severe the sexual dysfunction, the more the couple will need the therapist to keep them motivated and focused. In general, a broad-based sex therapy approach is more acceptable to women, due to its compatibility with the intimacy and pleasure-oriented approach of female sexual socialization. It is crucial for the therapist, regardless of clinician gender, to be empathic and respectful toward each spouse, and to routinely reinforce the personal responsibility-intimate team model.

Traditional male sexual socialization emphasizes the man as a strong, autonomous sexual performer who has no doubts or questions. He is embarrassed and feels stigmatized at having a sexual problem and needing help, whether from the spouse or therapist. He may worry that his wife and the therapist will collude in blaming him, or, even worse, pitying him. There are two typical patterns with male sexual dysfunction. The most common is the man with a primary premature ejaculation dysfunction who tries to deal with it himself by reducing arousal, which creates an erectile dysfunction. The anticipatory and performance anxiety increases so that each sexual encounter is a tense, pass-fail performance test. A successful sexual experience is more of a relief than a reinforcement of sexual confidence. Sex is contingent. He is always one failure away from feeling impotent and humiliated. This leads to self-consciousness, avoidance, and inhibited sexual desire. The second pattern is where the man has a sexual secret, including a history of sexual trauma, a variant arousal pattern (e.g., compulsive masturbation to cybersex or fetish object), an extramarital affair, or a homosexual/bisexual secret life. A central dynamic is the secrecy and fear that if his spouse knew she would be angry and might abandon him. These patterns reinforce the importance of conducting an individual sexual history interview, thus avoiding a sham therapy contract.

Almost all males have their first orgasmic experience during self-sex (masturbation or nocturnal emission), typically occurring between the ages of 10 and 14. In early couple sexual experiences, the most common problem is premature ejaculation. Men learn that sexual response is easy, automatic, predictable, and, most importantly, autonomous (he does not need anything from his partner in order to function sexually). This is not a good lesson for young males, and it becomes even more destructive during the middle years for married men. In therapy, these self-defeating attitudes need to be challenged and replaced by a cognitive, behavioral, and emotional system that values intimate, interactive couple sexuality. He needs to learn to enjoy intimacy and nondemand pleasuring. The most difficult change is to move away from pass-fail intercourse performance criteria toward a pleasure-oriented, variable, flexible approach to couple sexual satisfaction.

Healthy lessons are reinforced by sexual exercises and careful processing of attitudes and emotions during therapy sessions. These lessons are also reinforced by acceptance of the wife as an intimate sexual friend, not someone to perform for or to fear that he will disappoint. Two special exercises can be particularly influential learning experiences. An erotic exercise that maintains a prohibition on intercourse but removes the prohibition on orgasm can vividly illustrate the "give to get" pleasuring guideline extended to eroticism. Without the performance pressure of intercourse, he can experience being aroused by her arousal (including a realization that her arousal can be easier and more predictable), which is a bridge for his sexual desire and arousal. Especially with the aging of the couple and their marriage, his openness to her stimulation, arousal, and eroticism are a major source for his arousal. The second exercise involves the female's initiation of the transition from erotic stimulation to intercourse, with her guiding intromission. His receptivity and responsiveness to this flexible, variable couple sexual scenario successfully challenges his old belief that anything other than quick, autonomous, male-controlled intercourse is second class sex. The therapist's role is not to coerce a "politically correct" response, but to challenge the couple (particularly the man) to develop a way of thinking, talking, acting, and feeling about sexuality that promotes a healthy, realistic sexual relationship.

GUIDELINES FOR COUPLE SEX THERAPY

The therapist needs to adopt a conceptual and clinical strategy, which is individualized depending upon the couple and the sexual dysfunction. The theoretical orientation of the authors is social learning theory, and the clinical orientation is cognitive-behavioral therapy.

Basic sex therapy guidelines are applicable, but need to be flexible enough to be successfully utilized with different dysfunctions, types of couples, gender issues, and degrees of chronicity and severity. The chief guideline is the personal responsibility-intimate team model of understanding sexual problems and implementing change strategies. Use of semistructured sexual exercises is a core component in building comfort and confidence with psychosexual skills. The emphasis, through practice, on pleasure rather than performance, and the development of positive, nonperfectionist expectations is crucial in the creation of healthy sexuality. Another critical guideline is the continuum of touch, which emphasizes the value of all five dimensions of contact: affectionate, sensual, playful, erotic, and intercourse. For many couples (and many therapists) touch is either affectionate or intercourse. The concept of five gears of touch, or connection, is a method of breaking down the rigid, all-or-nothing approach to sexuality. It is also important for the couple to develop a sexual style that is compatible with their marital style (complementary, conflict-minimizing, best friend, or emotionally-expressive). The couple sexual style must involve a mutually comfortable level of intimacy, which facilitates sexual desire. The couple sexual style must address mutually agreeable initiation patterns, preferences for predictable versus variable sexual scenarios, preferences for multiple versus single stimulation, preferences for taking turns versus mutual stimulation, preferences for the role of intercourse initiation, functions and meanings of sexual experiences, and preferences for the inclusion of afterplay. A fundamental element in all types of sexual dysfunction treatment is an individualized couple relapse prevention program. Hoping that a sexual problem will not recur or treating sexuality with benign neglect is ineffective in maintaining therapeutic gains and a healthy sexual relationship.

MALE SEXUAL DYSFUNCTIONS

Premature Ejaculation

Premature Ejaculation (PE) is the most common male sexual dysfunction, affecting approximately 30 percent of adult men. Contrary to the pervasive belief that there is one cause (rapid masturbation learning) and one treatment (the squeeze technique), new research indicates nine possible causes for PE, and the need for a comprehensive treatment plan with a relapse prevention component. For the majority of men, PE is a primary dysfunction most commonly caused by a lack of psychosexual skills or an overly efficient neurological system ("hardwired" to rapidly ejaculate). Common causes of secondary PE are an untreated infection (particularly prostatitis), genital injury, drug side effects, psychological or relationship distress, or other sexual dysfunction (particularly erectile dysfunction). The most problematic yet common pattern is that the man attempts do-it-yourself control techniques, such as wearing two condoms, using a penile desensitizing cream, or thinking antierotic thoughts. These techniques do not improve ejaculatory control, but do decrease sexual arousal. Commonly, these techniques result in secondary erectile dysfunction and the beginning of a downward cycle of sexual embarrassment, avoidance, and inhibited sexual desire.

Understanding, assessing, and treating PE begins with the basic tenets of the personal responsibility-intimate team model of sexuality. He assumes primary responsibility for learning ejaculatory control, and she assumes the role of cooperative, intimate partner. He must identify the point of ejaculatory inevitability—after this, orgasm is not a voluntary process. Then he focuses on enhancing his ability to accept pleasure and arousal without moving toward ejaculation. The ejaculatory control strategy appears counterintuitive in that stimulation is increased rather than decreased. Ejaculatory control teaches the client to slow down and extend the eroticism and arousal process.

There are a range of skills and interventions that can be used, depending on the type of PE and its severity. Some couples require only one or two interventions and the change process is relatively simple. The vast majority of couples need to utilize a number of interventions; the change process is gradual, and fraught with challenges caused by miscommunications or difficulty with a technique. The most frequently used interventions are mental and physical relaxation techniques, identification and relaxation of pelvic muscles, identification of the point of ejaculatory inevitability using masturbation and partner manual stimulation, self-entrancement arousal, acceptance and adaptation to moderate and high levels of erotic stimulation, stop-go stimulation, the intercourse acclimatazation process, slow pacing and circular thrusting during intercourse, adoption of the idea that sex does not end with ejaculation, and enhanced enjoyment of afterplay. There are also a number of specific couple interventions, including increasing emotional intimacy, enhancing couple identity, valuing an intimate and interactive couple sexual style, adaptive coping with marital issues outside the bedroom, increasing couple cooperation and ability to process sexual exercises in a productive manner, and valuing sensuality and eroticism separate from intercourse. The integral role of the woman is reinforced by interventions that encourage her to develop her sexual voice, state her desire for intimate connection, asking for what she wants during sex, guiding penile intromission, controlling the rhythm of intercourse, greater awareness of her arousal and orgasm pattern(s), and the meanings and value of intimacy and sexuality for herself and the couple.

The sequencing of sexual exercises and interventions is important for successful treatment of PE. The typical therapeutic mistake is to move too fast and to focus on sexual performance, rather than sharing intimacy and promoting pleasure. Both public and mental health professionals have viewed PE as a simple, easy-to-cure problem. Although optimism about change is good, the danger of overpromising results looms large, and can result in a demoralized, blaming couple. The man may alternate between self-blame, spouse-blame, and therapist-blame. For therapy to be effective, the clinician needs to convey confidence in the strategies and techniques for ejaculatory control, without presenting one technique as a panacea.

As with other sexual dysfunctions, a relapse prevention program to generalize and maintain ejaculatory control gains is essential. A common mistake is the client's belief that he can return to normal intercourse—man on top, using short, rapid thrusts. This is the most difficult scenario in terms of ejaculatory control. The newly learned techniques, particularly pleasure-oriented intercourse, multiple stimulation, and slow, circular thrusting, are accepted as healthy, satisfying sex. The most important relapse prevention strategy is maintaining a regular schedule of intercourse. When couples are sexual less than twice a month, it is difficult to maintain ejaculatory control and self-confidence with psychosexual skills. Other helpful relapse prevention strategies specific to PE include using either the stop-go method or pacing technique at least once a month. If the couple have not had intercourse for 2 weeks or longer, and quick ejaculation occurs, they should purposefully practice an erotic or sensual afterplay scenario. They need not panic, but be aware that whether once a month or once a year, he will have a rapid ejaculation experience. The primary concern is preventing one lapse from becoming a relapse. The couple might also experiment with a new pleasuring or intercourse scenario at least once a year, so that they do not settle for a functional, but routine sexual life.

Erectile Dysfunction

Awareness of erectile dysfunction (ED) has exponentially increased since the introduction of Viagra in 1998. It is estimated that over 50 percent of men over the age of 50 have at least mild ED. Unfortunately, old myths and stigma of ED have given way to new performance myths and unrealistic expectations about the effect of Viagra.

The couple sex therapy approach to understanding, assessing, treating, and relapse prevention of ED emphasizes a comprehensive biopsychosocial model. Again, the key is to reject notions of autonomous, easy, automatic sex, and to adopt pleasuring as a mutual, interactive challenge. Typically, the man with ED is not open to the woman's pleasuring or erotic stimulation unless he is already panicking because of insufficient erection or lack of erection.

A significant component of therapy for ED is challenging male performance myths. The client must accept that his penis is part of who he is as a person, not a flawlessly performing sexual machine. Cognitively, one of the most difficult concepts for men to accept is that it is normal for 5 to 15 percent of sexual experiences to not culminate in successful intercourse. Male socialization emphasizes intercourse and orgasm as the only measures of sexual satisfaction, which is reinforced by adolescent and young adult experiences. However, by age 40, approximately 90 percent of males have had at least one experience where they did not have a sufficient erection for intercourse. So, the most feared male sexual experience, in truth, is an almost universal phenomenon. Males are not sexually honest with each other and do not discuss sexual questions, uncertainties, or negative experiences. Instead, men are socialized to brag about sex and to "one-up" each other. This is even truer of the media and advertising messages about male sexual performance. The data on Viagra, Levitra, and Cialis indicate that successful medication treatment results in a 65 to 80 percent success rate for attempts at intercourse. However, the advertisements lead one to believe that easy return to predictable, autonomous erections and 100 percent intercourse is the norm, thus creating an unrealistic, self-defeating expectation.

Behaviorally, the most important exercise/intervention involves waxing and waning of the man's erection. Almost all men prefer to go to intercourse on their first erection, so they panic if that erection wanes. Realizing that he can relax and be open to sensuous and erotic stimulation, which allows his erection to wax again, is a powerful lesson. Behaviorally, the man needs to establish comfort and confidence with his ability to get, lose, regain, and maintain an erection sufficient for intercourse the majority of times (perhaps 85 percent). He cannot fall into the trap of his erectile confidence being contingent on 100 percent intercourse success, because that leaves him one failure away from resensitized anxiety. In addition, the couple needs to develop comfort with two backup scenarios. The first is to be open to erotic stimulation (oral, manual, or rubbing) to orgasm for one or both partners. The second is a transition to a sensual scenario, so they end the encounter in a physically close and comfortable manner.

In the treatment of ED, a major assessment issue is whether to seek medical intervention. The three physiological factors most influencing erection are vascular, neurological, and hormonal. A number of diseases and drug side effects can negatively effect erections. These include diabetes (particularly with poor diabetic control), hypertension (partly due to hypertensive medications), depression and anxiety disorders, drug or alcohol abuse, surgery involving pelvic muscles or vascular function, multiple sclerosis, and other neurological disorders. Urologists and other sexual medicine specialists can utilize a number of sophisticated assessment techniques, especially nocturnal penile monitoring. By far the most popular medical intervention is Viagra, usually prescribed by the family practitioner or internist. Very seldom is the wife involved in the discussion or decision making. Viagra is a safe and effective drug, but as a stand-alone intervention it has high risks of discontinued use (dropout rates are estimated between 40 percent and 80 percent) and relapse to ED, as well as problems with sexual desire, sexual avoidance, and a nonsexual marriage.

Viagra, or other medical interventions, needs to be integrated into the comprehensive couple sex therapy approach in order to be truly effective. Otherwise, the man hopes that Viagra will miraculously return him to the easy, predictable, autonomous sex of his twenties. Successful use of Viagra requires his openness to her penile and erotic stimulation, and results in successful intercourse 70 to 80 percent of the time. In order to regain comfort and confidence, realistic expectations about Viagra are essential. Medications like Viagra are valuable adjunctive resources in the treatment of ED, but are generally ineffective without the therapeutic integration of intimacy, pleasuring, eroticism, and realistic sexual expectations.

One of the most helpful interventions for ED is the wax and wane exercise. In this procedure, the male is open to his partner's manual and oral stimulation. When he achieves a firm erection, stimulation is discontinued, allowing the erection to wane (become flaccid). Rather than panicking and attempting to force a return to erection, the man learns to relax and lie with his partner. Relaxation is the foundation of sexual response. In fact, Viagra works by relaxing the smooth muscles, allowing blood to flow to the penis, resulting in maintaining his erection. Learning that a relaxed state can be helpful in regaining erection, and that erections can return, is crucial in maintaining erectile confidence. Almost all men prefer to proceed to intercourse and orgasm with their first erection—which is fine, as long as it is not a source of pressure, performance anxiety, distraction, or panic if the erection is not perfect.

A crucial couple lesson is that the man needs intimate and interactive sex and that the woman's erotic response and arousal are a major source of his arousal. Cognitive and behavioral exercises can be designed to target cognitions surrounding male arousal, reinforcing his arousal from partner arousal and negating the performance demand for intercourse.

Another important exercise involves changing the erotic sequence so that the woman initiates the transition to intercourse and guides intromission. This exercise reinforces the woman as an active, intimate partner and reduces self-preoccupation and performance anxiety. Distraction is often a central element in maintaining ED. Distraction from sensuality, eroticism, and arousal, due to a focus on penile performance, prevents the experience of intercourse as a natural extension of erotic flow resulting in intromission at high levels of arousal. When intercourse is viewed as a performance, with catastrophic consequences for failing, the man and the couple lose the sense of intercourse as an integrated continuation of the pleasure/eroticism process.

Planning an erotic, nonintercourse scenario that incorporates high arousal and orgasm as well as a sensual afterplay scenario can be another useful exercise. This intervention allows both partners to be assured that if a particular encounter does not flow into intercourse, it is easy to transition into either an erotic or sensual backup scenario. Men over 40 should expect that 80 to 85 percent of sexual experiences will flow into intercourse, but 15 to 20 percent will not. It is normal to have a variable, flexible sexual repertoire that includes the woman being more aroused and orgasmic than the man, erotic, nonintercourse sex, and enjoyment of sensual experiences. The penis is not a perfect machine, but a positive, variable part of a man's humanity. Increased self-awareness and self-acceptance is vital in resolving ED and maintaining gains to prevent relapse.

Inhibited Sexual Desire

Male Inhibited Sexual Desire (ISD) is even more stigmatized than ED. When a man makes the decision to discontinue sex, it is usually because he finds it too frustrating and embarrassing, resulting in avoidance. ISD in males is almost always a secondary problem that is caused by another chronic sexual dysfunction, including ED, PE, and ejaculatory inhibition. The major cause of primary ISD is a sexual secret, such as homosexuality, a variant or deviant arousal pattern, or compulsive masturbation.

ISD increases with age. Middle-aged men believe the sexual lessons of their youth, and do not account for the natural changes in sexuality that come with an aging body and an aging marriage. Men who cannot transition from autonomous, automatic sex to intimate, interactive sex become vulnerable to secondary sexual dysfunctions, developing ED and subsequent secondary ISD.

Men tend to think of desire in terms of spontaneous and automatic erections. Erection becomes the cue for desire, rather than desire cueing the erection. The man learning to build bridges to sexual desire must develop openness to a variety of cues other than erection, including his partner's desire for connection, nondemand pleasuring, erotic fantasies, playful interactions, and a desire for intimacy. Sexual desire is an integrated part of the man and the marriage. Therefore, ISD can be challenged by turning the focus to sharing pleasure (not intercourse performance) and the need for emotional and sexual connection.

A highly effective exercise for ISD involves increasing comfort with touch—inside and outside the bedroom. The couple agrees to a prohibition on intercourse and orgasm, but are encouraged to explore clothed versus nonclothed touching, taking turns versus mutual pleasuring, verbal versus nonverbal connections, and sensual versus playful interaction. The theme of this intervention is that there are many ways to physically connect and be comfortable without the performance demand of intercourse.

He experimented with times, settings, types of touch, external stimuli, and initiation patterns which facilitate anticipation of a sexual encounter. Through this intervention, the man is learning to value a variable, flexible couple sexual repertoire rather than the all-or-nothing approach to sex.

In terms of vital, resilient male sexual desire, perhaps the most important exercise is to develop openness to his wife's erotic scenario(s). Men are socialized to believe that they should be more desirous and amorous than women. Yet, it is precisely this rigid view of male sexual identity that can lead to ISD. Exploring her sexual scenario, in which she is more desirous and aroused, can serve to increase his desire and erotic response (providing he is not intimidated). This intervention is especially useful if she enjoys erotic, nonintercourse scenarios, suggesting to him that there are times when intercourse is less effective in meeting their sexual needs than other desired scenarios.

Ejaculatory Inhibition

Ejaculatory Inhibition (EI) is the least discussed and researched male sexual dysfunction. The most common form of EI is the secondary intermittent pattern, which affects 10 to 15 percent of males over 50. EI is often misdiagnosed as ED. The primary difference between EI and ED is that the man loses his erection because he is unable to orgasm. EI can cause a self-defeating cycle of anticipatory anxiety, performance-oriented and frustrating sex, embarrassment and apologies, sexual avoidance, and, eventually, ISD. Men mistakenly blame EI on aging. It is true that after 60, men have less of a need to ejaculate at each sexual opportunity. Thus, it is normal to not ejaculate one out of four times. However, EI involves a significant number of incidents in which the man cannot reach orgasm, even though he is aroused and is driven to climax. In a particularly self-defeating pattern, the man may fake orgasm to try to hide EI from his partner.

The primary intervention with intermittent EI is to utilize multiple stimulation during intercourse. Most men believe that intercourse thrusting is and should be all that is needed for orgasm. After 50, the man may benefit from multiple stimulation during intercourse. Rather than moving to intercourse as soon as aroused and erect, he can benefit from additional manual or oral stimulation to reach high levels of arousal (at least a 7 on a scale of 10, with 5 being the initial erection and 10 being orgasmic) before transitioning to intercourse.

It is also helpful to identify "orgasm triggers" through masturbation. These triggers can be transferred to partner sex to use as multiple stimulation techniques.

Most men who experience EI do not have difficulty reaching orgasm during masturbation, probably due to comfort level, lack of pressure, confidence, and innate knowledge of his own triggers.

Examples of orgasm triggers are increasing muscle tension by stretching his legs or curling his toes, making sounds or breathing loudly and rapidly, increasing pelvic thrusting, verbalizing his level of arousal, and/or experiencing the culmination of his sexual fantasy and orgasm in reality. He is urged to verbally share orgasm triggers with his partner and then behaviorally play out those scenarios and techniques.

Multiple stimulation during intercourse is a strategy to increase eroticism so that it flows naturally into orgasm. The most common form of multiple stimulation is the use of erotic fantasies. Other techniques include the use of intercourse positions that allow greater freedom for manual stimulation of testicles or clitoris, kissing and stroking, buttock or anal stimulation, or verbalization of romantic or erotic feelings. Rather than trying to force orgasm, the focus is on increasing eroticism.

EI occurs in younger men, and involves an inability to ejaculate intravaginally, which is usually a primary dysfunction. The man is able to ejaculate during masturbation and usually with manual or oral stimulation, but not during intercourse. Careful assessment of cognitive, behavioral, emotional, and relational factors is crucial before developing an intervention plan. Typically, the young man quickly gets a firm erection, but his subjective arousal is low (2 or 3). As intercourse progresses, his subjective arousal may increase but not reach a high level (8+). In essence, his body is "lying," in that there is a continual incongruence between erection and feeling turned on. The most useful intervention is to focus on arousal and eroticism, not to try to force an orgasm. Utilizing multiple stimulation before and during intercourse, transitioning to intercourse at high levels of arousal, and using orgasm triggers are effective techniques. The basic strategy is to increase subjective arousal and erotic involvement with his partner. Orgasm can flow from high arousal, not forced at low levels of arousal.

FEMALE SEXUAL DYSFUNCTIONS

Inhibited Sexual Desire

It is estimated that one third of women suffer from inhibited sexual desire (ISD). The majority of female ISD is secondary, but primary ISD occurs in significant numbers. Originally, the focus of treatment for female sexual dysfunction was on orgasm, assuming that greater arousal and orgasm would remedy a lack of desire. The new paradigm emphasizes the centrality of desire, pleasure, and satisfaction in female sexuality (as well as male sexuality). Arousal and orgasm are integral to female sexuality, but do not solely define satisfaction.

Core cognitions of positive anticipation of sex, and feeling that she deserves sexuality to be a healthy part of her life and marriage are essential in overcoming ISD. Disappointment and resentment toward the spouse or marriage are major contributing factors in ISD. Typically, ISD is multicausal and multidimensional. Common causes include: anger, another sexual dysfunction (especially dyspeurunia), unresolved sexual trauma, medication side effects (especially SSRI antidepressants), not valuing sexuality, stress from balancing work and children, fear of unwanted pregnancy, reaction to spouse's sexual dysfunction, and guilt about past sexual experiences. Identifying and dealing with inhibitions is necessary, but not sufficient, to revitalize desire.

Two exercises are particularly helpful in resolving ISD. The first involves developing her sexual voice and building bridges to her sexual desire. Female socialization emphasizes intimacy and touching, but de-emphasizes sexual initiation and eroticism. Yet, couple sexuality is more vital and resilient when both the woman and man feel free to initiate a sexual encounter. Particularly important is the woman's understanding that she can initiate sensual, playful, erotic, and intercourse scenarios. Thus, her sexual voice is not limited to the dichotomies of affection or intercourse. Knowing that she can initiate an intimate physical connection, inside and outside of the bedroom, not necessarily culminating in intercourse, increases her sexual freedom and anticipation.

Common bridges to sexual desire include showering or bathing together, having 2 hours of quiet time while he takes over parenting and household chores, reading erotic or romantic fantasy material, together watching an R- or X-rated video, cuddling on the couch, receiving a whole body massage with lotions, or seductively waking the spouse by nibbling on his ear and stroking his penis. The role of the therapist is not to assign a bridge to desire, but to offer a plentiful array of scenarios, with the exercise of choosing one with which to experiment.

Awareness and acceptance of responsive sexual desire is another core concept in treating ISD. Rather than desire manifested as sexual thoughts or fantasies, a need for orgasmic release, or initiation of sex, for many women desire increases as the spouse initiates and she responds. As response and arousal increase, she experiences desire. Responsive desire is normal and healthy. The woman must identify her conditions to feel sexually receptive and responsive. Once these conditions are defined, how can the couple continue the scenario to enhance desire? Each woman and couple need to develop their own preferences and style, but a common request is not to transition to genital stimulation until responsiveness is at least a 3, and ideally a 5 (10 = orgasm). Another scenario is not to transition to intercourse until she has been orgasmic with non-intercourse erotic stimulation. If her preference is to be orgasmic with intercourse, then the transition to intercourse should not occur until arousal is at least a 7. Multiple stimulation during intercourse is another request, including kissing and caressing to increase pleasure, and clitoral, breast, or anal stimulation to increase arousal.

Spending time in afterplay can be a factor in increasing sexual desire. Enjoyable and bonding afterplay is an important ingredient in building or rebuilding a positive cycle of anticipation, pleasure-oriented sexual experiences, and a regular rhythm of sexual contact. Afterplay can be intimate, playful, or erotic. Some women find it easier to orgasm with afterplay. Her sexual voice, in terms of afterplay preferences and the fundamental belief that she deserves to be satisfied, are key.

Many of the exercises that build bridges to sexual desire for male ISD are useful in female ISD, such as increasing comfort, attraction, trust, and a personal style of initiation and eroticism. The focus is on feeling emotionally connected and safe, thus giving herself permission to integrate her erotic scenarios into their relationship, to talk about and experience a broad, flexible couple sexual style, and trust that her emotional and sexual needs are as important as his.

Nonorgasmic Response during Couple Sex

Since the 1960s there has been an inordinate emphasis on female orgasm as the key to sexual satisfaction. Couple sex therapy emphasizes sexual similarities between adult women and men, as well as the importance of a respectful, trusting, and equitable relationship. Orgasm is a healthy part of sexuality for both women and men. However, female orgasm is more complex and variable than male orgasmic response. This does not imply better or worse, but it does mean different. Only one in four women follow the male pattern of having a single orgasm during intercourse with no additional stimulation. Over 85 percent of women have experienced orgasm during couple sex. One in three women who are orgasmic during couple sex are never orgasmic during intercourse. This is not a sexual dysfunction, but rather a normal variation of healthy female sexual response. In fact, the majority of women find it easier, and some might say more satisfying, to be orgasmic with manual, oral, rubbing, or vibrator stimulation than during intercourse. Stimulation of the clitoris with her hands, his hands, or a vibrator is the most common means to facilitate orgasm during intercourse. In assessing the woman's arousal and orgasm pattern, the clinician needs to be clear about not only behavioral patterns, but also attitudes, feelings, preferences, and anxieties. For example, some women are able to be orgasmic on self-stimulation, possibly with the aid of a vibrator, but are embarrassed or inhibited to utilize these techniques during partner sex. Other women are very responsive and orgasmic during oral sex and might enjoy a multi-orgasmic response pattern, but feel inadequate because he wants her to be orgasmic during intercourse. Male sexual response is much more predictable; a single orgasm during intercourse. The male measure of satisfaction is orgasm. The current male model of orgasm and satisfaction is not the right model for females (and many sex therapists, including the authors, do not think it is a healthy model for men, especially those over 50). The woman may by nonorgasmic, singly orgasmic, or multi-orgasmic during a given sexual encounter. Orgasm might occur in foreplay, during intercourse, or during afterplay. Contrary to media myths, there is not one right orgasmic pattern. The performance criteria of vaginal orgasm, G-spot orgasm, multiple orgasms, and extended orgasms raise performance anxiety and reduce sexual desire, pleasure, and satisfaction for both genders.

There are a series of interventions to enhance female responsiveness, arousal, and orgasm. The format is to gradually increase comfort, psychosexual skills, exploration of preferences, ability to make sexual requests, and control of type and sequencing of pleasuring and erotic stimulation, including transition to intercourse via female guided intromission. Rather than reacting to his sexual scenario, she develops an intimate, interactive scenario, emphasizing her sexual voice and her flexible sexual repertoire.

A crucial cognitive change is the acceptance that it is normal to not be 100 percent orgasmic. Female sexuality is based upon desire, pleasure, and satisfaction. While female sexuality includes enjoying and valuing orgasm, it is not contingent on orgasm. Once she develops her desire/arousal/orgasm pattern(s), her partner accepts this, rather than comparing it with his own pattern or a mythical, ideal pattern.

Some women can be orgasmic by themselves, but not during couple sex. In assessing this problem, it is important to determine whether it reflects anxiety and inhibition or disappointment with and alienation from the spouse and marriage. If the former, the core intervention focuses on increasing comfort and sexual assertiveness. It is often helpful for the woman to watch a psychoeducational video such as *Becoming Orgasmic,* first alone and then with the spouse. Then, she works to implement the personally relevant components of the change program. Most commonly, this involves giving herself permission to use all of her erotic resources and to "let go" sexually. Behaviorally, it means deciding whether her preference is multiple stimulation and/or mutual stimulation. She also needs to identify and integrate her orgasm triggers. Just as for the male, orgasm becomes a natural progression of the pleasuring process, not a performance test.

In the last generation there has been a significant decrease in the number of women suffering from primary nonorgasmic response. Reasons for this include a greater awareness of female sexuality, female pre-orgasmic therapy groups, and use of the vibrator. Approximately 7 to 8 percent of adult women have never been orgasmic. The clinician needs to be respectful of the woman's comfort level and preferences for treatment. Some women are open to using a vibrator, self-help programs, or joining a 10-session pre-orgasmic group. Other women prefer individual therapy or couple sex therapy. One size does not fit all. Careful assessment of each individual and couple is not just desirable, but necessary.

Sexual Pain and Vaginismus

Sexual pain (dyspeurunia) and vaginismus are excellent examples of the need for a multicausal, multidimensional approach to assessment, intervention, and relapse prevention. Intermittent experiences of sexual discomfort or pain are an almost universal phenomenon for women over 40. However, severe pain or vaginismus (which refers to great difficulty with or impossibility attaining vaginal penetration) very much interfere with female and couple sexuality. Often, the cause of the initial pain problem (infection or tear in the vaginal wall) has been resolved, but other factors, including anticipatory fear, lack of lubrication, and vaginal tension maintain the pain dysfunction. Visits to the gynecologist result in, "I can't find a physical cause for your pain, it's a psychosomatic problem," leaving the woman feeling blamed and wondering if it is all in her head. In truth the pain is in her vulva—not in her head. Cutting-edge researchers dealing with chronic sexual pain suggest that this be approached as a pain problem rather than a sexual problem. They recommend a team approach to treatment, consisting of a sexual medicine specialist, a physical therapist with a subspecialty in pelvic musculature, and a couple sex therapist.

For the majority of women dealing with sexual pain, the most common exercise involves choosing a hypoallergenic, water-based lubricant for use before intercourse begins (not as a reaction to the pain). She should also control the transition to intercourse and guide intromission. Since she is the expert on her vagina, she is more likely to successfully control intromission and reduce or eliminate pain. For pain during thrusting, changing the intercourse position, varying types of thrusting, and increasing erotic stimulation can be helpful in managing the pain. The role of the partner is very important for the clinician to assess, especially if the partner has PE, ED, or EI. Other factors to assess include her fears or inhibitions about her vulva or sexuality, history of sexual trauma or STDs, feelings of intimidation by the spouse, fear of pregnancy, and feeling a lack of control.

RESISTANCE TO SEXUAL INTERVENTIONS AND EXERCISES

When couples avoid engaging in sexual exercises or ignore critical psychological issues, the therapist attempts to restructure the assignment, with a focus on smaller steps and a more comfortable manner of approaching the anxiety-provoking issue. The therapist tries to maintain a positive, encouraging stance, emphasizes a smaller number of interventions for the person and couple, and urges them to choose the interventions that would be personally relevant and helpful. The emphasis is on the 5 to 1 positive reinforcement approach, gradually building comfort and skills. However, if avoidance and/or blame continue, it is important to help each client and couple confront the inhibitions and fears that serve to block change. The exercises can serve a diagnostic function of identifying cognitive, behavioral, and emotional factors, which subvert the change process. At times it is valuable to have individual meetings (part of a session or an extra session) with a spouse to explore the avoidance or of feeling "stuck." Sometimes this will result in new information, which will change the treatment plan (e.g., decision to not try to revitalize marital sex, or disclosure of a sexual secret that must be processed). More commonly, this increases motivation to confront the sexual dysfunction.

───────────────── **Case Study** ─────────────────

The ideal sex therapy couple would be highly committed to facing a specific sexual dysfunction in its acute stage. Unfortunately, that seldom occurs in clinical practice. Diana and Art had been married for 9 years and had a 4-year-old son. Their sexual life had been troubled throughout the marriage and nonexistent since the birth of their son. Neither Diana nor Art were strangers to therapy, although this was their first experience with sex therapy.

Like many couples with chronic sexual dysfunction, Diana and Art recall their best sex in the first 6 months, when there was high romanticism, passion, and idealization of the partner and the relationship. During this time they had sex almost each time they were together, often more than once (Art reported better ejaculatory control the second time). Art was 27 when he met 28-year-old Diana, and felt she was the most attractive and sexual woman he had ever dated. Art was a handsome, athletic man who had a reputation as being very social and funny, but in fact had a number of emotional and sexual inhibitions. Diana always had boyfriends who she knew found her sexually attractive, but she was passive sexually and rarely orgasmic. Diana and Art were engaged after 5 months, and married 8 months later. Four months before their wedding, sexual frequency had reduced to less than once a week, but other than a few unkind jokes, Art and Diana were optimistic about being a couple.

The major sexual meltdown occurred on their 10-day honeymoon in Hawaii. They were tired from the wedding and the flight, but Art insisted they have intercourse. He ejaculated before intromission. Art apologized profusely, but insisted they try again so he could do better. From his perspective, the sex was better, but from Diana's it was a chore, and she felt some discomfort. This set the stage for continual sexual conflict over the course of their marriage. Diana complained to her individual therapist that Art's PE became much worse after marriage. The therapist suggested that PE was a symbol of an intimacy problem and that Art needed individual therapy. Art was a reluctant therapy client, who felt put on the defensive by the therapist and Diana. They then tried couple therapy. Although neither the quality nor frequency of sex improved, they enjoyed couple therapy, liked the therapist, felt an improvement in communication, and were pleased when Diana became pregnant. A planned, wanted child is both a celebration and a challenge for most couples. Unfortunately, Diana and Art could not meet this couple challenge, although they did well working as cooperative parents. Diana was bitter and disappointed with Art as a spouse and felt let down by their marriage. She frightened herself by responding to the attention of other men in the tennis group to which she belonged. She missed feeling desirable to men, which intensified her negative feelings toward Art. Art withdrew into the world of internet sex and pornography. Although they intermittently consulted their marriage therapist, and talked about their lack of emotional intimacy, sexual issues were avoided by all involved. The situation came to a crisis point when Diana found an overdue credit card bill (Art was the bill payer) that had over $300 a month in charges to various Internet pornography sites. This resulted in seeking couple sex therapy.

Although Art tried to minimize the problem and avoid disclosing details— making the situation worse—Diana established that over the past 3 years Art had spent $10,000 on Internet sex. Art was genuinely shocked at the figure, as he had rationalized that this was a private and harmless sexual outlet. The marital therapist suggested Art be referred for sexual addiction assessment, but the sex therapist suggested a more comprehensive couple sexual assessment. As part of the sexual history, compulsive sexual behavior would be carefully assessed (Art had three individual sessions rather then a single session).

Art and Diana were a demoralized couple, trapped in a nonsexual marriage. In the feedback session, the clinician recommended a therapy contract with two goals: building a mutually satisfying couple sexual style, and abstinence from Internet sex, with gradual reimbursement of the $10,000 to their son's college fund. Art agreed to complete Internet and credit card transparency; he would report any high-risk situation or acting-out to Diana within 24 hours (the "24-hour" rule) and would masturbate using only written, pictorial, or fantasy material. Art's masturbation frequency reduced to one to three times a week, and he realized that his secret sexual world had been serving a number of nonsexual motivations, including boredom, loneliness, and emotional self-soothing.

Rebuilding Art and Diana's trust bond was necessary but not sufficient to revitalize sexuality. Anger and alienation subverted intimate and erotic feelings. Diana was concerned about her ISD, sexual discomfort, and history of nonorgasmic response. Art was feeling guilty about his sexual acting out, worry over his PE, and hurt from Diana's anger and rejection.

Sex therapy began with intimacy and nondemand pleasuring exercises. The most difficult challenge for Diana was to take responsibility for her own desire, arousal, and orgasm, rather than blaming Art. The concept of integrated eroticism was motivating for Diana. Art focused on the attraction exercise, and Diana realized that he did view her as an attractive spouse and wanted a sexually satisfying marriage, which was both validating and motivating for her. Diana had always viewed Art as sexually selfish and too much of a "man's man." Realizing that Art was emotionally and sexually shy was freeing for Diana and made her more open to developing an intimate and interactive couple sexual style. Anger is the main emotion that inhibits desire. Diana was able to access the hurt underlying her anger. She made it clear that a regression to a secret world, more so than sexual misuse of the internet, would not be tolerated. Diana and Art accepted that enhanced intimacy is the best way to heal from the hurt.

Art had to confront his pattern of avoidance, his secret sexual world, and his apologizing for PE. These issues made the marital problems worse, and subverted the change process. Ceasing avoidance, sexual secrets, and apologizing were necessary but not sufficient. Art needed to share attitudes and feelings with Diana. He needed to move toward her, not hide from her. Art began to think of Diana as his sexual friend, not his worst critic. Art was able to learn the principles of ejaculatory control during masturbation by identifying the point of ejaculatory inevitability, relaxing his pelvic muscles, using stop-go stimulation, and using self-entrancement arousal. This increased Art's confidence that he and Diana could develop a cooperative, satisfying sexual relationship. Art was surprised and pleased that Diana took the initiative in nondemand pleasuring exercises and that she was responsive and orgasmic during the erotic, nonintercourse couple exercises. Although there were difficulties and setbacks, Diana and Art treated the ISD as a mutual enemy, broke their sexual hiatus, and learned to enjoy a functional, mutual marital sexuality.

Diana worried that they would fall into a rigid pattern of her being orgasmic during the pleasuring/foreplay phase, with Art feeling free to quickly have an orgasm during intercourse. Art was learning to be more emotionally expressive, and assured Diana that he valued a variable and flexible sexual repertoire. To put this into action, he initiated their first relapse prevention exercise—buying a special lotion and initiating an erotic, nonintercourse date. Diana wanted to be sure that Art would not lapse back into sexual avoidance and a marginal marriage. Diana was enjoying marital sexuality, which she found to be better than her premarital experiences, because it was intimate, sensual, and erotic. Art felt he was growing personally and maritally and felt proud that they had established a healthy marital, not just parental, model for their son. Art and Diana agreed to design an active relapse prevention program. For Diana the most important component was the agreement that if they went 2 weeks without a sexual encounter, Art would initiate. Art felt the most important component was his agreement not to apologize or withdraw if they had a dissatisfying or dysfunctional sexual encounter, but rather to hold Diana. Within the next 3 days, Art would initiate, to ensure their disappointed sexual feelings did not grow and fester.

BUILDING A FUNCTIONAL COUPLE SEXUAL STYLE

The primary function of couple sex therapy is to resolve sexual dysfunction. A second, essential function is to establish or reestablish a comfortable, satisfying couple sexual style. Clinical and research data emphasize a mutually comfortable level of intimacy that facilitates desire and emotional connection, rather than more intimacy necessarily being better. Ideally, there is congruence between a couple's marital and sexual style. If the couple adopts a complementary marital style, which balances autonomy and coupleness, their sexual style will allow both people to initiate affection and intercourse dates. Typically, conflict-minimizing couples follow more traditional gender roles, in which sex is the male's domain, and marital sexuality is not experimental. A particular challenge for best-friend couples is not to allow desire and eroticism to be smothered by too much closeness. Emotionally expressive couples have the most vital, playful, erotic sexual style, but are also the most explosive and divorce prone. Their challenge is to not allow conflicts and anger to cross personal boundaries. They can use sexuality as a way to heal from hurts and to increase resilience.

In addition to establishing a mutually enhancing level of intimacy, other components of a couple sexual style include: developing a sexual initiation pattern, finding a comfortable way to stay physically connected, agreeing on issues of conception and contraception, sexual trust, frequency and quality of sexual encounters, preferences for types of stimulation, erotic scenarios and techniques, the role of afterplay, and the meaning and value of marital sexuality. There is no one right way to be sexual. Sexuality fits each couple's personalities, feelings, values, and situation.

Couple sex therapy is a focused, time-limited intervention. After the 4-session assessment phase, therapy itself usually involves 6 to 20 sessions, from 4 months to 1 year. As therapy progresses, the therapist is less active and directive, giving greater responsibility to the couple. Sessions are scheduled on a biweekly basis and then gradually tapered off.

RELAPSE PREVENTION PROGRAMS

Relapse, both marital and sexual, is often ignored by couples and therapists. However, there is ample empirical evidence that relapse is a major problem in marital and sex therapy.

An obvious element of relapse prevention is comprehensive couple sex therapy, which carefully assesses and addresses a range of attitudes, behaviors, and feelings about intimacy and sexuality. Iatrogenic therapist behaviors include prematurely terminating therapy at the first functional sexual experience and telling the couple they no longer need to be concerned about sex. Sexuality cannot rest on its laurels; the couple has to continuously nurture intimacy and eroticism.

The last two therapy sessions emphasize relapse prevention, and 6-month follow-up sessions occur over the next 2 years. This facilitates the couple remaining accountable to each other and to the change process. Before termination, the couple are given a list of 10 relapse prevention techniques and encouraged to choose 2 to 4 that are personally relevant. Examples include saving therapy time and having a couple date, accepting that 5 to 15 percent of encounters will be dissatisfying or dysfunctional to prevent overreaction, coping techniques to prevent a lapse from becoming a relapse, and scheduling a weekend away from children at least once a year. In each follow-up session, the couple set personally relevant goals, including trying a new intercourse position, shopping for sexy clothing together, planning a week-long trip as a couple, and resolving extended family problems together. The goal is not only to maintain sexual gains, but also to reinforce and generalize healthy attitudes, behaviors, and feelings. The couple can use the session to discuss concerns and deal with problems when they are in the acute stage. If there is a problem, they can call for a booster session at any time.

CULTURE AND RELIGION ISSUES IN SEX THERAPY

Couples from different cultural, religious, educational, socioeconomic, racial, or value backgrounds will react differently to the role and meaning of sexuality and sex therapy. Certain religious groups, such as Mormons, Orthodox Jews, and Fundamentalist Protestants have strong norms involving marriage and sexuality. It is important that the therapist be cognizant and respectful of those religious values when planning interventions. Awareness of cultural and value issues are even more important if the couple comes from different backgrounds and/or are a nonmarried couple. The guideline is that the therapist works within the couple's value system and helps the couple clarify their views about sexuality. For example, a valuable resource is a referral to a minister of the couple's denomination, who assures them of the positive role of marital sexuality (almost all religions are pro-marital sex).

SPECIAL ISSUES WITH UNMARRIED COUPLES

Rates of sexual dysfunction and dissatisfaction are higher among unmarried couples than married couples. Couple sex therapy can be very relevant for dating and cohabitating couples. The same types of sexual dysfunction occur and the same sex therapy strategies and techniques are useful. However, there are special issues to be aware of and special assessments and interventions to use with this population.

A chief question is whether sex therapy is an appropriate intervention. The existence of a sexual dysfunction does not mean that sex therapy is necessarily the right treatment. A common joke is that the best way to break up a marginal or nonviable couple is to send them to sex therapy. The emotional intensity of sex therapy is too much for a tenuous couple. Some couples make getting married contingent on resolving the sexual problem. This usually is a poor therapy contract. Sex should not be a relationship "deal maker" or "deal breaker".

Reasonable criteria for couple sex therapy are that the couple have a serious, ongoing relationship, and have a sexual dysfunction that they are willing to address. Although we know of no empirical data, our clinical experience is that the majority of nonmarried couples do resolve sexual problems, but the resolution does not result in marriage. The partner of a sexually dysfunctional person who hopes that his or her cooperation will be rewarded by marriage is setting him- or herself up for disappointment. Of course, there are couples that increase respect, trust, and intimacy during their therapy experience and then commit to marriage. There are other couples that sexually improve moderately, or even minimally, but have a stronger bond and successfully marry. The senior author remembers a couple who did extremely well in sex therapy, improved their intimacy and communication, but who never married because of irresolvable religious and political conflicts. Many people are excellent as a dating couple but are not viable as a married couple. Remember the guideline that the essence of marriage is a respectful, trusting relationship, to which sexuality contributes 15 to 20 percent to relationship vitality and satisfaction. Sexuality is not a deal maker.

What about the man with primary PE who asks his girlfriend to help him learn ejaculatory control? In this case, improving ejaculatory control will be positive for both individuals and the relationship. However, having a functional sexual relationship does not predict marital viability or success.

An important factor to assess before beginning treatment and during therapy is the partner's ability to be cooperative and supportive. It is not uncommon for the partner of a woman with an orgasmic dysfunction to balk at moving at her pace or respecting her veto. He says she cannot expect so much from him. She feels betrayed, because she is trying to implement the therapeutic strategy of being responsible for herself and developing her sexual voice. Obviously, this could and does happen with married couples, but it illustrates the need for both partners in the relationship to commit the time and psychological energy needed to successfully resolve the problem.

SEX THERAPY WITH GAY COUPLES

Although there is a lack of empirical data, the estimate is that rates of sexual dysfunction are as high, if not higher, for gay couples relative to straight couples. However, gay couples are less likely to seek couple sex therapy. It is not easy for gay couples to access competent sexual help. Lesbian couples typically choose to work with a female therapist, whether straight or gay. The therapist needs to be competent in dealing with couple and sexual dysfunction issues, as well as be supportive and understanding of the gay community. Male couples vary in preference for a male or female therapist, as well as preference for a gay or straight therapist.

A particularly value-ladened, sensitive issue is whether the couple is monogamous, which brings up issues of HIV/AIDS and STDs, especially for male couples. Ideally, a couple with open values about monogamy would commit not to have affairs during sex therapy. The time as well as the physical and emotional energy required for couple sex therapy can easily be sabotaged by the ease of affair sex.

Data on sexual dysfunction among lesbian couples is very controversial. Most researchers believe that rates of ISD are high, while rates of nonorgasmic response and sexual pain are low. Lesbian theorists and clinicians believe this narrowly defines and stigmatizes lesbian sexuality. There is an obvious need for empirical research that is sensitive to lesbian culture and value issues while being honest and clinically relevant, rather than politically correct. It is especially important to attend to the meanings and values of lesbian sexuality, so that it plays that 15- to 20-percent positive role in the relationship. The focus in terms of exercises is not unlike those for straight couples, and includes building bridges to sexual desire, developing comfortable initiation patterns, and developing erotic scenarios and techniques.

Gay male couples have been found to struggle more with ED and EI, and less with PE. In addition, valuing and maintaining desire with one partner is a challenge, because traditional gay male socialization has valued variety and illicitness, not intimacy and security. Before HIV/AIDS, nonmonogamy was the valued norm.

One of the major assessment issues is how bonded the couple is and how bonded each partner would like them to be. In terms of ISD, primary interventions are to build bridges to sexual desire and establish erotic scenarios that are arousing to each partner. Each individual strives to play off the other's arousal. In general, the gay community is more accepting of scenarios that involve external stimuli, including sex toys, Viagra, or three-way sex.

The therapist helps the couple to establish conditions for good sex in terms of desire, arousal, and orgasm. A complex issue to address is making erotic scenarios compatible. For example, both partners may want to be passive in anal intercourse. It is therapeutically dangerous to minimize the hard issues or to be politically correct. The therapist needs to help the couple explore a range of alternatives, including one partner taking Viagra in order to be active in anal intercourse, the use of dildos, using manual or oral anal stimulation, or focusing on oral, manual, or rubbing erotic stimulation instead of anal intercourse. Once the couple has chosen what they are open to experimenting with, the therapist individualizes an exercise program to implement the behavior change. In confronting the dysfunction, the therapist needs to be empathic and respectful, but also encourage couples to make difficult cognitive, behavioral, and emotional changes.

SEX THERAPY FOR PEOPLE WITHOUT PARTNERS

Although there has been much media discussion of surrogate sexual partners, and sex magazines have ads for surrogate partners for $1,000 per weekend to cure sexual dysfunction, there is very little clinical use of surrogate partners. The couple sex therapy model is not the right intervention for people without partners. However, the single person with sexual dysfunction can benefit from sexual counseling. Examples include bibliotherapy, masturbation training, guided imagery, role-play of discussing sexual issues with a partner, and choosing a partner based on comfort, attraction, and trust. Many women are open to attending a 10-session, semistructured female sexuality group focused on either nonorgasmic response or on general issues of female sexual function. Male sexuality groups have generally not been successful, because males are extremely reluctant to become involved.

Telling a client you cannot help him or her until they have a partner, thus forcing them to pick a friend or new partner to attend therapy with, is potentially iatrogenic. Many males are so embarrassed by their dysfunction that they purposefully pick a woman that they are not attracted to, so they have a rationale for unsuccessful sex. Or, the man may choose a woman intent on playing the role of rescuer. Women find it easier to recruit a "sensitive man" who is confident he can "fix" her. Yet, when therapy is progressing slowly or she vetoes something, he turns on her instead of being the sexual friend. This results in the woman's further distrust of men and sex.

SENSITIVE AND SECRET ISSUES

There are a variety of sensitive and secret issues that come out in sex therapy, including past or present affairs, variant or deviant arousal patterns, conflict about sexual orientation, lack of attraction or love, history of child abuse or other trauma, present sexual harassment, dealing with a recurrent STD, and guilt over a sexual secret. Secrets can have a number of negative sexual effects, particularly poor sexual self-esteem, a guilt-ridden approach to sexuality, and inhibitions about sharing sexual communication and intimacy. People fear that if the spouse knew their secret, he or she would be appalled. Most sexual secrets, especially about past experiences, cause inappropriate and unnecessary guilt and shame. Usually, the spouse is less judgmental and more supportive than the person expected. The spouse can be a partner in healing, helping to cope with past negative experiences or trauma. A helpful cognition is that living well is the best revenge. The person can feel like a survivor, not a victim. Therapy sessions allow the client to process feelings about the past and plan how to develop a healthy sexual self-esteem, as well as an intimate and interactive sexual style. Experiencing healthy desire, arousal, orgasm, and satisfaction can be symbolic of freedom from a traumatic sexual past.

Present sexual secrets are more difficult and complex, but important to deal with in a therapeutic manner. Common present sexual secrets include an affair, a variant or deviant arousal pattern, a secret sexual life of cybersex or paid sex, homosexual encounters, lack of love or attraction, and guilt about masturbation or fantasies. The function and meaning of the sexual secret, as well as the person's motivation to address and change the problem, need to be carefully assessed. In some instances, such as an ongoing "comparison affair," gay sexual orientation, or unwillingness to confront a deviant arousal pattern, a couple sex therapy contract is not viable. The therapist does not disclose the secret without the client's permission, but would make recommendations for individual, couple, or sexual addiction treatment. The therapist will not engage the couple in a sham therapy contract.

Ideally, the client is willing to address the sensitive issues, and the problem is integrated into the couple feedback session with a recommended treatment plan. Hopefully, the spouse is supportive and an ally in helping the client make changes. The person with the secret needs to take primary responsibility for change, thus following the personal responsibility-intimate team model of change.

NEW DIRECTIONS IN SEX THERAPY

There is a dire need to address a multitude of clinical and research issues in sex therapy. Unfortunately, lack of research funding, except from drug companies, makes this exceedingly difficult.

A priority in sex therapy research is to examine the couple sex therapy model with a variety of populations, socioeconomic groups, religious groups, couples with and without children, age groups, couples with chronic medical or handicapping conditions, and alcohol- or drug-abusing couples. In addition, there is a need for both process and outcome data for gay couples and unmarried heterosexual couples. There is also little empirical data on the effects of sexual dysfunction on family functioning, particularly the effects on children. How does sexual dysfunction affect a parent's ability to be a sex educator for his or her child?

It is also of fundamental importance to evaluate the benefits and the iatrogenic effects of medical or other external interventions on couple sexuality. Increasingly, the culture has become interested in quick fixes and medical interventions, especially pills and patches. Viagra has been oversold as a magic pill, and has resulted in demoralized men and nonsexual marriages. There is a great need for clinical and empirical research on how to best utilize medical resources and integrate them into the couple sexual style. In terms of relapse prevention, how can a clinician differentiate between someone who can be weaned off a medication and those who must take the medication on a continuous basis?

There is also a pressing need for more information on sexual function, dysfunction, prevention, and treatment with understudied populations: couples with disabilities, minority couples, couples with histories of physical or sexual trauma, lower socioeconomic class couples, and multiproblem, high-risk couples.

Sexuality is a positive, integral component in people's lives and relationships. Sexuality and sexual dysfunction deserve much more research and clinical attention than currently received. Most marriage therapists will not choose to do sex therapy as a subspecialty, but marriage therapists should be comfortable and competent in giving prosexual messages, open to discussing sexual issues, able to provide scientifically accurate information about sexual problems, supportive of dealing with psychosexual issues, versed in suggestions for common sexual problems, and willing to refer clients for sex therapy when appropriate.

REFERENCES

Heiman, J. (2002). Sexual dysfunction. *Journal of Sex Research, 39,* 73–78.

Michael, R., Gagnon, J., Laumann, E., & Kolata, G. (1994). *Sex in America.* Boston: Little, Brown.

FURTHER READING

Basson, R. (2001). Human sexual response cycles. *Journal of Sex and Marital Therapy, 27,* 33–43.

Bergeron, S., Meana, M., Binik, Y., & Khalife, S. (2003). Painful genital sexual activity. In S. Levine, C. Risen, & S. Althof (Eds.), *Handbook of clinical sexuality for mental health professionals* (pp. 131–152). New York: Brunner/Routledge.

Foley, S., Kope, S., & Sugrue, D. (2002). *Sex matters for women.* New York: Guilford.

Heiman, J. & LoPiccolo, J. (1991). *Becoming orgasmic* video. Chapel Hill, NC: Sinclair Intimacy Institute.

Laumann, E., Paik, A., & Rosen, R. (1999). Sexual dysfunction in the United States. *Journal of the American Medical Association, 10,* 537–545.

Leiblum, S., & Rosen, R. (2000). *Principles and practice of sex therapy.* New York: Guilford.

Maltz, W. (2001). *The sexual healing journey.* New York: Harper-Collins.

McCarthy, B. (2001). Relapse prevention strategies and techniques with erectile dysfunction. *Journal of Sex and Marital Therapy, 27,* 1–8.

McCarthy, B. (2002). Sexual secrets, trauma, and dysfunction. *Journal of Sex and Marital Therapy, 28,* 353–359.

McCarthy, B., & McCarthy, E. (2002). *Sexual awareness.* New York: Carroll and Graf.

McCarthy, B., & McCarthy, E. (2003). *Rekindling desire.* New York: Brunner/Routledge.

Metz, M., & McCarthy, B. (2003). *Coping with premature ejaculation.* Oakland, CA: New Harbinger.

Metz, M., & McCarthy, B. (2004). *Overcoming erectile dysfunction.* Oakland, CA: New Harbinger.

Risen, C. (2003). Listening to sexual stories. In S. Levine, C. Risen, & S. Althof (Eds.), *Handbook of Clinical Sexuality for Mental Health Professionals* (pp. 3–19). New York: Brunner/Routledge.

PART IV
Relationship Difficulties in Families

CHAPTER 19

Family Therapy with Stepfamilies

James H. Bray

The call came late one morning. My secretary buzzed me and said there was some-one on the phone that wanted to talk with me "right now." That was our signal that we had a clinical situation that needed my immediate attention. When I asked Patsy Sanders how I could help her, she stated quickly, "Its not for me—I'm call-ing for help for Luke, my son. He's been acting strange lately and I'm afraid some-thing is really wrong with him. We just had a big fight and he ran out of the house." She sounded tense, and then blurted out, "Things had been going so well the last few years, I don't want them to get bad like they used to be," as her voice crack-led and sounded like tears on the other end of the phone.

I asked her to tell me a little bit more about what problems her son was having and about her family situation. She said Luke had "become sullen and withdrawn and was getting into fights with everyone in the family—especially with my hus-band, Mike." Ms. Sanders said that she was remarried and that her son, Luke, was 13 years old. At home were her second husband, Mike, Lauren, age 11, Cody, age 4, and Luke. She asked if she could be seen right away, and I scheduled an ap-pointment for that afternoon. I asked her to bring everyone in the family for the first session. Patsy repeated, "Everyone?" but sounded a bit relieved when I ex-plained that to best help Luke I needed input from all of the family.

After the call I began to wonder about her stepfamily and what might be going on. I realized I had a flood of questions about them—how long had she been re-married, how many times had she been married, which marriages did the children come from, what kind of relationship did Luke have with his stepfather, and what role did Luke's father play in their lives? I also began to think about my research on stepfamilies and how it might help me work with this family.

RESEARCH ON STEPFAMILIES

Stepfamilies have been around since at least Biblical times, but they have experi-enced an exponential increase over the past 25 years, due to the large divorce and remarriage rates and an increase in the number of children born outside of mar-riage (Bray, 1999; Bray & Hetherington, 1993). It is estimated that there are be-tween 15 and 20 million stepfamilies in the United States, and the number continues to increase each year. The rise in the number of stepfamilies is linked to major demographic changes: increases in cohabitation, with more childbearing outside of marriage, the high divorce rate, and the high remarriage rate. Although there is a high divorce rate, people appear to value the institution of marriage, as they continue to remarry. The divorce rate for second and subsequent marriages is higher than for first marriages, and has been partially attributed to the presence of children from previous relationships. It is estimated that between 65 to 75 percent of women and 75 to 85 percent of men will eventually remarry. Most adults remarry quickly, within 5 years of their divorce. White and Hispanic women are more likely to remarry than Black women. The first year is the most stressful; if the second marriage makes it through that year, then the probability of divorce drops to that of first marriages.

The term stepfamily originated in England (Bray & Kelly, 1998; Visher, E. B. & Visher, J. S., 1988). The prefix *step* is from the Anglo-Saxon word *steop,* meaning to bereave or to make orphan. This name was applied to children whose parents had died. Step-relations were primarily established because of loss through death. Although this still occurs, today a stepfamily is usually created after divorce (Bray, 1995). There are a variety of names for stepfamilies. Common names include re-married families, reconstituted families, REM families, blended families, binuclear families, second families, and/or two-fams. There are probably many other names, but these seem to be the most common.

The most common type of stepfamily is the divorce-engendered stepfather family in which a man, who may or may not have been previously married, marries a woman who has children from a previous marriage or relationship (Bray & Easling, 2005). However, it is much more common for stepmothers to seek out family therapy. Most stepfamilies are created after a remarriage, but with the current increase in cohabitation, many repartnered families are formed without the legal sanction of matrimony. Most research and clinical writings are about stepfamilies with minor children, but stepfamilies are created later in life, too (Hetherington, Henderson, & Reiss, 1999).

The socialization of our views of stepfamilies starts early, with the familiar fairy tales and folk stories of the "wicked stepparent." Family members, especially children, may enter a stepfamily with fears and anxieties that are unconsciously reinforced by descriptions and names for stepfamilies as a result of the prevailing myths and stories about stepfamilies. These perspectives are reinforced through our everyday language. Referring to the biological parents as "natural" parents implies that stepparents are somehow "unnatural." Referring to first-marriage, nuclear families as "regular" or "normal" families implies that stepfamilies are "irregular" or "abnormal." It is important to consider these negative overtones or implications and the impact they may have on the therapy process and life in a stepfamily (Bray, 2001, 1995).

My research and clinical interest in stepfamilies grew out of my general interest in family therapy and several encounters with stepfamilies during my professional training. As a clinical psychology intern, I was assigned an interesting family that was struggling with their attempt to form a new stepfamily. Because of my inexperience with stepfamilies I mainly gathered information and empathized with them during the first session. I looked for published material on stepfamilies, but in 1979 there was very little information about stepfamilies in the professional literature (Visher, E. B., & Visher, J. S., 1979).

After this case, I was invited to write a research proposal to develop a prevention program to help stepfamilies cope with their unique stresses and changes. The grant proposal was not funded by the federal funding agency. The reviewers thought the program was interesting, but they recommended against funding because they felt that it was not clear that there was a need for a special program for stepfamilies. There was no systematic research on stepfamilies that demonstrated how they were different from other types of families. One reviewer questioned whether there were enough children in these kinds of families to warrant such a program, and if so, why would stepfamilies need any different treatment than other types of families? We were perplexed by these comments, because we knew from our clinical experience that stepfamilies are unique and need special programs.

A few years later I decided to continue my research and clinical work with stepfamilies. At that time, research on divorce and remarriage indicated that 20 to 25 percent (it is up to 40 percent now) of all children in the United States would live in a stepfamily before they reach age 18. Millions of children would be directly involved in multiple family transitions from a first-marriage nuclear family, to a post-divorce, single-parent family, to a stepfamily. Some children would also experience other family changes because of their parents' multiple divorces and remarriages (Bray, 1999; Bray & Hetherington, 1993).

Joyce Ambler and Sandra Berger, two social workers, and I decided to study stepfamilies because of these increasing numbers. We started a developmental study on the nature of stepfamilies and how children grow and adjust within them. We needed this type of research so that better prevention and intervention programs could be developed for stepfamilies. Using my research expertise and Joyce and Sandra's clinical experience, we designed a study to investigate how stepfamilies functioned during the first 5 years after remarriage. The study was funded by the National Institute of Child Health and Human Development (NICHD) of the National Institutes of Health (NIH; Bray, 1988; Bray & Berger, 1993).

Our project was concerned with normal stepfamily life—to understand how stepfamilies operate and to document the family life cycle of stepfamilies. In addition, we were interested in how stepfamilies are unique from first-marriage families. Further, we wanted to know how life in a stepfamily impacts family members' adjustment and development, and how extended family relationships function in stepfamilies. We were also interested in which factors influenced the success or failure of a stepfamily.

We had several hypotheses when we began the Developmental Issues in Step-Families (DIS) Research Project that now seem unrealistic. With our limited knowledge about stepfamilies, we assumed that life in a stepfamily would be initially stressful, involve several short-lived changes for children and adults, and that children would respond to these changes with increased behavioral problems (Bray, 1999). There were larger amounts of stress and change, both positive and negative, after a remarriage than we estimated. Stressors often included moving to a new residence, usually better than the previous one because of the increased income available with two adults in the family. For children, moves were usually quite stressful, because they entailed losing old friends, changing schools, establishing new peer and family relationships, and, especially, getting accustomed to a new stepparent in the home. We also underestimated the influence that children had on the remarriage. In the case of stepfamilies, the children had a large influence on how the remarriage turned out.

We also assumed that within a year or two, stepfamily relationships adapt, and that they would be quite similar to those in nuclear families. Further, we believed that children's adjustment would improve, and there would be few differences between children in stepfamilies and children in nuclear families, after a couple of years in a stepfamily. We were incorrect about several of these ideas. First, we found that it takes a couple of years, not a few months, for stepfamilies to adjust. However, there continue to be unique aspects of stepfamily relationships and remarriages that are different from nuclear families, even 5 years after remarriage. While not as negative as some claim, we found that stepchildren continue to have more behavior problems than do children in nuclear families. And these problems reemerge during adolescence.

After following these families over time, we found that the children's adjustment continues to be impacted by these particular stepfamily relationships—stepfamily life is influenced by the developmental changes of children, especially during adolescence, and stepfamilies change in unique ways compared to nuclear families. We were surprised by some of our findings, because they were different from what we expected and different from some of the prevailing myths about the impact of divorce and remarriage. A summary of the findings of the DIS Research Project can be found in Bray (1999), Bray and Berger (1993), and Bray and Kelly (1998).

DEVELOPMENTAL-SYSTEMS FRAMEWORK FOR WORKING WITH STEPFAMILIES

Stepfamilies continue to evolve over time, and have their own developmental life cycles that are different from first-marriage families (Bray, 1999; Bray & Berger, 1992; Bray & Kelly, 1998; McGoldrick & Carter, 1988). Relationships in stepfamilies are influenced by previous individual and family experiences (i.e., the divorce experience), developmental issues within the stepfamily, and developmental issues for individual family members. When working with stepfamilies it is important to consider the multiple developmental trajectories of family members and the stepfamily life cycle.

Stepfamily life has three major transition points, and two of the three transition points can throw a family into temporary crisis (Bray & Kelly, 1998). Cycle one includes the first year- or year-and-a-half mark, and appears to be the most challenging time period. Cycle two includes the 3- to 5-year mark. During this cycle, families' identities and patterns are solidified and stress tends to decrease. Cycle three occurs after the first 5 years, during the children's adolescent years. This cycle is also challenging, as the adolescent's identity needs create new conflicts and challenges in the stepfamily.

A stepfamily is at greatest risk for divorce during the first 2 years (Bray & Kelly,

1998). Nearly a third of stepfamilies fail in this period. This finding also has a corollary, and it is noteworthy, because it illustrates the danger of applying a nuclear family map to stepfamily life. Typically, in a first marriage, marital satisfaction begins high, then declines. In a stepfamily marriage, the opposite flow occurs: Marital satisfaction starts low, then climbs (Bray & Berger, 1993; Hetherington & Clingempeel, 1992).

INTERVENTIONS WITH STEPFAMILIES

We use a developmental systems model to understand their current context and to work with stepfamilies (Bray, 1995; Bray & Harvey, 1995). We define context as family members' interactional patterns and styles, the expectations of family relationships, and the attributions or understanding that they make about family relationships and patterns. Strategic-intergenerational interventions are also used to facilitate change in family patterns, interactions, expectations, and meanings (Bray, 1995; Bray & Harvey, 1995; Williamson & Bray, 1988). These interventions are designed to consider the interactions between the life cycle tasks of the stepfamily and the individual family members.

Accurate Family Assessment

A first step in working with stepfamilies is to assess who are the relevant family members that are impacting the presenting problem. Stepfamilies are inherently more complicated than first-marriage families, because of the multiple family systems and contexts that impact their functioning. The stepfamily system is composed of the current residential stepfamily, the nonresidential parent's family system, and the stepparent's family system. Issues from the previous marital and divorce experiences, and particularly unresolved emotional problems and attachments, and issues from the family of origin are central areas of focus in our work with stepfamilies. We use genograms to conduct our family assessment (Bray, 1994). McGoldrick, Gerson, & Shellenberger (1999) provide an excellent overview of the use of genograms in family assessment, and Visher & Visher (1988) provide examples of how to use genograms specifically with stepfamilies. It is important to note that many children do not consider their stepparent as part of their family, even after living together for several years (Fine, Coleman, & Ganong, 1998). Thus, it is important to look at similarities and differences in the way family members define family membership. In addition to who is in the family, it is important to assess what kind of stepfamily we are dealing with. In our research we found that stepfamilies often fall into one of three categories: neotraditional, matriarchal, or romantic (Bray & Kelly, 1998).

Neotraditional stepfamilies are the most representative of the popular image of the happy stepfamily. The neotraditional family is typically a close-knit, loving family and functions well for a couple with compatible values. At the end of our study we found that, on average, our neotraditional couples scored very high on important markers of success like marital satisfaction and conflict resolution; the children in our neotraditional families also had a lower incidence of behavior problems. The adults remarry for a new family and a new marriage. Overall, they cope well with the stress and changes experienced in forming a stepfamily. That is not to say that they have less stress, they just seem to flow with issues more successfully. They also form a strong marital bond rather quickly, that supports the development of a parenting coalition. This helps the children adjust to the changes and results in fewer overall behavior problems for them.

Matriarchal stepfamilies are rarely mentioned in the popular literature. However, anyone familiar with stepfamily life will recognize them. The chief characteristic of the matriarchal family is the dominant role of the woman. Matriarchal women usually have powerful personalities, a high degree of domestic competence, and a strong desire to be the family leader. This stepfamily, which accounted for about 25 percent of our study sample, is also frequently successful if the matriarchal woman is married to a man with compatible values. The adults remarry because they love each other, but not because they want to have a family life together. These stepfamilies resemble single-parent families in the beginning, as the woman maintains her primary role as parent and keeper of the household, while the stepfather tends to be in the background and remains disengaged from the children. He is often viewed as a familiar stranger to the children. These families tend to do well, although over time they may run into trouble over two conditions. First, if the woman decides she wants her new husband to be more involved with the children and family, and he does not, this produces significant conflict and disharmony. Second, if the stepfather decides he needs to be more involved with the children (often after the birth of their own child), conflict then ensues, because he is now treading on his wife's turf with the children.

Romantic stepfamilies are sometimes seen in popular literature. Romantic stepfamilies often look like neotraditional stepfamilies in the months after remarriage. The adults remarry because they want a second marriage and family life. Romantics expect everything from stepfamily life that neotraditionalists do, but, unlike neotraditionalists, romantics expect everything immediately, and have many unrealistic expectations. They particularly suffer from the Nuclear Family Myth—which is that a stepfamily should be just like a nuclear family. They expect feelings of love and harmony and closeness to begin flowing as soon as the couple and the children become a stepfamily. This results in many unrealistic expectations. We found that the early, conflict-prone period of the stepfamily cycle is particularly difficult for romantic stepfamilies. Indeed, romantics had the highest family breakup rate in the project.

A third area to assess is the relevant developmental cycles of the family and family members. As discussed previously, there are life cycle issues for the stepfamily as a whole that interact with the individual life cycles of family members. It appears that it is easier to form a stepfamily with younger children than with adolescents (Bray, 1999), but all stepfamilies face a common set of developmental issues. Using psychoeducation is a useful technique to help stepfamilies understand their current situation and begin the change process.

Psychoeducation with Stepfamilies

Helping family members understand the context of stepfamily life through psychoeducation about divorce and remarriage is an effective intervention to normalize the experiences of family members and promote a context for change. Psychoeducation is the presentation of psychological or health information in a therapeutic context (Levant, 1986). Differentiating the unique issues encountered by stepfamilies from the expectations based on a nuclear family model is a frequent part of the normalization process in psychoeducation (Bray, 1995). In addition, it is useful to educate family members about developmental issues and sequences for all children, so that the problems are not labeled as created by the stepfamily (Bray & Berger, 1992). In the DIS project we identified common developmental issues that stepfamilies face. We use this information to educate stepfamilies about what to expect, and to begin the change process. The following is a brief overview of common developmental issues that we encounter in clinical work with stepfamilies. For a more complete discussion of these issues see Bray (1995, 1999, 2001) and Bray and Kelly (1998).

Planning for Remarriage

There are at least three central issues for families to consider as they plan for remarriage. However, it should be noted that most stepfamilies do not discuss these issues prior to remarriage, and they are common concerns that bring stepfamilies into therapy. These include preparing for the financial and living arrangements for the family, resolving feelings and concerns about the previous marriage, and planning for changes in parenting the children. Many couples that plan to remarry address these issues before marriage, but, unfortunately, many do not. Some couples discuss the remarriage with their children and include them in their plans, while in some families the children do not know about the wedding until after it has occurred.

The adults have to decide where they will live and how they will share money. In general, adults report that it is advantageous to move to a new residence, so that it becomes "their home." Living in the home of one of the adults, particularly if it was the home of the previous marriage, makes it more difficult to establish a new family identity. Families generally decide either to share all of their funds and be a "one pot family," or keep funds separate and be a "two pot family." Both methods can work, although couples using a "one pot" method generally report higher family satisfaction than couples using a "two pot" method. The most important aspect of sharing money is that the couple agrees how to do it—thus, the type of sharing seems to work if the couple does not fight about money issues. Over time, more stepfamilies become "one pot" families.

Post-Remarriage Issues

In the first few years of remarriage, stepfamilies face three main issues. First, the couple needs to form a strong marital bond. This is particularly challenging for stepfamilies with residential stepchildren, as the couple may not have the time and energy to nurture and attend to their marital and adult needs. However, we found that it is critical for success that couples form a good marriage, as it is difficult to handle other issues if the marriage is rocky. Helping couples develop a common ground and understanding in their marriage, taking time to meet their adult needs, and having fun and enjoyment in the marriage are essential. Homework assignments include scheduling regular dates and time alone without the children (at least once a week is recommended). Sometimes, household chores and responsibilities need to be more equally shared, in order for the woman to feel like she has time and energy to attend to the marriage. It is very important that couples actually schedule the time, as they often will not do it otherwise, because other issues and demands get in the way. Therapeutically, it is important to help parents deal with their common concern—that taking time away for their marriage is good for the stepfamily, and not destructive to the children.

Interventions developed from marital therapy research and practice (Gottman, 1994, 1999; Guerney, 1977; Hendrix, 1988; Jacobson & Margolin, 1979; Love, 1994; Renick, Blumberg, & Markman, 1992) are useful as long as they are done in the context of a remarriage and stepfamily.

In addition to forming a new marriage, remarriages have the added stress of bringing unresolved and old patterns from previous marriages into the current one. We call these issues "ghosts at the table," because they often operate in unseen ways and pop up to create problems in the relationship. Helping couples identify these "old ghosts," and how they operate in the current relationship, is an important step in getting rid of them, or at least changing them into "friendly ghosts."

The second issue is to develop a parenting plan. The biological parent and stepparent have to come to agreements about how to discipline and parent the children. As with first-marriage families, the essential part is that they *agree* with each other and support each other in the parenting. We found that in the early months after remarriage it is important for the biological parent to play the primary parental role and the stepparent to focus on developing a relationship with the stepchildren. Helping the biological parent monitor his or her stepchildren's lives is useful, but more active parenting and discipline by the stepparent usually needs to wait until there is a solid relationship between the stepparent and stepchildren. Helping parents in stepfamilies develop a consistent set of rules, and consequences for violating rules, is a key step in developing a parenting coalition. Bray (1995) and Visher and Visher (1988) describe exercises to help develop parenting plans.

A third issue is integrating the nonresidential parent and his or her kinship into the stepfamily. Unlike first-marriage families, children in stepfamilies live within two families, and can have up to four sets of grandparents. There is wide variety in visitation and access plans between nonresidential parents and children. However, even in cases where the nonresidential parent does not see the children often, the children will have loyalty feelings toward that parent. In addition, the children are sensitive to criticism of the nonresidential parent, and it is important not to denigrate that parent, because the children may internalize the negative perceptions or feel they need to defend that parent. Making transitions between households smooth and conflict free is very important for children's adjustment. This is often a source of problems in stepfamilies, and needs to be a focus of family therapy.

For stepfamilies with adolescents, there are two additional issues that are common. We found that children often suddenly erupt after several years of seemingly healthy adjustment to stepfamily life as they move through adolescence. The increased behavior problems for young adolescents were unanticipated in our research (Bray, 1999). It appears that adolescents are again struggling with their parent's divorce during early adolescence. These findings may be similar to what has been termed the "sleeper effect" of divorce, in which children who experience a parental divorce between the ages of 4 and 6 come to terms with it when they reach adolescence (Hetherington & Clingempeel, 1992).

Our ideas about the reemergence of behavior problems for adolescents in step-families relate to the struggle to individuate and develop autonomy during this period (Bray, 1999). Part of the individuation process is to interact with parents during identity formation (Steinberg, 2001). However, in stepfamilies, the nonres-idential parent, who is usually the father, is often not present. Thus, the individu-ation process is transferred onto the stepfather, and may become problematic, be-cause adolescents need their other parent to complete this process. We believe this may be why adolescents in stepfamilies have more behavior problems, stress, and conflict with parents than do adolescents in first-marriage families. As part of this process, it is common for children in stepfamilies to develop an increased interest in their nonresidential parent. We found that about 20 percent of adolescents tem-porarily or permanently changed residence from their mothers to their fathers during this period (Bray & Kelly, 1998).

A second issue during adolescence is sexuality. In stepfamilies, the usual sexual taboos for incest are not present, due to the lack of biological connection. Chil-dren in stepfamilies are at greater risk for sexual abuse (Finkelhor, 1984; Gar-barino, Sebes, & Schellenbach, 1984); the abuse may come from the stepparent or other nonbiological relatives. Sometimes, stepfathers become so concerned about the sexual abuse issue that it impacts the level of intimacy between stepparent and stepchild. Differentiating between appropriate emotional intimacy and inappro-priate intimacy (both physical and emotional) is an important consideration dur-ing family therapy. In addition, it is useful to counsel stepfamilies about appro-priate dress and privacy boundaries between parents and children. Making these issues explicit often makes it possible for concerns to be alleviated.

Therapeutic Orientation

Our therapy approach with stepfamilies is a brief therapy orientation, in which we try to help them as quickly as possible. Most stepfamilies attend between 6 and 8 sessions, but some come for longer periods, and many return at different develop-mental stages for additional help. We use a variety of interventions developed within the family therapy literature, including communication skills training, problem-solving training, reframing, behavioral tracking, parenting skills, family of origin work, and others. It is important to emphasize that all of these interventions need to be applied within the context of life in a stepfamily. Trying to make stepfamilies be like first-marriage families usually does not work well and results in treatment failure. For example, it is always important to remember the influence of the previ-ous marriage when helping remarried couples work on their marriage, as the unre-solved issues, or ghosts, are often operating in the present relationship. In addition to psychoeducation and other interventions, we ask family members to do home-work assignments outside of sessions to facilitate and speed up the change process.

───────────────────── **Case Study** ─────────────────────

Our goals during the first session are to start the family assessment and genogram, understand the presenting problems, decide which problems to focus on, begin at least one intervention, and assign some homework. We usually request that all members of the residential stepfamily come to the first session, to observe their interactions and understand their perspectives on the problem. After the first session we invite some or all of the family members back, depending on which issues we are working on.

The Sanders family initially appeared relaxed and almost jovial while I gathered background information and conducted the family assessment and genogram. The family was focused on the youngest child, Cody, who was quite active, intent on exploring everything in the office. The two older children watched over Cody and engaged him in the toys in the room. I learned that Mr. and Ms. Sanders had been married for about 5½ years. This was her second marriage and his first. Luke and Lauren were from Ms. Sanders' first marriage, which had ended in divorce a few years before Ms. Sanders remarried. Cody was from the current marriage. Luke's father, Johnny Wilson, lived in a nearby suburb and had been remarried for about 2 years. Ms. Sanders' parents and extended family lived in the area and she had regular contact with them. Mr. Sanders' parents lived in a different state, as did most of his other family members. He only saw them a few times a year, although visits with the grandparents had increased after the birth of Cody. Mr. Wilson's family also lived in the area, but did not see the children, except on holidays and special occasions.

The mood changed rapidly when I asked how I could help them. At this point, the parents became very serious, and Luke shoved back in his chair, as if to try to hide—all the while shooting venomous glances toward his mother and stepfather. Ms. Sanders started with a brief history of their family. She said the divorce had been very difficult for everyone in the family, especially Luke. Her former husband, Johnny, had left the family suddenly, and it had put a great deal of stress on her, both emotionally and financially. She said they initially moved in with her parents for about a year, and were then able to get their own place after she got back on her feet. She and Mike met at a church function soon after this move, and their relationship evolved into marriage. Luke's father had not been around much after the separation and divorce, and she said Luke was angry and belligerent, and that his grades dropped during the first year and a half. She said this was surprising, as the father had been close to the children during the marriage. As she related her story, Mr. Sanders generally nodded in agreement, while Luke frequently made faces or rolled his eyes. She admitted she often blamed these problems on Luke's dad, for leaving and the divorce.

After she mentioned the part about Luke's dad leaving, Luke jumped in with, "He didn't leave—you and Nanna (Luke's maternal grandmother) drove him away, with all of your bitching and complaining!"

She first glared at Luke and then retorted, "Luke, where do you get that stuff from? Is he filling your head with all of this?" She then turned to me with tears in her eyes and said, "See, Dr. Bray, whenever I say anything about Luke's dad, he defends him—lately, every time Luke comes back from his dad's house he acts this way."

Mr. Sanders added, "Lately Luke seems angry and unhappy with us all the time. It's worse after he sees his dad, but it happens other times too, so it's not just that. I know he's growing up and dealing with all of that adolescent stuff, but this seems more than that—what's really concerning me is how he is treating his mother and siblings—and now his grades are beginning to drop. I wonder if he is doing drugs or something."

Luke flashed back, "I ain't doing drugs—but I just might if you keep harping on me all the time. And this isn't my dad's fault either—why do you keep blaming everything that goes wrong on him? You even blame your fights on my dad—it ain't fair!"

Mr. and Ms. Sanders tried to jump in and respond to Luke, but I stopped them. I had seen enough of their family conflict patterns and wanted to know more about their family story, and when things had begun to change. I thanked them for sharing their family conflict with me so that I could understand their situation and start reframing this interaction. I also indicated that these are common problems for stepfamilies with adolescents, to begin educating them about common issues in stepfamilies.

Ms. Sanders continued by saying that during the 6 months before she and Mike married, Luke started doing a lot better—his grades improved, he seemed happier, and he and Mike seemed to really hit it off. But after they married, Luke returned to his old ways, and they did not understand the change. Luke got into trouble at home and school and he started being distant and fighting with Mike. I asked what changed after their remarriage and she said that they had moved from an apartment to a house, and this required a change in schools. Although both were better, she said Luke did not like the new school at first, and he was upset about leaving some of his friends. Luke nodded in agreement.

She said that about 5 months after the marriage, Luke's dad started calling and wanting to see the kids. She said they had some fights over this, because Mr. Wilson had not paid his child support, but she let him see the kids and they worked out something on the support. Luke's dad visited intermittently and started paying his child support. She said that things were tough during the first couple of years, and she had taken Luke to see a therapist for a few sessions. The therapist only saw Luke and the mother. The sessions seemed to help Luke, but he did not want to continue.

I asked them about their parenting, and what role Mr. Sanders played with the children. Ms. Sanders said that during her first marriage and after the divorce she had been the primary parent and support for the kids. She juggled work and parenting, and that was okay with her. Johnny, Luke's dad, moved to various jobs, and had a difficult time settling down and being a family man. What she liked about Mike was that he was most interested in her and the marriage, but would help out with the kids when she needed it. She said, "I think the kids liked Mike at first, because in some ways he was like a big brother to them—he didn't try to discipline or parent them—I did all of that." Ms. Sanders said that this changed after the birth of Cody. Mike wanted to be a more active parent with all of the kids. Mr. Sanders said that this caused some trouble in the marriage for a little while, because he felt like he was "treading on her turf," but they worked out their issues. Mike said that having Cody seemed to really bring them together as a family, which was echoed by the rest of the members. Ms. Sanders said this changed suddenly, about 6 months ago. The Sanders seemed to initially be what we call a matriarchal stepfamily and then evolved into a neotraditional stepfamily.

I asked when the current problems started. Ms. Sanders said that about 6 or 8 months ago, Luke started changing. At first she thought it was just being an adolescent, but the conflict escalated and Luke's grades began to drop. She said that about a year ago Luke's father moved back into town with his new wife. Luke wanted to see his dad more and his dad seemed more interested in being with Luke. Ms. Sanders said that Luke's dad seemed to be more mature and responsible and that she liked his new wife. Mr. Sanders said that Luke had been asking to see his dad more and also asking about his parent's divorce. Ms. Sanders said she did not know how much to tell Luke about what happened, and she wondered what Luke's dad was saying about her. Mr. Sanders said that Luke was more disrespectful and challenging of his parenting and discipline. He said that Luke started telling him things like, "I don't have to listen to you—you're not my real dad—I don't want to live with you anymore—I want to live with my real dad." Mr. Sanders said those statements really hurt, because he and Luke had developed what he thought was a close relationship over the years, while his dad had not been around that much. Mr. Sanders continued, "Patsy and I have had a couple of really bad arguments lately—and unfortunately Luke heard them."

Luke countered with, "Yeah, and you blame them all on me and my dad."

I said, "It is apparent that all of you have strong feelings about this and that your anger reflects some of the hurt and disappointment you might all be feeling." I continued with, "It is also clear to me that you really care a lot about each other. I am impressed about that and I compliment you for seeking some help to work this out." These statements were again to reframe the context into a caring and loving one and to be empathic about their problems.

I gave them the homework assignment of writing down the individual concerns they have within their family and to take notes about any arguments they might have this week. I also asked the parents to write down their rules and consequences for the children. I asked for the parents, Luke, and Lauren to return for the next session. It did not seem necessary to have Cody present.

This family illustrated some of our findings about stepfamilies with adolescents, which were surprising and unexpected (Bray & Berger, 1993; Bray & Harvey, 1995). The early behavioral problems that Luke displayed are common and expected, since children and adolescents react to the stress and early transitional phase of stepfamily formation with externalizing behavior problems. As stated previously, the reemergence of behavior problems during early adolescence is common and Luke appeared to be in the beginning stages of this shift.

In addition, a stepparent like Mr. Sanders may respond to increased behavior problems by disengaging, which further contributes to externalizing behavior by adolescents. Mr. Sanders made statements like, "I don't understand why he is suddenly sullen and rude with me. It seems like he is angry about something, but he won't talk with me about it." Further, the stepfather-adolescent conflict often bleeds over into the marriage, which results in increased marital conflict and stress (Bray, 1999; Bray & Jouriles, 1995). This seemed to be happening in the Sanders family.

When the Sanders returned, they stated that the week had gone much better, with no major fights or arguments. Ms. Sanders and Luke had done the homework of writing down issues and concerns, but Mr. Sanders and Lauren had not.

Ms. Sanders had also made a list of rules and consequences. Mr. Sanders said that he had been very busy that week, but "I have them all in my head and have thought about it all week." I find that it is very important to ask about homework at the beginning of each session—to reinforce the importance of it and to see about any barriers that might arise. I thanked Patsy and Luke for doing their assignments and told Mike that it was good that he at least thought about it, as we did not want to go too fast for the family in changing the situation. The major issues for the parents regard Luke's behavior toward them, their concern about the influence that Luke's father was having on Luke, and concerns about parenting. Mike also added that he did not have much time alone with Patsy anymore, especially since the issues with Luke came up. I provided the family with information about step-families in the first part of the session and we engaged in some give and take about this during the psychoeducation. I pointed out how they were dealing with many of the normal issues for stepfamilies with adolescents.

We spent the rest of the session focusing on the household rules and expecta-tions. We decided to focus on the household rules, as this was an important, but not too "hot" topic to deal with. The parents generally agreed on their rules and expectations. However, Luke complained that he was treated differently than Lau-ren and Cody, and that Cody was especially favored and was allowed to "get away with anything." Luke said that he really did not like it when Mike disciplined him, as he seemed harsher toward him than toward the other kids. I helped them con-solidate their rules, come to understanding about their parental expectations, and negotiate consequences for breaking the rules. It was important to get Luke and Lauren involved as a way of recognizing their developing autonomy and individ-uation. I asked the family to write the rules on a sheet of paper, with the conse-quences for breaking the rules, and put it in a public place in the house. I asked them to review these agreements a couple of times during the week and bring me back a progress report next session.

The next session started with additional psychoeducation about stepfamilies. We reviewed the rules and consequences, as there had been a couple of arguments about them that week. I used this discussion as an opportunity to teach and model effective communication and problem-solving skills.

The next session started off similar to the first—everyone was upset, and Luke was withdrawn and very angry. I explained about how relapses frequently occurred and that this is a normal part of the change process. Luke and Lauren had visited their father the past weekend. The father returned the kids late and this caused a scene when he dropped them off. The adults were yelling at each other and Luke got in the middle of it. Luke had kept himself locked in his room the past couple of days.

I asked what happened. Luke said they were having fun at the lake and lost track of time—to which Patsy said, "Why didn't you just call me? I thought some-thing terrible had happened—like your father was drinking again and had an ac-cident or something!"

Luke shouted, "There you go again bringing up old stuff—dad doesn't even drink anymore and we were just having a good time—what's wrong with that— you're just jealous!"

Ms. Sanders started to defend herself and I stopped the argument. I thanked them for bringing this important issue to therapy, as it sounded like something we should focus on. I pointed out that when they criticize Luke's father, that Luke hears this as criticism of himself, because he is half his father. So, Luke defends his father as a way of defending himself. I could see Luke nodding in agreement as I told the parents this. I told them that adolescents, and especially boys, who hear their nonresidential parent denigrated or criticized usually have lower self-esteem and more behavior problems. They stated that they had not realized this and certainly did not want to criticize Luke—they were only trying to be truthful about Luke's father. I responded by saying, "You can be more helpful to Luke by letting him figure this out himself, as he is old enough to do that—and any attempts to get him to see your truth about his dad will only make him defend his dad more and drive him away from you." The parents nodded and seemed relieved after this discussion.

We spent the rest of the session discussing ways to improve the relationships between the two families. I suggested that Patsy apologize to Luke and his father as a way to heal the situation. She was very resistant to this idea, but we discussed why this is important, and to follow the apology with a request: When you are going to be more than 15 minutes late, please call and let her know. Apparently, time boundaries had been a big issue during her first marriage, and this was an old ghost that needed to be put to rest. She said she would think about this, but would not commit to doing it—I followed with—"yet." We all laughed. The next session I requested to only see the couple, because I wanted to explore their relationship in more depth and to talk about more ghosts at the table. Their homework was to go out and have a date without the kids this week and report back about it.

Patsy started the next session by saying that she had apologized to Luke for blowing up and told him that she truly wanted him to enjoy his time with his father. She said that she thought about calling her ex-husband all week and finally got up the courage last night. She was shocked by his reaction—at first he seemed very reluctant to even come to the phone, but after she apologized for the argument, she said that he thanked her and apologized back—"the first time ever he had done that." She remembered to make the request and he said he would let her know if they were going to be late. She seemed empowered and elated about how it all went. Mike was also very pleased; he said that it seemed like a dark cloud had moved off of them.

We spent the rest of the session discussing how to nurture and improve their relationship. They had planned a date, but it had fallen through when Cody got sick. I complimented them on this and encouraged them to set another one. Patsy said she would like to be more available to Mike, but she was just overwhelmed with work, taking care of the kids and the house. I told them about John Gottman's research on happy marriages and how women were happier and more available when their husbands contributed more to housework. Mike balked at first, but Patsy retorted, "See, I told you that if you would help me I would do more for you—now it is official." I also talked with Mike about how he wanted to be more involved as a parent, and reminded him that part of parenting is to help with household chores. He said, "I tried that when we were first married, but Patsy made it clear that that was her territory and I should butt out." Patsy acknowledged this, but said she now needed the help. We spent the rest of the session discussing how to divide up the household chores, how to get Luke and Lauren to help, and then how they could spend more time together. They left the session with a plan to implement for the next week. As they were leaving, I reminded them of the date.

Next week the couple returned happier than I had ever seen them. They had started the household plan, discussed the issues with the kids, and were surprised that the kids were willing to do some of the chores so that Patsy and Mike could have some adult time. Patsy said that Luke gave her a sly smile when they talked about the need for adult time, and said, "Maybe if you get some you will be less grumpy." We spent the rest of this session discussing other couple issues, other ghosts at the table, and how to better handle them. They both reported that Luke was doing better, especially after she apologized, but they were not sure how long it would last. I reminded them that there may be a relapse, but that is normal. I requested that they bring Luke in for the next session with them. As it turned out, Mike was not available, so I met with Patsy and Luke.

I wondered if anything specific had occurred 6 to 8 months ago that started Luke's behavior change, so I requested to meet with him alone. When I asked Luke about what had happened, he got very nervous, wrapped his arms around himself and started shaking. It literally looked like he was being squeezed and I wondered what all of the emotion was about. Luke said that his father had mentioned about moving to another town a while ago, and this upset him. He also said that he felt pressure from his dad to move with him. Luke said that he felt very conflicted, as he loved his dad and their relationship, but he also really liked living with his mom, and liked his school and friends. Luke was caught in a loyalty bind between his parents—a triangulated relationship that was squeezing him.

He felt that he would really disappoint his dad if he told him this. The new job fell through, so the dad did not move, but Luke said he still felt pressure to go live with his dad. He felt he could not talk to his mom about this, as "She would go ballistic on me." There was no one else to talk to, either, and he had just kept it inside and worried about it. I asked him if he would like me to help him talk to his parents about this. At first he was reluctant, but with a little coaching, he agreed.

I brought his mother back into the room and Luke discussed the issue with her. At first she seemed upset, but with some coaching she was able to listen and be empathic to Luke. Toward the end, Patsy started to gently cry, and said, "Luke, I love you so much and I want only the best for you—if you would really be happier living with your dad, I won't fight you about it." Luke beamed and gave his mom a big hug, as tears came down for both of them.

We discussed different options for this. I talked to them about the law and how kids sometimes want to live with the nonresidential parent during adolescence. We ended the session with the assignment for them to continue to discuss this next week. I asked Luke to make a list of the disadvantages of moving with his dad. Thinking about the disadvantages often helps people get ready for a change. Luke did not want to talk to his dad about this yet, so that was the main agenda for the next session.

Patsy, Mike, and Luke returned the next week. Luke seemed happy and calm.

Patsy said that it had been a difficult week for her, but she had talked with Luke several times. Luke said he made his list of disadvantages. I asked the parents to step out to discuss the list. As soon as they left, Luke firmly stated, "I've decided—I don't want to move with my dad—but I am scared to tell him." We discussed the list and he said it helped him make up his mind. We then role played conversations that he could have with his father about this. I use reverse roleplays in this situation, in which I have the client, in this case Luke, pretend to be his father, and I pretend to be the client (Williamson & Bray, 1988). In this way, I can model different lines and statements. Based on their experience, the client will be able to respond as the other person might respond. This demonstrates how to handle the tough situations in more productive ways. We practiced several times, then I asked Luke if he would prefer to ask his father to come to a session so I could help them discuss it. He said he did not think his dad would come and that he would like to try it by himself. I told him I thought he could handle it on his own, too. I invited the parents back in and we talked some more about Luke's desires. Mike told a story about having to talk to his father about a tough issue, and this seemed to help Luke feel more confident. At the end, I reminded Luke that it was okay if he did not talk to his dad this week, and that we could always invite him into a session to discuss this. Luke smiled and said, "I think I can handle it now—but thanks for the offer—see you next week."

The family cancelled the next appointment. I was concerned that something had not gone right for Luke, but Patsy assured me that it was due to some other demands. The family returned, and I could hardly wait to hear what happened for Luke. He seemed to bounce into the room—more confident and happier than ever. He said that he had talked with his father, "Just like we practiced it." He said that his father was at first taken aback by Luke's view that he was pressuring Luke to come live with him, because that was not his intention. Luke said that his father apologized to him for this and told him that while he would love to have Luke live with him, he understood Luke's feelings. Luke then said, "He even complimented mom—said that she was doing a good job and he would never want to hurt her by taking him away from her." Patsy smiled and said, "I never dreamed he would ever say something like that—I guess I have been holding on to old stuff about him for too long." We spent the rest of the session discussing these issues and how they might help Luke be more comfortable living in the two families. At the end of the session, the family said they thought things were going well and would like to take a break. I suggested that they come back in about a month.

About 5 weeks later Luke and his family were still doing well. The parents reported that the relationship with the exspouse had continued to improve and Mr. Wilson had even called them twice to say that he was going to be late picking up and dropping off the kids. There had been some conflict around Luke and his friends. Luke had wanted to go out with a girl to the movies and there was an issue around curfew. I let the family know that these were normal adolescent issues and that the stepfamily issues seemed to be resolved or headed in the right direction. I encouraged the couple to keep up their dates and adult time, which had slipped a bit since the last session. I reminded them that they needed to schedule it just like any other important activity. They thanked me and agreed that this was important. They said they felt they had accomplished their goals and would call me if they needed more help.

Several months later I received a phone call from Patsy. She said she just wanted to let me know that things were going well, and that Luke had just brought home a report card with all As and Bs—the first time in years. She said that their relationship was going well, with the normal ups and downs, but the marriage was back on track and she and her husband had taken up a couple of hobbies to spend more time together—and of course Cody was still keeping everybody busy and laughing.

This stepfamily exemplifies many of the issues that remarried families face during their development and over the course of their life cycles. While this family had been together for some time, they encountered and reencountered various issues concerning loyalty, triangles, parent-child conflict, and marital conflict that are faced by all stepfamilies. The hidden and unspoken losses and hurts continued to have a significant impact, years after their occurrence—the ghosts of marriages past had not been put to rest. It appears that adolescents, in their developmental quest, resurrect some of these issues—and it is part of the normal process of stepfamily development.

Further, issues with children, including parenting, tend to greatly impact the marriage. The direction of effects of parent-child problems and marital problems tends to differ in first-marriage families and stepfamilies. In first-marriage families, problems in the marriage usually move downward and create problems with the children. However, in stepfamilies, the marriage is more independent of the parent-child relationships, and these relationships tend to have more impact on the marriage. This seemed to be the case with the Sanders family.

A stepfamily can help heal the scars of divorce. For the past decade, conventional wisdom has held that divorce permanently scars a child. Our data, however, paints a somewhat more complex picture. It affirms the work of other investigators who believe that a child is profoundly affected by family dissolution. But we found that a loving, well-functioning stepfamily can help restore a youngster's sense of emotional and psychological well being—as in the case of Luke.

We also found something else: A strong, stable stepfamily is as capable of nurturing healthy development as a first-marriage family. It can imbue values, affirm limits and boundaries, and provide a structure in which rules for living a moral and productive life are made, transmitted, tested, rebelled against, and ultimately affirmed.

The proposed developmental systems model fits well with several aspects of stepfamilies. First, it addresses the developmental issues in stepfamilies and their intersection with individual life cycles. Second, the model helps inform both clinicians and clients about potential stress points or areas of conflict, so that they can understand and hopefully plan for them. Finally, while we now know significantly more about stepfamilies, we still need much more research, particularly about stepfamilies from diverse ethnic and social backgrounds, so that we can develop more effective prevention and intervention programs.

REFERENCES

Bray, J. H. (1988). *Developmental Issues in StepFamilies Research Project: Final Report.* (Grant Number RO1 HD18025). Bethesda, MD: National Institute of Child Health and Human Development.

Bray, J. H. (1994). Children in stepfamilies: Assessment and treatment issues. In D. Huntley (Ed.), *Understanding stepfamilies: Implications for assessment and treatment* (pp. 59–71), Washington, DC: American Counseling Association.

Bray, J. H. (1995). Family oriented treatment of stepfamilies. In R. Mikesell, D. D. Lusterman, & S. McDaniel (Eds.), *Integrating Family Therapy: Handbook of family psychology and systems therapy* (pp. 125–140). Washington, DC: American Psychological Association.

Bray, J. H. (1999). From marriage to remarriage and beyond: Findings from the Developmental Issues in StepFamilies Research Project. In E. M. Hetherington (Ed.), *Coping with divorce, single-parenting and remarriage: A risk and resiliency perspective* (pp. 253–271). Hillsdale, NJ: Lawrence Erlbaum.

Bray, J. H. (2001). Therapy with stepfamilies: A developmental systems approach. In D. D. Lusterman, S. H. McDaniel, & C. Philpot (Eds.), *Integrating family therapy: A casebook* (pp. 127–140). Washington, DC: American Psychological Association.

Bray, J. H., & Berger, S. H. (1992). Stepfamilies. In M. E. Procidano & C. B. Fisher (Eds.), *Contemporary families: A handbook for school professional* (pp. 57–79). New York: Teachers College Press.

Bray, J. H., & Berger, S. H. (1993). Developmental issues in stepfamilies research project: Family relationships and parent-child interactions. *Journal of Family Psychology, 7,* 76–90.

Bray, J. H., & Easling, I. (2005). Remarriage and stepfamilies. In W. Pinsof and J. Lebow (Eds.), *Family psychology: State of the art* (pp. 267–294). Oxford: Oxford University Press.

Bray, J. H., & Harvey, D. M. (1995). Adolescents in stepfamilies: Developmental and family interventions. *Psychotherapy, 32,* 122–130.

Bray, J. H., & Hetherington, E. M. (1993). Families in transition: Introduction and overview. *Journal of Family Psychology, 7,* 3–8.

Bray, J. H., & Jouriles, E. (1995). Treatment of marital conflict and prevention of divorce. *Journal of Marital and Family Therapy, 21,* 461–473.

Bray, J. H., & Kelly, J. (1998). *StepFamilies: Love, marriage, and parenting in the first decade.* New York: Broadway Books.

Fine, M. A., Coleman, M., & Ganong, L. H. (1998). Consistency in perceptions of the step-parent role among step-parents, parents and stepchildren. *Journal of Social and Personal Relationships, 15,* 810–828.

Finkelhor, D. (1984). *Child sexual abuse.* New York: Free Press.

Garbarino, J., Sebes, J., & Schellenbach, C. (1984). Families at risk for destructive parent-child relations in adolescence. *Child Development, 55,* 174–183.

Gottman, J. M. (1994). *Why marriages succeed or fail.* New York: Simon & Schuster.

Gottman, J. M. (1999). *The marriage clinic: A scientifically based marital therapy.* New York: Norton.

Guerney, B. G. (1977). *Relationship enhancement.* San Francisco: Jossey Bass.

Hendrix, H. (1988). *Getting the love you want: A guide for couples.* New York: HarperCollins.

Hetherington, E. M., & Clingempeel, W. G. (1992). Coping with marital transitions: A family systems perspective. *Monographs of the Society for Research in Child Development, 57* Nos. 2–3, Serial No. 227.

Hetherington, E. M., Henderson, S., & Reiss, D. (1999). *Adolescent siblings in stepfamilies: Family functioning and adolescent adjustment.* Malden, MA: Blackwell.

Hetherington, E. M., & Stanley-Hagan, M. (1999). Stepfamilies. In M. E. Lamb (Ed.), *Parenting and child development in "nontraditional" families* (pp. 137–159). Mahwah, NJ: Lawrence Erlbaum.

Jacobson, N. S., & Margolin, G. (1979). *Marital therapy: Strategies based on social learning and behavior exchange principles.* New York: Brunner/Mazel.

Levant, R. F. (1986). An overview of psychoeducational family programs. In R. F. Levant (Ed.), *Psychoeducational approaches to family therapy and counseling* (pp. 1–51). New York: Springer.

Love, P. (1994). *Hot monogamy: Essential steps to more passionate, intimate lovemaking.* New York: Penguin.

McGoldrick, M., & Carter, E. A. (1988). Forming a remarried family. In E. A. Carter & M. McGoldrick (Eds.), *The changing family life cycle* (pp. 399–429). New York: Gardner.

McGoldrick, M., Gerson, R., & Shellenberger, S. (1999). *Genograms: Assessment and intervention.* New York: Norton.

Renick, M. J., Blumberg, S. L., & Markman, H. J. (1992). The Prevention and Relationship Enhancement Program (PREP): An empirically based preventive intervention program for couples. *Family Relations, 41,* 141–147.

Steinberg, L. (2001). Adolescent development. *Annual Review of Psychology, 52,* 83–110.

Visher, E. B., & Visher, J. S. (1979). *Stepfamilies.* New York: Brunner/Mazel.

Visher, E. B., & Visher, J. S. (1988). *Old loyalties, new ties: Therapeutic strategies with stepfamilies.* New York: Brunner/Mazel.

Williamson, D. S., & Bray, J. H. (1988). Family development and change across the generations: An intergenerational perspective. In C. J. Falicov (Ed.), *Family transitions: Continuity and change over the life cycle* (pp. 357–384). New York: Guilford.

CHAPTER 20

Integrative Family Therapy for Families Experiencing High-Conflict Divorce

Jay L. Lebow

Divorce is almost invariably a major life crisis for families. Divorce is associated with a multiplicity of stressors, making it among the most difficult life transitions that families face (Amato, 1994, 2001). Some of this stress has a structural foundation: A family must move from one structure of organization, in which all members reside in the same home, to another, in which there are two separate households and two distinct sets of rules and roles. Even under the best of conditions, such restructuring is a complex task that involves considerable negotiation and adaptation.

Other aspects of the life stress in divorce are emotional. Partings are often painful, and the chances for at least some degree of conflict between parents or between parents and children are high. Children experience numerous losses: the loss of one home, the loss of two parents working together, and, sometimes, the loss of a parent. Almost inevitably, at least one parent also feels hurt and left out.

And there are yet other repercussions that derive from the pragmatic changes that occur. For most families, divorce also means that everyone relocates to new home(s); for many families, this involves a substantial change in economic well-being. And, in terms of family development, divorce, for most families, is the first step in a complex, two-step process of moving into a transitional family structure, soon followed by a second, equally evocative transition into remarriage families (see the chapter by Bray in this volume).

Thus, there are many significant stressors facing almost all divorcing families. Yet, there is not so much one "divorce" experience, but many different variants on this experience. Although there are few "easy" divorces, many families negotiate this transition with relatively low levels of conflict, allowing the transition to two households to feel cooperative. At the other end of the spectrum, however, families remain mired in the zone between marriage and divorce for very long periods of time, during which there is high conflict, significant triangulation between family members, and what Johnston and Campbell (1986) have aptly called "tribal warfare" involving friends and extended family. Although there are universal challenges that accompany the transition through divorce, a one-size-fits-all approach to intervention makes little sense in this context. Most families have some difficulties, but negotiate this transition successfully with little or no help; for others, even with a great deal of intervention, the family continually totters on the verge of multiple disasters.

The domain of intervention for divorcing families is perhaps best viewed through the lens of a public health perspective. From this vantage point, divorce can be considered to be a potentially pathogenic factor in the lives of families, which can affect the mental health of the individuals in those families. And the extent to which the well-being of families is affected by divorce can be viewed as the product of a number of factors, including the level of conflict, triangulation of children, and individual vulnerability of the individuals in the family. For everyone experiencing divorce, it presents a challenge as a life transition. For those subject to fewer risk factors, the transition can be successfully negotiated with little long-term damage accruing, while for those who are subject to higher levels of risk, divorce can result in life-long trauma, for both the children and the adults going through the experience.

Taking this model one step further, it is possible to picture a graduated series of levels of intervention for those experiencing divorce, aimed at delivering service in a cost-effective way, much as is done in programs of intervention for dealing with physical pathogens that can impact public health. At one end of this continuum are low-intensity, preventive interventions, aimed at all families experiencing divorce. Such programs aim to educate people about how to successfully negotiate this developmental transition. Programs that offer psychoeducation to parents and children about the experiences and feelings likely to occur in the process of divorce, and about how to cope and to mitigate the negative effects of this experience, have been shown to have a substantial preventive impact (Emery, 1999). Such programs are frequently offered by schools (for children) and at religious institutions and community mental health facilities, and typically involve low cost, both in money and time. Several of these programs have been demonstrated to be both efficacious and cost-effective.

This level of intervention is sufficient for most of those going through divorce, but further intervention is needed under some circumstances; for example, when there are conflicts about issues of child custody or visitation, or for those who experience more troubling emotional reactions. Considerable research has confirmed that mediation can resolve a high percentage of difficulties surrounding arrangements between parents about custody, visitation, and financial matters, and help avoid problems (Emery, 1994). In mitigating these conflicts, mediation also serves the mental health of all family members.

For those for whom relational or individual difficulties persist at a level of concern despite efforts at psychoeducation and mediation (that is, where there is a greater than average amount of conflict or where there are more than transient symptoms of individual difficulties), the level of intervention is best increased to that of a brief, integrative, family-based therapy. Such an intervention utilizes multiple therapy formats (e.g., family, couple, individual) to help with the transition to a new family structure and to target the problem that has emerged in the family, be it a problem in the whole family, a subsystem, or an individual (Walsh, 1991). And, at the most intensive end of the spectrum, for those families engaged in intractable conflicts, a longer, more intensive course of therapy is needed. Sometimes, in order to be effective, these therapies need to extend years beyond the time of divorce.

This chapter focuses on describing a method for intervening with those families in high conflict, for whom more intense psychotherapy is the appropriate level of intervention in divorce; that is, the territory of the last level of intervention previously described. Although some of the intervention strategies remain similar in lower conflict divorce (such as the benefits of psychoeducation and mediation-like skills in therapy, attending to the narratives of all family members, and assuming a problem-centered stance), a description of intervention in lower-conflict divorce remains beyond the scope of this chapter, despite its obvious importance. The reader is referred to Walsh and colleagues (Walsh, Jacob, & Simons, 1995) and Emery and colleagues (Emery, 1994; Emery, Kitzmann, & Waldron, 1999) for examples of approaches to therapy and mediation, and to Braver (Braver & Griffin, 2000) and Pedro-Carrall (Pedro-Carrall, Alpert-Gillis, & Cowen, 1992) and colleagues for examples of prevention programs targeted at adults and children.

The approach to psychotherapy described in this chapter builds on a multidimensional, biopsychosocial understanding of human functioning, that adds components of intervention in relation to the nature and severity of the problems the family faces. Within the umbrella of this framework, treatment plans can be created for intervening across a wide range of levels of difficulty, and for specific problems. For example, a treatment can be constructed, following and adapting the principles stated in this chapter, that would speak to a situation in which a child or parent becomes depressed in the context of a less acrimonious divorce.

However, this chapter specifically aims to describe the treatment of a special population in divorce; those cases in which parents engage in intractable conflict over child custody and visitation. Because of the severity of the problems engendered through intractable conflict, these families present with a special need, and are very frequently referred for treatment.

DIVORCE

Even an amicable divorce presents a crisis for the lives of families. Although the percentage of children and adults for whom divorce has long-term, significant negative effects is relatively small, divorce is associated with increased risk for a variety of problems (Amato, 2001). Children and adults are particularly more likely to show physical or emotional problems during the time of divorce (Hetherington, Stanley-Hagan, & Anderson, 1989). For most, these problems typically diminish over time (Grych & Fincham, 1999, Hetherington et al., 1989), leaving relatively small differences between children and adults in divorced and intact families on long term follow-up (Hetherington, Law, & O'Connor, 1993, Ahrons, 1994). However, even if the long-term effects are less great than argued in some places (Wallerstein, 1998), divorce clearly presents a challenge for families. As Grych and Fincham (1999) suggest, "There is now widespread recognition that divorce is best understood as a process that begins prior to the physical separation of the parents and may even continue long after" (p. 97).

High conflict between parents significantly increases the risks of negative effects on both children and adults, during and after divorce. Such conflict is almost an inevitable consequence when there is a legal dispute over child custody and visitation (Doolittle & Deutsch, 1999; Johnston, 1994; Johnston & Campbell, 1988). Although there is little good research directly assessing adults and children in child custody conflicts, the implications about the deleterious nature of these conflicts for all parties clearly can be readily extrapolated from considering the research on high-conflict divorce.

High levels of parental conflict have consistently been shown to be among the most potent destructive factors in both intact and divorced families (Fincham, Grych, & Osborne, 1994; Grych & Fincham, 1990; Grych, Fincham, Jouriles, & McDonald, 2000). Amato (Amato, 1993, 1994, 2001) concludes that parental conflict is the single strongest predictor of child maladjustment in divorce. It also has been clearly documented that children themselves assess the conflict between their parents as one of the most stressful aspects of divorce (Wolchik, Ruehlman, Braver, & Sandler, 1989). Furthermore, the kind of hostile, aggressive, poorly resolved, and child-centered conflicts evident in these cases also has been shown to be the most upsetting parental conflict to children (Grych & Fincham, 1999). Buchanan, Maccoby, & Dornbusch (1991) found that the perception of being caught between parents accounted for the association between parental conflict and children's adjustment difficulties in divorce. And in a series of articles directly assessing the impact of child custody conflicts, Johnston and her associates have clearly documented the multiple, negative effects of these disputes on children (Johnston, 1993, 1994; Johnston, Campbell, & Tall, 1985; Johnston & Campbell, 1988; Johnston, Kline, & Tschann, 1989).

Such ongoing conflicts about child custody and visitation represent a major public health problem.[1] These conflicts present extremely difficult and anxiety-provoking circumstances for families, a context that clearly has negative effects on all parties involved, most especially on children (Galatzer-Levy & Kraus, 1999; Grych & Fincham, 1999; Johnston & Campbell, 1988). Conflicts frequently continue over a period of several years, leaving most family members in highly traumatic states over considerable periods of time (Doolittle & Deutsch, 1999). Triangulation of children into parental conflict occurs in most cases. Symptoms of traumatic stress, depression, anxiety disorders, and various kinds of acting out disorders are commonplace in both children and adults (Grych & Fincham, 1999). The wide array of specific symptoms that occurs in this context, coupled with the high percentage of these cases manifesting such symptoms, suggests that these cases are better understood in the framework of a relational diagnosis of Protracted Conflict over Child Custody and Visitation, rather than a *DSM-IV*-syndrome emphasis on individual psychopathology[2] (Kaslow, 1996).

---

[1] The term "visitation" traditionally is employed in the judicial system to describe time spent with the nonresidential parent. Although it is predicated on an out-of-date view of the postdivorce family, in which one parent has visits, and better terms are available, such as "time with each parent," because of its wide usage, for sake of simplicity, the term "visitation" is used throughout this chapter.

[2] This is not meant to minimize the presence of diagnosable *DSM-IV* disorders in this population, both as the result of these conflicts and as precursors to them.

Typically, parents, during and after divorce, create a clear structure for time with each parent and the sharing of authority.[3] Most parents create a structure for the time to be spent with each parent (typically referred to in the legal process as residence or residential custody and visitation) and for decision making (often referred to in the legal process as custody), allowing the family to build a new, binuclear family structure and move on with its life tasks. Often, this involves more mutual tolerance than active coparenting, but most families manage to move through life without being embroiled in a crisis about the structure of the lives of children.

This chapter focuses on the treatment of a special minority among divorcing and postdivorce families; those in which the parents are unable to reach the minimal level of agreement needed to allow for the stabilization of family structure. In these families, the judicial system looms as a constant preoccupation, and loyalty conflicts are inevitable. Approximately 10 percent of divorcing families engage in substantial conflict within the judicial system (Grych & Fincham, 1999; Maccoby, Depner, & Mnookin, 1990; Hetherington, Law, & O'Connor, 1993). In the Stanford Custody Project, Maccoby, Depner, & Mnookin (1990) found almost one-third of couples showed significant conflict 18 months after separation. These parents tended to have longer legal disputes, higher levels of hostility, concerns about the quality of the other parent's parenting, and younger children than other parents.

There is a clear need for a therapy paradigm for treating these families. Although there is no research assessing the impact of typical therapies not specifically tailored to deal with these problems, observation of the results of many of these therapies suggests that these interventions have little positive impact on such conflicts. Experience also suggests that, frequently, well-intended therapies with these clients degenerate into either sources of further acrimony, or, as is often the case in individual, nonsystemic therapy of these cases, become sources of perceived support on the part of the parties for continued conflict. Nonetheless, these families frequently do seek therapy: sometimes mandated by the court, sometimes referred by a concerned attorney, and sometimes self-referred because of their own pain. Although these families represent a small percentage of the divorcing/divorced population, they account for a disproportionate percentage of the time spent on cases of domestic relations court judges, family law attorneys, and child and family therapists.

This is a special population with special needs. The special configurations of family difficulties (e.g., high conflict between parents and the triangulation of children) and the special interface with the legal system that these cases present calls for a therapy approach tailored to the needs of these families (Doolittle & Deutsch, 1999; Grych & Fincham, 1999). Johnston & Campbell (1988) suggest that these families show a myriad of factors contributing to the impasse, including the changed nature of the marital interaction, the input from the social milieu, and issues of individual vulnerability, such as unmourned loss. This myriad of factors needs to be targeted in a multimodal treatment.

---

[3] Many parents engaged in these conflicts have never married, and some have never lived together. The terms "divorce" and "postdivorce" are used for simplicity, to speak to any situation involving parents who are no longer together.

The treatment model presented here, called Integrative Multilevel Family Therapy for Disputes Involving Child Custody and Visitation (IMFT-DCCV) is an open-ended, biopsychosocial, science-based method for working with these difficulties. The approach is open-ended in viewing therapy as a resource that can be utilized over time. The treatment is biopsychosocial in bringing a multilevel view to the understanding of problems and intervention. The approach is science-based in drawing extensively from research assessing families in shaping the specific intervention strategies. The IMFT-DCCV approach has been developed in my work with this population over 20 years. It applies an integrative, family systems framework to intervening with this population. The method has been shaped and augmented in relation to the experience of bringing this approach to several hundred cases.

There have been many efforts to help children and families with divorce, but few targeted to this population. Most divorce programs have been targeted at children and/or offered psychoeducation to parents. Although programs like The Children Of Divorce Intervention Project (Pedro-Carrall, Alpert-Gillis, & Cowen, 1992) that highlight coping skills have been shown to be effective (Grych & Fincham, 1999), these programs have not been targeted to the extreme situations that typify these families. Only Johnston's model for treating these families has received much attention (Campbell & Johnston, 1986; Johnston & Campbell, 1988; Johnston & Roseby, 1997) other than the approach described in this chapter. Grych and Fincham (1999) point to the paradox of the lack of family-based models of intervention in divorce juxtaposed with the substantial body of research pointing to the need for approaches to intervention.

FOCUSES FOR INTERVENTION

This model of intervention begins with a number of assumptions. Three of these assumptions are higher-order assumptions about the nature of these difficulties. These are:

1. *The Biopsychosocial base of behavior: a multilevel understanding of difficulties.* The essential elements underlying these disputes can reside at a multiplicity of levels. Some are biological, some are psychological, and some are social (Lebow, 1997; Pinsof, 1983). Individuals in these disputes often show biologically rooted difficulties, such as depression, psychological difficulties such as cognitive distortions, and social difficulties, such as inability to deal with the pressures from extended family. Each level contains potentially crucial factors in understanding these families and in constructing a pathway to ameliorate these problems. Difficulties are often experienced on multiple levels simultaneously.

2. *Circular causal pathways.* Understanding context and circular causal pathways is essential to understanding the behavior of the individuals in these disputes (Lebow & Gurman, 1995; Nichols & Schwartz, 1998). For example, a father's keeping his child out late while in his care may serve to reinforce a mother's belief about his incompetence as a parent and serve as a reason for restricting his access to the children. In turn, that mother's restriction of the father's access may be responded

to with other provocative behaviors by the father, including filing court petitions suggesting that the mother is undermining and alienating, and by keeping his child out even later the next time the child is in his care. The father's response then can lead to further limitation of access by the mother.

3. *The importance of individual personality and psychopathology.* Many of those involved in custody and visitation conflicts manifest patterns of behavior that clearly indicate significant, diagnosable individual difficulties (Grych & Fincham, 1999; Jenuwine & Cohler, 1999). Many meet criteria for Axis Two Personality Disorder diagnoses. Other parents show basic difficulties in functioning that directly or indirectly threaten children, including physical abuse, sexual abuse, depression, and drug or alcohol abuse (Jenuwine & Cohler, 1999). The children in these cases frequently also manifest their own psychopathology (Doolittle & Deutsch, 1999).

Thus, it is essential to understand the importance both of individual and systemic factors at work in the creation and maintenance of these difficulties. In most of these cases, at least some aspect of each is applicable.

Beyond these core assumptions, IMFT-DCCV posits a number of key areas for intervention, identified from patterns frequently encountered in these cases.

4. *Attribution.* Negative attribution plays an essential role in driving many of the interactions in these families. Each parent typically views the actions of the other through a negative filter; problematic actions by the other are invariably viewed as evidence of character flaws and/or hostile action, while constructive behavior is seen as disingenuous or transitory (Hooper, 1993). For example, a mother faced with evidence that her separated spouse had become abstinent in the use of alcohol and a faithful attendee of Alcoholics Anonymous attributed these changes to his desire to win his court case, remaining convinced that the alcoholic behavior would return as soon as the court proceedings were completed. When a child becomes ill or injured, typically the working assumption is that the other parent's behavior is to blame. Behavioral problems in children are similarly attributed to the expartner's contribution. The most frequently encountered negative attribution relates the difficulties children manifest in divorce, or at transitions between homes (e.g., not wanting transitions to occur from home to home, or feeling sad) to the behavior of the other parent. Children and extended family and friends in these cases often also become caught up in similar patterns of selective attribution (Johnston & Campbell, 1986). This is especially the case in instances where parental alienation (the promotion by one parent of a poor relationship with the other parent on the part of the child) plays a role (Gardner, 1998, 1999, 2002).

5. *Lack of parenting skill.* A lack of parenting skill is often evident in many parents in these disputes (Doolittle & Deutsch, 1999). Mothers and fathers may have little experience with successful parenting, or their individual difficulties may make them unsafe as parents.

6. *Communication problems.* Communication typically tends to be absent or pathogenic between parents in these disputes (Doolittle & Deutsch, 1999; Galatzer-Levy & Kraus, 1999; Grych & Fincham, 1999). In-person contact often leads to overt conflict, while e-mails and voice messages frequently come to be used as evidence in the legal disputes, leading to the lack of any reliable method of commu-

nication. A side effect of these problems is that children readily become triangulated in parental exchanges.

7. *Emotional flooding.* The interactions in these families frequently invoke memories of earlier traumas. Often, there are histories of highly emotional conflicts, of violence, or of betrayal in the relationship history of the parents (Galatzer-Levy & Kraus, 1999; Johnston & Campbell, 1988). The emotional flooding that occurs at moments of contact between former partners (or even in relation to some aftereffect of their behavior) vitiates any possibility for positive resolution. At times, there also are considerable risks of violence (Johnston, 1994; Johnston & Campbell, 1993).

8. *Parents' failure to separate their needs from those of their children.* Parents in these cases frequently cannot separate their own needs from their child's needs, to develop a positive connection with the other parent (Johnston, 1994; Johnston & Campbell, 1988).

9. *Remarriage family issues.* Some families begin to have conflicts, or have conflicts increase immeasurably, when one or both parents add a significant other (Lebow, Walsh, & Rolland, 1999). Alternatively, a parent, having been satisfied with a small amount of time with his or her children, may seek greater involvement after remarriage, and look to change the children's principal residence. The introduction of step- and half-siblings, with the predictable conflicts that emerge, may also strain family relationships.

10. *Multigenerational legacies and the influence of extended family.* Divorce invokes powerful, multigenerational legacies. Families of origin may also exert a powerful effect in present, ongoing interactions; many conflicts are fueled by strong feelings of betrayal by the family of origin of one of the partners (Doolittle & Deutsch, 1999; Johnston & Campbell, 1986).

11. *Gender politics.* Men and women typically fall into stereotypic positions relative to their parental rights. Women often believe children's lives should be grounded with their mothers, while men believe that parents should have coequal influence (Lebow et al., 1999).

12. *The interface with the legal system.* Behavior in these families must always be considered in relation to its frequent contacts with the legal system. The adversarial context of much of the judicial system provides endless opportunities for confrontations in pleadings, subpoenas, depositions, and court appearances, frequently engendering further conflict (Galatzer-Levy & Kraus, 1999). What transpires on these occasions becomes evidence for negative attribution. Children also can become highly polarized in the context of interviews with judges and attorneys regarding their best interests.[4]

CREATING A THERAPEUTIC CONTRACT

Work with these families necessarily begins with a need to create a clear contract for therapy. Typically, these families manifest a chaotic process in relation to the

---

[4] Although attorneys and judges do often intervene to mitigate conflict, such measures are frequently met with resistance in these families, sometimes even leading to parents engaging new attorneys or petitioning for changes in judges.

conflict. This chaotic process can readily be transferred, in an isomorphic manner, in the clients' relation to the therapy. Any vagaries about the structure of the treatment easily becomes occasions for disputes. Both parents and children in these cases often envision therapy as a place where they can gain support from the therapist for their parochial point of view. Some even enter expecting the therapist to transfer this support into the legal venues in which these families regularly engage, while others begin with a fear of any coordination of the treatment with any part of the judicial process. Some parents look to involve their children in the treatment process, while others avoid such contact. Core aspects of the therapy, which are not in writing, such as guidelines for the sharing of information, often are revisited, with the parties having divergent recollections.

Given this chaotic context of mixed motivations, IMFT-DCCV begins with a crisp and clear statement of the therapy contract. This contract builds on the broad understandings of contracts in psychotherapy (Orlinsky & Howard, 1987). Because of the ever-present interface with the legal system in these cases, and the complex motivations of clients, the written therapy contract must also contain more detail than typical agreements to participate in psychotherapy. To ensure clarity about these understandings, at the beginning of IMFT-DCCV a thorough discussion of the therapeutic contract is supplemented with written materials presenting details. This contract is not necessarily legally binding (as a technical matter, the court has ultimate decision power about many matters covered in the contract), but, in clearly laying out the assumptions of treatment, such contracts are rarely challenged in court, and almost never overruled. Wherever possible, the key elements about the therapeutic contract (e.g., who will participate, who will pay for treatment, expectations about confidentiality) should be reiterated in specific court orders about the treatment, so that there also will be clarity about these matters in the legal context.

The key matters to clarify in the contract include:

1. *The participation of various family members.* Typical contracts call for the participation of mother, father, significant others of the parents, and their children living at home, on the schedule to be suggested by the therapist. To the extent that others, such as extended family and stepsiblings, appear to have important roles in the family dynamics, their presence is also written into the contract.

2. *The frequency of meetings and who will participate in what session formats.* Frequency of participation is often a vital consideration in these cases. Often, one party will want to satisfy some minimal criteria—that they went to treatment without participating in a sufficient dosage of treatment to have any effect. The contract, therefore, contains a statement of expected frequency of meetings, constructed on a case-by-case basis.

3. *Confidentiality and who has access to information about the treatment.* The therapeutic contract specifies who has access to what information, how information will be shared across formats (i.e., between individual sessions with adults and with children), and about rules governing confidentiality with those outside the therapy, most especially with the judicial system. The contract in IMFT-DCCV calls for confidentiality to be maintained in relation to others outside the legal sys-

tem as it would in other cases, but for it to be understood that a special relationship will be established with the court and attorneys in the case. The contract specifies that the general level of cooperation of the clients will be reported to the court and attorneys, and that there will be more specific sharing about the status of the therapy and court case with the attorney for the children (if there is one), and about each adult client with their own attorney.[5]

In this way, the leverage available from the Court's support of the treatment can be invoked while leaving clients reassured that their sharing will not come to be used against them. Such leverage is often essential to progress in these cases. Clarity about the kinds of information which will be shared is essential, as is the signing of appropriate releases for the sharing of information. As Greenberg and Gould (2001) have suggested about the role of the treating expert who is primarily engaged as a therapist but who also might be looked to offer reports about progress to someone working in the judicial context (e.g., an attorney for the children or an evaluator), the key here lies in the therapist being forthright about the limitations on confidentiality with each family member and obtaining the appropriate waivers of confidentiality. Although some treatment goals can be accomplished without such waivers, the therapist will be limited in his or her ability to work with aspects of the problem without such a waiver, and will be unable to invoke important leverage. Furthermore, without such a waiver, therapists can expect a difficult interface with representatives of the legal system who are looking to them for a better understanding of the case.

4. *Fees.* Who will pay what fees needs to be clearly understood, even prior to the first session. These arrangements should be worked out by attorneys in the case. Typically, the parties divide the cost evenly. At times, all fees are paid by one party, with the clear understanding that this will have no effect on the course of treatment. Where the parties are not yet divorced, the payment often is made by one party, or from some shared account, with the costs ultimately being reconciled as part of the final divorce decree. Given the wrangling over monies so common in these families, payment is expected at the time of meetings.

ASSESSMENT

Assessment has a crucial role in IMFT-DCCV. What is the contribution of each family member to the problem? How much is it rooted in circular process and how much in individual behavior? Plans for intervention flow from the answers to these and similar questions. The intervention strategy varies in relation to key factors.

Sometimes, a child custody evaluation conducted by an evaluator who is not directly involved in treatment is available. When this is the case, such an evaluation can be enormously helpful in the construction of a treatment plan (Ackerman, 2001; Ackerman & Ackerman, 1997, 1999; Bricklin, 1995; Galatzer-Levy & Kraus, 1999; Gould, 1998, 1999; Gould & Stahl, 2000). Many allegations in these cases are often difficult to assess. How much danger does a father present for his children? A mother may suggest that the danger is great, because of the father's

---

[5] There is no sharing about the other parent with the particular parent's attorney.

violence, whereas the father denies any violent behavior. The custody evaluator, in the 20 or so direct contact hours devoted exclusively to assessment, can bring considerable resources to understanding the complex questions about individual character and circular pathways that unfold in these cases. When available, such reports can serve as blueprints for the changes needed in therapy. In such cases, IMFT-DCCV utilizes the report as the foundation for assessment, allowing for a shortened assessment phase.[6]

More typically, therapy must begin without the benefit of an independent child custody evaluation. IMFT-DCCV therefore begins with a structured assessment phase for targeting problems and treatment goals. This phase consists of a mini-evaluation, including separate meetings with each parent (with or without new spouses, depending on the issues involved), and children, along with a review of records and input from other involved professionals. This mini-evaluation seeks to elaborate the key factors to target. A case formulation is developed about the factors that appear to have generated and be maintaining the present problem.

From this brief assessment, a treatment plan is created for the format of future sessions—that is, who will participate in what combinations, at what time, focused on what issues. Strategies for intervention and session format flow from this formulation. The key question becomes, "What needs to change to allow this family to move beyond this developmental sticking point?"

Therapy follows the treatment plan, but the plan remains flexible; it is augmented and sometimes substantially altered as information accrues from the responses of various family members to intervention. Following one of Pinsof's (1995) concepts from Integrative Problem Centered Therapy, the formulation and consequent interventions are modified if new data emerges that changes the assessment as therapy evolves.

INTERVENTION STRATEGIES

IMFT-DCCV looks to identify the most salient factors at work in each case and to build a therapeutic plan based on these factors, rather than following an invariant method for treating those who present with custody and visitation disputes.

Choosing the Formats for Sessions

Following another tenet of Pinsof's Integrative Problem Centered Therapy (Pinsof, 1995), all family members are viewed as part of the client system—but who participates in sessions varies, based on the specific goals set in that case. Session formats are chosen based on an algorithm for which session formats impact most in relation to particular kinds of problems. For example, issues of parent-child cooperation are addressed principally in sessions between the children and a parent, adult psychopathology is most readily addressed in individual sessions with a parent, and parental communication is best addressed in conjoint sessions with both

---

[6] This presumes an unbiased report conducted by an evaluator appointed by the court or through agreement by both sides in the dispute; an evaluation that speaks to the issues that need attention; and that the report can be made available to the therapist in a timely manner.

parents. Some of the sessions are invariably with each parent individually, some with parents and children, and some with the parents together, but the proportion of sessions of each format varies from case to case.

Given the kind of pervasive and powerful problems presented in these disputes, choices about session formats are often not simple. Custody evaluations frequently suggest family therapy involving parents and children, sessions between parents, and weekly individual therapies for all parties. When the resources are available for such intense treatment, there is a great deal to be said for intense therapy for each subsystem (subject to there being coordination across the therapies; all the parties finding their own disconnected therapists seldom helps).

However, pragmatically few families can afford or are willing to participate in such multiple therapies. For most, the cost of the therapy becomes an issue. Family members are also usually willing to participate in only so much therapy. Most family members in these cases begin treatment at what Prochaska and DiClemente (Prochaska & DiClemente, 1982; Prochaska, Johnson, & Lee, 1998) call the pre-contemplative stage, where they cannot see that they have any problem. Therefore, choices about who should be in what kind of session must be made in a judicious way. Decisions to involve multiple therapists also must be made thoughtfully. There may be more than one therapist involved, given such factors as the value in some cases of children having their own special person with whom to work, but it is essential that there be one therapist coordinating the work.

The varying session formats in IMFT-DCCV are coupled with active efforts to minimize triangulation involving the therapist. Strategies for avoiding triangulation include emphasizing clarity about the goals for each kind of session, clear procedures for the handling of information across formats, refusing to participate in the sharing of secrets, and building strong alliances with all parties.

Alliance Building

Forging satisfactory therapeutic alliances with all parties is especially crucial in these families, because of the powerful splitting between good and bad objects that so often occurs (Doolittle & Deutsch, 1999). However, finding such a balance is difficult. Some participants typically enter therapy only because they have been court-ordered, or because of other pressures. Family members often have resentments about other mental health treatment and/or custody evaluations in which they have participated, leaving many quite suspicious. The task of building a multipartial alliance (Boszormenyi-Nagy, 1974) with all parties is further challenged by the many triangulations afoot; an alliance with one party is easily experienced as an alliance against another.

The therapist in IMFT-DCCV aims to establish the kind of multipartial alliance described by Boszorenyi-Nagy (1974). The goal is to be experienced as caring, fair, and involved. Achieving this goal is not an easy task, given the additional need for the therapist to bring issues into focus (these clients typically prefer to vent about the behavior of their former partner), and to label and work with the problems that require attention. The therapist provides honest direct feedback, but looks to reframe the changes sought in a way that will not unduly provoke resistance (Alexander, Waldon, Newberry, & Liddle, 1990). Similarly, a frame is established that highlights client strengths and that does not unduly pathologize family members (Walsh, 1998; Walsh et al., 1995). Problematic behaviors related to the conflict are directly confronted, but the positive intent of each client is always underscored. The therapist communicates that most difficult behaviors can be understood in the context of the stresses of family life and the ongoing, circular processes at work, simultaneously working to highlight alternatives. When presented in this context, clients much more readily accept their difficulties as appropriate targets for change in the setting of treatment goals.

Setting Realistic Goals

Goals in IMFT-DCCV are shaped to be realistic. Even successful outcomes typically end with less than an ideal postdivorce environment. Pragmatically, the central goal is to reduce the most damaging aspects of custody disputes: high conflict, triangulation, failure to arrive at an agreed-upon family structure, lack of safety, and inability to carry out ordinary life operations, such as visitation, without controversy.

One goal that comes into focus in almost every case is the creation of a respectful disengagement between the parents, in which contact is kept to the minimum needed to successfully raise their children. A key process goal invariably is to help family members each move one step at a time along the continuum described by Prochaska and DiClemente (1982) in motivation to change. First, clients must come to understand that there is something that they can do to improve the problem. Given the degree of dysfunctional behavior that typifies almost everyone involved in these conflicts, it is rarely difficult to find some immediate change that would be helpful for each client in the service of the ultimate goal of reducing conflict (i.e., even if an exspouse is acting like the world's worst person, there may not be much payoff in remaining obsessed with his or her behavior).

Moving from the Initial to the Intervention Phase of Treatment

The therapeutic contract is arrived at in the first meeting with each parent, and explained to the children in the first meeting with them. Assessment and alliance building are emphasized over the first few meetings, though these remain ongoing tasks as treatment develops and information accrues from various family members' response to interventions (Pinsof, 1995).

Once the therapeutic alliance has begun to be built and the therapist has a working assessment, the therapist forms a blueprint for intervention. Each blueprint typically includes a number of specific treatment strategies. Some strategies are utilized in all cases, whereas others are only utilized when suggested by behavior patterns that emerge from the assessment. The degree to which various strategies are emphasized depends on the case assessment and on the clients' response to these strategies.

Interventions Utilized in All Cases

IMFT-DCCV includes several intervention strategies that are incorporated into the treatment of each case.

Psychoeducation

Psychoeducation has been found to be a very potent intervention for helping clients resolve a wide range of difficulties (Lebow & Gurman, 1995). Psychoeducation has an especially important role in treating families in these disputes, given the many misunderstandings that frequently occur about what constitutes normative behavior in divorce and in disputes over custody and visitation.

Psychoeducation is employed in IMFT-DCCV in two distinct ways. One is to help family members better understand the challenges that accompany the transition through divorce and, most especially, child custody litigation. In the strange territory of these conflicts, where litigation can go on for years, even many professionals are likely to be unaware of the typical behavior patterns in these families.

One psychoeducational theme centers on what is ultimately "the best interests of the children" in child custody conflict. The goal here is to help the parents move outside of their own mindframe, and see their children's needs in a broader perspective. Data from research and clinical experience is presented to parents regarding the pernicious effects on children of protracted conflict, and the risks entailed (Doolittle & Deutsch, 1999; Grych & Fincham, 1999).

A related focus of psychoeducation centers on the reactions children have to divorce and to conflicts about child custody. From their narrow viewpoints, parents often envision their children's reactions as unique, or as reactions to the special negative qualities of their former partner. Children can be expected to often be stirred up, and transitions can be expected to be difficult, no matter how well parents parent. The inevitable losses that children must face in high conflict divorce are highlighted, as are the challenges that accompany these losses.

Another related theme centers on loyalty conflicts and triangulation. Parents are explained the ways children typically respond to these sorts of loyalty conflicts. This includes a discussion of how children can readily fall into patterns of showing one parent their loyalty through sharing problems occurring with the other parent. Commonplace behaviors, such as children telling parents that they don't want to leave their home, are also framed in the context of this understanding.

Yet another related target of psychoeducation lies in helping family members understand symmetrical escalation in these disputes, and the measures that can be taken to avoid such escalation. It is striking how rarely parents can see the provocative nature of their own behavior or that of their lawyer in these disputes.

Specific examples from each case are interwoven into these psychoeducational discussions. None of these explanations alone leads to magical insight, but the examples set the stage for a greater sense of ownership of the problem. Positive examples are offered of families who resolve their difficulties through de-escalating conflicts as are constructive ways parents can respond to these challenging situations.

Psychoeducation is also employed in IMFT-DCCV in another, quite different way. In those cases in which parents lack requisite basic parenting skills, psychoeducation focuses on helping parents learn these skills. Parents often need to learn to distinguish the ways children think about the world from the way adults think, to learn about how to set structure for children, to learn how and when to share their feelings, and to learn about how to physically care for their children. This type of psychoeducation not only helps the parent in question to act more competently, but the knowledge that this training is occurring often helps the other parent to more readily believe their former partner can become more competent as a parent.

Creating a Solution-Oriented Focus

Clients entering treatment in disputes involving custody and visitation almost always see themselves as right-minded and as victims of the difficulties presented by others. As noted earlier, they inevitably begin therapy at what Prochaska & DiClemente (1992) refer to as the precontemplative stage, having not yet identified any role they have in the problem or any personal goals for change. IMFT-DCCV employs solution-oriented language (Duncan, Hubble, & Miller, 1997) that conveys the possibility of building on strengths already present (i.e., caring about the interests of children) to resolve the difficulties and to help clients recognize that they do have some control over the problem. The goal here is to change the focus from who started the problem to how it can be resolved. A frequent theme in IMFT-DCCV centers on refocusing the attention of each parent away from the behavior of the former partner and onto the pernicious effects of the conflict on the children.[7] This refocusing brings into the center of attention an overriding concern (the children's welfare) that can ultimately motivate parents to change their behavior, even if they continue to remain justified in their positions.

Promoting Disengagement between Parents and Separation of Mom's House and Dad's House

Explicit coaching with each individual focuses on how to respectfully disengage from the ongoing conflict. Parents are helped to see disengagement as a goal through psychoeducation, framing such disengagement as a constructive step in the divorce process. Parents are also explicitly taught disengagement skills, and children are taught skills for avoiding triangulation into parental conflict.

Establishing Reliable, Rule-Driven Methods of Communication and Good-Enough Coordination

IMFT-DCCV works to build reliable and agreed-upon methods of communication and coordination between family members. The goal for these cases is for the households to function independently, with only a minimum of communication and coordination, except in those special circumstances that necessitate coordination. When differences between households present special difficulties (for example, when there are radical differences in family rules) or when children present with issues that render greater coordination imperative (as in ADHD or diabetes),

---

[7] The extent to which this makes sense, of course, depends on the risks presented by the other parent to the children. The safety of the children must always be the first consideration. When a parent presents dangers, the therapy begins with addressing these dangers, by supporting arrangements that protect the children and by direct measures to alter the dangerous behavior.

IMFT-DCCV works to create just enough coordination for children to successfully go on with their lives. Much of this coordination is done in sessions with both parents (and, regrettably, in some of these families, therapy sessions remain the only place for such communication, over time).

The therapist brainstorms with parents about possible ways of communicating when communication is needed. New technologies, such as e-mail and fax, are often very helpful, as long as there are clear rules for their use (for example, agreed arrangements to keep them from being used as evidence). A highly structured version of verbal communication is taught for those occasions when verbal communication is necessary between parents: a speaker-listener technique allowing for only a few, crisply delivered, rule-governed exchanges (Renick, Blumberg, & Markman, 1992). Too much communication often is as risky in these families as too little, degenerating into off-subject fights, frequently with the children involved. In successful outcomes, most of the parents rarely communicate with the other, except when absolutely necessary. These families need just enough communication between parents to serve the lives of their children.

Negotiation

The formal process of mediation, conducted by a trained mediator, often has an important role in resolving conflicts in custody and visitation disputes, especially when the mediation occurs early in the conflict process (Campbell & Johnston, 1986a, 1986b; Folberg, 1991; Folberg & Milne, 1988; Milne & Folberg, 1988). Many jurisdictions mandate some participation in mediation for families involved in disputes over child custody. When those involved in less severe conflicts enter mediation early in the conflict process, as many as 75 percent of the conflicts can be resolved (Emery, 1994).

IMFT-DCCV is designed for those for whom mediation fails or is simply not an option, due to the level of acrimony. Nonetheless, some of the negotiation techniques utilized in mediation remain important in IMFT-DCCV, especially structured efforts to reach mutually acceptable solutions to problems. Typically, this requires more than a simple generation of a compromise. Often, significant blocks to resolution must be worked through. The therapist frequently engages in shuttle diplomacy through individual meetings with parents before setting the stage for conjoint meetings. The goal is to create a working context for compromise. Nonetheless, often, even at the end of therapy, such compromises can only occur with the presence of the therapist.

Reattribution

Family members in these conflicts present with powerful stories of blame and victimhood. In IMFT-DCCV, drawing on techniques from cognitive and narrative therapies, the therapist intervenes to create new ways of thinking about the problems that are occurring (Beck & Freeman, 1990; Combs & Freedman, 1990). The process goal here is the creation of narratives describing events that are not blaming or destructive. Conflict promoting beliefs are actively questioned. For example, when a parent sees his or her child upset as directly a function of the other parent's behavior, but this interpretation does not appear accurate, the therapist reframes a new narrative, suggesting other possible sources for the child's distress, such as feelings about separation, the natural difficulties in learning to live in two households, or memories of old events.[8] The therapist actively questions dysfunctional beliefs and works to build new narratives.

Work with Children

Children in custody and visitation conflicts often have internalized the conflict between their parents. They frequently show many symptoms as well as provocative behaviors toward one or both parents. In individual or sibling meetings, children in IMFT-DCCV are helped to better understand what it means to be in a divorced family, to talk about their feelings about the conflict between their parents, and to find ways to insulate themselves from that conflict.

The specific intervention strategies utilized are tailored to the age of the children. For young children, stories that enable feelings to be processed in fantasy serve as launching points for exchanges. Direct discussion of the issues predominates in older children, drawing on cognitive techniques and psychoeducation. Children are explicitly coached in how to avoid becoming triangulated into parent conflict, and how to master living in two households that show little cooperation.

Building Parent-Child Understandings

Family sessions involving one of the parents (and possibly his or her new partner) and the children are organized around how to help the lives of the children work best in each household. These meetings also focus on helping to structure clear boundaries that limit the content of conversations about what is occurring in the other household.[9] In cases where children and a parent have high levels of conflict, meetings between that parent and child focus on reducing the level of conflict.

Working with the Judicial System

Families in the midst of disputes over child custody and visitation live with the legal system. It is a rare week when there is no direct contact with lawyers or the court. In IMFT-DCCV, therapists work closely with lawyers and judges to understand what is transpiring within the judicial process and to help the court understand the therapy. In working in concert, court appearances can be anticipated in therapy, and ways of dealing with these events developed to minimize the trauma that occurs around these events. Attorneys for the children, in particular, typically welcome such coordination and are prepared to actively intervene to support the therapy process. Attorneys for the parents, and the court, also frequently

---

[8] Again, such a reattribution is not therapeutic if the parent in question continues to present dangers for children; in that case, the focus must be on helping that parent to become less dangerous and helping the other parent and children to differentiate between which behaviors present threats and which do not.

[9] When there are concerns about behavior that endangers children, physically or psychologically, these avenues for sharing are left open, despite the difficulties entailed. To mitigate the potential problem of triangulation, the therapist also offers himself or herself as an alternative; someone the children can talk to about their concerns.

are prepared to provide such support. Coordination with attorneys and the court needs to be especially close when issues present as to the necessity for supervision of visitation, the initiation or discontinuation of visitation, or when children manifest parental alienation.

Interventions Utilized when Suggested by the Assessment

IMFT-DCCV also includes a number of intervention strategies that are not utilized in every case, but reserved for situations where the assessment points to a special need for these strategies.

Catharsis

Family members in these cases typically feel traumatized and injured. Many of these families have histories of violence, abuse, infidelity, and betrayal (Johnston & Campbell, 1988). When affects are so charged, therapy must attend to these powerful feelings and the accompanying attachment injuries. When client feelings are so charged, clients are given opportunities to vent; times where the therapist can bear witness to the power of those feelings. Individual sessions provide the best format for such sharing, where the expression of feeling is not contaminated by engendering further conflict. The client's anger and feelings of hurt can be brought into focus, leading to the possibility that an agenda might form for the client to master her or his feelings of hurt and anger (Greenberg & Paivio, 1997).

Anger Management

Anger management skills are taught when the assessment suggests that a parent or child has difficulty in modulating his or her anger. Anger management may involve learning to control indirect forms of provocation, such as passive-aggressive action, as well as angry outbursts.

When one or both partners present with histories of violence, special measures are introduced to minimize the contact between the parents, in and out of sessions. In these cases, there may be no meetings involving both parents. The therapist also works with the court to ensure the safety of children in situations where they are at risk.

Working with Significant Child Difficulties

When there are significant symptoms in a child or when there is evidence of parental alienation syndrome (Gardner, 1998, 1999, 2002), the work with that child becomes more intense. When children are symptomatic, treatment incorporates specific interventions aimed at ameliorating those problems, as well as efforts to coordinate parenting in relation to those problems. When it appears clear that these problems require more attention, referral is made for child therapy.

When children manifest parental alienation (Gardner, 2002), intense work with each subsystem aims at changing the powerful beliefs underlying this difficulty. Meetings with the child involved begin with the child's sharing his or her experiences and beliefs; followed by a supportive effort to help the child examine the basis for those beliefs. Meetings between the child and alienated parent similarly center first on the sharing of feeling, followed by efforts to problem solve and address the blocks to relationship. Work with the alienated parent alone aims at helping build that parent's understanding of behaviors that may contribute to the problem. Treatment sessions work to build enough of a parent-child alliance and enough of a quid pro quo between the parents so that visits, and their aftermath, can help enable attachment rather than promote further alienation.

Working with Extended Family

The extended families and new partners of parents also can have immense influence in these disputes (Johnston & Campbell, 1986). When these families of origin and/or partners have a powerful role in the conflict, sessions with these family members are held with the parent present attempting to bring them into the solution process. If families, after such efforts at intervention, still continue to fuel conflict, the focus of the therapy shifts to how the parent can better deal with the feelings of his or her family.

Exploration of Individual Issues

At times, progress can only be made with substantial work by one or both parents surrounding substantial issues of character, personality, or psychopathology. When this is the case, referral is made for individual therapy, specifically focused around the presenting set of issues. The goal of this therapy is not long-term change in personality, but instead to change as directly as possible those behaviors that appear to block progress, such as substance abuse or paranoid traits.

GENERAL CONSIDERATIONS ABOUT TREATMENT

The Timing of Interventions

The sequence for strategies of intervention is not invariantly prescribed in IMFT-DCCV. Strategies and sequence of intervention are adapted to the specific case, based on the assessment of that case and which intervention strategies prove to be most effective. However, there are some guidelines for when to do what. The therapeutic contract is negotiated in the first session with each parent, and a brief preliminary assessment is conducted over the first few meetings. Alliance building assumes central importance early in treatment, with considerable opportunities for the sharing of beliefs and affects. Psychoeducational and reattribution interventions almost invariably follow this period of alliance building. Meetings in which there are negotiations between parents are reserved for later; after the alliance with each partner has an opportunity to grow and after enough other positive change has preceded these sessions creating the possibility of a positive (if challenging) experience.

Meetings early in the treatment are held with each parent alone, each parent with children, and with the children. Although each session format continues to be utilized to some extent over the course of the therapy, the distribution of the session formats flows from the ever evolving blueprint suggesting the proximate goals of therapy.

Responding to Resistance

The preceding description of direct interventions aimed at behavior change should not be taken to suggest that change occurs in an easy and stepwise fashion in these cases. Typically clients respond to directives with considerable resistance. They typically want to refocus on their upset with the behavior of other family members, not on what they can do to improve the situation. Therefore, intervention with these families must focus considerable attention on recognizing signs of resistance, and intervening to minimize the forces working against change. Following Pinsof's (1995) problem-centered tenet, when significant resistance is encountered and an intervention strategy is not leading to treatment progress, the therapist alters the intervention strategy. This refocusing may involve reframing the therapy task in a more palatable way to make it more acceptable, exploring what lies beneath the resistance, or simply changing the intervention strategy.

The Open-Ended Strategy

IMFT-DCCV impacts substantially on the problems in these families, but rarely are the problems fully resolved after the 20 to 30 sessions of therapy that are typical. In that time, the treatment usually positively impacts on the presenting problems, but the future offers endless possibilities for the renewal of conflict, as children develop and new, potential issues emerge. In public health terms, disputes over child custody and visitation easily become a chronic condition. Therefore, in IMFT-DCCV, intervention is framed as not only dealing with the immediate presenting problem, but also as creating a vehicle that can be utilized to prevent and ameliorate future conflicts. Ideally, a return to therapy is written into divorce or postdivorce decrees as the first source of help when conflicts arise. Typically, courts regularly insist on some therapy around issues before being willing to reengage around further conflicts between parties. IMFT-DCCV works to reduce conflicts as much as possible in the context of short-term therapy, while creating a vehicle for further intervention when needed over time. The working assumption in IMFT-DCCV is that once a problem over child custody and visitation emerges, the likelihood of the return of related difficulties is high, even when intervention is successful. Therefore, at termination, a plan is formed for clients to return if problems begin to reemerge—before deep wounds are reopened.

Role of the Therapist

treatment of families manifesting child custody and visitation disputes is among the most stressful contexts for therapy. Therapists working with this population need to develop strong support systems, both in the therapy and legal communities. Beyond acquiring the requisite therapy skills, therapists need to learn how to comfortably interface with the judicial system and how to work with these families without burnout. They also must work assiduously for clarity as to their role in these cases, avoiding problematic dual relationships and fully understanding relevant professional guidelines (Greenberg & Gould, 2001). Therapists must become conversant with the ethical issues that emerge in work with these cases and the special ethical dilemmas and identity issues posed in working with cases that are also actively engaged in the judicial system (2001).

──────────────── Case Study ────────────────

Nancy and Steve had a cordial coparenting relationship during first 2 years following their separation. With the help of their lawyers, they formed a joint parenting agreement that gave them joint custody of their children Tim, age 6, and George, age 4. The children lived with Nancy during the week, visiting every other weekend and one night a week with Steve. They also arrived at a cooperative financial settlement, and divorced without much acrimony. In the first year after their divorce, they communicated frequently about the children and made decisions together about their schooling.

Nonetheless, difficulties developed when Nancy entered into a new relationship with Mark. Within one month of the time they began to date, Mark began to spend most of the time he was not working in Nancy's home. Mark was a blue-collar man who had dropped out of high school. Mark's personality was abrasive and outspoken. He was very unlike Steve, who was college educated and passive. Mark took the children to wrestling matches, would show them injuries he had gotten in fights, and would roughhouse with them each evening. Mark also frequently became angry, sometimes yelling at the top of his lungs in the home.

Tim and George became afraid of Mark, and carried this fear to their father. Steve shared his worries about Mark with Nancy, but Nancy told Steve that what Mark did was none of his business. Steve and Nancy began to argue regularly about these reports. The conflict escalated when Tim sprained his wrist while wrestling with Mark. Tim told Steve that Mark had become red-faced, and twisted his arm to the point where he thought it would fall off. Mark went back to his attorney, initiated an investigation by the local child protective services, and petitioned the court for Mark to be barred from the house, and for sole custody of the children. This set off a cycle of accusations and counter-accusations. Nancy filed a petition alleging neglect, because Steve would leave the children with his sister during some of his visitations. Steve filed to reduce child support due to Mark's presence in Nancy's home.

After innumerable court appearances and a failed effort at mediation, the children's attorney in the case referred the family for therapy. With my input, a court order was structured that mandated the participation of the parents, the children, and of Mark in the therapy. Because participation in therapy was a central concern of the court, as in many of these cases, all parties were fully cooperative with scheduling sessions once the order was entered.

The therapy began with an individual meeting with each of the parents. During these meetings, I listened to each of their narratives about the events that had been occurring, and outlined the therapeutic contract. All the parties would be involved in treatment. A schedule for the first few meetings was agreed, and I let them know about how the plan was likely to evolve over time. I described the ways information would be shared with the attorney for the children, their attorneys, and the court, and had the parents sign appropriate releases for this sharing of information.

The initial meetings with each parent were followed in short order by two meetings with the children and a meeting with Nancy, Mark, and the children. The primary goals for these initial meetings were to build an alliance with each of the parties, and problem assessment. It was strikingly easy to build a therapeutic alliance with Nancy and Steve. Both were very frustrated with their present circumstance and saw therapy as a place to vent their feelings and to gain support for their view of the conflict. Nancy and Steve were each in the precontemplative stage in assessing their roles in creating and maintaining the problem, but each were open to participating in therapy sessions. The children were also highly cooperative, if only to be able to reiterate the viewpoint they shared with their father about Mark. They repeated the history of their interactions with Mark much as Steve had related it, and expressed the desire to spend less time with Mark and have him be less angry. Mark was much more difficult to engage. He feared that the treatment process would be used against him. He obviously was only participating because of the court order and the considerable pressure that Nancy was putting on him to support her in her case.

My initial assessment was that Mark did not appear to present an ongoing physical threat to the children. The investigations by the child protective agency had judged the allegations of abuse to be unfounded. Moreover, in hearing about the injuries the children had suffered, these injuries seemed to be much more the result of an adult who was trying to be playful and did not fully understand the impact of his size and strength, rather than of physical abuse. Mark was actually in a process of building an attachment with the children that was easily observed when we had a session with Nancy, Mark, and the children. Nonetheless, it was equally clear that the relationship between Mark and Nancy posed considerable challenges for the children and father. Nancy had allowed Mark to move into the children's lives with the privileges of a parent before the children were ready to accept him in this role. Clearly, this also engaged profound feelings of loss and displacement on the part of Steve. Furthermore, Mark's temper presented a special problem, and Mark's ways were very different from anyone else in the family.

After these initial sessions I felt I had enough information to form an initial assessment. This assessment became the basis for the creation of a set of proximate and ultimate goals and a specific treatment plan for this family. At the systems level, there was a need to calm the frequent crises and break the circular chains of accusation and counter-accusation that were being unleashed. In turn, this depended on being able to create a mutual understanding about the next phase of life, in which there would be relationships with new partners, particularly in terms of how the children would be parented. To achieve this goal, Mark's behavior would need to be tempered, the children would need to build a trusting relationship with Mark, the parents would need to establish good-enough communication about these issues, Steve would need to process the changes occurring as less threatening, and Steve and the children would need to find ways to deal with the changes occurring other than engage in the triangulation pattern that was evident.

Since Mark's individual behavior played such a key role in the problem, and because the alliance with Mark in the therapy seemed as if it would benefit from more meetings with him, one initial proximate goal focused on building an alliance with Mark and having him begin to work on his aggressive behavior. Engaging Mark in therapy (at first with Nancy and ultimately in individual sessions) and in constructively working at his behavior, turned out to be much easier than one might have thought. Mark was a boisterous man, who, although he responded to directives with opposition, was highly cooperative when he felt understood. He saw himself as wanting to have a positive impact on the lives of Nancy and the children. His patterns of behavior with the children mostly represented his way of trying to get closer, and he had no trouble identifying a general problem with expressing of anger. Mark also was troubled by the ongoing conflict between Nancy and Steve, which was requiring a good deal of his time and his money. It helped that in my assessment I did not view Mark as the risk that Steve's attorneys had portrayed him as being. My relationship with his attorney also helped; he assured Mark that he would be fairly treated.

I was able to refocus Mark on his need to build his relationship with the children. Letting him know I thought he was not dangerous, but was rough for these children (my actual assessment, not a vacuous reframe), helped him engage in learning to develop better control over his behavior. He grasped that he was very different from anyone else who had spent time with these children, and how this presented issues for the children. He also understood that he had trouble controlling his anger. Mark agreed to work on anger management in individual sessions, and on setting rules governing his interactions with the children in sessions with Nancy and the children.

Mark, Nancy, and the children were seen for two family sessions that were focused on clarifying expectations about discipline and structuring a system of reward and punishment in relation to the children's behavior. Corporal punishment was clearly placed out of bounds.

Intermixed with these sessions, I met with Steve alone. I worked with Steve to help him take in the reattribution I offered about Mark's behavior: that he was rough but not dangerous. I described the circular causal chains that become unleashed in situations like this one, and tried to help him consider the possibility that what he had seen was a worst-case scenario. I also shared how I thought the children had been caught up in the difficulty because of their own complex feelings, and how we might move toward a more calming circular path of mutual reassurance. Steve was not convinced that Mark was safe for the children. The first time the reframe about Mark's behavior was raised Steve showed little change in his attitude. However, he trusted that I had his interests and those of the children in mind, and was calmed by the thought that I would be working with Mark on his behavior. With time, and no further incidents, Steve was able to accept the reframe about Mark, and that changes were occurring.

During two meetings with the children, interspersed with the other sessions, I focused on giving them an opportunity to speak their concerns and helping them grasp the changes toward which the treatment was aiming. The children showed a good deal of relief about the changes that were occurring. Just after these sessions with the children, in brief meetings between each parent and the children, we also developed guidelines for under what conditions it was appropriate and when not to talk about one parent with the other.

Two meetings were then held between Steve and Nancy, focused on rebuilding constructive communication between the parents. Convened at a point of there being some constructive possibilities for success, these meetings proved quite productive. These sessions produced an agreement about when to communicate about various issues to each other, and marked a return to better communication about matters such as illnesses and joint decision making, when needed. Building on their prior positive history of postseparation cooperation, they were able to go beyond the disengagement and mutual tolerance, which are more typical goals in disputes over child custody and visitation.

Significantly, after 3 months of treatment, the petitions in court for change of custody and residence filed by the father were withdrawn. Not only did this mark the success of the intervention, it also had a salutary effect on the process in these families. Mark even continued his work with me on his anger management for several months on an intermittent basis, extending his focus to situations that extended beyond the family. Anecdotal 2-year follow-up from reports from the clients and attorneys indicates the therapy successfully resolved the crisis, and moved the parties on to a life with minimal contact between the parents, yet with good-enough coparenting to allow for the children's development.

Evaluation of the Treatment

Integrative Multilevel Family Therapy for Disputes Involving Child Custody and Visitation is a treatment developed specifically for dealing with conflicts over child custody and visitation. It has been applied in over one hundred cases with considerable success. As yet, there is no outcome data assessing the efficacy of this method, but the outcomes attained in a number of clinical cases look promising. Although there are as yet no outcome data about this approach, it is grounded in the research describing typical challenges in divorce (Hetherington et al., 1993), characteristics and dynamics of this population (Johnston, 1994), effective treatments for high conflict (Christensen & Jacobson, 2000), and intervention strategies demonstrated to be effective in couples and families (Lebow & Gurman, 1995).

REFERENCES

Ackerman, M. J. (2001). *Clinician's guide to child custody evaluations* (2nd ed.). New York: Wiley.

Ackerman, M. J., & Ackerman, M. C. (1997). Custody evaluation practices: A survey of experienced professionals (revisited). *Professional Psychology—Research and Practice, 28,* 137–145.

Ackerman, M. J., & Ackerman, M. C. (1999). Custody evaluation practices: A survey of experienced professionals (revisited); notice of clarification to Ackerman and Ackerman (1997) article. *Professional Psychology—Research and Practice, 30,* 210–212.

Ahrons, C. (1994). *The good divorce.* New York: HarperCollins.

Alexander, J., Waldon, H. B., Newberry, A. M., & Liddle, N. (1990). The functional family therapy model. In A. S. Friedman & S. Granick (Eds.). *Family therapy for adolescent drug abuse* (pp. 183–199). Lexington, MA: Lexington Books/D. C. Heath.

Amato, P. R. (1993). Family structure, family process, and family ideology. *Journal of Marriage and the Family, 55,* 187–192.

Amato, P. R. (1994). Life-span adjustment of children to their parents' divorce. *Future of Children, 4,* 143–164.

Amato, P. R. (2001). Children of divorce in the 1990s: An update of the Amato and Keith (1991) meta-analysis. *Journal of Family Psychology, 15,* 23–38.

Beck, A. T., & Freeman, A. M. (1990). *Cognitive therapy of personality disorders.* New York: Guilford.

Boszormenyi-Nagy, I. (1974). Ethical and practical implications of intergenerational family therapy. *Psychotherapy and Psychosomatics, 24,* 4–6.

Braver, S. L., & Griffin, W. A. (2000). Engaging fathers in the post-divorce family. *Marriage and Family Review, 29,* 247–267.

Bricklin, B. (1995). *The custody evaluation handbook: Research-based solutions and applications.* Philadelphia: Brunner/Mazel.

Buchanan, C. M., Maccoby, E. E., & Dornbusch, S. M. (1966). *Adolescents after divorce.* Cambridge: Harvard University Press.

Campbell, L. E., & Johnston, J. R. (1986a). Impasse-directed mediation with high conflict families in custody disputes. *Behavioral Sciences and the Law, 4.*

Campbell, L. E., & Johnston, J. R. (1986b). Multifamily mediation: The use of groups to resolve child custody disputes. *Mediation Quarterly,*

Christensen, A., & Jacobson, N. S. (2000). *Reconcilable differences.* New York: Guilford.

Combs, G., & Freedman, J. (1990). *Symbol, story, and ceremony: Using metaphor in individual and family therapy.* New York: Norton.

Doolittle, D. B., & Deutsch, R. (1999). Children and high-conflict divorce: Theory, research, and intervention. In R. M. Galatzer-Levy & L. Kraus (Eds.), *The scientific basis of child custody decisions* (pp. 425–440). New York: Wiley.

Duncan, B. L., Hubble, M. A., & Miller, S. D. (1997). *Psychotherapy with 'impossible' cases: The efficient treatment of therapy veterans.* New York: Norton.

Emery, R. E. (1994). *Renegotiating family relationships: Divorce, child custody, and mediation.* New York: Guilford.

Emery, R. E. (1999). *Marriage, divorce, and children's adjustment* (2nd ed.). Thousand Oaks, CA: Sage.

Emery, R. E., Kitzmann, K. M., & Waldron, M. (1999). Psychological interventions for separated and divorced families. In E. M. Hetherington (Ed.), *Coping with divorce, single parenting, and remarriage: A risk and resiliency perspective* (pp. 323–344). Mahwah, NJ: Erlbaum.

Fincham, F. D., Grych, J. H., & Osborne, L. N. (1994). Does marital conflict cause child maladjustment? Directions and challenges for longitudinal research. *Journal of Family Psychology, 8,* 176–189.

Folberg, J. (Ed.). (1991). *Joint custody and shared parenting* (2nd ed.). New York: Guilford.

Folberg, J., & Milne, A. (Eds.). (1988). *Divorce mediation: Theory and practice.* New York: Guilford.

Galatzer-Levy, R. M., & Kraus, L. (Eds.). (1999). *The scientific basis of child custody decisions.* New York: Wiley.

Gardner, R. A. (1998). The parental alienation syndrome: What is it and what data support it?: Comment. *Child Maltreatment: Journal of the American Professional Society on the Abuse of Children, 3,* 120–127.

Gardner, R. A. (1999). Differentiating between parental alienation syndrome and bona fide abuse-neglect. *American Journal of Family Therapy, 27,* 97–107.

Gardner, R. A. (2002). Parental alienation syndrome versus parental alienation: Which diagnosis should evaluators use in child-custody disputes? *American Journal of Family Therapy, 30,* 101–123.

Gould, J. W. (1998). *Conducting scientifically crafted child custody evaluations.* Thousand Oaks, CA: Sage.

Gould, J. W. (1999). Scientifically crafted child custody evaluations: Part one: A model for interdisciplinary collaboration in the development of psychological questions guiding court-ordered child custody evaluations. *Family and Conciliation Courts Review, 37,* 181–187.

Gould, J. W., & Stahl, P. M. (2000). The art and science of child custody evaluations: Integrating clinical and forensic mental health models. *Family and Conciliation Courts Review, 38,* 92–103.

Greenberg, L. S., & Paivio, S. C. (1997). *Working with emotions in psychotherapy.* New York: Guilford.

Greenberg, J. W., & Gould, J. W. (2001). The treating expert. *Professional Psychology, 32,* 469–478.

Grych, J. H., & Fincham, F. D. (1990). Marital conflict and children's adjustment: A cognitive-contextual framework. *Psychological Bulletin, 108,* 267–290.

Grych, J. H., & Fincham, F. D. (1999). The adjustment of children from divorced families: Implications of empirical research for clinical intervention. In R. M. Galatzer-Levy & L. Kraus (Eds.), *The scientific basis of child custody decisions* (pp. 96–119). New York: Wiley.

Grych, J. H., Fincham, F. D., Jouriles, E. N., & McDonald, R. (2000). Interparental conflict and child adjustment: Testing the mediational role of appraisals in the cognitive-contextual framework. *Child Development, 71,* 1648–1661.

Hetherington, E. M., Law, T. C., & O'Connor, T. G. (1993). Divorce: Challenges, changes, and new chances. In F. Walsh (Ed.). *Normal family processes* (2nd ed.). (pp. 208–234). New York: Guilford.

Hetherington, E. M., Stanley-Hagan, M., & Anderson, E. R. (1989). Marital transitions: A child's perspective. *American Psychologist, 44,* 303–312.

Hooper, J. (1993). The rhetoric of motives in divorce. *Journal of Marriage and the Family, 55,* 801–813.

Jenuwine, M. J., & Cohler, B. J. (1999). Major parental psychology and child custody. In R. M. Galatzer-Levy & L. Kraus (Eds.), *The scientific basis of child custody decisions* (pp. 285–318). New York: Wiley.

Johnston, J. R. (1993). Children of divorce who refuse visitation. In C. E. Depner & J. H. Bray (Eds.), *Nonresidential parenting: New vistas in family living* (pp. 109–135). Thousand Oaks, CA: Sage.

Johnston, J. R. (1994). High-conflict divorce. *Future of Children, 4,* 165–182.

Johnston, J. R., & Campbell, L. E. (1986). Tribal warfare: The involvement of extended kin and significant others in custody and access disputes. *Conciliation Courts Review, 24,* 67–74.

Johnston, J. R., & Campbell, L. E. G. (1988). *Impasses of divorce: The dynamics and resolution of family conflict.* New York: The Free Press.

Johnston, J. R., & Campbell, L. E. G. (1993). A clinical typology of interparental violence in disputed-custody divorces. *American Journal of Orthopsychiatry, 63,* 190–199.

Johnston, J. R., Campbell, L. E., & Tall, M. C. (1985). Impasses to the resolution of custody and visitation disputes. *American Journal of Orthopsychiatry, 55,* 112–129.

Johnston, J. R., Kline, M., & Tschann, J. M. (1989). Ongoing postdivorce conflict: Effects on children of joint custody and frequent access. *American Journal of Orthopsychiatry, 59,* 576–592.

Johnston, J. R., & Roseby, V. (1997). *In the name of the child: A developmental approach to understanding and helping children of conflicted and violent divorce.* New York: The Free Press.

Keslow, F. W. (1996). *Handbook of relational diagnosis and dysfunctional family patterns.* New York: Wiley.

Lebow, J. (1997). The integrative revolution in couple and family therapy. *Family Process, 36,* 1–17.

Lebow, J., & Gurman, A. S. (1995). Research assessing couple and family therapy. *Annual Review of Psychology, 46,* 27–57.

Lebow, J., Walsh, F., & Rolland, J. (1999). The remarriage family in custody evaluation. In R. M. Galatzer-Levy & L. Kraus (Eds.), *The scientific basis of child custody decisions,* (pp. 236–256). New York: Wiley.

Maccoby, E. E., Depner, C. E., & Mnookin, R. H. (1990). Coparenting in the second year after divorce. *Journal of Marriage and the Family, 52,* 256–272.

Milne, A., & Folberg, J. (1988). The theory and practice of divorce mediation: An overview. In J. Folberg & A. Milne (Eds.), *Divorce mediation: Theory and practice* (pp. 3–25). New York: Guilford.

Nichols, M. P., & Schwartz, R. C. (1998). *Family therapy: Concepts and methods* (4th ed.). Needham Heights, MA: Allyn & Bacon.

Orlinsky, D. E. & Howard, K. I. (1987). A generic model of psychotherapy. *Journal of Integrative and Eclectic Psychotherapy, 6,* 6–27.

Pedro-Caroll, J. L., Allport-Gillis, L. J. & Cowen, E. I. (1992). An evolution of the efficacy of a preventive intervention for 4th and 5th grade children of divorce. *Journal of Primary Prevention, 13,* 115–130.

Pinsof, W. M. (1983). Integrative problem-centered therapy: Toward the synthesis of family and individual psychotherapies. *Journal of Marital and Family Therapy, 9,* 19–35.

Pinsof, W. M. (1995). *Integrative problem centered therapy.* New York: Basic Books.

Prochaska, J. O., & DiClemente, C. C. (1982). Transtheoretical therapy: Toward a more integrative model of change. *Psychotherapy: Theory, Research and Practice, 19,* 45–52.

Prochaska, J. O., Johnson, S., & Lee, P. (1998). The transtheoretical model of behavior change. In S. A. Shumaker & E. B. Schron J. K. Okene & W. L. McBee (Eds.), *The handbook of health behavior change* (2nd ed.; pp. 59–84). New York: Springer.

Renick, M. J., Blumberg, S. L., & Markman, H. J. (1992). The Prevention and Relationship Enhancement (PREP): An empirically based preventive intervention program for couples. *Family Relations: Journal of Applied Family and Child Studies, 41,* 141–147.

Wallerstein, J. S. (1998). Children of divorce: A society in search of policy. In M. A. Mason & A. Skolnick (Eds.), *All our families: New policies for a new century* (pp. 66–94). New York: Oxford University Press.

Walsh, F. (1991). Promoting healthy functioning in divorced and remarried families. In A. S. Gurman & D. P. Kniskern (Eds.), *Handbook of family therapy: Vol. 2.* (pp. 525–545). Philadelphia: Brunner/Mazel.

Walsh, F. (1998). *Strengthening family resilience.* New York: Guilford.

Walsh, F., Jacob, L., & Simons, V. (1995). Facilitating healthy divorce processes: Therapy and mediation approaches. In N. S. Jacobson & A. S. Gurman (Eds.), *Clinical handbook of couple therapy* (pp. 340–365). New York: Guilford.

Wolchik, S. A., Ruehlman, L. S., Braver, S. L., & Sandler, I. N. (1989). Social support of children of divorce: Direct and stress buffering effects. *American Journal of Community Psychology, 17,* 485–501.

CHAPTER 21

Differentiation and Dialogue in Intergenerational Relationships

Mona DeKoven Fishbane

THE PROBLEM AREA

This chapter addresses therapy with adult clients who experience distress in relationships with their family of origin, especially with their parents. Some people seek out this work directly, to improve or repair family relationships. For example, a client may call wanting to deal with unfinished business with an aging parent; adult siblings may seek help for tensions in their relationship; a parent and adult child may come together to resolve old issues. A family crisis, such as a death, illness, or other life cycle transition may precipitate the decision to seek therapy. Alternatively, this work may emerge more indirectly; in the midst of couple, individual, or family therapy, difficulties in the family of origin that are impacting the presenting problem or current relationships may become apparent.

Intergenerational family therapists have long noted that unfinished business in the family of origin affects individuals and their relationships for generations. Hidden legacies, loyalties, and secrets can haunt families in countless ways. Seemingly unrelated presenting problems, such as marital discord, depression, self-esteem problems, or difficulties managing relationships with children may reflect ongoing tensions with family-of-origin relationships. This can take the form of current tensions, for example, with parents or in-laws, or of inner struggles rooted in intergenerational relationships in the past. Adults may be stuck in either overaccommodating positions or resentful, blaming positions with their parents. Distressed contact with family of origin ranges from intensely involved to highly conflictual to distant, even cut-off relationships. The approach presented here addresses these dilemmas, and offers a path to more authentic relating and dialogue in family-of-origin relationships, especially between adult children and their parents. This type of therapy is particularly relevant with clients who carry a burden of resentment toward their parents. The clinical work usually is with the adult child directly; sometimes a mother or father is invited to a session with the client. In other cases the entire therapy includes both parents and adult child, and/or siblings. With divorce and remarriage, step-relations may also be addressed. Whether the work is conducted with one or more clients, a family systems lens is utilized in the therapy. As Bowen (1978), Lerner (1985), Szapocznik, Kurtines, Foote, Perez-Vidal, & Hervis, (1983) and others have observed, one person changing his or her part in the relational dance can be transformative for both the client and the family system. It is in this spirit that we explore facilitating both differentiation and dialogue between adult clients and their families of origin.

THE ROOTS OF THE TREATMENT APPROACH: A RELATIONAL, MULTIGENERATIONAL PERSPECTIVE

This chapter integrates the intergenerational insights and techniques of Bowen coaching (Bowen, 1978; Kerr & Bowen, 1988; Lerner, 1985; McGoldrick, 1995; McGoldrick & Carter, 2001), contextual therapy (Boszormenyi-Nagy, Grunebaum, & Ulrich, 1991), and the work of Framo (1976). These authors and others have demonstrated how important and clinically effective reworking relationships with one's family of origin can be; increasing differentiation of self within the family of origin and coming to a place of systemic understanding and reconciliation with family members may be more transformative than years of long-term individual psychotherapy. The theory and practice offered here build on the considerable contributions of these intergenerational theorists. This chapter is also informed by the relational theory of Jordan, Kaplan, Miller, Stiver, & Surrey (1991), which has conceptualized the individual as a self-in-relation, offering an alternative to the narrative of the separate, autonomous self which predominates in our culture and in much psychotherapy (see also Carter & McGoldrick, 1999; Fishbane, 2001; and Walsh, 1998). Relational theory highlights connection and interdependence as central features of human development and identity. The therapy described here is influenced as well by narrative and social constructionist theories, which consider the self as socially constituted, and challenge dominant cultural discourses around power and autonomy (White, 1989; McNamee & Gergen, 1992). Finally, this work is informed by the philosophy of Martin Buber, especially his insights about facilitating dialogical, I-Thou relationships, in contrast to objectifying, I-It relationships.

Intergenerational Narratives: Cultural Assumptions

Many systemic and intergenerational theorists have challenged Anglo-American cultural assumptions about autonomy, independence, and separation as the goals of adult development. The emphasis on individualism and the "self-made man" has been reflected in traditional individual psychotherapies that valorize personal autonomy at the expense of family connection; these therapies often entail parent-blaming, especially mother-bashing. Some psychodynamic theories have posited a rejection of parents in the turmoil of adolescence as part of normal development. Correspondingly, much individual therapy of adolescents and young adults maintains a pathologizing view of parents, often leaving clients holding a blaming, angry stance toward their parents.

By contrast, research on normal adolescent development has shown that most adolescents want to stay connected with and be understood by their parents, even as the relationship changes and the adolescent differentiates (Apter, 2004; Offer & Sabshin, 1984). In keeping with this finding, many family therapists work to facilitate parent-adolescent child dialogue; Weingarten's (1994) work on "mutual knowing" between adolescents and their parents is an example of this approach. Intergenerational theories, as well as more recent relational psychodynamic approaches, emphasize interdependence rather than independence as a developmental goal throughout the life cycle (Carter & McGoldrick, 1999; Stolorow & Atwood, 1992). Indeed, research on healthy intergenerational relationships identifies an ongoing connection between adult children and their parents (Fingerman, 2003; Galatzer-Levy & Cohler, 1993). Both the resilience-based approach of Walsh (1998) and contextual theory focus on strengths and "resources of trustworthiness" (Boszormenyi-Nagy & Ulrich, 1981), not just pathology, in families.

The contextual theory of Boszormenyi-Nagy and his colleagues highlights intergenerational processes of filial loyalty and obligation. According to this view, adult children owe their parents filial loyalty for the care the parents gave them over the years. If an adult son or daughter does not find a constructive way to repay that debt, through connection and care as the parent ages, contextual theory predicts that the individual will become mired in "invisible loyalty" (Boszormenyi-Nagy and Spark, 1973), living out a negative tie to parents in other areas of the adult child's life. Examples of invisible loyalty might include becoming reactive to one's spouse or children if they exhibit characteristics similar to one's parents; becoming like the parent in a negative way, for example, depressed or anxious; or looking to one's children to heal wounds from the family of origin.

In this contextual view, finding a way to express healthy filial loyalty to one's parents as they age is an important developmental task of the adult. In an introduction to a book about contextual theory, van Kilsdonk (1987) contrasts the myth of Aeneas with the myth of Oedipus. While the Oedipal myth, especially as taken up by Freud, emphasizes individual passion and competition, the Aeneas myth highlights intergenerational care and concern. Aeneas, fleeing burning Troy with his wife and young son, carries his blind, crippled father Anchises on his shoulders. The Aeneas story reflects the stage of adult development in which caring for elders and finding a way to honor them is considered a core task of the healthy individual.

Expectations of what is normal in adult child-parent relationships vary with different cultures; the value of honoring parents and elders is central in most traditional cultures, but is less the norm in the dominant Anglo-American culture. What one culture may consider enmeshed may be appropriate closeness in another culture. While enmeshment can occur to a pathological extent in relationships, the therapist must use caution in assessing this and other factors that are culture-specific. Balancing personal autonomy with loyalty to parents and family of origin differs among ethnic and cultural groups. Therapists, and clients as well, informed by the dominant discourse of separation and autonomy, may pathologize intergenerational loyalties and overlook resources within the family of origin.

Many cultures assume a normative reciprocity between the generations. Caregiving and generosity from parent to young child is transformed during the life cycle as both parents and children age, to a mutuality of care and concern. Ultimately, the roles may reverse as the adult child cares for the frail, elderly parent. Framo (1976, p. 198) suggests that "one of the deepest motives of people is to rescue or save parents." I have termed this "the protective urge," the instinct to protect and care for those we love, including our parents. While this can become distorted into parentification of the child, a healthy balance of give and take is a goal of intergenerational therapy (Boszormenyi-Nagy & Krasner, 1986). The negative side of a client's ambivalent feelings toward parents is often the focus of individual therapy. Contextual and intergenerational theories address the positive or protective side of the adult child's ambivalence as well.

The therapeutic techniques presented in this chapter build on contextual and resilience-based theory. Rather than viewing parents as toxic influences to be discarded, managed, or kept at a distance, this approach looks for the potential resources of trustworthiness in the parent-adult child relationship and other relationships in the family of origin. The therapy encourages a collaborative, respectful, dialogical relationship, both between therapist and client and between client and his or her family of origin.

Differentiation and Dialogue

Intergenerational family therapists coach clients to take differentiated positions with family-of-origin members. McGoldrick & Carter (2001, p. 289) define the process of differentiating: "It consists of developing personal and authentic emotionally engaged relationships with each member of the family and changing one's part in the old repetitious, dysfunctional emotional patterns to the point at which one is able to state, calmly and nonreactively, one's personal view of important emotional issues, regardless of who is for or against such a view. It involves learning to see your parents as the human beings they are or were, rather than as your 'inadequate parents', and relating to them with respect and generosity." Bowen coaching stresses the need for the individual to determine his or her own identity and boundaries vis-à-vis the family of origin, and to be able to connect with family members in a differentiated and respectful manner.

Contextual theory focuses on the obligations and balance of fairness in family life. Boszormenyi-Nagy and Spark (1973) propose the term "relational autonomy," which includes the capacity to think of the relational consequences of one's actions. Boszormenyi-Nagy was influenced by Buber, who emphasized the relational potential of persons in his articulation of the I-Thou (or I-You) relationship: "The I of the basic word I-You is different from that of the basic word I-It. The I of the basic word I-It appears as an ego. . . . The I of the basic word I-You appears as a person. . . . Egos appear by setting themselves apart from other egos. Persons appear by entering into relation to other persons" (Buber, 1970, pp. 111–112). The "person" in Buber's view is sufficiently differentiated that he or she can enter into dialogue with an other; reciprocal, genuine dialogue facilitates the differentiation of the self. The nuances of autonomy and relation, of differentiation and dialogue in intergenerational relationships, will be apparent in the clinical and theoretical discussions below. The premises informing this work are that identity and change are relational processes, and that both differentiation and dialogue between the generations are key for personal and family transformation.

INTERVENTION STRATEGIES

Clinical Challenges in Working with Clients "Under the Spell of Childhood"

Clients often describe their feelings about their parents in conflicted, resentful terms. An adult child may carry a sense of victimization from childhood, and may become stuck in blame in relation to parents. This is, of course, most dramatic when there was serious abuse or neglect; but even in families with moderate unhappiness, adult children often feel old wounds in the present and seethe with resentment or disappointment. Examples of such wounds include a sense that a parent preferred one sibling over another; parental criticism or perfectionism; parental insensitivity, neglect, or preoccupation with self at the expense of the children. The adult child, haunted by these old or ongoing issues with parents, may feel both helpless and angry in the intergenerational relationship. An individual carrying this chronic sense of blame may attribute significant power to the aging parent. At times, clients are encouraged to invite their parents to a session. From the powers attributed to these parents, the therapist might expect giants to walk into the office. Instead, in comes a little old lady and a stooped, elderly man, burdened with guilt and frightened of the blame they expect to hear from their child. It takes work for the client to see his or her old, vulnerable parent rather than the looming presence of the client's childhood.

When an individual is stuck in anger and blame with parents because of old wounds, and is still somehow hoping that the parent will one day wake up and "get it," becoming the parent the child always wanted, that adult child can be described as living "under the spell of childhood" (Fishbane, 1998). This psychological experience is quite common, even though in actuality the child may now be far taller and more powerful physically, fiscally, and cognitively than the parent. Much of the intergenerational healing work described in this chapter starts with helping the adult child "wake from the spell of childhood." This entails enlarging one's view of parents, coming to see them as distinct human beings, with their own strengths and limitations; it leads to seeing the parent as a "Thou" in Buber's terms. Waking from the spell of childhood also includes taking responsibility for one's own life.

Kohut (1977) has described the mirroring process between parent and young child that is basic to a healthy relational construction of self. In an attuned and affirming relationship, the parent mirrors back to the child aspects of the child's self with admiration and support. Many clients did not experience this attunement. They experienced their parents' mirroring as distorted, based on their parents' needs, or as neglectful or nonexistent. To please parents or to fit into parental expectations, many children deny their own needs or develop a "false self" (Winnicott, 1965). For these individuals, the original mirror was cracked or obscured; in adulthood, they often experience a yearning for the attunement and mirroring they lacked as children. The child may have felt frozen in the parental gaze, unable to grow and develop his or her own capacities.

The adult child may reciprocally view the parent through a distorted lens of anger and reactivity. The need for confirmation, so basic to our human experience

(Buber, 1965), is often frustrated for both offspring and parent, as the adult child "returns the favor" and deals with the parent through a disconfirming, I-It relationship of resentment or distance. Thus, the adult child may not see the parent evolving and dealing with his or her own life journey, separate from the child's expectations and disappointments. Family cutoffs exacerbate this distorted view of parents. When an individual cuts off all contact with parents, the adult child's view of the parents is frozen or crystallized, with no possibility for transformation of the perception or of the relationship.

While living under the spell of childhood, the individual experiences him- or herself as a helpless young child, and the parents as having the power to give or withhold, love or reject, comfort or frighten. The adult child may be hoping to finally get the right "blessing" or affirmation from the parents. Stories of children feeling wronged by parental blessings are at least as old as the biblical narratives of Genesis, in which sibling rivalry or hatred are the result of a parent preferring one child over another. Whatever the childhood wound, the individual living under the spell of childhood often hopes that the mother or father will finally become the parent one needed, or at least apologize for not having been a good parent. But this leaves the adult child in the victim position, giving all power and control to parents. The likelihood of disappointment is high. The individual is caught in a constraining narrative, a victim in his or her own story.

Being stuck in the blame or victim position takes a toll on one's life. Blame tends to beget blame. When persons relate to their parents primarily in a blame mode, they are likely to relate similarly to their partner or children. As we saw above, Buber finds that the "I" that says "It" to another is different from the "I" that says "Thou." The person who is an "It"-sayer with parents will often be an "It"-sayer in other relationships, because that individual has closed his or her mind and heart, and looks with resentful eyes at others (Fishbane, 1998). Carrying a chip on one's shoulders can make one stoop.

Contextual therapists point out that a person who feels like a victim may seek damages, but often at the wrong address—for example, with one's spouse or children. Innocent others are hurt in the process, as the "victim becomes a victimizer" through "a revolving slate of vindictive behavior" (Boszormenyi-Nagy & Ulrich, 1981, p. 167). Thus, the cycle of victimization is perpetuated. For example, a woman who is angry at her father for having been self-centered and unavailable when she was growing up becomes highly reactive to her adolescent son when he becomes distant and self-focused.[1] Prior to his teenage years the boy was close to his mother; she relished the connection, and felt it made up for some of the losses she experienced with her father. She looked to her son to heal her own childhood wounds. Now, rather than seeing her son's adolescent behavior as developmentally appropriate, she sees in him her narcissistic father, and becomes enraged at her son's thoughtlessness. This mother, a victim of her father's limitations, is now unwittingly victimizing her son, unable to guide him through the tumultuous challenges of adolescence or to maintain connection with him as he changes. Her resentment toward her father is echoed in her resentment to her son; through "invisible loy-

---

[1] All case examples are composites, and identifying information has been altered.

alty," she is living out her unresolved relationship with her father in her dealings with her child. The moral and psychological consequences of her unfinished business with her father are carried by her son.

Being mired in resentment with parents may also impair one's self-esteem. The very qualities persons hate in their parents are often the qualities they hate in themselves. (To borrow from a popular book title, this can be termed "My bad mother/My bad self.") For example, a man who blames his father for having been anxious and depressed throughout his childhood, himself becomes anxious and depressed as an adult. This negative identification with parents can be seen as another example of invisible loyalty between child and parent. According to contextual theory, this unconscious, insidious, self-destructive tie to parents becomes unnecessary once a person has loosened the grip of blame, and has found a way to express positive loyalty to parents.

Some adult children decide to "share" with their parents how the parents let them down or hurt them in childhood. This is not an uncommon event in the course of individual psychotherapy. Indeed, many parents, when they hear that their adult child is in therapy, assume that they will be blamed for the child's problems; parents then tend to become anxious, guilty, and defensive. If the child angrily confronts the parents with their flaws, the natural—and understandable—response of the parents is to become self-protective and defensive; to either deny or to counterattack. Some parents can take appropriate responsibility for their mistakes, apologize, and try to make amends. But many, in the face of the onslaught, fall back onto their own self-protective defenses, and are unable to see or hear their adult child as a full person. Such encounters are typified by "I-It" interactions. A vicious cycle of mistrust, blame, and defensiveness is generated. The intergenerational relationship is then fraught with suspicion and mutual recrimination, and becomes stagnant (Boszormenyi-Nagy & Ulrich, 1981).

Individual psychotherapy may exacerbate parent-blaming, if it sets up a loyalty conflict between the "good" therapist and the "bad" parents (Boszormenyi-Nagy & Ulrich, 1981). Therapists who were rescuers in their own families of origin may be especially tempted to "save" the client from the "bad" parents. Some therapists even encourage clients to cut off contact with parents. From a contextual view this is counterproductive and potentially harmful. Ultimately, the forces of family loyalty will prevail, and when the therapist allies with the client against the parents, the therapy will become stalled. What appears to be resistance in therapy is often a subtle expression of invisible loyalty, of the client maintaining ties to parents by not changing. When a client expresses hurt or anger about past or current interactions with his or her parents, the therapist must attend to the concerns and be empathic with the hurt; therapy offers a safe space to witness and work with the client's pain. At the same time, contextual theory holds that the therapist needs to acknowledge the client's attachment to the parents, and, utilizing a systemic view, to try to gain a perspective on the parent's experience as well. This is not to deny or whitewash the client's experience, but rather to hold a larger, intergenerational perspective. Using "multidirected partiality" (Boszormenyi-Nagy & Krasner, 1986), the therapist holds concern for the parent even while the primary focus is on the adult child's experience. Knowing that the therapist won't turn them against their family of origin, clients are often freer to explore their negative as well as positive feelings toward parents.

Many times, children blame themselves when there is unhappiness in the family. A young child needs to make sense of the world; if parents are depressed, alcoholic, abusive, or if they divorce, the child may blame him- or herself for the trouble. Children frequently hold themselves accountable if they have been unable to heal or make their parents happy. Through therapy in childhood or adolescence, the child may come to see that he or she is not to blame for family problems. In the process, however, the blame is often shifted to the parents. That child may appear in a therapist's office years later as a middle-aged adult, still stuck in a blame mode with his or her parents. What may have been a life-saving therapeutic intervention for the child has created iatrogenic problems for the adult.

Some clients who were parentified children haven't outgrown the overresponsibility or self-blame in the relationship with their parents. These individuals continue to overfunction and overaccommodate, and have difficulty setting appropriate limits. They may be resentful at siblings who are less responsible or don't contribute their fair share to the family. These overfunctioning clients may periodically erupt in anger at siblings or become impatient with parents; only in fury are they able to set limits or express their needs. These individuals tend to overfunction in other relationships as well, and often come to therapy angry at a spouse or child who is underfunctioning.

Differentiation: "Waking from the Spell of Childhood"

Much of the work in the relational intergenerational approach focuses on helping clients become more differentiated and empowered in their lives and in their relationship with their parents. This includes giving up the angry victim or overfunctioning position, and waking from the spell of childhood. It involves becoming the author of one's own life (White, 1989), and challenging the narrative in which one is helpless and parents have all the power. The work encourages clients to take responsibility for their own needs, feelings, and beliefs. The goal is to change oneself in the relationship with parents, not to change parents (Bowen, 1978; Lerner, 1985). It may feel like a revelation to a client that one can make a claim for oneself in a clear but firm "I" voice, without getting entangled in blaming interactions with parents (McGoldrick & Carter, 2001). The therapist encourages clients to "make a relational claim" (Fishbane, 2001) with parents. This involves speaking one's own needs, while taking into account the needs of the parent and of the relationship at the same time.

Many adult children assume that either they must do things the way their parents want, or they have to distance from their parents and push them away. One adult woman was fed up with her mother's attempts to get close and control the relationship. The daughter said, "I can't be the daughter my mother wants. So I can't be her daughter at all." The therapist replied, "What kind of daughter do *you* want to be? How would you like things to go?" This client was surprised that she could stay in contact with her mother *and* have some say in the relationship. Rather than become infuriated when her mother called at inconvenient times, or capitulate to her mother, the daughter was coached to call her mother at times that were good for her, and to set a comfortable time limit for the calls. She was also helped to become more empathic and curious about her mother's experience. This vignette highlights the process of the client's developing greater differentiation while at the same time facilitating dialogue and connection between mother and daughter. In some cases an explicit discussion of what parent and child each want in the relationship is helpful; in other situations, the relational negotiations are more indirect.

Rethinking Power

This intergenerational work calls for a reconsideration of power. The traditional notion of power, "power over" another, is the view many adult clients have with regard to their parents. Living under the spell of childhood entails seeing parents as having the power over the child, for good or for ill. Differentiation involves taking control and responsibility for one's own life and decisions. This is "power to" (Goodrich, 1991), not "power over"; it is the power to make decisions, to be the kind of person one wants to be. It is not a reversal of the power struggle with parents, this time with the adult child holding power over parents (e.g., by threatening to withhold contact with the grandchildren if the parent doesn't do things the way the child wants).

The shift to personal empowerment is not at the parents' expense. The therapist encourages clients to present claims for the self in a manner that allows for the dignity and power of the parents as well. Thus, what might have been a zero-sum, "power over" relationship with parents, evolves into a nonzero-sum relationship, in which there is room for "power with" or "mutual empowerment" (Jordan et al., 1991) of both parent and adult child. With mutual empowerment, there is room for both parties to make a claim, to speak and be heard; as a result, each experiences a sense of energy and well-being.

This notion—that one can achieve personal power without disempowering or having to be "one up" on another—differs from traditional notions of autonomy and the self. In a relational view, rather than focusing only on separation and independence, the developmental and life tasks of the individual are seen as relational processes, in which the self becomes more differentiated and complex *within* relationship. Relational intergenerational therapy helps the client shift from a *hierarchical* view of parents to a *generational* view (Fishbane, 1998). The hierarchical view of parents is one of "power over," with parents holding power over children. In this mode, an adult child may get caught up in a power struggle with parents, trying to wrench power and authority away from parents. In the generational view, the child sees that the parent was once a child, who learned to survive in certain ways; and the child/client is now an adult, perhaps also a parent, aware of the awesome responsibility involved in caring for a child. The generational view looks at intergenerational relationships in life cycle developmental terms. The adult child doesn't resign from the parent-child relationship in giving up a hierarchical view of parents. Rather, the shift entails reassessing how one can be an adult child to parents and honor them—including the obligations of care and loyalty—while at the same time respecting or honoring oneself (Fishbane, 1999).

The Fence Exercise

Entering into a more adult, dialogical relationship with parents, in which one is both authentic and able to accommodate the experience of the parent, requires the cultivation of respectful boundaries. In order not to get reactive with parents, an individual must know where the parent ends and the adult child begins. If the parent becomes upset, the child does not have to get "hooked" or reactive. Indeed, one's capacity for empathy with parents who are anxious or struggling is much greater if the boundaries are clear. Many clients have confused boundaries with their parents. They either push away with distance or get intertwined in their parents' concerns and agendas and lose their own.

A visual imagery technique which I call "the fence exercise" is helpful in addressing these boundary dilemmas. For example, Barbara, a 44-year-old woman, describes how reactive she gets to old—and ongoing—disappointments with her mother. The therapist suggests to Barbara that she imagine her mother as her neighbor, with a clear fence between their yards. The fence is symbolic—perhaps a picket fence—rather than a brick barricade. If her neighbor is planting flowers that Barbara thinks are inappropriate, for example, sun-loving flowers in a shady spot, Barbara might or might not choose to offer her advice to the neighbor. If the neighbor rejects the advice and has a poor outcome with her flowers, Barbara can still enjoy her own yard; she doesn't have to ruin her own summer in aggravation over her neighbor's flower bed. The therapist adds that if her neighbor is planting poison ivy that will creep into Barbara's yard, Barbara does need to protect herself and her property. In applying this analogy to their relationships with parents, clients find the fence exercise very useful. Barbara comes to see that she doesn't have to become upset and reactive over everything her mother does that disappoints her. The fence is her boundary to remind her that she and her mother are separate, and can relate safely and respectfully and tolerate their differences if they remember the boundary. The therapist helps Barbara see that her mother's behavior comes from the *mother's* anxiety and concerns, and is not necessarily about something Barbara is doing. Seeing this strengthens the boundary between them without leading to anger or distance on Barbara's part.

This boundary-strengthening work is particularly helpful with women who have been socialized to overaccommodate to others at the expense of self. A woman who has not learned to nurture herself in a relationship may either lose herself in empathy for her parents, or distance through withdrawal or anger to protect herself. The fence exercise helps her stay connected while maintaining differentiation.

Many women in heterosexual marriages take on both the care of and reactivity to their mothers-in-law, as the sons/husbands learned long ago to remove themselves from the emotional sphere of their mothers. Men are frequently in a protected position, while their wives fight it out, overgive, or negotiate with the husband's parents. In such an instance, the therapist encourages the husband to do his own work of differentiation and connection with his parents, so that his wife won't have to overfunction for him in this arena. To do this, the man may have to challenge his socialization as a male to stay away from feelings, caregiving, interpersonal conflicts, and especially from engaging with his mother (Bergman, 1991).

The therapist can suggest that he reconsider boundaries as places of "meeting or communicating" (Jordan, 1997a, p. 16), rather than as mechanisms of distance or rejection. Framing the capacity to connect and negotiate with family of origin (and other relationships) as a kind of relational empowerment tends to appeal to male clients. The therapist offers concrete relational techniques, "tools for your toolbox," to men who find the relational world mysterious and intimidating. Empathy training and role playing are particularly helpful techniques for such relational empowerment. This work is relevant to men, straight or gay, partnered or alone. Helping men take responsibility for their own relationships with their family of origin offers an alternative to the cultural expectation of women as "kinkeepers" (Fingerman, 2003) and men as peripheral in the family's emotional life.

Many clients of both genders have built solid brick walls rather than fences with their parents. Behind the high wall the adult child may be fearful of contact with parents. It is important for the therapist to work collaboratively with the client over the timing and pacing of attempts to reconnect or improve the relationship with parents. Otherwise, the client may feel unsafe, that the therapist is pushing too fast. Imagery is useful here as well. The therapist might say, "You have built a strong wall. It is yours to keep or modify. Would you be interested in adding a window, one you can close and lock, to see what's going on on the other side? Or might you want to add a door, one you can open or close, into the relationship with your parents?" Keeping the choice for change and the timing in the hands of the client eases the client's fear that he or she may be pushed to make changes before it feels comfortable or safe to do so.

If there is a danger of actual ongoing abuse or harm, clients might need to restrict contact with parents and attend to safety first—for themselves and their children. However, in our culture the term "abuse" is quite broadly applied; anyone in an unhappy relationship may be described as a victim of abuse. Many adult children would refer to their parents as unsafe or abusive; in the course of therapy, it may emerge that the client has not yet learned how to renegotiate a healthier relationship with the parent, and that the parent is not a source of actual danger. Or a parent, abusive in the past when actively alcoholic, might have changed in the context of sobriety and no longer poses a threat. The therapist, in such a circumstance, witnesses and works with the client's pain around old wounds, while at the same time helping the adult child separate the present from the past (Scheinkman & Fishbane, 2004). Utilizing the fence imagery and learning to make a relational claim are techniques that empower clients in the present to connect with parents in a safe and relationally competent manner.

Authorship

The adult child is encouraged to take authorship of his or her own life, and of the relationship with parents. It is more helpful to think of it as *co-authorship* of the relationship between adult child and parents. Differentiation of self is often described as differentiation *from* one's parents and siblings; I prefer the term *differentiation with* one's family of origin (Fishbane, 2001). In this view, the individual and family of origin coevolve, developing new skills, patterns and rules as they interact with each other. Rather than view this as a solo task vis-à-vis one's parents and siblings, the therapist can consider with clients the rich possibilities of speaking with members of the family of origin, where possible, about evolving relationships. In this view, differentiation develops in the context of dialogue.

The Challenge of the Parentified Child

This work encourages self-responsibility and thoughtfulness on the part of the adult child. Some clients, who were parentified children in their families of origin, initially balk at the notion that they need to be responsible in the relationship with their parents. Many feel they have done this their entire life, and view responsible functioning as if it were overresponsible overfunctioning. Such clients are likely to still be under the spell of childhood, hoping that their parents will now become the responsible ones. The therapist helps these clients separate the inappropriate parentification of themselves as children from the developmentally appropriate task of becoming self-responsible adults in their current relationship with parents.

For example, John's elderly father Henry is depressed, lonely, and self-absorbed after he moves into an assisted-living facility following the death of John's mother. He is irritable and frequently turns to John, the only child in town, with his complaints. John becomes reactive and annoyed with his father, and resents having to work so hard to help him, both practically and emotionally. John knows this is the right thing to do, but he is painfully reminded of his childhood; he was the parent to his parents from the age of 10, when his younger sister died of leukemia—his mother became depressed and his father was remote and self-absorbed. Only when his baby brother Matt was born 2 years later did the parents become more engaged; they poured all their love into their new baby, and John continued to feel neglected and overburdened in the family. In therapy, John explores his grief over his mother's death, and the old feelings this reawakens from his sister's death many years ago, when John felt alone and unable to process his pain with his parents. Sharing these old wounds in the context of an empathic therapeutic relationship helps John feel less alone and more resilient. The therapist works with John to distinguish his old feelings of loss and resentment for having had to overfunction as a child from the current existential challenge of helping his father transition to a new stage of life. John also addresses his sense of injustice that his brother Matt, living out of town, is oblivious both to the father's needs and to John's feeling burdened. The therapist coaches John on ways to discuss the situation with Matt without blaming him, speaking of his own struggles in an "I" voice. Matt agrees to come visit more often, but still limits his involvement. John learns to deal with his disappointments with his brother, and to accept Matt's limitations, forged in his role as indulged baby of the family. John considers ways he can help his father while setting limits, learning to balance his father's needs and his own. He determines a frequency of visits that is a compromise between what Henry would like and what John would prefer. John hires a caregiver to help his father with daily tasks, and encourages Henry to attend classes and activities at the assisted-living facility. He also helps his father get to a doctor who prescribes antidepressant medication, which improves his irritability and depression. Perhaps most important, John's annoyance at his father abates, and the son becomes curious about his father as a person. Over card games or lunch, feeling his son's interest, Henry begins to share stories from his own childhood and to ask more about John's life. Henry's vulnerability and increased sense of connection with his son allow him to soften and become more engaged than he had ever been as a father.

Grieving

Many clients carry a sorrow that their parents were not nurturing, understanding, or protective when they were young. As one wakes from the spell of childhood, lets go of anger at parents, and comes to accept their limitations, one may experience renewed sadness and even grief that the parents may never become who one wanted them to be. The therapist works with this grief in therapy, helping the client deal with this loss.

Internal Resources

In addition to mourning the lost wished-for parent, clients are helped to develop their own "inner good parent" resources. This intrapsychic work is an important part of intergenerational healing. In this regard the imagery work of Schwartz's (1995) Internal Family Systems (IFS) parts therapy is particularly useful. Clients learn, for example, to nurture their own vulnerable child part. Many clients are more nurturing of their children than they are of themselves. The therapist can build on this, asking them what they would do if their youngster were upset or frightened. Clients are then helped to transfer their own good parenting skills to the part of themselves that feels hurt or scared or neglected. As the client learns to "parent" him- or herself better, the dependence on and rage at the actual parents for failing the child become less compelling. This facilitates a more equal sense of power in the relationship, as the adult child can take better care of self in vulnerable situations.

Therapeutic Witnessing

In the process of helping clients differentiate, grieve lost dreams with parents, connect with and care for their own inner vulnerabilities, and connect with their family of origin, the therapist functions as a "secure base" (Byng-Hall, 1995) with the client. Whereas Bowen coaching work tends to be more cognitive and deflects intensity away from the client-therapist relationship (McGoldrick & Carter, 2001), the approach presented here builds on the attachment between therapist and client as a resource for change. The therapist's ability to witness and "hold" the client's vulnerabilities and intense feelings about the family of origin—without shaming the client—promotes safety in the therapy relationship. This, in turn, facilitates the client's explorations into change, both internal and in his or her relational world. The therapist's belief that differentiation and dialogue are mutually enhancing, and that the growth of the self and improved dialogue with family of origin are intertwined, gives courage to the client in the face of this often difficult intergenerational work. A powerful aspect of the therapeutic relationship is the witnessing of the client by the therapist. Relational and narrative therapists have identified how the therapist can reflect back to the client the possibility for a new self-story. As a client put it to Jordan (1997b, p. 53), "I know myself partly through your knowing me."

In intergenerational therapy, old assumptions or beliefs about self and family are re-examined, and often new narratives are constructed. For example, Helena came to therapy unhappy and self-deprecatory because she was so emotional. She had been taught by her parents that she was oversensitive, and her tears were seen as a sign of weakness. As she explored her family of origin with the therapist, she traced her parents' anxiety over her tears or unhappiness to her older brother's and paternal grandmother's bouts with serious depression. Her parents, especially her father, were vigilant for any sign of mental illness in their daughter. In that context, her emotionality was seen as dangerous. As Helena's sadness was explored in therapy, it emerged that she had no symptoms of clinical depression, but rather a tendency to feel deeply and to cry when she was emotionally touched. Her tears were reframed as a sign of her intense, passionate nature. Helena was tremendously relieved by this new view of herself. It allowed her to witness herself in a new way. She began a dialogue with herself in which she would notice her own alarm and self-criticism when she cried or felt blue; she learned to challenge her self-criticism and to normalize her own reaction. She began to see the value of her own passionate nature. She reported that she checked out her new self-perception with her friends and boyfriend; they agreed that her tears and her intensity were positive and healthy.

Helena's inviting significant others in her life to see and celebrate her changes points to an important aspect of change: Change occurs in a relational context. Helena's friends are her "chorus of advisors" (Fishbane, 1998); they were positive about her changes, and were additional witnesses to her new story. White & Epston (1992), in helping individuals resist the dominant discourse of the culture or of their lives that constrains them, encourage people to share the news with others, who can then support and affirm the change process. They call this the "recruitment of audiences for the authentication of change" (p. 16). Eventually, Helena will invite her parents to witness her changes. She will share with her parents her new view of her emotionality, and will ask them to support her in her endeavor to be less self-critical. This is the kernel of the "loving update," to which we will return.

Understanding and Forgiving Parents

While assuming responsibility for and authorship of his or her own life, the client is encouraged at the same time to come to understand the parents' lives from a new, adult perspective. Framo (1981) points to importance of seeing parents as real people. In seeing parents for who they are and not through the lens of one's own needs and distortions, one begins to view the parent as a full person, a "Thou" in Buber's term. This "Thou" is demystified and much less intimidating or dangerous; the parent-"Thou" emerges as a distinct other, a worthy and vulnerable human being. This shift allows the adult child to see the parent from a position of interest or curiosity, with the potential for a new narrative to emerge about the parent's own struggles and life journey. Michael Kerr (personal communication, 2003) suggests, "Think of your mother as your grandmother's daughter and get to know her that way." This reframe facilitates a shift from a hierarchical to a generational view of the parent. In particular, it focuses on the parent as a child, growing up in a family with its own challenges, norms, and limitations; the parent as child developed his or her own survival strategies, which then affected how that individual came to parent the client. Taking into account larger contextual factors in parents' lives, such as culture and gender constraints, further enlarges the parents' stories; experiences such as immigration, poverty, racism or sexism contribute to parental coping strategies and belief systems. There is often a sense of wonder and compassion at considering parents from these wider points of view. As a new narrative of the parent emerges, the self-story of the adult child may change as well. It is often helpful to invite parents to a session with their adult child to facilitate this process.

For example, Peter, a middle-aged man, described his mother as overbearing and intrusive. Peter had spent his entire adult life keeping his mother at a distance, fearing that she would suck him in with her neediness and desire for a close relationship. In the course of therapy he agreed to invite his mother, Maria, to a session. In walked the proverbial little old lady, frightened of her shadow, of her son, of this process. The therapist immediately put her at ease (as had been rehearsed with Peter ahead of time), relieving her of her fear that she would be blamed for Peter's problems. The therapist said that Maria had been invited to the session as a resource to her son, and that her perspective would be welcome on some of the issues Peter was working on in therapy. Maria immediately relaxed and let down her guard and defensiveness. She was thrilled to be invited to help her son. Encouraged to tell her own story, this mother explained that she had been severely neglected and abused as a child by the grandmother who raised her; her own parents were alcoholic and uninvolved in her life. What got her through her childhood was the determination that one day she would be a good mother, never abandon her child, and give to that child all the love and attention she herself never received. She also vowed never to tell her child about her own sorry childhood, as she didn't want to burden him. She heaped all her love on Peter, her only child; their bond became even more intense when her husband divorced her, when Peter was 5 years old. The son, now an adult client, was moved to tears by his mother's story. What he had experienced as his mother's smothering and overprotecting behavior was now seen as her courage and love in giving him what she never received, and in protecting him from her painful past. This reframe allowed Peter to begin to step out of his own narrative of victimization and resentment. In seeing his mother's love and devotion, and in understanding her own story in multigenerational terms, Peter's self-story began to change. In addition, mother and son began to coconstruct a better relationship, with clearer boundaries, and a way of both respectfully communicating their needs and hearing the other's needs. Maria came to see Peter's need for boundaries—which he learned to express more respectfully—as her son taking care of himself, rather than as a rejection of her. She saw that her desire for closeness was at times overwhelming to her son; feeling less rejected, she pursued him less intensely. Peter, in turn, experienced his mother as less intrusive and less demanding, and became more relaxed and generous with her.

Understanding and contextualizing parents' behavior—and the empathy that often ensues—leads some clients to a sense of forgiveness. Forgiveness is certainly facilitated when parents can apologize and take ownership of their limitations and the ways they may have hurt their children when they were younger. As Hargrave

(1994) points out, forgiveness is much easier if the offender can take responsibility, apologize, and make amends. However, even if parents are unable to do so, adult children may be able to forgive some childhood wounds once they come to understand their parents more fully. As much of the literature on this topic suggests, the person who benefits the most from forgiveness is the forgiver, as the heavy burden of anger and resentment is lifted.

This work may require forgiving oneself as well as parents. Many children blame themselves for what goes wrong in their family. Waking from the spell of childhood includes relinquishing the child's view that all that went wrong was the child's fault. Giving up the fantasy that one could make parents happy or assuage their pain is often a necessary part of this work.

Updating the Relationship

In addition to differentiating oneself in the relationship with parents, taking ownership and responsibility for one's own life, and coming to a more realistic and compassionate view of parents, intergenerational work may include an updating of the current relationship between adult children and their parents. This can take many forms. Often, it entails reworking roles, rules, and boundaries that are more suitable to the current needs of each party. As Carter & McGoldrick (1999) and Walsh (1998) have pointed out, the family's journey through the life cycle necessitates adaptability and flexibility to changing circumstances and needs of the various members. For example, a young adult in a serious love relationship or just married might need to discuss new boundaries with parents that acknowledge that the primary relationship is now between the adult child and a significant other. Later in life, the needs of elderly or frail parents may necessitate a closer relationship in which the child cares for the parent. Parents often need help conceptualizing their child as an adult and letting go of their own tendencies toward caretaking, control, or criticism. At the same time, it is helpful for the adult child to understand that many parents worry about their children throughout their lives; in therapy this can be framed as normal rather than pathological. Parents and adult children may carry wounds from awkward or hurtful transitions in the life cycle; for example, leaving for college, marriage, or having children. Resentment or unfinished business from one life cycle transition can negatively affect coping with later ones. Likewise, parents' difficulty with a particular life stage may reflect unfinished business with their own family of origin. Thus, a woman who became pregnant at 16 and gave up the baby for adoption becomes hypervigilant when her own daughter enters adolescence.

Balancing Needs

Intergenerational relationships often involve conflicting needs, desires, and values. One of the challenges of parent-adult child relationships is finding a way to deal with these differences respectfully, on both sides of the generation gap. Engaging in conflict constructively while staying connected is an important relational skill (Bergman & Surrey, 1997). The therapist helps the client learn how to make a relational claim, to have a voice while tuning in to the other. This involves articulating needs and different points of view without either imposing on the other or feeling bullied by the other.

Adult clients frequently report confusion over whether to take care of their own needs or attend to their parents' needs. Giving to parents at the expense of self can be overwhelming and lead to resentment. Figuring out the balance of honoring and caring for parents while honoring and caring for oneself can be a daunting challenge (Fishbane, 1999). It entails balancing filial loyalty (the loyalty a child owes a parent) with personal autonomy and other loyalties to spouse, children, or job. Some clients need help sorting out how much they can give to parents without depleting self, and how to protect themselves if parents become difficult, demanding, or abusive. Finding a way to protect the self without becoming reactive or nasty to parents is a complex skill inherent in healthy intergenerational relationships.

Rethinking Guilt

In sorting out competing loyalties and needs, clients often bump up against feelings of guilt. They may resent this, feeling somehow manipulated if they feel guilty in the relationship with their parents. As part of this work, clients are encouraged to rethink their assumptions about guilt. In some families, "guilt" is a verb with a direct object (as in, "don't guilt me" or "don't guilt-trip me!"). In this context, guilt is defined as bad, as a part of dysfunctional family life; the self is seen as a victim, a recipient of parents' guilt trips. Similarly, many therapists view guilt with suspicion, as if it were by definition a toxic emotion.

By contrast, Martin Buber (1957) challenges the assumption that guilt is necessarily bad, and differentiates between neurotic guilt and existential or real guilt. Buber notes that existential guilt is an appropriate and necessary part of human functioning; it is our conscience, activated when we have acted in a way that harms another. Neurotic guilt provokes excessive self-condemnation or self-hatred, and is associated with depression and poor self-esteem. When individuals wake from the spell of childhood, they have various means to differentiate between existential guilt and the neurotic or guilt-tripping variety. If a person's parents do attempt to "guilt-trip," one doesn't have to become reactive and defensive. The therapist can help clients in such a circumstance to assess whether they are living up to their own internal standards or values. This allows clients to take ownership of their own guilt, to develop an honest dialogue with their own conscience, and to sort out existential from neurotic guilt. Maintaining a healthy boundary or "fence" facilitates this process of sorting out conflicting needs and guilt.

Blessings

The intergenerational therapist encourages clients to look not only at problems in the relationship, but also at strengths and resources. One client, reciting a litany of his father's failings, said, "At least I know he loves me." The therapist helped him pause over what he had just said, and marvel at the blessing he had almost overlooked. Many people are unable to see the strengths or blessings in their relationship with parents because they feel the parent in childhood gave them the wrong blessing, or even a curse. Thus, for example, a young girl may have been told she is the pretty one, while her sister is the smart one. This girl grows up insecure about her intellect, not feeling parental encouragement to succeed academically or professionally. A boy may feel he failed to get his father's approval because he lacked athletic prowess, while he in fact had artistic talent. Even if the girl becomes a successful lawyer and the boy a renowned artist, each still carries inside an insecurity and resentment because their parents were unable to see and appreciate their gifts. In the context of sorting out these resentments, adult clients are helped to consider blessings they may not have identified in their family. These include parental loyalty, care, love, or providing for physical needs and safety.

It is often the case that an elderly parent, in the context of a life-review or thinking about his or her own worth toward the end of life, looks to the adult child for a sense of affirmation (Walsh, 1999). In this sense, we can say that the parent is looking to the child for a blessing, for a confirmation that the parent's life was worthwhile, that the parent was loveworthy. Clients report a sense of gratitude and relief when they have conveyed their love or appreciation to their parent before the parent's death. This intergenerational affirmation can take the form of a ritual, or simply a quiet conversation between parent and child.

The Loving Update

When a person is less reactive or angry with parents, and has come to a position of more thoughtful self-responsibility, he or she may choose to invite parents to a loving update of their relationship. This entails asking parents to witness the changes in the self, and in one's evolving narrative. It is also an opportunity for the child to see parents in a new light, and for the parent's own narrative to become more complex. The update often includes a respectful renegotiation of the current parent-adult child relationship, and a coconstruction of a new narrative between parent and child. While some clients prefer to initiate changes with their parents indirectly, without a discussion per se, others appreciate the opportunity to be more explicit in their conversation with parents. The timing of this intergenerational discussion is crucial. If it is done too early, before the anger is processed, it may turn into just another blame fest, and can do more harm than good. Furthermore, as Bowen (1978), Lerner (1985), and others remind us, the adult child needs to have realistic expectations of how parents might respond, and should be prepared for disappointment. It has been noted that "disappointment is wrought of misplaced expectations" (Ryan, personal communication, 1997). The parent, after all, has probably not been in therapy and is still working with the old rules. And since parents expect to be blamed in any conversation about the relationship with their child, they may come to the moment anxious and defensive. In preparing for the update the therapist can role play with the client scenarios in which parental reactions are anticipated and the client experiments with responses that promote more satisfying outcomes.

In the loving update, individuals attempt to bring more of themselves to their parents, to be more transparent. It goes something like this: "I know you love me, Mom/Dad, and I love you. I would like to be able to share more with you of who I am, I'd like to know you better, and I'd like us to have a better relationship." Many people are uncomfortable with this "love" language, and prefer an alternative formulation: "I want us to have a better relationship. Toward that end, I'd like to share more with you. . . ." Still other clients choose to appeal to parents' desires to be helpful: "I want to share some of my thoughts and personal issues with you. I could use your help and support. . . ." Whichever introductory frame is used, the update then becomes more specific; the adult child might talk about inner struggles, desires for better communication, or ways to restructure visits and time spent together. The update does *not* include blame or criticism of parents. Sometimes, the update occurs in a therapy session with parents; more often, clients are coached on ways to initiate the update with parents "out there," without a therapist present.

─────────────────────── **Case Study** ───────────────────────

Lana, an intelligent, attractive woman in her forties, was married with three daughters. She struggled with feelings of insecurity and jealousy, frequently comparing herself to other women. She worried when her husband as much as noticed another woman on the street. In working with the couple it became clear that her husband, Nick, adored her and had no interest in being with another woman. He was bewildered by her jealousy. The therapy included conjoint couple therapy and individual sessions with each partner. This vignette highlights part of Lana's intergenerational work in therapy.

Lana was comfortable in her relationship with her father, although they rarely talked personally. While Lana and her younger sister had been quite competitive as children, the sisters had become closer and supportive of each other as young adults. Lana was, however, very distressed in her relationship with her mother, Sarah. Lana had been keeping Sarah at arm's length for years, finding her overly critical. The mother-daughter relationship was stagnant and frustrating for both Lana and Sarah.

At one point in the therapy Lana and Nick agreed to join the therapist for a live consultation at a workshop with Michael White. In exploring Lana's jealousy and insecurity, Michael White highlighted her self-criticism. He asked Lana who was on the nurturing team and who was on the critical team in her life. Lana named Nick, her daughters, her father and sister, her close friends, and the therapist on the nurturing team, and her mother on the critical team. Michael White asked Lana if she would consider inviting her mother to join the nurturing team. Lana was intrigued, and agreed to try.

After the consultation, Lana focused in therapy on inviting her mother, Sarah, onto the nurturing team. This turned out to be no simple task. It took months before Lana was ready to have this conversation with her mother. In the interim Lana explored the history of criticism in her family throughout several generations, considering the sources of Sarah's own insecurities and desire for perfection. Seeing her mother as her grandparents' daughter—Sarah's parents were themselves highly critical people—helped Lana develop a new understanding of her mother. Exploring her mother's vulnerabilities and anxieties in light of Sarah's own life journey, Lana became less angry and more curious about her mother. Lana began to see her mother as a separate person with her own strengths and vulnerabilities, and to identify positive aspects of Sarah's mothering, including love, protectiveness, and a determination to give her daughter cultural and educational opportunities when she was growing up. Lana became less critical of Sarah, more compassionate and forgiving. Earlier in the therapy it was noted that Lana was critical like her mother; Lana's criticalness was aimed at herself and her mother. This was identified as a kind of invisible loyalty to her mother. As Lana shifted her own view of Sarah, and became less critical of her, Lana's own self-criticalness began to ease up as well. Furthermore, as Lana could see her mother more clearly as a separate person, the boundaries between them also became clearer.

As Lana felt less angry at her mother, clearer about boundaries, and more empowered in her own right, the therapy turned more explicitly to Lana inviting her mother to a joint project of improving their relationship. Lana roleplayed having a "loving update" discussion with her mother. In doing so, Sarah's possible reactions were anticipated, and Lana practiced how she might respond to them. This builds on Bowen's three-step work with intergenerational relationships, as described in Lerner (1985): As the individual plans to make a change in his or her own behavior with family members (step one), it is crucial to anticipate the other's response, including a negative one (step two); and finally, to consider what one might say or do following that response (step three). Lerner points out that family systems are very conservative, and when a member makes a change, other members often respond with a "Change back!" reaction, resisting the new behavior. Anticipating this and considering strategic ways to deal with it are part of planning for the loving update.

Lana worked on not becoming reactive if her mother responded in a negative or critical way, and visualized holding her own ground and remaining centered, even if she started to feel buffeted by Sarah's negativity. It helped Lana to see that her mother's criticism stemmed from Sarah's anxiety rather than from something wrong with Lana. Lana saw this as an example of the fence, a boundary between herself and her mother. Lana also worked internally on identifying when she felt hurt by criticism and how she could nurture the part of herself that felt so vulnerable. As she became clearer about her inner process, and more capable of self-soothing, she felt less wounded by criticism and more safe and protected interpersonally.

Finally, Lana was prepared to invite her mother to a more loving and mutually supportive relationship. She took her mother out to lunch, a rare occurrence. At lunch, Lana said, "You know, Mom, I've been in therapy working on my self-criticism." Her mother interjected, "I always said you were too self-critical!" Lana heard the critical tone in her mother's comment, but did not become reactive. She refrained from countering with, "There you go again, Mom! Always critical! Where do you think I got this from?"—which she would have said prior to the therapy. Lana had anticipated this response by her mother, and, through several roleplays, had found a way to remain calm when her mother said this. Lana replied, "You're right, Mom, and I'd like your help with my project." Sarah's ears perked up, and she sat up straighter in her chair. For years this mother had felt her daughter pushing her away, and she had been in great pain over the strained relationship with her child. She was sensing for the first time since Lana's adolescence that her daughter actually wanted her help. She replied, "Of course, Lana, anything I can do to help." Lana continued, "I have a tendency to get self-critical, and sometimes critical of others, too. If you see me criticizing myself, would you let me know? And if I get too critical of others, would you tell me that, too? Especially if you think I'm being critical of you, I'd like you to tell me." Sarah responded positively.

Lana then said, "And if I ever feel you're being critical of me, even if you don't intend to be critical, can I tell you?" Her mother, fully on board by now, said, "Of course, Lana. I want you to tell me if you think I'm being critical. I'd love to help you." Lana asked her mother about criticism in Sarah's family of origin, and mother and daughter reflected on the multigenerational impact of this trait in their family. Sarah shared how burdened she had felt by criticism as a child and an adult. Both reflected on how they could stand up to criticism, externalizing this quality and challenging it in their lives (White, 1989). Sarah also noted that she had been harder on Lana, her first born, than on Lana's younger sister. Sarah explained that with her first child, and with her own mother watching her critically, she had been determined to be the perfect mother and had been overcontrolling. Lana was relieved to hear this, as she had assumed as a little girl that her mother was so critical because there was something wrong with Lana.

Both Lana and Sarah left this "loving update" conversation feeling good. Lana had identified areas of concern to her mother in a gracious, nonblaming way. She felt heard, and saw that her mother was indeed taking the first steps to join the nurturing team rather than the critical team. Sarah felt grateful to finally be included in Lana's life. She felt connected, useful, and relieved that her daughter actually needed her. She did not feel threatened by Lana's comments, as Lana did not cast her as the bad mother who was always critical. The way Lana framed her comments, Sarah was able to be nondefensive and generous, and could even accept the reference to her own criticalness in a positive way. She felt Lana's genuine interest in Sarah's own experience of criticism.

The framing of Lana's side of this interaction was carefully crafted in therapy. The phrase about the mother's criticism, "even if you don't intend to be critical," was very important. It did not cast Sarah as an evil or mean criticizer; it suggested that despite good intentions, sometimes negative interactions occurred between mother and daughter and Lana would get hurt. Lana stated her experience without blame, and stepped away from a pathologizing view of Sarah's motivations. The daughter's formulation appealed to the mother's generous side, and gave Sarah the opportunity to be protective and loving with her daughter.

Some might say this careful phrasing is strategic, and therefore insincere or manipulatively paradoxical. I believe that strategy can coexist with honesty and collaboration. In this case, Lana wasn't trying to trick her mother into being noncritical; she was appealing to Sarah's noncritical, loving side, and her phrasing successfully elicited this from her mother. Lana's strategy included declining her own tendency to be blaming and critical of her mother's intentions. Because her formulation was the result of a deep process of soul-searching, understanding and forgiveness, Lana could pull off this loving update with a sincere heart.

This conversation between Lana and Sarah began a process of the two reworking their relationship. With the agreement forged at the meeting, a new contract was effectively in place. In the future, if Lana found her mother critical, Lana now had permission to challenge her mother in a way that wasn't critical or rejecting; Lana could simply refer to their new "deal." Eventually, she could even do this with humor, with a raised eyebrow, and both would understand. At times they would giggle when their old dance emerged.

The loving update is not a one-time event. It is part of a process of evolution, of ongoing refinement and communication between the generations. With the update as the frame, many difficult negotiations around expectations, rules, or boundaries can take place. Furthermore, it is important to understand that the update is not magic. A single conversation does not transform a relationship. There is ample opportunity for slipping into the old dance, the old dysfunctional interaction between parent and adult child, on both sides. The therapist anticipates with clients that this will probably happen. When it does, the client is less disappointed, because it has been anticipated. The therapist also suggests that a booster-session may be needed down the road; the client can revisit the update with the parent, going over the same territory or a new issue, to anchor the changes and return to a more constructive contract.

Old habits die hard. Lana and her mother had been doing a dance of criticism and counter-criticism/defensiveness for years. Their habitual responses, powered by automatic synaptic pathways in their brains, were hard to change. The work they did in the loving update created new synaptic pathways, new cognitive, behavioral, and emotional choices. But the old pathways are always available, and especially in times of stress or fatigue, they may come to the fore. At one point, when Lana and her mother fell back into their criticism and resentment with each other, Lana said to her mother, "Mom, I think we've gotten off track. I so cherish the work we did to improve our relationship. What do you think we can do to get back on track?" Her mother softened as she heard the word "we"; she saw that Lana considered them a team. Sarah said that she had been feeling down after her close friend died, and had felt hurt that Lana had recently been so preoccupied with her oldest daughter's college applications that she had no time to spend with Sarah. They were able to repair the hurt between them and find a way to balance their changing needs.

The impact on Lana's life of this intergenerational work with her mother was profound. Criticism—of herself, and of Sarah—no longer dominated Lana's experience. Correspondingly, she became more secure, and was no longer so jealous of other women. Lana's husband, sensitized in couple therapy to her feelings about this, was more tuned in to her and was less likely to eye other women when they were out together. While Lana's criticism had been directed toward herself and her mother, and not particularly toward her daughters, her work on differentiation and dialogue with her mother strengthened her ability to see her daughters in a more differentiated way. Lana worked on updating her relationship with her father as well. She began experimenting with speaking more personally with him, and he gradually became more open with her. Lana found that the ripple effect of the loving update with her mother extended to many contexts in her life, as she became less constrained by old assumptions and behaviors.

SPECIAL CONSIDERATIONS AND LIMITATIONS

Most clients engage in this differentiation and dialogue work with parents as adults, in their thirties or older. Having achieved some stability of adult identity and "filial maturity" (Fingerman, 2003) makes it more feasible for clients to engage in this process. Filial maturity, the capacity to see parents as separate human beings, is normally accomplished by the mid- to late-thirties (Fingerman, 2003). Research evidence that the prefrontal cortex, site of logical reasoning and judgment, is not fully developed until the mid-twenties (Apter, 2004) would support the view that this work is most successful after young adulthood. Furthermore, the readiness to explore intergenerational relationships with curiosity and compassion is often enhanced when the client becomes a parent or has experienced some of the challenges of building an adult life.

It is intriguing to consider whether younger clients can benefit from the approach described in this chapter. Individual differences as well as cultural variables may affect a person's capacity for filial maturity at a younger age. Indeed, this author has utilized this approach with clients in their twenties and even with some late adolescents in the throes of individuation. Establishing one's own identity and renegotiating a more adult and empowered relationship with parents can be mutually enhancing. While there may be limits on the developmental ability of a child to see parents as distinct individuals, it is possible that this capacity can be facilitated in the younger child or adolescent in a family that encourages dialogue and curiosity between the generations.

With regard to the loving update, there are situations in which this experience with parents may not be feasible. If parents have died, an update with them in life is no longer possible. However, as family therapists have demonstrated, it is still possible for the adult child to learn more about the parents' life journeys, through conversations with surviving relatives, and by reading old letters, documents, or newpaper accounts. Many individuals have been able to update the relationship with their deceased mother or father internally, through a more complex understanding and forgiveness of the parent. Visits to parents' graves offer an opportunity for ritual and emotional closure.

If parents are currently dangerous, actively abusing alcohol or drugs, or are severely impaired, it may not be safe to invite them to a discussion about the relationship. In that circumstance, the adult child can work on his or her own reactivity and find a respectful mode of relating to parents while protecting the self from harm. Similarly, if the parent is uninterested in meeting with the child or rejects any overture to discuss deeper matters, the adult child's own work on becoming less reactive may still lead to a changed relationship, as the child changes his or her part in the intergenerational dance. Parents who cut their adult children off pose a particularly painful challenge. Even in such circumstances, the adult child can do this work, finding a way to be self-protective while still reaching out occasionally to parents. In many cases, the parent eventually softens and the relationship improves. Finally, even if the parent is not available for any dialogue for change, doing the work of differentiation may suffice to stop the intergenerational transmission process of negativity and resentment, the passing on of invisible loyalties and hidden legacies.

Ethnic or social factors may impact on the nature of the loving update between the generations. Cultures that discourage direct negotiation or overt communication about relationships might not sanction an open discussion about the parent-adult child relationship. In such circumstances, the update would need to be more indirect, honoring cultural norms and values. Cultures that consider it a weakness to reveal vulnerabilities or disapprove of direct discussion of needs might also require a more subtle form of the update. Working with clients who are the children of immigrants can be particularly challenging, as the parents may be loyal to the culture of the old country while the child has taken on dominant American values. It is important that the clinician understand and honor the culture of origin of the client and his or her family, in order to frame suggestions and interventions sensitively and respectfully.

RESEARCH SUPPORTING THIS APPROACH

There is at this time no outcome research on therapy utilizing the particular relational, intergenerational approach described in this chapter.

CONCLUSION

The therapy discussed in this chapter promotes intergenerational reconciliation and generosity, as well as personal empowerment and relational competence in the adult client. It challenges cultural and therapeutic norms that assume that individual autonomy is purchased by rejecting and blaming parents, and takes the long view, a multigenerational systemic perspective. In addition to improving relations with parents, this approach helps clients consider which legacies from their family of origin they wish to continue in their own lives, and, if they are parents, what they want to pass on to their own children. In this manner, legacies, loyalties, and values are dealt with consciously, rather than affecting clients and their offspring in an indirect, insidious manner.

The techniques described in this chapter with respect to parent-child relationships can be applied as well to other relationships, such as with siblings, spouses, children, or friends. Like all differentiation-of-self work, these relational tools are useful in relationships in general, especially intimate relationships in which the individual feels disempowered or reactive. The emphasis is on strengthening the self while maintaining connection with others. This approach promotes collaboration rather than competition, and dialogue rather than debate, in human relationships.

REFERENCES

Apter, T. (2004). *You don't really know me.* New York: W.W. Norton.

Bergman, S. (1991). Men's psychological development from a relational perspective. Wellesley, MA: The Stone Center Work in Progress.

Bergman, S., & Surrey, J. (1997). The woman-man relationship: Impasses and possibilities. In J. V. Jordan (Ed.), *Women's growth in diversity: More writings from the Stone Center.* New York: Guilford.

Boszormenyi-Nagy, I., Grunebaum, J., & Ulrich, D. (1991). Contextual therapy. In A. S. Gurman & D. P. Kniskern (Eds.), *Handbook of Family Therapy, Vol. 2* (pp. 200–238). New York: Brunner/Mazel.

Boszormenyi-Nagy, I., & Krasner, B. (1986). *Between give and take: A clinical guide to contextual therapy.* New York: Brunner/Mazel.

Boszormenyi-Nagy, I., & Spark, G. (1973). *Invisible loyalties: Reciprocity in intergenerational family therapy.* New York: Harper & Row.

Boszormenyi-Nagy, I., & Ulrich, D. (1981). Contextual family therapy. In A. S. Gurman & D. P. Kniskern (Eds.), *Handbook of Family Therapy* (pp. 159–186). New York: Brunner/Mazel.

Bowen, M. (1978). *Family therapy in clinical practice.* New York: Jason Aronson.

Buber, M. (1957). Guilt and guilt feelings. *Psychiatry, 20,* 114–129.

Buber, M. (1965). *The knowledge of man.* New York: Harper & Row.

Buber, M. (1970). *I and thou.* New York: Charles Scribner's Sons.

Byng-Hall, J. (1995). *Rewriting family scripts: Improvisation and systems change.* New York: Guilford.

Carter, B., & McGoldrick, M. (Eds.). (1999). *The expanded family life cycle: Individual, family, and social perspectives.* Boston: Allyn & Bacon.

Fingerman, K. L. (2003). *Mothers and their adult daughters: Mixed emotions, enduring bonds.* Amherst, NY: Prometheus Books.

Fishbane, M. D. (1998). I, thou and we: A dialogical approach to couples therapy. *Journal of Marital and Family Therapy 24,* 41–58.

Fishbane, M. D. (1999). "Honor thy father and thy mother": Intergenerational spirituality and Jewish tradition. In F. Walsh (Ed.), *Spiritual resources in family therapy* (pp. 136–156). New York: Guilford.

Fishbane, M. D. (2001). Relational narratives of the self. *Family Process, 40,* 273–291.

Framo, J. (1976). Family of origin as a therapeutic resource for adults in marital and family therapy: You can and should go home again. *Family Process, 15,* 193–210.

Framo, J. (1981). The integration of marital therapy with sessions with family of origin. In A. S. Gurman & D. P. Kniskern (Eds.), *Handbook of family therapy* (pp. 133–157). New York: Brunner/Mazel.

Galatzer-Levy, R. M., & Cohler, B. J. (1993). *The essential other: A developmental psychology of the self.* New York: Basic Books.

Goodrich, T. J. (1991). Women, power and family therapy: What's wrong with this picture? In T. J. Goodrich (Ed.), *Women and power: Perspectives for family therapy* (pp. 3–35). New York: W. W. Norton.

Hargrave, T. D. (1994). *Families and forgiveness: Healing wounds in the intergenerational family.* New York: Brunner/Mazel.

Jordan, J. V., Kaplan, A. G., Miller, J. B., Stiver, I. P., & Surrey, J. L. (1991). *Women's growth in connection: Writings from the Stone Center.* New York: Guilford.

Jordan, J. V. (1997a). A relational perspective for understanding women's development. In J. V. Jordan (Ed.), *Women's growth in diversity: More writings from the Stone Center* (pp. 9–24). New York: Guilford.

Jordan, J. V. (1997b). Clarity in connection: Empathic knowing, desire and sexuality. In J. V. Jordan (Ed.), *Women's growth in diversity: More writings from the Stone Center* (pp. 50–73). New York: Guilford.

Kerr, M. E., & Bowen, M. (1988). *Family evaluation.* New York: W. W. Norton.

Kohut, H. (1977). *The restoration of the self.* New York: International Universities Press.

Lerner, H. (1985). *The dance of anger.* New York: Harper & Row.

McGoldrick, M. (1995). *You can go home again: Reconnecting with your family.* New York: W.W. Norton.

McGoldrick, M., & Carter, B. (2001). Advances in coaching: Family therapy with one person. *Journal of Marital and Family Therapy, 27,* 281–300.

McNamee, S., & Gergen, K. J. (Eds.). (1992). *Therapy as social construction.* London: Sage.

Offer, D., & Sabshin, M. (1984). Adolescence: Empirical perspectives. In D. Offer & M. Sabshin (Eds.), *Normality and the life cycle: A critical integration* (pp. 76–107). New York: Basic Books.

Scheinkman, M., & Fishbane, M. D. (2004). The vulnerability cycle: Working with impasses in couple therapy. *Family Process, 43,* 279–299.

Schwartz, R. C. (1995). *Internal Family Systems Therapy.* New York: Guilford.

Stolorow, R. D., & Atwood, G. E. (1992). *Contexts of being: The intersubjective foundations of psychological life.* Hillsdale, NJ: The Analytic Press.

Szapocznik, J., Kurtines, W. M., Foote, F., Perez-Vidal, A., & Hervis, O. E. (1983). Conjoint versus one-person family therapy: Some evidence for effectiveness of conducting family therapy through one person. *Journal of Consulting and Clinical Psychology, 51,* 889–899.

van Kilsdonk, J. (1987). Preface. In A. van Kilsdonk and E. van den Eerenbeemt, *Balance in motion: Ivan Boszormenyi-Nagy and his vision of individual and family therapy* (pp. ix–xi). New York: Brunner/Mazel.

Walsh, F. (1998). *Strengthening family resilience.* New York: Guilford.

Walsh, F. (1999). Families in later life: Challenges and opportunities. In B. Carter & M. McGoldrick (Eds.), *The expanded family life cycle: Individual, family and social perspectives* (pp. 307–326). Boston: Allyn & Bacon.

Weingarten, K. (1994). *The mother's voice: Strengthening intimacy in families.* New York: Harcourt Brace & Co.

White, M. (1989). The externalizing of the problem and the reauthoring of lives and relationships. In M. White, *Selected papers* (pp. 5–28). Adelaide, Australia: Dulwich Centre Publications.

White, M., & Epston, D. (1992). Consulting your consultants: The documentation of alternative knowledges. In D. Epston & M. White, *Experience, contradiction, narrative and imagination: Selected papers of David Epston and Michael White 1989–1991* (pp. 11–26). Adelaide, Australia: Dulwich Center Publications.

Winnicott, D. (1965). *The maturational processes and the facilitating environment.* London: Hogarth.

CHAPTER 22

An Integrative Approach to Health and Illness in Family Therapy

Anthony R. Pisani and Susan H. McDaniel

Every family that enters therapy has a health history that influences relationships and changes family life. Some families seek therapy explicitly to focus on illness, disability, or loss, while others have medical events that operate in the background as they focus on acute relational problems. Still others present with physical manifestations of emotional distress. Whichever the case, family therapists can be most helpful if we pay attention to the interplay among biological, psychological, and social processes.

Our aim in this chapter is to describe an integrative approach to health and illness in family therapy. We will describe the theoretical underpinnings of a systemic approach and outline specific therapeutic strategies for working with health-related histories and presenting problems. Throughout the chapter, we will point the reader to key resources for pursuing, in greater depth, the themes we highlight.

FOUNDATIONS: BIOPSYCHOSOCIAL SYSTEMS THEORY AND MENDING THE MIND-BODY SPLIT

Theoretical and Historical Foundations

Medical family therapy (McDaniel, Hepworth, & Doherty, 1992) is a practical application of the biopsychosocial model (Engel, 1977; Frankel, Quill, & McDaniel, 2003) and family systems theory (Bowen, 1978; Mikesell, Lusterman, & McDaniel, 1995), which both have roots in general systems theory (Bertalanffy, 1950; Wynne, 2003). The biopsychosocial systems approach draws our attention to different levels of human existence—from cellular and organ systems to the individual, couple, family, culture, and community. General systems theory addresses the interaction among levels. The medical family therapist is an expert on the interpersonal and family levels, working clinically to understand the influence of relationships on health and illness, and of illness and disability on primary relationships, and collaborating with other health professionals to implement a biopsychosocial approach to care.

In the 1950s and '60s, pioneers in family therapy such as Murray Bowen (1978),

Salvador Minuchin (e.g., Minuchin, Rosman, & Baker, 1978), and Lyman Wynne (2003) envisioned that family systems approaches would apply to both physical and mental health. With some notable exceptions (Bloch, 1984; Doherty & Baird, 1983; Penn, 1983; Gonzalez, Steinglass, & Reiss, 1989; Walsh, 2003), most latter-day family therapy theorists attended to the psychosocial level, and moved away from consideration of physical health or illness.

Over time, family therapists from a variety of theoretical and professional backgrounds recognized the opportunities that exist in medical settings, such as primary care, to help families that would not otherwise access mental health treatment. Primary care is the point of entry to mental health care for most patients. For a third to a half of all patients, it is the only place they receive such treatment; only a small percentage of patients with emotional distress seek help at specialty mental health clinics (Kessler, Burns, & Shapiro, 1987; Narrow, Regier, Rae, Manderscheid, & Locke, 1993; Regier, Goldberg, & Taube, 1978; Regier, Narrow, Rae, Manderscheid, Locke, & Goodwin, 1993). For this reason, primary care has been called the "de-facto" mental health care delivery system in the United States (Regier et al., 1993; Peek & Heinrich, 2000). In addition, many primary care patients present with somatic symptoms of unclear or psychological origins. In a study of the 10 most common physical complaints, Kroenke & Mangelsdorf (1989) found that 75 to 85 percent end up with no diagnosable organic etiology during a 3-year follow-up period. Although many physicians are highly skilled in working with psychosocial problems, most do not have sufficient training or time to conduct psychotherapy and assessment with the number and range of patients that present in their practices.

Medical family therapy developed in response to this need, drawing from research and clinical evidence to develop a metaframework for psychotherapeutic practice based on a biopsychosocial systems approach. The overarching goals for medical family therapy are *agency* and *communion,* taken from literature on psychology and theology (Bakan, 1969). Agency is a sense that one can make personal choices in dealing with illness and the health care system. For patients with medical illness, it means coming to grips with what they must accept while discovering what action they can take. Agency is a sense of activism about one's own health, in the face of all that is uncertain. The other goal, communion, refers to strengthening emotional and spiritual bonds that can be frayed by illness, disability, and/or contact with the health care system. It is the sense of being cared for, communicated with, and supported by a community of family members, friends, and professionals. Taken together, agency and communion reflect individual strength within a relational context (McDaniel et al., 1992). Of course, cultural values influence the balance of agency and communion, with different cultures prioritizing autonomy and community support in different ways and to different degrees. Nevertheless, Helgeson (1994), in a broad review of the literature, concluded that a *balance* of agency and communion is a foundation for mental and physical health. Individual agency, in the absence of communion, or an exclusive other focus without active autonomy, are related to poor health outcomes.

We conceptualize the scope of medical family therapy as encompassing the full range of presenting problems and family configurations. This broad purview follows naturally from the biopsychosocial perspective that all presenting problems—whether brought to professional attention as biomedical or psychosocial—are fundamentally both. Thus, any problem that could be the focus of family therapy is appropriate for a medical family therapy perspective. Of course, it is also true that some presenting issues or family health histories lend themselves more obviously to an approach that emphasizes health and illness in family life. When a family member faces illness, disability, or death, or a family has a recent history of health-related issues, a biopsychosocial focus seems most natural. However, our view is that expertise in assessing and working with the biopsychosocial context, and in collaborating with biomedical health care professionals, will enhance therapeutic effectiveness within a wide range of cases.

Empirical Foundations

An impressive body of research supports the biopsychosocial systems hypothesis: that health at somatic and at interpersonal levels is interrelated. Emotional support, family closeness, clear family organization, and aspects of marital quality are all associated with better overall health and illness survival rates. Conversely, individuals in families and marriages characterized by criticism, conflict, isolation, and rigidity are at greater risk of medical illness. (Weihs, Fisher, & Baird, 2002).

In a highly influential review article, House, Landis, & Umberson (1988) concluded:

> The evidence regarding social relationships and health increasingly approximates the evidence in the 1964 Surgeon General's report that established cigarette smoking as a cause or risk factor for mortality and morbidity from a range of disease. The age-adjusted relative risk ratios are stronger than the relative risks for all cause mortality reported for cigarette smoking. (p. 543)

Among family factors that have been examined in relation to health, the marital dyad often emerges as the most significant. Research has demonstrated a robust reciprocal link between close relationships and heath. Marital status, relationship quality, spousal support, nonhostile marital interactions, and having a nonanxious spouse are linked with outcomes as diverse as mortality rates, immune function, and pain behavior. Conversely, there is ample evidence that illness and injury profoundly affect relationships (see Kowal, Johnson, & Lee [2003] for a review of this literature and its implications for couples' therapy).

As one might expect from these findings, interventions focused on support from family relationships have proven to be effective in improving some health outcomes. Individual studies have demonstrated benefits of family and couple interventions (ranging from education to therapy) for individuals with diabetes, asthma, dementia, and some chronic childhood illnesses. (For a comprehensive review of family interventions for physical disorders, see Campbell, 2003.)

Researchers have not yet documented the possible benefits of medical family therapy, broadly speaking, on relational outcomes and overall family functioning. Obviously, family therapists have a keen interest in these outcomes, since most of our interventions occur at this level. Systematic intervention research in this area is needed. In the meantime, the persuasive body of research documenting reciprocal relationships between health and relationships provides a solid foundation upon which medical family therapists can build.

SPECIFIC INTERVENTION STRATEGIES FOR TREATING FAMILIES EXPERIENCING HEALTH PROBLEMS

Pre-Session Preparation

Who Is in the "Family"?

Before beginning therapy with any family, the therapist must determine which stakeholders to include. For many patients, "family" extends beyond those who are biologically related. For families living with illness or disability, health care providers, friends, personal assistants, and community agents form an identifiable system that interacts around the illness. Families whose presenting concern is not health related also have significant others who share in the experience of the problem and, potentially, in its solution. Thus, the ideal in deciding whom to involve in therapy is to match the treatment system as closely as possible to the "problem-determined system" of family, friends, and helping professionals (Anderson, Goolishian, and Winderman, 1986).

Of course, it is not always feasible to bring all of those involved with a particular problem into the therapy room. Some stakeholders will participate through phone or written contact, others by "conjuring" their presence in later sessions, by asking family members to give voice to absent members' perspectives. Nevertheless, therapists should explicitly encourage families to invite support persons to the first visit and, regardless of who is in the room, conceptualize the family as including these individuals and keep their potential contributions in mind.

--- **Case Study** ---

Ed was a 48-year-old candidate for bone marrow transplant (secondary to advanced-stage multiple myeloma). He was also a recovering alcoholic. Ed was referred for family therapy by the transplant team when it was discovered that his only possible donor match was his younger brother, from whom he had been estranged for 14 years. Accepting the marrow caused the patient significant distress, which, in turn, placed additional stress on his wife and his 6-year-old son. The family therapy team conducted 3 sessions with the immediate family before the transplant. Ed refused to invite his brother to these sessions. During the weeks of postoperative quarantine, the team continued to meet with the family and other caregivers (including staff from the hospital unit and a nurse from the transplant team), who would bring videotapes of the sessions to the patient in his hospital room. Eventually, the patient agreed to invite his brother to one of these videotaped sessions, which allowed him to hear his brother's sincere concern for him and begin to repair the relationship.

In this case, the question of who is in the family was central to the treatment. The donor match had ushered in a brother who had been previously cut off, and the patient's quarantine meant the patient could not physically attend sessions.

The family therapy team had to consider whom to involve and how, and sought to leverage each unique circumstance for therapeutic gain. Videotaping sessions for the ill patient meant that he could hear and process his brother's concern for him in a way that would have been unlikely in person, given his anger and defensiveness. The therapist's commitment to inclusion lead to a creative use of technology that reaped unforeseen benefits for the family. The participation by staff and nurses from the hospital also strengthened the patient's crucial connection with the medical team in charge of his care.

Framing Treatment for the Family and Treatment Team

The referral to family therapy is the first opportunity to model biopsychosocial integration and collaboration. For many families, referral to a mental health provider can feel intimidating or stigmatizing. For an individual presenting in a medical office with health-related problems, referral for family therapy can be misperceived as evidence that the provider thinks the problem is "in my head" or "my fault." In some cases, this perception is partially founded; medical providers who become understandably frustrated with some patients do offer psychotherapy referrals as a way of distancing themselves from difficult or frustrating patients.

To minimize this possibility, family therapists should seek to form ongoing relationships with medical providers in their communities, with whom they can develop a shared language and protocol for making referrals. While it is not always possible to influence how referrals are presented, many medical providers are eager for guidance about how to recommend therapy to their patients. The family therapist can offer collaborating providers general principles and concrete examples of effective referral language. In the transplant case previously discussed, the physician on the transplant team introduced the idea of a family therapy consult by saying, "In our experience, transplants of this nature place enormous stress on families. That stress can interfere with optimal postoperative recovery. In order to maximize our chances of success, I'd like your family to consult with a colleague of mine about the particular stresses this transplant places on your family." Glen (1987) and Blount (1998) provided other useful examples of referral language which we frequently modify to suit different settings.

> "The last few visits haven't resulted in as much relief for you as I would like, but I want to keep trying. I'd like to bring in Ms. Johnson. She is a family therapist who works with me quite a lot. Her job is to help physicians understand their patients better so they can find better ways to help them."

> "Your pain is obviously very real. I need to assess whether stress has a role in making it worse. I want to bring in Ms. Jones, a therapist on our team who is an expert on stress."

Proposing a team approach with patients and with medical providers models integration of emotional, relational, and physical health. As with any team, each player has a distinct role, but everyone knows what the other players are doing and each seeks to enhance the others' effectiveness. In this case, the family therapist's primary focus is the relational health of the family system, as part of a larger treatment plan that includes members' overall health. This teamwork benefits the patient and the professionals, who report higher satisfaction when collaborating on difficult cases (see Blount, 2003).

Once a referral has been made, the pretreatment contract with the patient should include a request for permission to exchange information with relevant medical providers. The format and style for explaining the need for sharing information will depend on both professionals' preferences. It is often helpful to provide a relational context for the release of information. For example, as part of the discussion about information exchange, the therapist might explain, "Dr. Howard asked you to see me because he is concerned about how your husband's death may be affecting your health. She has known you for a long time and I know she will want to stay informed about our work." The medical family therapist must balance emphasis on the importance of communication with the health care team with the need to provide opportunity for the patient to express concerns and reservations about information exchange. Most patients are pleased and relieved to see their health care professionals collaborating, and intuitively grasp how it can be helpful to them (see the following "Ethical issues: confidentiality and informed consent"). In some cases, the therapist may recommend having the first session at the physician's office, so that he or she can participate for all or part of the visit and directly help shape the therapeutic agenda.

When the presenting problem is directly related to a medical condition, the therapist should gather basic information from the medical provider about the condition, including prognosis and course. Therapists should not feel a burden to be an expert on the particular illness, but some information is important in order to understand a family's experience. The collaborating physician is an expert on the biomedical aspects of illness and can help inform the family therapist. For example, if a therapist will be seeing a family whose child has recently been diagnosed with acute lymphoblastic leukemia (ALL), it could be helpful to know that most children are diagnosed and immediately hospitalized for an extended course of treatment. They usually do not have time to go home or talk to friends before going to the hospital. It could also be helpful to know that the prognosis for this disease is fairly good compared to other forms of childhood cancer (95 percent of children with ALL achieve complete remission, and 70 to 80 percent live out a normal lifespan). With this kind of information, the therapist can more effectively grasp the biopsychosocial context of the family and establish credibility as a collaborating member of the health care team.

A therapist or clinic can communicate commitment to a wide view of involvement in therapy, from the first phone contact forward. When taking initial information from someone phoning our practice, we routinely ask, "What health care professionals, family members, clergy, or friends have been involved in helping you with this problem?" Because patients are rarely prompted by professionals to think systemically about their treatment, this question sometimes requires a brief explanation. For example, "In our practice, we strive to make your family's visits relevant to your life and effective for the problem you are facing. That often means drawing (directly or indirectly) on the wisdom of others who know and care about you. Sometimes it means helping people who impact your life see a problem or a family member from a different perspective, and vice versa." The therapist can then discuss which of these people might join the family for a first visit, which might be included at a later time, and which might be contacted beforehand to contribute.

Initial Sessions

Joining and Assessment

Successful joining with families around health-related issues requires many of the same skills that one would need to develop rapport under any family therapy approach. We will limit our discussion to aspects of joining that have particular relevance for health-related concerns.

Incorporate health from the beginning. Regardless of whether the initial presentation explicitly involves a medical problem, it is helpful to ask about health and illness in the first interview. Therapists can easily incorporate questions about family medical problems into genogram-based interviews, and can intersperse these concerns with questions about emotional and relational difficulties and strengths. By including health-related questions from the beginning, the therapist builds a bridge across the mind-body divide, and implicitly communicates a biopsychosocial approach. Some families whose immediate concerns are not health related are initially surprised when their therapist takes a family medical history, but most quickly see the wisdom of doing so when they begin talking about key health events and how they altered family life.

Solicit the "illness story." When medical issues are prominent, the next step in getting to know the family is to solicit the "illness story," the family's collective narrative about an illness, disability, or death. For many families, this will be the first time they have talked together about the experience. The day-to-day demands of illness or grief often crowd out discussions about feeling, meaning, and relationship. Empathy, curiosity, and a family resiliency approach (Walsh, 2003) should guide the therapist as the family story unfolds. The goal at this stage is to respect defenses, remove blame, and accept unacceptable feelings (McDaniel, et al., 1992). During this phase, the skillful therapist can actively notice themes of strength and possibility without imposing an interpretation of the experience that feels foreign to the family.

Case Study

The parents of a 5-month-old girl with Short Bowel Syndrome were referred for family therapy by the girl's pediatrician, who had concerns about the family's early adjustment to the infant's medical needs. Shortly after birth, physicians discovered that the girl needed emergency surgery to correct an imperforate anus and necrotizing enterocolitis (unhealthy or dead tissue in the intestinal lining). After a brief postoperative recovery period, she was discharged to home, requiring multiple cares, including special feeding procedures, ostomy care, and attention to a central line catheter. During her first few months, she developed several infections that required hospitalization.

At the first family therapy visit, the parents appeared weary, sad, and anxious. The couple had a close, supportive relationship, and loved their little girl (who slept peacefully through the visit). They had also grown increasingly frustrated with each other around their differing responses to their daughter's medical needs and crises. Whenever they had concerns about the girl's health, the mother became highly emotional ("berserk," in her words) and the father became cool and serious ("management mode," in his words).

The therapist asked them to share their story: "The three of you have been through so much together. I'd like to understand exactly what you've experienced with your daughter's health, starting with your pregnancy. It may take some time, but the details of your story really matter." They shared the story of the pregnancy, birth, and first few months living with their child's medical condition: They were thrilled to become pregnant, which they achieved with the help of fertility medications. They enjoyed an uncomplicated pregnancy, labor, and delivery, and were totally surprised when doctors told them that something was wrong and that their daughter would be immediately transferred from the community hospital where they delivered to a university medical center. They described the terror and anger they felt when doctors did not yet know what was wrong, or if their baby would be alright, and the arguments that arose between them during this crisis.

Throughout the illness story, the therapist asked questions designed to highlight the parents' strength and expertise. These questions included asking about the details of the medical cares they were responsible for performing with their daughter. Caregivers often accumulate formidable medical knowledge and technical skills related to their loved one's condition. Many parents and other caregivers feel good about this expertise. In this case, after describing her daughter's postoperative cares, the mother said, "I feel like I could teach a class in medical school about this. We know more about Jessica's condition than her specialists do, because they only know about their individual parts and we know the whole picture." Perhaps they never wanted to know this much about intestines, digestion, elimination, and infection, but this insider knowledge was a potential source of unity for the couple.

Sharing the story with an empathetic listener brought coherence to the experience. Doing this together brought cohesion to the couple. At one point while sharing these details the father observed, "I never really thought of it all in chronological order; it just seemed like one big blurry nightmare."

Consider the context. Health problems are embedded in a biopsychosocial-spiritual context. Assessment and conceptualization should take into account how contextual factors influence the family experience of illness or disability.

The historical context is the most obvious to consider. Premorbid individual and family functioning is an important predictor of how a family copes with illness or other disruptions. Without prior contact with a family, it can be difficult to distinguish problematic adjustment reactions from preexisting patterns or pathology. In addition to asking the family about previous treatment and examples of how they handled past trials, contact with a primary care professional is often invaluable in assessing premorbid history. Many physicians have known their patients and their families for years, and can help determine whether "This is how this family tends to handle crises" or "This isn't like them" (or some combination thereof).

The developmental context is also important. A family's experience of illness or death will be different at different stages of individual and family development (Carter & McGoldrick, 1998). This lens may be particularly salient for working with families experiencing health problem demands created by an illness that may be out of phase with the family's life cycle stage. For example, the parents of an older adolescent with a severe brain injury may need to monitor the appropriateness of the young person's social interactions, or help with basic decision making, during a time when other families with adolescents are preparing to launch their children and move on. This asynchrony with expected life stages can seem more pronounced if the family has other children who progress normally. Likewise, physically disabled parents often need help from their children in ways that the life cycle model does not predict, such as caring for their hygiene, performing daily household tasks for them, or acting as liaison to a society that is often not equipped for their needs. (For a thorough review of disability and the family life cycle see Marshak, Seligman, & Prezant, 1999).

The nature, course, and time of onset of the health problem is another context to consider. Like families, health problems have unique features that influence family experience and relationships. Rolland (1994) proposed a typology of illness and disability with four key dimensions: onset (acute or gradual), course (progressive, constant, relapsing/episodic, predictable/unpredictable), incapacitation (presence or absence and severity) and outcome (fatal, shortened lifespan, or nonfatal). The matrix formed by combining these dimensions helps to predict the pattern of psychosocial demands created by a particular illness. Parkinson's disease, for example, has a gradual onset, progressive, relapsing course, varying levels of incapacitation, and shortened lifespan. The caregiving demands and family dynamics of this terminal condition would be quite different from those associated with a spinal cord injury, which has acute onset, constant course, and nonfatal outcome.

Seaburn and Erba (2003) found that the time of onset in the history of a family also influences family dynamics. A medical condition that predates the inception of the family, such as when a person has epilepsy before he marries, become nested in family life; roles and relationships accommodate the needs of the disabled individual and caregivers. Caregiving routines become part of the rhythm of normal family life. When a disability occurs after a family is formed, such as a premature stroke, families must reorganize and redefine themselves. Often, families have difficulty making these adjustments. They can become stuck in a chronic state of crisis, so that individual and family development are disrupted or even frozen around the time of the disability (Penn, 1983).

Middle Stages

Avoiding Triangulation

At all stages, the family therapist should be careful to avoid triangulation with the medical professionals and family. Once family members realize that the therapist is in frequent communication with the medical professional, they may look to the therapist as a source for medical information: "Did the doctor say what we'll do if Mom doesn't respond to this new medicine?" They may also voice complaints or frustrations about the physician to the therapist. "I tried to tell him my head is still hurting, but he didn't have time to listen." The family therapist should gently redirect questions and concerns to the physician.

Some families require coaching on how to approach their physician with questions or concerns, especially if they harbor disagreements or doubts. Patients often worry that, if they annoy or anger the doctor, he or she may become less interested in helping. Such fears are understandable, given the life-or-death importance of the physician's involvement. However, many patients get stymied in relationships with professionals by the patterns similar to those that hinder their other relationships. For example, the family therapist may notice that members of a family who are afraid to disagree with their doctor tend also to avoid conflict in their interactions with each other, by masking disagreeable thoughts or feelings. Awareness of such parallel processes empowers the family therapist to choose at which level(s) of the biopsychosocial system to intervene. By working through the problem at the doctor-patient level, for example, the family can learn communication skills that generalize to family relationships; and vice versa.

In some cases, a care conference among the medical professional, therapist, and family is the best way to support the family's relationship with the health care team and to address family members' concerns (McDaniel, Campbell, Hepworth, & Lorenz, 2004). These conferences can be effective at key decision points, especially when family members seem split (among themselves or with medical providers) about what to do. Interdisciplinary meetings with families can be challenging to schedule and expensive to conduct, but there is often no substitute for a well-timed congregation of those who care. Family therapists are uniquely positioned among mental health providers to lead joint conferences because of their expertise in managing communication among multiple stakeholders in a system.

Communication among Family Members and with Health Care Providers

Direct family communication about an illness is one of the protective health factors clearly identified in the research literature (Weihs et al., 2004). Threats to physical health often give rise to particularly powerful protective impulses among members of a system. The desire to protect loved ones, self, or patients from distress can hinder communication about medical information, feelings, desires, and conflicts.

Medical information. Family therapists should pay special attention to communication of medical information among family members and with health care providers. Family members often have the instinct to keep potentially frightening or discouraging information from an ill loved one. They fear that bad news could cause the person to give up hope, thereby decreasing the chances for recovery. They may see attempts to share painful information (especially if it is seen as "beyond the person's control") with a patient as unnecessary, even inhumane.

The person with the health problem experiences similar protective urges. In addition, the patient may feel that health information is private, rather than a family matter. When this is the case, the medical family therapist helps the person to discern the difference between privacy and secrecy (Imber-Black, 1998).

———————————————— **Case Study** ————————————————

Maya had myotonic dystrophy, a rare, heritable genetic condition that progressively disables affected individuals with muscle weakening, cognitive deterioration, hair loss, and cataracts. She and her mother presented for therapy amidst conflict over whether and when Maya should disclose the genetic information to her fiancé, Cliff. Maya and her mother worried about Cliff's emotional devastation and feared that he would leave her (as a previous boyfriend had), especially if he knew that the illness typically worsens with each successive generation. Maya's mother's anxiety about this matter was so intense that she had asked her daughter's neurologist to write a letter to the fiancé minimizing the gravity of her daughter's condition. The neurologist declined and referred the family for therapy.

In one of the first visits, the therapist learned that Maya's best friend, Claire, was her most trusted confidante about this decision. With encouragement from the therapist, Maya invited Claire to join for two of their sessions. After the second of these, Maya decided to tell her fiancé about her condition. Cliff joined Maya for therapy following the disclosure. He responded to the news with sadness and remarkable acceptance. Surprising both the women and the therapist, he likened this trial to growing up with a deaf brother, and embraced his prospective role as caregiver. The therapist explored Cliff's reaction in subsequent visits, but was careful not to assault his defenses or to assume pathological origins of his apparently loving response. Instead, once the couple felt ready, the therapist terminated therapy, with a clear invitation to return when and if the couple found their feelings toward the illness hindering the relationship, or if, at any time, they needed additional help talking together about its implications for their lives. They later did return, to work through a decision to conceive a child through assisted reproductive technologies.

Hidden feelings, desires, and conflicts. Honest communication of feelings can be complicated when one member of a family is ill or disabled. Family members often feel as if they are walking on eggshells when one member of the family is ill, especially if the condition is disabling and/or life-threatening. This tension is sometimes related to the paradoxical position of vulnerability and power that the ill family member occupies. The patient may need to rely on family members more than ever, but also can make claims on them like never before. For example, a man confined to bed as a result of end stage liver cancer will need family caregivers to bring food, pain medicine, and sponge baths. At the same time, his disability entitles him to make requests that cannot easily be denied—"Would you stay home again tonight? I'm feeling lonely." This request may be entirely appropriate; but if the caregiver feels she cannot say "No," she may build up unspoken resentments toward him and/or his illness.

In these cases, the family therapist may need to play the role of truth teller, helping the family give voice to feelings or desires that are too painful or shameful to say. This role requires courage—to break family rules and to ask questions that family members dare only to think.

Case Study

A 67-year-old woman, Joan, with severe cardiovascular disease was referred by her primary care physician for family therapy. The physician requested help after receiving multiple phone calls from distressed family members, complaining the patient was not following through with medical recommendations. The woman, who lived with her youngest son, agreed, when in the doctor's office, to call him when her cardiac symptoms reached a certain threshold. However, each time the threshold symptoms appeared, Joan refused to call, for fear the physician will tell her to go to the hospital. The son with whom she lived felt angry and helpless at having to watch his mother get ill and not cooperate with the doctor's plan. His siblings, in turn, were angry with him for not getting their mother to the hospital.

The family gathered for a meeting conducted by a medical family therapist at the physician's office. Joan sat with her arms crossed, and calmly rebuffed her family members' repeated attempts to cajole and scold her toward agreeing to the doctor's plan. After a particularly heated exchange among family members, the therapist turned to Joan and asked, "Do you want to die at home?" A pause followed, then a chuckle from Joan and a burst of energy from family members. They smiled and relaxed and began to ask Joan how she wanted to handle her symptoms and her disease.

Here, the therapist observed the family stuck in a pattern of helpless advocacy and help rejection, and suspected that Joan was communicating something she could not say out loud by thwarting her family's attempts to help her. She tested this hypothesis by directly asking the patient about her wishes in the situation. The simple, direct question changed the rules of interaction and created space for direct and honest communication. In this case, the hypothesis was at least partially confirmed by Joan's chuckle, but the intervention could have achieved a similar outcome even if the patient had denied such a wish. The power of "saying the unsayable" is the directness and courage it models.

Maintaining and Adjusting Family Identity and Individual Self-Concept

Illness and disability necessitate adjustments in family routines, roles, and identity. Therapists can help families anticipate these changes and adjust to losses. Perhaps more importantly, therapists can encourage family members to discuss together which aspects of family life do not need to change and which changes could bring about growth or other gains for the family. In the first months and years after diagnosis of a chronic illness or disability, families can have a hard time seeing how life could be good without being normal or "how it used to be."

─────────────── **Case Study** ───────────────

Mark was a 14-year-old boy with a rare rheumatologic disorder, who was referred by a specialist to family therapy for depression and suicidal thoughts. The symptoms of his chronic condition included unpredictable episodes of arthritis and painful ulcers on his body and mouth. He had a close, mutually caring relationship with his mother, who was strong, sensitive, and highly protective of her son.

Several months into therapy, the mother voiced the depth of her discouragement for the first time: "It doesn't matter what we do. If his illness doesn't stay under control, it's all useless; he's never going to live a normal life." This confession proved to be a turning point in the therapy. The therapist accepted her feelings without judgment ("Wow. Yes, life will never be the same,") and slowly began to explore her son's reaction to them. He was sad and unsurprised: "I'm glad you finally said it. Why do you think I want to kill myself sometimes?" With little prompting from the therapist, this honest exchange freed the family to acknowledge for the first time how the illness they hated had actually taught and given them a lot. The therapist continued to develop this theme in subsequent visits, eventually helping the family incorporate the illness into the family identity, rather than considering it an invincible foe.

───

Routines and rituals are the visible outworking of family identity. When working with families who have experienced health-related stress, the middle stages of therapy often involve detailed attention to the adjustments family members have made (or refuse to make) in their daily routines. For example, medical professionals often counsel "lifestyle changes" as part of a treatment plan. Patients with cardiovascular problems often need to change their eating habits to reduce calories, sodium, and cholesterol. Such changes will rarely occur without commitment from families to change their cooking and eating habits, yet family therapists know from experience that well-worn routines do not easily give way to new demands. Healthy family members may resent having to eat less flavorful food, or a husband cooking differently for his wife's health may take personally her comments about having to eat "tasteless health food." (For an extended discussion of family routines and rituals, see the *Journal of Family Psychology* special section dedicated to this topic [Fiese & Parke, 2002] Imber-Black, Roberts, & Whiting, 1988; and Imber-Black & Roberts, 1998.)

─────────────── **Case Study** ───────────────

One married couple, Monty and Lila, in their mid-sixties, found themselves increasingly isolated from friends and family after Monty had most of his stomach resected to fight an aggressive stomach cancer. They presented as sad and discouraged at their family physician's office 8 months after the successful surgery.

They reported that most of their previous social activities revolved around eating—at restaurants and in other people's homes. Since Monty could no longer eat normally (and in fact, became violently ill if he tried), they had declined most dinner invitations and had stopped going on dates together. Monty felt self-conscious (and sometime nauseous) sitting at the table, watching everyone else eat. During a joint visit with their physician, Lila mentioned that her husband was an accomplished classical guitarist, though he hadn't played in several years. The doctor smiled, "Sounds like it's time to dust off the old ax and put on a concert." Within minutes, the couple remembered a fundraiser they had put on at their synagogue 30 years earlier, in which Monty entertained guests with guitar music while they ate. Within a couple of weeks they began what would become a monthly "guitar and goodies" dinner, to which they invited friends and family. Monty would play music (prepared with hours of practice each week) during the dinner, then retire with guests to converse in the living room, where guests were served coffee and Monty took his prescribed liquid meal in a coffee cup.

Termination

The relationship medical family therapists have with families over time resembles that which family physicians share with their patients. Medical family therapists see themselves as consultants who remain available for intermittent return visits or for more intensive courses of treatment at future transition points, or if problems recur. The end of an episode of care is better characterized as "punctuation" than "termination." The process shares many aspects of traditional termination— the therapist encourages the family to review progress, themes, and potential pitfalls. In addition, the therapist explicitly anticipates that the family may need to return as family members enter new stages of development or phases of illness. The skillful therapist projects confidence that the family will conquer the challenges that lie ahead, and acceptance that they may need help in doing so.

This longitudinal perspective reflects a philosophical commitment to longevity in the healing relationship and an embrace of the primary care model of continuity, that is, that patients remain with a practice and a professional over time. Your doctor is still your doctor, even when you're healthy. For therapists who practice onsite in medical settings this kind of ongoing relationship is reinforced by chance hallway encounters, or brief, previsit exam-room check-ins when the patient has come in for medical care.

SPECIAL CONSIDERATIONS

Collaboration

Experts in interdisciplinary collaboration have written a great deal about its challenges and rewards (see McDaniel & Campbell, 1986; Patterson, Peek, Heinrich, Bischoff, & Scherger, 2002; Seaburn, Lorenz, Gunn, Gawinski, & Mauksch, 1996; Strosahl, 1996; Strosahl, 2005). In this chapter, we will mention a few particularly salient points for family therapists.

Onsite versus Offsite

The ideal setting in which to practice medical family therapy is in an integrated healthcare setting (see Blount, 1998; Patterson et al., 2002; Peek & Heinrich, 2000). Integrated practice settings facilitate in-person case consultation and joint visits between mental health and medical professionals, and provide a continuous care experience for the patient and family. Furthermore, the presence of a family therapist in a medical setting symbolizes the biopsychosocial integration that our approach advocates. Thus, we strongly advocate that therapists interested in medical issues seek opportunities (large and small) for onsite collaboration. (For an example of how to start small with onsite exposure see Pisani, Berry, & Goldfarb, 2005).

Nevertheless, integrated health care settings remain relatively rare. Fortunately, most aspects of medical family therapy can be successfully adapted to offsite practice. In fact, almost all of the guidelines we offered in the previous sections can be followed in any practice setting. The medical family therapist practicing in a nonmedical setting, however, will need to overcome two main challenges. The first is establishing an identity with the patient, with medical providers, and with him- or herself as part of the health care team. The therapist practicing in a medical setting is not exempt from this challenge (the family therapist often needs to work harder to gain full and equal membership on the team), but the offsite provider faces additional barriers (see Driscoll & McCabe, 2004, for discussion of work with primary care as a private practice mental health practitioner). One key element in establishing this identity with others is how the therapist views her- or himself. Many family therapists have not been trained to think of themselves as health care professionals, per se. This may be especially true of those who see family therapy as their primary professional identity (in contrast, for example, to a psychiatrist or nurse, who is also a family therapist). For these individuals, memberships in interdisciplinary professional societies can help the process of forming a health-related identity, by providing an opportunity to meet like-minded colleagues, gain exposure to cutting-edge work, and link with training opportunities in collaborative health care (Harkness, Smith, Waxman, & Hix, 2003). The Collaborative Family Healthcare Association is an example of such an organization, dedicated to clinical innovation in interdisciplinary biopsychosocial care. (For information, see www.cfha.net.)

The second challenge is in the domain of communication and collaboration. It is simply harder to communicate across town than across the hall. Nevertheless, a responsive, proactive, and savvy family therapist can foster productive collaborative communication. First, family therapists should know that most medical providers value responsive mental health professionals. Physicians bear enormous responsibility for their patient's well-being and, therefore, are highly invested in knowing the outcome of their referrals to specialty providers. Historically, many psychotherapists have functioned in a more sequestered manner—therapy was the private sanctuary of the patient and therapist. While this model may be valid within the profession and is indicated in some cases, it can be frustrating and perplexing to other health care professionals who do not function with this kind of ethos (see

McDaniel & Campbell, 1986, for a humorous representation of this dilemma). Physicians often complain of a "communication black hole" they experience after referring a patient for mental health. As a result, family therapists who provide timely and consistent feedback quickly garner favor and appreciation from other health care providers.

Also, offsite family therapists should ask collaborating professionals about their communication preferences. An initial letter, containing assessment and treatment impressions after the first visit with a family, is a standard expectation among medical providers and should be part of every therapist's routine. The letter should be brief (usually no more than one page or three short paragraphs), signaling respect for the other professional's time. In that letter, it is also wise to indicate at what intervals the provider should expect updates (see the following for discussion of confidentiality in medical family therapy). The letter can also contain a sentence that alerts the provider that the therapist will be phoning to discuss the case. During this follow-up contact, the therapist can explicitly ask, "How do you prefer to exchange information or ideas about this case? Are letters or phone calls more useful to you?" The therapist can likewise state his or her preferences for contact.

Ethical Issues: Confidentiality and Informed Consent

One of the most sensitive and controversial areas for psychotherapists working in health care is the area of patient confidentiality. Psychotherapy is founded on a strict principle of confidentiality, providing the patient or family with a safe place to explore the most delicate and private matters of existence. Good therapists protect this patient privilege with great care. However, another principle of good psychotherapy is understanding the patient's context—her or his family, their workplace, their health care team, and so on. With regard to health and illness, collaboration with other health professionals is one of the single most valuable interventions that can be made in the treatment of a patient or family. For those patients facing health challenges, this collaboration allows for the development of an integrated, comprehensive diagnostic and treatment plan. It operationalizes a professional process that can help to mend the mind-body split.

Two different cultures, in health care and in psychotherapy, have evolved regarding the sharing of patient information. In health care, sharing information amongst specialists is often vital for the treatment of a patient. Confidentiality in this setting expands to the health care team, not just to a single professional. From the perspective of the physician, psychotherapists can appear irresponsible in the way that we may protect information and do not participate in the patient's wider care. On the other hand, many therapists are concerned that confidentiality is too loose in medical practices. Sharing information with a health care team leaves more opportunities for breaches of private information. Recognizing this concern, the U.S. Congress passed the Health Information Privacy and Portability Act, in part to protect the patient's right to confidentiality and to shore up these loose boundaries regarding sharing patient information. As a result of this law, sensitivity toward these issues has been substantially raised.

How can these two principles—the principle of privacy and the principle of collaboration—be reconciled? In practice, it usually is not difficult. Resolution comes through participation of the patient as part of the treatment team. Informed consent may begin with a statement to the patient like the following:

> "I understand that you're facing a difficult health problem. One of the most useful parts of my routine practice is collaboration with other health professionals. With your permission, I would like to contact your physician/nurse practitioner so that I can better understand your illness, its treatment, and its course. Do you have any concerns about that? This exchange may also help your physician to understand you better. I will not give that person information you have shared with me that is irrelevant to your health care. If there is something you're particularly concerned that I not share, that is your right; please let me know and we can discuss it further."

The vast majority of patients are very pleased that their health professionals consult with each other. Many have suffered in the past because information has not been shared and treatment has not been coordinated. Sometimes therapy may be advanced by including the patient in the conversation between professionals. Then, a joint session or a phone call using a speakerphone is very useful.

On the rare occasion when a patient is concerned about information being shared, the therapist must determine whether that information is truly private (i.e., not relevant to the patient's health or health care), or whether it is a secret (i.e., the information is relevant but the patient is opposed to sharing it with the health professional). For example, in an individual session, a patient in marital therapy revealed he was having frequent, anonymous homosexual encounters. Neither his wife nor his physician were aware of this behavior. In addition to the marital issues, a central part of that therapy was helping the man acknowledge the health risks in his behavior and discuss them with his physician. The right to confidentiality is the patient's (not the professional's), so reluctance to share relevant information must be worked through in therapy, like any other secret. (For additional discussion of confidentiality in medical settings, see Patterson, Peek, Heinrich, Bischoff, & Scherger, 2002.)

Somatization

Working with patients referred with suspected somatization is worthy of special mention because of the challenges associated with this population. Therapists should pay special attention to the therapeutic alliance when listening to the illness story of these individuals and their families. Acceptance and use of the patient's initial definition of the illness and the problem is crucial to the joining process. With some patients, it is tempting to interpret a physical complaint in terms of psychological distress—to try to force the emotional reality to the conscious. Therapists should resist this temptation and speak the language of the patient, keeping in mind that, if the patient or family could tolerate conscious experience of the emotional pain, the somatization for which they were referred would be unnecessary. The therapist should instead focus on demonstrating compassion and building trust.

Likewise, it is important to pay attention to how family members interpret the somatic complaints. Persistent physical symptoms with no diagnosable organic origin can be a source of contention between family members. Alliances and splits form around how much credibility the suffering patient is afforded. The therapist should frame family members' disagreements in terms of differences of perspective, such as, "Because you are not inside his body, it is difficult to know what it feels like, but from where you sit, it is hard to imagine that someone could look as healthy as he does and be in this much pain." (For a practical guide to working with somatization see Griffith & Griffith, 1994, and Watson & McDaniel, 2000).

Cultural Influences

Gender, race, and culture figure prominently in the assessment and treatment of any family. In medical family therapy, cultural influences are most salient in the domain of health beliefs. Health beliefs involve how people perceive health threats and their role in addressing them (Becker, 1974). Medical family therapists listen for ways in which a family's health beliefs shape the family's view of their role in causing a medical condition, interpretation of medical information, interactions with health care providers, and health-related behavior.

Case Study

A family physician trained in medical family therapy treated a young, professional couple who had immigrated to the United States from Brazil. Shortly after arriving in the country, the couple became pregnant, and then miscarried in the second trimester. During follow-up visits with the woman, their physician sensed tension and uneasiness beyond what she typically saw in families grieving after a miscarriage. The physician invited the woman to return with her husband for an extended office visit. During consultation, the couple slowly revealed a series of beliefs in their culture about what causes miscarriage, including attending a funeral or passing through a graveyard while pregnant. When they arrived in the United States, the couple had rented an apartment next to a cemetery, against the advice of their family members in Brazil. The couple articulately described their intellectual dismissal of these folk beliefs, but also the emotional power they nevertheless held. When the physician asked about how other family members had responded to the loss, the woman began crying, saying that her grandmother asked her in their last phone conversation if she and her husband were planning to move away from the cemetery. She had felt too ashamed to share this conversation with her husband, who, upon hearing about it, immediately leaned over to embrace and support her. This began an ongoing discussion between the husband and wife, and with the doctor, about how to grieve the loss, interact with family members, and, eventually, how to plan for the next pregnancy.

The key themes of medical family therapy also transcend gender, race, and culture. The vulnerability to disease and the experience of illness and death are universal. Every human culture at every time has faced loss, transition, caregiving, celebration, and survival. Indeed, these are at heart of culture. Thus, medical family therapy requires reverence and humility. It is a privilege to work with families around such fundamentally human experiences. Likewise, therapists must respect and support families' spiritual inquiry and resources, without overstepping our bounds as mental health professionals. Families are encouraged, when applicable, to include spiritual or religious leaders into their therapy. This invitation implicitly acknowledges that illness and health are multidimensional phenomena.

CONCLUSION

Family therapists are well positioned to contribute to the well-being of families as part of the biopsychosocial health care team. Full participation in health care requires some modification of how we, as individual professionals and as a field, think of ourselves and our work. The identity of family therapist as health professional implies a broadening of the definition of health to include both the impact of medical events on the family and the influence of close relationships on physical health. The systemic training and techniques that characterize family therapy are a natural fit for the multidimensional work that is always involved when it comes to health issues.

Expertise in family relationships will likely become even more valuable as technological and scientific advances change health care. The current explosion of knowledge about the role of genes in disease is revolutionizing the practice of medicine. The consequent focus on family history and genetic relationships highlights, and gives new metaphors for, family interconnectedness in health and illness (Miller, McDaniel, Rolland, & Feetham, in press). Other technological advances, such as new life-extending medicines for HIV patients, improved pacemaker technology for cardiac patients, and a thousand others give patients and families unprecedented opportunities and choices. Families need help sorting through feelings, decisions, and relational implications associated with these technological advances. Medical professionals are increasingly aware of the personal impact medical advances have on families, but a team approach will always be necessary to properly attend to intrapsychic and relational dimensions of health.

This chapter offers guidelines that operationalize the biopsychosocial approach for family therapy. This approach encourages discussion of health issues and collaboration with other health professionals at every stage of therapy—from initial planning and consultation, through termination. Family therapists in any setting can adapt the principles of medical family therapy and contribute to the overall health (physical and relational) of families. The approach is appropriate for a wide range of presenting problems, including those that do not ostensibly involve illness. The participation of family therapists in a wide range of health care settings can help or even heal some of the fragmentation that plagues the modern health care system. In summary, family therapists with a biopsychosocial approach can provide relevant help to families, support the work of colleagues, and enjoy the clinical and personal benefits of satisfying clinical teamwork.

REFERENCES

Anderson, H., Goolishian, H., & Winderman, L. (1986). Problem determined systems: Towards transformation in family systems. *Journal of Strategic and Systemic Therapies, 5,* 1–14.

Bakan, D. (1969). *The dual reality of human existence.* Chicago: Rand McNally.

Becker, M. 1974. *The Health Belief Model and personal health behavior.* Thorofare, NJ: Slack.

Bertalanffy, L. (1950). An outline of general systems theory, *British Journal for Philosophy of Science, 1,* 134–150.

Bloch, Donald A. (1984). The family therapist as health care consultant. *Family Systems Medicine, 2,* 161–169.

Blount, A. (1998). *Integrated Primary Care: The future of medical and mental health collaboration.* New York: W. W. Norton.

Blount, A. (2003). Integrated primary care: Organizing the evidence. *Families, Systems, and Health, 21,* 121–133.

Bowen, M. (1978). *Family Therapy in Clinical Practice.* New York: Aronson.

Campbell, T. L. (2003). The effectiveness of family interventions for physical disorders. *Journal of Marital & Family Therapy, 29,* 263–281.

Carter, B., & McGoldrick, M. (Eds.). (1998). *The Expanded Family Life Cycle: Individual, Family, and Social Perspectives* (3rd ed.). Boston: Allyn & Bacon.

Doherty, W. J., & Baird, M. (1983). *Family Therapy and Family Medicine.* New York: Guilford.

Driscoll, W. B., & McCabe, E. P. (2004). Primary care psychology in independent practice. In R. Frank, S. H., McDaniel, J. Bray, & M. Heldring (Eds.), *Primary Care Psychology,* pp. 133–148. Washington, DC: American Psychological Association.

Engel, G. L. (1977). The need for a new medical model: A challenge for biomedicine. *Science, 196,* 129–136.

Fiese, B. H., & Parke, R. D. (Eds.). (2002). Introduction to the special section on family routines and rituals. *Journal of Family Psychology, 16,* 379–380.

Frank, R., McDaniel, S. H., Bray, J., & Heldring, M. (Eds.). (2004). *Primary Care Psychology.* Washington, DC: American Psychological Association.

Frankel, R., Quill, T., & McDaniel, S. H. (Eds.). (2003). *The Biopsychosocial Approach.* Rochester, NY: University of Rochester Press.

Glenn, M. L. (1987). *Collaborative healthcare: A family oriented approach.* New York: Praeger.

Gonzalez, S., Steinglass, P., & Reiss, D. (1989). Putting the illness in its place: Discussion groups for families with chronic medical illnesses. *Family Process, 28,* 69–87.

Griffith, J. L., & Griffith, M. E. (1994). *The body speaks: Therapeutic dialogues for mind-body problems.* New York: Basic Books.

Harkness, J. L., Smith, A. L., Waxman, D. M., & Hix, N. V. (2003). Balancing personal and professional identities: The art of collaborative practice. *Families, Systems and Health, 21,* 93–99.

Helgeson, V. (1994). Relation of agency and communion to well-being: Evidence and potential explanations. *Psychological Bulletin, 116,* 412–428.

House, J. S., Landis, K. R., & Umberson, D. (1988). Social relationships and health. *Science, 241,* 540–545.

Imber-Black, E. (1998). *The secret life of families.* New York: Bantam Books.

Imber-Black, E., & Roberts, J. (1998). *Rituals for our times: Celebrating, healing, and changing our lives and our relationships.* New York: Aronson.

Imber-Black, E., Roberts, J., & Whiting, R. A. (1988). *Rituals in families and family therapy.* New York: Norton.

Kessler, L., Burns, B., & Shapiro, S. (1987). Psychiatric diagnoses of medical service users: Evidence from the epidemiologic catchment area program. *American Journal of Public Health, 77,* 18–24.

Kroenke, K., & Mangelsdorf, A. D. (1989). Common symptoms in ambulatory care: incidence, evaluation, therapy and outcome. *American Journal of Medicine, 86,* 262–266.

Kowal, J., Johnson, S. M., & Lee, A. (2003). Chronic illness in couples: A case for emotionally focused therapy. *Journal of Marital and Family Therapy, 29,* 299–310.

McDaniel, S. H., & Campbell, T. L. (1986). Physicians and family therapists: The risks of collaboration. *Family Systems Medicine, 4,* 4–8.

McDaniel, S. H., Campbell, T. L., Hepworth, J., & Lorenz, A. (2004). *Family-oriented primary care* (2nd ed.). New York: Springer-Verlag.

McDaniel, S. H., Hepworth, J., & Doherty, W. (1992). *Medical family therapy: A biopsychosocial approach to families with health problems.* New York: Basic Books.

McDaniel, S. H., Hepworth, J., & Doherty, W. (1997). *The shared experience of illness: Stories of patients, families, and their therapists.* New York: Basic Books.

Marshak, L. E., Seligman, M., & Prezant, F. (1999). *Disability and the family life cycle: Recognizing and treating developmental challenges.* New York: Basic Books.

Mikesell, R., Lusterman, D. D., & McDaniel, S. H. (Eds.). (1995). *Integrating family therapy.* Washington, DC: American Psychological Association.

Miller, S. M., McDaniel, S. H., Rolland, J., & Feetham, S. (in Press). *Individuals, families and the new genetics.* New York: Norton.

Minuchin, S., Rosman, B. L., & Baker, L. (1978). *Psychosomatic families: Anorexia nervosa in context.* Cambridge, MA: Harvard University Press.

Narrow, W. E., Regier, D. A., Rae, D. S., Manderscheid, R. W., & Locke, B. Z. (1993). Use of services by persons with mental and addictive disorders: Findings from the National Institute of Mental Health Epidemiologic Catchment Area Program. *Archives of General Psychiatry, 50,* 95–107.

Patterson, J., Peek, C. J., Heinrich, R. L., Bischoff, R. J., & Scherger, J. (2002). *Mental health professionals in medical settings: A primer.* New York: Norton.

Peek, C. J., & Heinrich, R. L. (2000). Integrating behavioral health and primary care. In M. Maruish (Ed.). *Handbook of Psychological Assessment in Primary Care Settings* (pp. 43–91). Mahwah, NJ: Lawrence Erlbaum.

Penn, P. (1983). Coalitions and binding interactions in families with chronic illness. *Family Systems Medicine, 1,* 16–25.

Pisani, A. R., Berry, S., & Goldfarb, M. (2005). A predoctoral field placement in primary care: Keeping it simple. *Professional Psychology: Research and Practice, 36,* 151–157.

Regier, D., Goldberg, I., & Taube, C. (1978). The de facto U.S. mental health system. *Archives of General Psychiatry, 35,* 685–693.

Regier, D., Narrow, W., Rae, D., Manderscheid, R., Locke, B., & Goodwin, F. (1993). The de facto U.S. mental health and addictive disorders service system. *Archives of General Psychiatry, 50,* 85–94.

Rolland, J. S. (1994). *Families, illness, and disability: An integrative treatment model.* New York: Basic Books.

Seaburn, D. B., & Erba, G. (2003). The family experience of "sudden health": The case of intractable epilepsy. *Family Process, 42,* 453–467.

Seaburn, D. B., Lorenz, A. D., Gunn, W. B., Gawinski, B. A., & Mauksch, L. B. (1996). *Models of collaboration: A guide for mental health professionals working with health care practitioners.* New York: Basic Books.

Strosahl, K. (2005). Training behavioral health and primary care providers for integrated care: A core competencies approach. In W. O'Donohue, M. Byrd, N. Cummings, & D. Henderson (Eds.), *Behavioral integrative care: Treatments that work in the primary care setting* (pp. 15–52). Brunner-Routledge: New York.

Walsh, F. (2003). *Normal family processes: Growing diversity and complexity* (3rd ed.). New York: Guilford.

Walsh, F., & McGoldrick, M. (2004). *Living beyond loss: Death in the family* (2nd ed.). New York: Norton.

Watson, W., & McDaniel, S. (2000). Relational therapy in medical settings: Working with somatizing patients and their families. *Journal of Clinical Psychology/In Session: Psychotherapy in Practice, 56,* 1037–1050.

Weihs, K., Fisher, L., & Baird, M. (2002). Families, health, and behavior—A section of the commissioned report by the Committee on Health and Behavior: Research, Practice, and Policy, Division of Neuroscience and Behavioral Health and Division of Health Promotion and Disease Prevention, Institute of Medicine, National Academy of Sciences. *Families Systems and Health, 20,* 7–46.

Wynne, L. C. (2003). Systems theory and the biopsychosocial model. In R. Frankel, T. Quill, & S. H. McDaniel (Eds.), *The biopsychosocial approach: Past, present, and future* (pp. 219–230). Rochester, NY: University of Rochester Press.

CHAPTER 23

Families in Later Life: Issues, Challenges, and Therapeutic Responses

Dorothy S. Becvar

Ours is an aging society, one in which the majority of the population soon will fall into the category of later life. Today, people tend to live much longer and stay far healthier than in previous eras. In addition, higher rates of divorce, remarriage and cohabitation, delayed and reduced fertility, as well as increased labor force participation are all factors that are having an impact on the experience of older adults (Davey, Murphy, & Price, 2000). Accordingly, the periods of both middle age and old age have lengthened and also have changed in character. As therapists, it is therefore becoming more and more likely that we will be working with individuals and families dealing with problems related to the latter stages of the family life cycle. At the same time, our understanding of the issues and challenges relevant to these stages may need revising.

In terms of demographic data, the population in the United States, like that in all modern nations, is becoming more mature. Indeed, the expectation is that by the year 2050, "there will be nearly two billion people in the world 60 years and older" (Dychtwald, 2000, p. 3), with the percentage of those 80 or older rising from 11 percent to 16 percent of the 60+ population. Further, while the older generations are growing in number, both their economic power and political influence are increasing. The baby boomers, those born between 1946 and 1964, tend to be better educated, more focused on self-discovery and lifestyle experimentation, more career-oriented, and more materialistic than their predecessors. As a dominant force in American society, the members of this group will continue to have a major impact as they enter the stages of later life. That is, they will consider themselves to be young and middle-aged longer, and to get old later (2000). Rather than retiring, retreating, and declining in the pattern of many of their parents and grandparents, those in midlife now are tending to experience great self-confidence, and to be active, healthy, productive, and very much involved as they focus on creating meaningful ways to enjoy what they look forward to as the second half of life. Given this shift in orientation, later life becomes a time for experimentation and exploration, rather than one of stagnation and deterioration.

The ramifications for family members of changes such as these are significant. For example, the likelihood that middle-aged adults will be called upon to deal with caretaking responsibilities for their elderly parents is increasing, while the availability of the former, in terms of free time to do so, is decreasing. Similarly, grandparents are becoming less and less likely to fulfill such traditional roles for their children as babysitters or providers of regular child care. Indeed, while retirement may occur earlier, given a general increase in affluence, it may take on a whole new meaning as mature adults return to school, start new careers, or simply are absorbed in enjoying a renewed sense of freedom. At the same time, as the French proverb goes, the more things change, the more they remain the same. Thus, those in the middle and older age groups may continue to face such classic tasks and issues as rebuilding and/or recreating marriages, realigning the family to include the spouses and partners of children and grandchildren, evaluating and rethinking career options, adjusting to retirement and old age, coping with the death of parents and spouses or partners, closing or adapting the family home, maintaining individual and couple functioning and/or dealing with illness, and supporting the younger generations (Becvar & Becvar, 1999). Keeping in mind this brief overview of some of the most salient issues, we turn now to an approach to working with individuals and families dealing with the various challenges currently associated with later life.

THEORETICAL ORIENTATION

The theoretical orientation underpinning this approach to families in later life is derived from a postmodern/second-order cybernetics perspective (Becvar & Becvar, 2006) that also is informed by theories of individual and family development (Carter & McGoldrick, 1988; Nichols, Pace-Nichols, Becvar, & Napier, 2001). Such an approach highlights sensitivity to such issues as middle-age children dealing with their elderly parents, aging partners supporting one another, and families dealing with the illness and death of one of their members. Pragmatically, the therapist participates in a process grounded in the assumption that change equals a change in context (Watzlawick, Weakland, & Fisch, 1976), with her or him engaging in conversations that facilitate the cocreation of the realities desired by clients. Indeed, according to Bonjean (1997), therapy with elderly adults that focuses on solutions may be useful in accessing their abilities and emphasizing their strengths. Given their greater length of life, their potentially rich history, and the likelihood that they will have experienced and survived many challenges, it is likely that the therapist may elicit many examples from the past of ways in which later-life clients have been successful in resolving problems. Clients then may be validated and recognized for their expertise when it comes to their own lives, and in the process, they may come to view themselves and their world in a much more positive manner.

Through the process of dialogue, clients dealing with later life issues thus are helped to expand their stories, or the systems of meaning that define their world, as well as their experience of it. An ongoing exchange of thoughts, feelings, and beliefs allows their personal histories and worldviews to be articulated, questioned, deconstructed, and reconstructed in the search for solutions to the problems they are experiencing. Such dialogue may be facilitated by means of a genogram, which has been found to be very appropriate with later life clients (Erlanger, 1990). Indeed, whether in oral or written form, a process that allows aging individuals to tell their story, and along the way to engage in a kind of life review, may increase the comfort level of potentially reluctant clients. At the same time, it also may provide important information, enabling the therapist to highlight significant moments as well as understand the clients' context.

Another important part of this process includes a concern for helping later life families to flourish by facilitating resilience (Walsh, 1998), the capacity of those who even under the most stressful circumstances are able to cope, to rebound, and to thrive. Thus, along with an awareness of a variety of family therapy approaches (Becvar & Becvar, 2006), the therapeutic conversation ideally incorporates knowledge about families in general (e.g., processes characterizing successful families, the expected and unexpected developmental challenges of later life), knowledge about specific families (e.g., the ramifications for families of variations in structure, ethnicity, and culture, the impact of gender differences), and knowledge about various family dynamics (e.g., communication, relationship skills, family enrichment, parenting, rituals and traditions, spontaneity and humor, goals, values and meaning, religion/spirituality). Finally, added to the mix are elements regarding therapist perspective and behavior.

Of great importance to this perspective is an awareness of theoretical relativity, and thinking in terms of both/and rather than either/or. Accordingly, it is assumed that all perspectives contain some degree of truth, and that the utility of a particular perspective can be decided only relative to context. Rather than operating according to a set agenda or a specific model, the therapist responds in the moment in ways that seem most appropriate for each unique client system. Thus, more important than the strategies or techniques is an orientation, or way of thinking about and being with later life clients. For example, it is essential for the therapist to be aware that believing is seeing, that her or his personal frameworks or stories influence her or his perceptions. Useful questions the therapist might ask are, "What am I telling myself about this client?" or "What other stories/theories might I tell myself?" In the attempt to be sensitive to and to acknowledge the influence of the observer on the observed, to recognize reciprocity and mutual influence, the therapist may consider such questions as, "How would my having a different story/theory change what I am seeing?" or "How might the client respond differently to my new story/theory?" Relative to the notion that the therapist is taking part in the creation rather than the discovery of realities, he might reflect on queries such as, "Can I recognize how I am participating in creating problems?" or "Can I recognize how I am participating in creating solutions?" Acting in a manner consistent with the behaviors desired is also important, prompting such considerations as, "What kind of response would I like to have from the other person?" and "What behaviors on my part are logical to the responses I desire?" Overall, the therapeutic stance is one of both respect for families dealing with later life issues and curiosity about their lives and what they would experience as meaningful.

Finally, given a systemic orientation, working with relationships is preferable, although working with individuals certainly is not precluded. However, even in the latter case it is important to think relationally and to consider the larger context.

Relative to issues of later life, it usually seems most appropriate to have the opportunity to interact with and observe the interactions of as many family members involved as possible. Indeed, intergenerational family therapy has been recommended for older clients (Davey, Murphy & Price, 2000), particularly those whose presenting problems revolve around role transitions. Accordingly, the therapist may be provided with more information and greater understanding, even as members of the younger generation may be able to become part of the process of finding and achieving solutions. A focus on strengthening connections and resolving old relationship issues also may become not only appropriate but also helpful to this end. Indeed, problems that emerge during the final stages of life often have multigenerational ramifications. In the experience of the author, it is not at all unusual to hear first from those in middle age who are attempting to deal with problems related to an elderly parent. The search for solutions therefore may be facilitated by greater systemic awareness and involvement. It is from such a theoretical orientation that specific strategies defining the realm of practical applications for working with families in later life emerge.

THE THERAPEUTIC PROCESS

Assessing, Analyzing, and Perturbing

A fundamental position of the therapist is one of suspending judgment (Becvar, 1996). That is, while socially undesirable and/or unacceptable behaviors may be recognized and certainly are not condoned, the therapist attempts to understand all behavior as somehow making sense, or being logical, in context. Thus, for example, she or he may search for the ways in which people have learned to behave in ways deemed unacceptable by others. The basic goodness of human nature is assumed—the therapist attempts to be compassionate and accept people where they are, while detaching from "shoulds," or ideas about how they are supposed to be. Similarly, the therapist is sensitive to and careful to avoid stereotypes about middle and old age, focusing on understanding each new client in his or her context. Further, it is important to postpone evaluations about behaviors and situations, recognizing that with time and perspective meanings may evolve and change, not only for the therapist but also for the clients. Indeed, as the therapist is able to be respectful of people and their problems, rather than judging, blaming, or condemning them, she or he is more likely to create an atmosphere of trust, so that the therapy process will proceed and continue and meaningful change can occur. The following case study provides an illustration:

―――――――――――――――――― **Case Study** ――――――――――――――――――

My first therapeutic encounter with Marcy focused on dealing with the emotional side effects of breast cancer and its treatment. During the time we originally worked together, I also had an opportunity to get to know her husband, Bill, as well as her three adolescent children. Therefore, when Marcy returned to therapy 10 years later, I already knew a great deal about her family and larger context. This time, however, she was requesting assistance in dealing with her mother, Ella. Ella had lived most of her life in another state. However, when her husband, Marcy's father, died from a sudden heart attack, Marcy persuaded her mother to come live with her and Bill. They had plenty of room, as the children were now gone and Bill and Ella got along well, so this seemed a good plan, and at first the new arrangement worked well. The dilemma evolved over time, as Marcy became more and more irritated by her mother's unwillingness to take care of herself appropriately, as well as by her general passivity relative to past unresolved issues with various family members. Marcy's relationship with Bill also became strained as he criticized her behavior toward her mother. As Marcy, now age 54, described this situation she became very tearful. She was torn between her desire to help her mother and her wish to behave as a loving daughter. However, it soon became apparent that an even greater issue for her related to fears that her mother was giving up on life, that she was going to die, despite the fact that at 76 years of age she was basically quite healthy.

As I reflected on the behaviors of Marcy, Bill, and Ella, they all made sense to me when considered in context. The story I told myself was that as a cancer survivor, Marcy was committed to life to the fullest, making the most of every day. Therefore, her mother's seeming lack of interest in life hit her in a very vulnerable spot, that also included her recognition that her mother was aging and that eventually she would die. I saw Bill's behavior as a reflection of his concern for Marcy, that above all he wished for her well-being, and worried that the tension with her mother would undermine the good health she had worked so hard to achieve. And I speculated that Ella, despite her daughter's good intentions, like many elderly persons, was probably having a difficult time adjusting to her new circumstances, having left her home, her friends, her sense of independence, and everything that was familiar behind when she moved in with Marcy and Bill.

It is important to note at this point that one of the major challenges to the functioning of older adults is the frequent need to accommodate role changes and transitions that may involve losses around money, autonomy, and relationships (Davey, Murphy, & Price, 2000). Thus, despite the best intentions of offspring, the process of providing care for aging parents, however that is arranged, can be challenging for everyone involved.

As conversations with clients continue, it is important for the therapist to be sensitive to language, being mindful about what someone or something is called. Accordingly, formal diagnoses are avoided whenever possible, with a preference for seeing specific behaviors rather than grouping them into a category that then becomes the focus of treatment. What is more, rather than *treating*, the therapist *interacts* and *works with*, assuming reality as socially constructed through language. The therapist also is aware that each of her or his questions or statements is a perturbation, and thus is careful about what she or he asks, says, and how questions and responses are framed. She or he also attempts to highlight skills and balance whatever assessments she or he may make to include strengths and talents as well as clients' perceptions about themselves.

The therapist also takes his or her cues about how to proceed from clients, asking what brings them to therapy, why now, and listening carefully to whatever it is they choose to share. In addition, he or she generally asks each individual or family member to provide a brief history, describing where each was born, the family each grew up in, the way parents related to each other, how each got along with parents and siblings, as well as various family, educational, relational, medical, spiritual/religious, or other experiences and milestones. At this point, the therapist also asks for information about and considers the cultural variables specific to the family. This verbal genogram process allows clients to tell and hear their stories at the same time that it enables them and the therapist to have a greater awareness of, and hopefully sensitivity to, the larger context within which various patterns and problems have emerged and become part of the fabric of the system.

Cocreating New Realities

In order to ascertain the goals for therapy, the therapist asks clients how they would like their lives to be, or more specifically, what would be going on at the end of their time of working together if therapy were successful. While clients generally are very articulate about their problems and what they don't like, it is not unusual, particularly for the elderly, to have difficulty describing what they would like. The therapist therefore might then ask them to think about particular behaviors that they would desire to experience for themselves or receive from others to replace those behaviors or situations about which they have complaints. Sometimes this process occurs in session, and sometimes clients are asked to go home and reflect on these questions and then return with a list outlining that which they desire.

The job of the therapist is to help clients get where they want to go. At the same time, as clients begin to focus on desired solutions, the therapist also attempts to help them understand the idea of recursion, or mutual influence, and reciprocal responsibility. They may be encouraged to recognize the degree to which the behavior of each has an impact on and influences the behavior of others. And, the therapist also recognizes that this same awareness applies to her or him, that resistance, for example, is a relational concept. In this way, a shift away from blame and guilt is facilitated along with awareness of the importance of paying attention to one's own behavior in order for change to occur. To encourage clients in this regard, the therapist may give homework assignments aimed both at experiencing new behaviors and generating a feeling of greater energy and a sense of mutual commitment to the process. The following case study provides an illustration:

─────────────── **Case Study** ───────────────

Like many of my clients dealing with later life challenges, Theresa and Joe, both retired schoolteachers, were struggling with the dilemma of redefining their relationship with each other and with their grown children, now that Joe had begun a second career as a real estate salesman. After they described an increase in tension and conflict during the past year, with Theresa noting that she felt ignored and Joe saying that he would like more support, I asked each of them to talk about how they would like things to be. Theresa expressed a desire to be able to spend more time relaxing and enjoying each other, perhaps pursuing a hobby together, and definitely traveling periodically and spending blocks of time with their four children, all of whom were married, had children, and were living in different states. While Joe certainly wanted to be with his wife and visit his children from time to time, he also wanted to be able to continue to focus on and become as successful as possible in his new business. And, he desired Theresa's support for his efforts in this regard, wanting particularly her understanding about the demands on his time.

Having already learned that Joe and Theresa had positive memories from the early days of their relationship, I asked them both to describe the things they had done for fun together during their courtship and the first part of their marriage, before the children were born. After hearing their descriptions of a wonderfully fulfilling time, I expressed my perception that they seemed to have a very strong foundation on which to rebuild and recreate their relationship, despite the degree of conflict they now were encountering. I also commented on their success over the years as they found ways to balance two careers and successfully rear four children. At the same time, I also noted that I didn't believe the problems they were experiencing would go away overnight, and that we would need to take some time to sort out the best ways to go. I suggested that while they certainly had known how to dance well together in the past, the music had changed, and both were feeling awkward and unsure, and as a result, were now stepping on each other's toes. As a first step toward regaining a better balance, I invited them to choose 15 to 30 minutes every day when both could be available to do something fun together. I also encouraged them to take turns being responsible for the activity of the day, with each selecting something the other would enjoy when it was her or his turn.

As part of the conversations and suggestions for homework, the therapist also may attempt to reframe (Watzlawick, et al., 1976) behavior in such a way that it may be understood and responded to in different, hopefully more useful, ways. Similarly, it may be useful to normalize whenever possible or appropriate, helping people to understand that what they are experiencing is not at all unusual, given their particular age or stage of life. In addition, the therapist speaks about stories, emphasizing differences in individual understanding and the role of perception in the creation of realities. He or she also externalizes problems (White & Epston, 1990), attempting to separate persons from behaviors. He or she is aware that in order to be effective, he or she must think creatively and speak carefully, choosing metaphors and other language that are meaningful to those with whom he or she is interacting.

Supporting and Validating

It is very important to respect and affirm clients, particularly those in the older generations. The therapist therefore acknowledges and validates whatever efforts clients may have made to solve problems in the past, as well as feelings of "stuckness" that they may express relative to the present. The therapist may commend clients for choosing to come to therapy, knowing that this is often a difficult step. In addition, in an effort to encourage success, she or he attempts to find out what success means to each individual, as well as what each individual would experience as encouragement. This is important information for both therapist and clients, enabling accomplishments to be acknowledged and validated in meaningful ways. Indeed, the therapist might suggest that relevant consequences be provided for appropriate behavior. And she or he certainly might seek out the causes of success, what helped a person to make a desired change. Similarly, she or he might engage in a search for talents, exploring hidden abilities and unique outcomes in an effort to help clients both to enlarge their stories about themselves and each other as well as to facilitate the expansion of their behavioral repertoires (White & Epston, 1990).

The therapist also may teach clients various communication skills, with a systemic awareness (Becvar & Becvar, 1997). For example, helping clients to learn how to speak in terms of "I" messages, to learn the utility of paraphrasing, and to be able to choose their responses rather than merely reacting to one another may be useful. Sometimes providing information about how to discuss difficult issues may be appropriate. Accordingly, the therapist may suggest that relationship pairs pick a spot where they can sit facing each other. Using a kitchen timer, each is allowed 5 minutes to speak her or his mind, without interruption from the other. They then must go away and think about their response for at least 30 minutes. They may return and have another 5 minutes each, followed by a 30-minute break, for as many times as it takes to resolve the conflict.

Clients also may benefit from an expression of the therapist's perception that they are responding to each other on the basis of the stories they are telling themselves about the other, rather than on the basis of what the other is actually doing or saying. This is a phenomenon particularly likely in the case of long-term relationships and much shared history, and awareness of it may change how family members respond to one another. In addition, the therapist is alert to instances when it is appropriate to talk about triangulation, a problem that often occurs at an intergenerational level, encouraging clients to find ways to avoid it in the future. A focus on this issue is illustrated as follows:

—————————————— **Case Study** ——————————————

Eileen and Sam, a middle-aged couple, came to therapy in great distress over the behavior of Eileen's mother, Katherine. Katherine, a divorcee of many years, had once been quite close to Sam, who had been more than willing to help his mother-in-law with household chores and errands as well as to provide financial advice. However, following a misunderstanding about how a gift of money was received, Katherine had turned on Sam, calling him selfish and interested only in himself, accusing him of wanting her money, and predicting that he was going to hurt Eileen. Katherine wrote several letters to Sam expressing her negative perceptions, and began telling some of her friends the same story. Sam, who was angry, hurt, and sad, made several attempts to talk with Katherine and straighten things out, sometimes alone and sometimes including Eileen in the discussions. He also asked

Eileen to talk with her mother about spreading lies, but all to no avail. Eileen also was angry at her mother, but felt obligated to remain in contact, and to do what needed to be done to help her since none of her siblings lived nearby. However, when Sam refused to have further contact with Katherine, Eileen became the recipient of the nasty letters and didn't know what to do. She tried to reason with her mother and she asked her siblings for help, but to no avail. At my suggestion, she took her mother for a checkup with her physician, to make sure there were no medical problems or cognitive impairment. She also asked their priest to speak to her, but Katherine remained adamant in her story.

Over time, Eileen learned to handle the letters by opening and reading them without comment, either to her husband or her mother. She also supported Sam's decision to absent himself from birthday and holiday observances with her mother, but worried about what to do if the topic of her husband came up in conversation with Katherine. In order to help her avoid being drawn any further into the middle, I suggested that Eileen respond to any mention of the situation by her mother with a totally unrelated comment, for example, "Can you believe the price of eggs?" or "I just love it when it rains!" (even if it isn't raining). I was encouraging Eileen to refuse to participate in any way in the triangle her mother was attempting to create, while successfully maintaining her relationships with both her husband and her mother.

In addition to learning how to detriangulate, clients also may benefit from recognizing that one acquires power by giving up power, that everyone makes mistakes from time to time, and that acknowledging both our own frailties and the strengths of others may be very empowering. Finally, a useful communication tool the therapist may offer is that of feedforward. Accordingly, rather than criticizing and shaming each other, clients may be invited to request the behavior desired of the other. In all of this, whether instructing or suggesting, the therapist also attempts to model respectful behavior by acknowledging both the humanness and the expertise of everyone involved.

Facilitating Resilience

Having an awareness of the traits and patterns characteristic of well-functioning individuals and families, the therapist seeks to highlight and encourage behaviors that fall into this category as part of the process of helping clients to achieve their goals. As exemplified in the homework assignment described in the case of Theresa and Joe, it may be important to encourage celebrating and having fun, taking advantage of opportunities to experience spontaneity and a sense of humor. Indeed, the more energy that is devoted to positive interactions, the less energy will be available for those interactions that would be experienced negatively. The therapist therefore may suggest the creation of rituals that might fill a void, or the recreation of traditions that no longer fit as individuals grow older and families mature. This may be particularly useful as a means of helping elderly adults accommodate the various changes with which they are likely to be faced.

In addition, a focus on such issues as goals and values, as well as a sense of meaning and purpose in life may be extremely useful and supportive of therapeutic goals. Not only is psychological well-being enhanced by a feeling that one is living, or has lived, a meaningful life, but shared goals and values may enhance the ability of clients to handle some of life's most challenging moments (Jones, 1995). This certainly may be the case when dealing with end-of-life issues and challenges, illustrated as follows:

Case Study

Helen and Harold, both aged 70, came to therapy following Helen's decision to terminate chemotherapy when her cancer was declared incurable and the treatments became intolerable. Helen had opted for quality rather than quantity of life. She knew she was dying, and wanted help both for herself and for Harold as she entered the final phase of her life. While Harold understood Helen's decision and supported her in every way possible, he was angry at the situation and was mourning the anticipated loss of his wife as well as of his dreams for their future together. He also was so focused on taking care of Helen and her needs that he was neglecting himself and his own needs, thus often becoming fatigued and irritable, not only with others but also with Helen.

Our conversations revolved around how Helen and Harold could make the best use of whatever time was left, so that quality of life really could be achieved. Together we made arrangements for both to receive massage therapy, and for extended family members and friends to provide assistance so that Harold occasionally could spend time going out and playing cards with friends. The therapy context provided a safe space in which Helen could discuss her fears and concerns about dying and Harold could speak about his sadness and anger. I stressed the importance of finding moments just to be together in enjoyable ways, outside of therapy. I also particularly encouraged them to make a video, to be shared with their children and grandchildren, in which they talked about the special relationship that was their marriage. Helen shared stories about significant moments in her life, and she articulated messages to each individual in the family. Having enlisted the help of one of their daughters to provide video equipment, they were able to work together to make the dying process more meaningful, in spite of the pain both were experiencing.

Given that a variety of issues related to death and dying are common elements in therapy with later life families, it is important to be aware of ways to support clients who are approaching the end of life and/or are grieving the loss of a loved one. The use of videography (Rigazio-Digilio, 2003), as in the previous example, certainly may facilitate one aspect of this process. In addition, it is essential that the therapist be comfortable with the topic of death, be aware that each experience of loss is unique, and recognize that the bereaved want to tell their stories and be heard (Becvar, 2001). Further, he or she must be sensitive to the fact that while grief may never end, this is not necessarily an indicator of pathology, nor does it preclude the possibility of also finding joy again in their lives.

Although not the case with Helen and Harold, conversations about meaning and purpose in life certainly may move into the realm of religion and spirituality. Among the elderly, given the likelihood of a preoccupation with death as well as questions about what comes after, it may be useful to explore various thoughts and concerns in this regard. The therapist therefore may ask clients where they are relative to spirituality and religion, what their beliefs and practices are, and consider ways in which resources in this realm may be incorporated into the therapy process. For example, she may suggest consultation with a clergy person or a spiritual guide, if this seems appropriate, and may encourage conversations about the ways in which various belief systems and practices may or may not have been helpful.

For those in their late middle years, the therapist also may wish to encourage a focus on ways to create an older age that is as enjoyable as possible. This often means revising the kinds of things clients say to themselves about what lies ahead. Given relatively new information derived from recent research on aging, the following are some suggestions that he or she may incorporate into various therapeutic conversations:

- Plan to live a very long life—80 or 90 years—and take steps now to guarantee the intellectual and social stimulation you'll want in your later years.

- Don't get trapped in yesterday's "linear" model of aging: Adjust your psychological, social, and financial expectations to support a "cyclic" lifeplan.

- Envision new career goals and challenges. Intellectual flexibility and the ability to learn new skills and technologies will be key assets in a more longevous era.

- Be prepared to reinvent yourself several times in adulthood—you may discover aspects of your potential you never knew existed. (Dychtwald, 2000, p. 110)

Being aware of such advice, and taking it to heart for oneself, is also very important for the therapist who works with later life clients.

SPECIAL CONSIDERATIONS

There are a variety of additional issues about which the therapist needs to be aware as she or he contemplates working with later life clients. First and foremost, she or he must be sensitive to her or his own biases, and work to check out preconceptions regarding the elderly. For example, Davey, Murphy, and Price (2000, p. 248) note the following:

Many therapists are reluctant to work with older people out of fear that they need some special skills. Other therapists may believe that older clients are fragile and not open to direct confrontation. . . . Still other therapists may have unresolved issues with their own older parents or grandparents. Even if therapy proceeds with older clients and a (presumably) younger therapist beyond these initial concerns, therapy can trigger therapists' own positive and negative memories of parents and grandparents. . . . Fears of death and dying may also be elicited for a therapist working with an older client.

In addition to being careful of this potential pitfall, the therapist also needs to be careful with regard to her or his assumptions about sexual activity among the elderly, checking with clients to learn where they are in this area and recognizing that, as with so many other issues, there is no one right way to be, nor do popular stereotypes necessarily fit.

Another area of importance relates to the perception of a stigma associated with therapy. Although it may not be the case by the time the baby boomers reach old age, currently many of the elderly may feel a sense of shame, or worry that their reputation will be tarnished, if they go to therapy. They therefore may be reluctant clients (assuming that they are willing to come at all), and the therapist may need to normalize the process and allay any fears about what it means to engage with a mental health professional. It may be particularly important to emphasize to clients that they are not crazy and that many others in their age group also have come to therapy, and to respond first to any questions and concerns clients may have, always maintaining a respectful posture.

It also is important to be aware of several issues related to physiology and physical well-being. Wheelchair accessibility in terms of stairs and restrooms is essential. And the therapist must be sensitive to the possibility that health issues and/or medications may be having an adverse impact on the behavior of elderly clients. In addition to recommending physical checkups or consultations, as mentioned in the case of Katherine, the therapist also might do well to understand the influence of normal aging processes as compared with the warning signs of Alzheimer's disease, which include the following:

- Memory loss
- Difficulty performing familiar tasks
- Problems with language
- Disorientation to time and place
- Poor or decreased judgment
- Problems with abstract thinking
- Misplacing things
- Changes in personality
- Loss of initiative

While the normal aging process typically includes some degree of loss or change in the aforementioned areas, further assessments by qualified professionals are definitely in order when difficulties with communication, learning, thinking, and reasoning interfere with work, social activities, and/or family life (Alzheimer's Association, 2003).

On the other hand, the therapist also needs to be aware of processes characterizing a healthy aging process. Indeed, offering suggestions and reinforcing life-enhancing behaviors as part of therapy also may support the achievement of clients' goals. Vaillant (2002) analyzed the data from three longitudinal studies of the aging process conducted over many years, and proposed that the characteristics of graceful aging could be summarized in the following manner:

1. Maintains social utility, open to new ideas, cares about others (within the limits of physical health).

2. Eriksonian Integrity—accepts the past and can take sustenance from past accomplishments.

3. Maintains other Eriksonian skills: Basic Trust (hope in life), sensible Autonomy, and Initiative. (In old age Industry, Generativity, and Intimacy are not always possible.).

4. Enjoys life, retains sense of humor, capacity for joy and play. (Since "old age is not for sissies," happiness may not be possible.)

5. Cheerful acceptance of "indignities of old age," graceful about dependency issues, takes care of self, and when ill becomes a patient that a doctor would want to care for.

6. Cultivates relationships with surviving old friends and is successful in making new ones. (Vaillant, 2002, p. 346).

As the therapist makes recourse to such information and encourages some of the above behaviors in appropriate ways, clients may feel a renewed sense of self as well as an enhanced ability to create realities that they experience more positively.

The therapist working with elderly clients also is advised to be aware of gender influences. For example, although this, too, may change in the future, currently it is likely that more women than men will be alone in the later stages of life. Not only do women continue to have a greater life expectancy, they tend to marry older men, and are likely to live longer than their spouses. Given that women in any age group are more comfortable with the idea of therapy, it therefore is highly likely that a large portion of one's elderly clientele will be comprised of females. And an important issue, particularly for widows, is the loss of both financial security and social support that may occur following the death of a spouse. Indeed, regardless of gender, a significant part of the therapy process may involve facilitating connections with a meaningful support system, as the loss of friends and family members becomes ever more common the older one gets.

Finally, the therapist needs to be aware of the tendency of older clients to be vague in their descriptions of problems and concerns, to gloss over potentially important details, and/or to have more than one complaint (Kane, Ouslander, & Abrass, 1994). Patience is therefore important, as clients are encouraged to articulate both their problems and their desired solutions in specific and concrete terms. Staying with a topic and probing more deeply also may elicit further information, relevant both to the potential for success and the breadth of perceived problems.

Case Study

The request for therapy came via a telephone call from Diane, a 60-year-old woman who desired help in dealing with the conflict she and her siblings were experiencing around how best to care for their mother, Sarah. At the time of the initial contact Sarah was 85 years old, had been a widow for 14 years, and was living on her own. Although quite independent, and adamant about remaining in the family home, Sarah had experienced a number of falls in recent months, and Diane was concerned. However, when she approached her older brother and two younger sisters regarding next steps, she was met with a variety of opinions and very little agreement about what to do. She was hoping that therapy might enable them to do a better job of dealing with what she was experiencing as a difficult situation. I encouraged Diane to invite all of her siblings as well as her mother to participate. After much juggling of schedules, a mutually acceptable date was arranged, with all family members agreeing to come, although the siblings had decided not to include their spouses, at least initially.

Session 1

Following the usual process of introductions, I asked each family member to share her or his thoughts about coming to therapy and what she or he was hoping to accomplish. I asked Diane to take the lead, as she had been responsible for organizing the meeting. Diane, who was happily married for the second time and the mother of two grown sons, spoke about her growing concern for their mother and her desire to be sure that her mother was as safe and well cared for as possible. Diane said that she typically spent at least one day a week taking her mother grocery shopping and helping her with other errands, as needed. She also spoke to her mother by telephone at least once a day and tried to be available to help out whenever possible. Given their frequent interactions, Diane was aware not only that her mother had experienced several falls recently but that she seemed to be growing more forgetful about appointments, about taking her blood pressure medications, and so on. Although she didn't want to alarm her mother, she felt the time had come to talk about alternative living arrangements. And she was very relieved that everyone had agreed to come to family therapy.

Diane's older brother, Mark Jr., age 62, spoke next. Mark, who lived about an hour away from his mother's home, said that he understood his sister's concerns but felt that she was exaggerating a bit. His perception was that their mother was fine, that it is not unusual for older people to fall occasionally and have memory lapses, and that he certainly had not noticed any other changes in Sarah's behavior. He noted that Diane had always had a tendency to worry more than most and also to catastrophize, and that he didn't want to act too hastily. In addition, he said that he had talked with his mother recently and since she had assured him that she was fine on her own, he felt they should respect their mother's wishes. He certainly was agreeable to coming to family therapy if that's what Diane wanted, but he wasn't sure it was necessary.

Julie and Janet, 58-year-old twins who were Sarah's youngest offspring, spoke almost as one unit, sharing similar thoughts and opinions and often finishing each other's sentences. Although both were married and had children of their own, they had remained very close over the years, lived near each other, and participated in many activities together. Both were annoyed about having to come to therapy, but had agreed because they didn't want their mother to think they didn't care about her. However, they felt that Diane was overreacting, as usual, and they resented her tendency not only to interfere but also to act as if she was the only one who knew what should be done. They didn't spend much time with their mother, but they believed that Sarah understood, because they had such busy lives and just didn't have the luxury of being as available as Diane, who was retired.

Sarah, who had been watching and listening very carefully, thanked her children for sharing their concerns and expressed gratitude that they would take the time to participate in therapy. She spoke about how difficult it had been when their father died, and how, at the age of 71, she had been forced to learn how to live on her own and take care of herself and their home. In response to a question from me, she indicated that her husband, an engineer, had died of lung cancer soon after the couple had celebrated their fiftieth wedding anniversary. She said that in spite of the challenges and the loneliness that followed, she was proud of what she had accomplished, and had come to appreciate the value of being independent and self-sufficient. She acknowledged that the time would probably come when she would no longer be able to manage on her own, but she felt that she wasn't there yet.

I complimented everyone for their willingness to participate, noting that the siblings all seemed to have their mother's best interests at heart despite the fact that they might be feeling differently about how to respond right now. I then proceeded by asking each person to describe what she or he hoped would be the outcome of therapy, what would be going on if things were the way each would like them to be. Julie and Janet said they felt that things were fine the way they were, and they wanted Diane to just back off and leave their mother alone. Diane wanted to be able to talk about selling the family home and making arrangements for their mother to live with one of them. Sarah was clear that she was not ready to sell her home, but that when she did, she wanted to go into an assisted living center rather than move in with one of her children. Mark wanted Diane to know he appreciated her efforts to be the major support for their mother but felt that it would be best if they allowed things to remain as they were for the time being.

Diane began to express her frustration that no one would take her concerns seriously. She acknowledged her tendency to be a worrier but felt that the others were in denial, refusing to take seriously the fact that her mother no longer seemed to be functioning as well as she had previously. She also was upset that her mother would choose to live in a facility rather than with one of her children. As the situation began to heat up, with several people responding and speaking at once, I asked if we could slow down a bit and begin to consider things a little differently.

I asked Sarah about her desire to move to an assisted living center and at what point she thought that would become appropriate. Sarah spoke eloquently about not wanting to be a burden on or an intrusion in the lives of her children, as she had so often seen happen with her friends. She also felt strongly that she wanted to maintain some semblance of independence, hence her decision. And, her plan was to live on her own for one more year and then start looking for an appropriate residential setting. At that point she assumed they could think about selling her home.

I asked Diane what kind of reassurance might be needed in order to allay her fears and to be able to accept her mother's desire to remain on her own for another year. Diane said that with a complete medical checkup and the approval of Sarah's physician that she would feel more comfortable. She also felt it would be important for Mark and Julie and Janet to spend more time, or at least have regular phone contact, with their mother, so that they would have a greater aware-ness of any changes as they occurred and she wouldn't always have to be perceived as the family doomsayer. And she wanted to start looking now for an assisted liv-ing center, so that when the time came, they would be prepared.

I asked the family members if this seemed like a reasonable plan. Sarah felt a medical checkup was unnecessary but she agreed to it, and everyone else con-curred. I wondered if any of the siblings would be willing to do some groundwork in terms of investigating locations and possibilities for assisted living, and Mark volunteered to undertake a search. Finally, I suggested that maybe they could cre-ate a regular schedule of visits and phone calls to enable everyone to be equally involved, complimenting them again for their care and concern for their mother. As everyone felt that they had reached a good place, we agreed that they would return on an as-needed basis.

Session 2

About 6 months later I received a call from Diane requesting an individual ses-sion. When she came in she reported that her mother had indeed seen her physi-cian right after the first session. The physician felt that Sarah was still basically healthy and well enough to be on her own, as long as family members checked in periodically. Although Diane was frustrated, she had gone along with the plan, but continued to worry. She said that very little else had changed, that neither her sisters nor her brother were in more frequent contact with their mother, and that when she had asked Mark about how the search for an assisted living center was going he had gotten angry with her and told her to get off his back, that he would take care of it in time. Julie and Janet had also gotten angry with her when she at-tempted to encourage them to visit their mother more often.

Diane's solution had been to increase her visits to her mother—to twice a week—and to hope things would be all right. She had asked her husband to help with the search for an assisted living center and she also had arranged with one of Sarah's neighbors to check in periodically and to let Diane know if anything seemed unusual. About one month previously the neighbor had called Diane to say that when she had visited Sarah, she noticed that the house was far messier than usual and that her mother seemed to be having difficulty walking. Diane im-mediately went to her mother's home and talked with her mother about what was going on. Although Sarah made light of the situation, she did agree to visit one or two of the centers that Diane's husband had located.

In the meantime, Mark had made one of his monthly visits to his mother and learned what Diane had been doing. He had called her in a rage, saying that as the oldest sibling and the one with his mother's power of attorney he needed to be consulted before Diane did anything. He also told her that she had no business pushing their mother, as Sarah apparently had reported she felt in response to Di-ane's actions. Diane had responded angrily to her brother's accusations, and when the argument began to escalate out of control, she had hung up on him.

Diane was frustrated at being considered the bad guy by everyone. She felt that she was the only one who was willing to look at the situation and acknowledge what was really going on. She was angry at her siblings for not honoring their commitments and she was especially hurt by her mother, whom she had been trying so hard to help. At this point she was unsure about what to do and wanted to sort things out. And her highest priority remained that of taking care of her mother.

I continued to affirm Diane for what she was trying to do. I noted that as the oldest daughter and the second child (Hoopes & Harper, 1987), it made perfect sense that she would be the one to take the lead in this situation. Then, I asked her to talk about her role in the family, starting when she was a young child. She said that she had always been the family worrier, and that she never felt like she quite belonged. She had been teased a lot, and her siblings also had been jealous of her academic success in their younger years. As they grew older, they had managed to create relationships that were comfortable, if not close. She said that her relationship with Mark had generally been better than those she had with her sisters, who seemed to live in a world of their own. She knew that Mark felt responsible to care for their mother, particularly after their father died, but that he was very busy with his career and couldn't seem to find time to do what needed to be done.

As Diane talked, she began to get a sense that perhaps some of Mark's extreme reaction might be a function of the guilt he was feeling about not fulfilling his responsibilities as well as he would like. She recognized that denial had always tended to be the means of survival for the twins. And she acknowledged that she, herself, could be pretty headstrong. I expressed my belief that if she continued to do what she felt needed to be done to care for their mother, she probably was going to have to experience the consequences in terms of the reactions of her siblings. However, I felt that perhaps another session with everyone involved might allow for a more productive discussion among them and perhaps ease some of the tensions. In addition, I noted that with everyone in the room, a continuation of the triangulation process that had occurred among Diane, Mark, and Sarah might be prevented. I suggested that Diane think about how she could speak not only about her own fears but also from a place of greater understanding of each of her siblings, as well as out of concern for her mother.

Session 3

I began the session by thanking everyone for coming again. With Diane's permission, and knowing that she had already informed them, I reiterated that we had had an individual session and that we both had agreed that it was important to have all of the family members participate in the conversation. Diane added her gratitude to everyone and asked if she could speak first. She talked about the fact that perhaps she had been out of line, at least from the perspective of everyone else, but that her intentions had been good. As she began to cry, she said that she just didn't want her mother to die, and that she had believed that somehow she could keep her mother safe and prevent that from happening. She apologized for being insensitive and said to Mark that she understood that he was doing the best he could and that she knew he was really carrying a huge burden. She told Janet and Julie that she could relate to their fears, and suspected that by staying away they could pretend that everything was all right. She told her mother how sorry she was if she truly felt pushed, although her mother had not expressed that feeling to her.

At this point, Sarah followed up by saying how much she appreciated the fact that Diane was willing to talk openly about her fears. She acknowledged that she, too, had been afraid to speak and to let her children know of her own mixed feelings. She said that she wanted to remain a strong presence for them but she also was feeling tired, and was looking forward to being with her husband again. She recognized that she had not been straight with either Diane or Mark about her true feelings. And she certainly didn't feel any animosity toward either Janet or Julie, understanding where they were coming from.

By now everyone was crying, but the feeling in the room had changed significantly. Each person was able to acknowledge a depth of emotion that previously had not been expressed, sharing feelings of sadness, fears, and much love. Eventually, the conversation shifted into a consideration of where to go from here, with Sarah saying she had really liked one of the assisted living centers, and asking if the others would go with her and Diane for a second visit. They also began to talk about making plans to sell Sarah's house once she moved. Finally, they expressed gratitude for the process and agreed to come back to therapy periodically to be sure that things remained on track.

CONCLUSION

Working with families in later life involves unique issues and challenges. At the same time, with an approach that is sensitive to the specific needs and concerns of middle-aged and elderly families and their members, the therapist may experience unique opportunities to assist clients in achieving their goals. They thus may succeed in contributing to the enhancement of the quality of life during what is often one of its most stressful phases.

REFERENCES

Alzheimer's Association. (2003). *Ten warning signs of Alzheimer's disease.* Retrieved at http:\\ www.alz.org/AboutAD/10signs.htm

Becvar, D. S. (1996). *Soul healing: A spiritual orientation in counseling and therapy.* New York: Basic Books.

Becvar, D. S. (2001). *In the presence of grief: Helping family members resolve death, dying and bereavement.* New York: Guilford.

Becvar, D. S., & Becvar, R. J. (1999). *Systems theory and family therapy: A primer* (2nd ed.). Lanham, MD: University Press of America.

Becvar, D. S., & Becvar, R. J. (2006). *Family therapy: A systemic integration* (6th ed.). Boston: Allyn & Bacon.

Becvar, R. J., & Becvar, D. S. (1997). *Pragmatics of human relationships: A guide to effective communication.* Iowa City, IA: Geist and Russell.

Bonjean, M. J. (1997). Solution-focused brief therapy with aging families. In T. D. Hargrave & S. M. Hanna (Eds.), *The aging family: New visions in theory, practice and reality* (pp. 81–100). New York: Brunner-Mazel.

Carter, E. A., & McGoldrick, M. (Eds.). (1988). *The changing family life cycle.* New York: Gardner Press.

Davey, A., Murphy, M. J., & Price, S. J. (2000). Aging and the family: Dynamics and therapeutic interventions. In W. C. Nichols, M. A. Pace-Nichols, D. S. Becvar, & A. Y. Napier (Eds.), *Handbook of family development and intervention* (pp. 235–252). New York: Wiley.

Dychtwald, K. (2000). *Age power: How the 21st century will be ruled by the new old.* New York: Jeremy P. Tarcher/Putnam.

Erlanger, M. A. (1990). Using the genogram with the older client. *Journal of Mental Health Counseling, 12,* 321–333.

Hoopes, M. M., & Harper, J. M. (1987). *Birth order roles and sibling patterns in individual and family therapy.* Rockville, MD: Aspen.

Jones, J. W. (1995). *In the middle of this road we call life.* New York: HarperCollins.

Kane, R. L., Ouslander, J. G., & Abrass, I. B. (1994). *Essentials of clinical geriatrics.* New York: McGraw-Hill.

Nichols, W. C., Pace-Nichols, M. A., Becvar, D. S., & Napier, A. Y. (Eds.). (2001). *Handbook of family development and intervention.* New York: Wiley.

Rigazio-Digilio, S. A. (2003). Videography: Re-storying the lives of clients facing terminal illness. In R. Neimeyer (Ed.), *Meaning reconstruction and the experience of loss* (pp. 331–344). Washington, DC: American Psychological Association.

Vaillant, G. E. (2002). *Aging well.* Boston: Little, Brown.

Walsh, F. (1998). *Strengthening family resilience.* New York: Guilford.

Watzlawick, P., Weakland, J., & Fisch, R. (1976). *Change: Principles of problem formation and problem resolution.* New York: Norton.

White, M., & Epston, D. (1990). *Narrative means to therapeutic ends.* New York: Norton.

Author Index

Subject Index